EL MIRADOR
NAKBÉ
RÍO AZUL
Carmelita
UAXACTÚN
TIKAL
EL ZOTZ
NAKÚM
YAXHÁ NARANJO
TOPOXTÉ
Lago Petén Itzá
El Remate
Melchor de Mencos
TAYASAL
IXLÚ
Flores
Río Mopán
CARRETERA AL PETÉN
El Subín
BELIZE
Sayaxché
CA 13
Belmopan
CEIBAL
AGUATECA
Poptún
NAJ TUNICH
Río de la Pasión
RN 5
CANCUÉN

Caribbean

Sea

Punta Gorda

Golfo

de

Punta de Manabique

Honduras

Puerto Cortés

Sebol
Fray Bartolomé de las Casas
Livingston
Puerto Barrios
Tela

Río Dulce
Sierra de Santa Cruz

El Estor
Lago de Izabal
Mariscos
Corinto
San Pedro Sula

Río Polochic
Río Motagua

Sierra de las Minas
QUIRIGUÁ
CA 4
CA 5

CA 14
CA 9
La Entrada

CARRETERA AL ATLÁNTICO
Río Hondo
Lago de Yojoa

Zacapa
El Florido
COPÁN
CA 4
Santa Bárbara
Siguatepeque
Comayagua

Chiquimula
Copán Ruinas
Santa Rosa de Copán

Río San José
CA 10
Gracias

Jalapa
Esquipulas

Angiatú
Nueva Ocotepeque
La Esperanza
CA 7

Río Paz
HONDURAS

CA 1

Ciudad Pedro de Alvarado
CA 4

CA 10
EL SALVADOR

CA 2
CA 1
San Salvador

Contents

Discover Guatemala

Guatemala has always been the stuff of legend. For me this was evident early on. Guatemala represented an exotic land with a palpable sense of magic and the source of my family's origins — a land of rugged mountain trails, exotic jungle ruins, and fascinating indigenous culture. I first visited Guatemala when I was three years old and was captivated by the country from the moment I set foot there. Some of my earliest memories are of mysterious Mayan Indians who giggled easily and carried baskets atop their heads while walking barefoot down dirt roads.

Wherever you go in Guatemala, you will sense this magic. When you leave its cosmopolitan capital, the green landscape unfolds before you from the window of a car, bus, or airplane. Its misty mountains, pine forests, and agricultural fields look like something out of a fairytale, populated by Maya people dressed in Technicolor attire. This magic strikes you as you watch a Maya woman weaving wonderfully intricate textiles on a backstrap loom or see a dozen enormous, 20-foot-in-diamater kites catching the light of the rising sun and turning it into a psychedelic dream. You might visit a highland market where Mayan crafts are sold, or climb an active volcano to witness a lava light show. Guatemala's conical volcanoes have been described by travel writers for centuries. Aldous Huxley called them "the beauty of witches," while a recent writer for *Condé Nast Traveller* said they "look absurdly like a volcano drawn by a small child, or by Hokusai."

Geography aside, perhaps most fascinating about Guatemala is its culture, history, and people. It's wildly diverse. Although Spanish is the official language, there are at least 21 other Mayan dialects spoken by the country's indigenous peoples. In Guatemala City, the remains of ancient Maya temples lie scattered among modern hotels, office buildings, and shopping malls housing Starbucks and U.S. fast-food franchises. In a fancy Antigua restaurant, you may dine beneath Spanish colonial arches set beside a gurgling fountain, as live music from modern dance clubs floats through the warm air.

Word of the magic that is Guatemala has gotten out. Come see it for yourself, and discover the mysteries of this ancient land that has gracefully adapted to modern life.

Planning Your Trip

▶ WHERE TO GO

Guatemala City

The largest city in Central America, Guatemala City has long history of being overlooked by travelers. Among its numerous attractions are recommended museums, vibrant nightlife, and a range of excellent restaurants and accommodations. The Zona Viva is the place to go for nightlife, pleasant streetside cafés, and some of Latin America's finest restaurants.

La Antigua Guatemala

La Antigua is a UNESCO World Heritage Site thanks to its sublime collection of convents, churches, and monasteries. It features Guatemala's loveliest town plaza, graced by the elegant facade of the Catedral de Santiago, and its pleasant cobblestone streets are lined with restaurants, accommodations, and shops housed in beautiful old colonial homes. The surroundings are perfectly suited to outdoor recreational activities.

The Western Highlands

The Western Highlands boast not only Central America's highest mountains and volcanoes, but also its most authentic and vibrant indigenous culture. You'll find colorful Mayan markets, quaint mountain villages, and gorgeous alpine scenery. On the shores of spectacular Lake Atitlán are three volcanoes and several Mayan villages. Guatemala's second-largest city, Quetzaltenango, is a popular language-school destination, while Chichicastenango is home to Guatemala's most famous market. An emerging eco- and cultural tourism scene can be found in the Ixil Triangle.

IF YOU HAVE . . .

- **A WEEKEND:** Spend your time in Antigua Guatemala.

- **ONE WEEK:** Add Pacaya Volcano and Lake Atitlán or Tikal.

- **TWO WEEKS:** Add Atitlán and Tikal; visit Quetzaltenango and Cobán, saving some time for the museums in Guatemala City. If Quetzaltenango is too chilly, head to the Pacific Coast.

- **THREE WEEKS:** Enjoy all of the above at a more leisurely pace, adding Río Dulce and Lívingston.

Catedral de Santiago in La Antigua

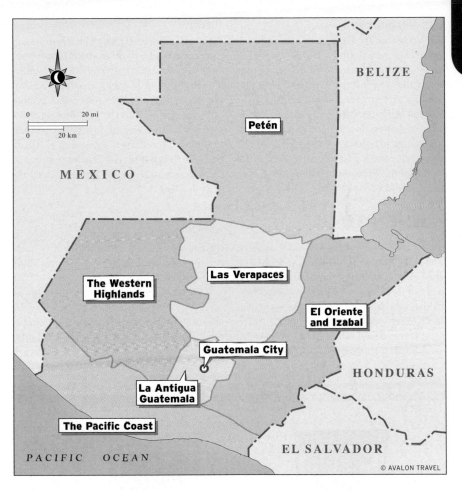

The Pacific Coast

On the western end of the Pacific Coast, Retalhuleu is a hot spot thanks to the twin theme parks of Xocomil and Xetulul. Bird-watchers and nature lovers will find several private reserves, including a fantastic lodge built on the ninth terrace of the Mayan site of Takalik Abaj. East along the coast, you'll find the small village of Sipacate, home to Guatemala's emerging surf scene, and Iztapa, Guatemala's sailfishing capital. Monterrico is the region's most popular resort town.

El Oriente and Izabal

The dry plains of El Oriente are populated by ladino cowboys and cattle ranchers. Just over the Honduran border is the site of Copán, with some of the Mayan world's finest stelae and best on-site museums. Heading east toward Izabal is the Caribbean town of Puerto Barrios, the gateway for adventures into untamed Punta de Manabique, the seaside Garífuna town of Lívingston, the Belize cayes, and tranquil Río Dulce.

Las Verapaces

Las Verapaces are Guatemala's green heartland. Here you'll find the country's best-preserved cloud forests in the Sierra de las Minas Biosphere Reserve, the Cloudforest Biological Corridor, which includes the Biotopo Mario Dary Rivera, and the pleasant town of Cobán. Nearby attractions include the spectacular limestone pools of Semuc Champey, white-water rafting on the Río Cahabón, the phenomenal Candelaria Caves, and splendid Laguna Lachuá.

Petén

Petén is to Guatemala what the Amazon rainforest is to Brazil. In this lowland jungle frontier are the remains of several Mayan cities. The best-known Mayan site is Tikal, a must-see. In addition to the impressive temple pyramids, Tikal and the neighboring Maya Biosphere Reserve harbor Mayan ruins and varied wildlife. Flores, occupying an island on Lake Petén Itzá, is a transportation and services hub rivaled by El Remate, along the road to Tikal.

► WHEN TO GO

Guatemala has two seasons—rainy and dry. The rainy season usually begins at the end of May; the summer months are characterized by short afternoon or early evening showers that clear up by nighttime. By September or October, however, the weather is often socked in for daysDuring these two months, many hotels offer discounts in hopes of filling their rooms. Some parts of the country, most prominently the Caribbean coast, are rainy throughout the year.

The dry season runs from November to early May. December through February are the coldest months, with cold fronts from the north bringing temperatures into the mid-60s for daytime highs in mountain areas such

a cyclist in Antigua Guatemala

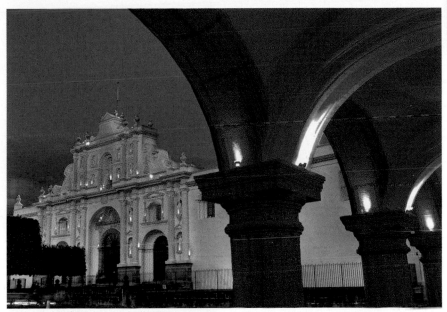

Antigua Guatemala's Catedral de Santiago

as Antigua, Quetzaltenango, and Guatemala City. Temps warm up dramatically in March and April. During this time, thick haze from heat, dust, and agricultural burning clouds the views of Guatemala's stunning mountain scenery.

The **high tourist season** runs from December to Holy Week (usually in April) with a **second high season** between mid-June and early September. **Language schools in** Quetzaltenango and Antigua are full with college students during the summer; rates go up accordingly. School lets out in mid-October, with **vacations** taking place until January. Families with children take over many of the popular destinations.

▶ BEFORE YOU GO

Passports

U.S. citizens will need a **passport** with at least six months' validity after arrival. Residents of other countries will also need **ticket documents** for onward or return travel.

Vaccinations

No vaccinations are required for entry into Guatemala, though it's a good idea to be up to date on rabies, typhoid, measles-mumps-rubella (MMR), yellow fever, tetanus,s and hepatitis shots.

Transportation

Guatemala City's modern **La Aurora International Airport** has several daily flights from numerous U.S. gateways. **Mundo Maya International Airport** serves the northern department of Petén and the ruins of Tikal.

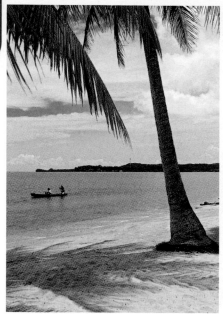

Playa Blanca in Lívingston is one of Guatemala's prettiest beaches.

a convent turned boutique hotel in Antigua Guatemala

The majority of inter- and intracity buses are recycled U.S. school buses known as "chicken buses" (cargo often consists of live animals); however, robberies and armed hijacking are increasingly common. Tourist shuttle buses are more expensive, but are recommended for safety reasons.

Rental cars can be rented in Guatemala City, Panajachel, Antigua, Quetzaltenango, Cobán, and Flores. Unless you plan to stick to urban areas such as Guatemala City and Antigua or along the Pan-American Highway, it's probably best to rent a four-wheel-drive vehicle. Taxicabs are available in almost any town or city. When in smaller towns, the best way to find a taxi is in the central square, or *parque central*. Otherwise, it's always best to call a cab rather than hail one from the street.

► WHAT TO TAKE

Dress in layers: Pack an assortment of short-sleeved T-shirts, sweaters, fleece jackets and/or a light rain jacket, shorts, and pants. Quick-drying synthetic fabrics wick away moisture during strenuous hikes in the backcountry. In jungle areas where mosquitoes are rampant, stick to light-colored and lightweight shirts with long sleeves you can roll up and lightweight travel pants. Also pack sunscreen, bug spray, and a wide-brimmed hat or ball cap. Footwear is extremely important. For serious jungle hiking, high, military-style boots protect against mud and snakes.

Explore Guatemala

▶ THE BEST OF GUATEMALA

If you have 10 days, you can enjoy the best that Guatemala has to offer. The following itinerary will help you see as much as you can in a short amount of time without running ragged. After all, it's a vacation.

Day 1

Fly in to Guatemala City around lunchtime. Take the afternoon to visit the **Archaeology Museum** or the **Museo Popol Vuh** and **Museo Ixchel** (next door to each other) for a crash course on the Mayan civilization. Enjoy dinner in one of Guatemala City's excellent restaurants.

Days 2-3

Take an early-morning flight out of Guatemala City to **Flores**, the gateway to the Mayan ruins of **Tikal**, in the northern Petén department. Tikal is the most famous of Guatemala's Mayan sites and boasts impressive temple pyramids. Spend all day exploring the ruins and enjoying the sublime jungle environment. You have the option of staying at the park and seeing the sunrise over the rainforest from the top of Temple IV or heading back south to **Lake Petén Itzá**, where you can stay at the ultrachic La Lancha. The lake, with its turquoise waters and tropical forest ecosystem, makes a good alternative to staying at the ruins. Fly back to Guatemala City on the afternoon of the second day. Upon arrival, grab a shuttle bus or taxi from the airport to **Antigua**, Guatemala's old colonial capital, and check in at any of the city's fine accommodations.

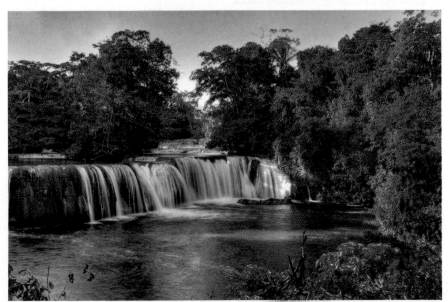

Las Conchas pools in Alta Verapaz, Las Verapaces

ANCIENT WONDERS OF THE MAYA

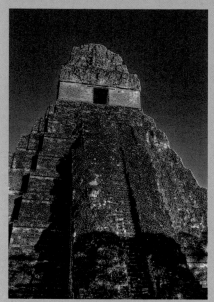

the temple at Tikal

In Guatemala, not only can you take in the ancient Mayan wonders from long before the arrival of the Spanish, you can also visit the Postclassic highland ceremonial sites that greeted the conquistadors upon their arrival in 1524.

Most of the Mayan ceremonial sites that were at their cultural zenith during these time periods can be found in the country's northern Petén region. Among the largest and most sophisticated cities from the Preclassic period is **El Mirador,** which flourished between 200 B.C. and A.D. 150. No self-respecting archaeology buff would come to Guatemala without visiting the ruins of **Tikal** at the center of a 575-square-kilometer (222-square-mile) national park protecting the historical site and surrounding rainforest ecosystem. Farther north is the interesting astronomical observatory at **Uaxactún.** West of Tikal are the sites of **Nakum** and **Yaxhá,** the latter of *Survivor TV* fame.

Real history buffs might want to check out the ceremonial sites found and subjugated by the Spanish at the time of the conquest, thus completing the picture of Guatemala's pre-Columbian archaeological heritage. When the Spanish arrived in Guatemala, they first secured an alliance with the Kaqchikel, who had their capital in **Iximché** in Guatemala's Western Highlands. The Spanish would eventually establish their first capital on the same site. You can visit the restored ruins of Iximché, very conveniently situated just a few kilometers from the Pan-American Highway about an hour from Guatemala City.

With the submission of the Kaqchikels, the Spanish were now free to turn on the K'iche', whom they met in battle near present-day Quetzaltenango. The K'iche' invited the Spanish to their mountain fortress at **K'umarcaaj,** the site of a failed ambush against the European invaders. Today, the largely unrestored ruins are still the site of Mayan rituals and feature a noteworthy underground cave tunnel.

Near the city of Huehuetenango, the inhabitants of the Mam ceremonial site of **Zaculeu** were done in by starvation after Pedro de Alvarado's brother laid siege to the city for two months. Northwest of Guatemala City, the ruins of **Mixco Viejo** were once the Poqomam capital and ceremonial center, falling to Pedro de Alvarado in 1525 after a typically ruthless attack. In addition to temple pyramids, the site has two ball courts decorated with twin serpent sculptures harboring human skulls in their open mouths, a rather unusual embellishment among Postclassic highland sites and further evidence of the Toltec and Aztec influences of the times.

Days 4-5

Grab breakfast or coffee from any of the coffee shops along the plaza. Café Condesa makes a fine choice for breakfast. Take some time to see Antigua's major sights. Return to your comfortable hotel room for some chill-out time before heading out to dinner. On the second day, head out to **Finca Filadelfia** for breakfast and take a tour of the coffee farm. Lunch is at your leisure, and you can also use the time to do some shopping. In the afternoon, head out with one of the groups making the **Pacaya Volcano climb** to see the lava light show. The trip returns late at night.

Days 6-7

Take a shuttle bus sometime around noon for **Panajachel,** on the shores of spectacular **Lake Atitlán.** You also have the option of continuing to nearby **Santa Catarina Palopó** or **Santa Cruz La Laguna** if Panajachel doesn't suit your style. The afternoon is yours to explore or simply relax. If possible, plan for

Day 7 to fall upon a Sunday or Thursday so you can grab a shuttle bus from Panajachel to Chichicastenango to see the colorful **Chichicastenango Market.** Return to Panajachel in the afternoon.

Days 8-10

It's up to you. Head to the other side of the lake to **San Pedro** or **Santiago** for some more highland Mayan culture amid splendid settings or any of the other Mayan villages around the lake. You can also stay right where you are and make day trips to the other villages. This will give you time to really enjoy the lake, as the pace of your visit to Atitlán thus far will have been a bit hurried. Take a shuttle bus back to **Guatemala City** on the afternoon of Day 9 and check in to your hotel. Savor the culinary delights offered at another one of the city's excellent restaurants before packing your purchases for the flight home the next day and turning in for the night. Be sure to leave room in your carry-on for the excellent duty-free shopping at La Aurora Airport.

colorful Guatemalan handicrafts

Antigua street scene

SURF AND TURF

La Reunión Antigua Golf Resort

Guatemala offers some of the best sailfishing in the world. Back on land, Guatemala City has at least four good golf courses—with another star player just one hour outside the city. Numerous sailfishing outfitters and accommodations can host your stay; virtually all of them have agreements with golf courses, allowing you to combine the two activities for a "surf and turf" vacation.

SAILFISHING AND WHALE-WATCHING

Your base for sailfishing will likely be Iztapa, about 90 minutes from Guatemala City. **Sailfish Bay Lodge** is among the best outfitters, with a lodge right on the beach. Another good option is **Casa Vieja Lodge,** near Puerto San José. You can fish from one to five days (or more) and then tack on an extra day or two for golf.

Guatemala is also a stopping point along the migration path of humpback whales, so you can take a morning for whale-watching in season. Other species you might spy include pilot whales, whale sharks, sea turtles, and bottlenose dolphins. Scheduled tours leave weekend mornings from Antigua Guatemala or Iztapa, beginning and ending in the Puerto Quetzal marina.

GOLF

Set on a former coffee plantation just 20 kilometers from Antigua, **La Reunión Antigua Golf Resort** is the only place in the world where you can enjoy a round of golf with a view of four volcanoes, two of which are active. Practice your swing at the driving range in the shadow of smoke-belching Fuego Volcano; its 18-hole, Pete Dye-designed Fuego Maya golf course takes its inspiration from the 19-month Mayan solar calendar. The adjacent 26-suite hotel offers fabulous accommodations and delectable culinary creations. You may never want to leave.

It's only an hour from La Reunión to Guatemala City, or 45 minutes to the Pacific Coast. You can easily combine a stay in Antigua or Guatemala City with some golf time; Guatemala's near-perfect climate makes golf possible almost any time of year. In the vicinity of Guatemala City, the best place to tee off is **San Isidro Golf Club.** The surrounding hillsides offer wonderful views of the city.

► WEEKEND ESCAPE

Guatemala's close proximity to U.S. shores and easy access by air (just 2.5 hours from Houston or Miami; 5 hours from New York) makes it a great candidate for an international weekend getaway.

Day 1

Plan this day to be a Friday or Saturday. There are nonstop flights from New York and Newark on Saturdays. Most other gateway cities have multiple flights daily.

Arrive in Guatemala City around noon. Grab a shuttle van or taxi to La Antigua and check into your hotel. Take the afternoon to explore the cobblestone streets and a museum or two, do some shopping, and get a bite to eat in one of the excellent restaurants. Grab drinks or dinner from Café Sky or Tartines and watch the sun set behind the volcanoes.

Day 2

Grab an early breakfast and then hike up to the **Cerro de la Cruz** for a wonderful view of the city with Agua Volcano in the background. Alternatively (between December and March), head out early to go **whale-watching** on the Pacific Coast (one hour away). Have lunch and an afternoon round of golf at **La Reunión Antigua Golf Resort** and spend the night there. From your Suite Gran Clase, enjoy views of Agua and Pacaya Volcanoes over your private plunge pool.

Day 3

Transfer to Guatemala City and its international airport. Depending on the time of departure, you may be able to visit one or several of the museums near the airport: the **Museo Nacional de Arqueología y Etnología** and the **Museo Popol Vuh** and **Museo Ixchel** (next door to each other). Allow some extra time at the airport for some duty-free shopping before you fly out.

Flowering bushes climb the wall along the road in La Antigua.

▶ ECOTOURISM TREKS

Community tourism initiatives, whereby local Maya guides take travelers to seldom-seen locales in Guatemala's rugged countryside, make for some extraordinary cross-cultural opportunities. You'll have the chance to stay in basic accommodations with Mayan families along the way, thus contributing directly to their economic well-being and greatly enhancing the cultural experience. Although many areas of Guatemala feature community tourism initiatives, this strategy details a selection from highland regions of the country.

Nebaj

There are several excellent treks leaving from the town of **Nebaj**, in El Quiché department's Ixil Triangle. Perhaps the most popular hike from here is a three-day **Nebaj-Todos Santos trek** across the Cuchumatanes mountain chain, where you'll encounter Andean scenery the likes of grassy plains strewn with rocky boulders in addition to Mam-speaking indigenous peoples herding sheep and llamas. Other overnight hikes from Nebaj lead west to picturesque lagoons near an area known as **Las Majadas** or to the villages of **Xeo** and **Cotzal**. Many hikers favor this route for the chance to get up close with the local culture in seldom-visited Mayan villages. The **Ixil Triangle**, as you may recall, was hard-hit during the country's civil war but is today one of Guatemala's best-kept secrets. The scenery alone makes the trip worthwhile, but the chance to take in the friendly indigenous Maya culture makes this trip memorable.

Uspantán and Around

This town lies along a back-door route between the departmental capital of Santa Cruz del Quiché and Alta Verapaz, to the east.

a wall mural in the highland village of Comalapa

Agua Volcano as seen from Santo Domingo del Cerro, La Antigua

a handmade Guatemalan *huipil*

Recreational opportunities include hikes through the backcountry to the wonderful waterfall of **Los Regadillos**, hikes to **Peña Flor** and the neighboring site of **Tzunun Kaab'**, and hiking or biking to the agricultural village of **Cholá**, where you can bathe in a refreshing spring-fed pool. You can also visit **Laj Chimel**, the birthplace of Nobel Peace Prize laureate Rigoberta Menchú and the gateway to Guatemala's fourth-largest cloud forest. You can try your luck at spotting the elusive quetzal (Guatemala's national bird) and other exotic species. Local Maya guides take visitors to far-flung locales such as **Mirador El Quetzal**, with spectacular views of the Ixil Triangle flanked by the Sierra de los Cuchumatanes, and lovely Laguna Danta. The community provides camping in a covered platform and basic lodging in an adobe guesthouse.

East of Uspantán, the town of **Chicamán** has also caught on to ecotourism and serves as the gateway to the seldom-explored **Rio Chixoy**. About 14 kilometers away, it's most easily visited from the hamlet of El Jocote via a community tourism initiative. A full day of river tubing includes three hours afloat on the cool, turquoise-colored river ending at a spectacular waterfall, a jungle hike, and lunch in a local community. You also have the option of staying overnight in a very comfortable and quaint wooden cabin.

Sierra de las Minas

Some of the best hiking anywhere in Guatemala, and Central America for that matter, can be found in the **Sierra de las Minas Biosphere Reserve**. Several trails wind through this remote wilderness, allowing the opportunity to spot Guatemala's national bird, the quetzal, and explore its unique cloud forest habitat. Starting in the village of **San Rafael Chilascó**, hook up with the local Community Tourism Organization for hikes to the nearby waterfall of **El Salto de Chilascó**, one of Central America's highest waterfalls. Longer, more challenging hikes take you up the mountain spine of **Lomo del Macho** and deep into the cloud forest to a research station at **Albores** and the **Peña del Ángel** rock formation.

▶ THE ROAD TO RUINS

On a map, several of the Maya sites in Guatemala's northern **Petén** department appear remote and completely off-limits. But appearances can be deceiving. Many of the **Maya Biosphere Reserve**'s most wonderful (and least visited) ruins can be reached during the March-April dry season via four-wheel-drive. Don't even think about trying most of these at any other time of year (unless indicated as year-round access). A recent attempt to visit some of these sites in January proved unfruitful, despite having four-wheel-drive vehicles equipped with winches and drivers armed with chainsaws to cut fallen trees. If you'd rather leave the driving (and cooking) to someone else, check out Antigua-based **No Limit Expeditions** for a 10-day itinerary covering remote sites in Guatemala and neighboring Belize.

If a guided tour isn't your thing, the easiest place to find a driver is through a local travel agency. They can contract a car and driver for you, or just a driver if you already have a car.

Yaxhá

The ruins of **Yaxhá** enjoy a spectacular location beside the site's namesake lagoon and provide commanding views of the surrounding forests. It is easily accessible via an unpaved all-season road and receives daily visitors who arrive by minivan. The site lies 11 kilometers down the unpaved road from a turnoff along the main highway leading east to Belize.

a dock on Lake Petén Itzá

Nakum and El Naranjo

The ruins at Nakum include an assortment of pyramids, plazas, and temples. From Yaxhá, the 17-kilometer-road to Nakum quickly deteriorates into a muddy mess. The main culprit is *bajo La Justa,* a low-lying marshland that must be traversed along the way. The road is narrow, with numerous fallen trees across the road. You'll need to bring a chainsaw. Another turnoff found shortly after embarking on the road to Nakum leads down a similarly rugged road east to El Naranjo, the third site in the Yaxhá-Nakum-Naranjo triangle.

Uaxactún and San Bartolo

Uaxactún can be reached via an all-season dirt road leading north from Tikal, but the adventurous like to take the rough, dry-season-only road that continues north from Nakum. From Uaxactún, you can also take a dirt road traveling east about 20 kilometers to the little-known Maya site of San Bartolo, home to some amazing Maya murals only discovered in the last 10 years. If the archaeologists are on site (mid-February to May) you'll be able to see the murals, but photography is forbidden. Otherwise, you'll need written permission from the Anthropology and History Institute (IDAEH) authorities in Guatemala City to see them. The park is heavily guarded. The road from Uaxactún is not well marked and there are numerous turn-offs. You'll need GPS and a map to plot points and ensure you're on the right path. The road passes a very swampy *bajo* along the way.

Dos Lagunas and Beyond

From Uaxactún, another rough dirt road heads north 50 kilometers to Naachtun-Dos Lagunas Biotope. The biotope protects abundant numbers of white-tailed deer and gets its name from the archaeological site of

Antigua Guatemala's ornate La Merced church

a Maya stela

BIRD'S-EYE VIEW

a scarlet macaw in flight

Guatemala's wide diversity of ecosystems makes it a birding hot spot – more than 700 species of birds can be found here. Avid bird-watchers consider this paradise, though novices can easily center an entire Guatemala vacation around birding.

With its own private reserve on the southern slopes of Atitlán Volcano, **Los Tarrales** harbors forests ranging in altitude from 700 to 3,000 meters (2,300-9,800 feet) that include broadleaf and cloud forests. Bird species are correspondingly diverse and include horned guan, long-tailed manakin, Pacific parakeet, orange-fronted parakeet, and several species of hummingbirds. Near Retalhuleu, **Reserva Patrocinio** lies south of Santiaguito Volcano at an altitude between 750 and 850 meters (2,500-2,700 feet). It is a good place for observing birds found in lowland and middle elevations. A substantial network of trails leads through protected patches of forest interspersed with coffee and macadamia plantations. Hawks, vultures, and falcons abound, as do parrots and woodpeckers.

On the Pacific Coast, the best places for birding are the vast **Manchón Guamuchal** wetlands and the canals and mangrove swamps bordering **Monterrico.** Species found in both parks include great egrets, roseate spoonbill, blue heron, and belted kingfisher.

On the moist Caribbean coast, the **Cerro San Gil Reserve** harbors more than 350 species of birds, including the black-and-white hawk eagle and keel-billed motmot. More than 90 neotropical migrants, including the wood thrush and blue-winged warbler, winter in the area. Also with more than 300 bird species is the remote peninsula of **Punta de Manabique,** a transit and wintering area for 25 Nearctic shorebirds. Notable bird species include the yellow-headed parrot, great curassow, and several species of herons.

Birding is excellent in the **Sierra de las Minas Biosphere Reserve,** particularly if you want to see Guatemala's national symbol, the elusive quetzal. If you'd like to bird-watch in the cloud forest while keeping a comfortable base to come back to after a long day, visit **Chelemhá Cloud Forest Preserve,** with its wonderful Maya Cloud Forest Lodge. The preserve lies at altitudes ranging from 2,000 to 2,500 meters (6,500-8,200 feet). Found within its forests are at least 14 bird species endemic to Central America's Northern Highlands. A total of 145 bird species have been recorded here to date.

In Petén, it's hard to beat **Tikal National Park.** You'll see oscillated turkeys along the forest floor as well as keel-billed toucans and Montezuma's Oropendola, among hundreds of other bird species, zipping about the forest canopy. The temple pyramids provide excellent vantage points for bird-watching. South of Tikal, on the shores of Lake Petén Itzá, **Cerro Cahuí** is also an excellent place for bird-watching with several waterbird species, including pied-billed grebe, herons, and northern jacana as well as the more typical rainforest birds such as toucans. Two trails wind through the forest with some excellent vantage points over the lake.

horseback riding near Copán, Honduras

Naachtun. Park guards come and go all year on foot or motorcycle, but four-wheel-drive vehicles should only attempt the trip during the March-April dry season. From the biotope, it's 25 kilometers east to **El Mirador** and its massive temples. This is an alternate way to arrive at remote El Mirador, as most visitors who arrive by land do so on foot from the village of Carmelita (further west). Part of the road to El Mirador from Naachtun–Dos Lagunas may be impassable by vehicle, even in the dry season.

From Naachtun–Dos Lagunas, it's 45 kilometers via (you guessed it) a rough dirt road to the very remote Maya site of **Río Azul**, which played an important part in the expansion of Tikal's dominance of the Petén area. The journey can only be done by vehicle in the dry season, though it can be made on horses or on foot at other times of year.

Doña Maria Gordillo candy store in Antigua

LIVING IT UP: HIP HOTELS AND RESTAURANTS

Guatemala has some of the hippest digs anywhere on the planet. Equivalent accommodations elsewhere in the world would cost twice as much. You also can find some of Latin America's best restaurants in Guatemala. After all, Guatemala's wealthy elite needs somewhere to spend its money. If you're sick and tired of hotels that all pretty much look the same and enjoy the opportunity to check out unique **boutique hotels** and **jungle lodges** near worthwhile attractions, then this list is for you.

GUATEMALA CITY

Otelito and the **Real InterContinental** are two of the city's hippest haunts. (George W. and Laura Bush stayed at the InterContinental during a visit in March 2007.) You can enjoy afternoon coffee at any one of the recommended Zona 10 cafés. For dinner, enjoy fusion cuisine at **Tamarindos** or **Jake's,** considered by *Travel + Leisure* magazine to be among the best restaurants in Latin America. You can also have dinner at **El Portal del Ángel** in the hills on the outskirts of town overlooking the city.

ANTIGUA

Be sure to eat at least one meal at **Mesón Panza Verde,** known for its phenomenal cuisine and wonderful atmosphere among baroque arches.

If you enjoy golfing (and even if you don't), head 20 kilometers outside of Antigua to **La Reunión Antigua Golf Resort** overlooking the Pacific Coast and in the shadow of four volcanoes. You won't want to leave, so plan on spending the night in one of the *Suites Gran Clase,* with a private infinity-edge plunge pool and views of Agua and Pacaya Volcanoes. When there's no reason to leave such a beautiful room, room service comes in handy.

LAKE ATITLÁN

My favorite Lake Atitlán hotel is **Casa Palopó,** just outside the village of Santa Catarina Palopó and overlooking the lake. Leave your cares behind and enjoy the excellent service, allowing plenty of time to watch the light change on the volcanoes or the wind dance across the lake throughout the day. If you've got the cash, rent out the entire **Villa Palopó,** higher up the hill. For a change of setting, stay at the lovely **Laguna Lodge** or **Villa Sumaya,** in Santa Cruz La Laguna.

THE PACIFIC COAST

On the ninth terrace of Takalik Abaj, **Takalik Maya Lodge** gives you the option of staying in quaint jungle cottages painted with yellow and green frescoes or on a converted coffee farmhouse overlooking a swimming pool and a coffee-drying patio. Explore the ruins by tractor-pulled trailer from the lodge. If you want to see Guatemala's version of Disney World, check out the well-executed **Xocomil** and **Xetulul** theme parks and stay across the street in the excellent **Hostal Palajunoj,** where you can choose among African, Indonesian, Mayan, and Southeast Asian-style accommodations. Eat at **Restaurante Kapa Hapa** overlooking the swimming pools. The Pacific Coast's most stylish digs are at **Dos Mundos Pacific Resort,** featuring cabanas with the feel of an exclusive Mexican beach villa. Along the road from Monterrico to neighboring Iztapa are the exclusive **Villa Los Cabos** condominiums, where you can rent a villa overlooking the enormous horseshoe-shaped swimming pool and the sea.

IZABAL

For the ultimate private getaway, head up the Río Tatín, a tributary of the Río Dulce, to **Rancho Corozal,** a sumptuous thatched-roof private villa beautifully furnished and decorated. Use the skiff to explore the surrounding jungle rivers or simply relax in the hammock lounge with a good book.

PETÉN

La Lancha, owned by movie director Francis Ford Coppola, is Petén's most exclusive hideaway. It enjoys a magnificent location on the shores of Lake Petén Itzá. Simply lounge by the pool overlooking the turquoise lake waters and beautiful jungle.

in the country is this striking contrast of wealth and poverty so evident. Look at a visit to Guatemala City as a glimpse into the country's culture, history, and politics, and a worthy introduction to a fascinating country of contrasts with unexpected surprises around every corner.

HISTORY

Guatemala City is in fact the fourth capital of Guatemala, the other three having been destroyed by natural disasters, including earthquakes and mudslides, or having been replaced by the establishment of Spanish-modeled urban centers, as in the case of the first highland capital Iximché. Like Iximché, the land now occupied by the modern-day urban center was once the site of a Mayan city that exercised considerable influence over trade routes for obsidian during Classic Mayan times thanks to an alliance with the Central Mexican powerhouse of Teotihuacán. Kaminaljuyú, as the city was called, was first settled sometime around 400 B.C. The early foundational cultures preceding the Mayan city established agriculture in the valley now occupied by Guatemala City and settled much of it, mostly in the western part of the valley. As with the other Classic Mayan sites, Kaminaljuyú was just a distant memory by the time the Spanish arrived on the scene in the 16th century.

The city's modern settlement dates to 1776, in the aftermath of the 1773 earthquakes of Santa Marta, which rocked the previous capital, now known as La Antigua Guatemala (The Old Guatemala, or "La Antigua" for short). Debate over whether or not to rebuild La Antigua raged on for a few years, but in the end it was decided to start all over again in the neighboring Valle de la Ermita (Valley of the Hermitage), as the valley was known. An edict by Governor Martín Mayorga made the move official. It took a while for the new capital to catch on, as many Antigua residents refused

to move despite Spanish decrees ordering the settlement of the new city. In 1800, the population of Guatemala City was only 25,000. The new city was laid out in a grid pattern, much like every other town established by the Spanish, with the construction of major public buildings including the Catedral Metropolitana (cathedral), Cabildo (Town Hall), and Palacio de los Capitanes Generales. Of these, only the cathedral remains standing.

In addition to resistance from Antigueños (residents of Antigua), the city's growth would be stifled by competition from the large highland urban center of Quetzaltenango. Indeed, it even threatened at one time to secede from Guatemala and become the capital of a new territory known as "Los Altos." In the end, however, nature took care of its secessionist dreams by dealing the city a massive blow with a 1902 earthquake that left it in ruins. Though it would be reconstructed, many of the city's wealthy elite opted to move to Guatemala City. The new capital would also experience its own series of destructive earthquakes in December 1917, lasting into February of the following year. By this time, it seems, the population had come to terms with the fact that its city was built upon one of the world's most active fault lines. The fault line would again create widespread havoc with another earthquake in 1976. Ironically, the earthquake triggered widescale migration into the city, resulting in the establishment of many slums lining the city's numerous ravines, or *barrancos*.

The city grew tremendously throughout the 20th century, spreading from its original core (now known as the Centro Histórico) and spilling out into the surrounding barrancos and up into the mountains lining the western and eastern edges of the valley. Much of the country's industry is concentrated here, fueling economic migration from other parts of the country. The population of Guatemala City's metro area now reaches over three million.

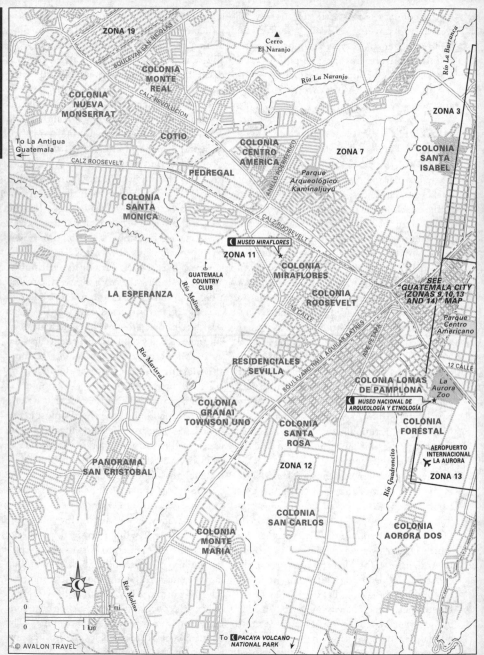

ZONA 19

BOULEVAR SAN NICOLAS

Cerro
El Naranjo

Río La Barranca

COLONIA
MONTE
REAL

CALZ REVOLUCIÓN

Río La Naranjo

ZONA 3

COLONIA
NUEVA
MONSERRAT

COTIO

To La Antigua
Guatemala

CALZ ROOSEVELT

COLONIA
CENTRO
AMERICA

ANILLO PERIFÉRICO

ZONA 7

COLONIA
SANTA
ISABEL

PEDREGAL

Parque
Arqueológico
Kaminaljuyu

COLONIA
SANTA
MONICA

CALZ ROOSEVELT

MUSEO MIRAFLORES

ZONA 11

GUATEMALA
COUNTRY
CLUB

COLONIA
MIRAFLORES

LA ESPERANZA

Río Molino

COLONIA
ROOSEVELT

1a CALLE

SEE
GUATEMALA CITY
(ZONAS 9,10,13
AND 14)" MAP

Parque
Centro
Americano

RESIDENCIALES
SEVILLA

BOULEVARD RAUL AGUILAR BATRES

AVE PETAPA

Río Marsical

12 CALLE

COLONIA LOMAS
DE PAMPLONA

La
Aurora
Zoo

COLONIA
GRANAI
TOWNSON UNO

MUSEO NACIONAL DE
ARQUEOLOGÍA Y ETNOLOGÍA

COLONIA
SANTA
ROSA

COLONIA
FORESTAL

PANORAMA
SAN CRISTOBAL

ZONA 12

Río Guadroncito

AEROPUERTO
INTERNACIONAL
LA AURORA

ZONA 13

COLONIA
SAN CARLOS

COLONIA
MONTE
MARIA

COLONIA
AURORA DOS

Río Molino

0   1 mi

0   1 km

To PACAYA VOLCANO
NATIONAL PARK

© AVALON TRAVEL

CLIMATE

Guatemala City enjoys a delightful climate almost year-round. Its location in a valley at an altitude of 1,493 meters (4,897 feet) above sea level ensures that it never gets excessively warm, as do some other, low-lying Central American capitals. This pleasant climate has earned it the nickname "Land of Eternal Spring." It should be noted, however, that the nickname was coined during a long-gone era before the city's exponential growth, which has given rise to urban microclimates such as the urban heat island. The latter is caused when the direct tropical sun heats large expanses of pavement, which in turn heat the surrounding air masses, causing a phenomenon not unlike a large convection oven. The truth is that it can get somewhat hot here during April and May, what locals generally call *verano,* or summer, with daytime highs in the mid- to upper 80s. Longtime residents frequently remark about the increasingly warm summers, which they say have become much warmer than what was once typical. This is also the driest time of year and the surrounding mountains can turn some rather parched shades of brown. Thermal inversions causing extreme haze are also quite typical this time of year, making Guatemala City look somewhat like a smaller version of Los Angeles. These occur frequently in valleys when a layer of warm air settles over a layer of cooler air lying close to the ground, holding this cooler air down and preventing pollutants from rising and scattering.

Between June and August, after the arrival of the rainy season, mornings are typically sunny and warm, giving way to increasing cloudiness and afternoon showers almost every day. September and October are increasingly rainy with entire stretches of cloudy or rainy days. In November the skies clear and become increasingly windy. Many people equate this time of year with kite flying, and indeed the giant kite festival in the nearby towns of Sumpango

and Sacatepéquez take place on the first of the month. December through February can be chilly here and elsewhere in mountainous parts of Guatemala with the arrival from the north of frequent cold fronts coinciding with the northern hemisphere's winter season. Bring some warm clothes if you're traveling to Guatemala City or elsewhere in the highlands during this time of year, as concrete houses with tile floors are the most popular form of architecture and aren't typically heated or carpeted, making it feel even colder.

PLANNING YOUR TIME

Upon international arrival into Guatemala, most travelers eager to make their way to the country's fascinating interior head straight to Antigua Guatemala, taking a shuttle bus from the airport and bypassing Guatemala City altogether. Whether at the beginning or end of your trip, a visit to the country's capital is crucial to understanding what makes this country tick. It is certainly worth spending some time here and it can be an extremely rewarding destination after weeks spent in the countryside, offering fine restaurants, excellent museums, and all the comforts that a modern capital city has to offer. Guatemala City is also the country's transportation and business hub, so if you are trying to get around the country or are in Guatemala on business, you will find yourself on its streets sooner or later.

Most of the major attractions can be seen in a day or two. If you have more than two days to spend in Guatemala City, you might consider staying in Antigua to make better use of your time. Exceptions to this would be those in town for business looking for things to do after hours without taking a trip out of the city. Zona 10, conveniently near the airport, has some fine hotels and is home to a number of highly recommended museums. It is also one of the city's most attractive commercial and financial districts. A day strolling down pleasant Avenida La

© AL ARGUETA

Zona 10 is Guatemala City's financial district.

Reforma and sampling the Zona Viva's cafés, bars, nightclubs, and restaurants is a great way to cap off your visit to Guatemala.

ORIENTATION

Guatemala City's sprawl occupies about 400 square kilometers, filling a large valley scarred by deep ravines (known locally as *barrancos*) and surrounded by mountains and volcanoes. Its terrain gives the city a patchwork kind of feel when viewed from the air, with parts of the city meandering fingerlike into the scarred landscape. The urban sprawl has also started migrating east and west into surrounding mountains. A large plateau atop the mountains abutting the city to the east is traversed by the Carretera a El Salvador (Road to El Salvador) and is one of the fastest-growing suburban sectors. The surrounding landscape is accentuated by the presence of active Pacaya volcano, often visible at night, to the south. To the southwest, the cones of Agua, Fuego, and

Acatenango volcanoes can be seen rising above the mountain separating Guatemala City from neighboring Antigua Guatemala.

The city itself is divided into 21 zones, or *zonas*. Only a few of these hold any interest for the foreign visitor or resident. Zonas 1 and 2 encompass the downtown sector, with Zona 4 serving as a kind of transition zone between the original city core and newer business and residential sectors. Zona 10 harbors the homes of wealthy elite, high-rise condominiums, hotels, restaurants, nightclubs, banks, and embassies. Moving south and abutting the airport, Zona 14 is home to a large concentration of wealthy neighborhoods and high-rise condos. To the east and heading up the slopes of surrounding mountainsides lie residential Zonas 15, 16, and Carretera a El Salvador. Several of the city's *zonas* are separated from each other by natural boundaries, such as forested *barrancos*.

Unlike Managua or San José, street addresses are very much in use here. Pay special attention when looking for street addresses, as the same street and house number can exist in more than one *zona*. Addresses usually begin with an avenue, or *avenida,* followed by a number with a dash. A typical street address would be something like: 7a Avenida 8-34 Zona 10. In this case, the "8" corresponds to the intersecting street number, or *calle.* The number after the dash is the house number. So the above address would be house number 34 between Eighth and Ninth Streets along 7th Avenue of Zona 10.

SAFETY

Guatemala City can be dodgy, though certain *zonas* are certainly safer than others. Most of the areas frequented by tourists are relatively safe, though the downtown area is considerably less safe than Zonas 10 and 14 and purse snatching and pickpocketing are serious problems. Exercise common sense and caution when in public areas. Riding public buses is not usually a good idea, though the newer Transmetro mass transit system has proven safer and is certainly more efficient. Transmetro buses are bright green and not to be confused with the Transurbano bus system (similar to the municipal buses).

Pay careful attention when using ATMs. Some thieves have been so ingenious as to set up keypads at the entrance to ATM kiosks asking cardholders to enter their PIN numbers in order to gain access to the machine. You should never enter your PIN number anywhere other than on the ATM keypad itself.

Watch out for another common scam, particularly in the vicinity of the airport, whereby a "Good Samaritan" informs you of a flat tire on your car. If that is indeed the case, pull over in a well-lighted, public place if you can but do not stop in the middle of the road to change the tire. He may try to carjack you. If you are able to make it to a public place such as a gas station, have someone in your party stay inside the car while another checks all four tires. If a tire is indeed flat, stay inside of or close to your car while someone changes the tire for you (it's common for gas station attendants to change tires in Guatemala). The important thing is not to lose sight of the inside of your vehicle for a moment. Thieves can be extremely crafty at distracting you and getting into your car while you take care of the urgent business at hand. Locked doors may be a deterrent but are not going to stop the thieves if they've targeted you. For information on other precautions and common scams to watch out for while traveling in Guatemala, see the State Department's Consular Information Sheet online at http://travel.state.gov.

Sights

Sights are listed by city zone, the official format for divvying up the city's land area. Most of the city's historic sites are found within the Centro Histórico. Some of the nicer museums are found near the airport in Zona 13 and in the Miraflores area west of the city center in Zona 11.

CENTRO HISTÓRICO

The original core of Guatemala City, dating to its foundation, is composed of 1a to 17 Calle and 1a to 12 Avenida, known today as the Centro Histórico. Most of the architecture is neoclassical, a sharp departure from the baroque architecture found in the previous capital of Antigua Guatemala. Few of the original buildings remain, having largely been destroyed by earthquakes in 1917 and 1976 or modified with the passing of time. Yet some excellent examples of the original architecture can still be found and there is an ongoing

THE FEEL AND VIBE OF GUATEMALA CITY

Your first glimpse of Guatemala City will most likely come from the window of an aircraft flying overhead in preparation of landing at La Aurora International Airport. Guatemala City tends to feel huge when first seen from the air. It might also feel quite intimidating and downright scary, depending on whether or not people have told you horror stories about the city's crime or its pollution and noise. While crime, pollution, and noise cannot be denied, you've made it this far, so you should probably check things out for yourself and see it through your own eyes.

Guatemala City is in fact quite large. It is Central America's largest city, with an approximate metro area population approaching four million inhabitants. The capital lies spread out across a broad valley surrounded by mountains and volcanoes and crisscrossed by ravines. Its setting is really quite spectacular. The good news concerning the city's size is that you really have no reason to venture into more than about a third of the city's area. Much of the sprawl composing the sizable metro area is found outside the official city limits and is composed of Guatemalan working-class subdivisions, industrial parks, and slums. The nicer parts of town are also conveniently located adjacent to each other, in the eastern third of the city near the airport. The downtown core lies to the north of the city's newer sectors.

Perhaps most fascinating about Guatemala City are the constant juxtapositions evidencing this vibrant capital's status as a microcosm of Guatemala's larger wealth and class disparities. Tin-roofed shacks cling to forested hillsides just out of view from the wooden decks of $500,000 homes. Buses trundle slowly down tree-lined boulevards while late-model BMWs zip by in the passing lane. Mayans from the highlands dressed in traditional garb wait for these buses under steel-and-glass bus stop shelters advertising French perfumes.

If you're coming from elsewhere in Central America or have been there recently (especially San José and Managua), you may be surprised to find that locations here have actual street addresses as opposed to general directions such as, "two blocks north of the pink church across from the house with purple bougainvillea." Guatemala City also tends to feel more like a real city and not an overgrown town (sorry, San José), with actual buildings occupying a somewhat impressive portion of the urban sprawl. These buildings house condos, banks, hotels, and office buildings, giving the city a very modern feel. You'll see Guatemala's well-to-do frequenting the cafés, bars, restaurants, and hotels found in these sectors, along with travelers and foreign residents. Guatemalans love to be seen dining out in fine restaurants and shopping at exclusive stores for the latest fashions.

A darker side of Guatemala City's flashy displays of wealth is the shotgun-toting guards you'll find stationed outside of banks, gas stations, and fast food franchises. The congregating of suit-wearing bodyguards outside gyms, restaurants, and private schools would be downright comical were it not such a flagrant reminder of the specter of extortionary kidnapping. And then there's the barbed wire—lots of it—and iron bars adorning many of the city's houses, which lie bunkered away in cordoned-off neighborhoods guarded by access gates staffed by security personnel. It all takes some getting used to, but we're fairly adaptable as a species.

Good or bad, love it or hate it, Guatemala City is what it is. If it all gets to be too much, just head up into the hills east of the city and look at it from above. It seems a lot more peaceful that way, framed by low-lying clouds and its gorgeous volcanic backdrop. Spend a few minutes picking out your favorite locations and seeing how many different parts of the city you can identify. It's a sight for sore eyes, believe me.

GUATEMALA CITY (ZONAS 1 AND 4)

ZONA 1

ZONA 2

ZONA 3

CENTRO HISTÓRICO

To Escuipulas, Cobán, Quiriguá, Livingston, and Copán

To Parque Minerva

EL CERRITO DEL CARMEN ★

PALACIO NACIONAL DE LA CULTURA

CATEDRAL METROPOLITANA ★

PARQUE CENTRAL ★

MERCADO CENTRAL ★

LIM CANOLA ■

MUSEO NACIONAL DE HISTORIA ★

TRANSPORTES ZACULEU FUTURA ■

IGLESIA SAN MIGUEL DE CAPUCHINAS ★

IGLESIA SANTO DOMINGO ■

PENSIÓN MEZA ■

POSADA BELÉN ●

PORTAL DEL COMERCIO LAS CIEN PUERTAS ★

CONGRESO DE LA REPÚBLICA ★

PALACIO DE CORREOS ■

HOTEL SPRING ●

MUSEO DEL MÚSICO INVISIBLE ■

CASA MIMA ★

EL PORTAL ▼

LOS CEBOLLINES ▼

REILLY'S ▼ GUATE CITY ■

HOTEL ROYAL PALACE ●

IGLESIA DE SAN FRANCISCO ♦

CUARTEL DE POLICÍA NACIONAL ■

HOTEL COLONIAL ●

PICCADILLY ▼

ARRIN CUAN ▼

LA CASA DE CERVANTES ▼

PARQUE CENTENARIO ↑

BIBLIOTECA NACIONAL ●

RESTAURANTE REY SOL ▼

EUROPA BAR ▼

ALTUNA ▼ EL GRAN PAVO ▼

LONG WAH ▼

CAFÉ DE IMERI ▼

EL GAZABO ▼

METROPOLE ▼

ARCHIVO GENERAL DE CENTROAMÉRICA ■

HOTEL PAN AMERICAN ●

BLUE TOWN ■

LAVANDERÍA EL SIGLO ■

CAFETERÍA PATSY ★

HOTEL QUALITY SERVICE ■

LA BODEGUITA DEL CENTRO ■

PASEO DE LA SEXTA

Parque Concordia

AVENIDA ELENA

AVENIDA ELENA

17 AVENIDA
16 AVENIDA
15 AVENIDA
15 AVENIDA (AVENIDA DE LOS ÁRBOLES)
14 AVENIDA
CALLE DE LAS TURCHEZ
5A CALLE
7A CALLE
8A CALLE
AVENIDA DE CANDELARIA
DIAGONAL 4
1A CALLE
2A CALLE
1A CALLE
12 AVENIDA
11 AVENIDA
10 AVENIDA A
10A AVENIDA
9A AVENIDA
8A AVENIDA
7A AVENIDA
6A AVENIDA
5A AVENIDA
4A AVENIDA
2A AVENIDA
1A AVENIDA A
1A AVENIDA
10A AVENIDA
9A CALLE
8A CALLE
7A CALLE
12 CALLE
11 CALLE
13 CALLE
14 CALLE
10A CALLE
11 CALLE
1A CALLE
2A CALLE
3A CALLE
4A CALLE
7A CALLE
6A CALLE
5A CALLE
7A CALLE
3A AVENIDA

GUATEMALA CITY

© AVALON TRAVEL

campaign to restore several historic buildings in the downtown core. This program, known as RenaCENTRO, is a collaboration between several entities, including the local municipality, INGUAT, the private sector, and Argentinean, Spanish, and French cooperation.

Guatemala City was once nicknamed "The Silver Teacup" for its urban Spanish Renaissance design and architecture, including elegant theaters, large colonial mansions, broad avenues, imposing churches, and charming side streets. Although they have aesthetically deteriorated, they are not beyond rescue. This is precisely RenaCENTRO's mission: a multifaceted, holistic approach to restoring the grandeur of Guatemala's colonial-era capital. The restoration inexorably hinges upon local economic reactivation. Given Guatemala's huge tourism potential, it seems only fitting that its capital would become a welcome stop along the visitor's path, although restoration remains an ongoing process.

Parque Central

In typical Spanish colonial fashion, the city was laid out around a central plaza with a Catholic church and government buildings surrounding it. It is also known as the Plaza de la Constitución. The central park encompasses a large area between 6a and 7a Avenidas and 6a and 8a Calles. Alongside it are the Palacio Nacional de la Cultura, Catedral Metropolitana, and Portal del Comercio. The park is usually abuzz with shoe shiners and folks enjoying a stroll through its grounds, now largely composed of concrete blocks with little greenery after being remodeled in the mid-1980s to include an underground parking lot. A large Guatemalan flag dominates the plaza near a small, sadly neglected monument to the 1996 peace accords; it consists of a glass case that once enclosed a flame, which has long since burned out. South of the park, heading towards 9a Calle is **Portal del Comercio,** a

commercial arcade recently restored as part of RenaCENTRO's ongoing gentrification projects. Novena Calle itself (between 6a and 7a Avenidas) has also been restored as a pedestrian thoroughfare known as Pasaje Aycinena.

【 Palacio Nacional de la Cultura

Boston's Fenway Park has its Green Monster and so does Guatemala City. The former presidential palace, built between 1939 and 1943 during the time of maniacal dictator Jorge Ubico, is a large, green stone structure with elements of colonial and neoclassical architecture. The 1996 peace accords between the government and URNG guerillas were signed here and the building was subsequently converted into a museum (tel. 2230-1020, 9 A.M.-noon and 2-5 P.M. daily, $5). It is also sometimes used to host visiting dignitaries such as former President George W. Bush and actor Mel Gibson. With most of Guatemala's presidents preferring to live in other parts of the city, it has not housed a president during a term in office since the early 1990s.

The palace is one of Guatemala City's most interesting attractions, as it affords the visitor a glimpse into Guatemala's colonial and dictatorial legacy. After all, Guatemala City was once the capital of the entire Central American isthmus and nowhere else in the region were colonial institutions so embedded in the national fiber. Similarly, Guatemala's *caudillos* (military strongmen) needed a residence befitting their status as rulers of a quasifeudal kingdom, to which end the palace served them quite well.

You can take a guided tour of the palace so as to better appreciate the intriguing architecture, including some Moorish courtyards, frescoed arches made of carved stone, and artwork by several Guatemalan artists of the 1940s. As you climb the wood-and-brass main stairway, you can admire a mural by Alredo Gálvez Suárez depicting a romanticized take on Guatemalan history. Stained-glass windows by Julio Urruela

Vásquez and Roberto González Goyri can be found in the second-floor banquet hall adorning the palace; they depict the virtues of good government. You might also be able to see the presidential balcony, which overlooks the plaza in classic dictatorial fashion.

A more modern-day attraction is the Patio de la Paz, where a stone sculpture of two hands commemorates the 1996 signing of the peace accords. A white rose held in the outstretched hands is changed at 11 A.M. daily by the palace guards or, on special occasions, by visiting dignitaries.

Catedral Metropolitana

The construction of Guatemala City's neoclassical cathedral (7a Avenida facing the plaza, 6 A.M.-noon and 2-7 P.M.) began in 1782 and was completed in 1815, though the bell towers would not be completed until 1867. It has survived two earthquakes, a testament to its

sturdy construction, though it isn't exactly the prettiest of Guatemala's churches. The pillars on the church's facade are adorned with the names of many of Guatemala's disappeared, etched into the stone as a testament to the desire for justice, whether in this lifetime or the next. Inside, many of the altars and paintings adorning the church were brought here forcefully when the capital, along with its institutions, was officially moved to its current site from Antigua. The standout is the image of the Virgen del Perpetuo Socorro, Guatemala's oldest, brought into the country by Pedro de Alvarado in 1524.

Parque Centenario

Adjoining the larger central plaza, to the west, is the smaller Parque Centenario, with the Biblioteca Nacional (National Library) and Archivo General de Centroamérica (National Archive) bordering it. It occupies the former site

© NATHAN GOLDEN

Guatemala City's Catedral Metropolitana

of the Palacio Centenario, built to commemorate 100 years of independence from Spain. It briefly housed the National Congress, whose building was burned to the ground in 1927. Its most interesting feature is a small acoustic shell amphitheater.

Mercado Central

Behind the cathedral is the city's central market (8a Avenida and 6a Calle, 6 A.M.-6 P.M. Mon.-Sat., 9 A.M.-noon Sun.). The basement harbors produce, while the top two floors have a varied assortment of textiles, leather goods, and various handicrafts. It's a bit dark and bunkerlike, with the stalls packed to the ceiling with all kinds of goodies. It's a bit overwhelming. The current market replaced the one destroyed by the 1976 earthquake. Be wary of pickpockets here.

Paseo de la Sexta

Historically, Sexta Avenida, otherwise known as "La Sexta," was the place to see and be seen. It was Guatemala City's most important thoroughfare, where the latest European fashions and luxury goods could be purchased from shops owned by Jewish, Spanish, and German immigrants. As the city expanded and its well-to-do moved south to Zonas 9, 10, and 13 during the 1970s, Sexta Avenida began a long, downward spiral.

As mentioned before, the downtown core of Guatemala City's historic Zona 1 has undergone urban renewal for some time now. In 2010 this process included the relocation of street vendors from the city's Sexta Avenida, at that time a disorganized mess choked by car traffic and sidewalks lined with street vendors hawking everything from pirated DVDs to knock-off designer sunglasses. Today, the car traffic is gone and Sexta Avenida, along ten blocks from the city's Plaza Central south to 18 Calle, has been re-named Paseo de la Sexta.

© AL ARGUETA

pedestrians along Sexta Avenida

An ongoing process, it has yielded remodeled art deco buildings, new lighting, sculptures, and a smattering of new cafés.

Although the area is much touted by the local media, don't expect to find a hip, trendy, and completely revamped downtown core. You also won't find cool streetside cafés or many good restaurants. This is Guatemala City, not Mexico City, and it's clear the wealthy prefer to stick to other parts of town. While you might expect to find new, slightly more upscale shops to line the newly upgraded streets of this pedestrian thoroughfare, the truth is the same shops continue to exist in slightly upgraded surroundings. If you're staying downtown, Paseo de la Sexta is worth a stop, but it's not exactly a popular attraction with foreign travelers. It is very much the haunt of working-class Guatemalans on weekends. It's still not the safest part of town for a stroll, so be extra careful if you do venture out this way, as it's known for assorted riffraff.

7a Avenida

Paralleling 6a Avenida is 7a Avenida, with a variety of architectural highlights. Among these is the splendid **Palacio de Correos** (Central Post Office, 8:30 A.M.-5 P.M. Mon.-Fri., 8:30 A.M.-1 P.M. Sat.), at the corner of 7a Avenida and 12 Calle, featuring a large archway that reaches over to the building across the street. Also attractive is the nearby **Tipografía Nacional** (National Printing Press), at the corner of 7a Avenida and 18 Calle. It dates to 1894 and somewhat resembles a gingerbread house.

Both 6a and 7a Avenidas continue their straight course southward through Zonas 4 and 9 before ending at a series of archways marking the northern extreme of the airport runway.

Museums

One block east of the market and one block south on 10a Avenida is the **Museo Nacional de Historia** (9a Calle 9-70 Zona 1, tel. 2253-6149,

9 A.M.-4:30 P.M. Mon.-Fri., $1.50) with historical documents, clothing, and paintings. Among the more interesting exhibits are some photographs by Eadweard Muybridge, who visited and photographed the country in 1875. The museum is housed in a very attractive colonial building.

Casa Mima (8a Avenida 14-12 Zona 1, tel. 2253-4020, 9 A.M.-12:30 P.M. and 2-6 P.M. Mon.-Fri., 9 A.M.-5 P.M. Sat., $2.50) offers a fascinating peek into the lives of Guatemala's upper middle class from generations past. The splendidly restored 19th-century townhouse is furnished in art deco, Victorian, and French neo-rococo styles. A quaint café on the back patio serves coffee and pastries. English-speaking guides are sometimes available to show you around.

La Casa de Cervantes (5a Calle 5-18 Zona 1, tel. 2232-5696, www.lacasadecervantes.com) showcases fair trade goods in Guatemala and has a gift shop, where you can purchase fair trade coffee, handicrafts, and other products. It also has periodic exhibitions and special events. It's more of an information and cultural center than a museum but is certainly worth a look.

Train enthusiasts will enjoy **Museo del Ferrocarril** (in front of the intersection of 9a Avenida and 20 Calle, tel. 2232-9270, ferroguat@hotmail.com, 9 A.M.-5 P.M. Tues.-Fri., 10 A.M.-5 P.M. Sat.-Sun., free), housed in a refurbished building that was once the city's train station. The state-run railways, known then as FEGUA, were privatized during the Arzú administration. Among the attractions are several steam engines, train cars, and exhibits of train paraphernalia, including some wonderful old photographs. Some cool classic cars are also on display here.

The city's newest and most offbeat museum is the **Museo del Músico Invisible** (Museum of the Invisible Musician, 13 Calle 7-30, Zona 1, 9 A.M.-6 P.M. Mon.-Fri., 9 A.M.-1 P.M. Sat., $2.50 adults, $2 students and children). The brainchild of Germán Rodríguez, the museum is the realization of a dream 15 years in the making and the product of a lifelong collection of antique musical instruments that began when Rodríguez was 11 years old. Among the items on display are harmoniums from the 1840s and '50s, phonographs, music boxes, player pianos, and antique radios. Most were acquired in Guatemala, though some were brought over from neighboring Mexico. Facilities include a theater for viewing movies or listening to musical performances. Rodríguez says he has many more instruments in his collection than what is on display and periodically changes the museum's exhibits.

Churches

Several of the city's downtown churches have been restored in recent years and might be worth a stop to admire their noteworthy architecture. Construction on **Iglesia de San Francisco** (6a Avenida and 13 Calle Zona 1, 7 A.M.-noon and 2-7 P.M.) began in 1800 and wasn't completed until 1851. Its charming light gray exterior has been worn down by the elements; inside are 18 altars of impressive quality. Another beautiful church is that of **Iglesia Santo Domingo** (12 Avenida and 10a Calle), constructed between 1792 and 1808. In addition to its attractive architecture, it is known for its paintings, including one depicting the apparition of the Virgin Mary to Santo Domingo de Guzmán, after whom the capital of the Dominican Republic is named. (It is believed he received the rosary from her.) **El Cerrito del Carmen** (12 Avenida and 2a Calle Zona 1, 7 A.M.-noon and 2-6 P.M.) denominates both the name of this hermitage and the hill on which it rests, with wonderful views of the downtown area. It dates to 1620 and is known for its image of a virgin of the same name embossed in silver, a gift from Carmelite nuns in the 17th century. Oil paintings by Tomás de Merlo adorn the inside of **Iglesia San Miguel**

de Capuchinas (10 Avenida 10-51 Zona 1, 6 A.M.-noon and 2-7 P.M.), with its transitional baroque-neoclassical architecture.

ZONA 2
Parque Minerva

As you head north along 6a Avenida and then Avenida Simeón Cañas, it's about 1.5 kilometers from the city center to Parque Minerva in the adjoining Zona 2 sector. The park here has some sporting facilities, including the **Estadio Nacional de Béisbol** (National Baseball Stadium), where there are games on weekends. Its informal atmosphere is a bit like that of old-time minor league parks in the U.S. Midwest. Baseball is nowhere near as popular in Guatemala as in other parts of Central America, namely Nicaragua, but if you're a fan of the game you might want to stop and check it out.

The park's main attraction, however, is also one of Guatemala's most unusual. The 2,000-square-meter **Mapa en Relieve** (Relief Map, 9 A.M.-5 P.M. daily, $2), is built to 1:10,000 scale and was created in 1905, well before the invention of Google Earth. It gives you a good idea of the country's mountain topography and the contrasting flatness of Petén and neighboring Belize, which, of course, is included as part of Guatemala in accord with the long-standing border dispute. The scale of the mountains is somewhat exaggerated, with the volcanoes and peaks looking steep and pointy. There are observation towers from which you can get a better vantage point. The rivers and lakes are sometimes filled with water from built-in taps, making for an even more authentic experience. It makes a good stop if you're in Guatemala City before heading out to the interior and want to get a feel for the country's unique geography.

ZONA 4

A revitalization program has given Zona 4 a distinct character in recent years with the establishment of a pedestrian thoroughfare known as 4 Grados Norte, lined with sidewalk cafés and restaurants during the day, doubling as bars at night. While it was a good idea in theory, it soon attracted a motley assortment of drug dealers and local riffraff. The restaurants and bars have mostly closed their doors, but the area is enjoying a renaissance as a center for technology-based businesses. The *New York Times* compared it to Silicon Valley in a 2011 story featuring the area's Campus Tec building. Plans are under way for a second building with three times the space.

The **Centro Cultural de España** (Vía 5 1-23 Zona 4, 4 Grados Norte, tel. 2385-9066 or 2385-9067, www.centroculturalespana.com. gt, 9:30 A.M.-1 P.M. and 2-7 P.M. Tues.-Thurs., 10 A.M.-7 P.M. Sat.) shows movies on Tuesday and Friday nights, hosts workshops and art exhibits, and has a small library.

Zona 4's other main attraction is a dilapidated bus terminal for second-class buses, though this was expected to fall into disuse with the municipal government's plans to move all bus traffic out of the city.

Centro Cívico

As you head south from the downtown sectors of Zonas 1 and 2, you'll come to a transitional area between the old city core and some of the newer parts of town. Some guidebooks refer to the latter as the "new city," which to the best of my knowledge has never been used by locals to describe their city layout. As the city spread south from the central area, urban planners and architects decided to build around a concept of a civic center to house some of the more important government buildings. Thus was born the Centro Cívico. Today it houses Guatemala's **Corte Suprema de Justicia** (Supreme Court), **Banco de Guatemala** (Bank of Guatemala), **Municipalidad de Guatemala** (City Hall), and the administrative offices of the **Guatemala Tourist Commission** (7a Avenida 1-17 Zona 4,

8 A.M.-4 P.M. Mon.-Fri.). There's the occasional exhibit in the lobby and you can get some tourist information, including maps, but you're probably better off picking these up at the information kiosks at the international airport.

Centro Cultural Miguel Ángel Asturias

Inaugurated in 1968 and named after Guatemala's Nobel Prize-winning author, the capital's national theater is built on a hill once harboring the fort of San José de Buena Vista, destroyed by artillery fire during the October Revolution of 1944. It consists of a **Gran Sala** (Great Theater) with a seating capacity of 2,041, an outdoor amphitheater seating 2,500, the 320-seat **Teatro de Cámara** (Chamber Theater), and several smaller venues. It has some interesting architecture designed by architect Efrín Recinos, and its hilltop location overlooking the rest of the civic center gives it an air of grandeur. The center still hosts frequent events, including ballet and theater productions. Check local listings for more information.

Iglesia Yurrita

This pretty rose-colored neo-Gothic chapel with ornate decor inside and out is one of Guatemala City's more quirky tourist attractions. It was commissioned by don Felipe Yurrita Castañeda, a wealthy Spaniard, as a thank-you offering to Our Lady of Anguish for sparing his life and that of his family in the 1902 eruption of Santa María volcano, which blanketed areas in rock and ash near his San Marcos coffee farm. It was completed in 1941 just five months before his death. Situated at Ruta 6 8-52 and usually open to the public (8 A.M.-noon and 3-6 P.M. Tues.-Sun.), it reflects an interesting mishmash of architectural styles that were in vogue at the time. Note the interesting crooked cross at top. A recent addition to the property is Restaurante Casa Yurrita (tel. 2360-1615).

kite-flying over a Kaminaljuyú temple mound

ZONA 7
Parque Arqueológico Kaminaljuyú
This Mayan site occupied the valley where Guatemala City now stands. It was first settled sometime around 400 B.C. and grew to house an abundance of flat-topped pyramids (with the remains of nobility buried underneath) by A.D. 100. The first inhabitants of the site appear to have been some early cultures (Las Charcas, Miraflores, and Esperanza, dating from 1500 B.C. to A.D. 150), which developed a foundation for the later development of the Classic Mayan culture here. These early cultures are characterized by the development of agriculture, weaving, pottery making, and ritual burial of the dead in temple mounds and shrines. Central to the city's rapid population growth was the development of a series of irrigation canals drawing upon the ancient lake of Miraflores. Eventually the lake began to dry out, leading to widespread migration out of the city. Its Chol-speaking inhabitants are thought

to have moved on to El Salvador and maybe even Copán, Honduras. The site's historical record fades out (momentarily) sometime between the 2nd and 3rd centuries A.D.

With the rise of Central Mexico's Teotihuacán in the 5th century, the Guatemalan highlands received a large influx of invaders from the north. Here the invaders established their regional capital, constructing new temples and structures, and flourished with the control of trade networks around highly prized obsidian and jade. It is thought that, along with its powerful neighbor to the north, Kaminaljuyú exercised considerable influence over the Petén lowland sites, in particular Tikal. One of Tikal's rulers, Curl Nose, may actually have come from here in A.D. 387.

The site was first excavated in 1925 and yielded potsherds and clay figurines from the early cultures. Its larger extent and importance were discovered in 1935 when a local football team uncovered a buried structure after cutting away the edges of two inconspicuous mounds to lengthen their practice field. Today the site is really no more than a series of mounds. Though the site is in Zona 7 proper, the best place to see it is actually near the Museo Miraflores in adjacent Zona 11, where you can tour the excellent museum and see some temple mounds.

ZONA 9
Part of the city's newer sector, Zona 9 adjoins Zona 4 and is crossed by 6a and 7a Avenidas. Along 7a Avenida, on 2a Calle, is an Eiffel Tower-like monument commemorating the rule of Guatemala's liberal reformer Justo Rufino Barrios (1871-1885), known as **Torre del Reformador**. Wonderfully illuminated at night with a large spinning spotlight at its top, the steel tower serves as a nice backdrop for an annual December fireworks show. A bell at top is rung every year on June 30 in remembrance of the Liberal victory in the revolution of 1871. It was a project of the Ubico administration

and was not a donation from France, as is commonly thought. The bell tower, however, was a gift from Belgium. Nearby, at the corner of 5a Calle and Avenida La Reforma is **Plaza Estado de Israel,** honoring the creation of the Jewish state with a giant Star of David sculpture.

Also along Avenida La Reforma, between 2a Calle and Calle Mariscal Cruz, is the **Jardín Botánico y Museo de Historia Natural** (Botanical Gardens and Natural History Museum, 8 A.M.-3 P.M. Mon.-Fri., 9 A.M.-noon Sat., $1.50), managed by the Universidad de San Carlos. It's really only recommendable for the botanical gardens, which offer a nice respite from the chaotic traffic just beyond its walls. The plant species are all labeled in Spanish and Latin. Give the natural history museum a skip unless you're really into bad taxidermy.

At 7a Avenida and 12 Calle is the **Plazuela España,** a circular miniplaza circumvented by traffic and featuring a pretty fountain built in honor of Spain's King Carlos III in 1789. It originally was in the city's central park, where it had a large equestrian statue that disappeared shortly after independence from Spain. Its current location was a move by the Ubico administration. Some very attractive tile benches are on the sidewalks opposite the fountain.

ZONA 10
Avenida La Reforma

Running between 1a Calle and 20 Calle, Avenida La Reforma is a classic example of the 19th-century trend, common throughout Latin America's major capitals, of emulating French architectural and urban design with wide, tree-lined boulevards adorned with statues. This broad thoroughfare separates Zonas 9 and 10 and features some of the city's better hotels, cafés, and restaurants along its path. The wide, grassy median contains some interesting sculptures and makes a great place for a stroll. La Reforma culminates at the spacious **Parque Obelisco,** featuring a large obelisk, a gigantic Guatemalan flag, palm trees, a fountain, and sitting areas.

❰ Zona Viva

Within Zona 10, east of Avenida La Reforma all the way to 6a Avenida and running north to south from 10a Calle to 16 Calle, the Zona Viva is Guatemala City's most pleasant commercial district, with a variety of hip cafés, trendy boutiques, lively bars and nightclubs, excellent restaurants, and expensive hotels. It's Guatemala City at its best and after long periods in the country's hinterlands, it can be downright refreshing.

Unlike in downtown Guatemala City, you'll find plenty of trees sheltering the streets from the harsh tropical sun in addition to wide, pedestrian-friendly sidewalks. Zona Viva's many high-rise buildings harbor banks, office buildings, the bulk of Guatemala City's international hotel chain properties, and condominiums. None of these buildings is more than 20 stories high, as the airport's proximity limits vertical expansion of the adjacent areas, giving the neighborhood a cosmopolitan feel without the claustrophobic concrete-jungle look found in larger international cities. Interspersed between office buildings are the area's many dining and entertainment options and tucked away into the side streets are some of Guatemala's nicest residences sheltered behind walls, barbed wire, and bougainvillea.

During the day, Zona Viva's streets are mostly the haunt of businessmen because of the area's prominence as the city's main financial district. By night, especially on weekends, it becomes the enclave of young folks heading to the area's bars and nightclubs or to dinner at a fancy restaurant. If you find yourself needing to spend a night or two in Guatemala City, you might make it a very enjoyable experience by checking into one of the area's attractive boutique or international chain hotels, eating at one of the recommended local restaurants, and

GUATEMALA CITY (ZONAS 9, 10, 13, AND 14)

© AVALON TRAVEL

ZONA VIVA

10a CALLE

3a AVENIDA
4a AVENIDA

AVENIDA LA REFORMA

TAMARINDOS ▼

11 CALLE
PECORINO ▼

EDIFICIO GÉMINIS ★   OTELITO/ OLIVVADA

MERCURE CASA VERANDA ●   IGUANA AZUL ■   ■ PLAZA FONTABELLA   ■ DHL
ZUMO ▼

CHINA TOWN ▼   BEST WESTERN STOFELLA ●   BRASS BEER CO.   ▼ DON EMILIANO

RADISSON   ■ SESTO SENSO   XAMANEK
▼ SHAKESPEARE PUB   ● STUDENT INN

CHEERS ▼   13 CALLE

HOLIDAY INN ●   SAN ▼ MARTIN & CO   ▼ TRE FRATELLI   BIG MOUNTAIN   ▼
CASA ▼   DONDE MIKEL
CHAPINA   ▼ KACAO   REAL INTERCONTINENTAL
▼ THRIFTY   ● GUATEMALA

14 CALLE

WESTIN CAMINO REAL   INKA ▼ GRILL   FRIDAS ▼   ● HOTEL VIVA CLARION SUITES   EL ▼ ESTABLO
★ MON ASTURIAS

BILTMORE   ■ WEB STATION
EXPRESS   15 CALLE
▼ KALHUA   ■ ● SANTANDER
DELTA   PLAZA
NYX ▼   AIRLINES
RATTLE N HUM ●

16 CALLE

0   200 yds
0   200 m

© AVALON TRAVEL   DAVID CROCKETT ●

taking in one or several of the nearby museums. The recent addition of a hostel to the area's accommodations means this is no longer just an option for wealthy travelers. It is also conveniently close to the airport.

€ Museo Ixchel

The city's most magnificent museum (6a Calle Final Zona 10, tel. 2331-3739, www.museoixchel.org, 9 A.M.-5 P.M. Mon.-Fri., 9 A.M.-1 P.M. Sat., $4.50 adults, $2 students), on the grounds of the Francisco Marroquín University, is dedicated to Mayan culture with an emphasis on weaving and traditional costumes. It's housed in a beautiful brick building built to resemble a Mayan *huipil*, or hand-woven, embroidered blouse. On display are Pre-Hispanic objects, photographs, hand-woven fabrics, ceremonial costumes, weaving tools, and folk paintings by Guatemalan artist Andrés Curruchich. You'll

find interactive multimedia displays, a café, bookstore, and *huipiles* for sale in the excellent gift shop. Displays are in English and Spanish. This museum is a must-see for anyone with even a casual interest in Mayan weaving, as it manages to condense the country's rich weaving heritage spanning a fairly vast geographical range into a single place with excellent displays and an attractive setting.

Museo Popol Vuh

Next door and also on the university campus is the similarly high-caliber Museo Popol Vuh (tel. 2361-2301, www.popolvuh.ufm.edu.gt, 9 A.M.-5 P.M. Mon.-Fri., 9 A.M.-1 P.M. Sat., $3.50 adults, $2 students). Started in 1978 with a university donation by private collectors, it has been in its current location since 1997. The museum houses an impressive collection from Guatemala's archaeological record grouped in different rooms denoted by Preclassic, Classic, Postclassic, and Colonial times. The highlight is in the Postclassic room with a replica of the *Dresden Codex,* one of only three Mayan books to survive their postconquest burning by the Spanish (the other two are the Paris Codex and the Madrid Codex).

ZONA 11
€ Museo Miraflores

The excellent Museo Miraflores (7a Calle 21-55 Zona 11, Paseo Miraflores, tel. 2470-3415, 2470-3416, 2470-3417, or 2470-3418, www.mcd.gob.gt, 9 A.M.-7 P.M. Tues.-Sun., $5 adults, $1 children and students) is dedicated to the history of the Mayan site of Kaminaljuyú. Just outside the museum's main entrance is a replica of an irrigation canal similar to those found throughout the Mayan city as early as 600 B.C. Inside, the large window panels provide fantastic views of the stark contrast between old and new, with the green temple mound of structure B-V-3 flanked by modern glass buildings in the background. Also at the entrance is a scale

Zona Viva street scene

model of what the city probably looked like in its heyday, built into the museum floor under a glass case. In the main exhibit area, you'll find a comprehensive history of Kaminaljuyú in English and Spanish as well as a burial display, pottery, jade jewelry, stone sculpture, and obsidian blades. There are also old photographs of the site's excavation and maps showing the large area once occupied by the ancient city. You are free to explore the temple mounds outside (steps are built into them). A few more temple mounds can be found in the vicinity of the museum, having been completely closed in by one of the city's larger shopping complexes. Among the latter are the ever-growing Galerías Miraflores, Paseo Miraflores, and Las Majadas.

ZONA 13

This area was once the site of a large farm known as La Aurora, which today gives its name to the zoo and airport. A future phase of the airport's renovation and expansion will

supposedly bring about the creation of a city park on the grounds of what was once a horse racing track. Details on the project are sketchy but it's expected to include sporting facilities and spacious grounds for strolling.

Zona 13 also houses a number of fairly good museums, all adjacent to each other in a large complex, and the city's zoo.

La Aurora Zoo

Guatemala City's La Aurora Zoo (Boulevard Juan Pablo II Zona 13, tel. 2475-0894, http://aurorazoo.org.gt, 9 A.M.-5 P.M. Tues.-Sun., $2.50 adults, $1 children) is modern and well run. Its grounds are a popular weekend destination for city dwellers from all walks of life. About 900 animals representing 110 species are housed in re-creations of their natural habitats, including African savannah, Asia, and tropical forest. There are leopards, lions, giraffes, Asian pachyderms, Bengal tigers, and jaguars and other species found in Guatemala's tropical forests. All

© AL ARGUETA

a Maya stela on display in Guatemala City's
Archaeology Museum

cages have been removed from the park so as to
provide visitors with the opportunity to see the
animals free of visual obstructions. Check out
the English tea house dating to 1924.

Children's Museum

Right across the street is the Museo de los
Niños (5a Calle 10-00 Zona 13, tel. 2475-5076,
www.museodelosninos.com.gt, 8 A.M.-noon
and 1-5 P.M. Tues.-Thurs., 8 A.M.-noon and
2-6 P.M. Fri., 10 A.M.-1 P.M. and 2:30-6 P.M.
Sat.-Sun., $5), housed in a pyramidal building,
with educational exhibits and hands-on learning on themes such as civic values and team-
work. You'll also find a giant jigsaw puzzle of
Guatemala, a music room, and trampolines.
It's closed from mid-December to mid-January
annually, but the rest of the year makes for a
popular school field trip.

◖ Museo Nacional de Arqueología y Etnología

The city's Archaeology Museum (6a Calle y 7a
Avenida Zona 13, tel. 2475-4399, www.munae.
gob.gt, 9 A.M.-4 P.M. Tues.-Fri., 9 A.M.-noon
and 1:30-4 P.M. Sat.-Sun., $7.50) houses an
outstanding collection of original monuments
from Guatemala's archaeological sites, including ceramics, carved rock sculptures and stelae
from Kaminaljuyú, *barrigones* (Olmecoid stone
figures with distended, bloated bellies) from the
Pacific Coast sites, and stelae from the Petén
sites. Among the latter are beautifully carved
stelae and a spectacular hieroglyphic bench
from Piedras Negras as well as stelae and hieroglyphic panels from Dos Pilas and Machaquilá.
Another of the museum's highlights is a splendid jade mask made famous on the cover of the
September 1987 issue of *National Geographic*.
The ethnology section has displays on traditional costumes and housing. The displays are
not quite as modern or well executed as those in
some other of the city's top museums, but the
sheer significance of the original pieces found
here makes a visit more than worthwhile.

Museo Nacional de Arte Moderno Carlos Mérida

Across the street is the city's Museum of
Modern Art (tel. 2472-0467, 9 A.M.-4 P.M.
Tues.-Fri., 9 A.M.-noon and 1:30-4 P.M. Sat.-
Sun., $1.50), which focuses largely on the work
of its namesake artist, including examples of his
Cubist art and large murals. He's Guatemala's
most celebrated artist; his work also adorns the
inside of several buildings in Guatemala City's
Civic Center, including City Hall, with a giant
mural known as *Canto a la Raza (Ode to the
Race)*, recently restored. Among the other in-
teresting works found here is one titled *La Peste
(Pestilence)* by Rodolfo Abularach, reminiscent
of Picasso's *Guernica*.

Museo Nacional de Historia Natural Jorge Ibarra

For all of Guatemala's rich ecology, it still lacks a comprehensive natural history museum to do it justice. The Natural History Museum (tel. 2472-0468, 9 A.M.-4 P.M. Tues.-Fri., 9 A.M.-noon and 2-4 P.M. Sat.-Sun., $1.50), around the corner from the previous two, makes an attempt but falls a bit short. You'll find plenty of taxidermy as well as exhibits on several of the country's ecosystems. A standout is the photo exhibit on the Atitlán pied-billed grebe, extinct since 1987, and the attempt in the mid-20th century to save it.

ZONA 14

Guatemala City's boom district, Zona 14 has grown by leaps and bounds in recent years thanks to a plethora of new condos and office buildings built in this area. The sector's main feature is Avenida Las Américas, which is really just a continuation of Zona 9/10's Avenida La Reforma and boasts the same sylvan landscaping interspersed with monuments to Columbus and other historical figures centered around wide plazas. At the end of this avenue is a steep drop-off and Plaza Berlin, from which there are good views of the city's southern sprawl and Pacaya Volcano, along with some simple snack and drink stands. An addition to this plaza are three pieces of none other than the now-absconded Berlin Wall, with a plaque commemorating liberty.

Avenida Las Américas parallels La Aurora Airport's runway. Branching off from the main artery are a number of side streets and residential areas. Two-story houses now share these streets with 20- and 30-story commercial and residential buildings. Between the airport runway and Avenida Las Américas is Avenida Hincapié, where the hangars of some of the domestic carriers and helicopter flights are housed just off its juncture with 18 Calle.

On Sundays, a stretch from Avenida Las Américas all the way to Avenida La Reforma's Plaza Israel is closed to pedestrian traffic, making for a very pleasant place to take a stroll.

Carretera a El Salvador

From Boulevard Vista Hermosa, the road winds out of the city and up a mountainside heading southeast, eventually making its way to neighboring El Salvador. The first 35 kilometers or so of this Carretera a El Salvador are Guatemala City's suburb extraordinaire. After climbing up the mountains to the east of Guatemala City, the road eventually traverses a plateau, providing the perfect topographic conditions for the establishment of a virtual satellite city. The area around Carretera a El Salvador is also prime agricultural farmland. You'll find countless subdivisions springing up all over this fast-growing area, giving it all the feel of a U.S. suburb. The plateau lies at an altitude of about 2,135 meters (7,000 feet), so it's a bit cooler than Guatemala City and it also receives more rainfall during the rainy season. Those familiar with San José, Costa Rica, might find this area very similar to the Escazú suburbs near that city.

Although it's very much a residential area, you may find yourself visiting friends or staying at one of the hotels in this neck of the woods. Catering to the ever-increasing numbers of Guatemala City residents migrating to the surrounding suburbs, the area has at least one sizable shopping mall in Pradera Concepción, which adjoins the Condado Concepción shopping district. Between them, they boast a number of restaurants, PriceSmart warehouse shopping, WalMart, Sears, banks, car dealerships, a Starbucks, and even an IMAX movie theater. The selection of goods in local supermarkets is more upscale (with prices to match), so a lot of folks looking for favorite import items do their shopping up here. This area is also home to two of Guatemala's most upscale golf courses and one of the city's finest hotels.

ZONAS 15, 16, AND CARRETERA A EL SALVADOR

COLONIA LA LIMONADA

ZONA 5

COLONIA VIVIBIEN

16 CALLE

27 CALLE

30 CALLE

COLONIA SARAVIA

CALLE DE LOS CIPRESALES

Río Negro

COLONIA LOURDES

CALZADA HOSPITAL MILITAR

SANTA ROSITA

1A AVENIDA

CALLE REAL ACATÁN

Río Negro

3A CALLE

COLONIA TECUN UMAN

7A CALLE

MUSEO IXCHEL

MUSEO POPOL VUH

ZONA 10

METRO BOWL

BULEVAR LANDIVAR

OAKLAND MALL

COLONIA OAKLAND

18 CALLE

16 CALLE

10 CALLE

Río Negro

4A CALLE

ZONA 14

GALERÍAS LA PRADERA

WORLD GYM

BULEVAR LOS PRÓCERES

PASEO CAYALÁ

UNIVERSIDAD DEL VALLE DE GUATEMALA

COLONIA VISTA HERMOSA TRES

Riachuelo de Santa Rosita

ZONA 16

SAN ISIDRO GOLF CLUB

28 AVENIDA

COLONIA VISTA HERMOSA UNO

BULEVAR VISTA HERMOSA

ZONA 15

MARGHERITA

COLONIA VISTA HERMOSA DOS

OLIVIA

COLONIA SAN LÁZARO

PORTAL DEL ANGEL

CARRETERA A EL SALVADOR

Río Pinula

ZONA 1

SANTA CATARINA PINULA

VISTA REAL

8A AVENIDA

0   500 yds

0   500 m

EL PUEBLITO

TUA

To Hotel San Gregorio and Pradera Concepcion

© AVALON TRAVEL

Entertainment

NIGHTLIFE

Guatemala City has a fairly lively nightlife scene with bars, clubs, and music found mostly in the Zona Viva and downtown. There are plenty of places to dance salsa and Latin beats in addition to rock and pop music. Electronica is also a big hit with Guatemalan partygoers. DJ Tiësto performed here in November 2004, February 2007, and March 2011.

Bars

A good mix of bars in the downtown area caters to the city's bohemian population as well as to international travelers. In Zona 10, the Zona Viva sector centered around 16 Calle is the place to go if you want to hang out with the city's wealthy elite in the hippest establishments.

Downtown, **El Portal** (Portal del Comercio, 9a Calle, between 6a and 7a Avenidas, 10 A.M.-10 P.M. Mon.-Sat.) is said to be the old stomping grounds of none other than Che Guevara, who lived in Guatemala City in the early 1950s. You'll find a long wooden bar and some wooden tables along with draft beers for about $2. The entrance is at the Portal del Comercio arcade entrance on the south side of the park along 6a Avenida. Nearby **Las Cien Puertas** (9a Calle between 6a and 7a Avenidas, Pasaje Aycinena, Zona 1, noon-2 A.M. Mon.-Sat.) is the city's quintessential bohemian hangout set in a restored colonial arcade. Enjoy tasty quesadillas and tacos when you get the munchies. **Europa Bar** (11 Calle 5-16, Edificio Testa, Local 201, tel. 2253-4929, 8 A.M.-midnight Mon.-Sat.) is a restaurant doubling as a bar that is popular with the expat crowd. CNN and sports are on the cable TV and the restaurant serves decent food, including the all-American staple breakfast of eggs, hash browns, bacon, and toast. The newest of the downtown venues

is **Reilly's GuateCity** (12 Calle 6-25 Zona 1, reillys.guatecity@gmail.com), a spin-off of the popular Irish pub in Antigua Guatemala.

Zona Viva's motley assortment of upscale bars is constantly in flux. New places open and close all the time, and it's hard to keep up with all the changes, even if you live in Guatemala City. A classic expat hangout, the **William Shakespeare Pub** (13 Calle and 1a Avenida, Torre Santa Clara II, Local 5, Zona 10, tel. 2331-2641, 11 A.M.-1 A.M. Mon.-Sat., 2 P.M.-1 A.M. Sun.) appropriately advertises, "No tragedy, no comedy, just good times." **Cheers** (13 Calle 0-40 Zona 10, tel. 2368-2089, 9 A.M.-1 A.M. Mon.-Sat., 1 P.M.-midnight Sun.) is the city's best sports bar with scrumptious buffalo wings, frosty beer on tap, dartboards, pool tables, foosball, big-screen TVs, and classic rock on the stereo. Another excellent brew pub, **Brass Beer Co.** (3a Avenida 12-48, Zona 10, tel. 2332-3329, noon-1 A.M. daily) offers a large selection of microbrews on tap and is one of the few places in Guatemala where you can order a ginormous beer. **Rattle N Hum** (4a Avenida 16-11 Zona 10, noon-1 A.M. daily) is a fun, Australian-owned place often featuring live music.

La Iguana Azul (12 Calle 3-46 Zona 10, tel. 2331-9866, 6 P.M.-3 A.M. Mon.-Sat.) is a Zona Viva hotspot popular with the younger crowd. The venue is built in contemporary style with steel and glass. Try the bar's signature drink, the Iguana Azul.

Nightclubs

Like the bars, nightclubs are in constant flux, but here are some options that have been around for a while and don't look to be going anywhere. In Zona 1, **El Gazabo** (6a Calle and 3a Avenida, 8 P.M.-1 A.M. Thurs.-Sat.) is a lively venue for dancing and nightlife in downtown

Guatemala City. Nearby is **Metropole** (6a Calle between 3a and 4a Avenidas, 8 P.M.-1 A.M. Thurs.-Sat.) which welcomes a mixed gay-straight crowd.

In Zona 10, **Kalhua** (15 Calle and 1a Avenida, Zona 10, 8 P.M.-3 A.M. Mon.-Sat., $5 cover) is one of Guatemala City's most popular clubs with a wealthy clientele and hip atmosphere spread out on four floors. In vogue with hip locals and international jet-setters is **NYX** (2a Avenida 12-52 Zona 10, 8 P.M.-1 A.M. Thurs.-Sat.).

Live Music

A popular place for live music in a wonderfully bohemian atmosphere is **La Bodeguita del Centro** (12 Calle 3-55 Zona 1, tel. 2230-2976, 8 P.M.-2 A.M. Tues.-Sat., $4 cover on weekends). Besides live folk, rock, and jazz music, there are poetry readings, forums, and movies some nights. The atmosphere features posters the likes of Bob Marley and Che Guevara, as well as tons of Che-related memorabilia. Food is also served, with tasty chicken sandwiches. Nearby is **Blue Town Café Bar** (11 Calle 4-51 Zona 1), with live bands and a younger crowd. **TrovaJazz** (Vía 6 3-55 Zona 4, tel. 2334-1241) has live jazz Thursday through Saturday evenings. It also serves food and coffee beverages. In Zona 10, check out **Sesto Senso** (2 Avenida 12-81, tel. 2361-6897) for its hip, lively atmosphere.

PERFORMING ARTS

The **Centro Cultural Miguel Ángel Asturias** (24 Calle 3-81 Zona 4, tel. 2232-4042, 2232-4043, 2232-4044, or 2232-4045) hosts ballet and a number of cultural events throughout the year. Check listings in the *Prensa Libre* newspaper or *Recrearte*, a free monthly publication widely available in tourist shops and hotels.

Somewhat less cultured but extremely hilarious (if you understand Spanish) are comedy productions featuring the antics of rural Guatemalans from the town of Huité starring comedian Hugo Aldana as the character Teco. The productions change from time to time but are usually in the same venue, the **Teatro de la Cámara de la Industria** (Chamber of Industry Theater, Ruta 6, 0-21 Zona 4, tel. 2334-4848 or 2331-9191, showtimes 8:30 P.M. Fri. and Sat., 5 P.M. Sun., $8).

For other cultural events, check the entertainment section of the useful Spanish-language website at www.deguate.com.

CINEMA

Guatemala City has a number of excellent movie theaters, with movies sometimes opening on the same day as their U.S. release. The city's IMAX movie theater can be found at **Cines Pradera Concepción** (tel. 2329-2550, circuitoalba.com.gt), located at the Pradera Concepción shopping mall along Km. 17.5 of Carretera a El Salvador, where you can have the IMAX theater experience for just $6. Located in one of the city's most popular shopping malls is **Cinépolis Miraflores** (Centro Comercial Miraflores, 21 Avenida 4-32 Zona 11, tel. 2470-8367, www.cinepolis.com.gt). Cinépolis (a Mexican chain) recently opened a second location in Zona 10's **Oakland Mall** (Diagonal 6, 13-01 Zona 10, www.cinepolis.com.gt). Five of Oakland Mall's theaters are VIP lounges, in which you can order a meal and/or drink while you watch a movie.

Not to be outdone, U.S. franchise Cinemark recently opened its first Guatemalan location at **Cinemark Eskala Roosevelt** (Calzada Roosevelt Km. 13.8 Zona 11, tel. 2250-7084, www.cinemarkca.com) featuring 3-D movies.

Check the *Prensa Libre* newspaper or the theaters' websites for showtimes. Movies at all of these venues generally cost between $4 and $5 and all have stadium seating.

Shopping

You can find almost anything you might possibly want or need in Guatemala City. In addition to many modern shopping malls stocked with the latest fashions and electronics, there are a number of department stores for household appliances and cosmetics. For grocery shopping, the local giant is Paiz, which was recently taken over by WalMart. U.S.-style warehouse shopping is available at PriceSmart or at a number of local chains. Guatemalans love U.S.-made goods, which is easy to see given their wide availability. For organic grocery shopping and natural foods, head to **Organica** (Diagonal 6 16-23 Zona 10, tel. 2363-1819 and Km. 15.5 Carretera a El Salvador, Condado Concepcion Fase 1 Local #21, tel. 6634-7077, 9 A.M.-7 P.M. Mon.-Sat.).

RETAIL DISTRICTS
Zona Viva
In line with its fashionable cafés and expensive hotels, the Zona Viva also features a number of attractive stores for window-shopping or picking up an outfit should you need something nice to wear for a fancy dinner or night out on the town. Two of the most fashionable retail outlets are the European chain **Mexx** (16 Calle 5-86 Zona 10, Plaza Magnolia, tel. 2368-0757, www.mexx.com, 10 A.M.-8 P.M. daily) and the European-inspired menswear store **Saúl Méndez** (12 Calle 1-25 Zona 10, Edificio Géminis, tel. 2379-8722, 10 A.M.-8 P.M. daily). Saúl Méndez, Mexx, and more recently, Zara, have locations in the following upscale shopping malls.

SHOPPING MALLS
Guatemala City has some excellent shopping malls carrying the most basic or most exclusive items one could need, in addition to fashionable boutiques and department stores.

None of the latter (curiously) seem to result from Guatemalan investment. These include Simán (El Salvador), Carrion (Honduras), Figaly (Panama) and Sears (United States). The city's largest shopping mall is **Pradera Concepción** (Km. 17.5 Carretera a El Salvador, 10 A.M.-7 P.M. Mon.-Thurs. and 10 A.M.-9 P.M. Fri.-Sat.), with a variety of familiar stores and restaurant chains including Sears and T.G.I. Friday's. It adjoins a smaller, open-air shopping center known as **Condado Concepción,** which features a Starbucks and an Applebee's in addition to several local chains. Opened in 2003 and expanded in 2006 and 2011, the sprawling **Galerías Miraflores** (21 Avenida 4-32 Zona 11, 10 A.M.-8 P.M. Mon.-Thurs., 10 A.M.-9 P.M. Fri.-Sat., 10 A.M.-7 P.M. Sun.) also harbors some of Guatemala's most exclusive stores, including a Simán department store, the international Zara boutique, and a L'Occitane store. There's also an IHOP if you need your pancake fix. Across the way is the **Parque Comercial Las Majadas** shopping center with a Sears, Fetiche perfume store, and a T.G.I. Friday's.

In Zona 10, east up the hill toward the Carretera a El Salvador, is **Galerías La Pradera** (20 Calle 25-85 Zona 10, tel. 2367-4136, 10 A.M.-8 P.M. Mon.-Sat. and 10 A.M.-7 P.M. Sun.), an upscale shopping mall remodeled in 2010-2011. Though not as upscale as its Zona Viva location might suggest, **Gran Centro Los Próceres** (16 Calle 2-00 Zona 10, tel. 2332-8742) nonetheless has some good shops and eateries and is conveniently situated near the major Zona 10 hotels.

Zona 10's newest and most upscale shopping mall is also Guatemala City's nicest. **Oakland Mall** (Diagonal 6, 13-01 Zona 10, www.oaklandmall.com.gt, 10 A.M.-8 P.M. Mon.-Thurs., 10 A.M.-9 P.M. Fri.-Sat. and 10 A.M.-7 P.M. Sun.) features 170 stores spread across three floors,

© AL ARGUETA

Carolina Herrera has a store at Plaza Fontabella.

in addition to several movie theaters. Among its stores and restaurants you'll find an aquarium, an impressive waterfall producing geometric shapes, and even a carousel imported from Italy. A Starbucks with plenty of outdoor seating fronts the street along its main entrance. Also in this sector is the very pleasant **Plaza Fontabella** (4a Ave. 12-59 Zona 10, tel. 6628-8600, www.plazafontabella.com), built as an outdoor mall in neo-colonial style, where you can enjoy Guatemala's spring-like climate and a decent selection of stores and restaurants while strolling the cobblestone pedestrian walkways. Guatemala's first Carolina Herrera designer handbag store opened here in 2011.

In Zona 16, you'll find another fine example of the recent trend toward construction of outdoor pedestrian malls in warm-weather locales. **Paseo Cayalá** (Ciudad Cayalá, Zona 16, www.paseocayala.com.gt) is housed in a sprawling collection of white-washed Spanish neo-colonial buildings. There are numerous specialty

stores in addition to cool restaurants and bars with outdoor patio seating fronting the cobblestone pedestrian thoroughfare. Three universities lie nearby and the shopping district is part of a larger residential complex encompassing homes and student apartments. There are lovely views of the city's downtown core, off in the distance.

HANDICRAFTS

You can shop the jam-packed stalls in downtown Guatemala City's **Mercado Central** (8a Avenida and 6a Calle, 6 A.M.-6 P.M. Mon.-Sat., 9 A.M.-noon Sun.) for textiles, *típica* clothing, and leather goods. A safer and more enjoyable option can be found near the airport and Zona 13 museums at the open-air **Mercado de Artesanías** (Boulevard Juan Pablo II, 8 A.M.-6 P.M. Mon.-Sat., 8 A.M.-1 P.M. Sun.), with a fairly wide assortment of handicrafts and tourist souvenirs.

Recommended retailers include **Lin Canola**

© AL ARGUETA

Paseo Cayalá has specialty stores, restaurants, and bars.

(5a Calle 9-60 Zona 1, tel. 2232-0858, www. lin-canola.com, 9 A.M.-6 P.M. Mon.-Fri.), where the assortment varies from home decorative items to jewelry and everything between. This store is especially recommended if you want to buy Guatemalan fabrics by the yard. Its Zona 10 location, **In Nola** (18 Calle 21-31 Zona 10 Boulevard Los Próceres, tel. 2367-2424, 8:30 A.M.-6:30 P.M. Mon.-Fri. and 8:30 A.M.-1:30 P.M. Sat.), is more modern and contains much the same in a better part of town.

Selling fashionable adaptations on traditional designs for the home, **Textura** (Diagonal 6, 13-63 Zona 10, tel. 2333-5496, 9 A.M.-5 P.M. Mon.-Sat.) is especially recommended for its beautiful and colorful hammocks.

ART GALLERIES

If you want to take in the work of local artists, head to Guatemala's oldest art gallery, **Galería El Túnel** (Boulevard Los Próceres 15-60 Zona 10, 2nd Floor, tel. 2363-4744, galeriaeltunel@

yahoo.com), featuring the work of more than 100 artists. Another good art gallery worth checking out is **el attico** (4a Avenida 15-45 Zona 14, tel. 2368-0853, elatticogal@msn.com). Next door to one of the finest restaurants in the city, **Carlos Woods Arte Antiguo y Contemporáneo** (10a Avenida 5-49 Zona 14, tel. 2366-6883/84, www.carloswoodsarte.com, 10 A.M.-8 P.M. Mon.-Fri. and 10 A.M.-2 P.M. Sat.) features a variety of exhibitions from local artists in a well-lit minimalist setting. Check the website for current exhibitions.

BOOKS

For a great atmosphere for unwinding with a cup of coffee or tea and a large selection of books (though mostly in Spanish), try **Sophos** (Plaza Fontabella, 4a Ave, 12-59 Zona 10, tel. 2419-7070, 9 A.M.-8 P.M. Mon.-Sat. and 10 A.M.-6 P.M. Sun.). Also with plenty of books in Spanish is **Artemis Edinter** (www.artemisedinter.com) with several locations including Galerías Miraflores, La Pradera, Pradera Concepción, and Oakland Mall.

A number of bookstores cater to the expat community, stocking a variety of English-language books on their shelves. **Vista Hermosa Book Shop** (2a Calle 18-50, Vista Hermosa II, Zona 15, tel. 2369-1003, vhbookshop@intelnet.net.gt, 9 A.M.-1 P.M. and 2-6 P.M. Mon.-Sat.) has books in English and Spanish and is in a quiet residential sector east of Zona 10. Another good option for books in English is **Géminis Bookstore** (3a Avenida 17-05 Zona 14, Edificio Casa Alta, tel. 2366-1031, geminisbookstore@hotmail.com, 9 A.M.-1 P.M. and 3-6 P.M. Mon.-Fri. and 9 A.M.-1 P.M. Sat.).

OUTDOOR GEAR

For anything you may have neglected to bring for your outdoor Guatemala adventures, head to **Big Mountain** (4a Ave. 13-45 Zona 10 local 7, tel. 2366-3122, www.bigmountainonline. com, 9 A.M.-8 P.M. Mon.-Sat.), offering a good assortment of hiking, climbing, mountain biking, and camping gear, and name-brand outdoor clothing.

Another option for outdoor gear is **The North Face** (2nd floor of the Oakland Mall, Diagonal 6, 13-01 Zona 10, tel. 2336-6881, 10 A.M.-8 P.M. Mon.-Thurs., 10 A.M.-9 P.M. Fri.-Sat. and 10 A.M.-7 P.M. Sun.).

Recreation

PARKS

The idea of a greenbelt is relatively new to Guatemalan city planners. Most of the city's parks tend to be plazas centered around churches. An exception is the **Campo Marte,** a relatively well-executed park with facilities for playing soccer, baseball, and basketball as well as running around its spacious grounds. It was previously the city's military barracks and is east of Avenida La Reforma along 2a Calle. A better option might be the planned **Parque Metropolitano,** tied closely to the project encompassing the airport's ongoing expansion in Zona 13. It should be the city's best park with plenty of space to get some fresh air and exercise, though it has yet to become a reality.

On Sunday mornings, parts of Avenida Las Américas and Avenida La Reforma (from Plaza Eucarística to Plaza Israel) are closed to car traffic as part of the municipality's **Pasos y Pedales** initiative. Pedestrians, cyclists, rollerbladers, and skateboarders take to the broad streets, while the green grass and plazas of the boulevards' wide central dividers serve as pleasant areas for rest and relaxation.

HEALTH CLUBS

There are a number of good gymnasiums, mostly U.S. franchises, where you can pay a day rate of about $7 to work out if you don't have a membership. **World Gym** (www.worldgym. com) has three locations to choose from. Its Calzada Roosevelt location (Calzada Roosevelt 21-09 Zona 7, Centro Comercial Gran Vía Roosevelt, tel. 2475-2856) is conveniently across the street from Galerías Miraflores and the Grand Tikal Futura Hotel. It also has a Zona 10 location (Boulevard Los Próceres 25-74 Zona 10, Gran Vía Pradera, tel. 2423-6000), and a third location in the southwest suburbs of San Cristóbal (tel. 2424-4848). All have a full gym and swimming pool. You can also work out at **Gold's Gym** (Pradera Concepción Mall, Km. 17.5 Carretera a El Salvador, tel. 6634-1240, www.goldsgym.com).

GOLF

Fans of golf will find some excellent golf courses in and around the city; those within private country clubs are usually still open to visitors. You can enjoy a round of golf

© AL ARGUETA

Bikers and pedestrians take to the Guatemala City streets during the weekly Pasos y Pedales.

surrounded by the country's spectacular mountain scenery as you play on narrow, sloping fairways lined with pine trees and a variety of other obstacles. Several of sport-fishing outfitters have combined fishing and golf packages. If interested, contact **The Great Sailfishing Company** (tel. 7832-1991, 5966-4528 Antigua, or 877/763-0851 U.S., www.greatsailfishing.com) or **Sailfish Bay Lodge** (tel. 2426-3909 direct or 800/638-7405 U.S. reservations, www.sailfishbay.com). It's also possible to arrange a round of golf through the concierges at some of the city's finer hotels, including the Marriott, Camino Real, and InterContinental. Entry to all of these clubs is by prior authorization only. You'll need to call ahead or email.

In 2006 and 2007, Guatemala City's San Isidro Golf Club hosted the **NGA/Hooter's Pro Golf Tour,** which has become an annual event between the last week of February and the first week of March. Guatemala is also a major stop along the annual **Tour de las Américas** in February.

San Isidro Golf Club

Still officially within the city limits in Zona 16, San Isidro Golf Club (Finca San Isidro, Zona 16, tel. 2419-1200, www.clubsanisidrogt.com) is the city's most modern and is in a quiet residential section in its eastern extremes. The 18-hole, par-72 course measures 6,640 yards and offers some truly spectacular views of Guatemala City flanked by Agua, Acatenango, and Fuego Volcanoes. Greens fees are $75, clubs rent for $15, a cart rental costs $20, and caddies are $15. The splendid facilities here include a restaurant overlooking the greens featuring a beautiful dining room with vaulted wooden ceiling, a gym, a squash court, and a swimming pool with lap lanes.

Hacienda Nueva Country Club

The 18-hole, 7,100-yard, par-72 golf course at

© AL ARGUETA

Alta Vista Golf and Tennis Club offers one of Guatemala's most challenging courses along with fabulous mountain views.

Hacienda Nueva Country Club (Km. 25, Ruta Nacional 18, Carretera a Mataquescuintla, San José Pinula, tel. 6628-1000, www.haciendanueva.com, $75 Tues.-Fri., $90 weekends and holidays) is just outside the city near the Carretera a El Salvador and is set beautifully on the grounds of a 16th-century Jesuit monastery. There's a small chapel with original artwork where Mass is still held weekly. Facilities include nine tennis courts, two squash courts, tennis and golf pro shops, and a swimming pool that has won international design awards. The clubhouse has three dining areas, including a poolside snack bar, a casual dining room serving international dishes, and La Pérgola, an outdoor steakhouse overlooking the 18th hole. Fees include $15 for caddie service and $25 for cart rental. A limited number of golf clubs are available for rental at $15. There are also a driving range and putting green.

Alta Vista Golf and Tennis Club

The most challenging course can be found just down the road from Hacienda Nueva at Alta Vista Golf and Tennis Club (Km. 27, Ruta Nacional 18, Carretera a Mataquescuintla, San José Pinula, tel. 6641-5058, www.altavistagolf. com.gt, 7 A.M.-8 P.M. Tues.-Sun., $75), where the 18-hole, par-71, slope-122 course is divided into two nine-hole sections. Additional challenges include 74 sand traps and two water traps with a route defined by 1,800 trees of varying species, adding a nice alpine touch to the incredible mountain views. The clubhouse is in a large and attractive three-story, English-style building with an elegant restaurant, a bar with pool table, an indoor swimming pool, three squash courts, and six tennis courts. Golf cart rentals cost $30, clubs are $15, and caddies $15.

Mayan Golf Course

South of the city in the neighboring district

of Villa Nueva, Mayan Golf Course (Finca El Zarzal, Villa Nueva, tel. 6631-0045, www.mayangolfclub.com, $75) is Guatemala City's oldest, dating to 1918. The facilities here feel somewhat dated but have been well maintained. The 18-hole, par-72 golf course has exquisite views of Lake Amatitlán and Pacaya Volcano along its 7,092-yard length. Rental clubs and golf carts are available and there is a café with a terrace overlooking the course. Additional sporting facilities include a bowling alley, tennis courts, a soccer field, volleyball court, and swimming pool.

BOWLING

Metro Bowl (2a Calle 15-93 Zona 15, on Vista Hermosa Boulevard, tel. 2243-2424, www.metrobowl.com.gt) is Central America's largest bowling alley, with 28 lanes. There are also eight pool tables and an area for video games. And, of course, there's a snack bar.

SPECTATOR SPORTS

Like other Latin Americans, Guatemalans are crazy about *fútbol*. The two most popular teams in the country's four-team national soccer league, denoted by the colors of their jerseys, are the Rojos (Municipales) and Cremas (Comunicaciones), who usually end up battling it out at the end of the season for the championship title. International games are also a big event, as Guatemala has never been to a World Cup. In recent years, it has gotten closer than it's ever been, and the postgame celebrations have spilled into the streets and lasted into the wee hours of the morning. Unfortunately, their high hopes have ended in bitter disappointment. Games can be seen at the **Estadio Mateo Flores** (10a Avenida, Zona 5), but be advised: The scene can get quite rowdy. In 1996, things got so out of hand that a stampede ensued when stands collapsed, killing 100 people. The soccer stadium has been remodeled in the aftermath. If you've always wanted to see a Latin American soccer match, you might want to check it out.

You can see baseball games at Parque Minerva's ballpark (Zona 2).

CITY TOURS

Traditional city tours can be arranged through any of the larger hotels or via **Clark Tours** (7a Avenida 14-76, Plaza Clark, Zona 9, tel. 2412-4700, www.clarktours.com). It has offices in the Westin Camino Real, Holiday Inn, and Barcelo.

Accommodations

Guatemala City has a wide variety of accommodations for all budgets. The major U.S. hotel chains have properties in Zonas 10, 11, and 13—close to the airport. Downtown is home to most of the city's budget accommodations.

CENTRO HISTÓRICO
Under $10

There are some real cheapies in downtown Guatemala City, traditionally the city's budget accommodation headquarters, though there are also some nice budget options outside the downtown area now, so you have to stay in this slightly dodgy part of town only if you really want to. A longtime favorite with the backpacker crowd, **Pension Meza** (10a Calle 10-17 Zona 1, tel. 2232-3177) has shared-bath doubles for $7 and rooms with private bath for $12 d. It's somewhat dilapidated, though the graffiti-strewn walls have a certain charm and the beds are good enough. You'll find a courtyard festooned with bougainvillea, table tennis, and a book exchange.

$10-25

Hotel Ajau (8a Avenida 15-62 Zona 1, tel. 2232-0488) has 44 rooms, including shared-bath doubles for $12 and doubles with private bath for $19. **Hotel Spring** (8a Avenida 12-65 Zona 1, tel. 2230-2858, hotelspring@hotmail. com) is a good value with clean, pleasant rooms. It has doubles with shared bath for $18, older doubles with private bath for $23, and quieter, newly remodeled doubles with private bath for $33. The architecture at **Hotel Colonial** (7a Avenida 14-19 Zona 1, tel. 2232-6722, www. hotelcolonial.net, $19-30 d) is just as its name implies, with tile floors, wrought iron, and dark hardwood accents. Its spacious rooms come with either shared or private bathrooms.

$25-50

On a quiet side street, a fine choice is **C Posada Belén** (13 Calle "A" 10-30 Zona 1, tel. 2253-4530, www.posadabelen.com, $49-60 d), an 1873 home converted into a lovely museum inn. It has 10 rooms with tile floors tastefully decorated with Guatemalan bedspreads, paintings, and weavings. Its gracious hosts, René and Francesca, speak English and can help you plan your journeys into Guatemala's rugged interior. Amenities include telephone and Internet access. All rooms have private bath and rates include breakfast. Other delicious homemade meals are available upon request. **Hotel Quality Service** (8a Calle 3-18 Zona 1, tel. 2251-8005, 2251-8006, or 2251-8007, www.qualityguate.com, $40 d) has 22 attractive tile-floor rooms with private hot-water baths, cable TVs, and desks. The hotel is housed in a cool art deco building. Rates include free Continental breakfast.

$50-100

Oozing with history is the landmark **Hotel Pan American** (9a Calle 5-63 Zona 1, tel. 2232-6807, $50 d), which was once Guatemala City's go-to property, having been established by its namesake airline. Rooms have tile floors and are nicely decorated with Guatemalan artwork and furnishings. The dining room, serving international and Guatemalan dishes, is well known for its antique charm and elegance, with waiters wearing traditional village attire. Another elegant downtown property is the **Hotel Royal Palace** (6a Avenida 12-66 Zona 1, tel. 2220-8980, www.hotelroyalpalace.com, $55-65 d), where the spacious, comfortable rooms have attractive traditional paintings, reading lamps, cable TV, and wooden furniture. There are standard rooms and larger junior suites to choose from. Other amenities include a workout room and an executive floor. Rooms facing the street have balconies and the property is wheelchair-accessible. There's also a restaurant that I can't bring myself to recommend.

ZONA 4
$50-100

Conquistador Hotel (Vía 5, 4-68 Zona 4, tel. 2331-2222) was formerly a Ramada property and has comfortable double rooms for $90 including breakfast. You'll find a lobby bar, the Café Jardín serving a breakfast and lunch buffet, and La Pérgola serving fine international dishes for dinner. Centered around a swimming pool in an art deco building with a newer motel-style wing is **Hotel Plaza** (Vía 7, 6-16 Zona 4, tel. 2332-7626, $65 d).

ZONA 9
$25-50

Hostal Plaza (6a Ave A 13-52 Zona 9, tel. 5417-2143, www.hostalplaza.page.tl, $30 d) features a great location close to the airport, Transmetro access, food, and entertainment. Run by friendly Guatemalans, all of the comfortable rooms have private hot-water bathrooms. There's a kitchen for guests' use and a nice little courtyard for lounging. Reservations are required, so call ahead.

$50-100

In this price category is the **Howard Johnson**

Inn (Avenida La Reforma 4-22 Zona 9, tel. 2360-7188 or 2361-6566, www.hojo.com, $70 d), with all the standard amenities you would expect from this international hotel chain, including air-conditioning, fan, nice wooden furniture, phone, and TV. Airport transfers are included and there's a small restaurant in the lobby. Try to get a room facing the outside street. Just one block west of Avenida La Reforma is the excellent-value **Hotel Residencia del Sol** (3a Calle 6-42 Zona 9, tel. 2360-4823, www.residenciadelsol.com, $60-70 d). It has comfortable, carpeted rooms, some with city views and windows shaded by trees, with private baths and in-room Internet.

$100-200

Among Guatemala City's numerous international hotel chain options is the [**Barceló Guatemala City** (7a Avenida 15-45 Zona 9, tel. 800/227-2356, www.barceloguatemalacity.com, $91-177 d), with six different room types to choose from and all the standard comforts usually found in the Spanish hotel chain's properties. American and United Airlines have offices in the lobby of this former Marriott property.

The Guatemala City location of a Guatemalan luxury hotel chain enjoying success throughout Central America, **Hotel Princess Reforma** (13 Calle 7-65 Zona 9, tel. 2334-4545, www.hotelesprincess.com, $120 d) is a winner for its sophisticated old-time ambience. Amenities include a swimming pool, gym, restaurant, and English pub-style bar. Its 110 rooms have air-conditioning. It is curiously the only of its Central American counterparts that is not part of the Hilton chain.

ZONA 10
Under $50

Zona 10 offered strictly high-budget options until the appearance of **Xamanek Hostel** (13 Calle 3-57 Zona 10, tel. 2360-8345, www.mayaworld.net/xamanek, $20 p/p in dorms,

$50 private doubles), a friendly sort of place with clean dormitories sharing spotless bathrooms and two guest rooms with private baths. Services include laundry, airport pickup, Internet (in lounge area only), bag storage, and free use of the kitchen. Room rates include a small breakfast and coffee. There are two gardens and a living room for chilling out. It's a good option if you're on a budget and don't want to stay downtown. Its Zona Viva location is excellent. The current Guatemala City favorite of the backpacking crowd is the Australian-Guatemalan owned [**Quetzalroo Hostel** (6a Avenida 7-84 Zona 10, tel. 5746-0830, www.quetzalroo.com). The owners take great pride in sharing their vast knowledge and enthusiasm for Guatemala and its capital city with visitors. For $18, you get a comfortable bed in a dorm room, shared bath, free wireless Internet, continental breakfast and free shuttle transport to and from the airport nearby. Private rooms with shared bath cost $35 per night. The hostel is conveniently situated in the heart of the Zona Viva. A fun historical tour of downtown Guatemala City includes a stop at the Gallo brewery and costs just $5.

$50-100

Oozing with old time atmosphere and housed in a restored French-style palace built by a late 19th century Guatemalan president is **La Casa Grande** (Avenida La Reforma 7-67 Zona 10, tel. 2332-0914, www.casagrande-gua.com/web/index.htm). There are comfortable rooms and spacious grounds for enjoying the spring-like Guatemalan climate. An attractive courtyard restaurant serves breakfast, lunch, and dinner. It's a block from the U.S. embassy. **Best Western Stofella** (2a Avenida 12-28 Zona 10, tel. 2410-8600, www.stofella.com, $65-100 d), a solid choice for business travelers, has rooms with fan or air-conditioning with breakfast included in the nightly rate. You'll find a lobby lounge, a fitness room with whirlpool tub, a bar, and in-room Internet connection. **Santander Plaza** (15 Calle 3-52 Zona 10, tel. 2333-5857, www.santanderplaza.com, $100 d) has 26 comfortable rooms with stylish, well-appointed furnishings in executive rooms and junior and master suites. It has a lobby bar and restaurant. Guests enjoy access to the wonderful Hacienda Nueva Country Club (Km. 25, Ruta Nacional 18, Carretera a Mataquescuintla, San José Pinula, tel. 6628-1000, www.haciendanueva.com, $75 Tues.-Fri., $90 weekends and holidays). Offering many of the same services as its pricier sister hotels under the management of the Camino Real chain, **Biltmore Express** (15 Calle 0-31 Zona 10, tel. 2338-5000, www.caminoreal.com.gt) offers corporate rates for $65 d, including continental breakfast, and has comfortable rooms with broadband Internet. Guests can enjoy use of the nearby Westin Camino Real's swimming pool, whirlpool tub, and tennis and racquetball courts for an additional $10 a day.

$100-200

Otelito (12 Calle 4-51 Zona 10, tel. 2339-1811, www.otelito.com, $120-160 d) is cool and hip but a bit noisy for some people's taste on account of a popular lobby lounge. There are 12 rooms, all named after local produce, housed in a modern home turned upscale hotel. The decor is minimalist with a different color scheme in evidence during each of the year's four seasons. It offers chill-out music playing on the speakers throughout the property, wireless Internet throughout, a business center, and a book exchange. Movies are shown nightly. The hip, frosted-glass lounge and restaurant (lunch and dinner daily, $7-12) mean you don't even have to leave your hotel to enjoy some of Zona Viva's best food in a delightful atmosphere. Popular Plaza Fontabella shopping mall is right across the street.

Rooms feature nice artwork, 300-thread-count Egyptian cotton sheets, down pillows,

air-conditioning, flat-screen cable TV, hardwood floors, and in-room chill-out music. Some have a mini fridge. Walk-in showers feature tempered glass in lieu of shower curtains.

Another top choice is the fabulous, 239-room 【 **Real InterContinental Guatemala** (14 Calle 2-51 Zona 10, tel. 2379-4548 or 888/424-6835 toll-free U.S., www.intercontinental.com, $125-485 d) with a wonderful lobby featuring Guatemalan paintings and sculpture, a sushi restaurant, a French café, and *boulangerie* and patisserie. The comfortable, stylish rooms feature in-room Internet access, down pillows, Egyptian cotton sheets, and flat-screen cable TV. Bathrooms have rain showerheads and the safe deposit boxes are large enough to accommodate a laptop. Guests have use of an in-room iPod. There are free airport shuttles and a pleasant swimming pool on a deck overlooking the city. President George W. Bush and his wife, Laura, spent the night here during their 24-hour visit to Guatemala in March 2007.

French chain Accor Hotels unveiled its Guatemala City property in March 2007. **Mercure Casa Veranda** (12 Calle 1-24 Zona 10, tel. 2361-0196, www.mercure.com, $100-150 d) features all the amenities you'd come to expect from a reputable international hotel chain. Among the unique features of the property's 99 spacious suites are hardwood floors, Persian rugs, wireless Internet and balconies with fantastic city views; some suites have full kitchens. The property also features a decent restaurant and bar.

A number of other international hotel chains are in this price category. Among them is the ever-reliable **Holiday Inn** (1a Avenida 13-22 Zona 10, tel. 2332-2555 or 888/465-4329 toll-free U.S., www.holidayinn.com.gt, $120 d), the landmark 271-room **Westin Camino Real** (14 Calle and Avenida La Reforma Zona 10, tel. 2333-3000, www.caminoreal.com.gt, $120-160 d), and the business traveler-oriented **Viva** view from a room at Mercure Casa Veranda

Clarion Suites (tel. 2421-3333, www.clarion-guatemala.com, $105-125 d), which also has some good packages for couples traveling to Guatemala to adopt children.

The all-suite **Radisson** (1a Avenida 12-46 Zona 10, tel. 2332-9797 or 800/333-3333 toll-free U.S., www.radisson.com, $120 d) has a Family Floor with rooms specially equipped for couples adopting children, including cribs and carriages, bottle sterilizers, and nanny service (at extra cost). There's also a floor exclusively for women with the business traveler in mind, featuring a beauty salon and free transportation to area shopping malls, among other perks. All rooms have a minibar, in-room safe, large windows with great city views, and in-room Internet access. There are also a gym, sauna, business center, and sushi restaurant/bar open 11 A.M.-midnight daily.

Conveniently located near the U.S. embassy in a building oozing with European charm, **Hotel San Carlos** (Avenida La Reforma 7-89,

Zona 10, tel. 2332-6055, www.hsancarlos.com, $90-175 d) offers 23 modern, comfortable rooms. The spacious suites are a good value and have hardwood floors and kitchenettes. There are also one- or two-bedroom apartments.

ZONA 11
$100-200
Formerly the city's Hyatt Regency, the **Grand Tikal Futura** (Calzada Roosevelt 22-43 Zona 11, tel. 2440-1234, www.grandtikalfutura.com.gt, $90-600 d) maintains high-quality standards and has comfortable, well-furnished rooms varying from standard rooms to stunning Diplomatic Suites. All have splendid views of the city and surrounding mountains. Restaurants include elegant La Molienda, serving international and Guatemalan dishes for breakfast, lunch, and dinner and the excellent Asia Grill and Wok serving lunch and dinner in a tropically inspired, casual atmosphere. There is a lobby bar, a fitness center with health-food bar, and a covered swimming pool with poolside service and city views.

ZONA 13 (AIRPORT)
Under $50
A number of inexpensive hotels all offering similar services are centered in a middle-class neighborhood near the airport. All offer free transport to and from the terminal as well as breakfast, though this varies from continental minimalist to a full-on Guatemalan feast. **Guatefriends B&B** (16 Calle 7-40 Zona 13, Aurora 1; tel. 5308-3275, www.guatemalahostal.com, $18) is run by a friendly couple. The rooms and property are decorated in bright colors that nod to Guatemala's bright textiles and vivid Maya culture. Among the nice extras are Bath & Body Works toiletries and tasty home-cooked meals. **Dos Lunas Guest House** (21 Calle 10-92 Zona 13, Aurora II, tel. 2334-5264, www.hoteldoslunas.com) has

© AL ARGUETA

The modern Grand Tikal Futura hotel contrasts with Mayan temple mounds in Guatemala City's Zona 11.

nine basic rooms, all with shared bath, for $12 per person including a breakfast of eggs and toast. Reservations are necessary, as it's usually booked. **Hostal Los Lagos** (8a Avenida 15-85 Zona 13, tel. 2334-5311, www.loslagoshostal.com) has cheerful rooms with colorful paintings and several beds each. You can share a room and a bathroom for as little as $15 or share a room with private bathroom for $20. A double room with one bed and private bathroom costs $35. All rates include a complete breakfast of eggs, beans, cereal, toast, juice, and coffee or tea. You'll find Internet, cable TV, laundry, and baggage storage as well as two sitting rooms with bamboo furniture.

Hostal Los Volcanes (16 Calle 8-00, Colonia Aurora I, Zona 13, tel. 2261-3040, www.hostallosvolcanes.com) has seven rooms with private or shared bathroom. Rates start at $10 per person in a dormitory bed. There are private shared-bath singles for $20. A room

with private bathroom, large bed, and cable TV costs $25 for a single or $40 for a double. The pleasant house in which the hostel is based has a lovely garden patio with a colonial fountain, a balcony with volcano views, a living room with cable TV, VCR, games, a library, Internet, and free drinking water. It also provides rides to the bus terminals.

A notch above the rest of the lodgings in the airport neighborhood is **Hostal Villa Toscana** (16 Calle 8-20, Aurora I, Zona 13, tel. 2261-2854, www.hostalvillatoscana.com, $49-61 d), a bed-and-breakfast where there are large, well-decorated rooms with private bathrooms and wireless Internet—there is even a suite with a balcony and volcano views. **Hotel Casablanca** (15 Calle "C" 7-35, Aurora I, Zona 13, tel. 2261-3116, www.hotelcasablancainn.com, $35-50 d) is another good choice with pleasant, simply decorated rooms with big beds, reading lamps, and shared or private bathrooms. There is wireless Internet throughout and a pleasant patio bar.

$100-200

The 183-room ◖ **Crowne Plaza** (Avenida Las Américas 9-08 Zona 13, tel. 2422-5000 or 800/835-4654 toll-free U.S., www.cpguatemala.com.gt, $105-150 d) features rooms with the chain's Sleep Advantage, including deliciously comfortable beds, fine duvets, and your choice of seven different pillows. The seventh floor is designated as a "Quiet Zone," with TVs that reach only a certain volume and a relaxation kit with aromatherapy products. The ninth floor is an all-suite executive floor. The staff assures me you can drink the tap water and everything, including the hotel food, is certified to the highest standards of hygiene. It has a business center with wireless Internet, a huge gym with excellent city views from the top floor, a sports bar with video poker and slot machines, and a heated pool with whirlpool tub. The Los Volcanes restaurant, on the ground floor, serves international and local dishes à la carte or buffet style. There's a piano player at night. Video Lotería Monte Carlo (video gambling, 1 P.M.-3 A.M. daily) is also based on the ground floor, featuring video poker and slot machines. Proceeds benefit the environmental foundation Monte Carlo Verde.

CARRETERA A EL SALVADOR (SUBURBS)
Over $100

Although a bit far from the action, the all-suite ◖ **Vista Real Guatemala** (Km. 8.5 Carretera a El Salvador, tel. 2420-7720, www.vistareal.com, $109-190 d) scores big points for its location on a bluff overlooking the city and its neocolonial architecture featuring Mexican artistic touches. Its 129 rooms are all comfortable and well furnished with some truly splendid features, including vaulted wooden ceilings and neocolonial archways in some rooms. The Suite Gran Clase rooms are a good value and substantially nicer than the Master Suites, which are only slightly less expensive. The Suite Presidencial ($799) is one of the nicest rooms in Guatemala. Check the website for special deals. Wireless Internet is offered throughout the property. There is a pleasant, though unheated, garden swimming pool. Its Restaurante Las Ventanas is one of the city's most exclusive, with a variety of international dishes served in an elegant dining room overlooking the hotel's gardens. Its well-stocked Bar Quinta Real is open 5 P.M.-1 A.M. Monday-Saturday.

Well outside of Guatemala City but entirely worth the trip, ◖ **San Gregorio Hotel & Spa** (Carretera a Santa Elena Barillas Km. 29.5, tel. 6634-3666, www.sangregoriospa.com, $120 d) is a modern, eco-chic facility with 10 stylish rooms featuring hardwood floors, flat-screen TVs, Guatemalan textiles, wood accents, and views over Guatemala City valley to Lake Amatitlán and Agua Volcano. There's an indoor/outdoor swimming pool; the hotel's eco-chic status is punctuated by the use of solar panels for water heating and rainwater collection for landscape irrigation. To get here, take the Carretera a El Salvador to a turnoff at Km. 25. You'll see a Texaco gas station; follow the road to Santa Elena Barillas, another 4.5 kilometers. A sign for San Gregorio indicates the intersection where you'll make a right-hand turn to the lodge.

Food

Cosmopolitan Guatemala City features a variety of excellent eating establishments for every taste and budget, as well as some more familiar U.S. franchises. In recent years, Jake's received a spot on *Travel + Leisure* magazine's list of Top 10 Restaurants in Latin America.

CAFÉS

A profusion of new cafés has come and gone in the downtown area in recent years. Among those still in business is **Café de Imeri** (6a Calle 3-34 Zona 1, tel. 2232-9008), which enjoys a loyal following owed to its delightful old-fashioned atmosphere and efficiently elegant service. The cakes and baked goods are top-notch, and there are good breakfasts, tacos, pasta, and salads. It makes a great place for lunch with a set menu for $3.50.

Café Saúl (several locations throughout the city in Miraflores, Oakland Mall, and Paseo Cayala, www.estilosaul.com, $8-15) is a local chain of cafes serving delicious sweet and salty crepes, ice cream, sandwiches, salads, smoothies, and coffee in an eclectic atmosphere with relaxing music. Beer and wine are also served. **Caffé dei Fiori** (15 Avenida 15-66 Zona 10, tel. 2363-5888, www.caffedeifiori.com, $3-8) has been around since the 1970s in three prior Zona 10 locations. Its current incarnation features a pleasant covered patio where breakfasts, pizzas, pastas, salads, and sandwiches are served. Desserts include delicious tiramisu and *empanadas de piña*. Great espresso drinks round out the meal.

There are a number of local coffee shops with a widespread presence throughout Guatemala City. These include **& Cafe** and **Cafe Barista**. If you must, there are three Starbucks locations in upscale Guatemala City shopping malls.

LIGHT MEALS AND SWEETS

For healthy vegetarian fare, check out **Restaurante Rey Sol** (11 Calle 5-51 Zona 1, 8 A.M.-5 P.M. Mon.-Sat., $4-8) serving tasty spinach lasagnas, whole-wheat bread sandwiches, salads, and smoothies. It also sells soy milk, granola, and herbal teas. Popular with Guatemalans, **San Martin and Company** (13 Calle 1-62 Zona 10 and various locations in upscale shopping malls, www.sanmartinbakery.com/english/principal.htm, 6 A.M.-8 P.M. Mon.-Sat.) is a bakery and café with pleasant outdoor seating on a terrace or ceiling fan-cooled dining room inside. There are scrumptious croissant sandwiches for breakfast as well as a variety of sandwiches, salads, and soups for lunch and dinner in the $3-5 range.

Chocolate lovers will find bliss at **Xocoli** (6a Avenida 9-19 Zona 10, tel. 2362-3251, www.xocoli.com). The Maya world is, after all, the birthplace of chocolate, dating back to the use of cacao beans as currency in Maya times.

SPANISH

At **Tapas y Cañas** (13 Calle 7-78 Zona 10, tel. 2367-2166 or 2366-7970, lunch and dinner daily) you can savor delicious Spanish tapas. Try the *pinchos españoles* or the *albondigas de lomito*. A longtime local favorite, **Altuna** (5a Avenida 12-31 Zona 1, tel. 2251-7185 and 10a Calle 0-45 Zona 10, tel. 2332-6576, www.restaurantealtuna.com, noon-10 P.M. Tues.-Sat., noon-5 P.M. Sun., $7-22) is also one of the city's fanciest offerings with impeccable service and an elegant atmosphere. Specialties include fish and seafood dishes, including paella and lobster, but the restaurant also serves land-based fare, including *jamón serrano* and chorizo. **La Paella** (12 Avenida 17-64 Zona 10, tel. 2368-2368, lunch and dinner daily, $10-20) specializes in Paella Valenciana.

STEAKHOUSES

You'll find a variety of excellent steakhouses in Guatemala City, including **Hacienda Real**

© AL ARGUETA

Guatemala City has a number of familiar food and beverage chains.

(5a Avenida 14-67 Zona 10, tel. 2380-8300, www.hacienda-real.com, lunch and dinner daily, $10-20), where the meals are served with tasty tortillas and savory side sauces. Try the peppered steak. There are other locations at Condado Concepción and Las Majadas. For prime cuts of U.S. beef, head to **David Crockett** (5a Ave. 16-28 Zona 10, tel. 2368-1845, www.davidcrockettgt.com, lunch and dinner daily, $20-75). For absolutely astounding views of the city from its perch along Carretera a El Salvador, you can't top **El Portal del Ángel** (Km. 11.2 Carretera a El Salvador, tel. 2369-6007, noon-9 P.M. Mon.-Thurs., noon-10 P.M. Fri.-Sun., $8-35). The food is just as good as the views and the tasteful decor, with walls in vivid hues adorned with cool paintings of Catholic saints, make this place truly heavenly. It is also in Zona 11 at Paseo Miraflores and Zona 10 at Plaza Fontabella, minus the city views. **Don Emiliano** (4a Ave. 12-70 Zona 10,

Oakland Mall; tel. 2362-3005, www.donemiliano.com.gt, noon-9 P.M. Mon.-Thurs., noon-10 P.M. Sun., $25) is another fine steakhouse with additional locations at Miraflores and the Mercado de Artesanías in Zona 13. It scores big points for its modern atmosphere and the beautiful presentation of its dishes. Try the tasty steak salads.

MEXICAN

Always a popular downtown favorite, **El Gran Pavo de Don Neto** (13 Calle 4-41 Zona 1, tel. 2232-9912, 7 A.M.-11 P.M. daily) serves a wide variety of authentic Mexican dishes at reasonable prices. It has live mariachi music on weekends and another location at 6a Avenida 12-72 Zona 10 (tel. 2362-0608 or 2362-0609). Also with several locations is **Los Cebollines** (6a Avenida 9-75 Zona 1, tel. 2232-7750 and Condado Concepción, at Km. 15.5 Carretera a El Salvador, tel. 6634-5405; www.cebollines.com, 7 A.M.-11 P.M. Mon.-Thurs.,

POLLO CAMPERO AND THE CULT OF FRIED CHICKEN

If, like most people traveling home from Guatemala, you fly out on a commercial airline, don't be surprised by the distinct smell of fried chicken onboard your aircraft. One look at the overhead bins will quickly reveal that they are crammed tight with boxes of fried chicken. Meet Pollo Campero, which, along with coffee and bananas, may be one of Guatemala's main exports.

Guatemalans have always had an affinity for the stuff. It's actually quite good, though I've never taken it along as a carry-on. Many travelers take a box home for homesick relatives craving a taste of the land they left behind. Although Pollo Campero has opened up shop in recent years in several U.S. cities, expatriate Guatemalans still make a point of stopping at the store in La Aurora Airport to pick up a box. To illustrate the utter hold it has on the Guatemalan masses, the airport shop operated out of a street-side trailer during the airport's recent renovation at a time when all other businesses were simply closed.

You may be asked by U.S. Customs if you're carrying food and this question might specifically address your smuggling of Pollo Campero. Rest assured, Customs officials are happy to let the cooked chicken cross the American threshold after applying the requisite X-rays. Some Newark Airport Customs officers even claim to have the uncanny ability to distinguish chicken from a Guatemalan Pollo Campero versus that of a San Salvador outlet, though I've never taken them up on offers to verify their claims.

Pollo Campero is becoming more than just a Guatemalan phenomenon, however. An aggressive company expansion includes the opening of numerous new locations throughout North America, Europe, and even Asia in the coming years. In 2007, Campero opened outlets in Jakarta, Indonesia, and Shanghai, China, with ambitious goals to open 500 more restaurants in China by 2012. Campero already operates 220 restaurants in 10 countries, including 38 in the United States. It employs more than 7,000 people and is the largest fast-food chain in Latin America. With such aggressive expansion plans, Pollo Campero may be headed for a location near you, and I don't mean seat 25F.

7 A.M.-midnight Fri.-Sat., 7 A.M.-10 P.M. Sun.), serving tasty grilled meats, enchiladas, and tacos you can wash down with refreshing lemonades, smoothies, or cocktails. Try the delicious *tacos de pollo pibil*. Along with its branch in Antigua, **Fridas** (3a Avenida 14-60 Zona 10, tel. 2367-1611/13, www.lasfridas.com, lunch and dinner daily) serves Mexican dishes that include tasty fajitas and flautas at fairly reasonable prices ($5-10). The chicken in mango sauce is delectable and the bar makes excellent margaritas. Pick your poison from the long list of tequilas ($4-12). The most casual of all the Mexican food options is **Ta'contento** (2 Av. 14-06 Zona 10, tel. 2363-5028, 11 A.M.-midnight Tues.-Sun., $3-7), where you can eat tasty tacos al fresco fronting a lively Zona Viva street.

FRENCH

There has always been considerable French influence on Guatemalan culture, which is also evident in the city's culinary offerings. Among the excellent options are **Saint-Honoré** (14 Calle 2-51 Zona 10, tel. 2379-4548, 11:30 A.M.-11 P.M. daily), inside the InterContinental hotel, a typical French bakery serving cakes and some of Guatemala's best coffee. Also in the hotel lobby is the excellent **[Café de la Paix** (6 A.M.-11 P.M. daily), the only franchise of the famous Parisian brasserie chain outside of France, serving heavier meals, including entrecôte and onion soup ($12-25).

[Jean Francois (Diagonal 6, 13-63 Zona 10, tel. 2333-4785, noon-3 P.M. and 7-10:30 P.M. Mon.-Fri., noon-3 P.M. Sat., $8-25) is a longtime favorite with Guatemala's

© AL ARGUETA

tacos de pollo pibil **from Los Cebollines**

wealthy elite and is arguably one of the finest restaurants in Latin America. The atmosphere is elegant with tablecloths and flowers adorning the tables and antique colonial furniture in the lounge. Entrées include snook in a cream and lemon sauce with fine herbs and steak *bondelaise* with porcini mushrooms. Try the fantastic cold lemon soufflé with caramel sauce for dessert.

A more casual French dining option is **La Maison de France** (13 Calle 7-98 Zona 10, tel. 2337-4029, info@lalanchavino.com, lunch Mon.-Tues., lunch and dinner Wed.-Fri., $6-11) with a set lunch chalkboard menu and à la carte dinner options. Choose from a mix of homemade semi-Guatemalan and French dishes and wash them down with all-natural fruit juices or a bottle of wine from the extensive wine list.

With pleasant indoor and outdoor seating at Plaza Fontabella, **Clio's** (4a Avenida 12-59 Zona 10, tel. 2336-6949, www.cliosbistro.com, 12:30-3:30 P.M. and 6:30-10:30 P.M. Mon.-Sat.,

12:30-3:30 P.M. Sun., $25) serves classic French cuisine in a tasteful atmosphere.

GUATEMALAN

For gourmet Guatemalan cuisine served in a wonderful atmosphere accented by a high-roofed thatch ceiling, head to **◖ Kacao** (2a Avenida between 13 and 14 Calle, Zona 10, tel. 2337-4188/89, lunch and dinner daily). You can try a variety of traditional Guatemalan dishes, including spicy beef and chicken dishes in *pepián* and *jocón* sauces as well as corn-based delicacies such as *chuchitos* and tamales. In the downtown area, another popular place for Guatemalan cuisine is **Arrin Cuan** (5a Avenida 3-27 Zona 1, tel. 2238-0242, or 16 Calle 4-32 Zona 10, tel. 2366-2660, www.arrincuan.com, lunch and dinner daily, $5-10), with many dishes from the Cobán region, including *kakik* stew, but also some less adventurous recipes such as chicken in apple sauce. The atmosphere is charmingly simple. Another good place for hearty Guatemalan fare is **Casa Chapina** (1a Avenida 13-42 Zona 10, tel. 2367-6688 or 2368-0663, lunch and dinner daily, $8-20), serving well-presented Guatemalan dishes such as *pollo en salsa de loroco* accompanied by fresh avocado and corn on the cob.

ASIAN

Sushi places seem to have sprung up all over town recently—even the Holiday Inn and Radisson each have their own sushi restaurants in their respective lobbies. The best of the hotel lobby sushi places, however, is **Tanoshii** (14 Calle 2-51 Zona 10, tel. 2379-4548, noon-3 P.M. and 6:30-11 P.M. Mon.-Sat.), inside the InterContinental hotel, also serving Japanese dishes in a hip, ultramodern setting. Also in Zona 10 is **Sushi Itto** (4a Avenida 16-01 Zona 10, tel. 2474-5812, www.sushi-itto.com, lunch and dinner daily). The city's best Thai restaurant, **Khawp Khun Kha** (13 Calle A y 7a Ave. Zona 10, Centro Comercial Plaza Tiffany, tel. 2367-1719 and 2363-6422, noon-3 P.M. and 7-10:30 P.M. Tues.-Sat., $7-15) features tasty pad thai but also has a number of other great dishes such as chicken satay, beef in coffee sauce, and hearty soups. **J.K. Ming** (4a Avenida 12-59 Zona 10, tel. 2385-4626, $25) is a gourmet take on Asian cuisine. It gets high marks for impeccable service, cool Asian decor, and flavorful cuisine.

For Chinese food, downtown there's **Long Wah** (6a Calle 3-75 Zona 1, tel. 2232-6611, lunch and dinner daily) with reasonably priced staple dishes you can eat in or take out. It's the best of several Chinese places west of the central plaza. **China Town** (13 Calle and Avenida La Reforma Zona 10, tel. 2331-9574, lunch and dinner Mon.-Sat.) delivers to the Zona 10 hotels, or you can enjoy your meal in its pleasant atmosphere.

AMERICAN

You'll find a number of familiar restaurant chains in Guatemala City, including Applebee's, T.G.I. Friday's, Chili's, and Tony Roma's. For a local take on American fare, check out **Frisco Grill** (4a Avenida 12-59 Zona 10, Plaza Fontabella; tel. 2336-7147, 11 A.M.-11:30 P.M. Mon.-Sat., 7 A.M.-10 P.M. Sun., $15). There's outdoor patio seating and tasty American favorites such as nachos, burgers, steak sandwiches, fish and chips, and quesadillas. I'm a big fan of their margaritas.

ITALIAN

Pecorino (11 Calle 3-36 Zona 10, tel. 2360-3035, www.ristorantepecorino.com, noon-1 A.M. Mon.-Sat.) is an excellent choice for its authentic Italian food, including brick-oven pizza, seafood dishes, steak, pasta, salads, and *panini* served in an attractive Old World atmosphere. There's also a huge wine selection. In a more modern setting with attractive blue-and-white-checkered tablecloths, **Tre Fratelli** (2a Avenida 13-25 Zona 10, tel. 2366-2678, www.trefratelli.com, noon-1 A.M. daily) serves ample portions of very good food in a lively atmosphere with prices in the $5-10 range. It's part of a growing chain of restaurants with locations in the United States, Mexico, and Central America. Other Guatemala City locations can be found in Zona 11 and Carretera a El Salvador.

Downtown, **Restaurante Piccadilly** (6a Avenida and 11 Calle Zona 1, tel. 2253-4522, 7 A.M.-10 P.M. daily, $5-10) has a great selection of Italian and Guatemalan dishes in a pleasant family atmosphere. It also has beer on tap and a second location in Zona 9 at the Plazuela España (tel. 2334-7442).

My new favorite pizza place is **Margherita** (16 Calle 4-32 Zona 10, tel. 5151-0110 and Boulevard Vista Hermosa 23-41 Zona 15, tel. 4999-0500; www.pizza.com.gt, lunch and dinner daily, $10-20). There's phenomenal brick-oven pizza prepared New York-style, thin crust, Neapolitan, or Sicilian. There are tasty salads, antipasti, and calzone that you can wash down with beer or wine. The atmosphere is modern and casual with indoor or outdoor seating and electronica music on the stereo. You can dine in or carry out. Another good option for brick-oven pizza served in a casual atmosphere is **Pizzeria Vesuvio** (18 Calle 3-36 Zona 10 and three other locations, tel. 2323-2323, lunch and dinner daily, www.vesuvio.com.gt, $7-15).

FUSION CUISINE AND FINE DINING

Many Guatemalan chefs study overseas early in their careers, which is clearly evident in the international influence permeating the city's excellent fusion cuisine. In other cases, talented chefs from New York and other international cities have set up shop in Guatemala, completely raising the bar for everyone else. Such is the case of **(Jake's** (17 Calle 10-40 Zona 10, tel. 2368-0351, noon-3 P.M. and 7-10:30 P.M. Mon.-Sat., noon-4 P.M. Sun., $10-25), started by New York City artist-turned-chef Jake Denburg. Several unique features come together to make a visit to Jake's something truly special. For one, it has a wonderful atmosphere in a converted house with tile floors and wooden ceilings, eclectic decor, interesting photography, and tables covered in butcher paper (crayons supplied). But nothing tops the exquisite food. The wine list is also impressive, and rounding out your meal with one of the delectable homemade cheesecakes is a must.

Housed in the Otelito hotel, **Olivadda** (12 Calle 4-51 Zona 10, tel. 2339-1811, lunch and dinner daily, $7-12) serves sushi and exquisite international dishes with Guatemalan flair in a wonderful garden courtyard. Try the *caldo de tortilla Moreno.* **Oliva** (Boulevard Vista Hermosa 23-80 Zona 15, Edificio Avante; tel. 2385-7969, all meals daily, $8-20) fuses Mediterranean and Peruvian cuisine in a modern atmosphere that puts large, floor-to-ceiling windows to their full advantage. Try the tenderloin with rosemary honey while enjoying

jazz and bossa nova on the stereo amid the cool furnishings.

Also serving as a culinary school, **Camille** (9a Avenida 15-27 Zona 10, tel. 2368-0048 or 2367-1525, noon-3 P.M. and 7-10 P.M. Tues.-Fri., 7-10 P.M. Sat., $10-15) serves creatively prepared fish, chicken, and seafood dishes. The steak in chipotle sauce served on a cheese *pupusa* (Salvadoran cheese-filled tortilla) is truly extraordinary. The atmosphere is pleasantly cozy with carbon sketches etched on the white plaster walls and also on ripped-out pages from spiral bound notebooks framed and hung.

A longtime favorite is **(Tamarindos** (11 Calle 2-19A Zona 10, tel. 2360-2815, reservaciones@tamarindos.com.gt, 12:30-3 P.M. and 7:30 P.M.-1 A.M. Mon.-Sat., $10-20), which makes some fine sushi and does an excellent job of combining Thai, Italian, and Guatemalan flavors into some irresistible dishes. There is pleasant indoor and outdoor garden patio seating and the hip ambience is set by postmodern decor and electronica music on the stereo. Try the vegetarian pad thai or the four-cheese gnocchi.

(Zumo (1 Av. 12-16 Zona 10, tel. 2334-6316, www.zumo.com.gt, noon-3 P.M. and 7-10 P.M. Mon.-Fri., 7-11 P.M. Sat.; $25) is another one of the city's culinary hotspots, with a wonderful ambiance and great food to match. I'm a big fan of mangoes so I love the shrimp in mango sauce with avocado butter. Naturally, I order the mango mousse for dessert. There's a cool wine cellar from which you can choose a bottle of wine to accompany your meal. Three fountains grace the premises and there's pleasant outdoor or indoor seating. The decor is Asian-inspired, evoking Turkey and the Philippines.

A newer addition to Zona 4's old Iglesia Yurrita is **Restaurante Casa Yurrita** (Ruta 6 8-52, tel. 2360-1615, lunch and dinner daily, $7-15), serving up fancy dishes such as duck in hibiscus (*Rosa de Jamaica*) sauce and fish al pesto. Zona 14 also has some highly recommended

© AL ARGUETA

Tamarindos is one of Guatemala City's finest restaurants.

restaurants. Amid spacious gardens is █ Ambia (10a Avenida 5-49 Zona 14, tel. 2366-6890 or 2366-6897, lunch and dinner Mon.-Sat., lunch Sun.), where the emphasis is on New Age cuisine consisting largely of Asian recipes, including Thai chicken and shrimp recipes, pad thai ($10-12), excellent soups, Italian pastas, and lobster Thermidor ($26). There are decadent desserts, including black-and-white chocolate mousse and pears in red wine. The wine list, incidentally, is extensive and includes a $278 bottle of Spanish Vega Sicilia Valbuena.

In the suburbs just east of the city, █ Tua (Km. 14.5 Carretera a El Salvador, Centro Comercial Escala; tel. 6637-5443 or 6637-5444, $30) is a bistro serving wonderful cuisine that is on par with the fabulous volcano

views off in the distance. It's definitely a place to choose outside seating, but the inside is modern and attractive as well, with dramatic high ceilings. I like the tuna tataki and coconut-breaded shrimp. The lamb chops and chipotle chicken are also fabulous.

In the city center and recommended more for the historical atmosphere than the somewhat overpriced, uninspired food is **Casa del Callejon Castillo Hermanos** (2a Ave. "A" 13-20 Zona 1, tel. 2366-5671, $15-35). Set in an old colonial home brimming with charm, the museum-like locale documents the life and times of the city's wealthy Castillo family, of Gallo beer fame. Interspersed with elegant dining areas are old photos, family heirlooms, and cool antique furniture on display. It makes a perfectly good place for a drink in a fancy, old-fashioned atmosphere. The best nights to visit are those featuring special performances of live jazz and tango, as dinner is often included in the admission price and tends to include better fare.

SEAFOOD

Donde Mikel (6a Ave. 13-32 Zona 10, tel. 2363-3308, lunch and dinner Mon.-Fri., lunch Sat.) serves some of the city's best seafood and grilled steak in a casual atmosphere. Its surf-and-turf plates are a popular favorite. Although officially Peruvian food, the menu at **Inka Grill** (2a Avenida 14-22 Zona 10, tel. 2363-3013, noon-10 P.M. Sun.-Wed., until 11 P.M. Thurs.-Sat.) is heavy on delicious seafood, including several types of grilled fish and a Chinese-Peruvian blend of flavors, as in the case of its tasty wonton soup. **La Perla** (13 Calle "A" 7-19 Zona 10, Plaza Tiffany; tel. 2366-1544, $12-25) serves a somewhat limited but delicious and original menu of creative seafood dishes in a modern atmosphere. They have a fabulous Saturday brunch.

Information and Services

TOURIST INFORMATION

The main office of the Guatemala Tourist Commission (INGUAT) is at 7a Avenida 1-17 Zona 4, and it is open 8 A.M.-4 P.M. Monday-Friday. Your best bet, however, is to stop by its kiosk in the airport arrivals area, which is open 6 A.M.-9 P.M. It also has smaller offices inside the Palacio Nacional de la Cultura (Parque Central, tel. 2253-0748), which keeps odd hours, and the historic Palacio de Correos (Main Post Office, 7a Avenida 11-67 Zona 1, tel. 2251-1898, 9 A.M.-5 P.M. Mon.-Fri.).

MAPS

The best maps of Guatemala are *Mapas de Guatemala* (www.mapasdeguatemala.com), a series of beautifully illustrated, full-color maps of Guatemala's main tourist regions that also include helpful information on local businesses. The free maps are available at INGUAT and at tourist gift shops and restaurants seemingly everywhere. You can also find interactive versions on their website. ITMB Publishing (530 W. Broadway, Vancouver, BC, Canada, 604/879-3621, www.itmb.com) publishes an excellent *International Travel Map of Guatemala* ($10.95), which is weatherproof and can be found at well-known bookstores in the United States.

COMMUNICATIONS

The main post office (8:30 A.M.-5 P.M. Mon.-Fri., 8:30 A.M.-1 P.M. Sat.) is downtown at 7a Avenida 11-67 Zona 1. There are also branches at the airport and the corner of Avenida La Reforma and 14 Calle Zona 9 with the same hours. It's called El Correo. Now you can find post office locations and even track packages online via their website at www.elcorreo.com.gt.

For faster service, many people prefer to use one of the international couriers, including FedEx (14 Calle 3-51 Zona 10, dificio Murano Center Local No. 1, tel. toll-free from Guatemala 1-801-00-333-39, www.fedex.com), UPS (13 Calle "A" y 7a Ave. Zona 10, Centro Comercial Plaza Tiffany, tel. 2421-6000, www.ups.com), and DHL (12 Calle 5-12 Zona 10, tel. 2332-7547, www.dhl.com). For an all-in-one shipping locale, try Fast Mail (5a Avenida 7-42, Zona 14, tel. 2246-4646, www.fastmailcenter.com, 8:30 A.M.-5:30 P.M. Mon.-Fri., 9 A.M.-1 P.M. Sat.).

MONEY

You can exchange dollars and cash travelers checks at virtually all of the city's banks, including the one in the arrivals hall of the international airport. ATMs linked to international networks can be found all over the city. Be especially careful when withdrawing money at ATMs in the downtown area. The safest places to hit up an ATM are the Guatemala City shopping malls and hotel lobbies.

You can search for Visa ATM locations in Guatemala City online at http://visa.via.infonow.net and MasterCard ATMs at www.mastercard.com/atm. A useful listing of Banco Industrial Visa ATM machines throughout Guatemala can be found at www.bi.com.gt.

The American Express Agent in Guatemala City is Clark Tours (7a Avenida 14-76, Plaza Clark, Zona 9, tel. 2412-4700, www.clarktours.com). It also has offices in the Westin Camino Real, Holiday Inn, and Barceló.

LAUNDRY

You can do laundry at some of the budget hotels, including the Xamanek Student Inn (13 Calle 3-57 Zona 10). Otherwise, downtown there's Lavandería El Siglo (12 Calle 3-42 Zona 1, 8 A.M.-6 P.M. Mon.-Sat., $4 per load). In Zona 10 is Lavandería Obelisco (Avenida La Reforma 16-30), where self-service laundry costs about $3 per load to wash and dry.

STAYING SAFE IN GUATEMALA CITY

Guatemala City can be a dodgy place, though some *zonas* are certainly more prone to crime than others. Most of the areas frequented by tourists are relatively safe, though the downtown area (Zona 1) is by far the country's purse-snatching and pickpocketing hub. Exercise common sense and caution when in public areas. Never leave valuables in a parked car and avoid flashing expensive items such as laptops and cell phones in public places.

Pay careful attention when using ATMs. Some thieves have been so ingenious as to set up fake keypads at the entrance to ATM kiosks asking cardholders to enter their PIN numbers in order to gain access to the machine. You should never enter your PIN number anywhere other than on the ATM keypad itself.

Riding public buses is not usually a good idea, though the new transit system, the Transmetro, has proven much safer. If driving, it's a good idea to keep the car doors locked and the windows rolled all the way up. (Make sure your car's air-conditioning system is working properly so as to avoid the temptation to roll down the windows when it gets hot out.) Avoid talking on a cell phone while driving; it will keep you alert to your surroundings and will not draw undue attention from potential thieves. Cell phones are a favorite target, as is flashy jewelry. Recently, some parts of the city have become prone to robberies whereby the perpetrators (usually on motorcycles) target cars stopped at traffic lights. In most cases, the victims have been talking on their cell phones or are women traveling alone and wearing expensive jewelry. For this reason, many Guatemalans tint their windows to keep prying eyes away from the contents of their car. If you are

the victim of a robbery or witness one, dial 120 from any phone.

Watch out for a common scam, particularly in the vicinity of the airport, whereby a "Good Samaritan" informs you of a flat tire on your car. If you can confirm that you indeed have a flat, pull over in a well-lit, public place. Do not stop at the side of the road to change the tire. If you are able to make it to a public place such as a gas station, have someone in your party stay inside the car or keep an eye on it yourself while you a gas station attendant changes the tire for you. The important thing is not to lose sight of the inside of your vehicle for a moment. Thieves can be extremely crafty at distracting you and getting into your car; locked doors may be a deterrent but will not stop thieves if they've already targeted you. For information on other precautions and common scams while traveling in Guatemala, see the State Department's Consular Information Sheet online at http://travel.state.gov.

In November 2008, the U.S. Embassy issued safety warnings for certain Guatemalan roads. Among the areas mentioned was the road east of kilometer 13 of Carretera a El Salvador. Due to its popularity with the city's wealthy residents, it appears this sector has become the scene of several violent robberies, carjackings, and kidnappings. The embassy recommends avoiding travel beyond kilometer 13 between 9 P.M. and 6 A.M. The document also recommends avoiding travel on the following roads outside Guatemala City: Routes 4 and 11 in the vicinity of Lake Atitlán and Route 14 between Antigua and Escuintla.

For this and other pertinent information, visit http://guatemala.usembassy.gov.

MEDICAL SERVICES

Guatemala City is becoming a destination for medical tourism, with many excellent private hospitals. Public clinics such as the Clínica Cruz Roja (Red Cross Clinic, 3a Calle 8-40 Zona 1, 8 A.M.-5:30 P.M. Mon.-Fri., 8 A.M.-noon Sat.) offer free or low-cost consultations. Private clinics with doctors who speak English include the highly recommended 24-hour Hospital Centro Medico (6a Avenida 3-47 Zona 10, tel. 2279-4949, www.centromedico.com.gt) and the Hospital Herrera Llerandi (6a Avenida 8-71 Zona 10, tel. 2384-5959 or 2334-5955 emergencies, www.herrerallerandi.com). Grupo Hospitalario Guatemala (www.hospitalesdeguatemala.

com) also has a good network of hospitals in the Guatemala City metro area.

EMERGENCY

Dial 120 from any phone for the police (6a Avenida and 14 Calle Zona 1). For emergency medical assistance, dial 125 for the Red Cross. For the fire department, dial 122 or 123,

IMMIGRATION

The offices of Migración (tel. 2361-8476, www. migracion.gob.gt) are on the second floor of the INGUAT building at 7a Avenida 1-17 Zona 4 and are open 8 A.M.-2:45 P.M. Monday-Friday.

TRAVEL AGENTS

For booking plane tickets and onward travel within Guatemala, a good choice is Viajes Tivoli (6a Avenida 8-41 Zona 9, tel. 2386-4200, or 12 Calle 4-55 Zona 1, Edificio Herrera, tel. 2298-1050, www.tivoli.com.gt), as is Clark Tours (7a Avenida 14-76, Plaza Clark, Zona 9, tel. 2412-4700, www.clarktours.com). Clark Tours also has offices in the Westin Camino Real, Holiday Inn, and Barceló.

Getting There and Around

GETTING THERE
Air

The once-wonky **La Aurora International Airport** (GUA) underwent a major expansion and renovation in 2007 and is now one of Central America's largest and most modern airports. Services include a bank, ATMs, various restaurants, excellent duty-free shopping, souvenir shops, and a post office. Members of United Airlines' United Club enjoy access to the airport's *Copa Club,* a lounge operated jointly with Copa Airlines and located next to gate 14. It's also open to First Class passengers traveling on United, Copa, or Star Alliance partners. Not traveling in first class? You can pay a day fee to visit ($50) if traveling on any of these airlines. Guests enjoy a TV lounge, free cocktails, Wi-Fi, and space to relax before the flight.

There is a $2.75 (Q20) departure tax levied on international and domestic flights leaving the airport, which must be paid in cash. This is paid at the bank downstairs from the check-in lobby and just before entering the security screening area. An additional departure tax of $30 is collected for international flights, though this is included in the taxes paid when purchasing your ticket.

Immigration, customs, and baggage claim are on the main building's first floor, while departures and check-in counters are located on the third floor. There are technically two adjacent terminals, though they are merged into one large facility. The first area, known as *finger central,* consists of six gates for wide-body aircraft. It fronts the main terminal, which is all that remains of the original facility dating to the 1960s. The second terminal, known as *finger norte,* consists of gates 7 to 19 and is seamlessly integrated into the rest of the terminal building. There is a food court on the fourth floor of the main terminal building overlooking the check-in counters. Additional restaurants can be found past the security checkpoints leading to the two *fingers.*

Immigration and customs procedures at La Aurora Airport are very straightforward. Customs (known as SAT) will look at your declaration paperwork (to be filled out on the airplane prior to arrival) and will either put you in a line where your bags will be searched and applicable duties (if any) collected or will simply wave you on. Most foreign travelers are waved on, as what they're mostly looking for are arriving Guatemalans with loot from stateside

La Aurora International Airport

shopping sprees. A disproportionate number of bags per traveler are usually a sure tip-off.

Taxis are easily booked from a kiosk inside the airport terminal, as are rental cars. A taxi from the airport costs $8-20 depending on what part of town you're going to. Avis, Budget, Hertz, and National have kiosks inside the airport terminal. Their lots are across the road fronting the airport's three-level parking garage. If you're arriving on a later flight and have never driven Guatemala City's chaotic streets before, it might make more sense to take advantage of free airport shuttles to Zona 10 hotels and have the rental car company drop off the vehicle at your hotel the next morning. You could also just as easily take a cab or shuttle from your hotel to the airport the following day and pick up the car at that time.

If most of your travel involves the Guatemala City and Antigua area, my advice is to forgo a car rental in favor of taxis and shuttle buses. You can also hire a driver to take you around for about US$75-100 a day. Local hotel concierges can usually recommend someone for you. Doing so will allow you to get a feel for the city without the stress of having to drive on its unfamiliar streets. It will also allow you to get acquainted with the particular style of Guatemalan urban driving you'll need to adopt if you do end up driving here.

If you're bypassing Guatemala City altogether, you'll find shuttle vans to Antigua (about $15) are easily booked upon arrival at the airport. There is also a very helpful INGUAT (Instituto Guatemalteco de Turismo) information desk just after passing customs. It's staffed by English-speaking agents who can help you get your bearings.

It's not a good idea to ride a public bus into the city, especially at night. The Transmetro is perfectly safe and efficient, but its coverage area is limited. It will not get you to or from the airport, though the newer *eje central* route can get you as close as Bulevar

Liberacion, which fronts the airport runway's northern extreme.

Several U.S. and foreign carriers fly daily into Guatemala City. Most of these airlines have city ticket offices, including **American Airlines** (Barceló Guatemala City, 7a Avenida 15-45 Zona 9, tel. 2422-0000), **United Airlines** (18 Calle 5-56, Edificio Unicentro, Local 704, Zona 10, tel. 2385-9610 or 801/812-6684 toll-free), **Delta** (15 Calle 3-20 Zona 10, Centro Ejecutivo, Primer Nivel, Zona 10, tel. 2337-0642), **TACA** (Avenida Hincapié 12-22, Zona 13, tel. 2470-8222), and **Iberia** (Avenida La Reforma 8-60 Zona 9, tel. 2332-0911). American Airlines and United Airlines passengers can check bags in the day before their flight at service centers in the Barceló Guatemala City hotel (7a Avenida 15-45 Zona 9).

The only **domestic service** is to Flores, near the ruins of Tikal, though other routes may open if government plans to revamp several smaller airports throughout the country ever come to fruition. The only airline leaving from the main terminal for domestic flights is TACA, with several daily flights to Flores. Local carrier **TAG** (Ave. Hincapie y 18 Calle Zona 13, tel. 2380-9494, www.tag.com.gt) offers service from the other side of the runway at its private hangar.

The airport is located 6 km south of downtown Guatemala City and 25 km from Antigua.

Bus

Guatemala City's unattractive Zona 4 bus terminal is being phased out thanks to a long-overdue plan to bring order to the chaos traditionally characterizing the state of public transportation, both within and into and out of the city. Accounting for 80 percent of the bedlam were buses arriving from and departing to the Western Highlands and the Pacific Coast. Buses to and from both of these regions are now based out of the **Central de Transferencias (CENTRA)** in Zona 12, on the

southern outskirts of the city. From there, a series of modern, bright green interconnected buses known as *buses articulados* take passengers on a new system called the **Transmetro** into the city center. Centra Norte (CA-9 Norte 40-26 Zona 17, Km 8.5, tel. 2329-9977) is currently under construction and will serve as the hub for buses heading out along the highway leading east to Izabal and Las Verapaces. The city's public transportation system, meanwhile, is being replaced entirely by the Transmetro, a sort of surface metro, which will cover the entire metropolitan area by 2020 (or so they tell us).

A number of the (mostly) **first class buses** still leave from their own depots spread throughout the city, and this will probably continue to be the case for some time. Here is the information on some of the more popular first-class bus routes:

To Chiquimula (3.5 hours, $4, 170 km): **Rutas Orientales** (19 Calle 8-18 Zona 1, tel. 2253-7282), departures every half hour 4:30 A.M.-6 P.M., or **Transportes Guerra** (19 Calle 8-39 Zona 1, tel. 2238-2917), every half hour 7 A.M.-6 P.M.

To Cobán (4.5 hours, $5, 213 km): **Transportes Escobar Monja Blanca** (8a Avenida 15-16 Zona 1, tel. 2238-1409) has hourly buses 4 A.M.-5 P.M., stopping at El Rancho and the Quetzal Biotope.

To Esquipulas (4.5 hours, $5, 222 km): **Rutas Orientales** (19 Calle 8-18 Zona 1, tel. 2253-7282), has departures every half hour 4:30 A.M.-6 P.M.

To Flores (eight hours, $10-30 depending on service level, 500 km): Options include **Línea Dorada** (16 Calle 10-55 Zona 1, tel. 2232-5506, www.tikalmayanworld.com), with luxury buses departing at 10 A.M. and 9 P.M. ($30), or a more economical overnight bus leaving at 10 P.M. ($16). **Fuentes del Norte** (17 Calle 8-46 Zona 1, tel. 2251-3817) has about 20 daily departures ($10-20).

To Huehuetenango (five hours, 266 km):

Los Halcones (7a Avenida 15-27 Zona 1, tel. 2238-1929, $5), departs at 7 A.M., 2 P.M., and 5 P.M. **Transportes Velásquez** (20 Calle 1-37 Zona 1, tel. 2221-1084, $4) has nine buses daily. **Transportes Zaculeu Futura** (9a Calle 11-42 Zona 1, tel. 2232-2858, $5), has buses at 6 A.M. and 3 P.M.

To La Mesilla (seven hours, $6, 345 km): **Transportes Velásquez** (20 Calle 1-37 Zona 1, tel. 2221-1084, $5.50), every two hours 5:30 A.M.-1:30 P.M.

To Panajachel (three hours, 148 km): **Transportes Rebuli** (21 Calle and 4a Avenida Zona 1, $2) has hourly buses 5:30 A.M.-3:30 P.M.

To Puerto Barrios (five hours, 295 km): **Litegua** (15 Calle 10-40 Zona 1, tel. 2220-8840, www.litegua.com) has 16 buses daily 4:30 A.M.-7 P.M.

To Quetzaltenango (four hours, $4.50, 205 km): **Transportes Álamo** (21 Calle 0-14 Zona 1, tel. 2251-4838) has six buses a day 8 A.M.-5:30 P.M. **Líneas América** (2a Avenida 18-47 Zona 1, tel. 2232-1432) has seven buses a day 5 A.M.-7:30 P.M. **Transportes Galgos** (7a Avenida 19-44 Zona 1, tel. 2253-4868) leaves seven times daily 5:30 A.M.-7 P.M. The newest option is a nonstop bus on an ultraluxurious coach aboard **Línea Dorada** (16 Calle 10-03 Zona 1, tel. 2220-7900 or 2232-9658, $6) at 8 A.M. and 3 P.M.

To Río Dulce (six hours, $6-21, 280 km): **Línea Dorada** (16 Calle 10-55 Zona 1, tel. 2232-5506, www.tikalmayanworld.com) has luxury buses departing at 10 A.M. and 9 P.M. ($21), or a more economical bus leaving at 10 P.M. ($11). Both continue to Flores. **Litegua** (15 Calle 10-40 Zona 1, tel. 2220-8840, www.litegua.com) has buses at 6 A.M., 9 A.M., 11:30 A.M., and 1 P.M.

To Zacapa (three hours, $3.50): **Rutas Orientales** (19 Calle 8-18 Zona 1, tel. 2253-7282) has 15 buses daily.

International Bus

To Copán, Honduras (five hours, 238 km, $35):

Hedman Alas (2a Avenida 8-73 Zona 10, tel. 2362-5072, 2362-5073, or 2362-5074, www.hedmanalas.com) departs daily at 5 A.M. and 9 A.M.

To San Salvador, El Salvador (five hours, 240 km): **Melva Internacional** (3a Avenida 1-38 Zona 9, tel. 2331-0874, $15) departs hourly 5 A.M.-4 P.M., with more expensive *especiales* ($20) leaving at 6:45 A.M., 9 A.M., and 3 P.M. **Tica Bus** (Calzada Aguilar Batres 22-55 Zona 12, tel. 2473-1639, www.ticabus.com, $20) leaves at 1 P.M. **King Quality** (18 Avenida 1-96 Zona 15, tel. 2369-0404, $30) has luxury buses departing at 6:30 A.M., 8 A.M., 2 P.M., and 3:30 P.M. **Pullmantur** (1a Avenida 13-22 Zona 10, Holiday Inn, tel. 2367-4746, www.pullmantur.com, $30-46) offers the most luxurious service on this route with double-decker buses and a choice of fare classes, departing at 7 A.M. and 3 P.M. daily with additional buses Fridays at noon and Sundays at 4 P.M.

To Tapachula, Mexico (seven hours, 290 km): **Transportes Galgos** (7a Avenida 19-44 Zona 1, tel. 2253-4868, $22) has departures at 7:30 A.M. and 2 P.M. **Línea Dorada** (16 Calle 10-55 Zona 1, tel. 2232-5506, www.tikalmayanworld.com, $22) departs at 8 A.M.

GETTING AROUND
Taxi

Getting around by taxi can be tricky, as there is really only one reliable taxicab company in the city and it requires you to call for a pickup if you wish to hire its services. **Taxis Amarillo Express** (tel. 2332-1515) is also one of the only companies to use meters. Otherwise, the airport taxis and those at the Zona Viva hotels are generally reliable. It's not usually a good idea to hail a cab from the street, as some of these are gypsy cabs and robberies do sometimes occur. If you find a reliable cab driver, you can always ask for a business card and hire his services for the rest of your stay or ask him to refer you to another reputable driver.

Car Rental

Several car rental agencies operate out of

TRANSMETRO EJE SUR

CENTRO CÍVICO

BOLÍVAR

SANTA CECILIA

TRÉBOL

PROGRESO

MARISCAL

REFORMITA

EL CARMEN

LAS CHARCAS

JAVIER

MONTE MARÍA

CENTRA SUR

NOT TO SCALE

© AVALON TRAVEL

TRANSMETRO CENTRAL

18 CALLE

PLAZA BARRIOS

EL CALVARIO

CENTRO CÍVICO

21 CALLE

9A AVENIDA

BANCO DE GUATEMALA

6A AVENIDA

7A AVENIDA

4 GRADOS SUR

RUTA 2

4 GARDOS NORTE

EXPOSICIÓN

RUTA 6

PLAZA DE LA REPÚBLICA

TERMINAL

TORRE DEL REFORMADOR

2A CALLE

INDUSTRIA SUR

SEIS 26

5A CALLE

IGSS ZONA 9

TIVOLI

12 CALLE

MONTÚFAR

PLAZA ESPAÑA

6A AVENIDA

7A AVENIDA

ACUEDUCTO

LOS ARCOS

BLVD LOS PRÓCERES

© AVALON TRAVEL

NOT TO SCALE

the airport and nearby Zona 10, including **Advantage** (Avenida La Reforma 8-33 Zona 10, tel. 2332-7525 or 2362-7202 or 800/777-5500 U.S. toll-free, www.advantagerentacar.com), **Avis** (6a Calle 7-64 Zona 9, tel. 2324-9000 or 800/331-1212 U.S. toll-free, www.avis.com.gt), **Dollar** (Avenida La Reforma 8-33 Zona 10, tel. 2385-8728 or 800/800-4000 U.S. toll-free, www.dollar.com.gt), **Budget** (6a Avenida 11-24 Zona 9, tel. 2332-7744 or 800/472-3325 U.S. toll-free, www.budget.com or www.budgetguatemala.com.gt), **Hertz** (7a Avenida 14-76 Zona 9, tel. 2470-3700 or 800/654-3001 U.S. toll-free, also with offices inside the Westin Camino Real,

Intercontinental, and Barceló, www.hertzguatemala.com), and **Thrifty** (7a Avenida 14-28 Zona 13, Aeropuerto La Aurora; tel. 2379-8747 to 52, or 800/847-4389 U.S. toll-free, www.thrifty.com).

Public Buses

Guatemala City's chaotic public bus transportation is not recommended for international travelers, mainly for safety considerations, as armed robberies and purse snatchings are frequent. Buses are also particularly susceptible to the city's increasing gang-related violence and drivers are often harassed for money by gang members.

© AL ARGUETA

Guatemala City's Transmetro is a safe and efficient means of transportation.

Transmetro

A glimmer of hope for the city's mass transit system emerged in 2007 with the unveiling of the Transmetro, a completely revamped public transportation system, which should be in full operation by 2020. The first phase, including the first transfer center (in Zona 12) for buses coming in from other parts of Guatemala, is already up and running and a second branch was scheduled to go into service at time of publication. Bus service via long, train-like interconnected green units brings travelers from the transfer center to the downtown area. More transfer centers are in the works.

The system promises to provide Guatemalans (and foreign travelers) with a safe, comfortable, and fast option for getting around the city. Buses stop at designated locations, drivers no longer trundle the streets competing for passengers, a prepaid system eliminates on-board cash, and buses and stations are guarded by cameras and plainclothes police officers. It costs Q1 to ride the Transmetro and the system only accepts one-Quetzal coins. Drop your coin in the slot, push past the turnstile, and wait for the next bus under a covered, raised platform.

For now, the Transmetro's routes include the *eje sur,* starting at the CENTRA and heading downtown to Zona 1's Plaza Amate, and the newer *corredor central.* The *eje sur* makes 12 stops along the way, including at the Centro Cívico (Plaza Municipal) and El Trébol. The *corredor central* route runs the length of 7a Avenida from Zona 1 to Zona 13's Avenida Las Americas all the way to Plaza Berlin, stopping at Zona 4's bus terminal and Cuatro Grados Norte along the way. The bus terminal's status as the transportation hub for many bus lines will probably remain in place pending the gradual transition to the new system based on transfer centers. Direct Transmetro buses (no stops) heading from downtown to CENTRA leave from **Plaza Amate** (4a Avenida and 18 Calle Zona 1, 5-9 A.M. and 4-9 P.M. Mon.-Fri.).

Near Guatemala City

South of the city along Calzada Aguilar Batres, the city sprawl continues into the adjacent district of Villa Nueva, a suburban housing and industrial area that has been swallowed by the larger city. From here, the Carretera al Pacífico, or Pacific Highway (CA-9) leads south to Escuintla and the Pacific Coast.

LAKE AMATITLÁN

Amatitlán lies 30 kilometers south of Guatemala City on the road to the Pacific Coast. The lake is in the process of being rescued from what would have been certain ecological death caused by wastewater from nearby industry and uncontrolled urban growth. A new sewage treatment plant now filters the filthy waters of the Río Villalobos, which once flooded untreated sewage into the lake. Trees have been replanted and the lake is being pumped with oxygen and cleaned of plants in an effort to reverse its eutrophication. It's still not possible to swim in the lake's waters, though it may be some day.

Recreation

The public beach of **Las Ninfas** was being remodeled by tourism authorities to include boat docks (for sailboats and motorboats), new food stalls, walkways, and landscaping. The long-closed **Teleférico** (Aerial Tram, 9 A.M.-5 P.M. Fri.-Sun., $2 adults, $0.85 children) was reopened in 2006, kicking off the rebirth of one of Guatemala City's oldest recreational enclaves. The funicular climbs 350 meters up a mountainside along a 1.5-kilometer route. There's a lookout point at the top of the mountain where you can get out, appreciate the view of the lake and Guatemala City, and grab a bite to eat at a small cafetería serving tacos, hot dogs, chicken wings, and salads.

Another recreational option is **rock climbing**

on the rock cliffs overlooking the lakeshore on 20 different routes ranging in difficulty from 5.8 to 5.13. **Vertical Expeditions** (tel. 5801-6871, www.verticalguatemala.com) does full-day climbing trips for $35 per person with a three-person minimum, including guide, gear, and transportation. It also offers a one-day rock climbing school for $50, covering all aspects of safety, equipment, and climbing techniques. Further options include climbing (5.8 to 5.13) and rappelling along a 70-meter (230-foot) waterfall in the eastern province of Jalapa, 100 kilometers from Guatemala City. You can also rappel down the actual waterfall, a practice commonly referred to as canyoning. Day trips cost $65 per person with a four-person minimum and include guide, transport, and gear. Antigua-based **Old Town Outfitters** (5a Avenida Sur #12C, tel. 5339-0440, www.bikeguatemala.com) also offers rock-climbing day trips to Amatitlán for $35 per person, including all gear, and can provide instruction.

If you'd rather just soak your weary bones in the warm waters of some pleasant hot springs, you can do that at **Kawilal Spa** at Baños Termales Santa Teresita (tel. 6633-0225, www.santateresita.com.gt, 8 A.M.-6 P.M. daily), where you can enjoy a private steam bath or a soak in a private tub filled with steaming hot water to your taste ($5). Several outdoor pools of varying temperatures are also available and there's a restaurant serving grilled meats and chicken, salads, sandwiches, and seafood. Rounding out the list of offerings is a spa, where you can enjoy a one-hour massage for about $20. A luxury hotel is planned to open here in Spring 2013.

Parque Nacional Naciones Unidas

This 491-hectare park near the lakeshore is managed by private conservation group **Defensores de la Naturaleza** (tel. 6630-6421

FIRE ON THE MOUNTAIN

Guatemala is one of few places in the world where you can get up close and personal with an active volcano in relative ease. While the climb is not for the faint of heart, adventurous types will find it to be a worthwhile endeavor. From the town of San Francisco de Salas, the 3.7-kilometer trail up Pacaya Volcano (2-3 hours) climbs gradually through cornfields and secondary forest before arriving at a vast volcanic wasteland of old lava flows. After crossing a barren ridge, the trail then winds up the slopes of the volcanic crater itself. Hiking up the loose ash will give you the sensation of taking two steps forward and one step back. It's a good workout but worth the effort. At the summit, you're treated to a fine view of the main vent spewing lava, rocks, and ash. It may sometimes feel too close for comfort, as large chunks of lava rock often land nearby. Take a moment to glimpse Guatemala City, the Pacific Coast, and some of the neighboring volcanoes from here. At the summit, avoid breathing in the clouds of sulfuric gases. Be especially careful where you step, as there are some hot zones and sometimes some slow-moving lava flows. The skilike descent down the same sandy ash can be tricky and you should exercise due caution to avoid a nasty face-plant into the jagged lava rocks alongside the trail.

If hiking during the day, bring plenty of sunscreen along with a hat, preferably with a chin strap that will prevent it from blowing away at the windy summit. Water and some snacks are always a good idea. Try not to carry excessive amounts of cash, but just what you'll need for the park admission, guide tip, and a drink and/or snack when you arrive back at the base of the trail. Rain gear (depending on the season) and some good, sturdy boots are also important. You'll especially appreciate the latter because you'll need ankle support and it's easy to get rocks and sand in your shoes, which can be extremely uncomfortable, during the final ascent up the sandy crater.

or 6630-6153) and is open 8 A.M.-4 P.M. Monday-Friday and 8 A.M.-5 P.M. Saturday and Sunday. Admission is $3.50. Facilities include picnic areas with barbecue pits, hiking and mountain biking trails with lookout points over the lake, basketball courts, and soccer fields. A five-platform, 400-meter canopy tour, and rappelling were added in 2008.

Getting There

You'll probably need to rent a car to get to Lake Amatitlán, though you could also hire a cab to take you there from Guatemala City for about $25. If you're driving, take the Pacific Highway (CA-9) south out of the city. The main entrance to the Amatitlán lakeshore is at Km. 26. You'll see signs. The exit veers off from the right side of the highway. From the exit ramp, you'll come to a Shell gas station, at which you turn left. Follow the road until it dead-ends just past the soccer fields on your left. Turn left at the dead end. You'll pass a bridge over the Río Michatoya on your right. The next left will take you to the Teleférico and farther up that same road is Parque Nacional Naciones Unidas. Turning right onto the bridge over the Río Michatoya followed by an immediate right will bring you to the Santa Teresita hot springs.

◖ PACAYA VOLCANO NATIONAL PARK

Looming over Lake Amatitlán is this 2,552-meter-high active volcano (www.volcandepacaya.com) spewing lava and ash for the amazement of tourists and locals alike. Its current active phase began in 1965 and has barely ceased since. Activity varies from quiet gas, lava, and steam emissions to full-scale explosive eruptions hurtling rocks into the sky. It sometimes spews large ash clouds that prompt the closure of Guatemala City's La Aurora International Airport, as was the case when a 1998 eruption blanketed the airport runway in fine volcanic sand and again in May 2010.

The volcano makes a convenient day trip from Guatemala City (45 minutes) or Antigua (1 hour). Logistically, it makes more sense from Guatemala City, but the tour operators offering the trip are almost entirely based in the old colonial city. It's possible to make the trip on your own, though going in a group with a local guide is highly recommended.

The volcano's national park status dates to 2001. A visitors center and ticket booth can be found at the trailhead in the village of San Francisco de Sales. Admission to the park is $5. You can also hire a guide here. There is safe parking for vehicles in San Francisco de Sales and the well-maintained trail has good signage, rest stops with trash receptacles, and outhouses. The trails are patrolled by park rangers and incidents of robbery, which once plagued this otherwise wonderful place, have become virtually unheard of in recent years.

To get here on your own steam, follow the CA-9 highway past Amatitlán to a signed turnoff at Km. 37.5. Head east eight kilometers to the village of San Vicente Pacaya, where you'll find the park entry station and information center. The road continues from here another 10 kilometers to San Francisco de Sales (turn left at the fork in the road just past San Vicente Pacaya). For an excellent map detailing the route of ascent, see the interactive map online at *Mapas de Guatemala* (www.mapasdeguatemala.com/mapas).

Guide Companies

Recommended companies (all based in neighboring La Antigua Guatemala) include **Old Town Outfitters** (5a Avenida Sur #12C, tel. 5339-0440, www.bikeguatemala.com, $30 including lunch), which leaves earlier than most other companies to avoid the crowds. **Adrenalina Tours** (5a Avenida Norte #31, tel. 7832-1108 or 5535-6831) leaves daily at 6 A.M. and 1 P.M. The trip costs $10-20 depending on whether or not you want a meal with your climb. The more expensive VIP trip has a four-person minimum and also includes the $5 park admission fee. **O.X. Outdoor Excursions** (1a Avenida Sur #4B, tel. 7832-0074 or 5801-4301, www.guatemalavolcano.com), offers well-guided trips. All outfitters use local guides, as required by the community of San Francisco de Sales.

Parque Natural Canopy Calderas

Three kilometers from San Francisco de Salas is the wonderful, privately owned Parque Natural Canopy Calderas (tel. 5538-5531 or 2369-7218; www.parquecalderas.com.gt, 8 A.M.-6 P.M. daily, $10 admission), where you can explore a volcanic caldera. Activities on and around the jungle-clad lagoon include cruising along a zipline through the forest canopy between six platforms ($10), four-wheeling ($13 per hour), horseback riding ($8), mountain biking, kayaking ($3.50), sailboarding ($7), rappelling, and guided hikes along nature trails or to the volcano. You can also safely camp beside the lake ($7) in your own tent or rent one (an additional $7).

LA ANTIGUA GUATEMALA

Its name means "the old Guatemala," and this is in fact what it is. The former capital of Guatemala was destroyed by an earthquake in 1773. Rather than rebuild, the country's aristocracy opted for a fresh start in the neighboring Valley of the Hermitage, the current site of Guatemala City. And so, by decree, the city and its inhabitants moved on. Still, some Antigueños stayed behind, choosing to live among the ruins, coffee farms, verdant hillsides, and sentinel volcanoes. The city's colonial architecture was maintained, as there were no plans to rebuild, and its ruined churches and convents remained just that. It is said the remaining residents of Antigua were so poor that they had to subsist on avocadoes, earning them the nickname Panzas Verdes (Green Bellies).

Today, Antigua (as it is more commonly referred to) is a UNESCO World Heritage Site and is home to much of Guatemala's expatriate population along with scores of international students studying in its many Spanish schools. Its brightly colored houses and cobblestone streets harbor some of Guatemala's finest restaurants, shopping, and art galleries in a fantastic mountain setting that has inspired artists, writers, and wanderers for centuries. Antigua is a pleasant mixture of Mayan and Spanish colonial influences and is an excellent base from which to explore other parts of the country.

Antigua lies 45 kilometers from Guatemala City via a good, paved highway. Its setting is

© AL ARGUETA

HIGHLIGHTS

LOOK FOR 🌙 TO FIND RECOMMENDED SIGHTS, ACTIVITIES, DINING, AND LODGING.

🌙 **Parque Central:** You can't miss the town's central plaza, easily Guatemala's loveliest, and the heart and soul of Antigua (page 89).

🌙 **Arco de Santa Catalina:** A beautiful colonial archway, which is also one of Antigua's most photographed landmarks, provides a suitable frame for views of Agua Volcano (page 90).

🌙 **Cerro de la Cruz:** This large stone cross on a hill overlooking the valley and volcanoes makes for a good afternoon stroll. Bring a camera (page 90).

🌙 **Iglesia y Convento de las Capuchinas:** One of Antigua's best-preserved colonial monuments has many interesting features, including a tower and 18 nuns' cells built around a patio (page 90).

🌙 **Centro Cultural Casa Santo Domingo:** The city's finest museum lies on the grounds of a fantastic restored monastery, which now

functions as a five-star hotel (page 93).

🌙 **Casa Popenoe:** This fully restored colonial mansion offers a rare glimpse into the life of a royal official in 17th-century Antigua in addition to wonderful city views from the second-story terrace (page 93).

🌙 **Volcano Climbs:** Antigua's fantastic mountain scenery is dominated by the presence of Agua, Fuego, and Acatenango Volcanoes, affording excellent opportunities for mountaineering at a variety of difficulty levels. Active Pacaya Volcano, though not within sight of town, is not too much farther and is another popular day trip. It is also the easiest of these to climb (page 100).

🌙 **Centro Cultural La Azotea:** This three-in-one coffee, music, and indigenous costume museum has excellent displays and offers an interesting glimpse into many aspects of modern-day Mayan culture (page 121).

spectacular, flanked on its southern extreme by the towering 3,750-meter (12,325-foot) Agua Volcano. The colossal 4,235-meter (13,900-foot) Acatenango and active Fuego Volcanoes lie to the west. The surrounding hillsides provide wonderful views of the valley and the

volcanoes, and are excellent terrain for recreational pursuits such as hiking and mountain biking. The climate is similar to that of Guatemala City, as Antigua lies at about the same altitude, just over 1,500 meters. Days are warm and nights are pleasantly cool.

LA ANTIGUA GUATEMALA

IGLESIA NUESTRA SEÑORA
DE LA CANDELARIA

CALLE DE LA NOBLEZA

LOS HERREROS

4A AVENIDA N

IGLESIA SANTA
ROSA DE LIMA

1A CALLE O

CENTRO LINGÜÍSTICO
INTERNACIONAL

CALLE DE SANTO DOMINGO

3A AVENIDA N

IGLESIA Y CONVENTO
DE LAS CAPUCHINAS

CENTRO CULTURAL
CASA SANTO DOMINGO

To Guatemala
City

2A CALLE O

2A AVENIDA N

ENVÍOS ETC

INGUAT

ANTIGUA TOURS

10

PALACIO DEL
AYUNTAMIENTO

POLICÍA TURÍSTICA
MUNICIPAL

CENTRO
COMERCIAL
LA FUENTE

MUSEO DE LA
SEMANA SANTA

JADES
S.A.

CASA
ANCESTRAL

CITIBANK

VIAJES
TIVOLI

ANGELINA

4A CALLE O

HAMLIN Y
WHITE

LA ANTIGUA
GALERÍA DE ARTE

PARQUE
CENTRAL

JOYERÍA
DEL ÁNGEL

LA TIENDA
DE DOÑA
GAVI

CATEDRAL DE
SANTIAGO

5A CALLE O

1A AVENIDA S

MUSEO DE
ARTE COLONIAL

CASA POPENOE

3A AVENIDA S

PALACIO DE
LOS CAPITANES
GENERALES

O.X. OUTDOOR
EXCURSIONS

6A CALLE O

GUATEMALA VENTURES
AND SKIN DEEP

4A AVENIDA S

QUICKBOX

IGLESIA Y
HOSPITAL
SAN PEDRO

IGLESIA Y CONVENTO
DE SANTA CLARA

AVENTURAS
VACACIONALES

Río Pensativo

2A AVENIDA S

7A CALLE O

CALLE DE LOS PASOS

IGLESIA DE
SAN FRANCISCO

LA FÁBRICA

8A CALLE O

A LA CARTA
TOURS

ACADEMIA DE
ESPAÑOL
GUATEMALA

CALLE DE HERMANO PEDRO

9A CALLE O

CALLE DE FRAY RODRIGO DE LA CRUZ

To San Juan del Obispo,
VOLCANO CLIMBS,
Santa María de Jesús,
and Agua Volcano

IGLESIA ESCUELA
DE CRISTO

0   100 yds

0   100 m

HISTORY

The former capital of Guatemala, now known as Ciudad Vieja, was the first of Guatemala's capitals to suffer merciless destruction at the hands of nature. It was built on the slopes of Agua Volcano; an earthquake on the evening of September 10, 1541, unleashed a torrent of mud and water that came tumbling down the volcano's slopes and destroyed the city. The new Muy Leal y Muy Noble Ciudad de Santiago de los Caballeros de Goathemala, as it would officially come to be known, was established on March 10, 1543, in the Panchoy Valley. The new capital would be no stranger to the ravages of nature; its first earthquake occurred only 20 years after the city's founding.

An earthquake in 1717 spurred an unprecedented building boom, with the city reaching its peak in the mid-18th century. At that time, its population would number around 60,000. Antigua was the capital of the Audiencia de Guatemala, under the jurisdiction of the larger Viceroyalty of New Spain, which encompassed most of present-day Mexico and all of Central America as far south as Costa Rica. The Viceroyalty's capital was in Mexico City, which along with Lima, Peru, would be the only other New World cities exceeding Antigua's political, cultural, and economic importance. Antigua boasted Central America's first printing press and one of the hemisphere's first universities and was known as an important center of arts and education. Among its outstanding citizens were conquistador and historian Bernal Díaz del Castillo, Franciscan friar and Indian rights advocate Bartolomé de las Casas, bishop Francisco Marroquín, artist Tomás de Merlo, English priest/traveler Thomas Gage, and architect Juan Bautista Antonelli.

Antigua's prominence came crashing down in 1773. The city was rocked throughout most of the year by a series of earthquakes, which later came to be known as the Terremotos de Santa Marta. Two earthquakes occurred on July 29th. The final blows would be delivered on September 7 and December 13. The city was officially moved the following year to its present location in modern-day Guatemala City.

Antigua lay in ruins occupied mainly by squatters, its monuments pillaged for building materials for the new capital. It wasn't until the mid-19th century that it became once again populated and its buildings restored, in part with the money from the region's newfound coffee wealth. The city was declared a national monument in 1944 and came under the protection of the National Council for the Protection of Antigua Guatemala in 1969. It was declared a UNESCO World Heritage Site in 1979. The council has done a fairly decent job at protecting and restoring the city's cultural and architectural heritage, though building code violations are not at all unheard of. Still, many power lines have gone underground and truck traffic has been effectively banned from the city's streets, greatly reducing noise pollution.

PLANNING YOUR TIME

A week in Antigua would give you ample time to explore the town, its ruins, museums, and churches, maybe climb a volcano, visit a coffee farm, and do some shopping. Depending on whether or not you plan to study Spanish, you could easily spend several weeks in Antigua. Some choose to study Spanish for a week just to brush up on their skills or get a very basic foundation before moving on to other parts of Guatemala. At the minimum, you should plan on spending two nights here. Some have even recommended Antigua as a long weekend getaway from cities such as Miami, Atlanta, Houston, and Dallas because of its proximity and ease of access. The Guatemala City international airport is about a 45-minute drive away.

ORIENTATION

Getting around Antigua is fairly straightforward. True to its colonial foundations, it was laid out in a grid pattern surrounding the central plaza with *calles* running east-west and *avenidas* running north-south. The plaza is bounded by 4a Calle and 5a Calle to the north and south, and 4a Avenida and 5a Avenida to the east and west. Street addresses are labeled according to their direction relative to the plaza: Norte (North), Oriente (East), Sur (South), and Poniente (West). Most streets are known by this method, though all have names dating to colonial times. Only a handful of streets are known solely in this manner.

Sights

Antigua is fascinating and easily manageable, as most everything you might want to see and do lies within a radius of a few miles.

◖ PARQUE CENTRAL

Antigua's central plaza is easily the most beautiful in the country and is the hub of activity for shoe shiners, strolling lovers, tour groups, ice cream vendors, and foreign visitors. Gracing the central part of the square is a lovely fountain dating to 1936, a re-creation of an earlier version from 1738 destroyed by earthquakes. It is bordered by the Catedral de Santiago, Palacio de los Capitanes Generales, Palacio del Ayuntamiento, and a commercial arcade known as the Portal del Comercio. The *parque* makes a great place for a stroll or people watching from its park benches. At night, the surrounding buildings and monuments are beautifully illuminated.

Catedral de Santiago

On its eastern side, the plaza is dominated by the beautiful Catedral de Santiago (9 A.M.-5 P.M.). It is wonderfully lit up at night. Its history, as is much of Antigua's, is one of constant destruction and reconstruction. The first cathedral built on this site dates to 1545, but its shoddy construction caused its roof to come crashing down during an earthquake in 1583. It was decided to build a new cathedral in 1670, a task that would require 11 years and the conscripted labor of indigenous Mayans. The scale of the new structure was astounding, with 18 chapels, a huge dome, five naves, and a large central chamber measuring 90 meters by 20 meters. It was graced by paintings and artwork of renowned European and colonial artists; its altar was inlaid with silver, ivory, and mother-of-pearl. Although it withstood the earthquakes of 1689 and 1717, it finally succumbed to the earthquake of 1773.

The current church is not really a cathedral in the strict sense of the word, as it consists of two restored chambers known as the Parroquia de San José. You can visit the interesting interior entering from 5a Calle Oriente ($0.50), where you'll find splendid arches and towering columns. There is also a sculpted black Christ similar to the highly revered statue found in Esquipulas, both carved by Quirio Cataño. The remains of the rest of the colonial structure can also be seen here, a moss-covered mass of stones and rotting beams. The remains of some of the major players from colonial days are said to be buried beneath the church altar, including Don Pedro de Alvarado, his wife, Beatriz de la Cueva, Guatemala's first bishop, Francisco Marroquín, and conqueror/chronicler Bernal Díaz del Castillo. Steps behind the main altar lead to the former crypt, now a chapel, harboring the black Christ statue.

Palacio del Ayuntamiento

Found on the north side of the plaza, this large structure functioned as the town hall, also known as the Casa del Cabildo. It has miraculously withstood the test of time, resisting damage from earthquakes until the most recent one in 1976, despite its construction dating to 1740. Some fantastic views of the cathedral and Agua Volcano are framed by the building's beautiful arches from its second-floor balconies. Today the building houses the town municipal offices as well as the **Museo de Armas de Santiago** (tel. 7832-2878, www.museoscentroamericanos.net, 9 A.M.-4 P.M. Tues.-Fri., 9 A.M.-noon and 2-4 P.M. Sat.-Sun., $1.50 admission), set in the city's former town jail. It houses colonial artifacts, weapons, paintings, and furnishings. Perhaps a bigger draw than the museum itself is the quite interesting colonial fountain embossed with the emblem of Santiago (St. James), found in a quiet courtyard. Next door, the **Museo del Libro Antiguo** (Antique Book Museum, tel. 7832-5511, 9 A.M.-4 P.M. Tues.-Fri., 9 A.M.-noon and 2-4 P.M. Sat.-Sun., $1.50 admission) features exhibits on colonial printing and binding processes. There's a replica of the country's first printing press, brought to Guatemala in 1660 from Puebla, Mexico.

Palacio de los Capitanes Generales

On the south end of the plaza, the Palace of the Captains General dates to 1558 and was once the seat of government for the entire Central American territory from Chiapas to Costa Rica, of which Antigua was the capital, until 1773. Its imposing architecture is dominated by a row of 27 arches on both of its floors. It once housed colonial rulers, the royal mint, the judiciary, and tax offices, among other things. It has been recently restored and is beautifully lit at night, though there is ongoing debate as to what its new function will be.

◖ ARCO DE SANTA CATALINA

Three blocks north of the park along 5a Avenida Norte (also known as Calle del Arco) is one of Antigua's most recognizable landmarks, the Santa Catalina archway. It is all that remains

of a convent dating to 1613. As the convent grew, it expanded to include a structure across the street. The arch then was built to allow the nuns to cross to the other side while avoiding contact with the general populace in accordance with strict rules governing seclusion. Its current version with a clock tower is a reconstruction dating to the 19th century, as the original was destroyed in the 1773 earthquakes. The clock is a French model, which needed to be wound every three days. It stopped working after the 1976 earthquake but was repaired in 1991. Looking south through the archway, you'll find some nice framing for an unobstructed view of Agua Volcano. The archway is practically an Antigua icon and is beautifully painted in a rich orange hue with white accents that have become delightfully aged.

◖ CERRO DE LA CRUZ

In the hills north of the city stands this giant stone cross, from which there are sweeping views south over the city with Agua Volcano in the background. Robberies were once frequent here until the creation of the tourism police, which began escorting visitors to the site and pretty much put an end to these crimes. It's still a good idea to go along with a police escort and to visit during daylight hours. Escorts are available free from the tourism police near the central plaza. You'll want to bring along your camera and some water. It's about a 30-minute walk from the plaza. From the top of the hill, you can see the entire Antigua Valley and the cross makes for a nice foreground element.

CHURCHES AND MONASTERIES
◖ Iglesia y Convento de las Capuchinas

The Las Capuchinas Convent (2a Avenida Norte and 2a Calle Oriente, 9 A.M.-5 P.M. daily, $4) was abandoned after being destroyed in the earthquake of 1773. Restoration began in 1943 one of the fountains at Convento de las Capuchinas

and is still being carried out today; the convent now also serves as a museum. The convent's foundation dates to 1726, making it the city's fourth, and is the work of renowned Antigua architect Diego de Porres. There are beautiful fountains and courtyards flanked by sturdy stone pillars with stately arches and flowering bougainvillea. It is certainly the most elegant of Antigua's convents and well worth a look for those with even a casual interest in colonial Latin American architecture. The convent was the haunt of the Capuchin nuns from Madrid, a rather strict order limiting its numbers to 28 and requiring the nuns to sleep on wooden beds with straw pillows and sever all ties to the outside world.

The church consists of a single nave lacking side aisles. There are two choir areas, one adjacent to the altar on the ground floor and another on the second floor at the end of the nave.

After the 1773 earthquakes and the subsequent transfer of the Guatemalan capital to its new location, many of the convent's historical artifacts were likewise transferred to their new home in the San Miguel de Capuchinas convent in modern-day Guatemala City.

Iglesia y Convento de Santa Clara

The Santa Clara Convent (2a Avenida Sur #27, 9 A.M.-5 P.M. daily, $4) originally dates to 1702, with its current incarnation having been inaugurated in 1734 and destroyed in 1773. Its ruins are also pleasant for a stroll and in front of its main entrance is **Parque La Unión** with several wash basins, known as *pilas*, where women gather to do their laundry. The park's other outstanding feature is a large stone cross, a gift from the city of Santiago de Compostela, Spain. The church is beautifully floodlit at night.

Iglesia de San Francisco

Southwest on 1a Avenida Sur, the church of San Francisco (8 A.M.-6 P.M. daily) is one of Antigua's oldest, dating to 1579. It once harbored a hospital, school, printing press, and monastery, among other things. Its main claim to fame nowadays is the tomb of Central America's first saint, **Hermano Pedro de San José de Betancourt,** a Franciscan monk who came to Antigua from the Canary Islands and founded the Hospital de Belén. He is credited with miraculous healings. The **Museo del Hermano Pedro** (8 A.M.-5 P.M., $0.50) is found on the south side of the church along with the ruins of the adjacent monastery. It houses church relics and some of Hermano Pedro's well-preserved personal belongings.

Iglesia y Convento de Nuestra Señora de la Merced

Known more commonly as **La Merced,** this is one of Antigua's most beautiful churches, painted in a bright yellow and adorned with white lily motifs on its columns. Inside are the ruins of its old monastery (5a Avenida Norte

and 1a Calle Poniente, 9 A.M.-6:30 P.M., $0.50 admission) with the Fuente de Peces, said to be the largest in Latin America and interestingly in the shape of a water lily. The pools were once used for breeding fish. The upper level affords some wonderful city views and the fountain just outside the church is also worth a look.

Iglesia y Convento de la Recolección

On Avenida de la Recolección, this large church built between 1701 and 1715 was heavily damaged in 1717 in the same year it was inaugurated. The earthquake of 1773 finished the job and it has lain in ruins ever since.

MUSEUMS
Museo de Arte Colonial

On the former site of San Carlos University, the Colonial Art Museum (5a Calle Oriente #5, tel. 7832-0429, 9 A.M.-4 P.M. Tues.-Fri.,

La Merced is one of Antigua's most beautiful churches.

9 A.M.-noon and 2-4 P.M. Sat.-Sun., $3.50 admission) harbors sculptures of saints, murals, furniture, and colonial paintings by Mexican artists. A beautiful Moorish courtyard dominates the surviving architecture.

◖ Centro Cultural Casa Santo Domingo

Antigua's finest museum is housed inside the Casa Santo Domingo hotel (3a Calle Oriente #28, tel. 7832-0140 or 7820-1220, www.casasantodomingo.com.gt, 9 A.M.-6 P.M. Mon.-Sat., 11:15 A.M.-6 P.M. Sun., $5). The site was once the city's largest and wealthiest monastery, with a church completed in 1666, but it was damaged and eventually destroyed by the 18th-century earthquakes. Several museums are housed within the same complex, including the **colonial museum** harboring Catholic relics, among them an old Roman coin found during the excavations for the hotel's construction. Other highlights of this wonderful historic complex include a gorgeous monastery church, cleared of rubble and restored in the early 1990s. It is now frequently used for weddings. Below this area are two crypts. The first of these, the **Cripta del Calvario,** has a well-preserved Crucifixion mural. The other crypt harbors two graves with human bones.

There is also a small archaeological museum, but the highlight here is the **Museo Vigua de Arte Precolombino y Vidrio Moderno,** a fantastic, well-presented juxtaposition of colonial and pre-Columbian artifacts mixed with glass art. Rounding out the impressive list of attractions is the Casa de la Cera, an elaborate candle shop.

Museo de la Semana Santa

Antigua's elaborate Holy Week celebrations have their own museum, housed in the restored **Convento de Sor Juana de Maldonado** (4a Calle Oriente No. 45 "A", 9 A.M.-4 P.M. daily, free). There are samples of the festive sawdust-and-flower carpets that adorn the city's streets during Holy Week, as well as exhibitions on other aspects of Catholicism and Lent.

◖ Casa Popenoe

Authentically restored to recreate the living conditions of a 17th-century official, Casa Popenoe (1a Avenida Sur #2, tel. 7832-3087, 2-4 P.M. Mon.-Sat., $1.50) was originally built in 1636 by Don Luis de las Infantas Mendoza. Like much of Antigua, it was left abandoned after the 1773 earthquakes until Dr. Wilson Popenoe and his wife, Dorothy, bought it in 1929. Dr. Popenoe, an agricultural scientist, worked with the United Fruit Company for much of his career and had a long history of adventures in plant collecting and botany in addition to his painstaking restoration of this fantastic cultural monument. He died in 1975, but two of his daughters still live in the house, one the noted archaeologist Marion Popenoe Hatch. You'll see paintings of Bishop Francisco Marroquín and fierce conqueror Pedro de Alvarado. Also on display are the wonderfully restored servants' quarters and kitchen. A narrow staircase leads up to the roof terrace, from where there are gorgeous views of Antigua and the volcanoes off in the distance.

SEMANA SANTA IN ANTIGUA

Semana Santa, or Holy Week, runs from Palm Sunday to Easter Sunday and is one of the best times to visit Antigua for the elaborate Catholic pageantry surrounding these holy days. Visitors come from around the world to see the colorful, solemn processions in which life-sized images of Christ and other Catholic icons are paraded through the city's cobblestone streets. Before the processions pass through, Antigueños design and produce exquisite, though ephemeral, *alfombras*, or carpets made of colored sawdust and flowers. The parade floats, or *andas*, pass over the carpets, forever erasing their elaborate patterns under the feet of faithful *cucuruchos*, purple-clad bearers who carry the floats. The floats can weigh up to 3.5 tons and require 80 men to carry them. The bearers are accompanied by Roman soldiers and other robed figures who carry swaying, copal-laden incense burners. It can be quite a moving experience to see the swaying floats with images of a cross-bearing Christ bearing down on the men amid thick smoke.

A highlight of the week's festivities is a Good Friday event occurring at 3 A.M. in which Roman soldiers on horseback gallop through the streets proclaiming Christ's death sentence. Though several local churches participate in the festivities, the largest procession is the one leaving from La Merced on Good Friday with the 17th-century image of Jesús Nazareno (Jesus of Nazareth). Another well-known procession is that of the Escuela de Cristo, which features some striking images on its parade floats.

For specifics on Holy Week events, head to the INGUAT office (corner of 2a Calle Oriente and 2a Avenida Norte, 8 A.M.-12:30 P.M. and 2:30-5 P.M. Mon.-Fri., 9 A.M.-12:30 P.M. and 2:30-5 P.M. Sat.-Sun.) on the central plaza, where you'll find free maps and event schedules. If you plan to take in the festivities, book far in advance, as word about Antigua's Holy Week events has been out for quite some time and accommodations fill up several months ahead with foreign visitors and vacationing Guatemalans.

© JENNIFER KEDDIE DE COJON/123RF.COM

17th-century image of the resurrected Christ in an Easter Day procession

Entertainment

NIGHTLIFE

Antigua has a lively nightlife scene, particularly on weekends when wealthy youths from Guatemala City flood the city streets in search of a good time.

Bars

The daytime version of the ever-popular dance venue La Casbah, **The Terrace** (5a Avenida Norte #30, tel. 7832-2640, www.lacasbahantigua.com, noon-8 P.M. Tues.-Sun.) is a classy second-floor patio bar serving a varied menu. **El Muro** (3a Calle Oriente #19, tel. 7832-8849, 6 P.M.-1 A.M. Mon.-Sat.) is popular with the American expat crowd. It has cool chalk art on the walls and basic snacks for when the munchies set in, including pizza, grilled chicken, and hot dogs. You can also order food from Ni-Fu Ni-Fa next door. Also popular with the American expat crowd is **Café No Sé** (1a Avenida Sur #11C, tel. 5501-2680, 9 A.M.-1 A.M. daily), where you can enjoy drinks in a rustically charming setting, often with live music. There's also good pub grub, though the main attraction is the tequila/mezcal bar, featuring their very own brand, Ilegal Mezcal. The second-hand bookstore next door is open until 4 P.M.

Just a few doors down, **Nokiate** (1a Avenida Sur #7, tel. 7821-2896, www.nokiate.com, 6:30 P.M.-1 A.M. Tues.-Fri., noon-3 P.M. and 6:30 P.M.-1 A.M. Sat., noon-9 P.M. Sun.) features a hip fusion of Japanese and Latin American styles in its very attractive, well-executed sake bar and lounge. Antigua's Irish pub is **Reilly's** (6a Avenida Norte #2, noon-1 A.M. daily), where there's also decent pub food, including fish 'n chips. You won't find Guinness on tap, however. You'll have to settle for a can ($8).

Monoloco (5a Avenida Sur #6, 11 A.M.-1 A.M. daily) is also wildly popular and lively. It's set on two floors, and you can drink al fresco on the second-floor terrace. Reasonably priced burgers, nachos, and pizzas are served and there are sports on the downstairs TV.

A great place to grab a drink and watch the sunset with nice volcano views is the rooftop bar at **Café Sky** (corner of 6a Calle and 1a Avenida, tel. 7832-7300, 8 A.M.-1 A.M. daily). In addition to the rooftop terrace café bar, there's the downstairs Sky Lounge and Bamboo Bar, where you can enjoy drinks and a full menu of tasty food that includes sandwiches, lasagnas, and quesadillas.

The ever-popular **Riki's Bar** (4a Avenida Norte #4, tel. 7832-1327, www.la-escudilla.com, 6 P.M.-1 A.M. daily) can be crowded and noisy at times. Locals tend to avoid it, but it is a major stop with the backpacker crowd, particularly for its 7-9 P.M. happy hour. Housed in the same garden courtyard complex is **Cielos Lounge Bar** (6 P.M.-1 A.M. Tues.-Sat.), where you can enjoy Arab and Cuban beats as well as live music in a more comfortable setting. Another popular watering hole, **the ocelot bar** (4a Avenida Norte #3, tel. 5658-9028, 12:30 P.M.-1 A.M. daily), enjoys a prime location across the street from Riki's. There's often live jazz and blues in addition to a weekly Sunday evening pub quiz. Upstairs and under the same ownership is **Lava Terrace Bar,** with nice views of the surroundings from shady patio umbrellas and scrumptious gourmet burgers made from imported Angus beef. Happy Hour is at 5 P.M. daily.

A few blocks south of the park, **La Sala** (6a Calle Poniente #9, tel. 7832-9524) hosts a fun mix of Guatemalans and foreigners. The ambiance is modern with a splash of Guatemalan color. There's also a varied menu that runs the gamut from Indian chicken dishes to bangers 'n mash. Next door is **La Esquina** (tel. 7882-4761), a wonderful courtyard bar also serving a varied menu of Asian and Latin-inspired dishes. There are unique handicrafts for sale.

Dancing

Antigua's most popular and dependably fun disco is the two-story **La Casbah** (5a Avenida Norte #30, tel. 7832-2640, www.lacasbahantigua.com, 8 P.M.-1 A.M. Mon.-Sat., free admission Mon.-Wed., $4 cover Thurs.-Sat.), where you can dance the night away in a classy atmosphere popular with the wealthy Guatemala City crowd. The admission price includes one drink. **La Sin Ventura** (5a Avenida Sur #8, tel. 7832-0581) is a popular disco bar with mostly Latin music and dancing on weekend nights.

Live Music

A recent addition to Antigua's nightlife scene is **JP's Rum Bar** (7a Calle Poniente and 5a Avenida #11, tel. 7882-4244, 6 P.M.-10:30 P.M. Mon.-Tues., Thurs., and Sun., 6 P.M.-midnight Fri.-Sat.). **Restaurante Las Palmas** (6a Avenida Norte #14, tel. 7832-9734, www.laspalmasantigua.com) has live jazz music on Wednesday nights, as does **Mesón Panza Verde** (5a Avenida Sur #19, tel. 7832-2925, www.panzaverde.com). **La Peña de Sol Latino** (5a Calle Poniente #15C, tel. 7882-4468, www.lapenaantigua.com) is the place to catch Andean music played on pan flutes, Latin guitar, and Cuban trova.

CINEMAS

Antigua has several cinemas where you can enjoy a movie along with dinner and drinks. You'll see weekly listings with schedules posted all over town. Features include Hollywood, art-house, and Latin American releases. The best place to do dinner and a movie is **Cine Lounge La Sin Ventura** (5a Avenida Sur #8, tel. 7832-0581, from 9 P.M. Tues.-Sun.). **Proyecto Cultural El Sitio** (5a Calle Poniente #15, tel. 7832-3037, www.elsitiocultural.org) sometimes shows art-house movies for $2.

Shopping

Antigua is one of Guatemala's top places for shopping, with a wide assortment of excellent shops carrying quality items not found elsewhere in Guatemala. You'll be hard-pressed to find the same variety of home decor, textiles, clothing, and jewelry anywhere else. Don't feel you have to confine your purchases to what you can fit in your checked airline baggage allotment, as there are a number of local companies that can help you ship your loot home.

HANDICRAFTS

Antigua's **Mercado de Artesanías** (4a Calle Poniente Final, 8 A.M.-7 P.M.) is an attractive, safe place to shop for textiles, handicrafts, and souvenirs among several stalls. There is also an adjacent outdoor market selling fruits, vegetables, and wonderful fresh flowers. **Casa del Tejido Antiguo** (1a Calle Poniente #51, tel. 7832-3169, www.casadeltejido.com, 9 A.M.-5:30 P.M. Mon.-Sat., $1 admission) is entirely run by Mayan weavers selling and exhibiting authentic textiles and exclusive handicrafts. **Textura** (5a Avenida Norte #33, tel. 7832-5067, 10 A.M.-5:45 P.M. Mon.-Wed., 10 A.M.-6:45 P.M. Thurs.-Sat., 10 A.M.-5 P.M. Sun.) sells stylish home furnishings in updated versions of Mayan textiles, including gorgeous hammocks and table dressings. Selling similarly exquisite home furnishings is **El Telar** (5a Avenida Sur #7, tel. 7832-3179), with another location across the street from the Hotel Posada de Don Rodrigo at 5a Avenida Norte #18.

Nim Po't (5a Avenida Norte #29, tel. 7832-2681, 9 A.M.-9 P.M. daily) has a large selection of traditional Mayan dress items, including colorful *huipiles* (blouses), *cortes* (skirts), and *fajas* (belts). There is also a wide variety of artwork,

© AL ARGUETA

Doña Maria Gordillo candy store in Antigua

masks, and other wooden carvings in the spacious warehouselike setting. Just down the street, **Nativo's** (5a Avenida Norte #25B, tel. 7832-6556, 10 A.M.-7 P.M. daily) also sells textiles and has some extremely rare, beautiful, and no-longer-produced textiles in the $600 range. Ask to see them. **Quinta Maconda** (5a Avenida Norte #11, tel. 7832-1480, www.quintamaconda.com, 9:30 A.M.-1 P.M. and 2-7 P.M. daily) sells its own brand of high-quality handcrafted leather travel gear and handwoven Guatemalan brocades in beautiful muted hues and earth tones. It also has a fine collection of Southeast Asian antiques and wooden furniture in its by-appointment-only showroom. One of my favorite shops for high-quality (though somewhat expensive) crafts and textiles is **Colibrí** (4a Calle Oriente #3B, tel. 7832-5028, textilescolibri@turbonett.com, 9 A.M.-6 P.M. daily). I particularly like their bedspreads, though a Queen size will set you back about $200. For one-of-a-kind handbags in Guatemalan styles, check out **Purpura & Te** (1a Avenida Norte #12, tel. 7832-4860, 10 A.M.-6 P.M. Tues.-Sun.).

JEWELRY

Guatemala produces some of the world's finest jade, including rare black jade, found only in this part of the world. You can buy fabulous jade jewelry here tax-free. The best store for perusing wonderful jade creations in colorful hues, including emerald, yellow, and lilac, is **Jades, S.A.** (4a Calle Oriente #34, tel. 7832-0109, www.jademaya.com, 9 A.M.-7 P.M. daily), where you'll find a vast array of items varying from 18-karat gold/jade earrings to a unique $3,800 jade chess board. All of the jade found here is mined from a quarry in eastern Guatemala. The store doubles as a jade museum and you can also visit the factory behind the shop. Guided tours are available in German, Spanish, English, French, and Italian. For fashionable and exotic jewelry, handbags, and sunglasses, visit **Joyería del**

Ángel (4a Calle Oriente #5A, tel. 7832-5334, 9 A.M.-6 P.M. daily). For silver jewelry, check out **Pablo's Silver Shop** (5a Calle Poniente #12C, tel. 7832-8960).

BOOKS

Hamlin y White (4a Calle Oriente #12A, tel. 7832-7075, 9 A.M.-6:30 P.M. daily) has a good selection of books and international magazines. Under the same ownership is **Tiempo Libre** (5a Avenida Norte #25, tel. 7832-1816, 9 A.M.-7 P.M. daily), with a wider assortment of books in English and Spanish, including Moon Handbooks. On the west side of the plaza in the Portal del Comercio, **La Casa del Conde** (5a Avenida Norte #4, tel. 7832-3322, 9 A.M.-7 P.M. Mon.-Sat., 10 A.M.-7 P.M. Sun.) sells an assortment of travel guides in addition to material specifically relating to Guatemala, Central America, and the Mayan world, mostly in English. A few doors down in the same complex, **Un Poco De Todo** (tel. 7832-4676, 9 A.M.-1:30 P.M. and 3-6:30 P.M. daily) also sells books, though mostly in Spanish.

ART, ANTIQUES, AND FURNITURE

Panza Verde (5a Avenida Sur #19, tel. 7832-2925, www.panzaverde.com) is a gallery housed inside its namesake restaurant/hotel; a new exhibit usually opens every second Wednesday of the month. **La Antigua Galería de Arte** (4a Calle Oriente #15, tel. 7832-2124, www.art-intheamericas.com, 9 A.M.-7 P.M. Mon.-Sat.) exhibits the work of numerous local and international artists in a large building surrounding a pleasant courtyard. **El Carmen Galería de Arte** (3a Avenida Norte #11D, tel. 7832-5620, www.elcarmengaleriablogspot.com, 9 A.M.-7 P.M. Mon.-Sat.) is small but features the fine work of local and international artists in its pleasant space. **Galería de Arte GO** (4a Calle Oriente and 1a Avenida Norte, tel. 7832-0618, 9 A.M.-7 P.M. Mon.-Sat., 10 A.M.-2:30 P.M.

Sun.) also showcases a good mix of local and international artists' work.

For antique furniture and architectural accents, a good bet is **Ritual** (7a Calle Poniente #30 and 5a Avenida Norte #18, tel. 7832-4767). A modern twist on traditional and tropical furniture can be found at **Mezzanine Home** (4a Calle Oriente #30, tel. 4472-4242, www.mezzaninehome.com, 8 A.M.-5 P.M. Mon.-Fri.). **Differenza** (5a Avenida Sur #24C, tel. 7832-1851, pierre@conexion.com.gt, 9 A.M.-6 P.M. Mon.-Sat.) features the work of French sculptor and designer Pierre Turlin. Among the unique finds are raku sculptures and bowls, blown-glass stemware and decanters, and wooden furniture. The store also carries extraordinary handcrafted jewelry from two other Antigua resident artists. **Casa Chicob** (Callejón de la Concepción #2, tel. 7832-0781, http://casachicob.com, 9 A.M.-6 P.M. Mon.-Sat.) features a wonderful assortment of Guatemalan-inspired home decor. **Angelina** (4a Calle Oriente #22, tel. 7832-1812, 10 A.M.-6 P.M. daily) sells primitive antique furniture, reproductions of colonial columns, and contemporary sculpted furniture. **La Casa de las Escudillas** (6a Avenida Sur # 4, tel. 7832-9257, 9 A.M.-8 P.M. daily) sells antique furniture and ceramics. The best place for antiques is **Casa Ancestral** (4a Calle Oriente #46, tel. 7832-9740, 9:30 A.M.-6 P.M. Fri.-Wed.).

COFFEE AND TOBACCO

For coffee, head to **Tostaduría Antigua** (6a Calle Poniente #26). You can buy Cuban and Honduran cigars, as well as enjoy them in a comfortable lounge, at **Antigua Tabaco Compañía** (main store, 5a Avenida Norte #32B, tel. 7882-4228; cigar lounge, 3a Calle Poniente #12, tel. 7832-9420).

WELLNESS

One of Antigua's most interesting stores is **La Tienda de Doña Gavi** (3a Avenida Norte #2, tel.

7832-6514, noon-7 P.M. daily), where you can pick up a number of natural remedies, including Jacameb, a powerful concoction created from the jacaranda flower that does the trick on amoebas and assorted other parasitic problems.

(Friendly Doña Gavi also serves the tastiest mango ice cream I've ever had.) Organic groceries, natural foods, and eco-friendly products can be found at **Organica** (5a Calle Poniente #6, tel. 7832-6533, 8 A.M.-6 P.M. daily).

Recreation

HEALTH CLUBS

Antigua's Gym (6a Calle Poniente #31, tel. 7832-7554, 7 A.M.-8 P.M. Mon.-Fri., 8 A.M.-2 P.M. Sat.) offers spinning, Tae Bo, cardiovascular equipment, free weights, and some weight-lifting machines. **La Fábrica** (Calle del Hermano Pedro #16, tel. 7832-0486) also has cardiovascular machines and weights in addition to aerobics and martial arts.

SPAS AND YOGA

Casa Madeleine (Calle del Espíritu Santo #69, tel. 7832-9348, www.casamadeleine.com) offers complete spa packages along with its swanky boutique accommodations. Services include massage, reflexology, aromatherapy, mud therapy, pedicures, manicures, and deep facial treatments. **Skin Deep** (1a Avenida Sur #15, tel. 7832-7182, 8 A.M.-8 P.M. daily) is a well-run day spa and salon housed in the same building as Café Sky offering the usual assortment of spa services in a pleasing environment.

There are quality yoga classes by trained U.S. instructors available in Antigua. **YogAntigua** (tel. 5251-4809, lizzieyogini@gmail.com) offers classes every morning inside Galería Panza Verde (5a Avenida Sur #19) and afternoons at Antigua Center (7a Calle Poniente #11, Mon. and Thurs. at 5 P.M.). Vinyasa and Hatha yoga classes start at $6 for drop-in or $50 for a 10-class pass.

MOUNTAIN BIKING

Antigua's mountain terrain and the variety of trails traversing it make mountain biking a popular recreational activity. **Old Town Outfitters** (5a Avenida Sur #12C, tel. 5399-0440, www.bikeguatemala.com, $35 half day) is a highly recommended outfitter offering rides for all skill levels. Half-day options include easy rides in the Almolonga Valley or in and around a coffee plantation to edge-of-your-seat single-track rides careening down volcanic slopes or along narrow mountain ridges with fantastic views. Its equipment is top-notch and well cared for. **Guatemala Ventures** (1a Avenida Sur #15, end of 6a Calle Oriente, tel. 7832-3383, www.guatemalaventures.com) is another recommended outfitter for tackling the rugged terrain around Antigua by mountain bike. It also rents out mountain bikes for $8 a day. Both companies also offer a lot of other recreational options in addition to mountain biking, as you'll see by the frequency with which they are mentioned here.

BIRD-WATCHING

Just a 20-minute walk from Antigua's central park (or a ten-minute *tuk tuk* ride) is **Finca El Pilar** (tel. 7832-4937, fincaelpilar@live.com, 7 A.M.-5 P.M. daily). The reserve protects a large area that includes dry forest, pine oak, and cloud forest. Among the bird species you can expect to find are numerous types of rare and endemic hummingbirds, Emerald Toucanet, Golden-browed Warbler, Highland Guans, and Blue-throated Motmot. There is a system of trails throughout the reserve and altitude ranges from 5,250 to 7,870 feet. To get here, walk south from the central plaza toward

7a calle until you reach San Francisco Church. Behind the church, you'll find the path leading to neighboring Santa Ana. Look for El Calvario church, where you'll turn left and continue all the way to the end of an uphill path, passing San Cristobal El Bajo church along the way. **Cayaya Birding** (tel. 5308-5160, www.cayaya-birding.com) does guided trips to the reserve.

HIKING

There is no shortage of rugged hiking trails for enjoying the spectacular mountain scenery and peaceful mountain villages found near Antigua. The same recommended mountain biking outfitters can point you to the best hiking trails. A guide is highly recommended, as robberies of solo hikers along remote mountain footpaths is sometimes an issue in rural Guatemala. The bulk of the hiking done around Antigua involves one of the volcanoes towering ominously over its streets.

◖ Volcano Climbs

At 3,750 meters (12,325 feet) **Agua Volcano** is one of the most popular climbs because of its proximity to town, from which it invites hikers to attempt an ascent of its steep slopes to the near-perfect crater ringed with various radio antennas. The trailhead is in the nearby village of Santa María de Jesús, from where it's a five-hour ascent; be aware, however, that numerous tourist robberies have occurred through the years in the vicinity of this town. **Guatemala Ventures** (1a Avenida Sur #15, end of 6a Calle Oriente, tel. 7832-3383, www.guatemalaventures.com) drives farther up the road to a spot two hours from the summit and is the recommended way to go. A day trip costs $40 with this outfitter.

Just shy of 4,300 meters (14,000 feet), **Acatenango Volcano** is a safer and somewhat more interesting climb, as it has twin craters and often affords fantastic views of nearby **Fuego Volcano,** which entered a phase of increased activity in 1999. **Old Town Outfitters** (5a Avenida Sur #12C, tel. 5399-0440, www.bikeguatemala.com) offers a one-day ($75) or overnight ($95) trip to the volcano starting in the village of La Soledad, from where it's a 5-6-hour hike through cornfields and pine forests to the first crater. The overnight trip camps on the second peak, which stands at 13,900 feet. Guatemala Ventures (www.guatemalaventures.com) also does this trip, driving to within two hours of the first summit for the one-day and overnight trips.

By far the most popular volcano trip is to active **Pacaya Volcano,** near Lake Amatitlán and closer to Guatemala City. There's no shortage of outfitters offering this trip, which generally leaves in the afternoon and costs $7-30 per person. Recommended companies include **Old Town Outfitters** (5a Avenida Sur #12C, tel. 5399-0440, www.bikeguatemala.com, $50 p/p including lunch with 4 person minimum), which leaves earlier than most other companies to avoid the crowds. **Adrenalina Tours** (5a Avenida Norte #31, tel. 7832-1108 or 5535-6831) leaves daily at 6 A.M. and 2 P.M. The trip costs $10 and includes roundtrip transportation and local Spanish-speaking guide. The more expensive VIP trip costs $75 and leaves whenever you want it to. The VIP tour includes bilingual and local guides, transportation, park admission and breakfast.

Recommended by readers for all of the above trips is **O.X. Outdoor Excursions** (1a Avenida Sur #4B, tel. 7832-0074 or 5801-4301, www.guatemalavolcano.com), offering well-guided trips to the Antigua area volcanoes. The Spires of Fire trip is a five-day adventure climbing Guatemala's three active volcanoes (Fuego, Pacaya, and Santiaguito); it costs $500.

CANOPY TOURS

The zipline madness that seems to have gripped almost every tourist town in Central America has not bypassed Antigua. If you want to monkey around, zipping from tree to tree, your best bet is **Antigua Canopy Tours** (tel. 4010-6592, www.antiguacanopytours.com, $50-75). For the ultimate adventure, try its Canyon Express tour across a canyon in two stages (520 and 430 meters long) while dangling 150 meters above the ground. The zipline tour is located on the property of Finca Filadelfia, near Jocotenango.

HORSEBACK RIDING

In the nearby village of San Juan del Obispo, toward Agua Volcano, **Ravenscroft Riding Stables** (2a Avenida Sur #3, San Juan del Obispo, tel. 7832-6229) offers three-, four-, or five-hour rides in the hills and valleys near Antigua for $15 per person per hour.

CITY TOURS

A La Carta Tours (8a Calle Oriente, inside Porta Hotel Antigua, tel. 7832-9636, www.

A photo tour is a great way to capture some memorable vacation pictures like this one.

alacartatours.com) offers creative thematic walking tours at 9 A.M. and 2:30 P.M. Monday-Saturday centered around subjects that include shopping, art, food, photography, and religious celebrations, among others. Prices range $14-39 per person. Practically an Antigua institution, **Antigua Tours** (3a Calle Oriente #22, tel. 7832-5821, www.antiguatours.net) are guided by Elizabeth Bell (author of *Antigua Guatemala: The City and Its Heritage*) Tuesday, Wednesday, Friday, and Saturday at 9:30 A.M. Tours on Monday and Thursday at 2 P.M. are guided by Roberto Spillari. All tours meet at the fountain in Antigua's central park and cost $20. There is also a guided tour of nearby villages, including San Antonio Aguas Calientes, San Pedro Las Huertas, and San Juan del Obispo, going out at 2 P.M. Monday-Friday and lasting three hours. It costs $35 per person with a two-person minimum.

Martha Hettich (1a Avenida Sur #4A, tel. 7832-2134 or 5792-2459, www.marthahettich. com) does recommended guided historical and shopping tours of Antigua and the highlands; by appointment only. She can also tell you stories garnered from years spent in Guatemala and is a wealth of historical information.

GOLF

Antigua is home to Guatemala's newest—and nicest—golf course, the 18-hole Pete and Perry Dye-designed **Fuego Maya Golf Course** (La Reunión Antigua Golf Resort, RN-14 Km. 93, Alotenango, tel. 7873-1400, www.lareunion. com.gt). The 72-par, 7,560-yard course is one of the country's most challenging and is the only golf course in the world with a view of four volcanoes (Agua, Fuego, Acatenango, and Pacaya). Its designers gleaned inspiration from the Mayan Solar Calendar, which consists of 18 20-day months; each of the course's 18 holes is named after the corresponding month on the Mayan calendar. (The last month, Wayeb, is a five-day month and gives its name to the 19th

© AL ARGUETA

Chateau DeFay vineyards

hole.) The golf course is 11 miles from Antigua and 40 miles from Guatemala City. Facilities include a driving range, putting green, chipping green, practice bunker, and pro shop.

WINE TASTING

Ever exciting and brimming with new leisure opportunities, Antigua Guatemala now boasts Guatemala's first winery. **Chateau DeFay** (tel. 7832-5078 or 5883-3911, www.chateaudefayvineyards.com), on the slopes of Agua Volcano in neighboring Santa María de Jesús, is a 3,000-case winery and vineyard. Its owners, Jacques and Angie Defay, purchased a former coffee farm and converted part of the land into vineyards using plants brought in from Washington state. The farm also grows asparagus. Jacques, a former economist with the International Development Bank (IDB), retired to Guatemala from Falls Church, Virginia in 2002 after numerous visits to the country.

The winery is open for tastings Saturday and Sunday from 10 A.M. to 4 P.M. Chateau DeFay wines come in several varieties, including Angie's Blend, Chardonnay, White Merlot, a Cabernet Sauvignon/Merlot, and Bruno's Favorite. The latter is named for resident winemaker Bruno Coppola.

The first year of wine production was 2008. A bottle of wine costs Q149, or about $20.

Accommodations

UNDER $10

Antigua has a number of excellent hostels offering comfortable accommodations at budget prices. One of the city's newest offerings is friendly 【 **Terrace Hostel** (3a Calle Poniente #24B, tel. 7832-3463, www.terracehostel.com, $8.50 in shared-bath dorm to $35 d in room with private bath). Included are the usual amenities found in most hostels such as luggage storage, wireless Internet, TV, DVD collection and library, but Terrace Hostel goes the extra mile with free breakfast, a welcome cocktail, and a fun rooftop bar and restaurant. There's a nightly barbecue featuring hot dogs, burgers, and chili you can wash down with local microbrews. On Wednesdays and Sundays you can partake in a communal dinner featuring a more elaborate mix of grilled favorites for around $5. **Hotel Mochilero's Place** (4a Calle Poniente #27, tel. 7832-7743, $14 d shared bath, $16 d private bath) is a well-known establishment with 10 large, clean rooms. Among the amenities are free coffee and tea, laundry sinks, and luggage storage. The rooms facing south have decent views of Agua Volcano. Reservations are necessary, as it's very popular. **Hostal Día Verde** (1a Calle Poniente #14B, tel. 7832-3402) has seven clean rooms with shared bath ($7 p/p) or private bath ($8 p/p). Rates include breakfast and one free hour of Internet. Another popular choice is **Yellow House** (1a Calle Poniente #24, tel. 7832-6646), where the mattresses are somewhat soft but the attractive, private shared-bath rooms ($16 d) are well decorated and have cable TV. Dorm beds go for $8 p/p. The single rooms are very small. Rates include breakfast and half hour of Internet daily. Guests have free use of the kitchen.

Ever-popular with Antigua's budget scene is the attractive **Black Cat Hostel** (6a Avenida Norte #1A, tel. 7832-1229, www.blackcathostels.net), where there are shared-bath dorm beds ($8) and private doubles ($20). Amenities include wireless Internet, a substantial free breakfast, a movie lounge with more than 350 DVDs, a living room and hammock patio for hanging out, a restaurant serving breakfast and light meals (8 A.M.-11 P.M.), and a full bar. **Jungle Party Hostel** (6a Avenida Norte #20, between 3a and 2a Calle Poniente, tel. 7832-0463) is a lively backpacker hangout with clean dorm rooms and shared baths for $6-8 p/p. There's a fun communal area that doubles as a bar and snack stand. The cheerfully painted, tiled-floor **UmmaGumma Hostel** (7a Avenida Norte #34, tel. 7832-4413) has a wide range of accommodations, including dorms ($5 p/p) and private rooms with ($13 p/p) or without ($8 p/p) private bath. Guests enjoy use of two fully equipped kitchens, communal lounge areas with DirecTV, laundry service, wireless Internet, international phone calls, and luggage storage. The staff can also help with travel arrangements.

Conveniently located near some of the town's favorite watering holes, **El Hostal** (1a Avenida Sur #8, tel. 7832-0442, www.el-hostal.hostel.com) has cozy private rooms with shared bath ($15 d) or clean dormitories ($10 p/p) in a remodeled colonial house that includes a pleasant little courtyard. Guests won't find electric water heaters here (yippee!), but rather the hot-water showers many visitors are used to. You can book and pay online in advance; wireless Internet is available throughout the house.

$10-25

A rooftop chill-out area with wonderful views of Agua Volcano and a friendly, feel-good vibe make **Holistico Hostal** (1a Calle Poniente #6B, tel. 4531-8959, www.hostalholistico.com, $10 p/p to 30 d) a popular choice. The nightly rate includes breakfast, served in its small cafe. There is free Wi-Fi, a movie lounge, and tours to local attractions can be arranged. A well-established budget hotel is the very pleasant and friendly **Posada Juma Ocag** (Calzada de Santa Lucía #13, tel. 7832-3109, www.posadajumaocag.com, $20 d) with seven tastefully decorated, well-furnished rooms featuring wrought-iron headboards, mirrors, and reading lamps, all with private bath. It has a rooftop patio and garden as well as some nice extras like free drinking water. It's also conveniently situated near the bus terminal.

A step above its sister property, **The Black Cat Inn** (5a Calle Poniente #11A, tel. 7832-0374, www.blackcathostels.net, $25 d) is a bed-and-breakfast with well-decorated rooms and private bathrooms. There's a rooftop restaurant and bar and youthful patrons that might keep you up at night.

One of my favorite budget-friendly places is the cozy and welcoming **Hotel Mi Casa** (1a Avenida Sur #4B, tel. 7832-1735, $25 d), where it feels more like staying at a friend's house than a hotel. The comfortable rooms (some with wood floors) have nice furnishings and attached, shared bathrooms. Guests have use of the kitchen, but the hotel is well located next to some of my favorite feeding troughs. **Posada La Merced** (7a Avenida Norte #43, tel. 7832-3197, $20-25 d) is another good choice offering nicely decorated, furnished rooms with private or shared hot-water bathrooms. It features a courtyard where you can help yourself

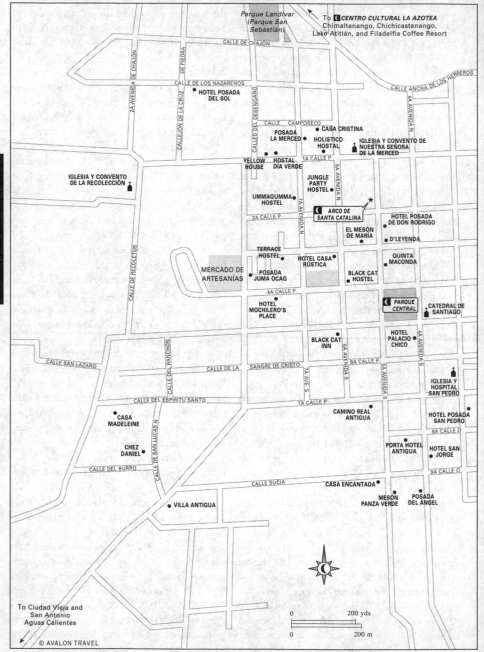

Parque Landívar
(Parque San
Sebastián)

To **CENTRO CULTURAL LA AZOTEA**
Chimaltenango, Chichicastenango,
Lake Atitlán, and Filadelfia Coffee Resort

CALLE DE CHAJÓN

CALLE DE LOS NAZARENOS

HOTEL POSADA
DEL SOL

2A AVENIDA DE CHAJÓN

CALLEJÓN DE LA CRUZ

DE PIEDRA

CALLE DEL DESENGAÑO

CALLE ANCHA DE LOS HERREROS

4A AVENIDA N

CALLE   CAMPOSECO

POSADA
LA MERCED

CASA CRISTINA

HOLISTICO
HOSTAL

IGLESIA Y CONVENTO DE
NUESTRA SEÑORA
DE LA MERCED

YELLOW
HOUSE

HOSTAL
DÍA VERDE

1A CALLE P

6A AVENIDA N

IGLESIA Y CONVENTO
DE LA RECOLECCIÓN

JUNGLE
PARTY
HOSTEL

UMMAGUMMA
HOSTEL

2A CALLE P

7A AVENIDA N

ARCO DE
SANTA CATALINA

HOTEL POSADA
DE DON RODRIGO

EL MESÓN
DE MARÍA

D'LEYENDA

TERRACE
HOSTEL

HOTEL CASA
RÚSTICA

QUINTA
MACONDA

CALLE DE RECOLETOS

MERCADO DE
ARTESANÍAS

POSADA
JUMA OCAG

BLACK CAT
HOSTEL

4A CALLE P

HOTEL
MOCHILERO'S
PLACE

PARQUE
CENTRAL

CATEDRAL DE
SANTIAGO

CALLE SAN LÁZARO

CALLE DEL RANCHÓN

BLACK CAT
INN

HOTEL
PALACIO
CHICO

6A AVENIDA S

CALLE DE LA

SANGRE DE CRISTO

7A AVE S

6A AVENIDA S

6A CALLE P

5A AVENIDA S

CALLE DEL ESPÍRITU SANTO

7A CALLE P

IGLESIA Y
HOSPITAL
SAN PEDRO

CASA
MADELEINE

CALLE DE SAN LUCAS N

CAMINO REAL
ANTIGUA

HOTEL POSADA
SAN PEDRO

8A CALLE O

CHEZ
DANIEL

PORTA HOTEL
ANTIGUA

HOTEL SAN
JORGE

CALLE DEL BURRO

9A CALLE O

CALLE SUCIA

CASA ENCANTADA

MESÓN
PANZA VERDE

POSADA
DEL ÁNGEL

VILLA ANTIGUA

To Ciudad Vieja and
San Antonio
Aguas Calientes

© AVALON TRAVEL

0   200 yds

0   200 m

LA ANTIGUA GUATEMALA

to purified drinking water, baggage storage, and a communal kitchen. Candles add a nice touch in the evening.

$25-50

Just one block from the central plaza, **Hotel Casa Rústica** (6a Avenida Norte #8, tel. 7832-3709, www.casarusticagt.com, $26-36 d) has comfortable rooms with shared bathroom or private bathroom, with or without cable TV and garden view. Rates include breakfast, filtered drinking water, and use of the kitchen. It also offers laundry service, bag storage, and wireless Internet. There are nice gardens and hammocks for lounging. The excellent value **Casa Cristina** (Callejón Camposeco #3A, between 6a and 7a Avenida, tel. 7832-0623, www.casa-cristina.com, $27-40 d) has beautifully decorated, colorful rooms with wrought-iron accents, Guatemalan bedspreads, tile floors, and private hot-water bathroom. Pricier "standard plus" rooms have cable TV, while deluxe rooms also have gorgeous volcano views and mini-fridges. Room rates include unlimited use of wireless Internet, purified drinking water, coffee, and tea. **Hotel Posada del Sol** (Calle de los Nazarenos #17, tel. 7832-6838, $40) is housed in a pretty yellow house just outside the city center and has six spacious, well-furnished rooms with orthopedic beds and private hot-water bathrooms. There's laundry service and the friendly staff can help you plan onward travel throughout Guatemala. The excellent-value **Hotel Posada San Pedro** (3a Avenida Sur #15, tel. 7832-3594, www.posadasanpedro.net, $41 d) is also stylish and comfortable, featuring 10 spotless rooms with firm beds, tile floors, wooden furnishings, attractive tile bathrooms, and cable TV. Guests also enjoy use of a living room and full kitchen. The staff here is friendly and the place is well-run with a laid back but efficient atmosphere. There's a second location at 7a Avenida Norte #29 (tel. 7832-0718, $46 d) with slightly higher rates for newer rooms. **Hotel Santa Clara** (2a Avenida Sur #20, tel. 7832-0342, www.hotelsantaclaraantigua.com, $50 d) features 19 rooms, some with cable TV, and all with private bathroom, colorful decor, and wooden furniture set around a courtyard. Newer rooms with less character, but slightly more cheerful, are at the rear.

$50-100

One of the city's best values is **C Chez Daniel** (Calle de San Luquitas #20, tel. 4264-1122, chezdanielantigua.blogspot.com, $54 d). It's 7 blocks from the central square in a quiet neighborhood, in a large house fronting a green lawn. The comfortable, high-ceilinged rooms have flat-screen TVs and large bathrooms with shower tubs. They are wonderfully decorated with Guatemalan knickknacks and amazing photography depicting the country's vivid Maya culture. Amenities include a dining room, fully equipped communal kitchen and rooftop terrace with volcano views. **Hotel San Jorge** (4a Avenida Sur #13, tel. 7832-3132, www.hotelsanjorgeantigua.com, $61 d) has attractive rooms centered round a garden courtyard with a fountain and patio furniture. The well-furnished rooms are carpeted and have private hot-water bathroom, Guatemalan bedspreads and accents, chimney, cable TV, and reading lamps. Rates include a continental breakfast and guests enjoy free use of the nearby Porta Hotel Antigua's sprawling swimming pool. Featuring many of the fine decorative touches and amenities of its pricier boutique counterparts **C El Meson de María** (3a Calle Poniente #8, tel. 7832-6068 or 7832-0520, www.hotelmesondemaria.com, $85-140 d) is a good value. Its 20 brand-new, well-appointed rooms are attractively decorated with Guatemalan fabrics and beautifully carved wooden headboards. You'll feel the antique charm as soon as you enter the doorway of your room framed with antique wooden beams. Rooms on the second floor have skylights and some of the spacious tiled bathrooms have whirlpool tubs. There are gorgeous views of the town and volcanoes from the delightful third-floor terrace. Rates include breakfast at the nearby La Fonda de la Calle Real. Rates are higher on weekends. Outside the city center on the way to Santa Ana is **Hotel Quinta de las Flores** (Calle del Hermano Pedro #6, tel. 7832-3721/25, www.quintadelasflores.com, $75-140 d), another excellent value. The lodge was built on the site of what were once public baths and you can still hear the soothing sounds of tinkling fountains throughout the property. The charming rooms, built around a peaceful and spacious garden, feature tile floors, chimneys, cable TV, Guatemalan bedspreads, and nice accents and furnishings along with a small porch with sitting area. Larger two-bedroom casitas comfortably sleep five and have living room, dining room, and fully equipped kitchen. There's a large outdoor swimming pool just next to the hotel's restaurant, which serves Guatemalan dishes, including delicious *chuchitos* and *tostadas,* or salads, steak, and chicken. It's a good choice for vacationing families.

Posada de Don Rodrigo (5a Avenida Norte #17, tel. 7832-0291, $68 d) is one of Antigua's classic hotels, well situated near the Arco de Santa Catalina. Housed in a very old house, the inviting rooms have been updated with all the comforts of a modern hotel. The staff wears traditional costumes and marimba music can often be heard in the main courtyard. **Hotel Casa Noble** (2a Avenida Sur #29, tel. 7832-0864, www.hotelcasanoble.com) has 11 beautifully decorated rooms, some with views of Agua Volcano, featuring electronic locks and cable TV starting at $98 d. There's a pleasant garden courtyard with tables. For a phenomenal location at an incredible price, it's hard to beat **C D'Leyenda Hotel** (4a Avenida Norte #1, tel. 7832-6194, www.dleyendahotel.com, $70-100 d). The hotel is located less than a block from the central square. Its somewhat smallish but comfortable rooms are named after different Antigua ghost legends and include flat-screen cable TV, safe deposit box, and Wi-Fi. Three of its six rooms have bathtubs and fireplaces. A fountain graces the ground floor courtyard opposite a spiral staircase leading to a second-floor terrace with lounge chairs, tables, a hot tub, and volcano views. It bears mentioning that there's a popular watering hole next door, as that may or may not suit your style. Did I mention the staff is extremely friendly?

OVER $100
Resorts

Antigua's newest resort hotel is the **C Camino Real Antigua** (7a Calle Poniente #3B, www. caminoreal.com.gt, $135-210 d). The chain hotel has cozy rooms with high, wood-beamed ceilings and some of the most delicious beds I've ever slept on, as well as all the amenities you would expect. The **Soleil Antigua** (9a Calle Poniente, Carretera a Ciudad Vieja, tel. 7879-4444, www.gruposoleil.com, $145-280 d) has 139 rooms and 45 suites, all of which are spacious and equipped with chimney, cable TV, and wonderful garden and volcano views. It has a swimming pool, restaurant, and all the usual amenities found at a large resort. It is the oldest of Antigua's resorts and ironically the one with the least colonial charm because of its more modern architecture. Part of the excellent Villas de Guatemala chain, **Villa Colonial** (Alameda del Calvario #28, tel. 7832-2039 hotel or 2334-1818 reservations, www.villas-deguatemala.com, $104-134 d) has 50 rooms housed in colonial buildings charmingly built to imitate a colonial Spanish town, complete with cobblestone streets, a town square garden, and fountain-style swimming pool. Rooms are tastefully decorated with Guatemalan fabrics and include cable TV in addition to the usual resort amenities. There are standard rooms and larger junior suites with a separate living room.

A *Condé Nast Traveler* Gold List property, **C Porta Hotel Antigua** (8a Calle Poniente #1, tel. 7832-2801, www.portahotels.com, $150-225) has 77 sumptuous rooms with chimneys, colorful walls with faux finishes, Guatemalan decor, and charming stained hardwood floors in its standard and deluxe rooms and suites. It features a restaurant serving excellent Guatemalan and international dishes overlooking the swimming pool set amid tropical gardens, as well as a fully stocked, quaint wooden bar. Candles provide atmosphere at night and a colonial fountain graces the entrance to the hotel. The service is excellent, as is the courteous and friendly staff. Another property that has put Antigua on the map of the world's finest accommodations is the exquisite **C Hotel Casa Santo Domingo** (3a Calle Oriente #28, tel. 7832-0140, www.casasantodomingo.com. gt, $150-550 d), built in the ruins of an old Dominican monastery. Its 125 rooms have all the comforts you could wish for and effortlessly merge colonial charm with modern comfort. Some rooms have a chimney and there are some newer rooms with chic glass and wooden showers. Other amenities include a charming swimming pool and a location just steps from the city's best museum and wonderful colonial ruins. The restaurant here is also highly recommended.

Boutique Hotels

Antigua has an astounding assortment of boutique properties offering comfort and privacy in an atmosphere of elegance and style. Spending a night in one of Antigua's boutique properties is the real deal and can feel like waking up in a museum chock-full of interesting knick-knacks and artwork. President Clinton chose **C Posada del Ángel** (4a Avenida Sur #24A, tel. 7832-5303 Antigua or 305/677-2382 U.S., www.posadadelangel.com, $165-240 d) for his 1999 visit to Antigua for a summit meeting with Central American leaders. If you'd like

© AL ARGUETA

Posada del Ángel's exterior offers a glimpse of the character found inside.

to follow in his footsteps, stay in the exquisite Rose Suite, the largest of the lodge's five, with a private balcony offering gorgeous volcano views and fine antiques. Each of the suites is different but all are truly charming and include wood-burning fireplace, cable TV, and fresh flowers. Rates include a delicious breakfast served in the dining room looking out to the hotel's small lap pool. A luxurious private inn, **Quinta Maconda** (5a Avenida Norte #11, tel. 5309-1423 Antigua or 866/621-4032 U.S., www.quintamaconda.com, $130-165 d) has four comfortable bedrooms, all with private bath, tastefully decorated with rare textiles, colonial antiques, and primitive art that are the collection of long-term Antigua resident and world traveler John Heaton. Rates include breakfast served in a pleasant garden patio or in a formal dining room oozing with character and charm. Lunch and dinner are available upon request. There is wireless Internet throughout the house and gracious hosts Catherine and John arrange

fabulous custom-tailored travel to explore any and all aspects of Guatemala's unique offerings in comfort and style, drawing on years of experience and first-hand knowledge.

Mesón Panza Verde (5a Avenida Sur #19, tel. 7832-2925, www.panzaverde.com, $75-200) exudes a distinct European atmosphere with an eclectic array of decor that includes Persian rugs, wrought-iron works, chandeliers, fresh flowers, Guatemalan textiles and wooden furniture, and tile or hardwood floors. There are nine suites, including the splendid Grand Suite, and three double rooms. There are wonderful private patios in some of the rooms and one of Antigua's finest restaurants is in the lobby. The 10 cozy, white-walled, wood beam-ceilinged rooms at **Casa Encantada** (9a Calle Poniente #1, tel. 7832-9715 Antigua or 866/837-8900 U.S., www.casaencantada-antigua.com, $75-225 d) are a more modern take on European decor with Guatemalan flair. Stylish accents include framed Guatemalan *huipiles,* oriental rugs, wrought-iron beds, feather and down comforters, and fine Italian linens. There is a rooftop bar perfect for enjoying the sunset over the colonial city streets. All rates include a scrumptious full breakfast, also served on the rooftop patio.

Like its sister hotel in Guatemala City, **Vista Real** (3a Calle Oriente #16A, tel. 7832-9715 or 7832-9716, www.vistareal.com, $150-225 d including breakfast) offers colonial style with distinction, excellent service, and attention to detail. Each of the five luxurious suites features four-poster beds, artwork, chimney, telephone, a private patio, and large bathroom decorated with Spanish tiles.

One of Antigua's most elegant properties, **(Posada de los Leones** (Las Gravileas #1, tel. 7832-7371, www.lionsinnantigua.com, $165-250 d) is set amid coffee trees and tropical gardens. Its six spacious, absolutely gorgeous rooms feature high ceilings, hardwood floors, and a delightful array of classy European and Guatemalan decorative touches. On the house's second floor is Antigua's loveliest terrace overlooking tropical gardens, the surrounding coffee plantation, and the volcanoes off in the distance. You can enjoy drinks on the terrace in addition to a lap pool, a comfortable living room, and library. There is wireless Internet throughout the house, which is sometimes the haunt of international celebrities.

Nearby is the phenomenal **(Un Paseo Por La Antigua** (Calle de los Duelos, Las Gravileas #7 and 8, tel. 7832-3354, www.unpaseoporlaantigua.com, $135 d with breakfast), run by a friendly French couple that have lived in Guatemala for many years. With the experience gleaned from running Petén's La Lancha (subsequently acquired by Francis Ford Coppola), they've managed to successfully create a unique, tastefully executed hideaway. Each of the five rooms is eclectically decorated with a different theme. There's a lovely rooftop patio where you can enjoy your meals with outrageous volcano

views. Set in a quiet residential neighborhood, you might find yourself sleeping in well past your normal wake-up time.

If you're looking to combine your stay with an excellent spa experience, **Casa Madeleine** (Calle del Espíritu Santo #69, tel. 7832-9348, www.casamadeleine.com, $105-240 d) is the place for you. Its six comfortable rooms feature wrought-iron beds and lamps and are decorated in different hues with Guatemalan bedspreads and artwork. Complete spa packages are available and services include massages, reflexology, aromatherapy, mud therapy, pedicures, manicures, and deep facial treatments. Room rates include a full breakfast you are welcome to enjoy in the comfort of your own room at no extra charge.

Casa Quinta (5a Avenida Sur #45, tel. 7832-6181, www.hotelcasaquinta.com, $125-180 d) was brought to my attention by a reader with discriminating taste. The rooms gracefully meld modern comforts with wonderfully dilapidated antiques and traditional furniture. View all of the rooms online and pick your favorite. An excellent value in this category, **Hotel Cirilo** (Calle de los Duelos #11, tel. 7832-6650, hotelcirilo.com, $100 d) combines modern touches with the charm and history of La Antigua. Built on the grounds of an old hermitage, the property features spacious gardens, old ruins, and a wooden-decked swimming pool. Glass doors provide wonderful views of the grounds from the comfortable living room and breakfast areas. Some of the comfortable rooms are literally built around the old ruins and you can have the old architecture all to yourself. Other room features include *retablo* headboards, a fireplace, and flat-screen TV.

OUTSIDE OF TOWN

On a working 40-acre avocado farm, **Earthlodge** (tel. 5664-0713 or 5613-6934, www.earthlodgeguatemala.com, dorms $5 p/p to $32 d in cabin) is a sure bet for wonderful volcano views and the chance to get away from it all at a reasonable distance from town in the surrounding hillsides. Accommodations include a shared-bath, eight-bed dormitory, three A-frame cabins, and a tree house. The private cabins and tree house are wonderfully secluded in a grove of Spanish oaks and have fabulous views of the valley and surrounding mountains. Each has a large double bed. Bathrooms are shared.

Delicious vegetarian dinners are served family-style for $5, though carnivores need not despair as meat options are also available, including a fun weekend barbecue. Breakfast items include eggs, bacon, sausage, pancakes, and fresh fruit. Heaping sandwiches and salads are served for lunch. You can relax in a hammock and take in the valley views, hike nearby trails, or sweat out any remaining First World stress in the stone-and-mortar sauna. There are also books, movies, music, and games on hand should you need further entertainment. Spanish classes are also available and the owners accept volunteers to help out with chores in exchange for reduced rates on food and bed. The lodge is run by a friendly Canadian-American couple who will pick you up in town in their green VW Bug with prior notice for a nominal gas charge, as they come into Antigua almost daily. Alternatively, you can hitch a chicken bus to the village of El Hato for about $0.50 or flag a pickup truck heading this way.

In nearby Santa Ana, **Posada El Ensueño** (Calle del Agua, Callejón La Ermita Final, Santa Ana, tel. 7832-7958, www.posadaelensueno.com, $95-115 d) is a splendid bed-and-breakfast in a quiet setting. Run by American expatriate Carmen Herrerias, the lodge has three tastefully decorated rooms with garden showers, one of which is a suite. It's a great place to relax away from the action in Antigua. Breakfast and home-cooked meals are served poolside, and Carmen loves to cook for her guests. There's also a small heated lap pool and bikes to get around. It's about a 25-minute walk to Antigua's central park.

Just minutes from Antigua in neighboring San Felipe de Jesús, **◖ Filadelfia Coffee Resort and Spa** (150 meters north of the San Felipe de Jesús church, tel. 7728-0800, hotel@rdaltoncoffee.com, $211-449 d including breakfast) is a working coffee farm where you can stay in a splendid neocolonial building harboring luxurious accommodations. The 20 spacious rooms have tile floors, king- or queen-sized beds, classy Guatemalan furnishings, cable TV with DVD player, large two-sink bathrooms, glass showers with antique tiles, and nice patios with furniture. There are four standard rooms, 14 deluxe doubles, and two master suites with island kitchen and a living room with leather sofa and large desk. Coffee machinery and wooden carvings adorn the public areas, while the main building harbors a cozy lobby adorned with Persian rugs. Activities include twice-daily coffee tours lasting two hours each at 9 A.M. and 2 P.M. ($15), mule riding ($20), and a four-hour hike to a lookout point ($50, including sack lunch). An elegant restaurant in the main lodge serves international dishes with flair.

Closer to the farm's main entrance is **Cafetenango** (tel. 5219-9291, 7:30 A.M.-7 P.M. Mon.-Sat. and 7:30 A.M.-6:30 P.M. Sun.), offering a more casual dining atmosphere in a country setting with lovely volcano views. It serves eggs, fruit, and yogurt for breakfast ($4), and grilled meats and sandwiches for lunch and dinner ($6-12). Traditional Guatemalan dishes ($10) include *pollo en jocón* and *pepián de pollo*.

Antigua now has its very own golf resort, thanks to forward-thinking Guatemalan investors willing to plunk down $80 million to provide Antigua with something its world-class offerings once lacked. Opened in 2008, **◖ La Reunión Antigua Golf Resort** (Km. 91.5 Carretera CA-14, tel. 7873-1400, www.lareunion.com.gt, $220 d) lies 17 kilometers from Antigua in neighboring Alotenango on the road to the Pacific Coast. The hotel setting and its Pete Dye-designed 18-hole golf course is truly spectacular, flanked by four volcanoes and lush green fields. The larger Suites Gran Clase are worth the splurge (an extra $30), for their private infinity-edge plunge pools and a hot tub with stunning volcano views (Agua and active Pacaya). The luxuriously well-furnished rooms have L'Occitane bath products, air-conditioning, and satellite TV. Plans call for the existing 26-room boutique hotel to be joined by a 125-room hotel managed by an international hotel chain. For now, La Reunión remains wonderfully peaceful. The only sounds you'll hear are the chirping of birds, the occasional roar of a distant lawnmower, and, once in a while, a landing helicopter announcing the arrival of Guatemala City's business elite coming in for a round of golf. It's all par for the course.

Food

Antigua's status as one of Guatemala's main tourist destinations is evident in the variety and number of excellent restaurants for every taste and budget. The mix here is rather eclectic and restaurants can often be classified into more than one category. While the presence of a McDonald's in town hardly constitutes anything worth writing home about, Antigua's golden arches are the focus of some local lore completely in line with the magic seemingly everywhere in Guatemala. According to local urban legend, the Ronald McDonald sitting on the bench outside Antigua's McDonald's has at least on one occasion crossed its legs and come to life, scaring unsuspecting passersby out of their wits.

CAFÉS AND LIGHT MEALS

The Refuge (7a Avenida Norte #18A, www.refugecoffeebar.com, 7:30 A.M.-7 P.M. Mon.-Sat., $2) is an independent coffee shop serving phenomenal coffee and espresso beverages at very reasonable prices in a quaint, intimate atmosphere. Also recommended for its high-quality coffee is **Tretto Caffe** (4A Calle Oriente #10, Local 28, tel. 5050-1021). For coffee on the go, **Café Barista** (on *parque central's* northwest corner) serves a variety of favorites, including caramel macchiato, mochas (hot or iced), and tasty pastries. It's part of a chain popular throughout Guatemala. One of Antigua's best-known cafés, **Doña Luisa Xicotencatl** (4a Calle Oriente #12, tel. 7832-2578, 7 A.M.-9:30 P.M. daily) serves delicious breakfasts, snacks, pastries, and light meals in a delightful garden courtyard. There are fresh-baked breads and cakes available all day from the bakery at the front of the building. Next door, **La Fuente** (4a Calle Oriente #14, tel. 7832-4520, 7 A.M.-7 P.M. daily) is a good place for breakfast and vegetarian fare as well as for a cup of coffee accompanied by an ever-so-sinfully delicious chocolate brownie topped with coffee ice cream and chocolate syrup.

On the west side of the central park, **Café Condesa** (Portal del Comercio #4, tel. 7832-0038, 7 A.M.-8 P.M. Sun.-Thurs., until 9 P.M. Fri.-Sat.) is a great place to get some pep in your step with an early breakfast and coffee or to refuel later in the day. There are excellent cakes, pastries, sandwiches, and salads served in a pleasing garden atmosphere or you can enjoy the all day breakfasts. A Sunday brunch is served 10 A.M.-2 P.M. and includes scrambled eggs, home-fried potatoes, silver-dollar pancakes, quiche, homemade bread, and muffins, just to name a few items. If you're on the go, grab a cup of the excellent coffee at the **Condesa Express** next door.

For fresh bagels, bagel sandwiches, and great coffee, stop at **The Bagel Barn** (5a Calle Poniente #2, 6 A.M.-10 P.M. daily). There is wireless Internet if you're traveling with a laptop and movies are shown in the afternoons and evenings. Another Antigua standby is the **Rainbow Café and Bookshop** (7a Avenida Sur #8, tel. 7832-1919, all meals daily), serving delicious menu options including eggs Florentine, Israeli falafel, and the chocolate bomb for dessert. Try the outstanding Greek chicken fillet stuffed with spinach, bacon, raisins, feta cheese, and covered with a creamy oregano and lime sauce ($8). Live music, poetry readings, and other cultural events are held on-site. On the pricier side, **Caffé Opera** (6a Avenida Norte #17, tel. 7832-0727, www.cafe-opera. com, closed Wed., $6-15) is a popular place serving some delicious coffee frappé beverages in an eclectic atmosphere stuffed with opera-themed posters and artwork. The *panini* are recommended. Under the same ownership as the Café No Sé (which is a bar), **Y Tu Piña También** (corner of 6a Calle Oriente and 1a Avenida Sur) is a juice bar also serving snacks, pastries, and light meals. The mango chutney chicken is good if you're on the hungrier side. Finally, a trip to Antigua wouldn't be complete without a stop for some *dulces típicos* (typical Guatemalan sweets) from **Doña María Gordillo** (4a Calle Oriente #11).

Antigua's finest delicatessen is **Epicure** (3a Avenida Norte #11 B, tel. 7832-5545, 10 A.M.-10 P.M. daily, $5-12), serving phenomenal sandwiches and deli items. The owners prefer that patrons dine onsite rather than carry out, and the pleasant outdoor area centered around a lovely garden courtyard and the remains of an old aqueduct makes that request easy to accommodate. A second location (6a Avenida Norte #35 A, tel. 7832-1414) is only open until 7 P.M. Monday-Saturday (until 6:30 P.M. Sun.).

STEAKHOUSES

Ni-Fu Ni-Fa (3a Calle Oriente #21, tel. 7832-6579, noon-10 P.M. Sun. and Mon., noon-10:30 P.M. Tues.-Thurs., noon-11 P.M. Fri. and

To Chimaltenango, Chichicastenango,
Lake Atitlán, and ((*CENTRO CULTURAL LA AZOTEA*

((CERRO DE
LA CRUZ

LA ANTIGUA GUATEMALA
FOOD AND NIGHTLIFE

CALLE ANCHA DE LOS HERREROS

CALLE DE LA NOBLEZA

6A AVENIDA N

IGLESIA Y CONVENTO
DE NUESTRA SEÑORA
DE LA MERCED

DON
MARTÍN

1A CALLE P   EL SERENO

1A CALLE O

HÉCTOR'S ▼
QUESO Y VINO ▼

LA CASBAH ▼

6A AVENIDA N

4A AVENIDA N

3A AVENIDA N

2A AVENIDA N

CALLE DE SANTO DOMINGO

▼ FRIDAS

ARCO DE
SANTA CATALINA ★

7A AVENIDA N

LA COCINA
DE LOLA ▼

((IGLESIA Y CONVENTO
DE LAS CAPUCHINAS

((CENTRO CULTURAL
CASA SANTO DOMINGO

To Guatemala
City

2A CALLE P

CAFFÉ
OPERA ▼

HOTEL POSADA
DE DON RODRIGO ▼

2A CALLE O

EPICURE ▼

CASA SANTO
DOMINGO ▼

LA FONDA DE
LA CALLE REAL ▼

EL SABOR
DEL TIEMPO ▼

3A CALLE O

3A CALLE P

REILLY'S ▼

RIKI'S BAR ▼

LA FUENTE ▼

EL MURO ▼ NI-FU NI-FA

▼ LA CASSEROLE

L'ESPRESSO ▼

LA FONDA DE
LA CALLE REAL ▼

CAFÉ
▼ BARISTA

DOÑA LUISA
XICOTENCATL ▼

NICOLAS ▼

CALLEJÓN DE LA CONCEPCIÓN

4A CALLE O

4A CALLE P

▼ TARTINES

DOÑA MARÍA
GORDILLO ▼

BISTROT
CINQ ▼

WELTEN ▼

▼ PAPAZITOS

RESTAURANTE ▼
LAS PALMAS

CAFÉ
CONDESA ▼

((PARQUE
CENTRAL

((CASA POPENOE
★

ORGÁNICA ▼

5A CALLE P

BAGEL
BARN ▼

CATEDRAL DE
SANTIAGO

LAS
ANTORCHAS ▼

5A CALLE O

▼ NOKIATE

RAINBOW CAFÉ
AND BOOKSHOP ▼

LA SIN
VENTURA ▼

EL MIX ▼

CAFÉ
FLOR ▼

Y TU PIÑA
TAMBIÉN ▼

▼ CAFÉ NO SE

6A CALLE P

5A AVENIDA S

4A AVENIDA S

3A AVENIDA S

2A AVENIDA S

CAFFÉ
▼ MEDITERRÁNEO

6A CALLE O

▼ CAFÉ SKY

LA SALA ■

DINEMA
BISTRO ▼

Río Pensativo

7A CALLE P

IGLESIA Y
HOSPITAL
SAN PEDRO

7A CALLE O

IGLESIA Y
CONVENTO
DE SANTA CLARA

JP'S
RUM BAR ▼

IGLESIA DE
SAN FRANCISCO

8A CALLE O

CALLE DEL HERMANO PEDRO

9A CALLE O

CALLE SUCIA

CALLE DE LOS PASOS

MESÓN PANZA
VERDE ▼

SANTA ANA

To San Juan del Obispo,
((*VOLCANO CLIMBS,*
Santa María de Jesús,
and Agua Volcano

© AVALON TRAVEL

Sat., $5-22) is a genuine Argentinean steakhouse serving tasty grilled meats on a pleasant raised wooden deck surrounded by lush gardens. **Restaurant Las Antorchas** (3a Avenida Sur #1, tel. 7832-0806, www.lasantorchas.com, 11 A.M.-3 P.M. and 6-10 P.M. Mon.-Fri., 11 A.M.-4 P.M.and 6-10 P.M. Sat.; 11 A.M.-5 P.M. Sun., $8-31) offers a more elegant setting and a menu that includes grilled onions, cheese fondue, tortellini, salmon in orange sauce, and well-presented grilled steak and chicken dishes.

MEXICAN

Just like its Guatemala City counterpart, **Fridas** (5a Avenida Norte #29, tel. 7832-0504, www.lasfridas.com, lunch and dinner daily, $4-10) serves scrumptious Mexican classics such as fajitas, flautas, tacos, burritos, enchiladas, and nachos in addition to the best margaritas and *mojitos* in town, all in a lively atmosphere.

CONTINENTAL

Antigua is full of hidden gems. One of these is ◖ **Hector's** (1a Calle Poniente #9A, tel. 7832-9867, lunch and dinner, $7-17), tucked away on the street fronting *Iglesia La Merced*. It's a simple, bistro-style kind of place with half a dozen tables and a bar. The menu rotates but includes amazing open-faced sandwiches, homemade pasta, seared duck, and beef tenderloin. You can watch your meal being prepared in the open kitchen. Olives make a wonderful starter to pair with a glass of wine. For French food, **La Casserole** (Callejón de la Concepción #7, tel. 7832-0219, noon-3 P.M. and 7-10 P.M. Tues.-Sat., noon-4 P.M. Sun.) is hard to beat. In an appealing garden patio with a dozen or so tables, there are tasty soups, well-prepared pastas, and fish and chicken or meat dishes to satiate your hunger. For dessert, there are excellent crepes, tiramisu, sorbet, and mousse. For Spanish food, head to **La Cocina de Lola** (2a Calle Poniente #3, tel. 7832-6616, noon-3 P.M. and 6-10 P.M. Tues.-Fri.,

noon-10 P.M. Sat., noon-9 P.M. Sun., $5-10), where there are several rooms around a garden patio. You can feast on classic Spanish dishes the likes of paella, seafood, and grilled steaks. Just down the street from the Arco de Santa Catalina, **El Sabor del Tiempo** (Calle del Arco and 3a Calle, tel. 7832-0516, lunch and dinner daily, $5-11) offers a casual dining atmosphere and creatively prepared dishes, including rabbit steak, pastas, *panini,* and tasty Greek burgers. ◖**Como Como** (6a Calle Poniente #6, tel. 7832-0478), specializes in Franco-Belgian cuisine and enjoys a loyal following thanks to consistently great food and a pleasant atmosphere that includes a lovely garden patio. **Sobremesa** (4a Calle Oriente #4A, tel. 7832-3231, www.alexferrar.com, $8-13) is a restaurant doubling as an art gallery. The art is fabulously eclectic but the food is not to be outdone. Menu highlights include phenomenal Croque Monsieur, delicious Unicorn Steak (tenderloin medallion in a wine and Dijon reduction) and yummy Japanese Plum Chicken. For dessert, savor exotic ice cream flavors the likes of strawberry merlot and jasmine blackberry.

ITALIAN

Antigua has a number of Italian restaurants popular with travelers and locals alike. **Quesos y Vino** (1a Calle Poniente #1, tel. 7832-7785, noon-3 P.M. and 6-10 P.M. Wed.-Mon., $5-10) has delicious pizza, pastas, and cheeses in addition to Chilean and Spanish wines. **Caffé Mediterraneo** (6a Calle Poniente #6A, tel. 7832-7180, noon-3 P.M. and 6-10 P.M. Mon. and Wed.-Sat., noon-4:30 P.M. and 6:30-9 P.M. Sun., $7-12) is small but serves excellent Italian food, including homemade pastas and delightful antipasti in addition to a good assortment of wines. For gourmet pizza, try **Papazitos** (4a Calle Oriente #39, tel. 7832-5209, 11:30 A.M.-11 P.M. daily). It also serves nachos, *panini,* calzones, pastas, vegetarian dishes, wine, and beer. It offers free delivery with a minimum $7 purchase; 10- to 18-inch pizzas go for $9-16.

GUATEMALAN AND LATIN AMERICAN

Another one of Antigua's legendary restaurants is **La Fonda de la Calle Real** (3a Calle Poniente #7, tel. 7832-0507, noon-10 P.M. daily; 5a Avenida Norte #5, tel. 7832-2629, noon-10 P.M. daily; 5a Avenida Norte #12, tel. 7832-3749, 8 A.M.-10 P.M. daily, $5-12), with three branches, the nicest of which is the one on 3a Calle Poniente. There is a varied menu of Guatemalan favorites, including *chiles rellenos* as well as tasty grilled meats. If you can't decide, do as President Clinton did and order the filling sampler menu. **Don Martín** (4a Avenida Norte #27, tel. 7832-1063, 6-10 P.M. Tues.-Sat., 1- 9 P.M. Sun.) features creative Guatemalan dishes, including *pepián* (a spicy meat or chicken stew), and has an international touch with pasta dishes. For a lively atmosphere and great food, **Restaurante Las Palmas** (6a Avenida Norte #14, tel. 7832-9734, www.las-palmasantigua.com, 9 A.M.-10 P.M. daily, $7-12) makes a fine choice. Among the varied menu items are fish in cilantro sauce, spinach lasagna, shrimp with pasta in Alfredo sauce, and filet mignon. There are whirring ceiling fans, a fully stocked bar, and vibrant tropical Latin decor.

ASIAN

Café Flor (4a Avenida Sur #1, tel. 7832-5274, 11 A.M.-11 P.M. daily, $6-12) does a reasonably good job with Thai food, though it won't taste familiar to fans of Asian cuisine. Other dishes include Thai curries, rice dishes, and Indian tandoori recipes. The portions are adequate, but not huge, either. A baby grand piano adds to the eclectic ambiance. With a Far Eastern "cool Zen" atmosphere, **Nokiate** (1a Avenida Sur #7, tel. 7821-2896, www.nokiate.com, 6:30 P.M.-1 A.M. Tues.-Fri., noon-3 P.M. and 6:30 P.M.-1 A.M. Sat., noon-9 P.M. Sun., $5-10) pulls it off beautifully. The hip lounge, sake bar, and wonderful Asian garden patio make a suitably glamorous backdrop for enjoying the best sushi in town. For your standard Chinese food, head to **Su Chow** (5a Avenida Norte #36, tel. 7832-1344, noon-10 P.M. daily, $5-10). Su Chow also delivers. For Indian food, check out **Abassi con Curry** (4a Calle Oriente #14, tel. 7832-4518, $4-10). You'll find several of your Indian favorites, including samosas, Vindaloo, chicken korma, and shrimp masala, though Tandoori chicken and chicken tikka masala are oddly missing from the menu. There are, of course, numerous vegetarian options. You *will* find chicken tikka masala and Tandoori chicken on the menu at **Pushkar** (6a Avenida Norte #18, tel. 7882-4098, lunch and dinner daily, $4-11), along with meat or vegetable samosas and seafood curries. There's also pleasant patio seating.

FINE DINING

One of the city's most atmospheric restaurants, **El Tenedor del Cerro** (tel. 7832-3520, 7 A.M.-10 P.M. Mon.-Sat., 7 A.M.-5 P.M. Sun., $4-15) features fabulous views of the Antigua valley and its volcanic backdrop, along with a well-rounded menu that includes hearty breakfasts, salads, pasta, pizzas with an interesting array of international flavors, steaks and decadent desserts. Many of the fresh ingredients come straight from the onsite garden. The views of Agua, Fuego, and Acatenango volcanoes are fully appreciated with outdoor seating on a pleasant patio. The main restaurant features a high canvas ceiling and floor-to-ceiling windows. The eatery is part of a larger complex known as Santo Domingo del Cerro, by the same owners as the city's Casa Santo Domingo hotel. There are a separate patio lounge, gift shop, aviary, and sculpture gardens to enjoy, along with rotating art exhibits. To get here, follow the winding road to the top of the hill. The entrance is found just before Antigua's main entrance, on the left, on the road from Guatemala City.

© AL ARGUETA

the restaurant at Casa Santo Domingo

With a long tradition of excellence, **Welten** (4a Calle Oriente #21, tel. 7832-0630, www. weltenrestaurant.com, noon-10 P.M. Mon.-Sun and Wed.-Thurs., until 11 P.M. Fri.-Sat., $13-22) is one of Antigua's well-established dining options serving an impressive menu of gourmet Guatemalan, French, and Italian specialties in an elegant atmosphere. Menu highlights include creamy peppered steak (filet au poivre), seafood fettuccine, and fish fillet in a traditional salsa. There are delicious homemade ice creams for dessert. ◖**Mesón Panza Verde** (5a Avenida Sur #19, tel. 7832-2925, www. panzaverde.com, lunch and dinner Tues.-Sat., brunch and lunch Sun., $10-20) is easily one of Guatemala's finest restaurants, with outstanding food and sophisticated European ambience. The mostly French cuisine is heavy on meat and fish dishes. The wine list is impressive, as are the desserts. A Sunday brunch is served 10 A.M.-1 P.M. You can enjoy your meal in the main dining room surrounded by fine

art under a vaulted ceiling or al fresco in La Cueva, a covered patio beneath baroque arches beside a fountain. *Chacun à son goût.*

On par with the exclusive digs in this landmark Antigua hotel, the restaurant at **Casa Santo Domingo** (3a Calle Oriente #28, tel. 7832-0140, www.casasantodomingo.com.gt, $15-25) serves delicious Guatemalan and international fare in the restored ruins of an old monastery. It makes a great spot for a romantic candlelit dinner. The town's most authentic hotel restaurant can be found at ◖ **Hotel Posada de Don Rodrigo** (5a Avenida Norte #17, tel. 7832-0291, all meals daily), which is popular with Guatemalans who come here for its stellar service, wonderful ambience overlooking the hotel gardens and consistently delicious Guatemalan and international cuisine. The tortillas are made fresh on the premises and you can watch the dough being patted and placed on the *comal,* where it is cooked over a fire. There is sometimes live marimba music to complete the authentic Guatemalan feel.

A longtime favorite is ◖ **El Sereno** (4a Avenida Norte #16, tel. 7832-0501, www. elsereno.com.gt, lunch and dinner daily). The restaurant dates to 1980, but the wonderfully old colonial building in which it's housed dates to the 16th century and once housed the Spanish priests who built La Merced church. You can dine on gourmet international dishes in the elegant main dining room, in a romantic cavelike candlelit room, or al fresco either in a delightful covered garden patio or on the rooftop terrace.

A wonderful addition to Antigua's restaurant scene is **Tartines** (4a Calle Oriente #1C, tel. 7882-4606 or 7882-4607,

11 A.M.-7 P.M. Tues.-Wed., 11 A.M.-10 P.M. Thurs.-Sat, 11 A.M.-4 P.M. Sun., $5-20). On the menu you'll find crêpes, paninis, pasta, and very tasty duck. Enjoy your meal from the rooftop patio overlooking the ruins of the Catedral de Santiago.

Last but certainly not least of the fine dining options is ◖ **Bistrot Cinq** (4a Calle Oriente #7, tel. 7832-5510, www.bistrotcinq.com, noon-10:30 P.M. daily, $9-25). The emphasis is on French cuisine; dishes include chicken scaloppine and trout Armandine, but with take-out or delivery items such as scrumptious half-pound burgers and steak *frites* also on the menu. The bar is top-notch and includes absinthe.

Information and Services

TOURIST INFORMATION

The INGUAT office (corner of 2a Calle Oriente and 2a Avenida Norte, 8 A.M.-12:30 P.M. and 2:30-5 P.M. Mon.-Fri., 9 A.M.-12:30 P.M. and 2:30-5 P.M. Sat.-Sun.), also known as Casa del Turista, has friendly, helpful staff who can help steer you in the right direction as well as provide free maps, bus schedules, and other useful information. A useful website with lots of information on hotels, restaurants, shops, and services is www.aroundantigua.com. Another useful publication is the monthly *Revue* magazine, available free at many hotels, restaurants, and shops. Another publication, *Qué pasa en Antigua,* has very complete information on all that's going on.

COMMUNICATIONS

Antigua's main post office is near the bus terminal on the corner of 4a Calle Poniente and Calzada de Santa Lucía and is open 9 A.M.-5 P.M. There are also various international couriers with offices here, including UPS (6a Calle Poniente #34, tel. 7832-0073) and DHL (6a Avenida Sur #12, tel.

7832-1696). A number of companies can also help you ship home any purchases you're unable to fit in your check-in baggage allotment. These include Quickbox (6a Calle Poniente #7, tel. 7832-3825) and Envíos Etc. (2a Calle Poniente #3), which is also the local representative for FedEx.

Conexion (4a Calle Oriente #14, Centro Comercial La Fuente, tel. 7832-3768, 8:30 A.M.-7:30 P.M. daily) offers fast Internet on new machines with flat screens for $1.50 an hour. It also offers printing, photocopying, and CD-burning in addition to phone and fax services. Enlaces (6a Avenida Norte #1, tel. 7832-5555, 8 A.M.-7:30 P.M. Mon.-Sat., 8 A.M.-1 P.M. Sun.) is another good setup offering many of the same services. Funky Monkey (5a Avenida Sur #6) is housed in the same complex as the Monoloco bar and has a decent Internet connection for about $1 an hour. Strictly for phone calls, your best bet is Australis Telecom (4a Calle Poniente #15, tel. 2381-0698, 8 A.M.-8 P.M. daily), where you can pretty much call anywhere on the planet for $0.09-0.10 a minute from a nice

CHOOSING A LANGUAGE SCHOOL

Antigua has close to 100 language schools, and the task of choosing the right one can seem downright daunting. It really boils down to the quality of individual instructors, though some schools are definitely better than others. Look around and ask plenty of questions. If you decide midway through a weeklong course that you're just not jiving with the instructor, don't hesitate to pull out and ask for a new one. That being said, the following websites can help you out in your search: www.guatemala365.com and www.123teachme.com. Both have surveys and rankings of individual schools in Guatemala.

Among the recommended Antigua schools are **Academia de Español Antigueña** (1a Calle Poniente #10, tel. 7832-7241, www.spanishacademyantiguena.com), a small, well-run school with space for 10 students at a time. I've personally had the pleasure of working with **Spanish School La Unión** (1a. Avenida Sur #21, tel. 7832-7757, www.launion.edu.gt). They offer quality one-on-one instruction and are involved in a variety of social projects. **Escuela de Español San José El Viejo** (5a Avenida Sur #34, tel. 7832-3028, www.sanjoseelviejo.com) has its own very attractive campus where you can stay in comfortable accommodations with facilities that include a tennis court and swimming pool amid lovely gardens and coffee trees. A longtime student favorite is **Christian Spanish Academy** (6a Avenida Norte #15, tel. 7832-3922, www.learncsa.com), a very well-run school set in a pleasant colonial courtyard. Antigua's oldest language school is **Proyecto Lingüístico Francisco Marroquín** (7a Calle Poniente #31, tel. 7832-2886, www.plfm-antigua.org), run by a nonprofit foundation working toward the study and preservation of Mayan languages. It comes highly recommended. **Academia de Español Probigua** (6a Avenida Norte #41B, tel. 7832-2998, www.probigua.conexion.com) is run by a nonprofit group working to establish and maintain libraries in rural villages. Another good choice with comfortable accommodations across the street from the school is **Centro Lingüístico Internacional** (1a Calle Oriente #11, tel. 7832-0391, www.spanishcontact.com).

The recommended schools range in price $140-225 per week, including 20-35 hours of instruction and a stay with local family. While the schools provide everything you will need to learn the language, it might be a challenge to have a total language immersion experience because of the overwhelming presence of foreigners in Antigua. If this is an issue for you, consider taking Spanish classes in Cobán or Petén.

soundproof cabin. Most hotels and decent restaurants nowadays offer free Wi-Fi.

MONEY

Banco Industrial (5a Avenida Sur #4), just south of the plaza, has a Visa/Plus ATM. There is also an ATM on the north side of the plaza next to Café Barista. Another ATM may be found on the plaza's west side next to Café Condesa (Portal del Comercio #4). Just off the square at the corner of 4a Calle Oriente and 4a Avenida Norte, Citibank changes U.S. dollars and can cash travelers checks. Avoid any and all BAC ATM machines, as there have been incidents of card cloning originating at their Antigua locations.

LAUNDRY

Detalles (6a Avenida Norte #3B, tel. 7832-5973, 7:30 A.M.-6:30 P.M. Mon.-Sat., 8 A.M.-4 P.M. Sun.) does dry cleaning and has coin-operated laundry machines. Lavandería Dry Clean (6a Calle Poniente #49, 7 A.M.-7 P.M. Mon.-Sat., 9 A.M.-6 P.M. Sun.) charges about $4 a load. Quick Laundry (6a Calle Poniente #14, tel. 7832-2937, 8 A.M.-5 P.M. Mon.-Sat.) charges about $0.85 per pound.

MEDICAL SERVICES

Casa de Salud Santa Lucía (Calzada de Santa Lucía Sur #7, tel. 7832-3122) is a private medical hospital with 24-hour emergency services.

Hospital Nacional Pedro de Betancourt is a public hospital two kilometers from town with emergency service. For serious issues, your best bet is to go to Guatemala City.

EMERGENCY

For Asistur (Tourist Assistance) dial 1500 from any phone or call 2421-2810. For the Bomberos Municipales (Municipal Fire Department), dial 7831-0049.

TRAVEL AGENCIES

Travel agencies are ubiquitous in Antigua. Among the recommended companies for shuttle buses is Atitrans (6a Avenida Sur #8, tel. 7832-3371 or 7832-0644, www.atitrans.com). For plane tickets and general travel needs, recommended travel agents include National Travel (6a Avenida Sur #1A, tel. 2247-4747), Viajes Tivoli (4a Calle Oriente #10, Edificio El Jaulón, tel. 7832-1370), and Rainbow Travel Center (7a Avenida Sur #8, tel. 7832-4202, www.rainbowtravelcenter.com). Specializing in student and youth travel is STA Travel (6a Calle Poniente #21, tel. 7892-3985).

Sin Fronteras (5a Avenida Norte #15A, tel. 7832-1017, www.sinfront.com) is another good all-around agency with package deals to Tikal in addition to local tours. It rents cars through Tabarini Rent A Car. Another good agency for packages to Tikal or other parts of Guatemala is Adrenalina Tours (5a Avenida Norte #31, tel. 7832-1108, www.adrenalinatours.com). It also has daily shuttle service to Quetzaltenango at 8 A.M. and 2:30 P.M. for $25 per person. Bon Voyage Guatemala (6a Avenida Norte #3A, tel. 7823-9209, www.bonvoyageguatemala.com) is a good source of travel information and acts as a booking agent for various transportation providers. The company also runs daily shuttles at 8 A.M. for El Salvador beaches. Also recommended for country-wide tours from Antigua is Guinness Travel (6a Avenida Norte #16, tel. 4623-6297, www.guinness-travel.com).

VOLUNTEER WORK

Proyecto Mosaico Guatemala (3a Avenida Norte #3, Casa de Mito, tel. 7932-0955, www.promosaico.org) places volunteers with organizations working to make Guatemala a better place. It also provides resources to more than 60 ongoing projects. Amerispan Guatemala (6a Avenida Norte #40A, tel. 7832-0164, www.amerispan.com) can also get you connected to volunteer opportunities throughout the country for a $60 fee. If you're interested in working with impoverished children, check out The God's Child project (Carretera a San Felipe #106, tel. 7832-4678, www.godschild.org).

COOKING SCHOOL

If you acquire a taste for traditional Guatemalan cuisine and want to re-create the country's myriad flavors at home, check out **El Frijol Feliz** (4a Avenida Sur #1, tel. 7832-5274, www.frijolfeliz. com, $45 per class). The school is open every day and there are classes available in the morning or afternoon. The class includes instruction on the preparation of one main dish, two side dishes and a dessert. More focused classes include instruction on the preparation of typical Guatemalan sauces such as mole and salsa verde. Dishes include *pepián, chiles rellenos,* and *chuchitos* (the author's favorite).

Getting There and Around

BUS

The main **bus terminal** is found next to the market, three blocks west of the central plaza. It is separated from the heart of town by a broad, tree-lined street. There are connections to the highlands available by taking one of many frequent buses up to Chimaltenango (every 15 minutes, half-hour travel time) along the Pan-American Highway and a requisite stop for buses trundling along to the highlands from Guatemala City. You can also catch one of the slightly less frequent buses to San Lucas Sacatepéquez, which is closer to Guatemala City. There may be more seats available on the buses plying the same highway en route toward Chimaltenango. Buses for Guatemala City leave every 15 minutes or so 4 A.M.-7:30 P.M., taking about an hour and costing about $1.25. There is also a direct bus to Panajachel at 7 A.M. leaving from 4a Calle Poniente #34 (two hours, $5).

Otherwise, buses leave every 15 minutes for San Miguel Dueñas ("Dueñas," 30 minutes, $0.50) stopping along the way in Ciudad Vieja. There are also buses every 30 minutes for San Antonio Aguas Calientes and Santa María de Jesús.

SHUTTLE BUS

Many travelers opt for the comfort, convenience, safety, and hassle-free experience aboard one of the numerous shuttle buses. Destinations include frequent runs to the Guatemala City airport, at least one bus daily to Monterrico and Cobán, several daily to Panajachel and Quetzaltenango, and less frequently to Río Dulce. Recommended shuttle companies include **Atitrans** (6a Avenida Sur #8, tel. 7832-3371 or 7832-0644, www.atitrans.com) and **Adrenalina Tours** (5a Avenida Norte #31, tel. 7832-1108, www.adrenalinatours.com).

TAXI

Taxis can be found on the east side of the park next to the cathedral by the bus terminal. The former is probably a safer place to board one. A ride to Guatemala City should cost around $30. You'll also see *tuk-tuks* (motorized rickshaws) throughout the city, costing considerably less and recommended for short distances.

CAR RENTAL

Hertz (7a Calle Poniente #3B, inside Camino Real Antigua hotel, tel. 7968-6156) has opened an office in Antigua. **Tabarini** (6a Avenida Sur #22, tel. 7832-8107) rents cars from its own office and also handles bookings via **Sin Fronteras** (5a Avenida Norte #15A, tel. 7832-1017).

BICYCLE RENTAL

Don Quijote Cruisers (7a Avenida Norte #2, tel. 7832-9427, www.donquijotecruisers.com, 9 A.M.-5:30 P.M. Tues.-Sun., $25 full day) sells and rents bikes for touring around town. For mountain bikes, check out **Old Town Outfitters** (5a Avenida Sur #12, tel. 5399-0440, www.bikeguatemala.com).

Near Antigua Guatemala

Antigua is surrounded by a number of picturesque towns and villages built in the midst of the Panchoy valley and on the slopes of neighboring volcanoes. You'll find plenty of recreational opportunities in these parts—enjoy the region's natural backdrop, surrounded by coffee farms and even a winery.

JOCOTENANGO

Jocotenango lies just 3.5 kilometers northwest of Antigua. A pretty, pink stucco church adorns the main square. In colonial times, the town served as the official entry point into neighboring Antigua.

◖ Centro Cultural La Azotea

The town's main attraction is La Azotea Cultural Center (Calle del Cementerio, Final, 8:30 A.M.-4 P.M. Mon.-Fri., 8:30 A.M.-2 P.M. Sat., $4 adults, $0.85 children), which functions as a three-in-one coffee, costume, and music museum. The music museum, **Casa K'ojom** (www.kojom.org) features a wonderful assortment of traditional Mayan musical instruments, including *marimbas,* drums, a diatomic harp, and flutes in addition to masks and paintings collected by its dedicated administrator, Samuel Franco. There is also an audiovisual room where you can watch a video on traditional music as it would be played in Mayan villages. Traditional costumes and crafts of the Antigua Valley are exhibited in a separate room dedicated to Sacatepéquez department.

The adjoining **Museo del Café** covers the history and evolution of coffee cultivation and is available as a self-guided or guided tour. You can see coffee beans in varying stages of production from recently harvested to fully roasted. The well-illustrated displays include information on wet and dry mills, some old

roasters, and machinery. You can then tour an actual plantation on-site. There is also a shop where you can buy CDs, DVDs, handicrafts, and of course, coffee.

Also found here is the **Establo La Ronda** (tel. 7831-1120, www.centroazotea.com), where you can ride around the grounds on horseback for an hour in the mornings ($3). Call ahead.

You can get to Jocotenango by taking any Chimaltenango-bound bus leaving from Antigua's bus terminal. Buses leave every 20 minutes; you can also take a *tuk-tuk* or taxi.

SAN JUAN DEL OBISPO

Although this town itself is unremarkable, it bears mentioning for the impressive **Palacio del Obispo,** the original home of Bishop Francisco Marroquín, which was restored in 1939. Though it's now used as a place for spiritual retreats, the nuns living there are happy to show you around if you ring the bell at a reasonable hour. The entrance is on the street behind the attached church. Marroquín arrived with Alvarado and temporarily assumed government leadership in the wake of the death of Alvarado's wife, Beatriz de la Cueva, who assumed power after his death. He also assumed a great deal of responsibility for the construction of the new capital at Antigua. The palace interior is quite lovely and still contains original furniture in addition to a 16th-century portrait of Marroquín and religious artwork imported from Europe. There is also an ornate baroque chapel. There are some nice views of Antigua and the valley from here, just south of town. Buses leave hourly from the Antigua bus terminal, taking about 20 minutes to get here.

CIUDAD VIEJA

Ciudad Vieja served as Guatemala's colonial capital before its destruction by mudflows from

THE GIANT KITE FESTIVAL

If you're visiting the Antigua or Guatemala City area around November 1, you should certainly plan a trip to either of the highland Mayan towns of Santiago Sacatepéquez or Sumpango, home to the annual Giant Kite Festival. In addition to the lively atmosphere of a typical Mayan fiesta, you'll be treated to an awe-inspiring display of larger-than-life kites, typically 20-50 feet wide. The kites are painstakingly crafted from tissue paper and bamboo reeds incorporating colorful and elaborate designs. Preparations typically begin six weeks in advance, in mid-September, with teams working extended hours as the deadline for completion draws closer. Judges are on hand at the festival to name the best entries in a variety of categories.

Kites under 20 feet in diameter are flown over the town cemetery later in the day and are believed to be a vehicle for speaking with the souls of departed loved ones. The flying kites are representative of the floating spirits of the dead. Larger kites are only for show and typically carry a message or theme, sometimes overtly political in nature. The weather is typically windy during this time of year, with the surrounding hillsides still tinged with verdant hues thanks to the recently ended rainy season. The colorful cemetery structures and the typical native dress of the Mayan people cap off a Technicolor dream of a day.

The festival in Sumpango, the larger of the two towns, takes place in a broad field adjacent to the cemetery. Santiago Sacatepéquez has a somewhat more cramped setting, its cemetery being perched on the edge of a plateau and extending down a gently sloping hillside.

Many Antigua travel agencies have special trips to both towns on these days, or you can go by bus. Santiago Sacatepéquez lies a few kilometers off the Pan-American Highway. You can take a direct bus from Antigua or get off from any Guatemala City-bound bus at the junction and continue from there. For Sumpango, your best bet is to get to Chimaltenango, also on the Pan-American Highway, and connect from there.

one of the smaller kites at the Giant Kite Festival

© AL ARGUETA

Agua Volcano in 1541, after which the capital was moved to present-day Antigua, six kilometers north. Its former glory is long gone, its only outstanding landmark being the colonial church on the plaza. Beatriz de la Cueva, Don Pedro de Alvarado's second wife, perished in the ruins of a nearby chapel while seeking refuge from the storm, which brought mud and water clambering down the slopes of the volcano.

Just beyond Ciudad Vieja, on the road to San Miguel Dueñas, **Estación Experimental Valhalla** (Km 52.5 Carretera a San Miguel Dueñas, tel. 7831-5799, www.exvalhalla.net, 8 A.M.-5 P.M. daily) is an experimental macadamia nut-farming operation. You can tour the organic plantation, sample macadamia chocolates and macadamia oil skin-care products, or eat delicious macadamia nut pancakes served with blueberry jam and macadamia butter 8:30 A.M.-3:30 P.M. The owner is a visionary who sees macadamia trees as a sustainable agricultural and ecological alternative to coffee harvesting and may be on hand to show you around.

SAN ANTONIO AGUAS CALIENTES

This town is well known for its wonderful weavings incorporating geometric/floral patterns and for handicrafts, including *petates* (reed mats), wooden masks, reed dolls, and kites. At the time of its founding in the 16th century, San Antonio and other adjoining communities were lakeshore villages on Lago Quinizilapa, which has long since been drained. The town's prominence as a handicrafts production center has made it relatively prosperous and it enjoys one of the highest literacy rates in the Guatemalan highlands. There are frequent buses to San Antonio, just six kilometers from Antigua. **Antigua Tours** (3a Calle Oriente #22, tel. 7832-5821, www.antiguatours.net) includes a stop in San Antonio Aguas Calientes as part of its "Antigua Villages" tour.

THE WESTERN HIGHLANDS

The Western Highlands are probably the region most travelers familiar with Guatemala think about when daydreaming about a trip to this country. The region is home to quaint and colorful mountain villages, highland lakes, pine forests, and the majority of Guatemala's indigenous peoples. Although other parts of Central America offer attractions similar to those found elsewhere in Guatemala, nowhere else in the region are age-old traditions, exquisite Mayan culture, and a history both proud and painful so remarkably evident and incredibly alive. From the Indian markets in Chichicastenango and the Mayan practices of the *costumbristas* (shamans practicing traditional Mayan rituals) in the hills just outside of town to the all-day November 1 horse races of Todos Santos, the region is steeped in rich culture.

In the Western Highlands, you'll find the ruined cities of the highland Mayan tribes encountered by Pedro de Alvarado and the Spanish when they arrived in 1524. The sites are still places of pilgrimage for the modern-day descendants of the various linguistic groups populating this part of the country. Traversing the pine tree-peppered mountain scenery, you'll also come across the region's spectacular volcanic chain, which runs like a spine heading west from Antigua all the way to the Mexican border. The water-filled caldera of an extinct volcano forms the basis for one of the country's most outrageously beautiful natural attractions,

© AL ARGUETA

HIGHLIGHTS

LOOK FOR 【 TO FIND RECOMMENDED SIGHTS, ACTIVITIES, DINING, AND LODGING.

【 **Iximché:** Conveniently situated close to the Pan-American Highway about an hour outside of Guatemala City, the ruins of the former capital of the Kaqchikel kingdom is worth a look to see what the Spanish encountered when they first arrived in Guatemala. It is the most easily accessible of all the highland Mayan centers brought under Spanish dominion at the time of the conquest (page 130).

【 **Reserva Natural Atitlán:** Lake Atitlán is one of Guatemala's greatest natural wonders, and this private nature reserve offers a unique glimpse into its ecosystems. There are trails, waterfalls, plenty of animals, a butterfly farm, and a private lake beach in addition to comfortable accommodations (page 133).

【 **Chichicastenango's Market:** Don't miss the chance to barter for goods and take in the chaotic atmosphere of this colorful Sunday and Thursday market at the center of a K'iche' town (page 164).

【 **Acul:** One of the so-called "model villages" established by the military, Acul has come into its own in the aftermath of the armed conflict. It makes an excellent hike from Nebaj, though the pastoral scenery and Swiss-like ambience found in some of the local accommodations will probably have you planning on staying the night (page 180).

【 **Laguna Chicabal:** Near Quetzaltenango, this enchanting, bowl-shaped crater lake makes a worthy day hike. Mayan rituals still take place here, and the site is equally fascinating for the spectacular natural surroundings (page 213).

the singular Lake Atitlán. In addition to water-based recreational activities, unlike any other lake in Central America, it offers the opportunity to observe and interact with the fascinating highland Mayan people inhabiting the dozen or so villages along its lakeshores. Farther west is Guatemala's second-largest city, Quetzaltenango, which has become a popular place for Spanish-language study as well as a hub of NGO activity in the aftermath of the civil war. It boasts some outstanding nearby natural attractions of its own and the cosmopolitan feel of a European city.

Throughout the highlands, you'll encounter the after-effects of Guatemala's bloody civil war, which affected this region more than any other. But, like a brilliant springtime flower emerging through fertile soil from winter's icy chill, the highlands and its people are fast changing and rising from the ashes of the armed conflict. There's a new feeling in the air. Where once there was fear and apprehension (and rightfully so) on the part of its Mayan inhabitants, there is now curiosity and a desire to build a new future while holding on to the culture that is their inheritance. You are a big part of this, as your presence in these parts is a catalyst to substantial progress along the lines of sustainable development with tourism at the forefront. There are many community-based tourism projects in this area and your visit helps provide needed income but also positive interaction with the outside world.

It is so refreshing, years later, to be able to travel to areas that were once bombed out and cleared of vegetation but are now green and vibrant again. This painful legacy intertwined with optimism is most evident in the Ixil Triangle, which stands poised to become a mecca for cultural and ecotourism, overseen by and to the benefit of, its Ixil inhabitants. Despite having suffered some of the most horrendous atrocities during the civil war, still they smile, a testament to their fortitude. Farther west toward the Mexican border, the department of Huehuetenango boasts fascinating Mayan villages of its own in addition to some seldom-visited natural attractions along the Sierra de los Cuchumatanes mountain chain. It's only a matter of time before visitors to Guatemala put this vast wilderness on the map.

PLANNING YOUR TIME

The Western Highlands are home to many of Guatemala's main attractions and there is plenty here worth seeing. Although distances on a map may be short, the rugged mountain terrain means getting to places that look close on a map will often take longer than expected because of twisting mountain roads, some of which are not even paved. You could easily spend several weeks here or longer, as attested to by the sizeable expat population living on the shores of Lake Atitlán. But, since most folks tend to be on a tighter schedule you'll probably

THE WESTERN HIGHLANDS

Yalombojoch

Bulej

San Mateo Ixtatán

Barillas

Playa Grande (Cantabal)

Parque Nacional Laguna Lachuá

Santa Eulalia

San Miguel Acatán

Soloma

San Juan Ixcoy

ALTA VERAPAZ

Sierra de Chamá

Río Negro (Chixoy)

QUICHÉ

Todos Santos Cuchumatán

Salquil Grande

THE IXIL TRIANGLE

San Gaspar Chajul

San Juan Cotzal

Cobán

Río Ixcán

Río Xacbal

SIERRA DE LOS CUCHUMATANES

ACUL

Santa María Nebaj

Uspantán

Chicamán

San Cristóbal Verapaz

To Guatemala City

Chiantla

Aguacatán

ZACULEU

Huehuetenango

Sacapulas

BAJA VERAPAZ

To Salamá

Parque Nacional Riscos de Momostenango

Momostenango

San Pedro Jocopilas

Cubulco

Rabinal

Santa Cruz del Quiché

K'UMARCAAJ (UTATLÁN)

Chinique

Zacualpa

Sierra de Chuacús

El Chol

TOTONICAPÁN

San Francisco El Alto

Chiché

Joyabaj

CUATRO CAMINOS

Totonicapán

Chichicastenango

CHICHICASTENANGO'S MARKET

Pachalum

MIXCO VIEJO

LOS ENCUENTROS

CHIMALTENANGO

GUATEMALA

Quetzaltenango

CA 1

Zunil

SOLOLÁ

Sololá

IXIMCHÉ

Tecpán

San Juan Sacatepéquez

To Cobán and Río Dulce

Volcán Santa María 3,772m

RESERVA NATURAL ATITLÁN

Panajachel

Comalapa

San Pedro La Laguna

Volcán San Pedro 3,020m

Lake Atitlán

Patzún

Patzicía

Chimaltenango

GUATEMALA CITY

CA 1

Santiago Atitlán

Volcán Tolimán 3,158m

San Lucas Tolimán

SACATEPÉQUEZ

Parque Nacional Naciones Unidas

SUCHITEPÉQUEZ

Volcán Atitlán 3,537m

La Ántigua Guatemala

To San Salvador

Mazatenango

To Cocales and Santa Lucía Cotzumalguapa

To Escuintla

Lake Atitlán

end up choosing among the many wonderful attractions.

The region is traversed in several parts by the Pan-American Highway, meaning that if you're on a limited schedule, you should stick to areas near this paved main road. Along this road, coming up from Guatemala City or Antigua, you may want to spend an hour or so at the ruins of Iximché, the former Kaqchikel capital, which also served as the first capital of Guatemala when the Spanish set up shop here after the conquest. If you have only a few days, you should certainly not miss a visit to Lake Atitlán, staying either in the large tourist and services hub of Panajachel or taking a boat across the lake to the village of your choice. Each has its own characteristics and tends to attract a certain crowd.

After the lake, you can continue along the Pan-American Highway to Quetzaltenango,

Guatemala's second-largest city, where you can take in area villages or natural attractions, including the fantastic crater lake atop Chicabal Volcano. It's also a great place to sign up for a week (or more) of Spanish lessons if you have the time. If you can work it in to your schedule, plan on visiting the market (Sundays and Thursdays) in the K'iche' town of Chichicastenango, which is easily accessible from Quetzaltenango and Panajachel. If you have more time, head north from Chichicastenango into the hills of Quiché department to the Ixil Triangle. You certainly won't be disappointed.

If you have still more time, consider heading west to Huehuetenango from the branch road in the town of Sacapulas (Quiché department) or east to Cobán and the Verapaces via a spectacularly scenic, and equally rugged, dirt road.

Chimaltenango Department and Vicinity

Although its namesake departmental capital is a collection of houses, bus depots, and businesses lining the side of the Pan-American Highway, the rest of the Chimaltenango Department is nonetheless a worthy destination. Along the road traversing the region's highland plateaus, you'll find plenty of pine-studded landscapes, agricultural fields, and even some Mayan ruins of note.

CHIMALTENANGO

The departmental capital of Chimaltenango is a major transit point between Guatemala City/Antigua and the highlands. You may find yourself changing buses here if you're heading up from Antigua going east to Guatemala City or west to the highlands, including Chichicastenango, Lake Atitlán, Quetzaltenango, and Huehuetenango. There's little else to keep you in this busy commercial town and transportation hub.

TECPÁN TO LOS ENCUENTROS

A much more pleasant alternative to the noise and pollution of Chimaltenango is a stretch of the Pan-American Highway (CA-1) heading through the Western Highlands from the town of Tecpán, about an hour from Guatemala City, all the way west to the Los Encuentros junction, from where a turnoff leads to a vertiginous drop down the sides of an extinct volcanic caldera to out-of-this-world Lake Atitlán. Another road leads north from Los Encuentros to the department of El Quiché, with its colorful markets and highland villages. Along the road from Tecpán to Los Encuentros, you'll find some interesting Mayan ruins and good eats, should you need to stop for sustenance or simply want a break from the drive to enjoy the wonderful sylvan settings.

Tecpán

The town of Tecpán proper is about half a kilometer from the main highway via a signed turnoff, though few people actually go into the town unless they're en route to the ruins of Iximché. You'll find plenty of roadside restaurants along this stretch of the highway, many with nearly identical menus. Some of these, such as **Katok** (Km. 87.5, tel. 7840-3384, www.ahumadoskatok.com, $8-20) and **Kape Paulino's** (Km. 87.5, tel. 7840-3806, www.kapepaulinos.com, $8-20), are perennial favorites with Guatemalans and are usually very busy, serving a variety of grilled steaks, chicken, Guatemalan dishes, and cured meats in a log cabin atmosphere.

If you're not a big fan of crowds, just across the road is the usually emptier and somewhat more charming atmosphere of **Hacienda Tecpán** (tel. 7840-3780, haciendatecpan@yahoo.es). The large, hacienda-style building is set among sprawling landscaped grounds traversed by small streams and grazed by sheep and goats. The pleasant dining room overlooking the grounds features tablecloths and somewhat more upscale country decor than its neighbors, with the emphasis on Guatemalan dishes.

At a turnoff from the main highway at Km. 90.5 heading to the village of Santa Apolonia, **El Pedregal** (tel. 7840-3055, $8-12) has pleasant grounds in a country setting away from the noise of the busy Pan-American Highway. It also makes a great place for kids, with ducks, cows, and other farm animals for them to enjoy. Delicious home-cooked meals including steaks, sandwiches, fresh bread, and cakes are served in a lovely covered patio fronting the gardens. The food here is homemade and tastes like it. It's worth getting off the main highway, just about 1 km or so away. There is beer, but no wine. **La Cabaña de Don Robert** (Km. 93.5 Carretera Interamericana, tel. 4285-4039, $8-15) is another Guatemalan

© AL ARGUETA

the ruins of Iximché

favorite, serving typical Guatemalan dishes in a wooden cabana surrounded by well-manicured gardens. Farther along the road at Km. 102, **Restaurant Chichoy** (also at Km. 78 in the village of Chirijuyú) is another good choice, serving breakfast, lunch, and dinner. It was originally started by a cooperative of widows from the civil war.

The nicest place to stay in the Tecpán area is undoubtedly ◖ **Casa Xara** (www.casaxara. com). Set amidst the sprawling grounds of Molino Helvetia (an old flour mill), there are two lodging options to choose from. The larger Casa El Molino ($300, $200 for 10 people or $60 per room) is set in the original house and sleeps 17 guests. Up the hill is the newer Casa Xara ($275), which sleeps 9. Both houses are made of wood (a rarity in highland Guatemala) and are charmingly decorated with lovely old knickknacks. A creek runs behind the original house and there's a network of small trails leading into the forest just past an old wooden

chapel. It's wonderfully peaceful, though it can get cold at night. Space heaters are provided and both houses have fireplaces. It makes a phenomenal weekend getaway. Food can be ordered from nearby El Pedregal restaurant and friendly manager Lucy Haase is onsite to cater to your wishes.

◖ Iximché

Faced with the increasingly belligerent expansionist aims of their K'iche' rivals, the Kaqchikel moved their capital from present-day Chichicastenango to the more easily defended site of Iximché, surrounded on three sides by ravines, sometime around A.D. 1470. Like many other Mayan sites, it bore strong influence from present-day Mexico, an influence evident in its Nahua name, Cuauhtemallan, a derivative of which eventually gave the country its modern-day name meaning "land of many trees." Societal organization here was based on lineages, with evidence of bitter rivalry between different lineages including ritual cannibalism and human sacrifice. The new capital had been established for only about 50 years before the arrival of the Spanish, who would enlist the Kaqchikels as allies in their quest to conquer the K'iche' and other Mayan peoples of the Western Highlands.

After the highlands were fully conquered, the Spanish established the first capital of Guatemala here on July 25, 1524. Alvarado, however, began demanding excessive tribute and the Kaqchikels soon revolted, eventually fleeing the town after Alvarado finally burned it to the ground. From the surrounding countryside (demonstrating a remarkable symmetry to the country's more recent history), the Kaqchikels launched a guerrilla war against the Spanish that lasted until 1530.

Iximché is the most easily accessible of Guatemala's highland Mayan ceremonial sites and makes an interesting stop for those with an interest in Mayan culture and history because of the differences it exhibits from the lowland Mayan sites of Petén, which date to much earlier times. Like many of its more remote highland counterparts (Mixco Viejo, K'umarcaaj, and Zaculeu), it was built on an isolated bluff surrounded and protected by ravines. Its smaller structures also exhibit much more Mexican influence, attesting to the population of the Guatemalan highlands by Toltec groups coming from the area near present-day Veracruz.

In March 2007, Iximché made a convenient stopover for President George W. Bush, the first lady, Laura Bush, and their Guatemalan hosts Oscar and Wendy Berger on their way back to Guatemala City from a visit to a nearby vegetable farming cooperative. They received a red carpet welcome of sorts, entering the ruins' main plaza on a specially made *alfombra* similar to the ones created for Antigua's Holy Week processions. They were also treated to a marimba band, an exhibition of the Mayan ball game, and a traditional dance performed by local children. In an impromptu display rarely seen in international protocol, Presidents Bush and Berger even attempted to play some ball of their own before members of the Secret Service rushed them on to the next order of business.

Of the ruined temple pyramids, only a few features stand out. The small altar at the base of Temple II, on Plaza A, has faint traces of murals. Other features include two ball courts and Plaza B, which housed royals. The museum has some interpretive displays predominantly on Pedro de Alvarado and the Kaqchikel uprisings. There's also a 1:200 scale model of Iximché based on an 1882 map created by Alfred Maudslay. The ruins are open 8 A.M.-5 P.M. daily. Admission is $3.50. To get here, turn off the main highway to Tecpán. From the town center there are buses, minibuses, and taxis heading out to the ruins, less than 10 minutes away.

Los Encuentros

The road diverting to El Quiché department is found at this junction and, about one kilometer farther down, is the turnoff for the road to Lake Atitlán. The Pan-American Highway (also known as the Interamericana) continues west to Quetzaltenango and Huehuetenango through lovely alpine scenery.

Accommodations and Food

West of Los Encuentros at Km. 145 of the Pan-American Highway, **Corazón del Bosque** (tel. 7723-4140 or 5299-6915, www.corazondel-bosque.com, $0.65 admission) is a community tourism initiative consisting of rustic wooden cabins, a *temascal* (Mayan sauna), plant nursery, and nature trails. There's also a restaurant and bar serving typical Guatemalan fare and highland Mayan alcoholic concoctions such as *kusha*. The quaint wooden cabins ($27 d) are well furnished and have nice views in addition to private wooden patios. True to its name, meaning "Heart of the Forest," it enjoys a sublime setting amid pine forests. The site is just 15 minutes from Los Encuentros, 45 minutes from Panajachel, and 1.5 hours from Quetzaltenango.

Panajachel and Lake Atitlán

From Los Encuentros, the road descends through beautiful agricultural fields tended by Mayan Indians, many of whom still wear traditional dress. After passing the departmental capital of Sololá, the road becomes steeper, descending to the Lake Atitlán shoreline with gorgeous views of the large, crescent moon-shaped lake bounded by three volcanoes on its southern shore. You'll also pass a waterfall or two along the way. For centuries the beauty of Lake Atitlán has captivated travelers, including Aldous Huxley, who compared it to Italy's Lake Como "with the additional embellishment of several immense volcanoes." Words cannot begin to describe the magic felt when seeing the lake for the first time, its waters shimmering in the afternoon light. Lake Como, as beautiful as it is, doesn't have volcanoes, tropical vegetation, and quaint Mayan villages lining its shores.

Lake Atitlán's origins can be traced back 85,000 years to a volcanic eruption that created the collapsed caldera the lake now fills, also spreading ash over a 1,000-mile radius. The lake was created when drainage to the Pacific Ocean was blocked after the emergence of the more recent Tolimán and Atitlán Volcanoes. It covers 125 square kilometers, being 30 kilometers long and 10 kilometers wide. Its maximum depth is more than 320 meters, though the 1976 earthquake that rocked much of Guatemala may have opened a drainage point somewhere, as the water level

Guatemala's gorgeous Lake Atitlán

© AL ARGUETA

has been gradually declining ever since. A third volcano, San Pedro, which is just under 3,000 meters high, is somewhat lower than the other two but still offers a challenging climb on a path straight up its slopes.

The lake's main tourist town has always been Panajachel, once a requisite stop along the "Gringo Trail," as it was known in the 1960s, the path of American and European backpackers making their way down to South America. There are incredible views across the lake from "Pana," as it's often referred to by locals, though in recent years several of the outlying villages have started receiving their own fair share of visitors. Many foreigners like the more peaceful atmosphere of the other villages surrounding the lake. As one expatriate living in San Pedro put it, "Twenty minutes in Panajachel is enough for me." Still, Pana is worth at least a night's stay for the excellent shopping and decent restaurants.

Lake Atitlán has begun exhibiting signs of eutrophication, with a green gulag of cyanobacteria making its first widespread appearance on the water's surface in October 2009. A legacy of Hurricane Stan was the destruction of a wastewater treatment plant that was never rebuilt. Adding to the raw sewage streaming into the lake from the towns and villages on its shores are phosphates from agricultural fertilizers. The race to save Atitlán is on, with numerous grassroots organizations working hand-in-hand with government agencies to clean up algal blooms and cease the indiscriminate pollution of the lake's waters.

Orientation

Pana's main street is Calle Principal. Most buses coming in to town stop at the intersection of Calle Principal and Calle Santander, which leads directly to the lakeshore. Santander is lined with a plethora of banks, shops, restaurants, hotels, and other tourist services. You'll find that many of these don't use street addresses. The town hall, church, market, and a few other restaurants and hotels are found a half kilometer northeast along Calle Principal from the Calle Santander junction. East of Calle Santander and running parallel is Calle Rancho Grande, which also has some accommodations. Running roughly between the two along the lakeshore is Calle del Lago.

SIGHTS
Museo Lacustre Atitlán

Atitlán's Lake Museum (inside Hotel Posada de Don Rodrigo, Calle Santander, 8 A.M.-6 P.M. Sun.-Fri., 8 A.M.-7 P.M. Sat., $5 admission for nonguests) has well-displayed exhibits on the geological history of Lake Atitlán and its creation, along with subaquatic Mayan archaeology, including ceremonial urns and incense burners, mostly from Late Preclassic and Classic times.

Casa Cakchiquel

This arts and cultural center (Calle 14 de febrero, tel. 7762-0969, casadeche@gmail.com, 10 A.M.-6 P.M. daily) is housed in a former hotel that once played home to Che Guevara. There are rotating exhibits on issues from women's rights to Maya heritage and a permanent exhibit of historical photos of the lake and Panajachel. It makes a nice introduction to the local culture. A gift shop sells unique crafts made from recycled materials.

◖ Reserva Natural Atitlán

Just outside of town 200 meters past Hotel Atitlán, this wonderful nature preserve on the grounds of a former coffee farm offers myriad attractions including a visitors center, a zipline between trees in the forest canopy, a butterfly farm, a lakeside beach, and well-designed nature trails with hanging bridges leading to waterfalls, where you can spot monkeys and coatis (pizotes) along the way. The park (tel. 7762-2565, www.atitlanreserva.com, $5 adults, $2 students/children) is open 8 A.M.-5 P.M. daily.

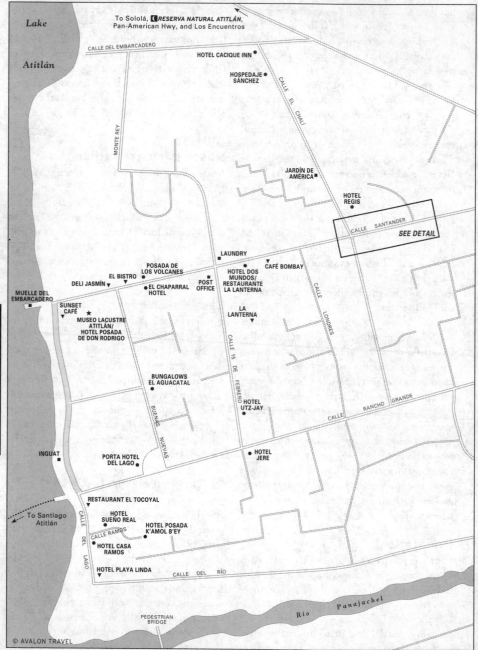

Lake

Atitlán

To Sololá, ◖RESERVA NATURAL ATITLÁN,
Pan-American Hwy, and Los Encuentros

CALLE DEL EMBARCADERO

HOTEL CACIQUE INN

HOSPEDAJE
SÁNCHEZ

CALLE EL CHALÍ

MONTE REY

JARDÍN DE
AMÉRICA

HOTEL
REGIS

CALLE SANTANDER

SEE DETAIL

LAUNDRY

CAFÉ BOMBAY

POSADA DE
LOS VOLCANES

EL BISTRO

DELI JASMÍN

EL CHAPARRAL
HOTEL

POST
OFFICE

HOTEL DOS
MUNDOS/
RESTAURANTE
LA LANTERNA

LA
LANTERNA

MUELLE DEL
EMBARCADERO

SUNSET
CAFÉ

★ MUSEO LACUSTRE
ATITLÁN/
HOTEL POSADA
DE DON RODRIGO

CALLE LONDRES

BUNGALOWS
EL AGUACATAL

CALLE 15 DE FEBRERO

BUENAS NUEVAS

HOTEL
UTZ-JAY

CALLE RANCHO GRANDE

INGUAT

PORTA HOTEL
DEL LAGO

HOTEL
JERE

CALLE

RESTAURANT EL TOCOYAL

HOTEL
SUEÑO REAL

To Santiago
Atitlán

CALLE RAMOS

HOTEL POSADA
K'AMOL B'EY

HOTEL CASA
RAMOS

CALLE DEL LAGO

HOTEL PLAYA LINDA

CALLE DEL RÍO

PEDESTRIAN
BRIDGE

Río Panajachel

© AVALON TRAVEL

PANAJACHEL

BUSES RÉBULI

BUS STOP

Mercado Municipal

SOLOMON'S PORCH/
BANCO DEL COMERCIO

CASABLANCA

ARBOLES

AV LOS

CHEZ
ALEX

BANCO
AGROMERCANTIL

EL
ALEPH

CHAPITEAU

TOLIMÁN
EXCURSIONS

LA TERRAZA

DHL

RUMBA
BAR

ATLANTIS
CAFÉ BAR

CIRCUS
BAR

PANA
ROCK CAFÉ

JABEL
TINAMIT

IGLESIA
SAN
FRANCISCO
DE ASÍS

BUS STOP

PANAJADNEL
MEATS

CENTRO
DE SALUD

HOTEL
MAYA KANEK

CALLE PRINCIPAL

HOTEL
LAS CASITAS

CAFÉ PULCINELLA

CALLE DE LA NAVIDAD

MÜLLER'S
GUEST HOUSE

RANCHO
GRANDE INN

SCALE NOT AVAILABLE

EL AMATE

To San Lucas
Tolimán and Cocales

FRUTALES

THE WESTERN HIGHLANDS

PIZZERIA FLORENCIA

DELI LLAMA
DE FUEGO

LAS CHINITAS

RESTAURANTE
ORALE

GUAJIMBO'S

UNIÓN
TRAVEL

SERVICIOS
TURÍSTICOS
ATITLÁN

ATI
DIVERS

AMÉRICO'S
TOURS

EL PATIO

INGUAT

MARIO'S
ROOMS

HOTEL
KAKCHIQUEL

LAUNDRY

MAYANET

TELGUA

CALLE SANTANDER

SCALE NOT AVAILABLE

© AL ARGUETA

visitors center at the Reserva Natural Atitlán

Spacious and attractive accommodations are available for up to six people with decks overlooking the surrounding forests. Rates vary from $65 (s/d) during the week to $80 (s/d) on weekends. Splurge for the better views. You are also welcome to camp here for $14; tent rentals cost $4.50 per person.

ENTERTAINMENT
Nightlife

Pana is a popular weekend playground for folks from Guatemala City and things are usually hopping on Friday and Saturday nights. There's a smattering of bars and dance places along Calle de los Arboles, which breaks off from Calle Principal just past its junction with Calle Santander. It's hard to beat the lively bohemian atmosphere at **Circus Bar** (Avenida Los Arboles, tel. 7762-2056, www.circusbar.com.gt, noon-midnight daily), popular with locals and foreigners alike. There are circus posters adorning the walls, a wide selection of drinks,

and tasty food. Its pizzas are highly recommended. There's live music 8-11 P.M. nightly. Across the street and under the same ownership is **Chapiteau,** a lively dance club open until 1 A.M. **El Aleph** is also along this corridor and worth checking out.

As you head back toward Calle Santander, on Calle Principal is **Rumba,** a dance club frequented by a younger crowd for its Latin pop and merengue beats. On Calle Santander, **Pana Rock Café** (tel. 7762-2194, www.panarockcafe.com, 8 A.M.-1 A.M. Wed.-Sun., 4 P.M.-1 A.M. Tues.) serves Tex-Mex food, including delicious burritos, has live music daily, and a lively happy hour. There's also wireless Internet. On the lakeshore at the end of Calle Santander is **Sunset Café** (tel. 7762-0003, 11 A.M.-midnight daily), with live music every night. It makes a great place to enjoy a cocktail while watching a gorgeous Lake Atitlán sunset. Decent tacos, nachos, quesadillas, burritos, and fajitas are served.

Cinemas

With a balcony overlooking Calle Principal, **Solomon's Porch** (http://solomonsporchpana.com, tel. 7762-6032, noon-10 P.M. Tues.-Sat.) shows digitally projected movies on its giant screen with surround sound. It also has an extensive DVD collection of movie titles available for rent. Complementing the audiovisual facilities are a full coffee bar and billiards.

SHOPPING

Pana is one of Guatemala's best places to shop for handicrafts; several shops line Calle Santander. Stalls also line the street jam-packed with goods from wall to wall. Street sellers expect you to bargain. Start at about half the asking price and work your way up from there. There are some nice, though somewhat pricier, shops in the small Centro Comercial Siquín on Calle Santander across the street from El Bistro.

RECREATION

The lake and mountainous surroundings afford a variety of recreational opportunities. Panajachel's public beach is not, at the moment, suitable for swimming pending the rebuilding of a water-treatment plant destroyed by Hurricane Stan in 2005. Some of the beaches in neighboring towns make much better places for swimming, though much of this depends on the presence of the lake's recently exhibited algal growth. Keep in mind the waters of this highland mountain lake tend to be a bit chilly. They also tend to get a bit rough in the afternoon because of the presence of a wind phenomenon known as the Xocomil. If you stop to look closely, you'll see it blowing across the lake, turning the glassy-smooth surface choppy in a matter of minutes.

Kayaking

Los Elementos Adventure Center (www.kayakguatemala.com, tel. 5359-8328) offers multi-day, round-the-lake kayaking trips that cover 50 miles of paddling in 5 days, along with a climb of San Pedro Volcano, among other activities. Trips begin and end in neighboring Santa Cruz La Laguna.

Cycling

Hotel Utz-Jay (2-50 Calle 15 de Febrero, tel. 7762-0217, www.hotelutzjay.com) rents mountain bikes and also organizes mountain-biking trips on trails around the lake. Antigua-based **Old Town Outfitters** (5a Avenida Sur #12, Antigua, tel. 5399-0440, www.adventureguatemala.com) runs a highly stimulating two-day Pedal and Paddle tour, dropping you 2,000 vertical feet along 20-25 miles of single track followed by sea kayaking across the lake for about four miles. You can add a third day of rock climbing and rappelling or climb San Pedro Volcano. The two-day trip costs $175 or $250 for three days.

Hiking

Tollmán Excursions (Calle Santander 1-77, tel. 7762-2455 or 7762-0334) offers guided hikes up San Pedro Volcano across the lake, leaving early in the morning (6 A.M.) and returning late afternoon around 6 P.M. The trip costs $39 per person including food, transport, guide, and park entrance fee. The possibilities for hikes to surrounding towns and villages are virtually limitless, though you should never hike alone and always inquire about the security situation with the local tourist office before heading out.

Scuba Diving

Although based in the nearby town of Santa Cruz, **ATI Divers** has an office in Panajachel on Calle Santander in Plaza los Patios (tel. 7762-2621, ati_divers@yahoo.com). You can do a fun dive for $25 or take the PADI open water course for $205. A high-altitude diving certification course is $75. You'll have to spend at least one night at lake altitude before your first dive to avoid decompression sickness. The

THE WESTERN HIGHLANDS

high-altitude lake offers a unique diving experience, including the chance to see underwater volcanic rock formations and a fault line where you can see and feel hot volcanic mud.

Paragliding

If you're the type who likes to fly by the seat of your pants, contact Canadian **Roger Lapointe** (tel. 5595-7732, panajaro@yahoo.ca) for exhilarating tandem paragliding from the lake's steep mountainsides, costing $90.

Fishing

The waters of Lake Atitlán have been stocked with largemouth bass since 1958 thanks to the efforts of tourism promoters at now-absconded Pan American Airways. These same largemouth bass were also largely responsible for the extinction of the rare Atitlán pied-billed grebe, which disappeared in the late 1980s as their young increasingly fell prey to the large fish. In any case, you can try your hand at catching one of these elusive bass. Most of the fish caught are in the five-pound range, though there are supposedly 20-pound fish here. The lake's 1,550-meter (5,100-foot) maximum depth further complicates matters, as the bigger fish tend to hang out at greater depths during the annual spring spawn. Your best chance of landing "the big one" is between March and May, before and after the spawn. If you're interested in learning more about Lake Atitlán largemouth bass fishing, email bass@panajachel.com.

ACCOMMODATIONS
Under $10

Mario's Rooms (Calle Santander, tel. 7762-2370, $9-11 d) is a long-running favorite with basic, clean rooms with shared bath. Rooms with private bathroom (really just a built-in cubicle) are just slightly more. **Hospedaje Sánchez** (Calle El Chalí, one block from Calle Santander, tel. 7762-2244, $5 p/p) is basic but clean and quiet. Try for an upstairs room with

lake breezes from the back window. There's a nice view from the rooftop. Another well-run family-owned budget choice is **Villa Lupita** (Callejón Don Tino, tel. 7762-1201, $5 p/p), right in the town center. Its 18 rooms have good beds, rugs, reading lamps, clean shared hot-water bathrooms, and nice views from the property's terrace. Free coffee and drinking water are available. **Hospedaje El Amanecer** (Calle Ramos, tel. 7762-0636, $8-16 d) is a new hotel with two shared-bath rooms and four pricier rooms with private hot-water bathrooms and TV. All of the rooms are spotless.

$10-25

Near the lakeshore on Calle Ramos, **Hotel Casa Ramos** (tel. 7762-0413, $20 d) has 18 sparkling clean rooms with warm Guatemalan wool blankets set in a small, plant-filled courtyard. Along the same street, **C Hotel Sueño Real** (tel. 7762-0608, $24-33 d) is an excellent value featuring comfortable rooms beautifully decorated with Guatemalan accents, private hot-water bathrooms, fans, and TV. There's a lovely second-floor terrace and Internet access on the first floor. The nicest room is on the second floor, just off the patio. The place and its guests are lovingly and well cared for by Pedro and Catarina Ramos, a charming Mayan couple. Well-situated on a quiet side street near the lake and Calle Santander, **Hotel Utz-Jay** (2-50 Calle 15 de Febrero, tel. 7762-0217, www.hotelutzjay.com, $30 d) has comfortable rooms housed in garden cottages decorated with traditional Guatemalan fabrics and equipped with fans and private hot-water bathrooms. There are good breakfasts (price not included) and the friendly, knowledgeable owners speak English, French, and Spanish. You can also enjoy a traditional Mayan sauna, or *chuj*, here. Internet access is available and you can rent mountain bikes for getting around or go mountain biking along the lake on an organized trip. **Hotel Jere** (Calle Rancho Grande, tel. 7762-2781,

$12-15 d) has nine cheerfully decorated rooms with woven blankets and private hot-water bathrooms; some guest rooms have TVs. You can book shuttle buses from here. If you want to be closer to the action along Calle Santander, there's **El Chaparral Hotel** (Final Calle Santander, one block from the lake, tel. 7762-0540, $24 d), in a multistory neocolonial structure. The comfortable rooms with private bathrooms are well furnished with basic wooden furniture and cable TV.

$25-50

If you don't mind being a little far from the lakeshore, a good choice in the main town is **Hotel Las Casitas** (Calle Prinicpal, near the market, tel. 7762-1224, www.hotellascasitas. net, $36 d including breakfast and taxes) with attractive rooms featuring traditional furnishings and vaulted wooden ceilings along with private hot-water bathroom. **Posada de los Volcanes** (Calle Santander 5-51, tel. 7762-0244 or 7762-1096, www.posadadelosvolcanes. com, $35-43 d) is an excellent value hotel in a neocolonial three-story building with spotless rooms, including tile floors, cable TV, patio furniture for relaxing on the balcony in front of your room, and private hot-water bathrooms. Rooms on the top two floors are more expensive. The owners, Julio and Jeannette, are friendly and knowledgeable. They can arrange pickup from Guatemala City upon your arrival and bring you to Panajachel for $25 per person. The same service costs $12 from Antigua. **Hotel Playa Linda** (Calle del Lago, tel. 7762-0096) is just off the public beach and has spacious though somewhat spartanly decorated rooms for $40 d or $55 with lake views. **Müller's Guest House** (Calle Rancho Grande, tel. 7762-2442) has three comfortable rooms set around a pleasant garden with hot-water private bathrooms and attractive wooden floors and ceilings. Rates include breakfast. **Hotel Posada K'amol B'ey** (Calle Ramos, tel.

7762-0219, hotelkamolbey@yahoo.com) is a large property with two different sections and prices ranging from $30-40. The clean rooms have TV and private bathrooms. Fronting attractive gardens, there's a spacious apartment that sleeps five people including a living room, kitchen, dining room, cable TV, and private bathroom for $78.

$50-100

◖Rancho Grande Inn (Calle Rancho Grande, tel. 7762-2255, www.ranchograndeinn.com, $55-77 d) dates to the 1940s and has 12 attractive rooms, suites, and cabins housed in faux-thatched-roof villas fronting a well-manicured lawn and tropical gardens. There's a nice kidney-shaped swimming pool with a partial wooden deck. Rates include a deliciously filling breakfast featuring pancakes, eggs, beans, and good, strong coffee to put some pep in your morning step. **Hotel Cacique Inn** (Calle El Chalí 3-82, tel. 7762-2053, $60 d) fills up with vacationing Guatemalans during holidays and weekends. It has 34 rooms built around a garden swimming pool; rooms feature Guatemalan blankets, weavings, and fireplaces. **Hotel Regis** (Calle Santander 3-47, tel. 7762-1152, $65 d) is set away from the street and has 25 comfortable rooms housed in a neocolonial building. The main attraction here is a hot spring set in the garden out back. **Hotel Dos Mundos** (Calle Santander, tel. 7762-2078, www.hoteldosmundos.com, $60 d) has comfortable rooms with tile floors and Guatemalan bedspreads set away from the street near a garden swimming pool. There's a recommended Italian restaurant on the premises as well as a street-side café and bar on Calle Santander. Also on Calle Santander, in a modern multistory building, **Hotel Kakchiquel** (tel. 7762-0634, www.hotelkakchiquel.com, $50 d and up) has spacious modern rooms with a separate living room area, a heated pool and whirlpool tub, and Internet access.

$100-200

Outside of town on a lovely and quiet lakeside plot, **☪ Hotel Atitlán** (tel. 7762-1441, www.hotelatitlan.com, $120-190 d) does a wonderful job of combining old-school charm with modern amenities in its well-furnished, tastefully decorated rooms featuring tile floors, antiques, and colorful textiles. All rooms have balconies with gorgeous lake views. There are extensive tropical gardens, an attractive swimming pool, and boat docks. The hotel's restaurant is a favorite with well-to-do Guatemalans. **☪ Hotel Posada de Don Rodrigo** (at the lakeside end of Calle Santander, tel. 7762-2326, www.posadadedonrodrigo.com, $100-110 d) has rooms in two separate areas, one of which is more modern and is worth the extra splurge for the splendid lake views. The rooms are comfortable and well furnished. The restaurant/bar serves excellent Guatemalan and international dishes in a pleasant dining room with views to the lake and the swimming pool below.

The resort-style **Porta Hotel del Lago** (www.portahotels.com, $220 d all-inclusive) is an all-inclusive affair housed in a modern five-story building overlooking the public beach. The recently renovated rooms have all the usual amenities and the remodeled pool area has a pleasant deck for lounging and enjoying your favorite cocktail. Outside of town just past the Hotel Atitlán, **San Buenaventura de Atitlán** (tel. 7762-2559, hotelsanbuenaventura.net, $105-262) has quaint rooms housed in buildings with domed ceilings and adobe and brick walls with an upstairs kitchen or slightly less attractive one- or two-story concrete structures, also with kitchen. You can rent out the whole structure for 4-6 people or a single or double room. There's plenty to keep you busy, including a beautiful private beach with kayaks available for rent, a pool and hot tub, and bike rentals. It's a good choice for families. Farther along the same road, **La Riviera de Atitlán** ($122-342 d) is a resort-style hotel in a large high-rise building reminiscent of Acapulco. The 16-story building had stood abandoned for decades under a previous owner, but it has now been finished. There are 82 comfortable rooms with all the usual amenities among standard rooms and suites. The lobby has a nice terrace bar with a happy hour 7-8 P.M.

FOOD
Cafés and Cheap Eats

In a pleasant garden patio decorated with Asian-style spherical paper lamps, **☪ Deli Jasmín** (Calle Santander, close to the lakeshore, tel. 7762-2585, 7 A.M.-6 P.M. Wed.-Mon.) serves delicious all-day breakfasts, including bagels and English muffins in addition to healthy fare such as tofu and vegetarian dishes. It sells teas, jams, whole wheat bread, and cookies for you to take away. Farther up Calle Santander and under the same management is **Deli Llama de Fuego** (tel. 7762-2586, 7 A.M.-10 P.M. Thurs.-Tues.), with much the same menu and surroundings. Another good place for breakfast is **El Patio** (tel. 7762-2041, 8 A.M.-9:30 P.M. daily), set in a sunny patio right next to the street about halfway down Calle Santander.

El Bistro (Calle Santander, closer to the lakeshore, tel. 7762-0508, 7 A.M.-10 P.M. daily, $5-10) is a pleasant, shady café and bar serving steak, pasta dishes, and sandwiches in the $5-10 range. Try the fettuccine with spicy tomato sauce. For tasty, reasonably priced Mexican dishes and steak there's **Restaurante Orale** (Calle Santander, tel. 7762-0017, lunch and dinner daily), popular for its friendly service and lively streetside atmosphere.

For American-style deli sandwiches and imported items you might miss from home, check out **Pana Super** (Calle Principal, next to Casablanca, tel. 7762-0852, 8 A.M.-8 P.M. Mon.-Sat., 8 A.M.-5 P.M. Sun.). The meats and cheeses are imported and the breads are baked fresh daily.

Italian

€ Circus Bar (Avenida Los Arboles, tel. 7762-2056, www.circusbar.com.gt, noon-midnight daily) has the best pizza in town as well as excellent pasta and seafood. There's a relaxed vibe and colorful decor that conveys the feeling of being under the big top. A reasonable alternative for pizza, particularly for carryout or delivery, is **Pizzeria Florencia** (Calle Santander, across from Telgua, tel. 7762-1055), where you'll also find Argentinean empanadas and cheeseburgers.

For authentic Italian food, head to **Restaurante La Lanterna** (inside Hotel Dos Mundos, Calle Santander, tel. 7762-2078), where there's excellent homemade pasta and a nice assortment of Italian wines. The large dining room has one of Panajachel's most pleasant atmospheres and the service is impeccable.

Pan-Asian

For scrumptious Pan-Asian cuisine, check out **Las Chinitas** (Calle Santander, tel. 7762-2612, 8 A.M.-10 P.M. daily), where you can savor Malaysian curries and Thai dishes, among other dishes, at moderate prices. It's a busy spot for dinner. A perennial favorite, **Café Bombay** (Calle Santander, 100 meters from the lake, tel. 7762-0611, 11 A.M.-9 P.M. Wed.-Mon., $2-7) is an inexpensive vegetarian restaurant serving a varied menu that includes tasty falafel, pita sandwiches, lasagna, burritos, curries, pad thai, and miso soup.

American and European

On Calle Santander, closer to Calle Principal, is La Terraza (Edificio Rincón Sai, tel. 7762-0041, lunch and dinner daily), with a second-floor balcony overlooking the street below and serving steaks, lake fish, and European fare including Spanish tapas.

Halfway down Calle Santander, Guajimbo's (tel. 7762-0063, 7 A.M.-10 P.M. Fri.-Wed.) serves South American-style *parrilladas* (barbecued meats) including steaks, chicken, and sausage. There are also vegetarian dishes and good breakfasts. On Calle Principal, close to the intersection with Calle de los Arboles, **Atlantis Café Bar** serves a good mix of international dishes, including decent burgers, pasta, pizza, and sandwiches along with a wide range of cocktails from its elegant wooden bar. The decor is eclectic and there are also some good desserts.

There are a number of eateries on Calle del Lago with similar seafood- and meat-based menus and outrageous decor, none of which I can bring myself to recommend. An exception is the well-staffed **Restaurante El Tocoyal** (Calle del Lago, 8:30 A.M.-5 P.M. Sun.-Fri., 8:30 A.M.-8 P.M. Sat., $3-13), which also has some vegetarian fare.

Fine Dining

Duck, escargot, lamb chops, and Wiener schnitzel are on the menu at **Chez Alex** (halfway down Calle Santander, tel. 7762-0172, noon-3 P.M. and 6-10 P.M. daily) in a tasteful atmosphere with prices in the $10-12 range. **€ Casablanca** (at the intersection of Calle Principal and Calle Santander, tel. 7762-1015, www.panajachel.com/casablanca.htm, 11 A.M.-11 P.M. daily, $8-22) serves delicious pastas, chicken, meat, and seafood dishes accompanied by Chilean wines in a sophisticated atmosphere. The dining room at the **€ Hotel Atitlán** (tel. 7762-1441, www.hotelatitlan.com, 6:30 A.M.-10 P.M. daily, $7-20) makes a fine place for a splurge, surrounded by pleasant gardens overlooking the lake and fabulous views. Patrons enjoy free use of the swimming pool and there are Guatemalan and international dishes on the menu. There is a Sunday breakfast buffet for around $15.

INFORMATION AND SERVICES
Tourist Information

The INGUAT information office (Calle Santander, tel. 7762-1392, 9 A.M.-5 P.M. daily) has basic hotel information, transportation schedules, and friendly staff who can answer your questions.

Communications

The main post office is on the corner of Calle Santander and Calle 15 de Febrero. DHL is in Edificio Rincón Sai at the northern end of Calle Santander.

Telgua (7 A.M.-midnight) is halfway down Calle Santander near the junction with Calle 15 de Febrero. There is no shortage of Internet cafés along Calle Santander for making international phone calls. Typical rates are $0.30 per minute to North America and $0.50 per minute to Europe.

There are Internet setups all over town. Among the best are MayaNet (halfway down Calle Santander, tel. 7762-2092) and Café Pulcinella (Calle Principal 0-72). Both are open 9 A.M.-9 P.M. and charge about $1 per hour.

Money

About halfway down Calle Santander, Banco Industrial has a Visa ATM and can cash U.S. dollars and travelers checks. There's a MasterCard/Cirrus ATM outside Banco Agromercantil on the corner of Calle Principal and Calle Santander. Banco del Comercio is on the ground floor of the same building as Solomon's Porch, on Calle Principal. It has an ATM that accepts both Visa and MasterCard.

Laundry

With Lake Atitlán's future at stake, it has become more important to choose environmentally friendly coin laundromats, where the detergents used are biodegradable. To that end, I highly recommend Il Bucato (Comercial El Dorado, at the junction of Santander and Calle Principal, 9 A.M.-6:30 P.M. Mon.-Sat.), where you can wash up to 12 pounds for $2.50. They will also wash 6-12 pounds of laundry for you for $6. All the detergents used are

non-toxic; hypo-allergenic detergent is also available. Other options include Lavandería Viajero (Calle Santander, Edificio Rincón Sai, 8 A.M.-7 P.M.); it charges about $0.50 per pound. Lavandería Automático (Calle de los Arboles 0-15, 7:30 A.M.-6:30 P.M. Mon.-Sat.) charges $4 for a full load.

Medical Services

Panamedic Centro Clínico Familiar (Calle Principal 0-72, tel. 7762-2174) has round-the-clock emergency medical attention. Doctors Francisco and Zulma Ordoñez both speak English. For an ambulance, dial 7762-4121.

Emergency

In case of an emergency, contact Asistur (Tourist Police, Calle Principal, in the town hall, tel. 7762-1120 or 2421-2810).

Travel Agencies

There are a number of travel agencies along Calle Santander that can book airline tickets, shuttles, and onward transport to other parts of Guatemala. Among the recommended agencies are Atitrans (Edificio Rincón Sai, tel. 7762-0146 or 7762-0152, www.atitrans.com), Unión Travel (corner of Calle Santander and Calle El Chali, tel. 7762-2426, www.igoguate.com), Servicios Turísticos Atitlán (Calle Santander, tel. 7762-2075), and Tolimán Excursions (Calle Santander 1-77, tel. 7762-2455 or 7762-0334).

Language Schools

There are a few language schools in Panajachel, including **Jardín de América** (Calle 14 de Febrero, 3a Avenida Peatonal 4-44, tel. 7762-2637, www.jardindeamerica. com) and **Jabel Tinamit** (Calle Santander, tel. 7762-0238, www.jabeltinamit.com). Rates are about $150 per week for four hours of one-on-one instruction Monday-Friday, including homestay with a local family at either school.

GETTING THERE AND AROUND

Bus

Buses stop at the junction of Calle Santander and Calle Principal both leaving and arriving in Panajachel. Direct buses leave for Antigua ($5, 2.5 hours) at 10:45 A.M. daily except Sunday. You can also take a Guatemala City-bound bus ($4, 3.5 hours) and change at Chimaltenango. There are 10 daily buses to Guatemala City between 5 A.M. and 2:30 P.M. Six buses leave daily to Quetzaltenango ($4, 2.5 hours) and there are eight daily buses to Chichicastenango ($3, 1.5 hours).

Shuttle Bus

The convenience and, most of all, safety of shuttle buses cannot be overstated. In the course of researching and writing this book, it seemed that not a week went by without newspapers reporting some sort of incident aboard Guatemala's second-class buses, including armed robberies turning into shoot-outs between passengers and would-be thieves or tragic accidents on twisting mountain roads. That said, there are frequent shuttle buses to Antigua, Chichicastenango (on market days), Quetzaltenango, and Guatemala City. Recommended shuttle agencies include **Atitrans** (Edificio Rincón Sai, tel. 7762-0146 or 7762-0152, www.atitrans.net) and **Servicios**

Turísticos Atitlán (Calle Santander near Calle 15 de Febrero, tel. 7762-2075).

Boat

There are two different boat docks for getting around to the surrounding villages. The first of these is at the end of Calle del Embarcadero and is for boats to Santa Cruz (15 minutes), Jaibalito (25 minutes), Tzununá (30 minutes), and San Marcos (40 minutes). Some boats continue to San Pedro, across the lake (just under an hour, with stops), but there are also direct boats from Pana taking about 20 minutes. All of the aforementioned routes are serviced by small, fast *lanchas*. The second boat dock is at the end of Calle Rancho Grande and is for ferry (one hour) and *lancha* service (25 minutes) to Santiago Atitlán. Expect to pay anywhere between $1.50 and $3 for the ride. Locals pay less than visitors. Ask around for the time of the last boat back to Pana from the outlying villages. Some may be as early as 4:30 P.M. **Lake tours** ($10, full day) from Pana visiting San Pedro and Santiago also leave from the second pier and can be booked at any travel agency.

Tuk-tuk

Tuk-tuks can get you anywhere in town for about $0.75. For longer trips to surrounding villages, such as Santa Catarina Palopó, expect to pay about $4 for the 20-minute ride.

Lake Atitlán Villages

Lake Atitlán is surrounded by a number of smaller villages, each with its own distinct feel. Across the lake, only San Pedro La Laguna rivals Panajachel in popularity. The other villages remain fairly quiet, though tourism has become a significant presence in almost all of them. Heading east of Panajachel along the lakeshore, the first village of note is Santa Catarina Palopó.

SANTA CATARINA PALOPÓ

Five kilometers east of Panajachel is the quaint lakeside village of Santa Catarina Palopó, a collection of adobe houses with tin and thatched roofs built into the surrounding hillsides. The streets near the church and the road leading to the lakeside are excellent places to pick up some of the colorful textiles and handicrafts

LAKE ATITLÁN

To Pan-American Hwy, Los Encuentros, Guatemala City, and Chichicastenango

SOLOLÁ

Santa Lucía Utatlán

RESERVA NATURAL ATITLÁN

San Jorge la Laguna

Santa Cruz la Laguna

San Andrés Semetabaj

Jaibalito

Panajachel

San Marcos la Laguna

San Pablo la Laguna

Santa Catarina Palopó

To Guatemala City

Godínez

Lake

San Juan la Laguna

San Antonio Palopó

San Pedro la Laguna

Atitlán

Volcán San Pedro 3,020m

Cerro de Oro

Río Madre Vieja

CHUITINAMIT

Santiago Atitlán

Volcán Tolimán 3,158m

San Lucas Tolimán

Bahía de Atitlán

Río la Vega

LOS TARRALES RESERVE

0   2 mi

0   2 km

Volcán Atitlán 3,537m

To Cocales

© AVALON TRAVEL

produced here. Many of the villagers still sport the traditional attire.

As elsewhere on Lake Atitlán, many well-to-do Guatemalans (and increasingly, foreigners) have bought property and built houses on the slopes just outside of town.

Accommodations and Food

Santa Catarina is the site of a few moderate to high-end hotels offering some of the lake's best accommodations. On the road between Panajachel and Santa Catarina, and under the same ownership as Antigua's Mesón Panza Verde, **Casa B'alam Ya** (tel. 7832-2925, www.panzaverde.com, $150-400 d) encompasses two villas. The first of these has two bedrooms, a hot tub, a spacious kitchen, and a deck fronting the lake. The smaller junior villa has one bedroom, a deck, and a kitchen. There are kayaks for guests' use. You can arrange for a local chef to cook your meals or have the kitchen stocked with everything you need to cook your own. Just off the street leading from town to the lakeshore, the 36-room **Villa Santa Catarina** (tel. 7762-1291 or 7762-2827, www.villas-deguatemala.com, $68-104 d) has attractive rooms and junior suites with gorgeous lake views, tile floors, TV, hot-water private bathrooms, telephones, and some rooms with ceiling fans. There are lovely antique furnishings throughout the property, a swimming pool and the excellent **Restaurante Las Playas** (7 A.M.-10 P.M. daily), serving Guatemalan and international dishes in an attractive dining room overlooking the swimming pool. Meal prices are in the $5-10 range. Along the road leading out of town toward neighboring San Antonio Palopó, **Tzam Poc Resort** (tel. 7762-2680, www.atitlanresort.com, $85-170 d) has accommodations varying from standard and deluxe rooms in Mediterranean-style, thatched-roof villas to an entire, fully furnished villa for $400-1,000 per night. The beautiful rooms are nicely decorated. The resort's centerpiece is an exquisite infinity-edge swimming pool overlooking the lake below. There are tropical gardens throughout. Other amenities include a tropical lounge, sauna, and solarium. Credit cards are accepted but incur a 7 percent service charge. A fabulous new addition to the area's offerings is **C La Casa Colibri** (Km 6.7 Via Rural a San Antonio Palopo, Entrada a Tzampoc Casa #4, tel. 5353-5823, http://emmaspencerliving.com/guatemala-vacation-accommodations/, $395-595 per night). The five-bedroom villa is built in Mediterranean style with lovely tropical touches that include thatch-roof terraces, bamboo accent walls and typical Guatemalan decor. Rooms have big wooden beds and awe-inspiring views of the lake and volcanoes. Amenities include a wooden-decked swimming pool, plenty of sun-lit patio space, a hammock deck, Wi-Fi, flat-screen TVs and a DVD player. A private chef is available at additional cost, though the room rate includes a light breakfast. For budget accommodations, **Posada Don Vitalino** (at the entrance to town coming from Panajachel, tel. 7762-2660, $20 d) makes a fine choice with basic, clean rooms and hot-water showers.

The most splendid of the lake's accommodations is **C Casa Palopó** (Km. 6.8 Carretera a San Antonio Palopó, tel. 7762-2270, www.casapalopo.com, $140-347 d), with rooms housed in a beautiful colonial-style villa featuring floor-to-ceiling windows with magnificent lake views. The rooms and common areas are loaded with antiques, brightly painted walls, exquisite furnishings, and wonderful extras such as Italian cotton sheets and Aveda bathroom products. There's also a charming swimming pool with peaceful angel carvings looking on from an adjacent wall. Farther up the hill is the even more alluring **Villa Palopó**, decorated with a tasteful mix of African tribal relics and Indonesian hardwood furnishings. There are hardwood floors and ceilings and phenomenal lake views from each of the two suites ($206-447 d). You can rent the whole villa for $803-1,368, depending on the season. The villa has its own lap pool, also overlooking the lake, and butler service.

Casa Palopó's restaurant, **6.8 Palopó,** is a bit on the expensive side ($15-30 for a typical meal), but the food is certainly some of the best you'll find on the shores of Lake Atitlán, with spectacular lake views from an airy terrace. If you're not staying there, it makes a great place to stop for a drink and watch the sunset or enjoy a romantic candlelit dinner.

SANTA CRUZ LA LAGUNA

West of Panajachel and accessible only by boat is the quiet village of Santa Cruz La Laguna, more commonly referred to simply as "Santa Cruz." There are a number of good accommodations here with a range of prices for every budget. It's understandably extremely popular with the backpacker crowd.

Recreation

Housed inside the Iguana Perdida lodge, **ATI Divers** (ati_divers@yahoo.com) is a PADI-certified **scuba diving** operation offering

© AL ARGUETA

the villa at Casa Palopó

Altitude Specialty certifications for $75, fun dives for $25, or PADI open water certifications for $205. Due to altitudinal pressure changes and the lake's location at just over 1,500 meters above sea level, you'll have to spend at least one night at lake altitude before your first dive to avoid decompression sickness. The lake offers a unique diving experience, including the chance to see underwater volcanic rock formations and a fault line where you can see and feel hot volcanic mud.

Los Elementos Adventure Center (www. kayakguatemala.com, tel. 5359-8328) provides myriad recreational options, including volcano climbs, a round-the-lake kayak trip, cliff jumping, and rock climbing using local guides. Proceeds from Los Elementos support nonprofit Amigos de Santa Cruz, focused on improving the nutrition and education of the local Maya. For utter relaxation and wonderful lakeside massages, check out their **Los Elementos Day Spa** (tel. 4095-3751).

Locally-guided tours are also offered by **Tours Atitlan** (www.tours-atitlan.com, tel. 5355-8849). Owned by a young Maya couple, tours encompass the Lake area and even involve treks to such far-away locales as the Ixil Triangle.

Options for exploring on your own include **hikes** up the hill to the village proper (20 minutes) to see the town church in addition to hiking along a trail skirting the lakeshore to the neighboring village of Jaibalito (45 minutes) or San Marcos (three hours).

Accommodations and Food

The town's original hotel, **El Arca de Noé** (tel. 5515-3712, www.atitlan.com/arca.htm, $17-47 d) is still going strong. The delightful lodge has 10 rooms, half of them with private bathrooms. Three of the rooms are lovely stone-and-wood cottages. All of the rooms are rustic but nicely decorated with Guatemalan fabrics. Delicious breakfasts and lunches are served à la carte. Guests are treated to delicious meals consisting of Guatemalan and European specialties for around $10 (dinner), served family-style. The lodge is solar-powered.

Just next door is one of Guatemala's quintessential backpacker hideaways, **La Iguana Perdida** (tel. 5706-4117 or 7762-2621, www.laiguanaperdida.com, from $5 p/p in dorms to $40 d with private bath), which has recently added some very attractive private rooms for those of us who have gotten just a bit older. There are three dormitories with a total of 22 beds and rooms with or without private bathrooms. Electricity was finally installed after years of making do without it and I am happy to report that now hot showers and Internet access are available. Still, the electricity can be spotty and kerosene lamps are on hand to provide agreeable ambient lighting after dark. Breakfast and lunch are served 8 A.M.-3 P.M., featuring delicious sandwiches, salads, crêpes, and other yummy dishes prepared by a staff of indigenous women. Dinner is a family-style affair and is a three-course spread, including soup and homemade bread, a main course, and dessert. Vegetarian options are always available. The dinner atmosphere is lively and it makes a great place to meet fellow travelers. The crowd is decidedly young. In addition to scuba diving, there are Spanish lessons available for $150 per week with dorm accommodations (upgrades available), a tandem kayak and snorkeling equipment for rent, waterskiing, and tons of board games. On Saturdays, there's a fun dress-up dinner party where you can eat chicken or veggie burgers and jam to a guitar and drums. If you get bored here, you should probably check your pulse.

Farther along the lakeshore heading back east toward Panajachel is **La Casa Rosa** (tel. 5803-2531, www.atitlanlacasarosa.com, $22-35), with modern, clean, and comfortable rooms with shared or private hot-water baths in addition to two suites housed in bungalows. An apartment with kitchen is available for rent for $120 per week or $350 per month. There are homemade jams and bread in addition to Guatemalan, international, and vegetarian dishes served in the main floor dining room. Spanish classes are also available for $150 per week.

You might stumble upon a few private villas as you make your way farther east a few hundred meters to the lovely, American-owned (**Villa Sumaya** (tel. 4026-1390, www.villasumaya.com, $68-115 d). There are 16 beautiful rooms, all named after jungle animals. Some are housed in a thatched-roof complex; others are farther up the hill in separate cabins. All of the spacious rooms have private hot-water bathrooms, warm Guatemalan wool blankets, and patios with furniture and lovely hammocks. The rooms up the hill have mosquito netting and larger bathrooms with tubs, one of which is impressively built into the side of the mountain with lava rock adorning the semioutdoor shower. There's an impressive, hardwood-floor and thatched-roof yoga center, which is often booked months in advance by groups from the United States. Other amenities include a massage parlor, library, and two hot tubs. The restaurant here is correspondingly excellent, consisting of vegetarian selections as well as fish, meat, and chicken dishes prepared by two talented chefs. Delicious baked goods are also produced daily. Breakfast and lunch are à la carte. Dinner is a set menu served family-style. The outdoor café is housed in a pretty wooden patio overlooking the lake.

A fabulous addition to Santa Cruz's hotel offerings is (**Laguna Lodge** (tel. 7823-2529, www.lagunalodgeatitlan.com, $240-370 d), built in eco-friendly style on the lakeshore and on its very own 100-acre nature preserve. The beautiful suites feature Guatemalan hardwoods and adobe walls, along with solar-heated showers and low-flow toilets. The restaurant and Lava Bar have phenomenal lake views and feature a delightful array of vegetarian dishes

© AL ARGUETA

Laguna Lodge

($25 set menu). A trail winds through the property's nature preserve and includes a lookout high atop a steep hill. There are several common areas at the lodge where you can laze the day away in a hammock or read a book. You can also enjoy a relaxing dip in a hot tub or sweat away your cares in a Mayan sauna.

From the main dock in Santa Cruz, heading west to Jaibalito, it's 400 meters to the private dock of **[Islaverde Hotel** (tel. 5760-2648 or 5964-7419, www.islaverdeatitlan.com, $35-65 d), with 11 comfortable, wooden A-frame cabins with wonderful lake views and shared or private bath. Two larger cabins ($75-125) with six beds apiece can accommodate families or groups. There are pretty gardens with plumeria flowers, a beautiful wooden deck, a restaurant, a lounge with books and games to keep you entertained in addition to a sauna, hot tub, and meditation and massage platform. All of the food served at the lodge is fresh and well prepared. The expanded beach includes a

sitting area. The property is the culmination of 12 years of travel by a young Spanish and British couple, who have put many of the ideas found along the road into this splendid place they see less like a hotel and more like a garden of delights.

Getting There

Santa Cruz is reached exclusively by boat. Boats leave from the dock at the end of Calle del Embarcadero in Panajachel. For the intrepid, there's a foot path from the departmental capital of Sololá.

JAIBALITO

West along the shoreline from Santa Cruz is the village of Jaibalito, which is even smaller than Santa Cruz and is also accessible only by boat or foot trail. A number of lodges have sprouted here in recent years, taking advantage of the remote location to offer a comfortable stay in a quiet environment.

Accommodations and Food

Wildly popular, 🎇 **La Casa del Mundo** (tel. 5218-5332 or 5204-5558, www.lacasadelmundo.com, $34-72 d) is a charming inn built into the side of a rocky cliff. There are rooms with shared or private bathrooms, all housed in wonderful stone cottages with outrageous lake views and decorated with tasteful Guatemalan accents. There's excellent swimming in a rocky cove where the water is an exquisite shade of emerald. There are kayaks for rent ($4-7) and mountain biking can be arranged via Antigua-based Old Town Outfitters with at least two days' notice. The trail to Santa Cruz or San Marcos passes right outside the lodge's back door. Meals are served at set times in a small dining room on the ground floor of the main house. Dinner is served family-style and costs $10. The service here is excellent and the Guatemalan-American owners are very friendly. In the village proper and away from the lake, **Vulcano Lodge** (tel. 5410-2237, www.vulcanolodge.com, $39-70 d) is a Norwegian-owned lodge with five guest rooms, all smartly decorated and featuring private baths. The largest is a family-size villa, which sleeps five and has a living room, kitchen, and a nice big terrace with lake views. The restaurant serves tasty meals for breakfast and lunch, with dinner ($12 for four courses) served family-style. Many of the fresh ingredients, including bananas, avocadoes, and limes, come right from the on-site garden plot. Jaibalito's budget accommodations are at **Posada Jaibalito** (tel. 5598-1957, www.posada-jaibalito.de, dorms $4 p/p with use of kitchen, $7-11 d with private bath and kitchen), offering basic but pleasant rooms located in the heart of the village.

For utterly delectable food, refreshing cocktails, and killer lake views from its infinity-edge swimming pool, head to 🎇 **Club Ven Acá** (tel. 5051-4520, www.clubvenaca.com, 11 A.M.-5 P.M. Wed.-Sun., $4-15). The fun staff will keep you entertained and fill your belly with delicious fish tacos, burgers, salads, BBQ sandwiches, and steaks. Try the signature beverage, the Jaibalito Mojito, made with basil instead of mint leaves.

West along the shore, the next village is Tzununá, home to the agreeable **Lomas de Tzununá** (tel. 5201-8272 or 7820-4060, www.lomasdetzununa.com, $85 d including breakfast and tax), high atop a steep hill. You can call the lodge for a pickup from the hotel's pier or make the 100-meter trek up the slope. Run by a Belgian-Uruguayan couple who discovered Guatemala while working with the United Nations, the lodge features 10 lovely stone-and-wood bungalows with tile floors and lake views greatly enhanced by their sheer height above water. Amenities include Internet, a lap pool, library, board games, and a crafts shop. Meals are served al fresco on a wooden patio with superb lake views. Just the views of the volcanoes reflected in the placid swimming pool high above the lake are worth the price of admission.

SAN MARCOS LA LAGUNA

San Marcos is a unique lake town in that it harbors a strangely esoteric vibe, aided by its prominence as Guatemala's New Age center. It's about a three-hour walk from Santa Cruz and two hours from San Pedro. Most visitors arrive at a boat dock beside Posada Schumann, though boats stop first at the main dock a few hundred meters east. A road runs beside the lodge into town, which together with a parallel street 100 meters west, form the main pedestrian arteries into town.

Sights and Recreation

Among the spiritually inclined attractions is **Las Pirámides** (tel. 5205-7302 and tel. 5205-7151, www.laspiramidesdelka.com), offering a variety of New Age alternative psychology courses, including a one-month "moon course" beginning with the full moon and culminating in a full week of fasting and silence. With

THE WESTERN HIGHLANDS

© AL ARGUETA
the dock at San Marcos la Laguna

completion of the moon course there's further study, including a three-month sun course, featuring elements of Kabbalah, tarot reading, and lucid dreaming. Nonstudents can join in on hatha yoga sessions at 7 A.M., classes on various spiritual topics at 10 A.M., and meditation techniques at 5 P.M. Sessions range $5-13. To get here, follow the path up the hill past Posada Schumann and then turn left along the signed pathway. It's about 200 meters on your left.

Back toward Posada Schumann is **San Marcos Holistic Centre** (www.sanmholisticcentre.com, 10 A.M.-5 P.M. Mon.-Sat.), offering a wide assortment of massages and holistic therapies. There are training courses in Reiki, shiatsu, massage, reflexology, and Bach flower remedies. English, Spanish, German, and French are spoken. A typical treatment costs somewhere around $15.

It's not recommended, but you can **hike** from San Marcos east to Tzununá and Jaibalito. Check on the safety situation with local sources, as hiker robberies between here and Tzununá have been frequent in the past. Going west to Santa Clara La Laguna is a safer bet. If you do go, leave your valuables behind. Until recently, the waters here were excellent for swimming, when the lake was nice and clean. In the aftermath of Atitlán's recent cyanobacteria algal blooms, you may be hard-pressed to find a decent place to swim.

Kayaks are available for rent next door to the Aaculaax hotel and cost $3 per hour. The owners of Tul y Sol restaurant (tel. 5293-7997) can arrange **paragliding.**

Accommodations

Posada Schumann (tel. 5202-2216, www.posadaschumann.com, $15-50 d) is the first place you'll come across if, like most people, you arrive into town at its dock. Most of the comfortable, well-furnished, and tastefully decorated rooms are housed in quaint stone-and-mortar cottages. An excellent value, room number

12 is a deluxe second-floor wooden bungalow ($25-36 d, depending on season) with its own deck. Numbers 8 and 10 have awesome volcano and lake views. The restaurant overlooking the well-tended gardens serves sandwiches, smoothies, and Guatemalan fare for breakfast and lunch, though the service can be slow.

West along the lakeshore past Las Pirámides is one of Guatemala's most unique hotels. **Aaculaax** (tel. 5577-5072, www.aaculaax. com, $26-140 d) is a work of art constructed out of recycled building materials, including glass, carved pumice stones, and colorful papier-mâché. Each of the seven rooms (two suites and five double rooms) is unique, though all have private bathrooms with composting toilets and lovely terraces. A newer addition includes five budget rooms costing $13 per person. The rooms are literally built around the rocks of the surrounding hillsides, which are prominently displayed in the architecture of some of the suites. The glasswork in evidence throughout the property is simply delicious, as is the food served in its Restaurante Las Mañanitas (8 A.M.-4 P.M. daily, $2-5). A gorgeous second-floor terrace lounge caps off the hotel's atmosphere quite nicely.

The footpath continues farther west to **Jinava Bay** (tel. 5299-3311 or 5406-5986, www.hoteljinava.com, $20-38 d), on the edge of town right on the lake in a quiet bay with its own beach. The five rooms are housed in Spanish-style whitewashed, tiled-roof villas with private terraces and have private or shared bathroom and attractive decor with tile floors and colorful textiles. The restaurant serves decent meals, including Thai, Indian, Mexican, Greek, Italian, and Guatemalan dishes. There's also a full bar.

Up the path into the main part of town is budget-friendly **Hotel Restaurante El Quetzal** (tel. 5350-0610, $10 d) with clean shared-bath rooms, good-value food, hot water, and a nice patio for lounging. Further up the path is **Hotel Unicornio** (tel. 4289-4754, $7 pp with shared bath), an eclectic sort of place with firm beds housed in simple but brightly painted A-frame cottages. There's a Guatemalan mail (*El Correo*) drop-off here. Closer to town is pleasant **Posada del Bosque Encantado** (tel. 5208-5334, www.hotelposadaencantado.com, $20 d), with rooms housed in a charming adobe structure and surrounded by tranquil gardens. The rooms have Guatemalan furnishings and vaulted ceilings; some have an extra bed on a second floor loft.

Near the top of the path leading straight up the hill from the dock at Posada Schumann is **Hotel y Restaurante Paco Real** (tel. 4910-3855, www.hotelpacoreal.com, $17-25 d), with simple but comfortable rooms and shared or private bath. The wooden, thatched-roof cabanas include Guatemalan furnishings and woven reed floor mats in a peaceful garden setting. There's a restaurant and bar on the premises where the highlights include Mexican dishes, seafood, and curried pineapple chicken.

Food

Word has gotten out concerning San Marcos's culinary hot spot, **F'e** (tel. 5994-4320, 7:30 A.M.-midnight daily, $8-20), where you can feast on curries, pastas, meat, and fish dishes in a sublime garden atmosphere accented with Guatemalan textiles. There's a covered second-floor patio bar.

Enjoying a wonderful lakeside location west of Posada Schumann is French-owned **Tul y Sol** (tel. 5293-7997 or 5854-5365, all meals daily) offering decent sandwiches served on thick slices of bread, grilled fish, and pasta. Located up the path toward town from Posada Schumann, **Il Giardino** (tel. 7804-0186, 4 P.M.-midnight Thurs.-Sun.) serves delicious burritos, pizza, and spaghetti dishes in a tranquil garden setting. It also has Internet access. Next to Las Pirámides, **Il Forno** (dinner only) is another recommended

Italian restaurant. For breakfast all-day, your best bet is **Restaurante Las Mañanitas** (at Hotel Aaculaax, 8 A.M.-4 P.M. daily, $2-5), where you'll find the usual staples such as eggs, fruit smoothies, granola, and pancakes in addition to more exotic cravings such as *shakshuka* (a spicy Israeli egg-and-tomato dish similar to *huevos rancheros*). Heading into the town center from the lakeshore and crossing the main road through town, you'll find **⟨ Blind Lemon's** (tel. 5540-0399, www.blindlemons.com, 11 A.M.-10 P.M. Mon.-Sat.), inspired by blues musician Lemon Jefferson and housed in a pleasant colonial-style courtyard. Tasty burgers, pizzas, steaks, chicken, and pasta are on the menu. There's live blues on Fridays starting at 8 P.M. (or whenever friendly owner Carlos wants to play for you) and movies are shown on a big screen almost every night.

Information and Services

Casa Verde Tours (tel. 5837-9092 or 7721-8344, www.casaverdetours.com), of San Pedro fame, also has an office in San Marcos and can arrange transport and local hikes. They are located at the top of the hill along the trail that leads straight into town from Posada Schumann. Another option is the newly formed **Jóvenes Mayas** (tel. 5527-2017), composed of local community guides offering English/Spanish guided hikes to local waterfalls, San Pedro, and the Pakachelaj forest reserve. They are also located on the path into town from Posada Schumann, near Il Giardino.

There are no banks or ATMs in San Marcos.

SAN JUAN LA LAGUNA

Serene San Juan La Laguna is a relative latecomer to the tourism scene and makes a good stop if you'd like to see a fairly sizable lakeside village that remains largely untouched by international tourism. It's accessible by boat or via a road that branches off from the Pan-American

Highway, subsequently twisting and turning down the surrounding mountainside. If you'd like to stay here, **Uxlabil Ecohotel** (tel. 5990-6016 or 2366-9555, www.uxlabil.com, $48-72 d) has comfortable, tastefully rustic rooms housed in a large building overlooking the lake. There's a large dock for swimming among plentiful grass reeds dotting the lakeshore here as well as a sauna, whirlpool tub, kayaks for rent, and horseback riding available on request.

SAN PEDRO LA LAGUNA

On the lake's southwest corner and accessible by frequent boats or road, San Pedro is second in popularity only to Panajachel and has a hip international atmosphere. The place has grown by leaps and bounds, from a once-scruffy village to a rather pleasant lakeside town with a solid international presence. You'll see signs in English, Spanish, French, and even Hebrew as you walk along the paths winding through town. The atmosphere in San Pedro embraces a simpler state of being and you'll have no trouble slowing down to the local pace of life amidst the serene tropical foliage.

The town flanks the northern slopes of San Pedro Volcano, a popular climb for which the town is ideally suited as a base. It has increasingly become home to a number of language schools, some of dubious quality, collectively offering some of Guatemala's least expensive tuition rates. While it was originally a backpacker Shangri-La, there have been recent additions to the hotel infrastructure, making for suitable accommodations to house the non-backpacker crowd.

The bulk of the tourist hotels and services are between two docks, on the southeast and northwest sides of town, and in the areas adjacent to them. The first one serves boats to/from Panajachel and the rest of the lake towns; the other is for boats to Santiago Atitlán. They are about one kilometer apart. The area between them is known as El Otro Lado (The Other

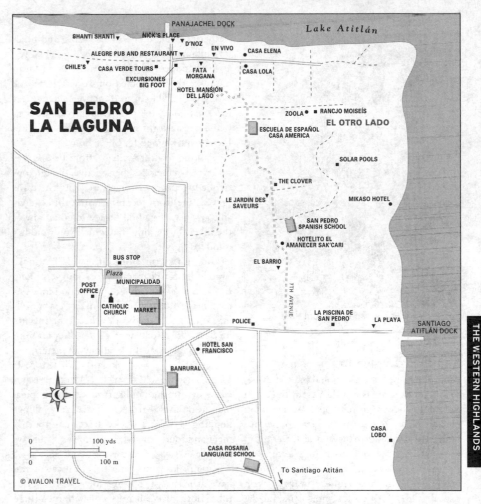

PANAJACHEL DOCK

Lake Atitlán

SHANTI SHANTI ▾   NICK'S PLACE ▾

D'NOZ ▾

ALEGRE PUB AND RESTAURANT ▾   EN VIVO ▾   CASA ELENA ●

CHILE'S ▾   CASA VERDE TOURS ■

EXCURSIONES BIG FOOT

FATA MORGANA ●

CASA LOLA ●

HOTEL MANSIÓN DEL LAGO ◆

SAN PEDRO
LA LAGUNA

ZOOLA ●   ■ RANCJO MOISEÍS

EL OTRO LADO

ESCUELA DE ESPAÑOL CASA AMERICA

SOLAR POOLS ●

THE CLOVER ▾

LE JARDIN DES SAVEURS ▾

MIKASO HOTEL ●

SAN PEDRO SPANISH SCHOOL

HOTELITO EL AMANECER SAK'CARI ●

BUS STOP ■

EL BARRIO ▾

Plaza

POST OFFICE ■   MUNICIPALIDAD

7TH AVENUE

CATHOLIC CHURCH   MARKET

LA PISCINA DE SAN PEDRO ■

POLICE ■

LA PLAYA ▾

SANTIAGO ATITLÁN DOCK

HOTEL SAN FRANCISCO ●

BANRURAL

CASA LOBO ■

0   100 yds

0   100 m

CASA ROSARIA LANGUAGE SCHOOL

To Santiago Atitán ▾

© AVALON TRAVEL

Side). Street numbers and names are not generally in use here. From the Santiago dock, go up about 50 meters and turn right on the footpath known as 7th Avenue to get to El Otro Lado and continue to the Panajachel boat dock. From the latter dock, go up one block and turn left to get to the other side of town. Numerous hand-painted signs will direct you almost anywhere you want to go.

In recent years there's been some tension in San Pedro due to the proliferation of evangelical churches and their congregants who sometimes look upon San Pedro's foreign presence as an unwelcome, "sinful" hindrance. On at least one occasion, congregants have surrounded a well-known bar and forced it to shut down for the night. The *palapa* lounge at the Israeli-owned Zoola restaurant and hotel has been burned down twice, leading some to wonder if the attacks were perpetrated in the name of anti-Semitism. The lounge has since been replaced with a less flammable canvas substitute.

© AL ARGUETA

San Pedro Volcano, as seen from Santiago Atitlán

San Pedro Volcano

The volcano became a national park in 2006, so it is hoped that, as was the case with Pacaya Volcano, its newly protected status will result in greater police presence and an end to the robberies that frequently happen near the summit. For now, check with locals before heading up the volcano. Under no circumstances should you attempt this hike alone. Always go with a local guide. There is a visitors center at the trailhead, which is just off the road to Santiago. The hike is fairly strenuous, as the trail runs straight up the mountain with very little in the way of switchbacks. It takes about 4-5 hours to reach the summit, which is still very much covered in thick cloud forest. There's a small gap in the trees at the top from which there are views of Santiago and the lake. Start your hike early in the day to avoid the midday heat and the clouds that typically gather at the summit of the lake's volcanoes in the afternoon.

Recreation

Activities include horseback riding and hikes up a mountain known locally as "Indian Nose," as its shape resembles the profile of a Mayan nose like those depicted on stelae. Horseback riding is available from **Rancho Moiseís** (next to Zoola hotel, tel. 5967-3235). Next door to Chile's restaurant on 8a Calle, Restaurante Elena rents **kayaks** for $2 an hour.

Walking to other villages from here makes sense from a logistical perspective, though too-frequent reports of robberies along the trails prevent me from recommending this as a viable activity. If you do decide to go on any of the hikes, bring only that which you wouldn't mind losing.

You can swim from either of the docks (watch out for boat traffic) or anywhere along the lakeshore, though recent pollution concerns have made a dip in the lake much less appealing. Your best bet to beat the heat is **La Piscina de San Pedro** (on the street heading up from the Santiago boat dock, about 50 meters, tel. 4708-3905, 11 A.M.-dusk daily), where it costs $2.50 to swim (children $1.25) in a pleasant, clean swimming pool surrounded by tropical plants and mural art. A lively bar keeps things hopping. There's a weekly bocce ball tournament and southern-style barbecue on Saturdays starting at 1 P.M. and costing about $8.

If you like your water bathtub-warm, you have at least two options for soaking in hot tubs. Both places feature concrete tubs filled with water that is solar-heated in black plastic tubing and pumped into reservoirs of various sizes. (You'll need to call ahead or visit with at least one hour's prior notice so they can draw the bath.) It costs $7 for one person, but you can split the cost with others sharing the same pool. The first of these, **Solar Pools** (7a Avenida 2-22, Zona 2, tel. 5770-5119, solarpools04@gmail.com, 8 A.M.-11 P.M. daily), is located on the main strip of El Otro Lado. Of the two, Solar Pools holds the slight edge in landscaping and it has an adjacent snack bar, Tzan Saqarib'al, serving light fare. You can reserve by phone. Closer to the lakeshore and a short walk down a side path is **Los Termales** (8:30 A.M.-11:45 P.M. daily), the town's self-proclaimed original hot tub operation. Its biggest draw is the sylvan lakeside setting. They prefer that you pre-book your tub in person.

Guide Companies

Excursiones Big Foot (tel. 7721-8202), on the main drag as you come up the hill from the Panajachel dock and turn left, is San Pedro's most reliable outfitter and has been in operation since 1995. It offers trips to San Pedro Volcano with knowledgeable guides and security for $14, including park admission. Big Foot can also guide you to Indian Nose with a four-person minimum for $5 p/p. **Casa Verde Tours** (www.casaverdetours.com, tel. 5837-9092 and 7721-8344) just down the street from the Panajachel boat dock, is the town's other recommended outfitter. They also have a variety of daily shuttle departures.

Entertainment

San Pedro is a lively town harboring several bars where the party goes on until about 1 A.M. A great place for happy hour is **Chile's** (tel. 4222-8292), with a large wooden deck overlooking the lake. Happy hour runs 6-8 P.M. and includes 2-for-1 drink specials.

Just to the left of the dock and directly above Nick's Place, **D'Noz** is a lively bar with good food, including baguettes and croissants, where movies are shown nightly at 8:30 P.M. In the center of town between the two docks, the ever-popular **Buddha Bar,** housed in a three-level building with a cool Asian atmosphere, has pool tables and dartboards on the first floor. For live music, check out **En Vivo** (up the street from the Panajachel dock and left). Closer to the Santiago dock, your best bet is **La Playa,** a British-owned sports bar with indoor and outdoor seating along with four big screen TVs. The town's neighborhood bar is **El Barrio** (7th Ave., 5 P.M.-1 A.M. daily) in the heart of the tourist zone. Happy hour is 5-8 P.M. and includes 2-for-1 drinks. They also have tasty burgers.

Accommodations

For budget accommodations, your best bet is **Yo Mama's Casa** (El Otro Lado, tel. 5755-4540, yomamas.sanpedro@gmail.com, $3.75 dorms, $8 d private room). All rooms have shared bath and there is a movie room, pool table, and hammock lounge to enjoy. Guests have free use of the kitchen. The dorm rooms all have footlockers to secure valuables. Another decent budget choice is **Hotel Pinocchio** (tel. 5845-7018) where spartan but clean rooms built around a garden run $4.50 for dorms or $6.50 per person with a private bathroom. There's a hammock on the patio fronting each room. To get here, take 7th Avenue and follow the signs heading towards El Otro Lado.

A popular favorite with travelers of all sorts is **Casa Elena** (tel. 5310-9243, $10-25 d), found by turning left at the first corner as you come up the street from the Panajachel boat dock. Housed in a large peach-and-white building, it has clean rooms with shared or private bathroom. Two larger rooms on the top floor face the lake and have nice patios with hammocks, tables, and chairs. The hippest place in town is the friendly, Israeli-owned **Zoola** (tel. 5534-3111, agmon2003@yahoo.com, $4 dorms, $13 d with private bath), found along the trail heading into El Otro Lado. It has eight rooms, half with private bathroom, and dorm beds. There is a movie lounge, book exchange, purified water from its own well, and a massage room, but the crowning achievement is the beautiful canvas-roof hammock lounge with comfortable pillows on woven floor mats. Around the corner is **Jarachik** ($4 p/p with shared bath, $10 d with private bath), an acceptable budget choice with clean but spartanly decorated rooms. In the small private bathrooms, the shower is practically on top of the toilet and lacks a shower curtain. **Hotelito El Amanecer Sak'cari** (7a Avenida 2-12 Zona 2, tel. 7721-8096, www.hotelsakcari.com, $26 d) feels a bit like a motel, though the rooms on the second floor have nice lake views with hammocks out front. All rooms have a private bathroom. The owners had added a small snack bar during my last visit.

Just up the street from the Panajachel boat dock, **Hotel Mansión del Lago** (near the Santiago dock, tel. 7721-8041, www.hotelmansiondellago.com, $20 d) has clean, pleasantly painted rooms in shades of blue, most with balconies where you can take in the lake views from a rocking chair. One of the largest places in town is **❰ Mikaso Hotel** (tel. 5973-3129, www.mikasohotel.com, $8 p/p in dorm, $25-45 d) with 11 rooms and a dormitory housed in an attractive Spanish neocolonial-style building fronting the lakeshore. Rooms have tile bathrooms, ceiling fans, tile floors, and tasteful decor. The rooftop restaurant here is also quite smart, serving Mediterranean Spanish food, including delicious *bocadillos* (sandwiches), and open 7 A.M.-10 P.M. Movies are shown three times a week on Wednesday, Friday, and Sunday nights. About two kilometers outside of town on the road to Santiago Atitlán, **❰ Casa Lobo Bungalows** (tel. 5950-9294, http://casalobo.org, $37-59 d) offers comfortable lakeside accommodations housed in stone cottages with Spanish tile roof. Rooms have high wooden ceilings and are well equipped with stove and refrigerator. Pleasant patios have lake views. The hotel has its own boat dock with kayaks for rent.

Food

To the left of the Panajachel boat dock, the first place you'll come across is **Nick's Place** (tel. 7721-8065, 7 A.M.-midnight daily, $4-8), serving good-value Guatemalan and International dishes inside or outside on the terrace. One

block on the left as you head up the street into town, the **Alegre Pub and Restaurant** (tel. 7721-8100, 5 P.M.-1 A.M. Mon., 9 A.M.-1 A.M. Tues.-Sat., 9 A.M.-11 P.M. Sun.) serves authentic pub grub, including Indian curry, Cajun fare, chili, baked potatoes, and fish 'n chips. There's a nice rooftop garden. Just around the corner is the best place for light fare on this side of town, **❰ Fata Morgana** (7:30 A.M.-10 P.M. Thurs.-Tues., $4-8). You'll find sandwiches, baguettes, pizza, pasta, fruit smoothies, and a wide selection of teas. They roast their own local coffee.

Up the street from the Panajachel dock, if you make the first right, the first place of note is **Shanti Shanti** (8a Calle 3-93 Zona 2, tel. 5561-8423, 7 A.M.-11 P.M. daily), with wonderful lake views, chill music, Israeli food, sandwiches, smoothies, and delicious breads and cakes. Just down the street, **❰ Chile's** (tel. 4222-8292, 7 A.M.-11 P.M. daily, $4-7) is wildly popular for its wonderful wooden deck fronting the lake and good Pan-Asian cuisine that includes pad thai, *paneang gai,* and tandoori chicken. The French-press coffee is also quite good. Hookas and salsa lessons round out its list of offerings.

There are a number of good eateries in the part of town inland between the two docks known as El Otro Lado. Among them is **Zoola** (all meals daily), housed in its namesake lodge and serving freshly prepared food, including vegetarian fare, though chicken salads and meat lasagnas are also on the menu. You can dine under a pleasant open-air, thatched-roof structure. Nearby is **The Buddha** (tel. 5967-6810, noon-1 A.M. daily), housed in a three-level building with a pool table and darts on the first floor, a dining area and chill-out lounge on the second floor, and a rooftop terrace bar. The restaurant serves authentic Asian and Guatemalan fusion cuisine with a variety of rice, noodle, and curry dishes, sushi, soups, wraps, and tasty desserts at reasonable prices. There's a hookah water pipe smoking lounge.

Also in this neck of the woods is the popular **Jarachik** (all meals daily), though the recipes of its late Dutch owner, including burritos, curry, kebabs, and Asian dishes, are now spread out in restaurants all over town. Still, it makes for pleasant dining in a garden patio setting. A popular addition to San Pedro's culinary offerings is **The Clover** (7th Ave., 8:30 A.M.-midnight daily, $4-7), a restaurant and bar on a nice patio overlooking the lake serving good sandwiches and Pan-Asian inspired dishes such as scrumptious mango curry. Across the way, **Le Jardin des Saveurs** (9 A.M.-9 P.M. Thurs.-Tues., $4-7) takes its inspiration from its French owners and offers a variety of tasty European-inspired dishes. Try the chicken in Dijon mustard sauce.

Last are a pair of offerings owned by the same couple. **Ventana Blue** (7th Avenue, tel. 5284-2406 or 4050-0500, 6-10 P.M. Tues.-Sun.), featuring a small dining room painted in blue hues, prides itself on creative Asian/Guatemalan cuisine. There are only four tables in this tiny hidden gem, so get there early or call ahead. Along the beach near the Mikaso Hotel, **Café La Puerta** (tel. 5098-1272, www.cafelapuerta.com) is the place to go for excellent homemade pasta.

Information and Services

There's a Banrural (with ATM) in the heart of town, reached by heading straight up the street from the Panajachel dock for about a kilometer. You'll pass the town market on your right, two blocks before the bank, which will be on your left. From the Santiago dock, head up the street and turn left at the market. There's also an ATM machine just off the Panajachel dock.

For Internet and phone calls, D'Noz is just off the Panajachel dock, or you can head up the street one block to **Casa Verde Tours** (www.casaverdetours.com, tel. 5837-9092 and 7721-8344), your all-in-one stop for Internet, laundry, international calls, and full-service travel

agency including shuttle buses to Antigua, Guatemala City, and Xela. On the main drag, turning left at Casa Verde as you come up from the Panajachel dock, you'll find Café Jardín (7:30 A.M.-9 P.M.), serving breakfast and snacks in addition to offering Internet access. Both charge about $1 for an hour online.

Recommended language schools include the following: **Casa Rosario** (Canton Sanjay, tel. 7613-6401, www.casarosario.com) and **Corazón Maya** (first left up the street from Santiago dock, tel. 7721-8160, corazonmaya.com). Also along this street is **Sol de Oro Spanish School** (tel. 7614-9618). In the El Otro Lado sector between the two docks are **Escuela de Español Casa America** (tel. 7767-7718, casaamerica@hotmail.com), **Mayab' Spanish School** (tel. 7815-7722, www.mayabspanishschool.com), and **San Pedro Spanish School** (tel. 7721-8176, www.sanpedrospanishschool.org).

Getting There

There are boats every half hour to Santiago (30 minutes, $2) from the dock at the northwest part of town. *Lanchas* also leave throughout the day for the lakeshore villages of San Marcos ($1.50), Jaibalito ($2), Santa Cruz ($2.50), and Panajachel ($3). All leave from the dock on the southeast side of town. The last boat going in either direction usually leaves around 5 P.M.

There are buses to Quetzaltenango ($3, 2.5 hours) leaving from in front of the church in the main part of town at 4:30, 5, 5:30, 6, 7, 8, 10:30, and 11 A.M. Monday through Saturday. On Sundays these buses leave at 5, 5:30, 6, 8, and 11 A.M. There are buses to Guatemala City from San Pedro departing Monday through Saturday at 3:30, 4, 5, 5:30, 6, 8, and 10 A.M. Afternoon buses depart at noon and 2 P.M. on the same days. Sunday departures for Guatemala City are at 6 and 7 A.M. and noon, 1, and 2 P.M. There are frequent pickups to the villages as far as the road goes to San Marcos along the main street coming up from the boat dock, which is lined with art galleries and craft shops. On display is a very distinct form of painting depicting various elements of indigenous life such as agricultural harvests and festivals.

Santiago suffered greatly during the civil war, as the area was a hotbed of activity for ORPA guerrillas, who established themselves in this strategic area between the highlands and the Pacific Coast. The Guatemalan military established a base here and began systematically searching for guerrilla sympathizers, killing hundreds. As the civil war waned, the military's presence became increasingly unnecessary, as was the case throughout much of Guatemala, and villagers became increasingly resentful of its presence. The massacre of 12 unarmed villagers (including three children) in 1990 unleashed a flood of local and international pressure to close the military garrison. A petition presented to the Guatemalan government asking for the base's closure was soon granted.

More recently, Santiago made world headlines in October 2005 after a number of devastating mudslides in the wake of Hurricane Stan left close to 1,000 victims. The neighboring village of Panabaj was completely wiped out by the mudslides, and the scars can still be seen on the mountainside. Many international organizations are still working in the area and Santiago has become a popular center for volunteer activities in the tragedy's aftermath.

Another Santiago curiosity is the presence of a highland Mayan deity known as Maximón, housed in the home of a different member of the local cofradía, or Catholic brotherhood, every year. The effigy is a wooden figure clad in colorful silk scarves and a Stetson hat, smoking a big cigar and receiving offerings of moonshine, cigarettes, and rum. Local village children will offer you their services to go see the idol, which you can photograph for a fee. It is not surprisingly a sore point between the Catholic syncretists and the increasingly prominent Evangelical

and in the other direction to Santiago. Shuttle vans ($25) leave from San Pedro (Casa Verde) at 9 A.M. daily for Antigua and Xela.

SANTIAGO ATITLÁN

Santiago Atitlán is a more traditional sort of place and has a very different feel from San Pedro. It's spectacularly set in an inlet with gorgeous views of San Pedro Volcano just across this small body of water. Atitlán and Tolimán Volcanoes rise behind it. It is the main enclave of Guatemala's Tz'utujil-speaking Mayans, whose wonderful painting and handicrafts can be seen

Christian churches, which have won over many of Santiago's residents.

You will probably be approached by innocent-looking children as soon as you arrive from the boat dock offering any of a number of services, including a guided trip to see Maximón or assistance in finding accommodations. You have the right to politely refuse, but you might be surprised at the colorful language they can resort to (in English) if they're unhappy with you for not hiring their services or if you fail to provide an adequate tip. Internationally recognized finger gestures are also not out of the realm of possibility.

Sights

Santiago's colorful market really gets going on Fridays and Sundays, when the town's streets are filled with vendors and Mayan women dressed in the town's spectacular purple costume. The men wear interesting striped shorts, though it seems in fewer numbers every year. Standing prominently in the central plaza, the Iglesia Parroquial Santiago Apóstol was built between 1572 and 1581. Inside lining the walls are wooden saints dressed in clothes made by local women and renewed yearly. At the far end of the church are three sacred colonial altarpieces refurbished with more Mayan-inspired motifs by two local brothers between 1976 and 1981. The altarpieces represent the three volcanoes in the vicinity of Santiago, which are believed to protect the village. Local creation myths distinguish them as the first dry land to emerge from the early seas. The wooden pulpit has interesting carvings, including corn and animal figures. The town's newest attraction is the Museo Cojoyla (9 A.M.-4 P.M. Mon.-Fri, 9 A.M.-1 P.M. Sat., free), a block up the street from the main dock, on the left, with displays on Santiago's artful legacy of traditional backstrap weaving.

Local women make robes for the saints in Santiago's church.

Recreation

Atitlán and Tolimán Volcanoes are tempting climbs from town but unfortunately have been the scene of robberies, a problem that unfortunately seems endemic in the Lake Atitlán area. Check with the local lodges on the security situation and for reliable guides who might be able to take you there, should you wish to venture on the path less traveled.

Jim and Nancy Matison (tel. 5811-5516 or 5742-8975, wildwestgua@yahoo.com, $60 full-day) offer recommended horseback riding and wilderness hikes throughout the area, though they no longer offer trips to San Pedro Volcano because of the state of the trail in the aftermath of Hurricane Stan.

Accommodations and Food

Santiago's nicest accommodations are at the charming 🄲 **Posada de Santiago** (tel. 7721-7366, www.posadadesantiago.com, $15 p/p to $135 d) with a variety of room types in comfortable stone cabins featuring tasteful Guatemalan decor. It has adjusted well to the recent influx of missionaries and volunteer groups, offering rooms for 4-5 people at budget prices. The lodge is run by Dave and Susie Glanville, a gracious American couple who have lived in Santiago for years. Ironically, the hotel originally opened just weeks before the installation of the defunct local military garrison. It was closed for 10 years and did not reopen until June of 1991. If you're interested in the hotel's interesting history be sure to ask for Dave's "Smart Aleck Interview," which should answer most of your questions. The restaurant here is one of the lake's finest. Breakfast, lunch, and dinner are served at set times throughout the day. Dinner costs $8-21 and includes Cajun, Asian, and continental cuisine. All of the sauces, breads, pastries, and ice cream served here are homemade and the Glanvilles grow, process, and roast their own coffee. Activities include fishing or kayaking on

the lake, Thai or deep tissue massages, lounging by the pool in a hammock overlooking the lake, and swimming. There is wireless Internet in the lodge.

Just outside of town, another nice place to stay is **Hotel and Restaurant Bambú** (tel. 7721-7333, www.ecobambu.com, $55-65 d) with two bungalows, eight rooms, and a villa housed in pretty thatched-roof stone cottages with fantastic lake and volcano views fronting beautifully landscaped grounds. The rooms are cheerful and bright with beautiful Guatemalan furnishings. There are a very nice swimming pool, a private dock, and kayaks available for rent at $5 an hour. The restaurant serves tasty international and Spanish cuisine. Be sure to take a taxi or *tuk-tuk* if you decide to go into town at night, as robberies have been reported on the isolated paths from the hotel into town after dark.

A decent budget choice is **Hotel Chi-Nim-Ya** (turn left at the first intersection after coming up from the dock, tel. 7721-7131, $10-13 d) with 22 simple and clean concrete-floored rooms built around a central courtyard with shared or private bathroom. Another budget choice is **Hotel Tzutuhil** (four blocks up the hill from the dock, then left, tel. 7721-7174, $8-11 d) with basic, clean rooms housed in a five-story building.

For lake fish, snacks, sandwiches, and light fare, a good choice is **Restaurante El Pescador** (two blocks up the street from the dock, tel. 7721-7147, 7 A.M.-9 P.M. Mon.-Sat., 7 A.M.-4 P.M. Sun.).

Services

There's a Banrural right on the plaza where you can exchange dollars and travelers checks.

Getting There

Ferry service ($2.50) departs Santiago for Panajachel at 6, 7, and 11:45 A.M.; 12:30, 1:30, 2, and 4:30 P.M. The ferry crossing takes about an hour and there is also faster *lancha* service. There are also frequent boats to San Pedro from here. There are seven daily buses leaving from the central plaza for Cocales and Guatemala City between 3 A.M. and 3 P.M. in addition to pickups for San Lucas Tolimán. Frequent pickups to San Pedro leave from Hotel Chi-Nim-Ya.

SAN LUCAS TOLIMÁN AND VICINITY

San Lucas is probably the least attractive of the lakeside villages, though the adjacent area is as gorgeous as the rest of the lake. It makes a good place to get away from it all. If you're looking for comfortable accommodations to host your escape, you might want to check out **Hotel Tolimán** (6a Avenida 1-26, tel. 7722-0033, www.hoteltoliman.com, $50-95 d) on a sprawling lakeside ranch run by a wonderful Guatemalan couple. The 22 comfortable rooms, including some splendid suites, all have private bathroom and a 17th-century hacienda ambience enhanced by numerous decorative touches that include delightful furniture and antiques. Hotel amenities include a swimming pool, Wi-Fi, and a restaurant.

Just a few kilometers along Ruta Nacional 11, leading from San Lucas to the coastal town of Cocales, this is a gem of a place to stay. **Los Tarrales** (Km. 164.2 RN-11, tel. 2478-4867 or 5208-0940, www.tarrales.com, $44-76 d) is a private reserve on the southern slopes of Atitlán Volcano named after the abundant bamboo trees that grow here. Altitudes range 700-3,000 meters (2,300-9,800 feet), providing for a wonderfully diverse array of ecosystems. Several locals are employed by the reserve, working on its coffee farm or in the ecotourism business and the lodge runs a school for local children. Activities include hiking and bird-watching with naturalist guides, climbing Atitlán Volcano, mountain biking, canoeing, horseback riding, and visits to the working coffee farm. Accommodations include shared-bath rooms, beautiful rooms with private bathroom, or wonderful tree house cabins. Excellent, home-cooked meals are served ($6-8) for breakfast, lunch, and dinner including fresh salads, vegetarian and meat dishes, and bread from the on-site bakery. Buses heading to Cocales pass right by the entrance to the reserve, which is 15 minutes from San Lucas and about 45 minutes from Santiago.

Nearby, in the adjacent municipality of Pochuta, Chimaltenango, **El Retiro Finca and Lodge** (Finca El Retiro, Pochuta, tel. 2365-4468, www.elretirofinca.com, $35 d) is another wonderful place to stay with four comfortable rooms and a larger wooden cabin, all with private hot-water bathroom. The lodge is on the grounds of a working organic coffee and banana plantation and the surrounding cloud forests harbor trails leading to waterfalls and pristine mountain streams for you to explore. Horseback riding and mountain biking are also available. Meals are served in a charming wooden dining room and there's also a bar and swimming pool.

To get here, follow RN-11 south toward Cocales, turning left at the junction for the road heading east to Pochuta. It's about a 45-minute drive from San Lucas Tolimán.

THE WESTERN HIGHLANDS

WAKE UP AND SMELL THE COFFEE, THEN PICK SOME BEANS

© AL ARGUETA

coffee pickers in Huehuetenango

Guatemala is known around the world for its excellent coffee. A recent trend in Guatemala's growing list of recreational alternatives is the opportunity to stay on a working coffee farm in comfortable accommodations. The farm provides a rare glimpse into the inner workings of one of the country's principal economic activities and an industry that largely shaped Guatemala into the nation it is today. Guatemala's coffee farms are largely centered in the Western Highlands, though coffee is also grown on the Pacific slopes, the Verapaces, and the Eastern Highlands.

If you've always wanted to see the origins of the potent potable that provides the pep in your step, you'll want to check out one or more of the coffee farms covered throughout this book, including: **Los Tarrales** (Km. 164.2 RN-11, tel. 2478-4867 or 5208-0940, www.tarrales.com) and **El Retiro** (Finca El Retiro, Pochuta, tel. 2365-4468, www.elretirofinca.com), both near Lake Atitlán; **Reserva Patrocinio** (tel. 7771-4393 or 5203-5701, www.reservapatrocinio.com) and **Takalik Maya Lodge** (tel. 2333-7056 or 2337-0037, www.takalik.com), near Retalhuleu; **Finca Filadelfia** (www.rdaltoncoffee.com) near Antigua; **Centro Cultural La Azotea** (Calle del Cementerio) in Jocotenango; and **Finca El Cisne,** near Copán, Honduras.

Activities include touring the coffee plantation as well as observing the process from harvest to roasting. Some properties are on large private reserves and combine bird-watching, hiking, and other outdoor activities with the visit to the coffee farm.

For a fascinating read on the myriad ways in which coffee cultivation has affected Guatemala's history and societal relations, including events in the civil war as they took place on a plantation caught in the crossfire, check out Daniel Wilkinson's excellent book, *Silence on the Mountain.*

Chichicastenango

At Chichi, tourism became voyeurism. There was always so much going on—the crowded, noisy market, the rituals on the steps of Santo Tomás, a ceremonial dance outside El Calvario chapel, the explosion of firecrackers in the morning, a procession—that it was easy to think it all a show put on for the tourists' benefit. But in Chichi it was not a show. The "spectacle" was part of daily life for the Indians, ritual that must be performed in spite of, not because of, the tourists. Wherever tourists went in Chichi they were treading on and through someone else's devotional rites. Two different worlds whirled past each other, momentarily inhabiting the same space but unable to comprehend each other. Bizarre scenes resulted from this encounter: a Quiché man walked on his knees over rough cobblestones, crying out his agony, while a tourist trailed behind him, filming the man's act of penance on a camcorder; a tourist group climbed the crowded steps of Santo Tomás, hoping to get a photo of the plaza from atop the church's platform, and in the confusion a heavy-set tourist kicked over an incense burner, apologized loudly in English to the woman kneeling there, then fumbled in her purse and waved a ten-quetzal note at the Indian woman; a cofrade, a member of a brotherhood devoted to the worship of a particular saint, was standing outside El Calvario, wearing the traditional outfit indicative of a special occasion and holding an ebony and silver staff, the symbol of his office, when a tourist approached and asked him how much he'd take for the staff: the tourist's money belt was already open when the cofrade without a word turned and disappeared into the sanctuary.

—Stephen Connely Benz,
Guatemalan Journey

While you may or may not witness such blatant disregard for the local culture,

Chichicastenango (Chichi, for short) will surely provide you with an opportunity to take in a unique highland market experience. There are certainly other, more authentic markets in highland Guatemala, at least one of which is larger, but Chichi's popular Sunday and Thursday market is unique in that it includes allowances for the very strong foreign presence here. It is the only highland market where you'll see large tour buses packed with camera-toting tourists negotiating the hairpin, dizzying mountain switchbacks along the road from Antigua and Guatemala City. The road to Chichi diverts from the Pan-American Highway at the Los Encuentros junction, along Km. 127.5.

The market, and Chichi's status as a bona fide tourist attraction, got their start in the 1930s when enterprising Alfred S. Clark opened the Mayan Inn and started busing folks in from the capital for a look at an authentic highland Mayan village. Chichicastenango, originally known as Chaviar, was an important Kaqchikel trading town long before the arrival of the Spanish. The Kaqchikel went to war with their K'iche' rivals based in K'umarcaaj (near present-day Santa Cruz del Quiché, 20 miles north) in the 15th century, moving their capital to the more easily defended site of Iximché. Spanish conquistador Pedro de Alvarado would play the K'iche'-Kaqchikel rivalry to his advantage, using the latter as allies in his final push against the K'iche', who comprised the only real opposition to Spanish conquest. Chichicastenango got its name, meaning "place of the nettles," from Alvarado's Nahuatl-speaking Mexican allies after the town's reestablishment here after the defeat of the K'iche' capital in 1524.

Today, Chichi is still very much a K'iche' town with strong adherence to the old ways. Its traditional fiesta, the **Fiesta de Santo Tomás,** takes place December 14-21. There are plenty of loud fireworks, traditional dances, moonshine, and the fascinating *palo volador* ritual in which men spin from ropes attached to a 20-meter pole.

SIGHTS
◀ Chichicastenango's Market

If you're a big fan of outdoor markets, you'll certainly enjoy this one. In addition to the crowds of vendors and potential buyers you'll find a dizzying array of good-quality weavings, pottery, fabrics, gourds, and masks, to name just a few. On the stairs of the adjacent church of Santo Tomás, you'll see Mayans waving incense burners, filling the air with the pungent smell of *corozo* palm and adding an additional aura of mystique to this chaotic market that is a feast for the senses. There are certainly more authentic indigenous highland markets, but what makes Chichi unique is its accommodation of visitors' needs and desires for traditional handicrafts into a twice-weekly event (Sunday and Thursday) that would otherwise continue undeterred for the benefit of the locals it has always catered to.

Most of the better handicrafts are found in the central part of the plaza, but be prepared to rummage through piles of lesser-quality stuff, which is readily in abundance. In addition to the main part of the plaza, there are stalls peddling tourist-oriented trinkets along the streets to the north of it. The streets to the south and the *centro comercial* on the plaza's north side are home to the everyday items villagers come to market for, including fruits and vegetables, clothing, spices, household items, and baked goods. As in all of Guatemala's markets, haggling is in order. The best time to get a good deal on anything that might have caught your fancy is after 3 P.M., when the market starts to wind down. You can often score substantial price reductions simply by walking away and feigning disinterest. It's all a very complex game. For fair trade goods, visit **Ut'z Bat'z** (on the square next to El Calvario church, 8a Calle 3-14 Zona 1, www.enmisala.com) where you'll find export-quality handmade goods.

Iglesia Santo Tomás

The town's oft-photographed church dates to 1540 and is the site of syncretic Catholic-Mayan rituals both inside and out. On the steps, you'll find *chuchkajaues*—indigenous people at prayer, swinging incense-laden censers (usually just metal cans punctured with holes) and reciting incantations. Take care to enter the church through the side door to the right, as the main entrance is reserved for religious officials and *chuchkajaues*. Inside you'll find an astounding number of lit candles lining the church floor along with pine boughs and offerings of liquor bottles wrapped in corn husks, flowers, and maize kernels in remembrance of departed relatives, some of whom are buried beneath the church floor. Photography is strictly prohibited inside the church.

Found beside the church is a monastery, where the *Popol Vuh* Mayan book was found among church archives by Spanish priest Francisco Ximénez in the early 18th century.

On the west side of the plaza is **Capilla del Calvario**, another whitewashed church somewhat like a miniature version of Santo Tomás and with much the same feel. There is a glass-encased Christ statue inside, which is paraded through town during Holy Week processions.

Museo Rossbach

This small museum (5a Avenida 4-47 Zona 1, 8 A.M.-noon and 2-4 P.M. Tues., Wed., Fri., Sat., 8 A.M.-4 P.M. Thurs., 8 A.M.-2 P.M. Sun., $0.75) harbors a collection of jade objects, including necklaces and figurines in addition to historical objects such as ceremonial masks, obsidian spearheads, and incense burners. It's named after Hugo Rossbach, a German who served as the town's Catholic priest for many years until his death in 1944.

CHICHICASTENANGO

To Santa Cruz del Quiché, Sacapulas, and Nebaj

3A CALLE

4A CALLE

4A AVENIDA

3A AVENIDA

3A CALLE A

6A AVENIDA

POSADA EL ARCO

ARCO GUCUMATZ ★

CHALET HOUSE

3A CALLE C

5A CALLE

5A AVENIDA

BUSES TO SANTA CRUZ DEL QUICHÉ

6A CALLE

2A AVENIDA

HOSPEDAJE GIRÓN

BUSES TO LOS ENCUENTROS, PANAJACHEL, GUATEMALA CITY

RESTAURANTE LAS BRABAS

HOTEL CHUGÜILÁ

CEMENTERIO MUNICIPAL

CHICHI TURKAJ TOURS

INTERNET DIGITAL

TZIGUAN TINAMIT

7A CALLE

LOS COFRADES

ACSES

6A AVENIDA

MAYA LODGE

BANRURAL

7A AVENIDA

LA VILLA DE LOS COFRADES

MAYAN INN

Parque Central

BANCO INDUSTRIAL

HOTEL SANTO TOMÁS

CASA SAN JUAN

CHICHICASTENANGO'S MARKET

CAPILLA DEL CALVARIO

INGUAT (PALACIO MUNICIPAL)

MUSEO ROSSBACH ★

IGLESIA SANTO TOMÁS

TELGUA

CORREOS (POST OFFICE)

9A CALLE

10A CALLE

11 CALLE

12 CALLE

HOTEL Y CAFETERÍA TUTTO'S

0   125 yds

0   125 m

HOTEL CASA DEL REY

To Pascual Abaj Shrine

To Los Encuentros, Pan-American Hwy, Lake Atitlán, Guatemala City, and Quetzaltenango

© AVALON TRAVEL

THE WESTERN HIGHLANDS

THE *POPOL VUH*

Believed to have been written by an unknown Mayan scribe in the 1560s, the *Popol Vuh* (Council Book), was found in the church archives in Chichicastenango early in the 18th century by parish priest Francisco Ximénez. Amazingly, it survived the burning and destruction most Mayan writings fell prey to at the hands of the Spanish and lives on as an important document recording K'iche' histories and legends. Ximénez painstakingly transcribed the document into Latin and then translated it into Spanish. It is now the only surviving copy of the Mayan text and resides in Chicago's Newberry Library.

The *Popol Vuh* contains the K'iche' peoples' creation myths as well as their history before the arrival of the Spanish. Although there are some striking similarities with Christian writings, including the Old Testament, scholars believe these are coincidences rather than evidence of overt Christian influence—this despite the fact that the text was written about 40 years after the conquest. It mentions Christianity only at its beginning and its end, framing the narration (as opposed to the events themselves) of the *Popol Vuh* as taking place within the context of the Christian era, for better or worse.

The book describes the moment of creation as having been spurred instantly by the words of the gods themselves describing the moments preceding creation with, "Whatever might be is simply not there: only murmurs, ripples, in the dark, in the night." It also describes how the gods attempt to create humans to give meaning to creation and have beings that can speak, praise, and keep the passing of time, first forming them out of earth and mud, which soon dissolves. The second version of humankind, the text relates, was created out of wood, but these beings were dull and could not speak in words. The gods decide to annihilate them by sending a flood and other devastations, including the revolt of the beings' own possessions, which turn and destroy their owners. The book explains that the remains of this previous version of humankind are the monkeys and humanlike creatures we see today. The gods finally create humankind using corn, which is not surprising given its importance as a Mayan subsistence crop to this day.

Other similarities shared with the Bible's book of Genesis include the explanation of astronomical features, including the Big Dipper, the assertion that woman was created after man, and the conclusion that man at one point had come too close to being like the divine, resulting in a confusion of languages to disperse humankind into different linguistic groups. The *Popol Vuh* is not without its own tales of heroics, the most prominent being the myth of the Hero Twins, who journey into the underworld (known as Xibalba), ruled by seven lords, and endure great hardships.

In addition to the interesting metaphysical speculation provided throughout the text, another fascinating feature of the *Popol Vuh* is that it may have served as a book of divination, with some hidden meaning if read in a certain way that allowed the reader to predict future events – hence its being referred to as the "Council Book." In a more literal sense, it also tells quite matter-of-factly of the impending difficulties that will arrive with the coming of "enemies, hidden behind mountains and hills," a possible allusion to the civil war and its atrocities. Despite the hardships, the book concludes that, "Our people will never be scattered. Our destiny will triumph over the ill-fated days which are coming at a time unknown. We will always be secure in the land we have occupied."

Pascual Abaj

On a hill just outside of town is this Mayan shrine dedicated to the earth god Huyup Tak'ah (Mountain Plain) where worshippers gather frequently to perform ceremonies. The idol is a blackened Pre-Columbian sculpture standing about a meter tall and lined with stones, candles, and sacrificial offerings of booze. It has been around for centuries. Ceremonies performed by a Mayan shaman usually involve much incense, liquor-drinking, chanting, and offerings of candles, flowers, and

Iglesía Santo Tomás

maybe even a sacrificial chicken. If you happen to stumble upon one of these ceremonies during your visit, be sure to keep your distance and refrain from taking photographs. You can always ask for permission, but don't be surprised if the answer is a firm "no." To get to the shrine, walk down 5a Avenida from the main plaza turning right onto 9a Calle. At the bottom of the hill found along this street, head left onto a path through the signposted *morerías* (mask workshops) found there. The path continues uphill from there to the hilltop site. It's best to go in a group and earlier in the day, as robberies of tourists along this route are not infrequent.

ACCOMMODATIONS
Under $25
Hospedaje Girón (6a Calle 4-52 Zona 1, tel. 7756-1156) has basic, passable rooms for $7 d with shared bath or $13 d with private bath. The rooms downstairs can feel a bit damp. Friendly **Hotel y Cafetería Tutto's** (12 Calle 6-29 Zona 1, tel. 7756-1540, $18 d) has spotless rooms with private bathroom and cable TV in addition to a downstairs café with beautiful mountain views. **Chalet House** (3a Calle "C" 7-44, tel. 7756-1360, $20 d) is on a quiet street and has pleasant rooms with private bathroom, warm wool blankets, and eye-catching textiles.

$25-50
The excellent-value **Posada El Arco** (4a Calle 4-36 Zona 1, tel. 7756-1255, $30 d) has friendly owners and seven spacious rooms with attractive Guatemalan decor, fireplace, and private hot-water bathroom; some have balconies with splendid mountain views over the well-tended garden. Some beds are firmer than others. The **Maya Lodge** (6a Calle "A" 4-08, tel. 7756-1167, $26 d) is rather "plain Jane," though it's right on the plaza. **Hotel Chugüila** (5a Avenida 5-24 Zona 1, tel. 7756-1134) has 15 rooms, all except one with chimney, and it is expanding. Rooms are set around a courtyard and have TV and nice patios.

$50-100
At the entrance to town on the left-hand side is **Hotel Casa del Rey** (Km. 144, entrance to Chichicastenango, www.hotelcasadelrey.com, tel. 7756-1053, $45-60 d) in simple motel style with a restaurant/bar and swimming pool. You'll see large tour buses parked here, as it's a favorite for folks on overnight package tours, giving the property some semblance of atmosphere. In the heart of town, 【 **Hotel Santo Tomás** (7a Avenida 5-32 Zona 1, tel. 7756-1051, $100 d) is a lovely colonial-style hotel with rooms centered around a graceful courtyard fountain complete with squawking macaws. There are a pool, hot tub, gift shop, a lively bar, and restaurant. A longtime favorite with travelers to Chichicastenango is the 【 **Mayan Inn** (8a Calle "A" 1-91 Zona 1, tel. 7756-1176, www.mayaninn.com.gt, $100 d), established by Alfred S. Clark, founder of

Clark Tours, in 1932. The 30 rooms are beautifully decorated with antique furnishings and have fireplaces. Most of the bathrooms have tubs. Each room has its own attendant dressed in traditional village costume, as there are no locks on the doors from the outside. Rest assured, you can lock yourself in at night. There's a good restaurant here. The market is literally at your doorstep.

FOOD

Tziguan Tinamit (5a Avenida 5-67 Zona 1, tel. 7756-1144, 7 A.M.-10 P.M. daily) serves a variety of light meals and has particularly tasty baked goods. **Los Cofrades** (corner of 6a Calle and 5a Avenida, tel. 7756-1647, 9 A.M.-10 P.M. Wed.-Sun.) has pleasant outdoor seating on a balcony overlooking the busy street below. There are delicious, large set-menu lunches and dinners for $5-7. **Restaurante Las Brasas** (6a Calle 4-52, Comercial Girón, tel. 7756-2226, 7 A.M.-10 P.M. daily, $4-9) is a good-value steak house also serving decent breakfasts. Beside El Calvario church, **Casa San Juan** (6a Calle 7-30 Zona 1, tel. 4090-4305) serves creatively prepared sandwiches and Guatemalan food in a stylish environment that includes wrought-iron chairs and artwork. **La Villa de los Cofrades** (6a Calle "A" and main plaza, tel. 7756-1643) is a café/restaurant serving good breakfasts, grilled meats, coffee, and even crepes. The town's most stylish eateries are at the restaurants housed inside the **Mayan Inn** and **Hotel Santo Tomás,** where a three-course meal runs in the vicinity of $15. The waiters at both places wear elaborate traditional costumes, though the food at Hotel Santo Tomás outshines that of its closest competitor, albeit slightly.

INFORMATION AND SERVICES
Communications
For post, you'll find Correos on 7a Avenida

between 8a and 9a Calles. ACSES (6a Calle 4-52 Zona 1) has Internet for $1.75 an hour, as does Internet Digital (5a Avenida 5-60 Zona 1).

Money
Conveniently, Chichi's banks stay open on Sundays. Among the options are Banco Industrial (6a Calle 6-05 Zona 1, 10 A.M.-2 P.M. Mon., 10 A.M.-5 P.M. Wed. and Fri., 9 A.M.-5 P.M. Thurs. and Sun., 10 A.M.-3 P.M. Sat.) with a VISA/Plus ATM. Banrural (6a Calle east of 5a Avenida, 9 A.M.-5 P.M. Sun.-Fri., 9 A.M.-1 P.M. Sat.) has a MasterCard/Cirrus ATM.

GETTING THERE
Bus
Chichi lacks a bus terminal, though bus arrivals and departures are centered around 5a Avenida and 5a Calle. There are buses to Guatemala City leaving every 30 minutes between 4 A.M. and 5 P.M. (three hours, $2), eight daily buses to Panajachel (1.5 hours, $1.50) between 5 A.M. and 2 P.M., and seven daily buses to Quetzaltenango (three hours, $1.75). Alternatively, you can take any of the above to the Los Encuentros junction and change there for connecting service. If you're heading north, there are frequent buses to the departmental capital of Santa Cruz del Quiché leaving every 30 minutes.

Shuttle Bus
Adrenalina Tours (www.adrenalinatours.com), with offices in Quetzaltenango and Antigua, offers shuttle service from Chichi to Panajachel, Antigua, Quetzaltenango, and Guatemala City on market days. **Chichi Turkaj Tours** (5a Avenida 5-24, tel. 7756-1579) offers departures to the above cities plus Huehuetenango, the Mexican border, and others, though it's best to inquire as to specific schedules and routes, as these tend to be somewhat elastic.

Santa Cruz del Quiché and Vicinity

The capital of the Quiché department holds little of interest for foreign visitors when compared to Chichicastenango, just 18 kilometers away, though facilities and services are adequate if you should find yourself needing to spend the night. There is quite a bit of history surrounding this town, including the old K'iche' capital of K'umarcaaj, also known as Utatlán thanks to Pedro de Alvarado's Mexican allies. It was here that Alvarado and his men were invited to sign a formal surrender by the defeated K'iche's after the showdown near Quetzaltenango. The surrender turned into wholesale slaughter when Alvarado suspected a trap and enticed the K'iche' rulers outside the safety of their city walls and then charged them with treason and burned them at the stake.

More recently, Quiché, as it's better known, housed an army garrison and the surrounding countryside was the site of intense battles between guerrilla and army forces during the civil war. The villages to the north suffered greatly during the conflict, particularly those in an area known as the Ixil Triangle. Today, the city serves mostly as a transit point for travelers heading north to these exquisite villages and their fantastic surroundings, which have become increasingly attractive in the advent of peace.

SIGHTS

The military barracks that once occupied the northeast corner of the plaza was closed in 2004. The plaza is dominated by, as usual, the church, said to have been constructed by Dominican friars using stones from K'umarcaaj's Templo Tohil. The local market is held on Thursdays and Sundays, just as in neighboring Chichicastenango. Other than that, there's little in the way of sights in the town proper.

K'umarcaaj (Gumarcaaj)

The former capital of the K'iche' empire enjoys

a splendidly sylvan setting surrounded by deep ravines, though little has been carried out in the way of restoration since it was destroyed by the Spanish conquerors in 1524. Only a few structures are still recognizable and the site consists mostly of unexcavated grassy mounds. The K'iche' established themselves here sometime around A.D. 1250 after a migration from the Gulf of Mexico lowlands (previously Toltec territory) to the Yucataán Peninsula and up the Río Usumacinta. They were able to dominate and subdue the less-complex highland societies they encountered along the way, eventually establishing a sizable kingdom that stretched as far east as the lands occupied by the Rabinal of modern-day Alta Verapaz, west to present-day Momostenango, north to the Sierra de Chuacús, and south to Chichicastenango. The population of the immediate urban area is thought to have numbered 20,000. The formal founding of K'umarcaaj, signaling the consolidation of K'iche' power, dates from about A.D. 1400. It fell briefly under the dominion of the Mexica (Aztec) of Central Mexico, with whom they maintained a peaceful coexistence, until the arrival of the Spanish two decades later.

Of the city's 80 structures, few are recognizable, these being limited to the area around the central plaza. The partially restored **Templo Tohil** is the site's tallest structure and featured a sacrificial stone altar that was once the site of ritual human sacrifice. It is dedicated to a deity of thunder and lightning. Modern-day worshippers still perform rituals here, as it remains an important site for the Mayans. Much of the temple's exterior stonework has been vandalized and removed for use in local construction. The circular foundations of **Templo K'ucumatz** can also be seen and are all that remains of a previous building about four meters in diameter with a doorway in the shape of a snake head.

THE HAUNTED HILL OF PACHALUM

Between Pachalum and the ruins of Mixco Viejo, the Río Motagua traverses forested hillsides and fields. One of these hills, **Cerro Potosí,** is thought by locals to be haunted. Townsfolk ascribe a number of mysteries to this seemingly innocuous hill, including the presence of animals seen but never heard, an airplane crash for which wreckage was never found, and the seeming disappearance of people who walk into the mountain's forests.

One of the most popular tales is that of a woman who decided to take a shortcut across the mountain while walking to her village, never to be heard from again. Family members and neighbors sent a search party but found nothing. Townsfolk also tell of a plane crash many years ago, clearly taking place on the mountain. When they went looking for the wreckage, there were no signs of the plane or its passengers. Although the hill is not very densely forested and

is covered mostly in scrub forest, locals often hear the sounds of turkeys, dogs, and roosters coming from the mountain. Some local hunters have even been lured into its expanses looking for animals they hear but can never find.

The secret to the origins of the strange happenings on this mysterious mountain may lie buried with its former landowner, Don Serbando Rosales, a wealthy man from Pachalum who is said to have worn only white and to have ridden only white horses. He was seen every Friday evening, villagers say, carrying a black chicken up the side of the mountain. Townsfolk also say black birds made of smoke flew over his house 40 days after he was buried and that during Rosales's burial, astonished funeralgoers realized he was no longer in his coffin.

Similar legends abound throughout Guatemala, a country with a long tradition of supernatural mystery, magic, and folklore.

A ball court lies to the east of here. Beneath the ruins on the site's southern escarpment is a long, 100-meter tunnel. It's debated whether it was built by the K'iche' to hide the women and children pending the Spanish arrival or as a representation of the mythical caves of Tula mentioned in the *Popol Vuh*. The site is revered by modern-day Mayans and is also a place for frequent rituals, including candle and flower petal offerings and chicken sacrifices. Bring a flashlight if you go into the cave, as there are a number of side tunnels, at least one of which ends in a dark, deep chasm. Watch your step.

The ruins are open 8 A.M.-5 P.M. daily and admission costs about $4. There's a small museum at the entrance with displays on the site's history, including a three-dimensional diagram of how it may have looked in its heyday. The easiest way to get here is to take a cab from the center of town, which should cost about $9 round-trip including an hour's wait time. You can also walk for about 45 minutes from the center of town, heading south from the plaza along 2a Avenida

and turning right onto 10a Calle, from where it's a straight shot to the ruins.

ACCOMMODATIONS

Quiché's basic smattering of accommodations includes **Hotel Rey K'iche'** (tel. 7775-0827, 8a Calle 0-39 Zona 5, $10-13 d), two blocks north of the bus terminal, where the 22 spotless rooms mostly have private hot-water bathroom and cable TV. There's also a decent cafeteria. Friendly **Hotel Maya Quiché** (3a Avenida 4-19 Zona 1, tel. 7755-1464, $10-13 d) is conveniently situated a block west of the plaza and has large rooms with or without private bathroom. With several rooms in a multistory building around a parking lot/courtyard, the 42-room **Hotel Monte Bello** (4a Avenida 9-16 Zona 1, tel. 7755-3948, $20-35 d) is a good value. There are rooms with shared or private bath and large in-room TVs for your entertainment. **Hotel San Pascual** (7a Calle 0-43 Zona 1, tel. 7757-1107, $7-13 d), between the bus terminal and central plaza, has clean rooms with or without private bathroom with the added bonus of pleasant plant-filled courtyards. The newest addition to the town's hotel offerings is ◐ **Hostal de Santa Maria Aparthotel** (7a Avenida 14-51 Zona 5, tel. 7755-0982, www. hostaldesantamaria.com, $50-300), with modern suites and one, two or three-bedroom apartments. The apartments come fully furnished and have full kitchens with modern cabinetry. There's in-room Wi-Fi in addition to the usual comforts found in more modern hotels.

FOOD

Casa Antaño (16 Calle 0-09 Zona 4, tel. 7755-3124, $7-10) serves decent-value grilled steak and chicken dishes in a pleasant colonial garden ambiance. **La Terraza de Martita**, on the west side of the plaza, serves tasty paninis and pizzas. There's a view of the plaza below, though it's somewhat obstructed by power lines.

If all else fails there's always Guatemala's ever-popular answer to KFC, **Pollo Campero** (2a Avenida 7-35 Zona 1), serving tasty fried or grilled chicken, sandwiches, and some decent breakfasts in a sit-down environment with wait staff. Pizza and pasta dishes have been added as part of a partnership with Spanish chain Telepizza.

SERVICES

Banrural, on the plaza's northwest corner, changes dollars and travelers checks and has a MasterCard ATM. Banco G&T Continental also has a location with a Visa/PLUS ATM machine just down the street from Pollo Campero.

GETTING THERE

The city bus depot is four blocks south and then two blocks east of the central plaza. Several of the buses heading to Chichicastenango from Guatemala City continue this way. There are buses every 30 minutes between 3 A.M. and 5 P.M. heading back toward Guatemala City, stopping at Chichicastenango and the Los Encuentros junction along the way. If you're heading north,

there are eight daily buses to Nebaj (2.5 hours, $3) between 8:30 A.M. and 5 P.M. All of these stop in Sacapulas (one hour, $1.50) along the way, meaning there is also hourly service to this city during the same period.

A road linking Santa Cruz del Quiché directly to Huehuetenango, to the west, may be a reality by the time you read this.

EAST OF SANTA CRUZ DEL QUICHÉ

The road east from El Quiché runs along the Sierra de Chuacús through some villages set in verdant agricultural fields and is newly paved, ultimately winding up in Guatemala City some 160 kilometers away. The first of these villages, 10 kilometers away, is **Chiché**, which shares similar characteristics with Chichicastenango and has a Wednesday market. Farther along are the towns of **Chinique** and **Zacualpa**. Known as Pamaca in Postclassic times, Zacualpa has Thursday and Sunday markets and features the restored **Iglesia del Espíritu Santo**, with an elegant facade featuring twin bell towers punctuated by a third atop a curved central rise.

Next along this road is **Joyabaj**, which was practically leveled to the ground in the 1976 earthquake. It was rebuilt and is the main regional market center. It is one of three places in Guatemala where you can witness the *palo volador* ritual in which two "dancers" twist around a pole while tied with ropes, eventually descending to the ground. The event takes place during the annual fiesta, usually the second week in August.

Pachalum

A highlight of this back-door route to Guatemala City is Pachalum, a prosperous town only 21 years old; it has become a development model for the rest of Guatemala, having received international acclaim for its widespread citizen participation in local government, decentralization of local political power structures, and financial transparency. It should be noted that much of this development has taken place with assistance from USAID, which chose Pachalum as a project site because of its young age and the chance to start off with a clean slate. Access to potable water, electricity, health care, and education are widely available and there are municipal offices dedicated to Women's Vocational Training and Children and Youth. The town even has its own website, found at www.pachalum.com. It is just 72 kilometers from Guatemala City and, while not necessarily a tourism destination in the traditional sense, it is certainly worth a look if you go this way, at least for the chance to see what a developed Guatemala might someday resemble.

Should you need to stay here, **Hotel Nancy** (northwest of the plaza) or **Hotel Posada del Sol** (150 meters from city hall on Avenida Los Geranios and Calle Las Ilusiones, Zona 4) are good, inexpensive hotels.

Mixco Viejo

The paved road from Pachalum to Guatemala City also provides convenient access to the site of Mixco Viejo, about 12 kilometers south of Pachalum and 59 kilometers northwest of Guatemala City. Situated on a promontory overlooking the Río Pixcayá and surrounded by spectacular ravines on all sides, Mixco Viejo is the former Poqomam capital and ceremonial center, consisting of several low-rise pyramids and two ball courts. There is only one way in or out of the city, this being a narrow causeway. Although it came under Kaqchikel influence shortly before falling to the Spanish in 1525, it shows heavy Toltec and Aztec influences, including a pair of sculptures of open-mouthed serpents with small human skulls adorning the ball court. The latter is a replica, with the original having been removed to Guatemala City.

The site, consisting of about 120 structures, was restored in the 1950s and '60s by a French expedition. It is thought to have harbored

a population of about 10,000 at the time of Spanish contact. According to Spanish accounts of the city's siege, the battle was fought in the plains near the city after Poqomam warriors from Chinautla attacked the Spanish from behind. The few survivors then pointed the way to a secret entrance to the city, which the Spanish entered practically unopposed to destroy and kill in a merciless fashion.

Mixco Viejo is open 7 A.M.-4:30 P.M. daily. Admission to the site is $3.50. To get here, hop on any of the buses headed to Pachalum from Guatemala City (four daily); they stop at the entrance to the ruins. It's also accessible from the town of San Juan Sacatepéquez, a satellite town of the capital, via pickups. It's about a 10-minute walk up the hill from the roadside drop-off point to the ruins.

NORTH OF SANTA CRUZ DEL QUICHÉ
Sacapulas

This town, on the banks of the Río Negro, sits at the crossroads of newly paved roads heading west to Huehuetenango, east to Uspantán and Cobán (partially paved), and north to Nebaj. If you need to spend the night here, a decent choice is **Tujaal** (tel. 5529-8609, $10 s/d), on the right side just before crossing the bridge over the river for the road to Nebaj. There's a restaurant on the ground floor serving basic Guatemalan fare. A second option is **Hospedaje y Restaurante Río Negro** (tel. 5410-8168, $3 p/p) with basic rooms and shared, cold-water bath. It's on the southern bank of the river next to the Cruz Roja (Red Cross).

If you should need to exchange cash dollars, Banrural is on the north side of the plaza uphill from the bridge.

From here, there are seven daily buses to Nebaj (1.5 hours), two buses to Huehuetenango at 4:30 and 5:30 A.M. (1.5 hours), and seven daily buses to Uspantán, in addition to pickups throughout the day. Buses leave from the north side of the bridge over the river.

SACAPULAS TO COBÁN

Uspantán

A very scenic road leads east toward Alta Verapaz. If you're traveling by bus, you'll probably need to overnight in Uspantán, a small town nestled in the Cuchumatanes Mountains, which is actually a very pleasant place with clean streets and friendly folk. Hoping you may wind up staying here by choice, the local government has installed a **Municipal Tourism Office** (Municipal Palace, 1st Floor, tel. 7951-8125, www.uspantan.com) to help you make the most of your visit. Recreational opportunities include hikes through the backcountry to the wonderful waterfall of **Los Regadillos,** hikes to **Peña Flor** and the neighboring site of **Tzunun Kaab'** along streams to another waterfall, witnessing a Mayan ceremony on the **Xoqoneb'** hillside just outside of town, and hiking or biking to the agricultural village of **Cholá,** where you can bathe in a refreshing spring-fed pool. Perhaps the most alluring option is a visit to **Laj Chimel,** the birthplace of Nobel Peace Prize winner Rigoberta Menchú and the gateway to Guatemala's fourth-largest cloud forest, where you can try your luck at spotting the elusive quetzal and other exotic birds. Locals guide visitors on far-flung adventures via mountain trails to such locales as Mirador El Quetzal, with spectacular views of the Ixil Triangle flanked by the Sierra de los Cuchumatanes, and lovely Laguna Danta. If you're interested in exploring the area, contact the local community tourism initiative (tel. 4909-7701, www.lajchimelecoturismo.com). Camping in a covered platform and basic lodging in an adobe guesthouse are also available, though there's no electricity. Be prepared for cold showers.

There are some good options for accommodations in Uspantán, all except one in the range of $10-15 d, including **Casa Blanca** (2a Avenida and 6a Calle Zona 3, tel. 7951-8049), where the rooms have cable TV and hot water.

There's also ample parking if you've brought a car. **Hotel Montana** (5a Avenida 4-60 Zona 3, tel. 7951-8025) has clean rooms with hot-water private bath and cable TV housed in a pleasant peach-colored building. Offering minibus service to Cobán at 5 A.M., **Hotel La Villa** (tel. 7951-8046) has rooms with private or shared bathroom centered around a patio/parking lot. Centrally located **C Hotel Posada de Doña Leonor** (6a Calle 4-09 Zona 1, tel. 7951-8045) has well-furnished rooms around a garden courtyard with shared or private bath and cable TV. Entirely with shared-bath rooms, a good budget option is **Hotel Uspanteka** (4a Calle 5-18 Zona 1, tel. 7951-8078, $6 d).

For food, there's **Café Don David** (5a Calle 3-27 Zona 1, tel. 7951-8169) serving light meals, dinners, and snacks that include sandwiches and Guatemalan food. **Comedor San Miguel** (4a Avenida 3-29 Zona 1, tel. 5592-1833) serving basic Guatemalan fare is another decent option. Across from the soccer stadium, **TV Café El Golazo** (tel. 7951-8027) is a good place for breakfasts, cakes, and sandwiches.

Banrural (7a Avenida Zona 4), two blocks from the central plaza, changes cash dollars.

Buses to Cobán (four hours, $4) leave early at 3 A.M. and 5 A.M. Heading west to Sacapulas are six daily buses continuing to El Quiché starting at 3 A.M. until about 4 P.M.

Río Chixoy Tubing

East of Uspantán, the town of Chicamán has also caught on to ecotourism and serves as the gateway to the seldom-explored **Río Chixoy.** About 14 kilometers away, it's most easily visited from the hamlet of El Jocote via a community tourism initiative. A full day of **river tubing** (tel. 5196-6519, www.guatetubing.com, $55 p/p with two-person minimum) includes three hours afloat on the cool, turquoise-colored river ending at a spectacular waterfall, as well as a jungle hike and lunch with a local community. Safety gear (helmet, life jacket, inner tube, dry bag) is included in the price. For an additional $22 per person (based on two people) you have the option of staying overnight in a comfortably quaint wooden cabin. It seems a bit hedonistic to have such comforts as cable TV and a DVD player out in this neck of the woods but they are nonetheless included, along with hot water showers, a fully equipped kitchen, laundry facilities, and lounge spaces.

The Ixil Triangle

North of Sacapulas via a newly paved road is the Ixil Triangle, a name given to the area comprising the villages of Santa María Nebaj, San Juan Cotzal, and San Gaspar Chajul. The scenery here is spectacular, as are the weavings made by its Ixil-speaking inhabitants. Set in the foothills of the lush Cuchumatanes, the area was the scene of heavy fighting during the country's civil war. Its inhabitants suffered greatly during the violence, undoubtedly more than any other region in Guatemala. Peace has returned, but the region remains remote, drawing visitors with its colorful traditional Mayan culture, some of the country's best hiking, and breathtaking scenery.

HISTORY

The area populated by the Ixil-speaking peoples shows signs of having been inhabited since the latter part of the Classic period, between the 6th and 9th centuries A.D., including various stelae, pyramids, and monuments unearthed in this region. The Ixil didn't come under Spanish authority until 1530, having managed to successfully repel earlier invasions from their fortresses in Nebaj and Chajul with help from their neighbors and allies in Uspantán. When the Spanish did finally conquer the region, they burnt Nebaj to the ground and enslaved its people. After Spanish priests felt confident they had secured the souls of the newly conquered peoples, the region fell into a period of neglect until Dominican friars arrived on the scene in the 19th century seeking to convert the remaining outlying mountain villages. Guatemala's burgeoning coffee trade and its insatiable need for cheap labor had become fully established by this time, and the region's inhabitants were soon conscripted to work on the coastal plantations using debt peonage, among other tactics.

By the mid-20th century several wealthy families had firmly established themselves in the lower elevations of the Ixil region, owning huge cattle, coffee, cacao, and sugar plantations. Among the local landowning families, the Brol and Arenas families were notoriously cruel masters and the subject of eventual retribution during the civil war. The Brols owned thousands of acres as far as Uspantán, employing as many as 4,000 resident and seasonal workers at their Finca San Francisco in the northern lowlands near Cotzal. Many of its workers were held captive to debt peonage.

The Ejército Guerrillero de los Pobres, or EGP, moved into the region in 1972, crossing the border from Mexico and finding in the Ixil a populace willing to cooperate with them in the hopes of being finally liberated from the tyranny of the landowning elite. The swift acceptance of the EGP in the hearts and minds of the Ixil was further aided by weak government and military presence throughout the region. Eventually, the Guatemalan military moved into the region and began indiscriminately executing and "disappearing" suspected guerrilla sympathizers.

Although the EGP quickly displayed the ability to enlist thousands of peasants to its cause, the ideological momentum was not matched with a logistical capacity to arm or

THE LIFE AND TIMES OF RIGOBERTA MENCHÚ

Rigoberta Menchú captured world attention in 1992 (the 500-year-anniversary of Columbus's landing in America) when she was awarded the Nobel Peace Prize for her work in bringing awareness to the plight of Guatemala's indigenous Mayan population. Her book *I, Rigoberta Menchú*, tells the story of her experiences growing up in a Mayan family in Guatemala's Western Highlands and of how several family members, including her father, mother, and brother, were murdered during the civil war at the hands of the military. Menchú herself had been persecuted by the military and eventually fled to exile in Mexico.

Much of her story was contested in author David Stoll's book *Rigoberta Menchú and the Story of All Poor Guatemalans*, published in 1999. After painstaking research and agonizing over whether or not to publish his findings, Stoll questions the veracity of several items appearing in Menchú's account. Among these are land conflicts with a neighboring ladino family, portrayed by Menchú as the product of class struggle which, according to Stoll, was more like a family feud between Rigoberta's father and his in-laws. The book also casts doubt on Menchú's claims that she personally witnessed the death of her brother, burned alive at the hands of the military in the village of Chajul, claiming she probably was not in fact there. Eyewitness testimony, meanwhile, contends the victims were machine-gunned to death. Underlying the issues of supposed embellishments and distortions was Stoll's contention that Menchú's autobiography served purposes aimed at gaining the support of the Mayan peasantry for the guerrilla movement. Stoll concedes that Menchú's story is valuable in that it is a compelling version of events that can be generally applied to the plight of Guatemala's Mayan population during the civil war. Somehow, Menchú managed to escape the controversy with her reputation largely unblemished. In any case, Menchú's book is a fascinating read, at the very least for the insights it provides into highland Mayan culture and the atrocities committed during the civil war.

More recently, Menchú's Rigoberta Menchú Tum Foundation presented former accusations of torture, murder, and genocide in a Spanish court against several prominent Guatemalan military officials for their role in the atrocities during the civil war. The case centers around the firebombing of the Spanish embassy, which killed Menchú's father, a prominent activist, after he and several other protesters occupied the foreign government outpost. In 2006, the Spanish court issued arrest warrants for the accused, including Efraín Ríos Montt and Oscar Humberto Mejía Víctores, after a fruitless visit to Guatemala by a Spanish judge to record eyewitness testimony. The accused presented injunctions preventing their court summons and have also presented various appeals to prevent the arrest warrants from being carried out. As is always the case in Guatemala whenever prominent figures are involved, they had some help from technicalities that prevented the courts from issuing warrants for their arrest because of a supposed mix-up in the paperwork coming from Spain, which mysteriously left out specific orders of apprehension for Ríos Montt and Mejía Víctores.

Menchú has also announced plans to form an indigenous political party to go along with her presidential aspirations, though she ran as a candidate for the Encuentro Por Guatemala party in the 2007 presidential election.

supply its followers. Villagers were soon caught in the middle of a scorched-earth campaign, with entire villages being massacred and destroyed, the guerrillas being largely unable to protect their followers.

An amnesty was declared under the subsequent government of Efraín Ríos Montt in 1982, bringing in thousands of refugees who had fled to the hinterlands trying to escape from the military. Between 1982 and 1984, 42,000 peasants turned themselves in. Other policies included the establishment of local Civil Defense Patrols, known as PACs, aimed at curtailing the influence of the guerrillas

© AL ARGUETA

splendid scenery along the road from Nebaj to Acul

among the local population, and the rounding up of displaced citizens into so-called "model villages" closely guarded by the military.

By the time democratic rule finally returned to Guatemala in 1986, the guerrillas had been pushed back to the northern reaches of the El Quiché department. There were occasional skirmishes until the signing of the 1996 peace accords. Almost all the smaller villages and hamlets of the Ixil Triangle and neighboring Ixcán were destroyed during the 1970s and '80s, with 25,000 Ixil murdered or displaced during the atrocities.

NEBAJ

Nebaj is the largest of the three villages and has grown substantially through the last few years since the end of the civil war. I still have pleasant memories of my first visit to this enchanting town, at the ripe old age of 18, riding on the roof rack of a crowded chicken bus on twisting mountain (dirt) roads. The location

of this hamlet, nestled in a valley among the Cuchumatanes mountain chain, is superb, and you'll surely remember the first time you see its quaint houses and whitewashed church coming into view from the mountains above. As elsewhere, the town is centered around the plaza with the church and government offices built around it. A peek inside Nebaj's church reveals a multitude of small crosses as a memorial to civil war victims.

During the worst of the violence Nebaj was pretty much off-limits, with military checkpoints in Santa Cruz del Quiché, Sacapulas, and along the road north keeping close tabs on the activities of sojourners to these parts. Today it's become increasingly popular with foreign volunteers working with one of many NGOs helping out with postwar reconstruction and community development projects throughout the area. Despite its violent history, the region is remarkably safe, with reports of tourist robberies in these parts being virtually unheard of.

The women of Nebaj wear one of the most colorful and beautiful of Guatemala's indigenous costumes; they're imbued with animal and bird motifs and worn with an elaborate headdress adorned with purple, yellow, and green pom-poms. You can pick up colorful weavings with these motifs from several stalls along the plaza and at some of the local restaurants.

Hikes

The opportunities for hikes around Nebaj are virtually limitless. Two of the nicest hikes are to the villages of **Acul** and **Cocop.** One of the easiest hikes is along green pastures and meadows to some nearby waterfalls known as **Las Cataratas,** about 20 meters (60 feet) high. There are also several sites that are sacred to the Mayans where you might witness ceremonies, though their locations are not well known and it's best to go with a guide. There are several multiday hikes offered by a number of outfitters that afford you the opportunity to really get off the beaten path. These include a fantastic three-day hike over the Cuchumatanes mountain range to the village of **Todos Santos,** hikes across highland plateaus dotted with meadows and lagoons, and two- or three-day treks to the remote villages of **Xeo** and **Cotzal.**

Another nearby attraction of sorts is an old military landing strip still pockmarked with bomb holes that was a settlement for displaced war victims. Found four kilometers west of town, it's also known by its Ixil name **Ak'txumb'al,** meaning "New Mentality," certainly as a way of adding insult to injury by its military creators.

Guide Companies

Because of the remoteness of most of the locales mentioned here, as well as the chance to contribute directly to the well-being of local inhabitants, guides are strongly recommended. Among the local outfitters is **Guías Ixiles** (3a

Calle Zona 1, tel. 5311-9100, www.nebaj.com/ixilguides.htm), housed inside El Descanso, which offers hikes to all of the above-mentioned locales. A share of the proceeds goes to finance community projects. Next door, **Pablo's Tours** (tel. 5416-8674) offers hikes to nearby waterfalls, a river cave near a magnificently pristine blue river, horseback riding ($5 per hour), and multiday hiking from Nebaj to Todos Santos. Quetzaltenango-based **Quetzaltrekkers** (Diagonal 12 8-37 Zona 1, inside Casa Argentinas, Quetzaltenango, tel. 7765-5895, www.quetzaltrekkers.com) is another recommended outfitter for the Nebaj-Todos Santos trek, with proceeds being donated to fund projects benefiting Quetzaltenango's street children. The six-day trip ($150) leaves from Quetzaltenango, though it might be possible to meet up with a group if you already happen to be in Nebaj. Trips leave every other Wednesday.

If you prefer to hike without a guide, pick up a copy of the very useful *Trekking en la Región Ixil* guide ($2) from Guías Ixiles.

Shopping

Nebaj's busy **market** is one block east of the church and sells basic items mostly of interest to local residents. It's substantially busier on Thursdays and Sundays, when merchants come from out of town peddling cheap First World goods. For weaving and handicrafts, there are several stalls near the church. Another good spot is the **Centro Cultural Ixil y Mercado de Artesanías** (3a Avenida Zona 1, right off the park), where you can shop for handicrafts in a pretty neocolonial courtyard.

Accommodations

Hotel Ilebal Tenam (Calzada 15 de Septiembre, Salida a Chajul, Cantón Simocool, tel. 7755-8039, $7-13 d) has rooms with shared or private hot-water bathrooms and basic furnishings centered around a courtyard. Rooms with

GUATEMALA: FAST-FORWARD

For decades, intrepid travelers have come to Guatemala to experience this mythical pocket paradise: a compact, diverse nation in the middle of the Americas with 33 volcanoes, Lake Atitlán ("the most beautiful lake in the world"), steamy jungles, ancient Mayan temples, and colorful indigenous villages.

The volcanoes are still here; the lake is still here; much of the steamy jungles are still here, with their enigmatic ancient Mayan temples. However, the villages of Guatemala's highlands are experiencing a major transition thanks to remittance money sent back from Guatemalans working in the United States.

Whitewashed adobe houses with terra-cotta-tiled roofs are being exchanged for concrete block walls and corrugated tin roofs. Electricity, indoor plumbing, rebar, satellite dishes, asphalt, and concrete are just some of the newcomers to these villages.

In one of my favorite, rather remote, highland villages, Chajul, young women in traditional regalia blithely sip colas and chat on cell phones in Ixil Mayan. Boys play soccer in the street wearing Beckham jerseys and Yankees baseball caps, calling to each other in Ixil, Spanish, and English. In Sololá, speakers broadcast evangelical radio shows that compete with hip-hop and rap coming from the local fruit market. It appears that more people own pickup trucks, cell phones, and televisions than toilets.

Why the dramatic change? Guatemala welcomes $3.5 billion annually from the Guatemalan workforce living in the United States. Thanks to these greenbacks, traditional, often indigenous communities are on fast-forward, hurtling into a brave new modern world.

Enrique V. Iglesias (former longtime president of the Inter-American Development Bank) lauds the direct and democratic attributes of remittances. However, witnessing remittances in action, I do not always find it pretty what they do to village life in Guatemala. It sounds so good on paper—courageous Guatemalans enter the United States, work hard, send money home, and help to sustain their country. It's direct, democratic, and family to family. However, early-stage capitalism produces the most voracious consumers and with limited leadership, law enforcement, zoning, education, or planning, these new dollars create new consumers who are left to learn as they go.

I have interviewed Guatemalans living in the United States who say (some with great relish, some with dejected nostalgia) that they no longer recognize their villages. They tell me that the families they left (to better support by working in the United States) have used their hard-earned cash to transform the highlands into something new. But few know just what that is.

The signs of progress are everywhere: A proud grandma's adobe house is now a three-story concrete house faced in shiny tile and paned with reflective glass. Old-time swimming holes have become water parks. Pagan shrines and rituals have diminished as evangelicals reweave the religious fabric and build Christian churches in these communities. A pickup truck is much easier to carry products with than a forehead tumpline—but one notices expanded waistlines. Televisions provide a window to the war in Iraq, China's environmental issues, American pop culture, and giraffes in Kenya. Women do not spend hours hand-spinning wool blankets anymore; the ones arriving from China are much cheaper and just about as warm.

After living in and writing about Central America for almost 10 years, I still encourage travelers to go to the Guatemala highland villages: Look, explore, listen, absorb—no longer for their simple charms, but as a fascinating window into the fast-changing lives and vernacular of Central America.

Contributed by Catherine Docter, writer and consultant, contributing editor, Departures *magazine, www.mesoamericanconsulting.com*

private bath have cable TV. The garden sitting areas with thatched-roof shelters for shade are a nice touch. Nebaj's attractive, hip hostel is **€ MediaLuna MedioSol** (tel. 5749-7450, $5 p/p in dorms or $7 p/p in private room), half a block from El Descanso on 3a Calle, with several amenities, including wireless Internet, a comfortable DVD lounge, a dartboard, table tennis, and a Mayan sauna in addition to clean rooms. Guests have use of the kitchen and you get the fourth night free if you spend three nights.

Hotel Shalom (corner of Calzada 15 de Septiembre and 4a Calle, tel. 7755-8028, $16 d) has spacious and attractive well-furnished rooms with private hot-water bathroom, cable TV, and wood-paneled walls. **Anexo Hotel Ixil** (tel. 7756-0036, corner of 2a Avenida and 9a Calle, $16 d) is basic but clean with rooms centered around a courtyard. All have private hot-water bathroom. The budget-friendly version of this property is **Hotel Ixil** (four blocks south of the plaza on 5a Avenida, tel. 7756-0036, $4 p/p) with simple shared-bath rooms. **Hotel Turansa** (corner of 5a Calle and 6a Avenida, tel. 7755-8487, $18 d) has a secured parking lot around which are centered 16 clean rooms with private hot-water bathroom and cable TV. The nicest place in town is **€ Hotel Villa Nebaj** (Avenida 15 de Septiembre, just north of the plaza, tel. 7756-0005 or 7755-8115, $30 d), where the comfortable rooms have big wooden beds with Nebaj quilts, private hot-water bathroom, cable TV, and tile floors. There's also plenty of parking. My new favorite option is **€ Hotel Santa María** (Calle Real, two blocks from the park, tel. 4212-7927 or 4621-9890, www.hotelsantamarianebaj.com, $30 d), built in neo-colonial style and harboring comfortable, clean rooms set round a small courtyard. The friendly innkeepers provide homecooked meals for their guests and there is parking.

Food
Local specialties in Nebaj include *boxboles,* an Ixil dish of steamed corn dough served with lemon and either tomato or peanut sauce.

A new addition to Nebaj is also an excellent value. Located on the way out of town towards Chajul and Cotzal and one block from the courthouse, **La Quinta de los Reyes** (tel. 7755-8098, $5) serves hearty, all-you-can-eat, buffet-style meals, including Guatemalan and International fare, as well as dessert and a drink. For tasty Guatemalan dishes and nice views overlooking the central plaza head to **Café Restaurante Maya Ixil** (tel. 7755-8168). It's also a good place for breakfast.

Nebaj's main gathering spot is **€ El Descanso** (3a Calle Zona 1, tel. 5311-9100, 6:30 A.M.-10 P.M. daily) where there are good Guatemalan dishes, sandwiches, nachos, and pastries. There is seating upstairs on a covered patio as well as a bar/lounge with comfy couches on the lower level. Movies are sometimes shown here and they serve *boxboles* on Thursdays. They also have free Wi-Fi. For decent pizza, there's **Pizza del César** (2a Avenida, tel. 7755-8095). Just off the square is **Papi's** (tel. 5906-5780), serving healthy American-style food the likes of soy burgers. The bread is freshly baked on the premises. For steaks, fajitas, and tasty sandwiches, **Restaurante El Rancho** (Cantón Xalacul, Barrio Tipepala, tel. 7755-8019 or 5715-5360, all meals daily) is a good bet and is popular with the NGO crowd. On the road out of town heading out to Sacapulas, **Asados El Pasabién** (tel. 5701-2222, noon-11 P.M. daily) serves scrumptious grilled meats and chicken in a simple environment.

Information and Services
Nebaj's de facto tourist information office is El Descanso (3a Calle Zona 1, tel. 5311-9100). It also serves as an all-in-one travel clearinghouse and services center providing Internet access ($1.50 per hour). Guías Ixiles is also based here and they run the very informative

the lovely countryside in Acul

© AL ARGUETA

website www.nebaj.com. The post office is at 5a Avenida 4-37, one block north of the central plaza.

For money, Banrural, on the north side of the plaza, has an ATM.

Established by the same folks who began El Descanso, **Nebaj Language School** (nebajlanguageschool.com) offers 20 hours of one-on-one teaching per week for $130, including homestay with a local family (includes two meals a day), two guided treks, and discounted Internet and food at El Descanso.

Getting There

Bus schedules in Nebaj, as in most small rural towns, are somewhat elastic. The bus depot is two blocks southeast of the plaza. There are several daily buses and minivans to Santa Cruz del Quiché, with the last bus leaving sometime around 5 P.M. All of these stop in Sacapulas along the way. There are frequent buses and minivans to neighboring Chajul, Cotzal, and Acul.

◖ ACUL

Originally established as one of the "model villages" under the authoritarian hand of Efraín Ríos Montt, Acul is starting to come into its own. It features friendly folk and a spectacular Swiss-like mountain setting enhanced by the presence of quaint dairy farms. There are fairly frequent buses and pickups heading out this way from Nebaj, though it seems most gringos prefer to walk out this way through the lovely countryside.

Accommodations

If you'd like to stay in town, there's **Posada Doña Magdalena** (tel. 5782-0891), with beds in the dorm for $4 p/p or in the private double room for $7 p/p. All of the simple rooms share a bathroom. The hostel is run by a friendly Nebajense woman who lived in Las Vegas and speaks English, Spanish, and Ixil. Meals here are served family-style. There are textiles for sale as well as a Mayan sauna, or *temascal,* out back.

Among the local dairy farms is **Finca San**

Antonio (tel. 5305-6240 or 2439-3352), started in 1938 by Italian immigrant José Azzari, who died in 1999. The finca Is a pleasant working farm run by Azzari's sons and grandsons and producing some delicious cheeses made using centuries-old methods brought over from the old country. They're happy to show you around and you're welcome to stay in the charming wooden cabanas featuring tile floors, simple but pleasing decorative touches, and shared ($11 p/p) or private hot-water bathroom ($13 p/p). One of the rooms upstairs has a deck with gorgeous views of the surrounding farmland. Activities include nature hikes in the surrounding countryside and there were plans to buy mountain bikes, maybe by the time of your visit.

Just next door along the road into town is ◖ **Hacienda Mil Amores** (tel. 5704-4817), also owned by members of the Azzari family. The four lovely, spacious tile-roofed cottages are a step above its neighbor's and are built of stone or wood. Each of the rooms is different and has elaborate tree-trunk or terracotta floors and private bathroom, some with chimney. Room rates are $47 d. The property has several connections with well-known tour operators and has no trouble filling its rooms, so book well in advance if you wish to stay here. This is also a working farm where you can buy cheeses. Kids will love the opportunity to see farm animals and even milk cows if they're so inclined. Other activities include hikes to neighboring villages and horseback riding. Meals are served family-style in the main farmhouse, which is beautifully decorated with orchids grown on-site and has wonderful views of the surrounding pasturelands from a pleasant wooden deck.

SAN JUAN COTZAL

Cotzal was the Ixil Triangle's largest town until the road to Nebaj was built in the 1940s. It's now rather small, though its setting is (as everywhere else in these parts) gorgeous,

surrounded by the imposing Cuchumatanes mountain chain. There's little to see in the town itself, though the weavings here are some of Guatemala's finest. Market days are Wednesdays and Saturdays. The **Iglesia San Juan** fronts a pretty plaza that has been remodeled and festooned with flowers and benches. The church's interior is not nearly as elaborate as that of neighboring Chajul, but its Christ statue curiously holds a staff with an Israeli flag. Jesus was a Jewish carpenter, after all.

Cotzal has been enhanced as of late by a community tourism project. **Tejidos Cotzal** (just behind the marketplace, tel. 5428-8218, www.tejidoscotzal.org) is a cooperative of 30 local weavers who retain traditional methods of weaving using natural dyes and backstrap looms. There are two-day guided tours to the weavers' homes, offering a wonderful opportunity to get out and meet the people who create these singular works of art. The trip costs $13 per person, with a minimum of two people, and can be combined with a visit to nearby waterfalls.

The paving of the road to Cotzal has opened it up to tourism and there is now at least one decent hotel in town. **El Maguey** (tel. 7765-6199, $12 d), two blocks north of the plaza, has clean, basic rooms with TV and shared bathrooms. The hotel's eatery offers good set menus for about $2.50. Enterprising weavers may also offer you a place to stay.

Chimel and Santa Avelina Waterfalls

Some pretty waterfalls out this way make a good day hike, 10 and 12 kilometers from town, though there are not as of yet any outfitters to take you here. You can take pickups or minibuses to the villages of Chichel and Santa Avelina, from where it's a much shorter walk to the falls. The first waterfall, near Chichel, is Chimel, which cascades down a rocky cliff into a small river. There are some tables and benches

© AL ARGUETA

Chajul's ornate church

You can ask any of the locals how to get here and they can point you in the general direction.

CHAJUL

About 15 kilometers northeast of Nebaj, Chajul is a picturesque collection of quaint adobe houses with tiled roofs. Of the three Ixil Triangle towns, it certainly has the most traditional feel, though the paved road to Nebaj has many traditionalists fearing the end is near for one of the country's most pleasantly isolated villages. In any case, it still offers spectacular weavings you'll undoubtedly see everywhere. Market days are Tuesdays and Fridays, though on any given day sellers will most certainly find you to offer their wares in brilliant hues of red and blue embroidered with animals and plants.

The main attraction here is the town's church, **Iglesia de San Gaspar Los Reyes,** one of Guatemala's most ornate, with wooden doors containing finely carved depictions of animals. Inside, an elaborate goldleaf altar guarded by two figures dressed in traditional garb surrounds its *Cristo de Golgotha* statue. Check out the cool wool red coats, which are now rarely seen on the town's male inhabitants. The church is a major pilgrimage site on the second Friday of Lent.

Chajul's plaza was also the site of a grisly public execution of EGP guerrillas carried out by the Guatemalan military in retaliation for the 1979 murder of landowner Enrique Brol, an event which is narrated in Nobel Peace Prize winner Rigoberta Menchú's autobiography. While the basic facts of the army's extrajudicial murders has not come into question, Menchú's testimony certainly has. An investigation by author David Stoll has since revealed Menchú may not have been there at all and is also at odds with her claims that the prisoners were burnt alive, claiming instead that they were mowed down with machine guns. The research and evidence supporting his claims and questioning much of Menchú's autobiography

in the surrounding grassy hillside beneath the falls and it makes a pleasant place for a picnic. You can drive part of the way on a rugged dirt road, but you'll find yourself hiking the last half mile or so to the falls through beautiful pastureland.

The second waterfall is reached by going a further two kilometers along the main road out of Cotzal to the village of Santa Avelina. The town is built on a hillside and if you go to the base of this hillside via the main road, you'll find the small *Tienda Lux* on the outskirts of town. You walk straight uphill from here on a very steep trail, turning left onto a smaller footpath, which eventually traverses cornfields for about 20 minutes to the falls. The water tumbles over a rock that is pitched just over the edge of the cliff and produces quite a bit of spray. There's a small tile-roofed changing room by the pool at the base of the falls and a friendly caretaker who will collect a $1 admission price.

are presented in his book, *Rigoberta Menchú and the Story of All Poor Guatemalans.*

Practicalities

There's not much in the way of accommodations in Chajul, though there is now at least one decent place to stay. **Posada Vetz K'aol** (tel. 7765-6114, $10 per person) lies about 300 meters south of the plaza down a dirt road turnoff from the main street. It's a bit hard to find, but any *tuk-tuk* driver can take you there for less than $1. Formerly housing a clinic, the building has large, clean rooms with bunk beds and wool blankets. There's also a pleasant sitting room with a fireplace and TV. Tasty meals cooked by the lodge's caretaker are available upon request.

You'll find a few simple eateries just off the plaza, the best of which is **Las Gemelitas,** two blocks downhill from the church. As in Cotzal, you will likely be approached by locals offering food and shelter in their homes.

There's a Banrural on the plaza for changing cash dollars.

THE IXCÁN

North of Chajul, foot trails lead to the summit of 2,700-meter (9,000-foot) **Cerro Bisís** and some hamlets scattered throughout a roadless wilderness that has been proposed for special protection. Beyond this lies the Ixcán, a jungle wilderness extending northwest to Huehuetenango and the Mexican border settled by landless peasants during the 1960s with the help of Maryknoll missionaries. It was hotly contested during the civil war with virtually every village being razed to the ground in a scorched-earth campaign by the Guatemalan military. Today it remains largely untamed and many settlers have moved back from exile in Mexico. An interesting read on this subject is *Paradise in Ashes,* by Beatriz Manz.

The region holds excellent possibilities for ecotourism and remains one of Guatemala's great wilderness areas. It's quite literally the end of the road. If you're the explorer type, you may want to head out this way and if you do, feel free to write in with your experiences.

Huehuetenango and Vicinity

Affectionately called "Huehue" (WAY-way) by locals, this somewhat busy coffee-trading town sits in a valley overlooking the glaciated peaks of the Sierra de los Cuchumatanes. Because of its location in the mountain chain's rain shadow, the town and surrounding areas are somewhat drier than the Quiché highlands to the east, which lie on the mountain chain's windward side. The departmental capital is busy with travelers heading to or from the western border with Mexico as well as with coffee farmers and traders heading to or from nearby farms. Since first coming here at the age of three, I watched the town grow up into a somewhat disorganized agglomeration of trade and commerce, though there has been a remarkable improvement in the level of its services.

It makes a great jumping-off point for deeper explorations of the very diverse department of Huehuetenango and even includes a worthwhile site of its own, this being the ruins of Zaculeu just outside of town.

Access to Huehue is mainly via the Pan-American Highway, with the turnoff into town at Km. 264, from where it's another three kilometers to its center via a boulevard. A recently paved road now also leads east to Sacapulas, passing the town of Aguacatán (and wonderful mountain views) along the way.

SIGHTS

As always, the town is centered on the *parque central,* which is actually one of Guatemala's

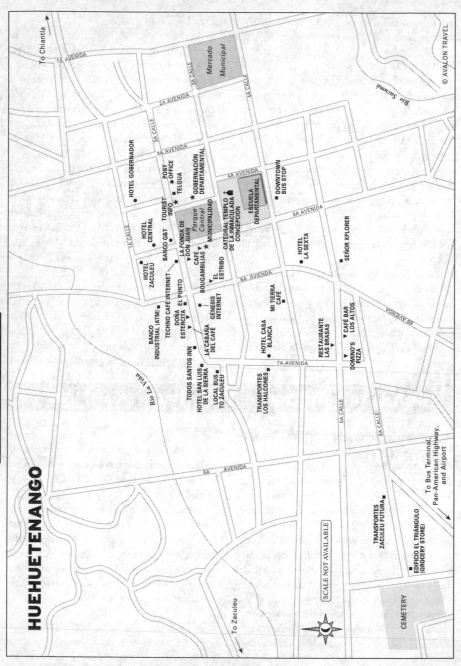

© AVALON TRAVEL

HUEHUETENANGO

To Chiantla

Rio Sacumá

Rio la Viña

To Zaculeu

To Bus Terminal,
Pan-American Highway,
and Airport

CEMETERY

SCALE NOT AVAILABLE

1A AVENIDA
2A AVENIDA
3A AVENIDA
4A AVENIDA
5A AVENIDA
8A AVENIDA

1A CALLE
2A CALLE
3A CALLE
4A CALLE
5A CALLE
6A CALLE
7A AVENIDA
8A AVENIDA

Mercado
Municipal

HOTEL GOBERNADOR

POST OFFICE
TELGUA
GOBERNACIÓN DEPARTAMENTAL

TOURIST INFO
PARQUE CENTRAL
MUNICIPALIDAD

CATEDRAL TEMPLO DE LA INMACULADA CONCEPCIÓN

ESCUELA DEPARTAMENTAL

DOWNTOWN BUS STOP

HOTEL CENTRAL

BANCO G&T

LA FONDA DE DON JUAN

CAFÉ BOUGAMBILIAS

EL ESTRIBO

HOTEL ZACULEU

HOTEL LA SEXTA

SEÑOR XPLORER

TECHNO CAFÉ INTERNET
EL PUNTO

DOÑA ESTERCITA

GÉNESIS INTERNET

MI TIERRA CAFÉ

CAFÉ BAR LOS ALTOS

BANCO INDUSTRIAL (ATM)

LA CABAÑA DEL CAFÉ

HOTEL CASA BLANCA

RESTAURANTE LAS BRASAS

DOMINO'S PIZZA

TODOS SANTOS INN

HOTEL SAN LUIS DE LA SIERRA

LOCAL BUS TO ZACULEU

TRANSPORTES LOS HALCONES

TRANSPORTES ZACULEU FUTURA

EDIFICIO EL TRIÁNGULO (GROCERY STORE)

church in Huehuetenango

prettiest. At its center is a colonial fountain along with well-tended gardens and even a **relief map** of the department of Huehuetenango. On the plaza's southern end, facing 5a Avenida, is its neoclassical church, the **Catedral Templo de la Inmaculada Concepción.** It dates to 1874. The town's **Municipalidad** (City Hall) is on the west side of the plaza and is curiously topped with an oyster-shaped band shell. On the park's eastern side, in early 20th-century architecture and notable for its clock tower, is the building housing **Gobernación Departamental,** the regional seat of government.

Zaculeu

Zaculeu (8 A.M.-6 P.M. daily, $3.50) was the principal Mam ceremonial site. Dating to the Early Classic period (A.D. 400-700), it shows signs of having been occupied for more than 1,000 years until it was conquered by Gonzalo de Alvarado, brother of Guatemala's other infamous conquistador, in October 1525. It was starvation that eventually did the local population in, as Alvarado and his troops simply staked out the fortified city (surrounded by ravines) for two months, cutting off rescue attempts from neighboring Mam villages with the help of the Spanish cavalry and 2,000 Mexica and K'iche' allies.

More than any of the other highland Mayan sites such as K'umarcaaj and Iximché, Zaculeu somehow manages to evoke the feel of the city as it might have looked in its heyday, thanks to a 1950s restoration project covering the restored temples in graying white plaster. At the same time, the temples lack the bright coloring they most certainly would have had and similarly lack any of their decorative details. The highest of its temple pyramids, **Structure I,** rises to about 12 meters. Another somewhat impressive structure is **Structure 13,** on the southeast corner of the main plaza. The site also has an interesting I-shaped ball court. There's an on-site museum with some interesting displays on the

© AL ARGUETA

the ruins of Zaculeu

siege of the city as well as burial pieces found beneath Structure I.

Snacks and refreshments are available from a couple of simple eateries across from the main entrance to the park.

To get here, you can hire a cab from the central plaza for about $6, which includes about an hour at the ruins. Otherwise, there are frequent, cheap local buses heading out this way from 2a Calle and 7a Avenida near Hotel San Luis de la Sierra.

GUIDE COMPANIES

Quetzaltenango-based Adrenalina Tours has closed the office it once had in Huehuetenango, though you can still hire the services of its knowledgeable local driver. **Mario Martínez** (tel. 5762-1903 or 7764-6897, mario_huehuetenango@yahoo.com), and his four-wheel-drive vehicle can take you to any of Huehuetenango's frontier attractions, such as the Paquix plateau and nearby villages.

NIGHTLIFE

When Huehuetecos want to party, they tend to head to Xela. Still, there are a few good places in town for enjoying an evening cocktail, including **El Estribo** (6a Avenida between 3a and 4a Calle Zona 1) and **Café Bar Los Altos** (5a Calle 6-85 Zona 1).

SHOPPING

You can pick up good-quality handicrafts at **Artesanías Ixquil** (6a Avenida, Cerrito del Maíz, Zona 4, tel. 5543-5661, ixquilhuehue@hotmail.com), which has a wide assortment of products representing the department's excellent weavings and singular traditional costumes. From the plaza, walk north up 6a Avenida to the top of a hill and then right on 1a Calle, where it's number 1-115. It's about a 15-minute walk.

ACCOMMODATIONS
Under $10

Hotel Gobernador (4a Avenida 1-45 Zona 1,

tel. 7764-1197, $7-12 d) is a solid family-run budget choice with good-size rooms, some with private bath. Some rooms are better ventilated than others. **Hotel Central** (5a Avenida 1-33 Zona 1, tel. 7764-1202, $6 d) is a reasonable budget option with large, if aging, rooms, all with shared bath.

$10-25

Friendly **Todos Santos Inn** (2a Calle 7-64 Zona 1, tel. 7764-1241, $10-16 d) has 16 rooms with shared or private bath cheerfully painted in hues of red and orange with passable mattresses and reading lamps, some with cable TV. There's an upstairs sitting area as well as a third-floor patio. Downstairs rooms are not as well ventilated and tend to feel moldy, a common issue throughout the highlands. Indifferent **Hotel La Sexta** (6a Avenida 4-29 Zona 1, tel. 7764-6612, $17 d) has stiff beds and small-ish rooms with cable TV and medieval-looking hot-water heaters. On the south side of the bus terminal, **Hotel Guatemex** (tel. 7769-0398, $10-20 d) is your best bet for late bus arrivals into town, with rooms in a variety of price categories, all with cable TV and good beds.

$25-50

Half a block north of the plaza, **Hotel Zaculeu** (5a Avenida 1-14 Zona 1, tel. 7764-1086, $37 d) has attractive ground-floor rooms with tile floors beside a garden courtyard. The top-floor rooms in a newer section have been upgraded with carpeting, accent lighting on the walls, and other pleasant decorative touches. All rooms have cable TV, great beds, and private hot-water bathroom. There's a dining room serving breakfast and dinner. Conveniently situated across from the Los Halcones bus depot, ◖ **Hotel Casa Blanca** (7a Avenida 3-41 Zona 1, tel. 7769-0777, $37 d) has personal sentimental value, as it was once my grandfather's home and office. All mushiness aside, there's plenty here to recommend it, including

attractive rooms in the original house (with plenty of character) or beside the back patio (more modern and spacious). All 15 rooms have hot-water private bathroom, phone, and cable TV. There are two restaurants, each fronting one of the house's two patios.

Just up the street, **Hotel San Luis de la Sierra** (2a Calle 7-00 Zona 1, tel. 7764-9217, hsanluis@intelnet.net.gt, $28 d) is lovingly cared for by María Rosa Calderón, a former grade-school teacher who once lived in Guatemala City and taught Spanish to a future Moon Handbooks author. The spotless rooms have fan, attractive furnishings, hot-water private bathroom, cable TV, and reading lamps. There's a dining room serving breakfast and dinner. ◖ **Hotel Premier** (2a Calle 5-37 Zona 8, tel. 7764-9200 or 7769-0927, http://huehuetenango.com, $33-85 d), on the way out to Zaculeu, has 36 rooms set around a pretty, opaque plastic-covered courtyard graced by a fountain. The rooms have the comfiest beds in town, tile floors, cable TV, wireless Internet, and hot-water private bathroom; some have views of the Cuchumatanes. The attractive lobby has a restaurant/bar serving international dishes.

There are a number of hotels along the entrance into town near the bus terminal, including the **Hotel California** (3a Avenida 4-25 Zona 5, Colonia Alvarado, tel. 7769-0500, $33 d), with clean, modern rooms with cable TV and private hot-water bathroom. There's also a dining room and lobby lounge. Don't let its name scare you; unlike the famous hotel in the Eagles tune, you can check out anytime you like and you can certainly leave. Also along the entrance into town is **Hotel San Francisco** (Km. 260, Cantón San José, tel. 7764-9987/88, $30 d), which is not as fancy as the armed guards posted at its doors would have you believe. It has 51 spotless rooms with somewhat bland decor and private hot-water bathroom and cable TV. There are an Internet center, a pool table, and a small gym as well as a restaurant next to the parking lot. The main lobby is housed under a pleasant opaque-ceiling courtyard, allowing for ample ambient light. The hotel's gardens are also the home of an unfortunate caged spider monkey.

FOOD

Conveniently situated across from the main plaza's cathedral, **Café Bougambilias** (tel. 7764-0105, 6:45 A.M.-9:30 P.M.) is a great place for a quick snack or cheap eat with set dishes that include steak or chicken, salad, and a drink for $3.50 or tortillas, burgers, and sandwiches for $1.50. The cooking is done on the ground floor, which you can see as you come in, with tables on the top two floors overlooking the park. Just off the square, **La Fonda de Don Juan** (2a Calle 5-35 Zona 1, tel. 7764-1173, 6 A.M.-10 P.M.) serves an excellent and varied menu including Italian, Mexican, and Guatemalan dishes the likes of pizza, pasta, and burgers in a lively atmosphere that includes checkered tablecloths. **Mi Tierra Café** (4a Calle 6-46 Zona 1, tel. 7764-1473, 7 A.M.-9 P.M. Mon.-Sat., 2-9 P.M. Sun.) is a friendly little restaurant that is ever-popular with locals, serving tasty nachos, pizza, and fajitas in addition to delicious breakfasts, including delectable croissant sandwiches. Try the "muffin ranchero," essentially a salsa-bathed egg sandwich with fried tortillas instead of bread. The strong coffee is locally grown and extraordinary. For steaks, seafood, and even some Chinese fare, check out **Restaurante Las Brasas** (5a Calle 6-104, on the corner of 5a Calle and 7a Avenida, tel. 7764-6200, 10 A.M.-11 P.M. daily, $4-15). There's even duck on the menu. **Domino's Pizza** is across the street.

Just down the street is one of the best places in town, **Hotel Casa Blanca** (7a Avenida 3-41 Zona 1, tel. 7769-0777, 6 A.M.-10 P.M.), where you can dine al fresco in the backyard garden or inside facing the house's original courtyard. On the menu are steaks, grilled

chicken, good soups, and salads as well as sandwiches. It makes a great place for breakfast. **Especialidades Doña Estercita** (2a Calle west of 6a Avenida, tel. 7764-2212, 8 A.M.-10 P.M. Mon.-Sat.) is the place to go for sweet or salty crepes, croissants, pies, empanadas, and sandwiches. Just a few doors down, **La Cabaña del Café** (2a Calle 6-50 Zona 1, tel. 7764-8903, 8 A.M.-9 P.M. daily) has probably the best coffee in town, including great espresso drinks, in addition to a range of light fare including sandwiches, breakfasts, and cakes, housed in a homey log cabin.

INFORMATION AND SERVICES
Tourist Information

Huehue's Centro de Información Turística (tel. 7694-9354, 8 A.M.-noon and 1:30-5 P.M.) is on 2a Calle housed inside the Gobernación Departamental building fronting the plaza. The staff speaks English and has a variety of maps and printed information that can help you get around town and explore the surrounding attractions throughout the department.

Communications

The central post office is at 2a Calle 3-54 Zona 1 just east of the plaza. Telgua has pay phones and international calling right next door.

With fast connections and abundant computers, Señor Xplorer (5a Calle 5-97 Zona 1, Centro Comercial La Plazuela Local 4, tel. 7768-1185/86) offers Internet service for about $1 an hour. Interhuehue (3a Calle 6-65 Zona 1) also charges about $1 an hour. Another large operation with about 20 computers is Techno Café Internet (2a Calle Zona 1, across from La Fonda de Don Juan, tel. 7762-6353, 9 A.M.-9 P.M. Mon.-Sat.). On 2a Calle next door to Especialidades Doña Estercita is El Punto (tel. 7764-7826), charging about $0.65 an hour. Across the street, Génesis Internet (tel. 7764-7021) charges the same.

Money

The ATM at G&T Banco Continental on the north side of the plaza fronting 2a Calle works with both Visa and MasterCard. Banco Industrial (6a Avenida 1-26 Zona 1) has a Visa/Plus ATM. Both banks can change cash dollars and travelers checks.

Language Schools

Huehue makes a good place to learn Spanish and become immersed in the language, as the gringo presence here is not as prevalent as in other parts of Guatemala. Its sole language school is **Academia de Español Xinabajul** (4a Avenida 14-14 Zona 5, Los Encinos, tel. 7764-6631, academiaxinabajul@hotmail.com), which charges $150 per week for 20 hours of instruction and stay with a local host family. It gets good marks from former students. For private lessons, contact Faby Castro at tel. 7762-7730 or 5348-1676.

GETTING THERE

The bus terminal is about two kilometers southwest of the city center, halfway along the boulevard leading out to the Pan-American Highway. There are frequent buses to many outlying towns and villages, most notably:

- **Aguacatán** (one hour, $1): 10 daily buses between 6 A.M. and 4 P.M.
- **Barillas** (seven hours, $4): 10 daily buses 2 A.M.-10 P.M.
- **La Mesilla (Mexican border)** (two hours, $2): 20 daily buses 6 A.M.-6 P.M.
- **Nenton** (three hours, $2): six daily buses between 3:30 A.M. and 1 P.M.
- **Sacapulas, Quiché** (1.5 hours, $2): at 11:30 A.M. and 12:45 P.M.
- **Soloma** (three hours, $2.50): 16 daily buses between 2 A.M. and 10 P.M.
- **Todos Santos Cuchumatán** (two hours, $2): leaving at 4:30 A.M., 5 A.M., 12:45 P.M., 1:30 P.M., 2:45 P.M., and 3:45 P.M. There may be others.

Frequent second-class bus departures also include **Guatemala City** (20 daily buses until 4 P.M., five hours, $5) and **Quetzaltenango** (16 daily buses until 2:30 P.M., two hours, $1.75).

Pullman bus service to Guatemala City is available via **Transportes Los Halcones** (7a Avenida 3-62 Zona 1, tel. 7764-2251, $5) at 4:30 A.M., 7 A.M., and 2 P.M. **Transportes Zaculeu Futura** (3a Avenida 5-25 Zona 1, tel. 7764-1535) has departures at 6 A.M. and 3 P.M. **Transportes Velásquez,** operating from the main terminal, is another option, with buses every half hour or so between 8:30 A.M. and 3:30 P.M.

NEAR HUEHUETENANGO

The following towns are close to the department capital and might make for interesting day trips if you lack the time to go deep into the heart of this remote corner of Guatemala.

Chiantla

Chiantla lies five kilometers north of Huehuetenango along a paved road that continues into the Cuchumtanes mountain chain. It was once a silver mining center and is known for its **Iglesia Nuestra Señora de Candelaria,** harboring the Virgen de Chiantla, adorned in the town's silver. There are some interesting murals in the church's nave depicting an *encomendero* watching over Mayan workers in the silver mine. The church is a pilgrimage site throughout the year, but especially on February 2 during the annual town festival. Chiantla's town center features two adjacent plazas, with one of them graced by a municipal building with a clock tower very much like the one in Huehuetenango. There are buses from Chiantla to Huehuetenango (and vice versa) about every 20 minutes. Heading out from Huehue, the buses stop at 1a Calle and 1a Avenida on the way out of town, which is much closer to the city center than the bus terminal.

Aguacatán

Heading east from Chiantla on the paved road toward Sacapulas, you'll pass this small agricultural town at the base of the Cuchumatanes. The village is the product of a merger of two distinct groups of people, the Chalchitek and Awakatek, into a single community by Dominican friars during colonial times. Today, they still speak separate languages. Gold and silver were mined here during colonial days, though nowadays its economic activities are centered around the production of abundant crops, most notably garlic. The weekly market is held on Sunday, with traders arriving and setting up shop on Saturday afternoon. The town's other claim to fame is the *nacimiento* (source) of the Río San Juan, which bubbles up from the underbelly of a rocky hillside about 20 minutes' walk outside of town.

For accommodations and food, your best bet is two blocks north of the plaza at **Hotel y Restaurante San Juan** (tel. 7766-0110, $7-15 d), with clean rooms with or without private bathroom.

El Mirador

The road winds its way out of Chiantla up the vertiginous face of the Cuchumatanes, with the superimposed quilt pattern of corn- and wheat fields upon the countryside transitioning to one of grasses and hearty maguey plants at about 2,700 meters (9,000 feet). At the top of the rise is a lookout point known as El Mirador or La Cumbre (The Summit), from where there are views of Huehuetenango and Guatemala's impressive volcanic chain to the south.

Huehuetenango Frontier

From the lookout, the road continues along the 3,300 meter (11,000-foot) Paquix plateau, characterized by smooth, rounded hills with scant vegetation that conjure images of the Peruvian Andes or Alaska. Windblown grasses, black granite rocks, sturdy maguey plants, and herds of sheep pepper the surrounding countryside with the occasional adobe house occupied by ruddy Mayans more closely resembling their South American Inca relatives. The recent introduction of llamas to these areas adds further similarity.

About one kilometer north from the lookout, a dirt-road turnoff heads east to the village of Chancol and the **Unicornio Azul** equestrian center. Back along the main (paved) road another nine kilometers or so is the **Paquix Junction,** with its westbound turnoff heading to the village of **Todos Santos Cuchumatán.** Its northbound turnoff leads to the villages of **San Juan Ixcoy,**

Soloma, Santa Eulalia, San Mateo Ixtatán and, eventually, **Barillas.**

UNICORNIO AZUL

Not so much a hotel as a professionally run equestrian center, ◖ **Unicornio Azul** (tel. 5205-9328, www.unicornioazul.com, $33 d) enjoys a spectacular location on the grassy plateau atop the rugged Cuchumatanes from where you can embark on horseback rides as short as one hour to as long as several days throughout the sprawling countryside. About 25 kilometers northeast of Huehuetenango, the operation consists of 11 well-cared-for horses, stables, and wonderful accommodations meticulously managed by its French-Guatemalan owners. Prices for rides range from $80 for one day to $970 for nine days, though they vary depending on the number of riders in a group. The accommodations here are rustically beautiful, consisting of five rooms housed in two

© AL ARGUETA

The rugged Huehuetenango highlands are among Guatemala's most beautiful.

separate tiled-roof houses. All of the rooms are distinctly decorated and furnished with unique touches such as gorgeous lamps fashioned from Honduran Lenca pottery. At night, gas lamps provide wonderful ambience, though there is electricity for showers and cooking. Room rates include breakfast and one hour of horseback riding. Lunch and dinner are served family-style and cost $7 each. If you're not keen on riding, there are also mountain bikes for exploring the rugged roads and trails all around.

TODOS SANTOS CUCHUMATÁN

Todos Santos sits on the dry western slopes of the Cuchumatanes. Remote and largely retaining its traditions, it is a fine place to take in Mayan culture, do some hiking, and shop for unique weavings. It is one of only a few places in the highlands where you'll still see men wearing traditional attire, consisting of bright red pants with thin white stripes paired with a zany striped shirt featuring oversize, elaborately embroidered collars. The costume also includes a straw hat with a wide, blue, grommeted ribbon. The women wear equally stunning purple *huipiles* and embroider many items with the town's signature designs. Contributing to the remarkable preservation of local customs and dress is the intense local pride of Todos Santos's Mam-speaking residents, who stand a full head taller than most other Mayan indigenous peoples.

The village first gained notoriety after social scientist and world traveler Maud Oakes spent two years here starting in 1945 and wrote two books about her experiences, *The Two Crosses of Todos Santos* and *Beyond the Windy Place*. The local Mam hold four local mountain peaks sacred and some of her neighbors reputedly believed the foreign-born female shaman to be the guardian of one of these.

The main market day here is Saturday. Don't be surprised to find inebriated men (mostly) stumbling through the streets or passed out

© AL ARGUETA

the church at Todos Santos

on the sidewalk, an unfortunately common sight throughout the highlands. As in the Ixil Triangle, the population here suffered greatly during the civil war. The army marched on the town in 1982 in the days following a brief occupation by EGP guerrillas, carrying out the torture, disappearance, and murder of suspected guerrilla sympathizers. Many villagers fled to the hillsides to wait out the troubles or went north to Mexico.

Todos Santos certainly remains very poor. Many of its residents have traditionally made ends meet by traveling to the Pacific lowlands to work in the annual harvests. Many Todosanteros now have family in the United States, a fact that becomes readily apparent as you walk the town's streets and see new construction funded with dollars sent from abroad by expatriate relatives. Despite its remoteness, it's not uncommon to see groups of villagers in their distinctive attire at Guatemala City's international airport waiting on the arrival of a returning family member. Huehuetenango

supposedly sends more of its inhabitants abroad than any other of Guatemala's departments.

As always, you should be careful not to photograph Mayan people (especially children) without permission, nor should you show undue interest. It can be tough at times, because Mayan children (and Mayan people in general) can provide some wonderful opportunities for portraiture. In 2000, a Japanese tourist and the Guatemalan tour bus driver who tried to protect him were lynched in Todos Santos by an angry mob after the tourist tried to photograph a child. The incident was certainly an isolated one and was attributed to a rumor about satanists who were supposedly in the area snatching local children at the time. If anything, it serves as a grim reminder that the old photographer's rule contending that it's easier to apologize (for taking a candid photo) than to ask permission doesn't really apply in Guatemala.

Sights

Museo Balam (tel. 5787-3598, 7 A.M.-9 P.M., $0.65) is to the left 150 meters off the main street one block from the park. Run by a friendly local family, it features marimbas, costumes for traditional village dances, and old leather sandals, bags, plows, and saddles, affording a glimpse into the town's history and traditions.

Todos Santos is one of very few places in Guatemala that still largely adheres to the 260-day Mayan calendar known as the Tzolkin. There are frequent rituals, including animal sacrifices, performed at a small Mayan site just above town known either as **Cumanchúm** or **Tojcunenchén.** The ruins look out onto the 3,650-meter (12,000-foot) **Chemal** peak (also known as "La Torre" for the radio mast atop it), which is the highest nonvolcanic peak in Central America. To reach the summit, hike or take a bus east to the neighboring village of La Ventosa, from where a trail leads past adobe houses through sylvan settings to the

ALL SAINTS' DAY IN TODOS SANTOS

If you're in Todos Santos around November 1 (All Saints' Day) and love a good party, you won't want to miss the three-day annual town festival, at the center of which is a series of horse races. There's plenty of drinking, dancing, and marimba music during this time. The race begins with costumed riders galloping from one end of the 600-yard course, drinking *aguardiente* upon their arrival at the course's other extreme before heading back once again. The back-and-forth pattern is a competition of survival of the fittest; riders struggle to hang on as the race (and drunken stupor) reach a crescendo. Traditionally, the riders hit the horses with live chickens, though in recent years they have used whips. The races sometimes continue well into the afternoon.

By the end of the day, most people are lying passed out in the streets or in bars (if they're lucky) in a drunken spectacle rivaled in few places in Guatemala. There are always a few drunken brawls and some folks who wind up in the town jail. The next day Is Day of the Dead, and the festivities transition to the local cemetery, where families visit departed relatives, marking their gravestones with candles and flowers. There's also more music and dance as part of the final day of celebration.

---

top, a journey of about 1.5 hours. Your reward on a clear day is a breathtaking view of Guatemala's volcanic chain from Tacaná on the Mexican border all the way east to Agua and Acatenango, near Antigua.

Todos Santos is well known for its annual November 1 horse races capping off weeklong festivities that include plenty of drinking, dancing, and general merriment.

Shopping

Housed in the Hotel Casa Familiar, **Artesanía Todosantera** (tel. 7783-0656) is a local weavers' cooperative displaying a fine array of handicrafts at reasonable prices. The gift shop is stocked with some of the region's most wonderful weavings and is almost an obligatory stop for anyone passing through.

Hiking

There are numerous opportunities for hikes. If you want a guide or printed information to make the most of your walk, head to either of the town's two language schools. One of the most popular walks is to the site of **Las Letras,** the town's equivalent of the "Hollywood" sign overlooking California's famous neighborhood.

The Todos Santos version is a series of white painted rocks above town, with an arrangement that might be illegible depending on when they were last reassembled. It's about a two-hour hike round-trip. From there, you can continue another five hours to the villages of **Tuicoy** and **Tzichim. La Puerta del Cielo** is another amazing lookout point accessible via a detour from Tuicoy. A five-hour trek from Todos Santos is the village of **San Juan Atitán,** up the ridge looming over the village and down into a valley, crossing streams and verdant forests along the way.

Accommodations

Most of the town's accommodations can be found in a cluster up the hill about a block from the plaza. Only a few have phones to contact for reservations. A virtual Todos Santos institution, **☪ Hotel Casa Familiar** (tel. 7783-0656 or 5580-9579, $6 p/p to $25 d) is a longtime favorite with travelers. Run by a local family, it has been remodeled to provide upgraded accommodations for visitors. Some of the new rooms have private bathrooms and patios; all have tasteful Maya-inspired decor. There is also a pleasant garden dining area. You can arrange guided hikes from here as well as reading lessons. Movies are shown daily at 4 P.M.

Another good choice is **Hotelito Todos Santos** ($5-15 p/p), also recently upgraded, with comfortable rooms featuring typical Guatemalan décor and a pleasant living room area where guests like to congregate. It also has a dining room serving basic meals. Next door is the bare-bones **Hotel Mam** ($4 p/p). Turning right up the hill at the end of this same street, you'll find **Hospedaje El Viajero** (tel. 7783-0705 or 5754-9760, $8 p/p), with basic, shared-bath rooms and hard beds.

Food

There are a few decent places for food along the main street heading out from the plaza toward the main road and Huehuetenango. Among these is **Restaurante Cuchumatlán**, serving pizzas ($8 for a large pie), curry dishes, and fruit smoothies. It also has a book exchange. The patio dining area at **Casa Familiar** (tel. 7783-0656, $3-7) is the best place in town to grab a bite to eat.

Information and Services

For your banking needs, Banrural is on the trapezoidal plaza at the center of town. The post office and police are also here. Along the main street leading out of town is **Café Internet** (tel. 5781-1059), charging $1.50 per hour for a somewhat slow Internet connection.

Todos Santos's two language schools charge about $120 per week for 4-5 hours of instruction per day plus homestay with a local family. Living conditions are very basic and most host families speak Mam, with a select few opportunities for homestay with Spanish-speaking families. Both schools also offer instruction in the local Mayan dialect. The two schools are **Academia Hispano Maya** (opposite Hotelito Todos Santos, www.hispanomaya.org) and **Nuevo Amanecer** (150 meters west of the plaza, escuela_linguistica@yahoo.com).

Getting There

There are seven daily buses to Huehuetenango (2.5 hours) that leave from the plaza, the last one leaving at 4:30 P.M.

SAN JUAN IXCOY TO BARILLAS

From the Paquix Junction, the spectacularly scenic road heads north to several mountain towns in the heart of the Cuchumatanes. Along the road are some exquisite pastures, which have been grazed since colonial times. Large, gray boulders are also strewn about and the frigid mountain scenery is at once beautiful and inhospitable. At the edge of the plateau, the road begins its steep descent shortly after passing a local limestone outcropping in the shape of two pointy teeth known as the **Piedras de Captzín**. The stones are sacred to the local Q'anjob'al.

San Juan Ixcoy is the first village you'll come across as you begin the descent from the plateau. Its women wear long, white *huipiles* with embroidery at the collar. In the vicinity of town are the **Los Jolotes** waterfalls, which got their name from a corruption of the Spanish word *tecolotes,* meaning "owls," which are said to be abundant in the surrounding forests. The waterfalls are part of the Río San Juan, a tributary of the Río Ixcán, which eventually flows into the mighty Río Usumacinta.

San Pedro Soloma

Another seven kilometers down the road is San Pedro Soloma, a fairly prosperous and surprisingly sizable town given its remote location deep in the mountains. It looks rather attractive from the surrounding mountainside as you descend into the green valley it occupies. The Mayans here also speak Q'anjob'al. Many of them have family members living in the United States, adding to the town's prosperity.

Soloma is a good place to break up the journey if you're headed north to Barillas. Among the options for accommodations is **Hotel Caucaso** (3a Calle 3A-37, tel. 7780-6179, $10 d), one block northeast of the plaza, with bare-bones rooms. The nicest place in town is **Hotel Don Chico** (4a Avenida 3-65 Zona 1, tel. 7780-6087, $20 d), where the comfortable rooms have hot water and cable TV. There's also underground parking and an Internet access center next door on the edge of a large parking lot bordering the hotel. Also found facing this lot is **Restaurante El Eden** (all meals daily), which serves good Guatemalan fare as well as pastas, sandwiches, and decent breakfasts. Another decent choice is **Restaurante Alma Latina,** on the plaza.

The pavement ends in Soloma, the rest of the way being a fairly well-maintained dirt road.

San Mateo Ixtatán

Continuing north, you'll pass the small village of **Santa Eulalia** before eventually arriving

© AL ARGUETA

the church at San Mateo Ixtatán

in the Chuj-speaking village of San Mateo Ixtatán, perched on the side of a mountain at 2,560 meters (8,400 feet). While the residents of neighboring villages travel to the coast for seasonal labor, those in San Mateo tend to work their own lands tending sheep and growing coffee, cardamom, and grains. Like most other towns in Huehuetenango, however, a large percentage of its men travel to the United States in search of work. Another source of local prosperity are the community-owned salt mines. The town is well known for the production of its exotic black salt and its very name is a derivation of the Nahuatl word Ixtatlán, meaning "abundance of salt."

The town's pretty **church** somewhat resembles a giant birthday cake and is supposedly painted every year in different bright colors. I remember catching my first glimpse of its Technicolor facade in a *National Geographic* magazine from the late 1980s, but on my recent visit it was painted a rather unremarkable cream and white. The traditional *huipil* worn by San Mateo's women is one of Guatemala's finest, with concentric woven star patterns in reds, purples, and blues that verge on the psychedelic. Some of the men still wear the *capixay,* a thick, black-wool, open-sided pullover. The town's annual fiesta runs September 17-21. Market days are Thursdays and Sundays.

Just below the village are the unrestored ruins of **Wajxaklajunh,** which look out to a valley and surrounding mountain ridges. There are a few temples, some stelae, and a ball court.

Hotels here are very basic. If you should find yourself needing to spend the night here, head to **Hotel Ixtateco** (tel. 7756-6586), which at the very least has hot water.

A good source of information on San Mateo is the website of the Ixtatán Foundation (www.ixtatan.org), a development organization that has helped the town build its very first high school and has a variety of other projects in the works. It also runs an Internet café, Wajxaklajunh.com, charging about $1 per hour.

Barillas

The road out of San Mateo Ixtatán heads east and descends 28 kilometers to the ladino frontier town of Barillas, which lies at about the same altitude as Guatemala City. The town itself is fairly unremarkable, though it's interesting in that it borders the Ixcán wilderness to the north and west. Should you need to stay or eat here, the best options are located just opposite the town's central square.

There is one daily bus and several pickups heading east to Playa Grande via a rough road. The government announced plans to construct a transversal highway stretching east to west from Izabal department through Alta Verapaz and Quiché all the way to Huehuetenango's Mexican border. It broke ground in November 2009.

WEST TO MEXICO
La Mesilla

Heading northwest from Huehuetenango, the Pan-American Highway leads to La Mesilla border and, beyond that, Mexico. Border formalities here are pretty straightforward, though the Mexican border crossing lies four kilometers away on the other side at Ciudad Cuauhtémoc, for which you'll need to take a collective taxi ($1) if you're not in your own car. There are basic services here, including banks, a post office, police station, and ubiquitous money changers. If you get stuck here, head to **Hotel Mily's** (500 meters uphill from the border, $15 d), with fan-cooled rooms, cable TV, and private hot-water bathroom. Another alternative is **Hotel y Restaurante Maricruz** (about 200 meters from the border, tel. 7685-0532, $10 d), also with private bathrooms.

Nentón to Gracias a Dios

A few kilometers east of La Mesilla along the Pan-American Highway, a turnoff branches north down a newly paved road to the town of Nentón and continues to a new border crossing at Gracias a Dios. Border formalities at Gracias a Dios are fairly straightforward and the friendly immigration agents might grant you a day pass to cross into Mexico to see the spectacular **Lagunas de Montebello**, a national park with pristine emerald lagoons surrounded by luxuriant forests.

Along the road from Nentón to Gracias a Dios, you could stop to admire **El Cimarrón,** a cavernous, 300-meter-deep limestone sinkhole harboring a forest at its base that has only recently been descended and explored. From the main road about three kilometers from the village of **La Trinidad,** 35 kilometers north of Nentón, a network of trails leads through surrounding farmland and cattle pastures to the sinkhole. It's about a 30-minute walk from the road.

From La Trinidad, a dirt road leads east to the village of **Yalambojoch,** where you can grab a pickup heading east to San Mateo Ixtatán. It also serves as the transit point for visits to the wonderful **Laguna Yolnabaj,** also known as Laguna Brava, five kilometers north of here. There are many returned refugees from Mexico living in these parts and you should be aware that the activities of foreign mining companies here and in other parts of northern Huehuetenango have locals a bit on edge. Exercise due caution. Better yet, go with a guide.

With help from local outfitter Unicornio Azul, the local community of Chaculá began hosting visits to the aforementioned attractions in 2009 as part of a community tourism program. Visitors stay at **Posada Finca Chaculá** (tel. 5205-9328, posadaruralfincachacula@hotmail.com, $40 d), a revamped old farmhouse where there are basic but clean, comfortable accommodations. The posada runs trips to El Cimarron and other nearby attractions, including Laguna Yolnabaj and the pristine Río Azul, which is a dazzlingly exotic hue of blue, as its name implies.

Quetzaltenango (Xela) and Vicinity

Head southeast from Huehuetenango on the Pan-American Highway, some 80 kilometers toward Guatemala City, to the highland city of Quetzaltenango. The country's second-largest city is the main population center of the country's K'iche' Mayans and an increasingly popular destination with language school students and NGO workers. Its original K'iche' name is Xelajú, still widely in use today, though in its abbreviated form, Xela. Set in a sprawling valley dominated by the near-perfect cone of 3,772-meter (12,375-foot) Santa María Volcano and the adjacent (active) Santiaguito, the city has a population of about 300,000. It sits at a rather high altitude of 2,400 meters (8,000 feet) and can be correspondingly chilly.

Xela is very cosmopolitan and has all the feel of a European highland city. It is considerably safe for a city of its size and has a lively cultural scene peppered by the presence of an ever-increasing number of foreign visitors. There are also good hotels and restaurants, along with interesting day trips to neighboring highland Mayan villages that still adhere strictly to the old ways. Nearby natural attractions include a wonderful crater lake, climbs to the surrounding volcanoes, and soaking in warm hot springs. If you really start to long for the warmer climates, the sweltering Pacific Coastal lowlands are just about an hour away and beaches lie not much farther.

History

Quetzaltenango was originally a Mam-speaking Mayan town before coming under the influence of the K'iche'-speaking Mayans of K'umarcaaj during their 14th-century expansionist wars. K'iche' leader Tecún Umán was defeated by Spanish conquistador Pedro de Alvarado in 1524 at a site known as Llano del Pinal, southwest of town at the base of Santa María Volcano. The town became quite prosperous during the 19th-century coffee boom. Its newfound prosperity, coupled with the abatement of Spanish power in the aftermath of independence, contributed to strong separatist sentiments shared with highland areas to the west. Guatemala City would bring the renegade region back into the fold in the latter part of the century, though Quetzaltenango remains a strong focal point for regional identity.

Like other Guatemalan population centers, it is no stranger to earthquakes, having been rocked by an earthquake and a volcanic eruption courtesy of Santa María Volcano in 1902. It was subsequently rebuilt, largely in neoclassical style. Its strategic location at a crossroads for trade and transport between the highlands and agriculturally rich Pacific slope have continued to ensure the city's prosperity despite any setbacks along the way. A regional railway once connected Xela to the Pacific slope, but natural disasters and political manipulation from Guatemala City made the railway, known as the Ferrocarril de los Altos, extremely short-lived.

Orientation

Quetzaltenango lies a few kilometers south of the Cuatro Caminos Junction, found along the Pan-American Highway. Its Zona 1 downtown core houses most of its important monuments, as well as the bulk of its tourist services, and is laid out in the standard grid pattern. Avenidas run roughly north-south and calles run east-west. Zona 2 covers an area to the northeast, while Zona 3 sprawls to the north and northwest. You'll find the city's bus station at this end of town.

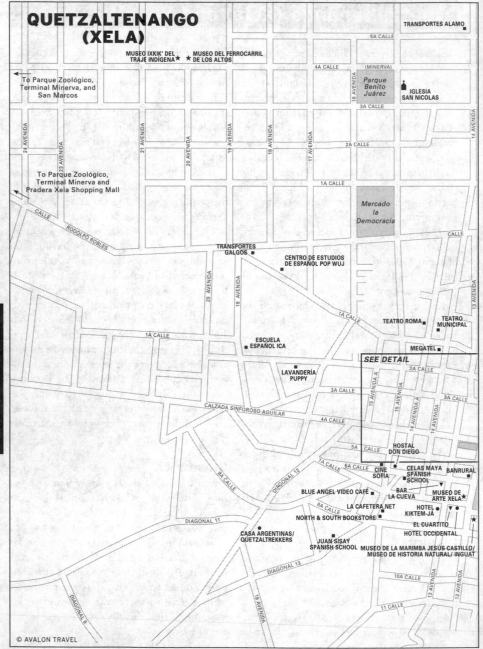

QUETZALTENANGO (XELA)

TRANSPORTES ALAMO ■

5A CALLE

MUSEO IXKIK' DEL ★ ★ MUSEO DEL FERROCARRIL
TRAJE INDÍGENA   DE LOS ALTOS

4A CALLE

(MINERVA)

Parque
Benito
Juárez   ✝ IGLESIA
                SAN NICOLAS

To Parque Zoológico,
Terminal Minerva, and
San Marcos

3A CALLE

2A CALLE

To Parque Zoológico,
Terminal Minerva and
Pradera Xela Shopping Mall

1A CALLE

CALLE
RODOLFO ROBLES

Mercado
la
Democracia

CALLE

TRANSPORTES
GALGOS ■

CENTRO DE ESTUDIOS
DE ESPAÑOL POP WUJ
■

TEATRO ROMA ■   TEATRO
                 MUNICIPAL ■

1A CALLE

ESCUELA
ESPAÑOL ICA ■

MEGATEL ■

SEE DETAIL

2A CALLE

LAVANDERÍA
PUPPY ■

3A CALLE

3A CALLE

CALZADA SINFOROSO AGUILAR

4A CALLE

HOSTAL
DON DIEGO ■

5A CALLE

7A CALLE   6A CALLE CINE
                     SOFÍA ■   CELAS MAYA
                                SPANISH ■   BANRURAL
                                SCHOOL

8A CALLE

DIAGONAL 12

BLUE ANGEL VIDEO CAFÉ ■

BAR
LA CUEVA ■   MUSEO DE
              ARTE XELA ★

LA CAFETERA.NET ■

HOTEL ●
KIKTEM-JÁ

8A CALLE

NORTH & SOUTH BOOKSTORE ■

DIAGONAL 11

EL CUARTITO

HOTEL OCCIDENTAL

CASA ARGENTINAS/
QUETZALTREKKERS ■

JUAN SISAY
SPANISH SCHOOL ■   MUSEO DE LA MARIMBA JESÚS CASTILLO/
                    MUSEO DE HISTORIA NATURAL/ INGUAT

DIAGONAL 13

10A CALLE

19 AVENIDA

DIAGONAL 8

11 CALLE

© AVALON TRAVEL

THE WESTERN HIGHLANDS

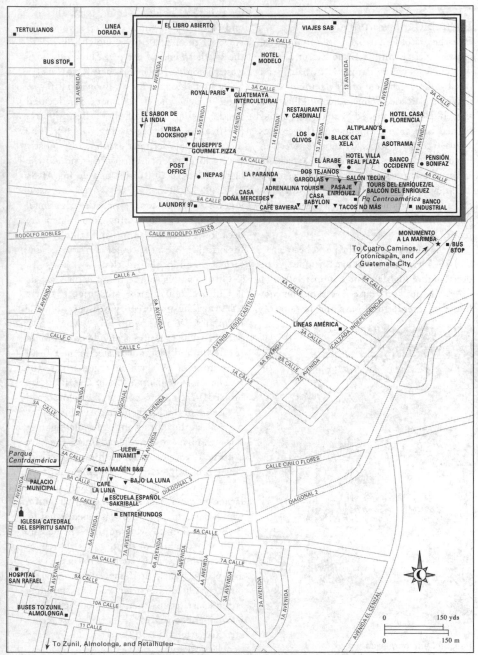

TERTULIANOS

LINEA DORADA

BUS STOP

13 AVENIDA

RODOLFO ROBLES

CALLE RODOLFO ROBLES

CALLE A

12 AVENIDA

10 AVENIDA

CALLE C

CALLE C

8A AVENIDA

AVENIDA JESUS CASTILLO

4A CALLE

5A CALLE

MONUMENTO A LA MARIMBA

BUS STOP

To Cuatro Caminos, Totonicapán, and Guatemala City

LÍNEAS AMÉRICA

3A CALLE

6A AVENIDA

7A AVENIDA

3A CALLE

1A CALLE

CALZADA INDEPENDENCIA

3A CALLE

DIAGONAL 4

7A AVENIDA

3A AVENIDA

CALLE CIRILO FLORES

3A CALLE

ULEW TINAMIT

CASA MAÑEN B&B

CAFÉ LA LUNA

BAJO LA LUNA

ESCUELA ESPAÑOL SAKRIBALL

DIAGONAL 3

DIAGONAL 2

ENTREMUNDOS

8A CALLE

8A CALLE

7A CALLE

Parque Centroamérica

3A CALLE

4A CALLE

11 AVENIDA

PALACIO MUNICIPAL

5A CALLE

6A CALLE

8A AVENIDA

6A AVENIDA

5A AVENIDA

4A AVENIDA

3A AVENIDA

2A AVENIDA

1A AVENIDA

IGLESIA CATEDRAL DEL ESPÍRITU SANTO

HOSPITAL SAN RAFAEL

9A AVENIDA

9A CALLE

10A CALLE

BUSES TO ZUNIL, ALMOLONGA

11 CALLE

↓ To Zunil, Almolonga, and Retalhuleu

AVENIDA EL CENZAL

0   150 yds
0   150 m

EL LIBRO ABIERTO

VIAJES SAB

2A CALLE

HOTEL MODELO

15 AVENIDA A

15 AVENIDA

ROYAL PARIS

GUATEMAYA INTERCULTURAL

3A CALLE

13 AVENIDA

2A AVENIDA

3A CALLE

EL SABOR DE LA INDIA

VRISA BOOKSHOP

GIUSEPPI'S GOURMET PIZZA

14 AVENIDA A

14 AVENIDA

RESTAURANTE CARDINALI

LOS OLIVOS

BLACK CAT XELA

13 AVENIDA

ALTIPLANO'S

HOTEL CASA FLORENCIA

11 AVENIDA

3A CALLE

ASOTRAMA

4A CALLE

POST OFFICE

INEPAS

LA PARANDA

EL ÁRABE

DOS TEJANOS

GARGOLAS

HOTEL VILLA REAL PLAZA

SALÓN TECÚN

PENSIÓN BONIFAZ

BANCO OCCIDENTE

4A CALLE

CASA DOÑA MERCEDES

ADRENALINA TOURS

PASAJE ENRÍQUEZ

TOURS DEL ENRÍQUEZ/EL BALCÓN DEL ENRÍQUEZ

5A CALLE

LAUNDRY 97

CAFÉ BAVIERA

CASA BABYLON

TACOS NO MÁS

Pq Centroamérica

BANCO INDUSTRIAL

SIGHTS
Parque Centroamérica

Like the rest of Guatemala's important urban centers, Xela is built around a central park. The city's sprawling Parque Centroamérica is lined with government offices, museums, and a shopping arcade, among other buildings, and is itself splendidly shaded by trees and adorned by neoclassical monuments and flower beds. It gives the city a decidedly European feel, enhanced by the presence of several Greek columns, and is a fine place for people-watching or enjoying the warm afternoon sun amid the surrounding buzz of activity. An artisans' market is held here the first Sunday of every month.

At the western end of the park, between 12 and 13 Avenidas, is **Pasaje Enríquez,** a pedestrian thoroughfare and commercial arcade originally built to house fine shops but now home to several good bars and restaurants.

One of these, Salón Tecún, is on the second floor, from which there are wonderful views of the plaza below. Downhill toward the southern end of the plaza but still on its western borders is the **Museo de Arte Xela** (7a Calle 12-12 Zona 1, 8 A.M.-noon and 2-6 P.M. Mon.-Fri., 9 A.M.-1 P.M. Sat., $1), located on the second floor of the Taller de Artes Plásticas, a building dating to 1909. The focus is on modern art exhibited by mostly young local talent. Also on this side of the park is **Centro Cultural Casa de los Altos** (6a Calle 12-32 Zona 1, tel. 7765-2226, casalosaltos@hotmail.com), where there is a small gift shop, café, and reading room. There are occasional poetry readings and talks by local historical figures; the center also provides information on local attractions.

On the park's southern end is the Casa de la Cultura, housing the **Museo de Historia Natural** (Natural History Museum, 8 A.M.-noon and 2-6 P.M. Mon.-Fri., 9 A.M.-1 P.M. Sat., $1). The museum is an odd collection of taxidermy and rooms dedicated to the Liberal Revolution of 1871 which, together with the **Museo de la Marimba Jesús Castillo** (also housed here), were collectively christened "Museum of the Kitchen Sink" by this guide's previous author for its antique dealer's garage sale feel. I have to concur, and unless you have a rainy afternoon with nothing else to do, you're probably better off skipping this one.

On the eastern end of the park is the original facade of **Iglesia Catedral del Espíritu Santo,** which dates to 1535 and was constructed by Bishop Francisco Marroquín. The facade is all that remains of the original church, as a new church was erected behind it in 1899 and was very heavily damaged in the earthquake of 1902. The current cathedral building is the latest reconstruction. The neighboring **Municipalidad** (City Hall) was likewise reconstructed after the 1902 earthquake in grand neoclassical style.

© AL ARGUETA

Parque Centroamérica

Outside the City Center (Zona 3)

The legacy of maniacal dictator Manuel Estrada Cabrera's quest to emulate all things European, the neoclassical **Templo Minerva** is a monument to the Greek goddess of wisdom. It stands at the corner of Calle Minerva and Calle Rodolfo Robles. The temple looks over the city's bus terminal and busy market. Farther along, in Parque Minerva proper, is the **Parque Zoológico Minerva** (9 A.M.-5 P.M. Tues.-Sun., free), where there's an unimpressive collection of animals housed in cages. Buses to this part of town leave from Pasaje Enríquez at 13 Avenida and 4a Calle Zona 1.

Formerly the Zona Militar 1715, the old building that once served as the train terminal for the defunct Ferrocarril de los Altos was slated to be the new home of the museum dedicated to its memory. The Museo del Ferrocarril de los Altos should be pretty spectacular, if a similar museum in Guatemala City is any indicator. (It's now known as the Centro de Desarrollo Intercultural y Deportivo de Quetzaltenango, and there are plans for several other museums to open here in the coming years.) The museum will be dedicated to the early 20th-century railroad that briefly connected Xela to the coastal town of Retalhuleu. Already housed in this complex is the **Museo Ixkik' del Traje Indígena** (4a Calle and 19 Avenida Zona 3, tel. 7761-6472, 9 A.M.-noon and 2-6 P.M. Mon.-Fri., $1), housing a collection of indigenous costumes.

ENTERTAINMENT

Bars

Beer drinkers will want to try Cabro, an excellent local brew sold widely in Xela. As for watering holes, the ever-popular **Salón Tecún** (Pasaje Enríquez, on the west side of Parque Centroamérica, tel. 7761-2832) is one of Xela's main gathering spots, with a great location, lively atmosphere, and funky decor. There's also outdoor seating fronting the attractive

Pasaje Enríquez

© AL ARGUETA

Pasaje Enríquez pedestrian thoroughfare. You can wash down your drink with menu items that include pizzas, pastas, vegetarian, and Thai dishes.

Gargolas (4a Calle 12-49 Zona 1, Pasaje Enriquez, 5 P.M.-1 A.M. daily) has a hip atmosphere and plays good music. You can drink at the bar or step into the stylish lounge areas to enjoy your evening under baroque, cathedral-like columns. A chill coffee bar also serving wine and cocktails is **La Pequeña Fonda** (15 Avenida 7-43 Zona 1, 3 P.M.-10 P.M. daily). There's live music some nights. The bar inside **Pensión Bonifaz** (4a Calle 10-50 Zona 1, tel. 7765-1111) is the place to go for high-brow socializing.

Nightlife

The town's local nightlife hotspots seem to change constantly, so you might be better off asking around. The city's so-called Zona Viva is centered between 12 and 15 Avenidas from 1a to 6a Calle in Zona 1. A walk around this part of town will surely yield some fun bar-hopping results. That said, **La Parranda** (14 Avenida 4-41 Zona 1, www.laparrandadisco.com, 8 P.M.-1 A.M. Wed.-Sat.) is a solid choice for dancing. For salsa and merengue dancing, check out **La Rumba** (at the corner of 13 Avenida and 7a Calle Zona 1, 6 P.M.-1 A.M. Mon.-Sat.).

Performing Arts

There are sometimes cultural performances at the elegant **Teatro Municipal** (1a Calle between 14 Avenida and 14 Avenida "A"), which dates from 1908.

Cinema

Blue Angel Video Café (7a Calle 15-79 Zona 1, 1-11 P.M. Mon.-Sat., 3-10 P.M. Sun.) shows movies at 8 P.M. nightly and serves vegetarian fare and smoothies. For the latest releases, head to **Cines Pradera Xela** (Avenida Las Américas y 7a Calle Zona 3, www.circuitoalba.com.gt, $4) inside its namesake shopping mall.

SHOPPING

Compared to Panajachel and Antigua, Xela is not a big shopping destination. A standout in this regard is **Asotrama** (12 Avenida 3-39 Zona 1, tel. 7765-8564), a women's cooperative of Mam, Cakchiquel, Ixil, Tzutuhil, and Quiché weavers that produces and sells high-quality products that are prewashed, preshrunk, and completely colorfast. There are scarves, purses, table runners, and some truly exquisite pillowcases for sale. For all your First World shopping needs, **Pradera Xela Shopping Mall** (10 A.M.-9 P.M. Mon.-Sat., 11 A.M.-8 P.M. Sun.) is on Avenida Las Américas between 7a and 8a Calles Zona 3, outside the city center.

Books

North and South Bookstore (8a Calle and 15 Avenida 13-77 Zona 1, tel. 7761-0589, 9:30 A.M.-6 P.M. Mon.-Fri., 9:30 A.M.-5 P.M.

Sat.) sells a good selection of books in English with subjects including Guatemalan politics and history, travel guides, birding manuals, maps, Spanish textbooks, and dictionaries. **Vrisa Bookshop** (15 Avenida 3-64 Zona 1, tel. 7761-3237, 9 A.M.-7 P.M. Mon.-Sat.) sells mostly used books with some new titles, mostly in English. **El Libro Abierto** (15 Avenida "A" 1-56 Zona 1, tel. 7761-5195, 9:30 A.M.-5:30 P.M. Mon.-Fri., 11 A.M.-5 P.M. Sat.) has a wide selection of books in English and Spanish.

RECREATION
Volcano Climbs

Accessible from Xela are a variety of volcano hikes, including **Tajumulco Volcano,** which is Central America's highest volcano, in the neighboring department of San Marcos. Closer to Xela is **Santa María Volcano,** affording excellent views all the way to Lake Atitlán as well as over its active, much smaller neighbor **Santiaguito Volcano.**

It is very easy to get lost on these peaks so a guide is strongly recommended. (Hikers have gotten lost on the slopes of Volcán Santa María.) Several local companies offer trips. Highly recommended for volcano climbs as well as excellent tours to area attractions is **Adrenalina Tours** (13 Avenida and 4a Calle Zona 1, Pasaje Enríquez, tel. 7761-4509 or 7767-2474, www. adrenalinatours.com). Trips leave with a minimum of four people and include Santa María Volcano ($20 p/p), Chicabal Lagoon ($20), the Santiaguito Volcano lookout ($20), Tajumulco Volcano ($43), and a rockin' three-day hike to Lake Atitlán ($67). Adrenalina Tours can also book plane tickets and Tikal tours. The company operates shuttle bus service to Antigua, Guatemala City, Panajachel, the Mexican border, and Chichicastenango.

Monte Verde Tours (13 Avenida 8-34 Zona 1, tel. 7761-6105, www.monte-verdetours. com) offers guided hikes to all of the Xela area volcanoes as well as to Laguna Chicabal and multi-day treks from Xela to Lake Atitlan ($75). Further afield, they run treks from Nebaj to Todos Santos Cuchumatan (4 days, $120).

With excellent guides and proceeds that go directly to fund projects that benefit Xela's street children, **Quetzaltrekkers** (Diagonal 12 8-37 Zona 1, inside Casa Argentinas, tel. 7765-5895, www.quetzaltrekkers.com) is highly recommended for its two-day volcano trips to Santiaguito and Tajumulco ($50), three-day treks to Lake Atitlán ($79), and a wonderful six-day highland trek between the villages of Nebaj and Todos Santos ($150). It also does a unique full-moon climb to Santa María Volcano to watch the sunrise ($17). Most trips leave on Saturdays and every other Wednesday depending on demand, but you can always get your own group together.

Other reliable options include **Altiplano's** (12 Avenida 3-35 Zona 1, tel. 7766-9614, www.altiplanos.com.gt) and **Icaro Tours** (15 Avenida 6-75 Zona 1, tel. 7765-8205, www.icarotours.com). Upcoming trips are prominently displayed on their websites, taking some of the legwork out of trying to get a group together if you are traveling alone.

Rock Climbing

The **Cerro Quemado**, near Xela, offers good rock climbing on its 45-meter (150-foot) rock faces known locally as "La Muela." Routes include traditional climbs as well as sport climbing and are rated 5.07 to 5.13. **Vertical Expeditions** (tel. 5801-6871, www.verticalguatemala.com) offers one and two days of climbing with a minimum of four people for $75 and $80, including transport from Guatemala City or Antigua, guide, gear, meals, and overnight camping on the latter option. Antigua-based **Old Town Outfitters** (5a Avenida Sur #12C, Antigua, tel. 5339-0440, www.bikeguatemala.com) does a two-day trip for $150, leaving from Antigua and staying overnight in a Xela hotel. Locally based **Quetzaltrekkers** (Diagonal 12 8-37 Zona 1, inside Casa Argentinas, tel. 7765-5895, www.quetzaltrekkers.com) does a day trip for $20 p/p (minimum of four) including gear, transport, food, water, and guides.

ACCOMMODATIONS
Under $10

An excellent choice for budget travelers, **Hostal Don Diego** (6a Calle 15-12 Zona 1, tel. 5308-3616 and 5308-1489, www.hostaldondiegoxela.com, $6.50 dorm, $12 d) has clean rooms and a choice of twin- or queen size-beds in private rooms, some with wood paneling. Xela now has its own version of the wildly popular Antigua equivalent, **Black Cat Xela** (13 Avenida 3-33 Zona 1, tel. 7761-2091, www.blackcathostels.net, $6 p/p dorm or $16 d private room). The comfortable rooms are centered round a two-story courtyard. **Hotel Quetzalteco** (12 Avenida, one block north of Parque Centroamérica, tel. 7765-8461, $9-13 d) is a decent-value hotel in an old colonial home where the 20 basic rooms have desks and reading lamps along with shared or private bathroom. The rooms upstairs are slightly nicer and there's a squawking parrot on the premises to keep you company.

Casa Argentina's (Diagonal 12 8-37 Zona 1, tel. 7761-2470, $3 in dorms, $4 p/p shared-bath room to $10 d with private bath) is a solid budget choice with 27 clean rooms. Some have cable TV and there are always tea, coffee, and purified water available. Guests have use of the kitchen. It's run by the very friendly and hospitable Leonor Morales and her charming mother. Quetzaltrekkers is housed here.

$10-25

◖ **Casa Doña Mercedes** (6a Calle and 14 Avenida 13-42 Zona 1, tel. 7765-4687, www.hostalcasadonamercedes.com, $25 d) has excellent-value rooms with tile floors, wood ceilings, Guatemalan bedspreads gracing the firm beds, and spotless shared bathroom. Another good choice is **Hotel Kiktem-Ja** (13 Avenida 7-18 Zona 1, tel. 7761-4304, $21 d), housed in an

CLIMBING SANTA MARÍA VOLCANO

© AL ARGUETA

Santa María Volcano

Santa María is one of the most popular volcano climbs from Xela, with spectacular views from its 3,772-meter summit. The trailhead is at the end of a paved road in the village of Llanos del Pinal. To get there, take one of the hourly pickups leaving from Xela's Cementerio General (General Cemetery) at 20 Avenida and 4a Calle 7 A.M.-5 P.M. Heading out of Llanos del Pinal, the road soon turns into a trail up the steep volcanic slopes, with painted arrows leading the way along this initial section of the footpath. About two hours from the starting point, you reach a flat grassy area known as "La Mesa," where the trail diverts to the right and then switchbacks up the mountainside through pine forests. This part of the climb is somewhat steeper, with the summit about three hours from this point. A few hundred meters from the summit, you'll see the end of the tree line and the summit itself, providing a much-needed mental boost for the end of your climb.

The best time to arrive at the summit is at sunrise, affording opportunities to take in the magnificent views before clouds start to roll in. From there, you can look southwest into the smoking crater of 2,500-meter Santiaguito Volcano, which has been belching out smoke and ash since its birth in 1902. To the east you'll see the cones of San Pedro, Tolimán, Atitlán, Acatenango, Agua, and Fuego. If you look west, you'll see the two highest volcanoes in Central America, Tajumulco and Tacaná, on the Mexican border.

Santa María's last major eruption took place October 24-25, 1902, when it coughed up 10 cubic kilometers of ash into the stratosphere, covering much of the Pacific Coast and destroying a large section of the volcano's south face. Ash from the eruption is reported to have reached as far north as California.

The safety situation on the volcanoes in Xela's vicinity is markedly better than on those around Lake Atitlán, though robberies are by no means unheard of. It's best to go with a guide. **Quetzaltrekkers** (www.quetzaltrekkers.com) runs a fantastic once-a-month overnight trip up the slopes of Santa María in the light of the full moon, arriving on the summit just in time for sunrise. If peering into the summit of smoking Santiaguito has you itching for more volcanic adventures, you'll be happy to know it also runs trips to the challenging, ashy slopes of this smaller active volcano.

old colonial building with wooden floors and a plant-filled courtyard. Some rooms have chimneys and desks; all have reading lamps, hotwater bathroom, and cable TV. Conveniently situated near Parque Centroamérica, **Hotel Occidental** (7a Calle 12-23 Zona 1, tel. 7765-4069, $20 d) has 10 spartanly decorated rooms with cable TV and private hot-water bathroom. Newcomer **GuateFriends Xela B&B** (42 Avenida 1A-08 Zona 8, Residenciales Luisa Fernanda; tel. 5308-3275, guatefriendsxela@ yahoo.com, $25 d) is a spinoff of successful hotels in Guatemala City and Coban. Its comfortable rooms are well-appointed and nicely decorated. An in-house chef prepares gourmet meals served in a pleasant dining room. There's also a nice sitting area with a warm fireplace. It's like staying with family.

$25-50

Los Olivos (13 Avenida 3-32 Zona 1, tel. 7761-0215 or 7765-3469, $27 d) is a good choice if you're traveling with a rental car, thanks to a large covered parking lot. All rooms have private hot-water bathroom and cable TV housed around a covered opaque-ceiling courtyard. Basic meals are also available and the owners are quite friendly. **(Hotel Modelo** (14 Avenida "A" 2-31 Zona 1, tel. 7761-2529, http://hotelmodelo1892.com, $40 d) is a well-situated, excellent-value hotel in an old colonial home run by a friendly Guatemalan family. The nicest rooms are in a section fronting the street and opening to a pleasant garden courtyard. All have private bathroom, hardwood floors and ceilings, cable TV, charming antique furniture, warm wool blankets to ward off the chill, and pleasantly hot showers. There's free Wi-Fi and the restaurant here serves good breakfasts. **Hotel Villa Real Plaza** (4a Calle 12-22 Zona 1, tel. 7761-4045, $43 d) is housed in a 19th-century building that once served as a prison. Some of the rooms tend to feel a little bit dark,

but that's a common thing in Xela's older constructions. All have private bath, cable TV, and closets. Some have a chimney. The lobby has a nice restaurant set in a courtyard under an opaque roof. There are rooms in a newer section with somewhat bland decor that tend to get loud thanks to the presence of the hotel's conference center in this part of the lodge. **Hotel Casa Florencia** (12 Avenida 3-61 Zona 1, tel. 7761-2326, $32 d) has nice, carpeted rooms with private bath, cable TV, wood paneling, tungsten reading lights, and nice extras such as shampoo and soap. The friendly innkeeper, Celeste, keeps it spotless.

$50-100

A gorgeous flower garden and rock waterfall set the mood as you enter Xela's most wonderfully atmospheric hotel, **(Casa Mañen B&B** (9a Avenida 4-11 Zona 1, tel. 7765-0786, www.comeseeit.com, $50-100 d), with nine tastefully decorated rooms featuring exquisite furnishings, wool blankets and throw rugs, terra-cotta floors, cable TV, and private bathroom. There's a rooftop terrace bar with wonderful city views. The delicious breakfast is served in a pleasant dining room looking out to the peaceful garden courtyard.

The haunt of Guatemala's oligarchy on visits to Xela, **(Pensión Bonifaz** (4a Calle 10-50 Zona 1, tel. 7723-1100, www.pensionbonifaz.com.gt, $65-100 d) is a beautiful hotel, though it tends to feel stuffy thanks to the pretentious front desk staff. It has spacious, well-decorated rooms with private bathrooms, desks, and cable TV. There are a restaurant, small gift shop, and a heated swimming pool in a pretty garden courtyard under an opaque ceiling letting in just enough sunlight. There's wireless Internet on the first floor and the rooms just above it (numbers 123-130) get a signal. More modern rooms are housed in a newer section, but those in the original building harbor all the charm.

Outside of Town

If you have your own car and find it more convenient to stay outside of town near the Cuatro Caminos Junction, your best bet is **Hotel del Campo** (Km. 224 Carretera a Cantel, tel. 7763-1665, www.hoteldelcampo.com.gt, $45 d), with cozy rooms equipped with hot-water private bathroom and cable TV. There's a business center with Internet, a pleasant dining room lined with overhanging ferns, and a heated, covered swimming pool. On the road leading out to Olintepeque, **Anna Inn** (Kilometro 3.5 Carretera a Olintepeque, tel. 7763-9280, www.annainnhotel.com, $100 d including breakfast) a pricier option that nonetheless feels a lot like a fancy U.S. chain hotel. Its comfortable and spacious non-smoking rooms feel brand new and include nice extras like reading lamps and cable TV. The lobby and public areas have nice wooden accents that add to the tasteful decor. There's a lobby restaurant and plenty of free parking.

FOOD
Cafés and Light Meals

⬛Café Baviera (5a Calle 13-14, tel. 7761-5018, 7 A.M.-8:30 P.M. daily, $3-5) has a decidedly German atmosphere chock-full of antiques where you can enjoy scrumptious pastries, sandwiches, crepes, and shakes in addition to some of the best coffee in town. **Café La Luna** (8a Avenida 4-11 Zona 1, tel. 7761-2242, 9:30 A.M.-9 P.M. Mon.-Fri., 4-9 P.M. Sat.-Sun.) is wonderfully decorated with an eclectic mix of antiques, including old signs, gas lamps, cash registers, and even pre-Columbian artifacts. Menu options include great coffee, snacks, and desserts and there are daily specials of various Guatemalan dishes, including delicious enchiladas on Sundays. Try the scrumptious chocolate cake.

Around the corner and under the same ownership is **Bajo La Luna** (tel. 7761-2242, 8 P.M.-midnight Tues.-Fri.), a cozy wine cellar with a charming Old World feel where there's a good mix of bottled wines ranging in price $9-50.

There are also various cheeses on offer. With wonderful views of Parque Centroamérica from its second-floor terrace, **El Balcón del Enríquez** (12 Avenida 4-40 Zona 1, tel. 7765-2296, all meals daily) is a good place to start the day or wind it up with a cup of coffee or cocktail while people-watching over the plaza below. There are good sandwiches, breakfasts, and pastries. For a quaint coffee-bar atmosphere, check out **El Cuartito** (13 Avenida 7-09 Zona 1, 11 A.M.-11 P.M. Wed.-Mon.), serving organically grown fair trade coffee, tea, and chocolate beverages in addition to tempting cookies and baked goods. There are books and board games to keep you entertained, free Wi-Fi and live music some nights.

Mediterranean

Your mouth will water as soon as you set foot inside **⬛ Casa Babylon** (corner of 5a Calle and 13 Avenida, tel. 7761-2320, 11:30 A.M.-11 P.M. daily); its ground-floor kitchen exudes the aroma of delicious meals being prepared. On offer are a variety of cocktails, a decent wine list, and nonalcoholic beverages, including fresh-fruit smoothies. Menu items include falafel, salads, tacos, quesadillas, burgers, pita pizzas, pastas, and vegetarian dishes. There are two more floors, including a nice third-floor lounge; you should call ahead and reserve on weekends, as it tends to get busy during dinner hours. **El Árabe** (4a Calle 12-22 Zona 1, tel. 7761-7889, noon-midnight daily, $4-10) serves delicious Middle Eastern fare, including fresh hummus and tasty falafel. It's conveniently situated just off the plaza and can also be a lively place at night.

Indian

Still going strong thanks to its Indian chef, **⬛Sabor de la India** (15 Avenida, off 4a Calle, 3-64 Zona 1, tel. 7765-2555, 12 P.M.-10 P.M. Tues.-Sun., $3-10) serves delicious vegetarian and non-vegetarian Indian dishes in generous portions.

Cuban

The rather simple **Cubatenango** (19 Avenida 2-06 Zona 1, tel. 5508-3348, 8:30 A.M.-9:30 P.M. Mon.-Sat.) features some tasty fare including such Cuban stand-bys as *ropa vieja* (shredded beef) and Cuban sandwiches. I also like their mojitos.

Tex-Mex

Xela boasts an excellent Tex-Mex restaurant in **Dos Tejanos** (4a Calle 12-33, Pasaje Enríquez, 7 A.M.-11 P.M. daily), where you can dig into authentic Texas barbecue ribs, chicken, and brisket.

Italian

For authentic Italian food in a wonderful Old World family atmosphere, head to **Restaurante Cardinali** (14 Avenida 3-25 Zona 1, tel. 7761-0922, 11:30 A.M.-10 P.M. daily). There's a large wine selection and various entrées in the $9 range. **Giuseppe's Gourmet Pizza** (15 Avenida 3-68 Zona 1, Edificio Santa Rita Segundo Nivel, tel. 7761-2521 or 7761-9439, 11 A.M.-9:30 P.M.) has fairly decent hand-tossed pizza and pastas.

Fine Dining

The dining room at the upscale **Pensión Bonifaz** (4a Calle 10-50 Zona 1, tel. 7765-1111, all meals daily) is a good place for a splurge with a variety of Guatemalan and international dishes served in a classy atmosphere frequented by the city's elite. **Royal Paris** (14 Avenida "A" 3-06 Zona 1, tel. 7761-1942, noon-11 P.M. Tues.-Sun., 6-11 P.M. Mon., $5-15) is a very popular, highly authentic French bistro with dishes that include crepes, baked camembert, and onion soup, as well as meat, chicken, fish, and pasta that you can enjoy accompanied by excellent wines. There's live music on Friday and Saturday nights and French or Italian movies are shown on Tuesdays at 8 P.M. Housed in a charming century-old mansion, **Tertulianos** (14 Avenida 5-26 Zona 3, tel. 7767-4202, www.restaurantetertulianos.com) serves a varied menu that includes meats, seafood, pasta and various types of fondue. Its quaint wine cellar is best reserved for a romantic dinner.

INFORMATION AND SERVICES
Tourist Information

The INGUAT tourism information center (tel. 7761-4931, 9 A.M.-5 P.M. Mon.-Fri.) is on the southern end of Parque Centroamerica next to Casa de la Cultura, though you might have better luck getting information from local travel agencies such as Adrenalina Tours just a few steps away in Pasaje Enríquez.

Useful websites with some helpful information include www.xelapages.com, www.xelapages.net, www.xelawho.com, and Spanish-language www.xelaenlinea.com.

Communications

The main post office is at 4a Calle 15-07 Zona 1. Couriers include DHL (corner of 12 Avenida and 1a Calle Zona 1, tel. 7763-1209). Some travelers have complained of incorrect import duties for packages shipped to Guatemala via DHL.

There are dozens of places where you can access the Internet in Xela, with most places charging somewhere around $1.25 per hour. La Cafetera.net (corner of 15 Avenida and 8a Calle Zona 1, tel. 7761-0588, 8 A.M.-8 P.M. daily) is an Internet café next door to the North and South Bookstore serving snacks, coffee, sandwiches, and breakfasts. Online access costs about $0.85 an hour. Celas Maya (6a Calle 14-55 Zona 1, tel. 7761-4342, 8 A.M.-7:30 P.M. Mon.-Fri., 9 A.M.-7:30 P.M. Sat.) is a Spanish school with an Internet café charging about $0.85 an hour for online access. Infinito Internet (7a Calle 15-16 Zona 1) provides phone service to the United States for about $0.25 a minute, $0.40 per minute to Europe. Megatel (1a Calle 14-35 Zona 1, 8 A.M.-8 P.M. Mon.-Sat., 8 A.M.-6 P.M. Sun.) has slightly higher rates.

Money

There are several banks, some with ATMs, on Parque Centroamérica, including Banco de Occidente, on the north end of the park, where you can change cash dollars and travelers checks. Banco Industrial, on the east side of the plaza, has a Visa ATM, while Banrural, on its west side, has both a Visa and MasterCard ATM.

Laundry

Near the post office, at the corner of 5a Calle and 15 Avenida, Laundry 97 (tel. 7761-7923, 8 A.M.-8 P.M.) charges about $0.65 per kilo to wash and dry. Lavandería El Puente (7a Calle 13-29 Zona 1, 8 A.M.-6 P.M. Mon.-Sat.) charges $2 for a four-kilogram load, washed and dried. Lavandería Puppy (2a Calle 16-61 Zona 1, 7:30 A.M.-5:30 P.M. Mon.-Sat., 9:30 A.M.-3 P.M. Sun.) charges similar rates for laundry washed, dried, and folded.

Medical Services

Private hospitals include Hospital Privado Quetzaltenango (Calle Rodolfo Robles 25-31 Zona 3, tel. 7761-4381/82), Hospital La Democracia (13 Avenida 6-51 Zona 3, tel. 7763-6760/62), and Hospital San Rafael (9a Calle 10-41 Zona 1, tel. 7761-4414 or 7761-2956), with 24-hour emergency service.

Emergency

For the firefighters *(bomberos)*, dial 122 or 7761-2002. For the Red Cross (Cruz Roja), dial 125 or 7761-2746. The Policía Nacional Civil (National Civil Police) can be reached at 120, 110, 7765-4991, or 7765-4992. The number for the Municipal Police (Policía Municipal) is 7761-5805.

Travel Agencies

Viajes SAB (1a Calle 12-35 Zona 1, tel. 7761-6402) is a good all-around agency for plane tickets, tours to Tikal, and the like. Adrenalina Tours (13 Avenida and 4a Calle Zona 1, Pasaje Enríquez, tel. 7761-4509 or 7767-2474, www. adrenalinatours.com) is also recommended for these and other services. Guatemaya Intercultural (14 Avenida "A" 3-06 Zona 1, tel. 7765-0040) is a good place for youth and student airfares as well as general travel arrangements.

Language Schools

Xela has become increasingly popular as a place to learn Spanish, even rivaling Antigua, and the days when Xela hosted few foreigners are long gone. Still, it's a much larger city than any other in Guatemala, save the capital, and affords an opportunity for the foreign population to more easily blend into their surroundings, providing an adequate Spanish-language immersion experience. Schools in Xela were charging between $135 and $180 per week for 25 hours of instruction and room and board with a local host family. Xela also tends to attract a rather humane crowd and so there are plenty of operations that allow you to combine your language instruction with some time working with charitable organizations. The following schools are recommended for their consistently good marks on student evaluations. If you're a college student, you may be able to get college credit with several of these language schools. Ultimately, you'll have to check the schools out to see which one works best for you. This is just one of the many things to consider when visiting potential schools. Rates go up between June and August, when college students come down in droves. Useful websites for checking out schools include www.123teachme.com and www.guatemala365.com.

   Proyecto Lingüistico Quetzalteco de Español (5a Calle 2-40 Zona 1, tel. 7763-1061, www.hermandad.com) is an extremely popular school often booked months in advance. Students have the opportunity to volunteer with the school's Luis Cardoza y Aragon Popular Culture Center, next door, providing art, music, and computer skill instruction to underprivileged local children. There are also opportunities to work in reforestation projects and meet with human rights workers, former guerrilla combatants and union leaders. **Celas Maya** (tel. 7761-4342, www.celasmaya.edu. gt) is another fairly popular school and is set around a pleasant garden courtyard. There's an adjacent Internet café.

Run by a cooperative of experienced teachers who are very active in social projects, **Centro de Estudios de Español Pop Wuj** (1a Calle 17-72 Zona 1, tel. 7761-8286, www.pop-wuj.org) is another highly recommended school. **Escuela de Español Sakribal** (6a Calle 7-42 Zona 1, tel. 7763-0717, www.sakribal.com), a school founded and run by women, has a project benefiting civil war widows and orphans. **Inepas** (15 Avenida 4-59 Zona 1, tel. 7765-1308, www.inepas.org) combines quality language instruction with a widely recognized service-learning program.

In business for more than 30 years, **Escuela de Español ICA** (19 Avenida 1-47 Zona 1, tel. 7763-1871, www.guatemalaspanish.com) runs social welfare projects that include a medical clinic, adult literacy education, and reforestation. **Juan Sisay Spanish School** (15 Avenida 8-38 Zona 1, tel. 7765-1318 or 7761-1586, www.juansisay.com) is named after a self-taught indigenous *primitivista* painter who was massacred in his home village on the shores of Lake Atitlán in 1989. It's run by a teachers' collective involved in numerous social projects. **Ulew Tinimit** (7a Avenida 3-18 Zona 1, tel. 7761-6242, www.spanishguatemala.org) is a good setup, allowing plenty of one-on-one instruction time with your individual teacher. Also recommended is **Madre Tierra Spanish School** (13 Avenida 8-34, Zona 1, tel. 7761-6105 or 5296-1275, www.madre-tierra.org/english).

Volunteer Opportunities

There are several volunteer opportunities available in and around Xela, as there's plenty of work to be done in Guatemala's impoverished Western Highlands. Any of the town's language schools can help you get plugged in to volunteer projects. A particularly helpful organization for volunteer opportunities is EntreMundos (El Espacio, 6a Calle 7-31 Zona 1, tel. 5606-9070 or 7761-2179, www.entremundos.org), which publishes a widely available free publication (*EntreMundos*) and has several resources on its website, including a database with contact information and descriptions for more than 150 NGOs in Xela and vicinity.

GETTING THERE AND AROUND
Air

Xela's airport terminal was upgraded a few years back as part of a Guatemalan governmental plan to revamp several domestic airports. It's anyone's guess as to whether scheduled flights will ever get off the ground.

Bus

Xela is a transportation hub for many buses heading to and from highland destinations. Upon arriving in town, you can avoid ending up at the Minerva bus terminal, which is well outside the city center, by getting off at a stop at 7a Avenida and 7a Calle. You'll see a giant monument to the marimba with a Mayan woman atop it at a traffic circle on Avenida de la Independencia. Most buses stop here and you can grab a taxi or minibus to the city center. If you do end up at the terminal, you can grab a taxi or bus into town from the south side of 4a Calle. Look for the bus labeled "Parque." As elsewhere, Pullman, or first-class buses, leave from their own stations throughout town. Second-class bus routes include the following:

- **To Antigua:** Take any bus heading to Chimaltenango (including first-class buses to Guatemala City) and change buses there.
- **To Chichicastenango:** 10 daily buses, 2.5 hours, $1.50.

- **To Coatepeque:** Buses every 30 minutes, just under two hours, $1.25.
- **To Guatemala City:** Frequent buses from 3 A.M.-4:30 P.M., $5.
- **To Huehuetenango:** Buses every 30 minutes 5 A.M.-5:30 P.M., 1.5 hours, $1.
- **To La Mesilla (Mexican border):** Six daily buses, 3.5 hours, $2.
- **To Momostenango:** Every 30 minutes 6 A.M.-5 P.M., 1.25 hours, $0.60.
- **To Panajachel:** Buses at 5 A.M., 6 A.M., 8 A.M., 10 A.M., noon, and 3 P.M., 2.5 hours, $2.
- **To Retalhuleu:** Every 30 minutes 4:30 A.M.-6 P.M., one hour, $1. The bus will most likely read "Reu."
- **To San Pedro La Laguna (Lake Atitlán):** Six daily buses, 2.25 hours, $2.
- **To Tecún Umán (Mexican border):** Buses leave hourly 5 A.M.-2 P.M., 3.5 hours, $2.50.
- **To Totonicapán:** Buses every 30 minutes 6 A.M.-5 P.M., one hour, $0.50.
- **To Zunil:** Every 30 minutes 7 A.M.-7 P.M., 30 minutes, $0.35.

First-class bus lines with service to Guatemala City include the following: **Líneas Américas** (7a Avenida 3-33 Zona 2, tel. 7761-2063), with six daily buses; **Transportes Alamo** (14 Avenida 5-15 Zona 3, tel. 7761-7117), six daily buses; **Transportes Galgos** (21 Calle 0-14 Zona 1, tel. 7761-2248), seven daily; and the ultraluxe, nonstop service of **Línea Dorada** (12 Avenida and 5a Calle Zona 3, tel. 7767-5198 or 7761-4509), with departures at 4 A.M. and 2:30 P.M.

Shuttle Buses

There are also a number of companies running shuttle buses to destinations that include Guatemala City, Antigua, Panajachel, the Mexican border, Chichicastenango, and Huehuetenango. **Adrenalina Tours** (13 Avenida and 4a Calle Zona 1, Pasaje Enríquez, tel. 7761-4509 or 7767-2474, www.

adrenalinatours.com) is recommended for dependable shuttle-bus service, as is **Monte Verde Tours** (13 Avenida 8-34 Zona 1, tel. 7761-6105, www.monte-verdetours.com).

Car Rental

Adrenalina Tours (13 Avenida and 4a Calle Zona 1, Pasaje Enríquez, tel. 7761-4509 or 7767-2474, www.adrenalinatours.com) rents vehicles, as do **Tabarini** (9a Calle 9-21 Zona 1, tel. 7763-0418, www.tabarini.com) and **Tours El Enríquez** (Pasaje Enríquez, tel. 7765-2296).

Bike Rental

For bike rentals, head to **Vrisa Bookshop** (15 Avenida 3-64 Zona 1, tel. 7761-3237, 9 A.M.-7 P.M. Mon.-Sat., $6/14/27 for daily/weekly/monthly rentals). **Monte Verde Tours** (13a Avenida 8-34, Zona 1, tel. 7761 6105, www.monte-verdetours.com) rents bicycles for $10 a week and offers guided bike trips ($20) to San Andres Xecul, Zunil, and the Fuentes Georginas hot springs.

NEAR QUETZALTENANGO

The towns and villages surrounding Quetzaltenango make for some interesting day trips. Found nearby are the Santa María and Santiaguito Volcanoes, hot springs, Indian markets, colorful churches, and an exquisite crater lake.

Almolonga

Just five kilometers southeast of Xela is the pleasant town of Almolonga, which has become quite prosperous by commercializing its excellent and abundant vegetables grown in a fertile valley. It has a lively market on Tuesdays, Thursdays, and Saturdays, where you can see its rich produce selection, including the largest carrots you've ever laid eyes on and baseball-size radishes. The cultivated plots here, as in neighboring Zunil, are irrigated by canals from which farmers scoop out water with large shovel-like contraptions.

The town's yellow and blue church, **Iglesia de San Pedro,** dates to 1608 and is now more of a tourist attraction with 90 percent of the local populace claiming conversion to Evangelical Christianity. The town was hard-hit by tropical storms during 2011's rainy season. Its annual **Festival de San Pedro y San Pablo** takes place from June 27 to 29. Buses leave Xela's Minerva bus station every 15 minutes for Almolonga.

Just below the village, the road passes several hot springs known as **Los Baños** and popular with locals, though I can't bring myself to recommend them, as they are rather dilapidated and dirty, and there are better places to soak farther along the highway.

Zunil

A few kilometers farther along the same road is the spectacularly set town of Zunil. You'll see the white **Iglesia de Santa Catarina** gleaming from a distance as it towers above the tiled-and tin-roofed houses around it. Lovely mountains flank its surroundings. Zunil is one of a handful of towns in Guatemala where there is still strong adherence to the worship of the **Maximón** idol, as in Santiago Atitlán. The idol's location is rotated yearly, but it's easy to find out its whereabouts from any local resident, assuming the local children don't first intercept you and offer their guiding services for a small tip. It's known locally as San Simón and, unlike elsewhere, visitors here can actually pour liquor offerings down the effigy's throat. You'll probably be charged around $1 to see it, more if you want to take photographs.

Zunil's annual fiesta takes place on November 25.

Las Cumbres

About half a kilometer south of town is **❰ Las Cumbres** (tel. 5399-0029 or 5304-2102, http://lascumbres.com.gt, 7 A.M.-7 P.M. daily), a

superb establishment harboring steam baths, beautiful accommodations housed in quaint red-tiled-roof cottages with mountain views, and a restaurant (all meals daily) serving mostly Guatemalan dishes but also sandwiches and wine. Its 11 rooms range $33-47 d and have nice wooden furnishings with warm wool blankets, private bathrooms, cable TV, CD player, and plenty of rustic charm. Some have their own in-room hot tubs. If you don't want to stay but just want a steam bath, you can have a private sauna for $3.50. Room rates include sauna access. There are also a squash court, pool table, and a small gym.

Fuentes Georginas

A popular day trip from Xela with locals as well as visitors, the Fuentes Georginas hot springs (office in Xela at at 5a Calle 14-08 Zona 1, tel. 5704-2959 or 7761-6547, www.lasfuentesgeorginas.com, 8 A.M.-6:30 P.M. Mon.-Sat., 7 A.M.-5 P.M. Sun., $6.50) were hit hard by Hurricanes Mitch and Stan but it was 2010's Agatha that dealt them the final blow. The first of these wiped out a Hellenic statue that once gazed upon the pools. The site re-opened in March 2011 and is again up and running, though the large main pool now has water so hot it's better suited for cooking lobster than for soaking. A medium-sized and small pool offer slightly more comfortable water temperatures. In addition to the wonderfully warm thermal pools you can enjoy a fairly decent restaurant serving cocktails overlooking the emerald-green waters surrounded by tropical ferns and flowers. There are also sheltered picnic areas with barbecue pits for which you'll need to bring your own fuel. Trails lead to the Zunil and Santo Tomás Volcanoes with guides available at the restaurant for about $15. The hikes require about 3-5 hours one-way. There are accommodations available but they are not recommendable.

To get here, you can first take a bus to Zunil

leaving frequently from Xela's Minerva bus terminal and then take a pickup the rest of the way (eight kilometers) to the hot springs. You can also walk from Zunil in about two hours. Head out from the plaza going uphill to the Cantel road (about 60 meters), turning right, and then going downhill to where you'll see a sign for the hot springs indicating their distance eight kilometers away. The easy way to get here is to book a trip through any of the local guide companies, including Adrenalina Tours, which runs transfers to the site at 8 A.M. and 2 P.M. for $16. Fuentes Georginas also shuttles visitors from its office in Xela for $16 departing at 9 A.M. and 2:30 P.M. The price includes entry fee.

Cantel

Along an alternate route heading from Xela to Zunil via Las Rosas junction and bypassing Almolonga, Cantel lies 10 kilometers east of Xela and about three kilometers east of Zunil. It became an industrial suburb and one of the principal economic engines behind Xela's late 19th-century prosperity with the establishment of the **Fábrica de Hilados y Tejidos de Cantel,** which was somewhat like a modern-day sweatshop providing European technology and production methods to an already established weaving tradition. It began operations in 1883 and once employed 500 workers from Xela's total population of 30,000 inhabitants. The textile factory closed in 2008.

Today the town is better known as the site of the **Copavic Glass Factory** (Carretera al Pacífico, Km. 217.5, Cantón Pasac II, tel. 7763-8038, www.copavic.com), found along the road to Zunil and producing outstanding hand-blown glass made exclusively from recycled materials and exported around the world. The factory is open for tours 10:30 A.M.-1:30 P.M. Monday-Friday and 10:30 A.M.-12:30 P.M. on Saturday. The sales floor is open 9 A.M.-6 P.M. Monday-Friday and 9 A.M.-1 P.M. Saturday.

Salcajá

Coming into Quetzaltenango from the Pan-American Highway, you'll pass this somewhat ugly town which nonetheless has a few noteworthy features. Among them is Central America's first Christian church, the **Iglesia de San Jacinto,** found two blocks west on 3a Calle from the main road (3a Avenida). It dates to 1524 and has a pretty facade with some interesting carvings. The interior boasts an ornate altar and some colonial-era paintings. Salcajá's other claim to fame is a pair of fermented beverages, including a uniquely fruity concoction made from pears, apples, peaches, and *nances* (white cherries), known as *caldo de frutas.* Its other adult beverage is *rompopo,* essentially a Mesoamerican eggnog made from egg whites, rum, sugar, crushed almonds, and assorted spices, including vanilla and cinnamon. It tastes much better than it looks. You can pick up small bottles of either of these drinks from local stores, including **Rompopo Salcajá** (4a Calle 2-02), a block east of the main road.

West to San Martín Sacatepequez

Head west from Xela 15 kilometers through the valley to the prosperous farming village of San Juan Ostuncalco, with a lively Sunday market. From the adjacent town of Concepción Chiquirichapa, the road climbs into the surrounding mountainside before once again descending into a fertile agricultural valley occupied by the village of San Martín Sacatepequez, also known as San Martín Chile Verde. Much of the land's fertility is owed to its proximity to Santa María Volcano, which provides ash-rich soil. It's a mixed blessing, however, as demonstrated by a 1902 eruption that buried the village in several feet of ash and volcanic rocks. San Martín, a Mam-speaking village, is a standout for its beautiful village costume consisting of a long white tunic with red stripes and elaborate embroidery around the cuffs, worn by village men. The look is completed with a bright red sash worn around the waist. The women wear bright red *huipiles* with blue *cortes*.

Laguna Chicabal

From San Martín, it's a two-hour hike to the magical Chicabal Lagoon (www.lagunadechicabal.com), ringed by lush cloud forest in a spectacular volcanic crater at an altitude of 2,700 meters (8,900 feet). It can be reached by taking the signed path on the side of the road from where the bus drops you off heading into town. From there you'll go uphill through fields, cresting and descending a hill. You'll soon see the rangers' station, where you pay a $2 park entrance fee. If you've driven out this way, parking costs an additional $1.30. There's a rustic visitors center here where you can get food. There are also some very basic bungalows with a (cold-water) shared bathroom.

Bring your own sleeping bag if you're thinking of staying here. You can camp on the shore of the lagoon for $1.30, though most folks end up camping at the visitors center.

From the visitors center it's about 45 minutes to an hour, uphill, to a wonderful lookout point where you might catch a glimpse of the fantastic crater lake ringed by verdant cloud forest. Most of the time, however, the clouds have the view completely socked in. Opposite of the lagoon lookout is another lookout towards Santa María and Santiaguito Volcanoes; both have covered observation platforms. From the lookout, a trail of stairs descends to the lakeshore and the gorgeous lagoon, which is caressed by wisps of cloud just barely glancing the waters' surface. You'll soon realize why it's considered sacred by modern-day Mayans and a central element of their creation myths. An annual event includes 40 continuous days of prayers for rain and healing, ending on May 3. During the last

© AL ARGUETA

Chicabal volcano's lovely crater lake

© AL ARGUETA

the church of San Andrés Xecul

Totonicapán

From the Cuatro Caminos Junction, the road heads northeast for 30 kilometers through pine-studded forests to the departmental capital of Totonicapán, also known as San Miguel Totonicapán. It's a fairly laid-back town with few foreign visitors. Sights include the ubiquitous town church, on a plaza superjacent to a second one below it harboring a statue of indigenous leader Atanasio Tzul, who led a peasant rebellion in 1820 spurred by government demands for taxation. Also on the upper plaza is a far less common **municipal theater,** built in 1924 in neoclassical style. It has been recently restored and painted in bright orange. The town's other main attraction is the **Casa de la Cultura Totonicapense** (8a Avenida 2-17 Zona 1, tel. 7766-1575), which was closed for remodeling. It should continue to house displays, including audiovisual presentations of local indigenous culture, history, and crafts, upon reopening. The visitors center also offers tours to local artisans' workshops and the opportunity to try some Mayan dishes in local homes.

Totonicapán is especially lively during its annual **Festival Tradicional de Danza,** usually late in October. It is also kicking during its annual fiesta dedicated to the archangel Michael from September 24-30. The day marking the apparition of said heavenly figure, May 8, is also celebrated with dancing and fireworks.

If you need to stay in Totonicapán, a good budget choice is just next door to the Casa de la Cultura Totonicapense. **Hospedaje San Miguel** (8a Avenida 7-49 Zona 1, tel. 7766-1452, www.hoteltotonicapan.com, $8-16 d) has rooms on the third floor with shared bath or on the second floor with private bathroom, TV, and slightly more cheerful surroundings. The 23 rooms are clean and have some furniture, including desks. Try to get a room facing the street. On the pricier side is the nicest place in town, **Hotel Totonicapán** (8a Avenida 8-15 Zona 4, tel. 7766-4458, $28 d), with

few days culminating on this date, the lagoon is essentially off-limits to outsiders so as to allow the ceremonies to proceed undisturbed. Bathing in the lagoon's waters is strictly off-limits at all times and, as always, you should be careful to respect the native culture by not photographing any ceremonies that might be in progress throughout the year. You'll find the locals extremely friendly and willing to answer your questions if you put forth the effort to inquire amicably. As always, a smile goes a long way.

San Andrés Xecul

A road branches off to the west from a crossroads between Salcajá and the Pan American Highway junction at Cuatro Caminos leading to San Andrés Xecul, home to a stunning Technicolor dream of a church festooned with vines, saints, and assorted other characters. It's easily one of Guatemala's most photographed churches, and certainly one of its most bizarre. It's certainly worth a look.

TOTONICAPÁN

TANQUE DE
LOS DRAGONES ★

17 AVENIDA

To Cuatro Caminos
and Quetzaltenango

16 AVENIDA

15 AVENIDA

14 AVENIDA

PENSIÓN ●
BLANQUITA ■

13 AVENIDA

■ TELÉFONO
COMUNITARIO

4A CALLE

2A CALLE

3A CALLE

HOTEL CHUIMEKENÁ ■

COOPERATIVA CDRO ■

SIAM CENTRO ▼

SAY MEIN CHEN ▼

COOPERATIVA
ARTESANAL
CHUIMEKENÁ ■

MODERIA NIMA K'ICHE' ■
(CASA DE LA CULTURA) ★

HOSPEDAJE
SAN MIGUEL ●

SALÓN MUNICIPAL
DE USO MÚLTIPLES ■

● TELE-ORO

1A CALLE

■ TIENDA
MAYA

IGLESIA SAN
MIGUEL ARCÁNGEL ■

TERMINAL
DE BUSES

LA HACIENDA
▼

■ TOTO
CAMBIOS

Parque
Central
Unión

HOTEL SHADAY ●

★ MONUMENTO
AL FERROCARRIL

TEATRO
MUNICIPAL ■

■ BANCO DEL
OCCIDENTE

● POST OFFICE

TERESA
HERNÁNDEZ ■
DE SON

● HOSPEDAJE
EL CENTRO

1A AVENIDA

2A AVENIDA

3A AVENIDA

4A AVENIDA

5A AVENIDA

6A AVENIDA

7A AVENIDA

8A AVENIDA

9A AVENIDA

10A AVENIDA

11 AVE

12 AVE

5A CALLE

6A CALLE

7A CALLE

8A CALLE

9A CALLE

To Santa Cruz
del Quiché

SCALE NOT AVAILABLE

© AVALON TRAVEL

THE WESTERN HIGHLANDS

well-furnished rooms painted in cheery yellow pastel tones housing handcrafted wooden furniture, cable TV, city views, and private hot-water bathroom. Its pleasant lobby restaurant serves Guatemalan and international dishes. Closer to the town center, a decent place to grab a bite to eat is **La Hacienda** (8a Avenida 3-25 Zona 1), a steak house also serving some lighter Guatemalan dishes.

San Francisco El Alto

Just north of the Cuatro Caminos Junction, San Francisco El Alto is the site of the country's largest market, an extremely authentic affair that takes place on Fridays. It is not at all a tourist market like the one in Chichicastenango and you'd be hard-pressed to find touristy handicrafts and *típica* here. But, if you're in the mood to see an authentic Indian market, this is certainly the place. An added bonus is the wonderful view of Xela from here, thanks to a splendid hilltop location overlooking the larger city. The best views are from the top of the town's church. The caretaker should let you up there.

Momostenango

Another few kilometers along a beautifully pine-forested mountain road brings you to the town of Momostenango, famous for its delightfully warm wool blankets, which you can shop for at the twice-weekly markets on Wednesday and Sunday. Adherence to the Mayan calendar and traditional Mayan ceremonies are still very much in evidence here.

Among the attractions here is an interesting geological formation known as **Los Riscos,** essentially like large outdoor stalagmites made of eroded clay and crystalized stone. They're worth a look, though you might find the litter in the vicinity of the rock formations a bit unnerving, as is often the case in rural Guatemala. They're about 500 meters outside of town. Anyone can point the direction, and there are signs to guide you once you're on the way.

Momostenango's annual fiesta, the **Octava de Santiago,** takes place July 28-August 2. There are also dances held a few times a year, most notably on Christmas and New Year's Eve, when townsfolk performing the displays dress up in devil costumes and drink copious amounts of liquor.

Momostenango is accessible via frequent second-class bus from Xela's Minerva bus depot as well as from the Cuatro Caminos Junction and San Francisco El Alto. If you need to spend the night, your best bet is **Hotel Estiver** (1a Calle 4-15 Zona 4, tel. 7736-5036, $5-7 d), which actually looks nicer from the outside. There are 12 spartan rooms with shared or private bath with hot water; some have balconies. A backup is the centrally located **Hospedaje Posada de Doña Pelagia** (2a Avenida "A" Zona 1, tel. 7736-5175, $2 per person), where you get a roof over your head and a room lit by a solitary lightbulb hanging on a wire. Bathrooms are shared. The rooms are centered around a courtyard and if you've brought a deck of cards you'll have to play elsewhere, as a sign clearly denotes that card-playing is strictly *verboten*. For food, there are a number of very basic *comedores* near the plaza.

THE PACIFIC COAST

Guatemala's identity as a mostly mountainous country of cool lakes, evergreen forests, and wandering rivers has meant the coasts (Caribbean and Pacific) have traditionally been omitted from the collective consciousness in favor of its better-known, more traditional attractions. Very few of the Pacific Coast's black-sand beaches are inhabited, the chief economic activities along the seaboard being fishing, shrimp farming, and loofah production. The actual sand beaches are separated, along much of the coast, from mainland Guatemala by a narrow channel known as the Canal de Chiquimulilla, running the length of the coast from the town of Sipacate east to Las Lisas, near the Salvadoran border, traversing Puerto San José, Iztapa, and Monterrico along the way.

Things have started to change in recent years with the growth of Guatemala's tourism industry, as visitors and foreign residents seek new places to explore beyond the well-trod path. The Pacific port of San José has always been popular with Guatemala City residents as a place for sun and surf, though foreign visitors will find more acceptable places to visit elsewhere along the Pacific seaboard; it's just 90 minutes from the capital via a four-lane toll road. Adjacent to Puerto San José is the newer Puerto Quetzal, best known for its cruise ship terminal hosting an increasing number of seafaring visitors to Guatemala. The Pacific Coast plains are bisected by Highway CA-2, which runs west to east from the Mexican border all the way to El Salvador.

The beaches found in and around the area

HIGHLIGHTS

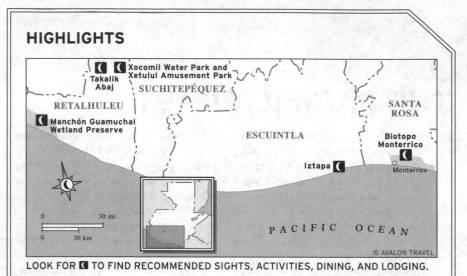

LOOK FOR **(** TO FIND RECOMMENDED SIGHTS, ACTIVITIES, DINING, AND LODGING.

(Xocomil Water Park and Xetulul Amusement Park: This amazing recreational center and its unique accommodations have quickly become Guatemala's top tourism draw and are certainly worth a stop if traveling to Guatemala with children—or if you just need to indulge your inner child (page 223).

(Takalik Abaj: This site spread over a series of terraces and coffee farms reveals interesting elements of Olmec influence in early Mayan culture. Adding to its allure is a wonderful lodge found on its ninth terrace (page 225).

(Manchón Guamuchal Wetland Preserve: These important protected wetlands are an excellent spot for bird-watching, which you can do along the canals lining the dense mangrove forests. The clean, gently sloping dark-sand beaches here are also among Guatemala's best-kept secrets (page 227).

(Iztapa: Guatemala is undoubtedly the sailfishing capital of the world, with several world records for single-day catch and release in the waters just off the coast of Iztapa. Several outfitters and lodgings have sprung up to accommodate the wishes of this very distinct class of adventure travelers (page 236).

(Biotopo Monterrico: Here is one of Guatemala's most popular, accessible beaches with a wide range of nearby accommodations. In season, you'll have the rare chance to spot a nesting sea turtle or interact with baby sea turtles at the local turtle hatchery before their initial voyage out to sea (page 242).

of Monterrico and its namesake sea turtle preserve have become the site of vacation homes and resort hotels. Nestled in between these two poles lies Iztapa, Guatemala's original colonial seaport, which in recent years has gained notoriety as word gets out about the world-class sailfishing in Guatemala's Pacific waters.

Guatemala is also Central America's surfing frontier, with some excellent breaks on many of the coast's empty beaches, particularly around the village of Sipacate and farther west toward Mexico. Things get more primitive the farther west you head from Sipacate, though the port of Champerico might soon become a magnet for tourism investment. Champerico is a satellite of nearby Retalhuleu, a haunt of the Pacific Coast's farming and ranching community and now the site of the large-scale Xocomil and

Xetulul amusement parks that are collectively Guatemala's most-visited tourist attraction. Other nearby attractions include the archaeological sites of Takalik Abaj, El Baúl, and La Democracia.

While many of the Pacific Coast beaches are not particularly good for swimming because of riptides, they are noteworthy because of their dark sand, the product of nearby volcanoes, which can be seen in the distance on a clear day. At the very least, the Pacific Coast offers the chance to enjoy a holiday in warm tropical weather, relaxing in a hammock strung between graceful coconut palms. This can be a welcome respite from an extended stay in the more temperate (and sometimes chilly) Guatemalan highlands.

Border towns, beginning with El Carmen and then moving south and east from the Mexican border, are generally unattractive and increasingly unsafe. There is no reason to linger in these parts.

PLANNING YOUR TIME

Two nights would be optimal to explore and enjoy the twin parks of Xetulul and Xocomil. A few hours is enough time to explore the ruins of Takalik Abaj, but the excellent accommodations at Takalik Mayan Lodge might keep you busy for another two days. From here or nearby Retalhuleu, you can explore the Manchón Guamuchal wetlands for some bird-watching or just unwind at its beautiful beaches. Retalhuleu also makes an excellent base for exploring some of the surrounding countryside by bike, thanks to the presence of an excellent outfitter based here.

If you are in search of sand and sun, you might find yourself spending several nights at Monterrico. If your interest lies in surfing,

you'll certainly want to spend a few days in Sipacate or Iztapa. For sailfishing, Iztapa is the place to go and you'll probably spend at least three days here. The 25-kilometer road between Iztapa and Monterrico is shaping up to be the closest thing to a Guatemalan Riviera and will certainly undergo some drastic changes in the next few years. For now, it's still a sleepy seaside area largely dedicated to the production of loofah. East toward El Salvador is another small seaside town, Las Lisas, with a couple of noteworthy accommodations, but unless you're heading out in this direction it's a bit out of the way.

WESTERN BORDER CROSSINGS

The northernmost and quieter of the two border crossings is found at **El Carmen,** where a bridge across the Río Suchiate connects it with Talismán, Mexico.

The more active (and preferable) border crossing is at **Ciudad Tecún Umán,** 39 kilometers south. A bridge links this city to its Mexican counterpart at Ciudad Hidalgo. There are frequent buses from here to points along the Pacific Coast Highway (CA-2) including Coatepeque, Retalhuleu, Mazatenango, and Escuintla. Buses also depart from here to Guatemala City and Quetzaltenango. You can connect to either of the latter two via Retalhuleu, a better place to linger if a bus is not immediately available.

Both borders are open 24 hours, but you should try to be out of border areas by dark. As elsewhere in Central America, border areas here are rife with crime thanks to immigrants trying to make their way northward and those who prey on them. There are some basic hotels and restaurants here.

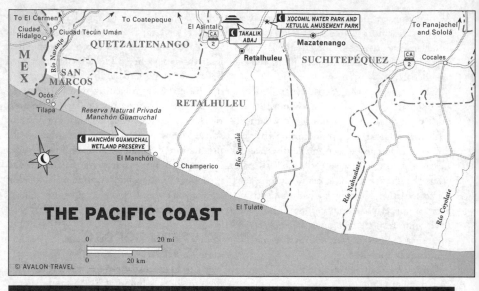

Retalhuleu and Vicinity

East from the Mexican border, the first town of any real interest to visitors is a rather pleasant place with a newfound importance as the gateway to some increasingly popular attractions. The most prominent of these are also Retalhuleu's newest: the twin amusement parks of **Xocomil and Xetulul,** just a few minutes outside of town. Adding to its prominence as the southern coastal region's new recreational hub is the proximity of the ruins of **Takalik Abaj** and some decent stretches of beach within a relatively short distance.

Commonly referred to as "Reu" by locals, the town has always been the playground of local coffee and sugarcane farmers, a fact that will be readily apparent by the prevalence of roadside hotels with sparkling swimming pools and pleasant outdoor restaurants. The weather here is warm year-round, but you can always find shelter from the scorching sun under the abundant palm trees, as you will see from the palm-lined boulevard leading to the town center from the main highway.

Reu is becoming increasingly attractive as a hub for exploring this seldom-visited area of Guatemala. Even if amusement parks aren't your thing, there is plenty to keep you busy here and very comfortable accommodations from which to base your explorations. At least one outfitter has begun to unravel the beauties of this pleasant sun-kissed stretch of the Pacific lowlands.

SIGHTS

Downtown Retalhuleu's main attraction, aside from the central square, is the **Museo de Arqueología y Etnología** (6a Avenida 5-68 Zona 1, 8 A.M.-5:30 P.M. Tues.-Sat., 9 A.M.- noon Sun., $1.50 admission) featuring archaeological relics on the ground floor and a collection of historical photographs from various stages of the city's past on the second floor.

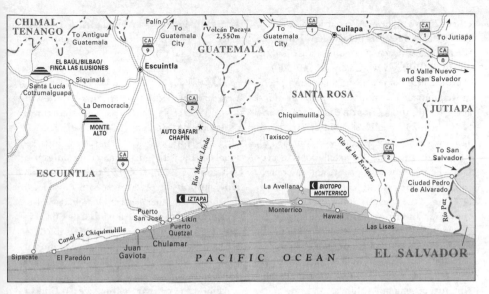

GUIDE COMPANIES

Retalhuleu is home to one of Guatemala's better outfitters. **Reuxtreme** (4a Calle 4-23 Zona 1, tel. 5202-8180 or 5205-1132, www.reuxtours.com) offers a variety of activities for the active traveler, including mountain biking to Champerico along the old railroad tracks passing over some very old bridges, kayaking in Manchón Guamuchal Wetland Preserve, treks to Quetzaltenango's Chicabal Volcano and Lagoon, coffee tours to local farms, and nighttime trips to Takalik Abaj. The outfit is run by Alejandro and María Mercedes Ravanales, a friendly Guatemalan brother-and-sister team who also manage the Hostal Casa Santa María.

SHOPPING

Retalhuleu's impressive outdoor shopping mall, **Centro Comercial La Trinidad,** is near the bus depot at 1a Calle and 5a Avenida "A" Zona 5, and has a modern grocery store, cell phone stores, banks, ATMs, and even a Radio Shack for all your technological needs while on the road. There's also a large condominium complex attached, attesting to the town's prosperity and its status as an enclave of the agricultural elite.

ACCOMMODATIONS

There are several motel-style places lining the main highway just outside of town where Guatemalan families like to stop and visit while en route from chillier locales in the highlands. These places tend to get a bit noisy on weekends, but during the week they tend to be quite silent. **Hotel La Colonia** (at Km. 178, Carretera al Pacífico, tel. 7772-2048 or 2426-3894) is an old standby with spotless, comfortable, air-conditioned rooms. There is a swimming pool with a pleasant restaurant and bar. Rooms in duplex bungalows go for $50 d on weekends and $32 d during the week. You can use the pool for the day at a cost of $1.25. At the intersection where roads split off toward Champerico and Quetzaltenango is **Hotel Siboney** (tel. 7772-2174 or 7772-2176, $40 d) with pleasant rooms centered around two swimming pools. All have air-conditioning, firm mattresses, cable TV, phone, hot water, and a desk. Rooms are in older and newer sections, so ask to see a room first. It costs $2 to swim here. Also outside of town are the excellent Hostales del IRTRA (Km 180.5 Carretera a Quetzaltenango por la Costa Sur, tel. 2423-9100, www.irtra.org.gt, $40-300).

In the heart of town, the most atmospheric of Retalhuleu's accommodations can be found at the family-run ☽ **Hostal Casa Santa María** (4a Calle 4-23 Zona 1, tel. 5202-8180 or 5205-1132, www.hostalcasasantamaria.com, $33 d), where eight tastefully decorated rooms in a colonial home come with private hot-water bath, cable TV, wireless Internet, air-conditioning, or ceiling fan. There is a nice breakfast room and a café and bar with Internet and book exchange. The young Guatemalan brother-and-sister team who own it also run Reuxtreme, Retalhuleu's finest outfitter, which operates weekend shuttles to Guatemala City and Antigua, among other things.

Another fine place to lay your head is the friendly ☽ **Posada de Don José** (5a Calle 3-67 Zona 1, tel. 7771-0180 or 7771-0841, donjose@terra.com.gt, $42-55 d), in an attractive two-story building centered around a small swimming pool and courtyard. Standard rooms are spotless and have good beds, cable TV, air-conditioning, ceiling fan, phone, and private hot-water bath. The larger suites have a sitting area and some nice furniture. The hotel's restaurant, managed by Don José's wife, serves some of the town's tastiest food. The Mexican consulate is also based here. Nearby, at the corner of 5a Avenida and 5a Calle, is the smaller **Anexo Posada de Don José** (tel. 7771-4182), run by the same owners, with pleasant double rooms for $25, breakfast included.

The well-furnished rooms in **Hotel Astor** (tel. 7771-0475 or 7771-2559, $45 d), are set in a colonial building and centered around a pretty garden courtyard and swimming pool. All rooms have air-conditioning, ceiling fan, and cable TV in addition to private hot-water bath. There is a restaurant in the lobby and a small sports bar. For budget accommodations,

try **Hotel Modelo** (3a Avenida "A" 5-14 Zona 1, tel. 7771-0256), where double rooms with ceiling fan and cable TV go for $15.

FOOD

A variety of decent restaurants are downtown. An excellent choice is the restaurant at ☽ **Posada de Don José** (5a Calle 3-67 Zona 1, tel. 7771-0180 or 7771-0841), serving international cuisine with Guatemalan flair. **Cafetería La Luna** (5a Avenida 4-97 Zona 1, all meals daily), just off the plaza's west corner, is a local favorite serving inexpensive Guatemalan fare. For a drink and pub fare, stop by **Lo de Chaz** (5a Calle 4-83 Zona 1). Reu's newest café is the **Café Rústico** (4a Calle 4-23 Zona 1 inside Hostal Casa Santa María, tel. 5202-8180), offering good coffee and snacks along with Internet access.

Among the culinary options you'll find in Centro Comercial La Trinidad is **Caffé Saúl** (1a Calle y 5a Avenida "A" zona 5, tel. 7771-7918, 10 A.M.-9 P.M. Mon.-Thurs., 10 A.M.-10 P.M. Fri.-Sun., http://latrinidadretalhuleu.com). There's also a **Domino's Pizza** and a **Tacos 3XQ10**. A large air-conditioned supermarket, **La Torre,** rounds out the list of options.

SERVICES

Banco Industrial has Visa ATMs at its locations on the central plaza (6a Calle 5-17 Zona 1) and at Centro Comercial La Trinidad (1a Calle and 5a Avenida "A" Zona 5). Banco Agromercantil, also on 5a Avenida facing the plaza, has a MasterCard ATM. Both banks change U.S. dollars and travelers checks.

For Internet access, check out Internet at 5a Calle and 6a Avenida, where an hour online costs $1.50. Hostal Casa Santa María (4a Calle 4-23 Zona 1, tel. 5202-8180 or 5205-1132) also has an Internet café.

GETTING THERE

Most buses plying the Pacific Coast Highway (Carretera al Pacífico) stop in Retalhuleu's main bus depot at 7a Avenida and 10a Calle. There are regular buses to Guatemala City, Quetzaltenango, the Mexican border, Champerico, and El Tulate.

NORTH AND WEST OF RETALHULEU
◖ Xocomil Water Park and Xetulul Amusement Park

The first of these, **Parque Acuático Xocomil** (Km. 180.5 on the road to Quetzaltenango, tel. 7772-5780, www.irtra.org.gt, 9 A.M.-5 P.M. Thurs.-Sun. Jan. 8-Oct. 31, Wed.-Sun. Nov. 1-Dec. 15, daily Dec. 15-Jan. 7, $13 adult, $7 children and seniors) is a wonderful water park on par with the world's best and a must-see if you are traveling with children. Among the attractions are 14 water slides, a wave pool, and a lazy river meandering through the complex of re-created Mayan ruins and monuments. The main restaurant showcases a Mayan pyramid painted in ochre, green, and yellow, as it would have looked in the Classic period. Additional food stands are scattered throughout the park.

The second phase of an eventual four-park plan is **Parque de Diversiones Xetulul** (tel. 7722-9450, www.irtra.org.gt, 10 A.M.-6 P.M. Thurs.-Sun. Jan. 8-Oct. 31, Wed.-Sun. Nov. 1-Dec. 15, daily Dec. 15-Jan. 7, $13 adult, $7 children and seniors; $19 admission to both parks for adults, $10 for children and seniors), where a variety of amusement park rides are spread out among seven plazas, each with its own restaurant and gift shop showcasing a variety of replicated world monuments. Among the highlights are Paris's Moulin Rouge, Rome's Trevi Fountain, and Guatemala's own Gran Jaguar Temple from Tikal. The park is also home to Central America's largest roller coaster.

A new convention center and 18-hole golf course were in the planning stages.

Hostales del IRTRA

Just across the road from the two theme

© AL ARGUETA

tubing at Parque Acuático Xocomil

well-designed architecture of hostel Palajunoj

parks are the lodgings created specifically to house visitors. The Hostales del IRTRA (Km 180.5 Carretera a Quetzaltenango por la Costa Sur, tel. 2423-9100, www.irtra.org.gt) encompass a virtual leisure city with various lodges, restaurants, bars, swimming pools, and a minigolf course. There are four separate lodging concepts ranging in price from $40 a night in the simplest accommodations without air-conditioning to $300 a night for a suite. The newest of the four *hostales,* ◖ **Palajunoj,** was inspired by the cultures inhabiting the world's tropical rainforests and is a popular favorite of guests. The five buildings in this complex each have a different theme: African, Polynesian, Thai, Indonesian, and Mayan. All rooms have air-conditioning, cable TV, a private bathroom, and wonderful wooden furnishings. The buildings housing the rooms at Palajunoj are worth a look for their unique architecture. The *hostales* outside this complex feature

Spanish Colonial, Greek, and rustic cabana architecture.

There are three restaurants, the nicest of which is **Restaurante Kapa Hapa,** inspired by the cultures of Asia and the Pacific. A beautifully luminescent Polynesian sailboat graces the entrance as you make your way up the stairs to the second-floor dining room. Try the chicken satay and wash it down with a Mai Tai. Main dishes cost $7-12. Outdoor seating overlooking the Moana swimming pools is also available and is a great place for breakfast, which includes a delicious menu of croissant sandwiches or lighter fare such as yogurt and pancakes.

Any bus traveling along the Quetzaltenango-Retalhuleu road can drop you off here.

Reserva Patrocinio

Farther north along the road heading to Quetzaltenango, in the area known as Las Palmas, lies ◖ **Reserva Patrocinio** (tel. 7771-4393 or 5203-5701, www.reservapatrocinio.com), an agro-ecological tourism destination. So-called "agritourism" is an increasingly popular form of recreation in Guatemala and encompasses natural areas adjacent to farms. The main attraction at El Patrocinio is bird-watching in and around its 25-hectare forest reserve. Other areas are dedicated to the cultivation of coffee, cacao, macadamia nuts, and exotic flowers, among others, which visitors are free to check out. There are three rooms in a comfortable, well-equipped farmhouse, each renting for $65 d with shared bath. The house has a kitchen and there is a separate and very pleasant open-sided dining room that fronts the coffee fields; meals can be prepared for you with advance notice.

The farm itself is on the slopes of Santiaguito Volcano and has outstanding views of its smoldering cone. It's a great place to get away from it all. For the best views of the surrounding coffee fields, mountains, and volcanoes, climb atop

the lodge at Reserva Patrocinio

Santa María and Santiaguito Volcanoes. The community received legal title to the land in 2004 after a drawn-out conflict with the farm's former owner who failed to pay workers' wages for 18 months and subsequently declared bankruptcy. The community received a loan to purchase the land and is actively making efforts to fund re-payment of the loan via numerous activities. These include ecotourism, production of bamboo furniture, sustainable energy production, and coffee and macadamia nut production.

Tours can be arranged via Quetzaltenango travel agencies or directly through the cooperative. You can stay in the community's comfortable lodgings in a hostel-style room with shared bath for $8 or in a private room with shared bath for $11. Meals cost $3-5 each. The community accepts volunteers for hostel maintenance, agricultural work, and community development.

Takalik Abaj

The site of Takalik Abaj (7 A.M.-5 P.M. daily, $3.50), meaning "standing stones," is particularly interesting because it reveals elements of Olmec influence in early Mayan culture. It made headlines as recently as 2002 with the discovery of an intact royal burial tomb thought to be that of the site's last Mayan ruler, a discovery featured in the May 2004 issue of *National Geographic.*

Formerly known as Abaj Takalik because of an error in translation, the site is spread out over 6.5 square kilometers along nine terraces. Its ceremonial center, at the city's core, is open to visitors but the remains of the city's outskirts are now on lands occupied by five coffee farms. One of these, on the ninth terrace, is home to an ecolodge.

In its heyday, between 800 B.C. and A.D. 200, Takalik Abaj was an important commercial and political center at the heart of a far-ranging trade network in which cacao and salt were exchanged for obsidian, quetzal feathers, pyrite, and jade.

the platform near the farmhouse. You can call the owner, Mario Aguilar, for a pickup ($12) or for directions from the Cuatro Caminos crossroads just outside of Retalhuleu; from there, it's another 14 kilometers to the farm. A detailed map is available on their website www.reservapatrocinio.com.

Birding packages can be arranged by booking in advance directly through Reserva Patrocinio or through **Cayaya Birding** (tel. 5308-5160, www.cayaya-birding.com).

Comunidad Nueva Alianza

Located about 45 minutes north of Retalhuleu, Comunidad Nueva Alianza (tel. 5801-7849, www.comunidadnuevaalianza.org) is a 300-acre organic coffee and macadamia plantation owned and operated by a cooperative of 40 Guatemalan families. Large tracts of tropical forest have been preserved on the property. A walk through the plantation will bring you to cascading waterfalls and wonderful views of

More than 275 structures have been unearthed here. Now being restored in an area once belonging to a private coffee and banana plantation is Structure 5, the tallest structure at 16 meters high. It occupies Terrace 3. East of here is Structure 7, thought to have been an astronomical observatory. Structure 4 contains some very clear engraving in Mayan style. There are many sculptures scattered throughout the site. Among them are smaller versions of the giant Olmecoid heads seen elsewhere, as well as the pot-bellied *barrigones* that are also typical of Olmec influence. Also noteworthy is Structure 12, the largest structure with a base measuring 56 by 42 meters and dating to A.D. 300. Standing before it are seven carved monuments, including Altar 8, and Stela 5, which shows two kings presiding over bound captives. Olmecoid heads and zoomorphs compose the other finely carved monuments at this structure. Structure 11 is similar, also with seven monuments before it.

Takalik Abaj was sacked sometime around A.D. 300 and its Mayan-style monuments were ritualistically defaced. Some were rebuilt after A.D. 600. The site is still an important ceremonial site and many highland Mayans perform ceremonies there.

To get to Takalik Abaj, drive or take a bus heading out from Retalhuleu to the town of El Asintal, 12 kilometers northwest of Reu and 5 kilometers north of the Carretera al Pacífico (Pacific Coast Highway, CA-2). The turnoff is at Km. 190.5. Buses leave from 5a Avenida "A" southwest of the town plaza about every half hour during daylight hours. From El Asintal, pickups cover the remaining four kilometers to the site. You can also take a taxi from Reu's main plaza for about $30 round-trip, including waiting time.

Takalik Maya Lodge

Just two kilometers up the road, on the site's ninth terrace, is the exquisite █ **Takalik Maya Lodge**

(Terraza 9 del Sitio Arqueologico Takalik Abaj, Km. 190.5 Carretera al Pacífico, tel. 2334-7693 or 2334-7694, www.takalik.com), where you have your choice between two different concepts, both on lands occupied by the working Montes Eliseos coffee farm. The **Kacike Maya** concept is built in a heavily forested area near the lodge's restaurant. There are two beautiful and comfortable rooms, each with unique interior paint and decor. Both have a winding staircase leading to a second-floor balcony, where you can lounge away soothed by the sounds of the surrounding jungle. The rooms are truly a work of art and the walls are painted with motifs inspired by the natural beauty all around. Indigenous bedspreads, gas lamps, and tile floors complete the ambience. You can stay at the Kacike Maya for $58 per person, but there are packages including one night's stay, three meals, and a tour to Takalik Abaj by tractor for $92 per person based on double occupancy.

At the **Paseo del Café,** just up the road, you can stay in the heart of a 19th-century coffee farm in comfortable wooden buildings with charming red tin roofs centered around a small plaza. The seven rooms here have electricity and share a bathroom. They are also just steps from a refreshing swimming pool surrounded by lush jungle and coffee bushes. Rooms here cost $38 per person and include breakfast. A package including two nights' stay, five meals, a coffee tour, and a visit to Takalik Abaj by tractor-pulled cart costs $125 per person in a double room. One-night packages are also available.

The restaurant, on the Kacike side of the lodge, serves a somewhat limited menu, though the food is quite good, with entrées in the $6-9 range that include kebabs and salads. The homemade lemonade is particularly thirst-quenching after a visit to the ruins.

Numerous nature trails wind their way through the farm and there is a small but refreshing waterfall just a 10-minute hike away. In addition to Takalik Abaj tours, the lodge

A GUATEMALAN TAKE ON DISNEY WORLD

The twin theme parks of Xocomil (Km. 180.5 on the road to Quetzaltenango, tel. 7772-5780, www.irtra.org.gt, 9 A.M.-5 P.M. Thurs.-Sun. Jan. 8-Oct. 31, Wed.-Sun. Nov. 1-Dec. 15, daily Dec. 15-Jan. 7, $10 adult, $7 children) and Xetulul (tel. 7722-9450, www.irtra.org.gt, 10 A.M.-6 P.M. Thurs.-Sun. Jan. 8-Oct. 31, Wed.-Sun. Nov. 1-Dec. 15, daily Dec. 15-Jan. 7, $27 adult, $13 children) sprouted seemingly out of nowhere just a few years ago on the outskirts of Retalhuleu along the road to Quetzaltenango. The first of these, Xocomil, opened its doors in 1997, with Xetulul being added in 2002. Both parks are operated by IRTRA, the Institute for the Recreation of Guatemalan Private Industry Workers, a private entity created by the Guatemalan Congress. This organization operates three other parks near Guatemala City.

Xocomil and Xetulul opened to much fanfare and are beloved by Guatemalans and foreigners alike for the quality of the parks' attractions, their cleanliness, and the friendliness of the staff. By any standard, the parks are impressive, and they are special because they showcase the excellent quality and amazing potential of the Guatemalan service sector. The theme parks and the accommodations built to house their guests truly have nothing to envy similar attractions in developed nations. If you are traveling in this part of Guatemala with children, a stop at Xocomil or Xetulul is almost obligatory.

Xocomil and Xetulul receive more than one million visitors annually, making them Guatemala's top tourist draw. There are plans to build two more parks in the lands adjacent to them. Retalhuleu itself has already begun a transformation inspired by the parks' creation. Though it has always been a regional recreational center, the arrival of more visitors to the area has vastly improved the quality of local hotels, though prices have likewise increased. In addition to its popularity with Guatemalans, visitors from Southern Mexico, El Salvador, and Honduras also flock to the parks in droves. There are plans to build an airport, allowing those visitors to arrive by plane on package tours.

All of this might sound suspect, like crass consumerism or the makings of mass tourism, brought home by the fact that the top tourism draw in a country of incredible natural beauty is a manufactured theme park. But you should keep in mind that it's a far cry from Las Vegas and it really goes to show that Guatemala, and her people, are entirely capable of competing with better-known tourism destinations and creating something that is professional, high quality, and yet entirely Guatemalan.

---

can also arrange bird-watching and visits to the Manchón Guamuchal Wetland Preserve and Chicabal Lagoon.

From Takalik Abaj archaeological site's roadside entrance, it's another two kilometers up the main road to Takalik Maya Lodge, about 30 minutes' walking.

Coatepeque

This rather unattractive town lies farther west toward the Mexican border and, as such, is the haunt of the usual rag-tag group of felons inhabiting shady border towns. It also doubles as a busy commercial center for the surrounding coffee farms. If you need to stay here, your best bet is the **Hotel Villa Real** (6a Calle 6-57 Zona 1, tel. 7775-1939, $30d), housed in a building dating to the early 1900s, featuring very clean rooms with ceiling fans, cable TV, and comfortable beds. There is also an *anexo* down the street with newer, single-bed rooms. The owner claims 80 percent of the local population is armed in this Guatemalan "red zone" and may be closing his doors in the next few years.

(Manchón Guamuchal Wetland Preserve

This wild, 13,500-hectare private wetland reserve harbors the last remaining undisturbed mangrove swamps in the country.

THE PACIFIC COAST

The Manchón Guamuchal is included in the Ramsar Convention on Wetlands, encompassing a list of globally important sites, particularly those that provide habitat for aquatic birds. The convention was adopted in 1971 and signed by more than 100 countries. Guatemala ratified the convention in June 1990, and in 1998 the Manchón Guamuchal was added to the list of sites with international importance.

According to a recent study by a Brazilian biologist, the wetlands are an important stop along the path of migratory birds coming from Canada and the United States. Among the varied bird life are 14 duck species, 12 of which are migratory, sparrow hawks, buzzards, falcons, and 20 species of egrets. Birds arrive sometime in October to November, leaving in March after wintering in the lagoons. In addition to birds, there are crocodiles, iguanas, and an abundance of fish.

The reserve is just now being made accessible to tourism, though access to the park is fairly straightforward. The only facilities are in the towns of Tilapa and neighboring Tilapita. You'll find several simple *comedores* lining a pleasantly clean stretch of black-sand beach in Tilapa. For tours of the mangrove swamps, negotiate with one of the local boatmen found at the dock.

You can catch a boat through the mangrove lagoons over to Tilapita for $0.50 or hire your own boat for about $3. There you'll find the wonderful **El Pacífico** beach hotel (in Tilapita village, tel. 5940-1524, $20 d) with large, screened-in rooms with fan and private bath. There's decent food on offer, including fresh seafood and cold beers.

To get to Tilapa, take one of the hourly buses leaving from Coatepeque. It's about a 1.5-hour drive from Retalhuleu, if you're driving. Take the Pacific Coast Highway (CA-2) west past Coatepeque and head south at the turnoff just past the town of Las Palmas.

The reserve is accessible on its eastern flank from Champerico along a dirt road heading west 25 kilometers to the village of El Manchón. There is one daily bus leaving for Retalhuleu at 5 A.M. and making the return journey to El Manchón at 3 P.M.

Outfitter **Reuxtreme** (tel. 5202-8180 or 5205-1132, www.reuxtreme.com) runs trips to the reserve for kayaking along the tranquil mangrove swamps and lagoons on this side of the park, where there is also a wide sandy beach.

SOUTH OF RETALHULEU
Champerico
Built as a shipping port during the late-19th-century coffee boom, this old port features a uniquely dilapidated wooden pier. The beaches here are not all that enticing, though there are some better ones nearby. Lining the beach in the area adjacent to the pier are a variety of cheap eateries serving mostly seafood. The old pier is worth a look and you can still walk on it for an out-of-this-century experience. Sportfishing outfitters and tourism authorities are trying to restore some of this town's old glory and infrastructure as a place from which to run deep-sea fishing trips. A new marina was built partially with Dutch capital.

A fun day trip from Retalhuleu is a 55-kilometer mountain-bike ride along old railroad tracks and wooden bridges. **Reuxtreme** (tel. 5202-8180 or 5205-1132, www.reuxtreme.com, info@reuxtreme.com) runs the trips, costing $30 per person and including all gear. It also offers surfing lessons.

For accommodations and food, your best bet is **Hotel Posada del Mar** (tel. 7773-7101, along the highway into town at Km. 222, $25 d), where the comfortable rooms have air-conditioning and cable TV. There is a restaurant serving mostly seafood dishes along with a swimming pool. Alternatively, there's the **Hotel Montelimar** (2a Calle and Avenida Coatepeque, tel. 7773-7231, $13 d), where the wooden bar outshines the small, dark rooms.

Playa El Tulate

A much better bet for hitting the beach near Retalhuleu is El Tulate, about an hour from town. The beach isn't as clean as the one at Tilapa, but there's at least one serviceable hotel here. The rooms at **Playa Paraíso** (tel. 5554-2715, $40 d) have big, cushy beds, ceiling fans, thatched roofs, and porch seating with bamboo furniture. There are two swimming pools and a restaurant.

To get to the beaches, you'll have to cross the **Canal de Chiquimulilla.** The cheapest crossing, if you're coming to Playa Paraío, is found by turning left when the main road dead-ends at the canal and continuing for 100 meters. It should cost about $0.25 to make the crossing. Local ferry boat operators will try to charge you $2 to cross closer to the end of the main road.

EAST TO ESCUINTLA

East of Retalhuleu along the Pacific Coast Highway to the department of Escuintla is

Mazatenango, a coffee and sugarcane hub with little of interest for the international traveler. If you need to stop for a bite to eat your best bet is Plaza Americas, a modern shopping center conveniently situated just off the Pacific Coast Highway outside the town center. Choose from Pollo Campero, Sarita, Pizza Hut, and Burger King. There's even a movie theater.

Río Nahualate

Further east along the highway, the town of San Antonio Suchitepequez serves as a convenient gateway for whitewater rafting trips to the class III Río Nahualate. There's a nice mix of exhilarating rapids, jungle scenery and more placid stretches of river to enjoy. The Nahualate is easily accessible from Guatemala City and La Antigua, making it a perfect day trip. Antigua-based **Rainbow Travel** (7a Avenida Sur #8, tel. 7931-7878, www.rainbowtravelcenter.com) runs one-day trips to the river.

Escuintla Department

Escuintla department is in many ways the gateway to the Pacific Coast, as it is easily accessed from Guatemala City and La Antigua. The departmental capital is a somewhat shady agglomeration of dilapidated houses and businesses serving mostly as a stopping point on the way elsewhere. (A toll road circumvents the departmental capital, so it's no longer even necessary to pass through it.) The department itself harbors the Pacific Coast's main ports, cruise ship terminal, and several seaside attractions.

SANTA LUCÍA COTZUMALGUAPA

In and of itself, the rather nondescript town of Santa Lucía Cotzumalguapa has little to recommend it. There are, however, some nearby archaeological attractions evidencing

the influence of the Olmec culture and its expansion into coastal Guatemala from lowland Mexico. They might be worth a stop if you are passing this way as you travel along the coast. The sites, in the cane fields just outside of town, can be a bit difficult to reach and you'll probably find yourself hiring a cab if you're coming from town on your own.

What you'll see here are the remains of the Late Classic Pipil culture, which flourished here between A.D. 500 and 700. In 1880 more than 30 of the large stones found at the site were removed, with nine of them being shipped off to Germany. Four sets of stones can still be found on-site. Unless you are a die-hard fan of pre-Columbian culture, I don't suggest traipsing through the cane fields to see them, as some of the highlights can be easily and conveniently viewed from museums on two different farms occupying the original site. In general, it's not a good idea to wander in and around the fields of tall sugarcane stalks, as they are prime territory for thieves and other assorted riffraff.

Museo El Baúl

Although parts of this site lie among the sugarcane fields of Finca El Baúl, the highlights can be seen at Museo El Baúl (tel. 5312-1073, 7 A.M.-5 P.M. daily, $1.50), an open-air, roofed-in exhibit housing Pipil stone sculptures, including a jaguar, several skulls, and a smiling head. The museum is being preserved as an eco-archaeological attraction by private landowners. The remains of old steam engines, one of which dates to 1914, can be found strewn about the grounds.

To get here, take the road heading north of town from El Calvario church. An intersection just past this landmark takes you about three kilometers to a fork in the road just past a bridge. The fork is marked by a sign, which reads "Los Tarros," where you make a left and follow the road another three kilometers to the headquarters of Finca El Baúl. An armed guard will greet you at the gate, where you'll have to identify yourself. Tell him you're visiting the museum. The museum is on the right another half kilometer or so past some old buildings. Buses carrying farm workers make their way out here from town at variable frequencies.

Museo Cultura Cotzumalguapa

On the site of Finca Las Ilusiones, the Museo Cultura Cotzumalguapa (7 A.M.-noon and 2-4 P.M. Mon.-Fri., 7 A.M.-noon Sat., $1.50) has a variety of obsidian arrow points, ceramic pots and figurines, and several monuments on display. Among these are several Olmecoid statues and a glass fiber copy of Monument 21—the original still stands among the sugarcane fields of Finca Bilbao. The stone depicts a scene involving a ball-game player, a shaman,

and a noble holding a heart. There are also photographs of stelae moved to Berlin's Dahlem Museum in 1880. The museum has some interpretive material and the caretaker is usually on hand to show you around.

The museum is one kilometer east of town along the Pacific Coast Highway. The signed entrance is on the left just before an Esso station. The turnoff leads another half kilometer to the museum along a dirt road.

Accommodations and Food

Along the highway on the western edge of town at Km. 90.4 of the Pacific Coast Highway is **Hotel Santiaguito** (tel. 7882-5435, 7882-5436, or 7882-5437, $26-50 d). The large, comfortable rooms have cable TV, phone, air-conditioning, and private bathroom set on spacious grounds with a swimming pool. Nonguests can use the pool for $3 and there is a good restaurant where fish, seafood, or meat dishes range $6-9. About 200 meters east along the highway is **Hotel El Camino** (tel. 7882-5316, $23-40 d), featuring bright rooms with tile floors, large bathrooms, balconies, cable TV; some have air-conditioning. Fan-cooled rooms on the first floor are less attractive but cheaper. There's also a decent restaurant here. Head east and then down a short signposted lane to **Hotel Internacional** (tel. 7882-5504, $20 d) with 14 large rooms and cold-water showers, fans, and cable TV. Try for an upstairs room.

Getting There

Most buses trundling along the Pacific Coast Highway no longer go into town thanks to a bypass constructed a few years back. If heading out here you might find yourself changing buses in Escuintla or Mazatenango. Santa Lucía is also accessible from Lake Atitlán via Cocales.

LA DEMOCRACIA

East from Santa Lucía Cotzumalguapa, a turnoff near the town of Siquinalá heads south to this small town. There's little to see and do other than admire the peculiar Olmecoid heads adorning the town's small central plaza. There is a certain Far Eastern mystique to these large, grinning heads with swollen eyelids, some of which are attached to smaller, rotund bodies and known as *barrigones* because of their swollen bellies. They bear a striking resemblance to Olmec sculptures found in the Mexican lowlands of Villa Hermosa, near the Gulf of Mexico. The stones date to the middle Preclassic period sometime around 500 B.C. and come from the nearby site of Monte Alto, located on the outskirts of town.

Also on the central plaza, a small museum, the **Museo Regional de Arqueología** (8 A.M.-noon and 2 P.M.-5 P.M. Tues.-Sun., $1.50) harbors some more stone heads, carvings, pottery, grinding stones, and an exquisite jade mask.

SIPACATE

If you continue south toward the coast from La Democracia you'll find Guatemala's surfing capital, Sipacate. Nowhere near as popular as in Costa Rica or even neighboring El Salvador, surfing nonetheless has some aficionados in this neck of the woods and there are some perfectly surf-worthy waves on the Guatemalan shores. International travelers are just now starting to get a clue, but in the meantime, a lucky few surfers can still ride these waves undisturbed by throngs of fellow wave enthusiasts, despite international travel magazines' best attempts to make these sites more widely known.

The drive south to Sipacate is almost as pretty as the beaches, with palmettos lining the road on either side of the well-paved, fast highway. Once in town, it should cost you about $1.40 to cross the Canal de Chiquimulilla over to the beaches. Sipacate's recommended accommodation, **Rancho Carrillo** (tel. 4579-2825 or 5413-9395, www.marmaya.com) is on a clean stretch of private beach. Rancho Carrillo offers a restaurant, pool, and bungalows with air-conditioning, private baths, minifridges, and cable TV. The bungalows house up to four people and cost $100 regardless of occupancy. A family-sized unit for up to eight people costs $130. Smaller, more basic rooms with air-conditioning, outdoor hammocks, and decks fronting the beach cost $64 for up to four people. There are deals available if you're here Sunday-Thursday.

El Paredón Buena Vista

East from Sipacate about five kilometers is the village of El Paredón Buena Vista, home to Guatemala's surfing mecca. El Paredón is inside **Sipacate-Naranjo National Park,** home to large extensions of mangrove forests. Little has been done to make the park an authentic ecotourism attraction. The emphasis at El Paredón is decidedly on the surfing aspects, though local lodges can arrange kayaking in the neighboring lagoons. El Paredón is accessible by boat from Sipacate or along a dirt road leading to the village. The turnoff for the final 14-kilometer journey is just past the luxury Juan Gaviota condominium complex.

Featured in *National Geographic Adventure* and *Outside* but still very much off the radar, **El Paredón Surf Camp** (tel. 7812-3387 or 5744-9342, www.surf-guatemala.com) is the Pacific coast's surfing hideaway. Rates range from $3.75 sleeping in your own tent to $40 in an equipped double-occupancy apartment. Other options include bunk beds ($6 p/p) and private rooms ($20 d). Meals ($3-5) are provided by a local family and are heavy on seafood. Surfboards are available for rent at $15 a day, though there is a $50 deposit. You can put them to good use on the sea, which dishes out 1.5-2-meter (5-6-foot) rollers opposite the lovely beach at your doorstep. The owners insist you book in advance. Transport from Antigua or Guatemala City takes two hours and costs $50-60 per person with a two-person minimum. It is highly recommended, as getting here by public bus involves changing buses four times.

YOU *CAN* SURF IN GUATEMALA

© AL ARGUETA

a surfer on Guatemala's Pacific Coast

While neighboring countries such as Costa Rica, Nicaragua, and even El Salvador have acquired relative status as Central American surf spots, Guatemala has remained somewhat obscure in this regard. Although the country's Pacific shores have perfectly surf-worthy breaks, the coast has always taken a back seat to the scenic and cultural wonders of the highlands, among other areas. A relative lack of tourism infrastructure in this region has also contributed to keeping the Pacific Coast on the periphery of Guatemala's emerging status as a destination for outdoor-loving, adventurous travelers.

The newfound popularity of beach destinations such as Monterrico and Iztapa has resulted in the corresponding development of coastal areas near these beach towns. As more and more people visit, locals and foreigners alike are discovering that you can, in fact, surf in Guatemala. The Guatemalan surfing community can be found mostly in small villages along the coast and numbers only about 100 people, according to local estimates. Surfing Guatemala's breaks means you won't have to share a wave with 20 other people, as is the case with other, more popular regions along the Central American coast. The best surfing beaches in Guatemala can be found at Iztapa and Sipacate, both of which have more-than-adequate accommodations.

United States travel magazines have put the word out concerning **El Paredón Surf Camp** (tel. 7812-3387 or 5744-9342, www.surf-guatemala.com), a bare-bones surfing paradise on one of Guatemala's best breaks. Still, you wouldn't know it cruising around the sandy streets of this quiet village where chickens roam freely. You can still show up on almost any given day with nary another surfer in sight.

The biggest waves can be found during swells occurring between mid-March and late October with wave faces sometimes as large as 18 feet. During other times of the year, waves average 3-6 feet with the occasional 10-foot swell.

If you want to check out the surfing scene in Guatemala, a useful website is www.surfinguatemala.com, established by Pedro Pablo Vergara, a local surfer who costarted Maya Extreme Surf School and offers trips to Guatemala's surf spots. The site lists about 20 breaks along the Pacific Coast with area maps to help you find them, along with information on accommodations ranging from budget surf camps to stays in private villas. The school can also arrange transportation for you and your surfboards to various surf spots from Guatemala City.

Along with Maripaz Fernandez, Vergara started **Maya Extreme Surf School** (www.mayaextreme.com) in 2001 and **Maya Extreme Surf Shop** (Centro Comercial Pradera Concepción Local 308, tel. 6637-9593) in 2005. The shop sells the company's own brand of "G-land surfboards" and is based in one of Guatemala City's nicest shopping malls. A one-day "learn to surf" package costs $125, including transfers, food, equipment, and instruction.

In 2006, Robert August (of *Endless Summer* fame) traveled to Guatemala with his crew to surf the Pacific Coast waves. The result was *The Endless Journey Continues,* a movie chronicling their trip to Guatemala.

Another option is **Paredón Surf House** (tel. 4994-1842, www.paredonsurf.com, $10 p/p in loft to $67 d in sea view suite). It's a stylish and yet simple seaside retreat perfect for surfers looking to be right on the beach in more private surroundings or anyone just looking to get off the grid for a bit. The raised-platform beachfront bungalows ($41 d) share a communal bathroom with the lofts. Spring for one of the seaview suites. There are boogie boards and surfboards for rent; surfing lessons are also available. A full restaurant and bar serves up good food and cocktails. Dinner is about $10. Transport from Antigua or Guatemala City is available.

ESCUINTLA

The departmental capital of Escuintla is a sweltering, busy place and mainly a pit stop along the road to the coast from Guatemala City, or if you're heading east-west along the Pacific Coast Highway. A four-lane *autopista* starts just outside of Guatemala City and leads from Palín to Escuintla, with inspiring views of Agua, Fuego, and Acatenango Volcanoes along the way. Another four-lane highway continues south from Escuintla to Puerto San José, Puerto Quetzal, and Iztapa. A bypass means you don't need to even pass through town unless it's absolutely necessary.

Your best bet for a decent cheap hotel is along 4a Avenida. Otherwise, try **Hotel La Villa** (3a Avenida 3-21 Zona 1, tel. 7888-0395, $30 d), containing adequate rooms with fans or air-conditioning, cable TV, and private bathrooms. A swimming pool and restaurant are also on the premises. Nicer accommodations with swimming pools popular on weekends with Guatemalan families can be found along Avenida Centro América in Zona 3. The best of these is **Hotel Sarita** (Avenida Centro América 15-32 Zona 3, tel. 7888-1959, $50 d), offering guest rooms with some of the usual amenities such as ceiling fans, cable TV, air-conditioning, and private hot-water bathrooms, all centered

around the swimming pool. The restaurant here is a favorite with Guatemalan families and has opened other locations throughout the country. Its menu is similar to that of U.S.-based Denny's and includes burgers, sandwiches, and grilled meats. There is another one in Escuintla on the *autopista* heading back toward Guatemala City, just past the northbound toll booths.

As for banks, Banco Industrial has a Visa ATM in its branch office at 4a Avenida 6-14 Zona 1. The main bus depot is on the southern end of town, at the end of 4a Avenida, from where there are half-hourly buses to Guatemala City, Puerto San José, and east toward El Salvador as well as hourly departures for Antigua. Buses coming into Escuintla sometimes leave you at the north end of town along 2a Avenida, meaning a long walk through the sweltering town center. Splurge for a cab ride if you need to get to the bus terminal.

Near Escuintla

East on the road to Taxisco is one of the most unusual attractions in Guatemala and indeed all of Central America, the **Auto Safari Chapin** (Km. 87.5 Carretera a Taxisco, tel. 5517-1705, www.autosafarichapin.org, 9:30 A.M.-5 P.M. Tues.-Sun., $8 adults, $7 children), where you can drive through grounds harboring a variety of animals, including zebras, hippos, rhinos, giraffes, and a lion. There are also local species such as macaws and monkeys, which you can see in a small zoo, and an aviary. There is a rest area partway through the drive where you can get up close and personal with the park's giraffes. A swimming pool and restaurant round out the list of amenities.

PUERTO SAN JOSÉ

Puerto San José is where Guatemala City dwellers escape to for a quick dip in the sea. Avoid coming here during Holy Week, as droves of Guatemalan families descend upon the town and its beaches like shoppers at a Filene's Basement day-after-Christmas sale, leaving a trail of trash in their wake. Otherwise, the town makes an acceptable place to enjoy some time by the sea, though nearby Iztapa and Monterrico are certainly better beach alternatives.

Once Guatemala's main shipping port, it has been displaced by the newer **Puerto Quetzal** just a few kilometers away along the same stretch of coast. Cruise ships dock at Puerto Quetzal, which has its own cruise ship terminal. Most visitors either stay at the terminal, where they can eat and shop, or are quickly whisked away on package tours to a local resort; others go sailfishing or visit Antigua for the day.

Ostrich Farm

If you're spending some time in Puerto San José or just passing through, you may want to stop by the local ostrich farm for a look. **Avestruces Maya** (tel. 5608-0835 or 5608-8075, 9 A.M.-6 P.M. Tues.-Sun., $3.50 adults, $2.65 children 10 and over, children under 10 free) occupies 27 acres, mostly devoted to raising ostriches, but also includes a small petting zoo, plant nursery, and riverlike swimming pool where you can relax in an inner tube.

A restaurant (open weekends) specializes in ostrich meat and a small shop sells ostrich-leather wallets, boots, purses, and assorted eggshell trinkets. The surprisingly supple leather can be very expensive.

The park is at Km. 100 along the old road from Guatemala City to Puerto San José. You can camp here for $3.25 per person. Bring your own tent.

Also at the farm, you'll find **light aircraft rides.** Contact Christopher at tel. 5651-6908 for details.

Aqua Magic

Another recreational option well suited to escaping the characteristic heat of Guatemala's Pacific plains is Aqua Magic (tel. 7881-1648,

10 A.M.-5 P.M. Wed.-Fri., 9 A.M.-6 P.M. Sat. and Sun., $8.75 adults, $6 children), where you'll find a small water park with numerous water slides, a wave pool, and beach access. There are also several restaurants and snack bars spread throughout. Though nowhere near as big or elaborate as Xocomil, in Retalhuleu, it is certainly adequate. You'll find the park by turning left after you cross the bridge across the Canal de Chiquimulilla leading to the beachfront part of town.

Accommodations

Most of the town's acceptable accommodations are, oddly, not found beachside. An exception is **Posada Quetzal** (along the main drag in Barrio Miramar, tel. 7881-1892 or 7881-2493, $65 d), where you'll find a pleasant beachside restaurant on a covered wooden deck, a swimming pool, and simple but clean bungalows with ceiling fans and cable TV. The beach fronting the property is somewhat dirty, as it's right in town.

Some nicer options can be found in the heart of town. **Turicentro Martita** (5a Calle y Avenida del Comercio, tel. 7888-4848, www.hotelmartita.com) has a very good restaurant with indoor or outdoor (poolside) seating and a varied menu of sandwiches, soups, grilled meats, and seafood. Its spotless rooms have comfortable beds, private bath, and air-conditioning, among other amenities. Rates vary, ranging from $75 (s/d) midweek to $90 per night (s/d) on weekends. Guests enjoy half-off admission to Aqua Magic water park.

Heading west outside of town along Km. 113 on the road to the beachside development of Chulamar, you'll find **Hotel Costa Verde** (Km 113 Carretera a Chulamar, tel. 2367-0571 or 7881-1161, www.hotelcostaverdeguatemala.com, $75-95 depending on day of week), a very nice property offering rooms with all the standard amenities as well as fully equipped suites. It also has a restaurant and a swimming pool.

Food

Turning right after the Chiquimulilla Canal bridge (coming from the mainland) into the beachfront part of town, you'll find **Rancho Costa Grande,** a popular place with a varied menu that is predictably heavy on seafood. All of the other recommended places to eat are in the hotel properties. The best restaurant in town is hands-down that of **Turicentro Martita** (tel. 7888-4848).

Getting There

Buses to Puerto San José leave Guatemala City's bus terminal every half hour or so. It's also possible to arrange a private transfer with almost any travel agency in Antigua.

Chulamar

West of Puerto San José, Chulamar is home to many of the weekend vacation homes of wealthy folks from Guatemala City. Here you'll find one of the Pacific Coast's most luxurious lodging options, built to satisfy the demands of the Guatemalan elite. The **☉ Soleil Pacífico** (tel. 7879-3131, www.gruposoleil. com), formerly a Radisson property, is a huge all-inclusive resort complex on a clean private beach with all the feel of an Acapulco beachside megaresort. Although it's popular on weekends, you may just have the place all to yourself if you visit during the middle of the week. There are two swimming pools and a variety of dining options. Double rooms start at $160 per room per night, all-inclusive, Sunday-Thursday or $200 on weekends. There are also deluxe suites and bungalows for $300 and $400 a night, respectively. You can get a day pass to enjoy the swimming pool and the hotel grounds for $50 per person, a popular option with cruise-ship passengers. Many of the sailfishing outfits also accommodate their clients here. Transport to the hotel is available from Guatemala City and Antigua with prior arrangement. Its sister hotel is the Soleil La Antigua.

Juan Gaviota

Juan Gaviota (www.juangaviota.com), a huge planned community spanning 15 kilometers of beachfront located 12 kilometers west of Puerto San José, is the newest enclave of Guatemala's elite and has all the feel of a Miami subdivision. The first of several construction phases encompassing this ambitious project is Marina del Sur, which features a central clubhouse with a restaurant fronting the Pacific Ocean, in addition to swimming pools, tennis courts, soccer fields, and beach volleyball courts. Juan Gaviota is equipped with a boat marina, and future plans call for a golf course, timeshare condos, and hotels. A few homes are available for rent. The best place to look for beach villa rentals in this neck of the woods is on the website of Antigua-based Century 21 Casa Nova (www.century21casanova.com). Homes here rent for about $700 a week, or $400 for a weekend. This is a self-contained, gated community and you won't find much outside of the private homes in the community.

PUERTO QUETZAL

The main attraction here is the **Puerto Quetzal Cruise Ship Terminal,** where an increasing number of boats calling on Guatemala's Pacific Coast make landfall. Within the larger terminal area is the **Marina Pez Vela** (tel. 2379-5790), harboring boats for sailfishing adventures. Cruise-ship passengers will find several amenities, including Internet access, telephone communications, and stands selling a variety of local handicrafts. You can also book sailfishing trips from here. **Guatemala Sport Fishing** (tel. 5709-8697) has a charter desk that operates out of the marina. There's also an excellent restaurant, **7 Caldos del Mar** (Seven Soups of the Sea, tel. 2361-8176, $10-30), run by the amiable Dimitris Moliviatis. You'll find more than seven soups on the menu—including *tapado, sancocho,* and *kakik*—as well as a variety of meat and seafood dishes, and a fully stocked

JUAN GAVIOTA: GUATEMALA'S PACIFIC PARADISE

While Guatemala's Pacific Coast hasn't yet attracted the attention of foreign investors, this doesn't mean the region lacks infrastructure comparable to that of its better-known neighbors. Local investors, as they always do in Guatemala, have stepped in to fill the void. The planned community of Juan Gaviota began in the late 1990s as the dream of a group of five Guatemalan investors who purchased a sizable land plot with 15 kilometers of beachfront.

The development essentially sprang up out of nowhere. A trail crisscrossing the property was upgraded to a serviceable road, a canal was dredged (and a bridge to cross it built), and electricity had to be brought in. The latter, at a cost of over $4 million, now benefits nearby communities in addition to residents of Marina del Sur. Wave breakers were installed in order to provide a safe haven for boats and facilitate the construction of the marina. Several thousand tons of rock were also brought in. The first phase of Marina del Sur alone is estimated to have cost over $130 million.

The project has a 20-year master plan, made in conjunction with a local consulting firm. The next phase encompasses a golf course and three hotels, opening Juan Gaviota to foreign investors and visitors. It is rumored the hotels are being built by a U.S. investment firm.

The community is in some ways an ecological preserve. Juan Gaviota's creators left local mangrove swamps undisturbed in their quest to maintain the local ecological balance. Poaching of sea turtle eggs and iguanas from the property is strictly prohibited. Private ownership of the vast property and the presence of private security forces to patrol it ensure closer compliance of these restrictions, something not easily replicated in coastal communities elsewhere in Guatemala.

Juan Gaviota's developers have placed their eyes upon Lake Petén Itzá and Antigua Guatemala as locales for future development projects on a similar scale.

bar. Order a Cuba Libre (rum and coke) with Guatemala's famous Zacapa Centenario rum.

◖ IZTAPA

Farther west along the coastline are the lovely beaches of Iztapa, which are remarkably clean, wide, and sandy. Although the town itself is a dilapidated old port town, it is becoming increasingly popular as the jumping-off point for some of the world's best sailfishing. Iztapa is Guatemala's original port, used by the Spanish conqueror Pedro de Alvarado to build boats and set sail for his onward journey to Perú. Anglers will find first-class accommodations to complement the world-class fishing just off the coast. Surfers will find plenty of waves to ride here, as there is a fairly decent break. A newer recreational offering is that of whale-watching tours during the winter months. All beach access in Iztapa is private and visitors have to cross the canal to get to the beaches. Your best bet is to stay at an area lodge.

Sailfishing Outfitters

A five-night fishing package (includes boat, captain, meals, transport from Guatemala City airport, accommodation in Iztapa and Antigua/Guatemala City hotels) generally starts at US$1,550 per person, based on a group of four. Add-ons include golfing in Guatemala City or La Antigua. Tips for the boat captain generally run about $100 per day per group.

Among the recommended outfitters is the American-owned and -operated **Sailfish Bay Lodge** (tel. 2426-3909 direct or 800/638-7405 U.S. reservations, www.sailfishbay.com). Packages include food and accommodations at a beautiful eight-room lodge right on the beach across the canal in Iztapa. Another option is the upstart **Buena Vista Sportfishing Lodge** (Calle Baja Mar, Aldea Buena Vista, tel. 7832-1991/05, www.buenavistasportfishing.com), owned by an American expatriate. Its developer sees huge potential along the Guatemalan coast after having drifted here from Costa Rica.

Based in Antigua, and a joint Guatemalan-American venture, is **The Great Sailfishing Company** (tel. 7832-1991, 5966-4528 Antigua or 877/763-0851 U.S., www.greatsailfishing.com). You can fish using conventional methods as well as fly-fishing and the company's informative website can point you in the right direction when planning a sailfishing trip to Guatemala. Guests stay at Villas del Pacífico Resort or a private villa within the same compound.

Under new ownership, **Pacific Fins Resort & Marina** (tel. 888/700-3467 U.S., www.pacificfins.com.gt) operates out of its very attractive namesake lodge and restaurant. They also offer whale-watching tours. **Guatemala Sport Fishing** (tel. 5709-8697) has a charter desk at Puerto Quetzal's Marina Pez Vela. It's a budget option with rates starting at $100 per person for Saturday fishing trips including roundtrip transportion from La Antigua.

Based in Florida and operating out of its namesake lodge one mile west of Puerto San José, **Casa Vieja Lodge** (tel. 866/846-9121, www.casaviejalodge.com) is one of the larger outfitters. Many of its staff members worked for Iztapa's original sailfishing lodge, Fins 'N Feathers. The lodge is in an old wood house (as its name implies) that has been wonderfully restored to afford anglers a comfortable place to come back to after a day of fishing. A more recent addition to the sailfishing scene enjoying very favorable reviews is **Blue Bayou Sailfishing** (tel. 5208-0098, www.bluebayouguatemala.com). Sailfishing trips include accommodations in a comfortable poolside villa inside a private compound near Marina Pez Vela. The company also offers fly fishing trips on Guatemala's Pacific Coast with accommodations in Rio Dulce.

Whale-Watching

Whale Watching Guatemala (tel. 2366-1026, www.whalewatchingguatemala.com, $175 per person) operates a six-hour tour. In addition to whales (humpback, short-finned pilot, finback, and whale sharks), you can expect to see bottlenose dolphins, sea turtles, and manta rays. Trips leave on weekends from December through April (at 7 A.M. from Aldea Buena Vista) and the cost includes breakfast, lunch, and drinks onboard the boat. Tickets for children are half-price; you can also charter a boat with a minimum of eight people on weekdays.

Accommodations and Food

In town, adequate accommodations can be found at **Sol y Playa Tropical** (1a Calle 5-48 Zona 1, tel. 7867-3847, www.hotelsolyplaya.com.gt, $40 d), which has rooms with private baths and ceiling fans or air-conditioning, situated around a nicely landscaped swimming pool area. A nicer option is **Hotel Suites Mar y Sol** (tel. 7934-2364, www.hotelmarysol.com, $70 d). Its spacious suites include a kitchen with microwave oven and refrigerator; rooms have cable TV and air-conditioning. There are two swimming pools and a swim-up bar. Across the Canal de Chiquimulilla and right on the beach, Iztapa's nicest accommodations are at the (**Sailfish Bay Lodge** (tel. 2426-3909 direct or 800/638-7405 U.S. reservations, www.sailfishbay.com, $125 d). Accommodations here are usually sold as part of a sailfishing package, but you are more than welcome to stay on your own. The Guatemalan Pacific Coast's best-kept secret is a modern, well-designed lodge featuring a thatched-roof seaside bar and swimming pool with whirlpool bath, comfortable oceanview rooms with all the usual amenities, and an excellent restaurant fronting the canal. You can enjoy phenomenal views of three volcanoes rising above the surrounding mangroves while you dine. The outstanding feature of this place is that it's the only lodge sitting right on the broad, black-sand beach. A number of luxurious beach villas are the only neighbors. There

THE PACIFIC COAST

THE SAILFISH CAPITAL OF THE WORLD

A unique swirling of ocean currents between Mexico and El Salvador creates an eddy unusually rich in pelagic fish (such as herring and mackerel) right on Guatemala's doorstep, where billfish, including sailfish and marlin, gather to feed along with large concentrations of dorado, yellowfin tuna, and wahoo. The result is some of the world's best sailfishing waters.

Enthusiasts of Guatemala's emerging sailfishing scene are quick to point out that it is the true "Sailfish Capital of the World" and have the numbers to back up their claims. The world records for conventional and fly-fishing single-day catches have been set here, at 75 and 23 respectively. In March 2006, a single vessel carrying five anglers caught and released a whopping 124 sailfish. While the records are indeed impressive, anglers plying the Guatemalan Pacific Coast need not worry about any "feast or famine" phenomenon, as catch-and-release numbers are quite consistent. In terms of billfish releases per angler, Guatemala ranks at the top (a statistic compiled by The Southwest Fisheries Science Center in California). Its Catch Per Unit of Effort (CPUE) for Pacific sailfish in 2005 was 5.83 compared to Costa Rica's 2.57 and Panama's 2.25. On average, you can expect to catch 15-20 fish per boat per day, but catches of 25 fish aren't uncommon.

Guatemala's strength is certainly in its numbers. Unlike most of its competitors, Guatemala's not known as a beach destination with impressive resort accommodations. All that is starting to change, however, and there are now some very comfortable accommodations where you can stay right on the beach and relax after a long day at sea. Some outfitters accommodate anglers in their own lodges; otherwise there are private luxury villas on the beach or the large Villas del Pacífico resort. Many outfits combine fishing packages with a round of golf on one of Guatemala City's excellent golf courses. All of the outfitters listed practice catch-and-release and use circle hooks, as mandated by Guatemalan law.

Fishing is active year-round, but most anglers come between November and May seeking a respite from colder climates. Prices for fishing packages vary by the size of the boat used and can be fairly expensive in Guatemala; boats generally travel 40-80 kilometers (25-50 miles) offshore to a deep, 600-meter (2,000-foot) basin where sailfish tend to congregate around its rim, translating into higher fuel costs. Boats heading out this way are usually in the 28-foot range, but there are also a few 42- and 43-foot boats. Expect to pay about $2,100 per person for two people on a two-day and three-night fishing package on a 28-foot boat. Most packages include food and drink, accommodations, boat and captain, gear, and transfers to and from the Guatemala City airport. Anglers often spend their last night in Antigua or Guatemala City.

are surfboards for guests' use. Transportation to the lodge from Guatemala City or Antigua is also available.

Another option is **Buena Vista Sportfishing Lodge** (Calle Baja Mar, Aldea Buena Vista, tel. 7880-4203/05 or 866/699-3277 U.S., www.buenavistasportfishing.com), housed in a large yellow villa fronting Chiquimulilla canal. Boats dock right in front of the property, so it's a quick trip to your shower or the lodge's swimming pool. The large somewhat spartan rooms feature air-conditioning and private baths.

Iztapa's best-known restaurant is popular with anglers and locals alike. **El Capitán** (tel. 7881-4403, 7 A.M.-9 P.M. daily) serves large portions of tasty seafood and meat dishes under a thatched-roof *palapa* facing the lagoon. It also has a lively bar.

Next door to El Capitán, the ◖ **Pacific Fins Resort & Marina** (tel. 888/700-3467 U.S., www.pacificfins.com.gt, $150-250 d) is an attractive lodge with six two-bedroom/two-bath villas with kitchenette and living room. Rooms include satellite flat-screen televisions, hardwood accents,

© AL ARGUETA

Sailfish Bay Lodge

ALONG THE IZTAPA-MONTERRICO ROAD

Heading east from Iztapa, a smooth paved road travels along the coastline for about 25 kilometers to Monterrico. A bridge from Iztapa's *Colonia 20 de Octubre* ($3 per vehicle) transports you across the canal to Puerto Viejo, from where the road begins. You'll see loofah farms lining the side of the road and the occasional turnoff toward the beach, where numerous small hotels have begun to spring up on what is probably the finest stretch of sand on Guatemala's Pacific shores. There are rumors of a luxurious 18-hole golf course planned somewhere along this route in the not-too-distant future.

Accommodations and Food

◖ **Cayman Suites** (Km. 10.5, tel. 5529-6518/19 lodge; 2362-1708 or 2362-1709 reservations, www.caymansuites.com.gt, $85-155 d) is set on a spectacular beach flanked by a kidney-shaped swimming pool and open-air *palapa*-roofed restaurant and bar. Its 22 rooms feature all the usual amenities, some with gorgeous sea views, and include deluxe rooms, junior suites, and spacious, fully furnished suites. All rooms have wireless Internet, DirecTV, and fine hardwood accents. The restaurant serves good international cuisine and seafood. ATVs are available for rent. Just one kilometer away, at kilometer 11.5, is the also stylish ◖ **Villa Los Cabos** (tel. 2363-4325, www.villaloscabos.com.gt, $275 per night). Although a private community, villa number 12C has been kept open for rentals. The horseshoe-shaped complex comprises three-story units built round a huge swimming pool overlooking the sea. The beautiful villa includes three bedrooms, two bathrooms, air-conditioning, a private patio with hot tub, and a living room, dining room, and full kitchen. It sleeps eight and comes fully equipped.

Closer to Monterrico, at Km. 14.5, is **Portete Beach Bungalows** (tel. 5411-9271, portete@intelnet.net.gt), with two simple beachfront

wireless Internet, and brand-new furniture. All rooms have air-conditioning. The bar and restaurant, facing the lodge's swimming pool, offer a varied menu that includes sandwiches, pasta, grilled, sautéed, or breaded fish, chicken Florentine, and Argentinean-style *parrilladas*. Stays at the resort are usually part of a multiday fishing package, but hosts are also open to receiving guests just looking for a place to relax in the tropical swelter. If you're not in Guatemala to fish and just want to stay here, your best chance of scoring a room is during the off-season (May-Oct.).

Getting There

The same buses that leave Guatemala City's bus terminal for Puerto San José more often than not continue to Iztapa. Most anglers arrive on all-inclusive packages booked directly through their operation of choice, covering transportation logistics.

THE PACIFIC COAST

© AL ARGUETA

oceanfront Cayman Suites, along the road from Iztapa to Monterrico

bungalows and a main house equipped with fan, refrigerator, private bath, and some decor. Each of the two bungalows can be rented for a weekend at a cost of $60 (d). The main house is available for $133. There is a small restaurant and bar. You might be able to get a deal for midweek stays and have the place all to yourself, though in that case, you might have to bring your own food.

Should you need to fill up, there is a gas station at kilometer 17. A good place to stop for a snack or pick up any needed groceries is **Las Garzas** (Km. 17.5, tel. 4073-1399, 7:30 A.M.-9 P.M. daily). The owners of this friendly roadside minimart can help you get your bearings. They also serve snacks, including pizza and sandwiches, which you can enjoy in a pleasant outdoor patio setting.

Another budget option (for this neighborhood) is found at **Hotel Villa Kairos** (Km. 20, tel. 5582-3767, www.hotelvillakairos.com, $44-56 d in standard rooms or $72-120 per

bungalow). The simple bungalows lack charm but front well-manicured lawns next to the swimming pool and overlook the sea. The standard rooms are a better value. The last place you'll come across on this road is **Utz Tzaba** (Km. 21.8, tel. 5318-9452, info@utz-tzaba. com, www.utz-tzaba.com, $89 d, $159 bungalow), which has 10 rooms in a large main building as well as four bungalows. All rooms have tile floors, private hot-water bathrooms, wireless Internet, air-conditioning, and ceiling fans. The bungalows include two bedrooms and a living room and come fully furnished with mini-fridge, gas range, kitchen sink, and dining room table. There is a bar by the infinity-edge swimming pool, along with whirlpool tub. The hotel's restaurant serves excellent meals, including sandwiches, pasta, and seafood in the $6-10 range. The lodge is closed yearly on Christmas Eve and Christmas Day. Call ahead, as it's also closed for fumigation about every two months.

Monterrico and Hawaii

Monterrico, once a sleepy fishing village with one hotel run by an ex-Peace Corps volunteer is fast becoming popular with foreigners looking to get some time by the beach on their trip to Guatemala. The village has grown considerably in the last few years, as has the quality of its accommodations. It is a popular weekend destination with folks from Guatemala City and students from Antigua's Spanish schools. The same architects who gave Xocomil and Xetulul Parks their outstanding visual appeal were hired by INGUAT and local tourism authorities to provide Monterrico with an urban facelift—complete with a tree-lined entrance to the main beach, pedestrian walkway, and a boat marina fronting Canal de Chiquimulilla. The pedestrian thoroughfare, officially dubbed Paseo de Don Pedro (after Pedro Cofiño Kepfer, a key player in masterminding Monterrico's urban facelift, who died in a tragic accident in 2007), has yet to attract the upscale businesses it seems to have been designed for. Nonetheless, it is a pleasant way to get from town to the beach.

Although it's easy to see Monterrico as a beach destination, it should be noted that it was a protected sea turtle nesting site long before it became the haunt of beach-seeking vacationers. Visitors can contribute to the conservation efforts of the local sea turtle conservation site via their paid admission to tour its grounds. As for the beaches in Monterrico, there are, in all honesty, better and cleaner stretches elsewhere along Guatemala's Pacific seaboard. The waves break very close to the sand here and the beaches slope dramatically downwards, which means you don't have a particularly wide stretch of beach, unlike at Iztapa or Tilapa farther west. The undertow, as along much of the Pacific Coast, is severe, and drownings are not uncommon. Exercise due caution.

In addition to the beaches, Monterrico offers the opportunity to interact with nature in some unique ways, whether it's touring the mangrove canals, holding a baby sea turtle in your hand before its maiden voyage out to sea, or watching a mother turtle come ashore to lay eggs in total darkness. Try to engage in at least one of these ecologically responsible activities while keeping in mind the ecological significance of this site. The sea turtles here have a fighting chance, though they are being wiped out elsewhere by the indiscriminate harvesting of their eggs. A newer threat to Guatemala's coastal ecosystems comes from Canadian and Australian mining interests, as its black-sand beaches are said to harbor 12 percent of the world's iron reserves.

Eight kilometers east along the sandy shoreline is **Parque Hawaii,** a more remote turtle nesting and iguana and crocodile breeding site on a pretty beach marked by the presence of sand dunes. **The Wildlife Rescue and Conservation Association** (ARCAS, www.arcasguatemala. com) has a sea turtle, crocodile, and mangrove conservation project here. Volunteers are welcome for a minimum one-week commitment ($80 per week for accommodations only) and assist in various projects, including animal care, construction projects, mangrove reforestation, environmental education, and turtle egg collection and hatchery management. Volunteers are also needed for another project in the neighboring village of El Rosario, six kilometers east. Turtle nesting season runs June-November with the peak of the action in August and September.

Hawaii is host to a few weekend homes for Guatemala's elite but has also added some recommended hotels of late. It has an online presence at www.hawaiiguatemala.com. You can get to Hawaii from Monterrico via public bus ($0.50), pickup ($5), or via a 20-minute boat ride through the canals ($20). Buses leave at 6 A.M., 11 A.M., 1:30 P.M., and 3:30 P.M.

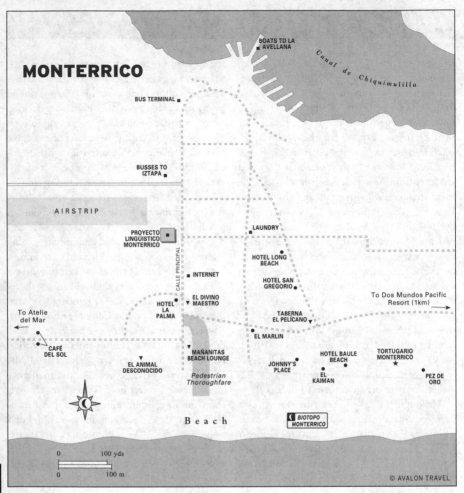

MONTERRICO

BOATS TO LA AVELLANA

Canal de Chiquimulilla

BUS TERMINAL

BUSSES TO IZTAPA

AIRSTRIP

PROYECTO LINGÜISTICO MONTERRICO

LAUNDRY

HOTEL LONG BEACH

CALLE PRINCIPAL

INTERNET

HOTEL SAN GREGORIO

To Dos Mundos Pacific Resort (1km)

To Atelie del Mar

HOTEL LA PALMA

EL DIVINO MAESTRO

TABERNA EL PELICANO

EL MARLIN

CAFÉ DEL SOL

EL ANIMAL DESCONOCIDO

MAÑANITAS BEACH LOUNGE

JOHNNY'S PLACE

HOTEL BAULE BEACH

TORTUGARIO MONTERRICO

EL KAIMAN

PEZ DE ORO

Pedestrian Thoroughfare

Beach

BIOTOPO MONTERRICO

0   100 yds
0   100 m

© AVALON TRAVEL

SIGHTS
◖ Biotopo Monterrico

This protected biotope (www.visitmonterrico.com) encompasses the beaches and mangrove swamps of Monterrico and those of adjacent Hawaii, which are the prime nesting sites for sea turtles on Guatemala's Pacific seaboard, including the giant leatherback and smaller olive ridley turtles. Locals are involved in a conservation project with the local turtle hatchery whereby they are allowed to keep half of the

eggs they collect from nests and turn in the other half to the hatchery. Sadly, leatherback turtle arrivals have declined dramatically in recent years.

In the heart of town and run by the San Carlos University Center for Conservation Studies (CECON), the **Tortugario Monterrico** (on the sandy street just behind Johnny's Place, 8 A.M.-noon and 2-5 P.M. daily, $1) encompasses a turtle hatchery right on the beach, where collected eggs are reburied and allowed

© AL ARGUETA

a baby sea turtle in Monterrico

to hatch under protected conditions. There's also a visitors center. In addition to baby sea turtles, the hatchery has enclosures housing green iguanas, crocodiles, and freshwater turtles bred on-site for release into the wild. The staff at CECON is always on the lookout for Spanish-speaking volunteers.

NIGHTLIFE

For a Central American beach town, the nightlife scene in Monterrico is pretty tame (weekends aside). This is certainly not your average spring break destination. Most places close at 10 P.M., with only a few exceptions. The liveliest place in town is **Johnny's Place** (right on the beach, tel. 4369-6900, www.johnnysplacehotel.com), where the party goes until 1 A.M. on weekends. Another hot spot is **El Animal Desconocido** (8 P.M.-1 A.M. Thurs.-Sat.), where you can chill out to an eclectic mix of dance and rock music in a colorful atmosphere. Behind Johnny's Place is **Taberna**

El Pelícano, but it also closes early. The poolside bar at **El Marlin** is another popular watering hole. It sometimes closes late. A great place to watch the sunset and enjoy a drink is **Mañanitas Beach Lounge** (tel. 5771-7768, 11 A.M.-1 A.M. daily), situated above the beach with a second-story patio.

RECREATION

You won't find a whole lot to do around here other than the beaches. Whether from a lack of entrepreneurial initiative or what have you, the recreational options aside from sunbathing and walking along the beach are pretty limited. Boat tours of the mangrove-lined canals are offered by ARCAS and CECON. They can often be arranged via the local hotels. You'll see plenty of birds and, with some luck, iguanas and anteaters. Antigua-based **Old Town Outfitters** (www.bikeguatemala.com) offers kayaking in the canals with prior arrangement. Monterrico's riptides and huge waves

THE PACIFIC COAST

MONTERRICO-HAWAII AND ITS SEA TURTLES

If you're traveling to the Monterrico-Hawaii area between June and December, you might have the opportunity to witness a sea turtle coming ashore to lay its eggs or watch baby sea turtles making their maiden voyage out to sea.

Turtle nesting peaks during August and September, when you might be able to glimpse a large leatherback (baule) or the smaller olive ridley (parlama) coming ashore to lay eggs. Unfortunately, locals are also on the lookout for egg-laying sea turtles to snatch up the eggs and sell them, but under an agreement with the CECON monitoring station at Monterrico and ARCAS in Hawaii, they donate part of their stash toward conservation efforts. Your best bet for seeing a nesting turtle is to go with one of the CECON-trained guides or volunteer with ARCAS.

Volunteers are welcome at both stations. Among the duties are the collection of turtle eggs after the mothers have come ashore and moving them to a protected nesting site, where they are reburied and allowed to hatch. Typical incubation periods for olive ridley eggs is 50 days, 72 for leatherbacks. After a few days in a holding pen, the young turtles are released, either at sunrise or sunset, and make their way across the sand and into the ocean. As the young turtles scamper across the sand, they are being imprinted with the unique details of the beach and its sand, where they will return and nest when they are adults. All this assumes they make it to adulthood, a big assumption when taking into account that only one turtle in 100 makes it to adulthood. Sea turtles are threatened not just by the collection of their eggs but also by fishing activities, where they often end up in nets, and sea pollution. Plastic bags, for example, are often mistaken for jellyfish by hungry sea turtles. The CECON station at Monterrico (www.visitmonterrico.com) releases about 5,000 sea turtle hatchlings per year. Turtle races, involving the release of new hatchlings on their maiden voyage to the sea, are no longer held because they were disruptive to the baby turtles' development and short-circuited the very conservation efforts they were meant to support. A newer initiative is the annual Festival de la Tortuga Marina, which takes place sometime during October or November. It features turtle releases, live music, and a surfing competition.

The ARCAS turtle hatchery in Hawaii also releases sea turtles. Visitors are allowed to witness turtle releases in limited numbers for a donation of about $3.25 (includes admission to the hatchery). If you're interested in volunteering with sea turtle conservation efforts, check out local grassroots turtle conservation group Akazul (http://akazul.org).

that literally crash onshore make swimming a perilous option.

ACCOMMODATIONS
Under $10

A good value in this price range can be found at ☖Hotel Long Beach (tel. 7848-1577 or 5867-3732, www.hotellongbeach.galeon.com), down the street from Taberna El Pelícano, with spotless rooms with firm beds built next to a pool for $10 per person. There are hammocks for lounging outside your door. Another recommended budget hotel is Hotel El Delfin (tel. 4661-9255, www.hotel-el-delfin.com). There are basic but clean rooms with shared bath for $5 per person or rooms with two king-size beds and private bath for $15. All of the beds, as in most Monterrico budget hotels, consist of a foam mattress on a concrete slab. There's a clean swimming pool, a bar and restaurant, and plenty of hammocks to lounge on. An old standby enjoying a new lease on life, thanks to savvy web marketing and new management, is Johnny's Place (tel. 5812-0409 or 4369-6900, www.johnnysplacehotel.com, $6 p/p in dorm to $120/bungalow) set right on the beach. The rooms are built so as to share a swimming pool with the unit next door and run the gamut from basic backpacker accommodations to souped-up bungalows sleeping up to 8. The basic shared-bath dorm rooms have foam beds and some spartan furnishings under a thatched roof. Middle-of-the-road accommodations include double rooms with ceiling fans and private bathrooms for $20 or $30 with air-conditioning (weekdays). Larger "deluxe bungalows" with air-conditioning, kitchen, living room, and cable TV go for $100 on weekdays. Room rates for weekend stays are about 20 percent higher. There's a restaurant and bar on the beach and a sand volleyball court. Johnny's is popular with the backpacking crowd.

Monterrico's original backpacker spot, **Hotel Baule Beach** no longer holds much appeal because of the availability of much better options. Beds in unattractive rooms consist of a concrete slab with thin cushioning. Numerous thefts have also been reported. Stay here only if in dire need. West from here, the next place over is **El Kaiman** (tel. 5617-9880), where for $7 per person you get a bed, a cold-water shower, and not much else. Upon last glance, the hotel pool looked somewhat funky.

$10-25

Set back a bit from the beach in Monterrico on a quiet side street, you'll find **El Marlin** (tel. 5715-4934), also seemingly popular with a younger crowd. There are a bar and a small pool with tables in the courtyard. The rooms have ceiling fan, private cold-water shower, cable TV, and thin mattresses. There are hammocks outside each door. Rates are $13 per person and it is open only on weekends outside of holidays.

Budget accommodations in neighboring Hawaii are somewhat more expensive than in Monterrico but the payoff is greater seclusion. **Villa Hawaii** (tel. 4146-8470, $20 d) offers basic, fan-cooled rooms in blue palapa-roofed structures situated around a swimming pool and fronting the ocean. It's owned by a local family and there's a basic *comedor* across the street.

$25-50

In Monterrico, west of Calle Principal along the beach you'll find pleasant **Café del Sol** (tel. 5050-9179 or 5050-9173, www.cafe-del-sol.com), where double rooms in the original building with cold-water showers in private bath, fan, and mosquito netting cost $30. There's a newer section behind the hotel across the street where slightly nicer rooms painted in cheerful yellows featuring some decor cost $33 (d). These rooms also have a small patio fronting the street. The restaurant here is quite good. East from Calle Principal, around the corner and down the street from Taberna El Pelícano, is **Hotel San Gregorio** (tel. 2238-4690 or 5204-2013, www.hotelsangregorio.com), with somewhat generic new rooms centered around a swimming pool for $40 (d), all with air-conditioning, some with fan. Along the beach heading east from Johnny's Place, you'll find **Hotel Pez de Oro** (tel. 2368-3684 reservations or 7920-9785 hotel, www.pezdeoro.com), an excellent choice with tastefully decorated rooms built around a swimming pool with wooden deck. The 11 attractive bungalows, all with private baths, feature terracotta floors, nice decorative accents, and firm beds. Rates for double occupancy are $40 on weekdays and $52 on weekends. The cost is the same for equally well-decorated and furnished raised-platform bungalows with nice decks (or patios) and hammocks in a separate area with its own swimming pool. The restaurant here is recommended.

In Hawaii, **Hotel El Camaron** (tel. 4084-4234, $40 d) has decent rooms with TV and private bathroom. There's an on-site restaurant and a sometimes-lively bar.

$50-100

West of the main street in Monterrico, about 200 meters from the pedestrian thoroughfare, **Atelie del Mar** (tel. 5752-5528, www.hotelateliedelmar.com, $60 d) has somewhat smallish rooms, all

Dos Mundos Pacific Resort

© AL ARGUETA

with air-conditioning and TV, centered around a sizeable swimming pool. The hotel is set away from the beach and there's a restaurant with spotty service. (Avoid the room directly above the kitchen, as smells tend to filter in.)

A newer option in this price range is found heading east toward Hawaii. (**Hotel Honolulu** (tel. 4005-0500, www.hotelhonolulu.com.gt, $80 d) is a comfortable beachfront hotel housed in quaint wooden cottages built round a pleasant swimming pool. It has a restaurant and bar serving mostly seafood dishes.

Over $100

Monterrico's most stylish beachside digs are at the Italian-owned (**Dos Mundos Pacific Resort** (tel. 7823-0820, www.hotelsdosmundos.com/monterrico, $122 d), located about one kilometer east of Monterrico, along the beach. This fabulous property features 14 luxurious beachfront villas with terra-cotta floors, hot-water showers, and air-conditioning housed in

ecochic thatched-roof structures with private patios. The bathrooms feature artsy ceramic sinks and oversized "rain" showerheads. The fine restaurant serves excellent Italian cuisine overlooking an infinity-edge swimming pool and the sea. Rates are about $30 lower during the week.

Another option in this pricier domain is located east of Monterrico in Hawaii. (**Casa Bella** (www.casabellamonterrico.com, $150 per bungalow) offers spacious one- or two-story bungalows (two or four bedrooms) with cable TV, full kitchens, and sitting areas featuring tropical rattan furniture. Each bungalow has a covered private patio with sea views. A pool and a restaurant are also on the premises. Also in Hawaii, **Hawaian Paradise** (tel. 5361-3011, www.hawaianparadise.com, $104 d) is another welcome addition to the area's hotel infrastructure. Comfortable air-conditioned rooms are housed in a cheerful yellow structure topped with a *palapa*-roof terrace. Spacious apartments with comfortable living room area ($200-300) sleep up to seven guests. The hotel fronts a swimming pool and the ocean. There are a restaurant/bar, hammock lounges, and a pool table. It's a good alternative if you're not into Monterrico's somewhat raucous weekend atmosphere and just want to get away from it all.

If you're looking to have a place all to yourself in Hawaii, your best option is to rent a villa. **Lahaina** (tel. 321/243-3555 U.S., www.vrbo.com/322283) is an American-owned seaside villa spread out over three floors. It comes fully furnished and equipped with air-conditioning, TV, and even Wi-Fi. There's a swimming pool overlooking the ocean. You can rent the first floor room next to the pool for $50 per night or the whole villa for $200. There are wonderful sea views from the third-floor patio.

FOOD

Most of Monterrico's hotels, particularly those that are on the beach, serve food. The following are the best of the hotel restaurants, along with a few non-hotel eateries serving decent food. **Café del Sol** (tel. 5810-0821, www.cafe-del-sol.com, all meals daily) serves excellent seafood dishes ($4-8) under an airy *palapa* or on a pleasant beachside patio. For Italian fare at affordable prices, you can't beat the atmosphere at **Pez de Oro** (tel. 7920-9785, www.pezdeoro.com, $5-7). On the pricier side, the restaurant at **Dos Mundos Pacific Resort** (tel. 7823-0820, www.hotelsdosmundos.com/monterrico, $10-35), overlooking both the sea and an infinity-edge swimming pool, is simply wonderful. Accompany your meal with a selection from the above-average wine list.

Hotels aside, there are also a few decent standalone eateries in town. On Calle Principal is **El Divino Maestro,** which does inexpensive seafood. Behind Johnny's Place, on the sandy street parallel to the shore, is **Taberna El Pelícano** (noon-2 P.M. and 6:30-9:30 P.M. Mon.-Fri., 6:30-10 P.M. Sat., noon-3 P.M. and 7-9:30 P.M. Sun.), where there are good pasta dishes and seafood ($4-8) and a fully stocked bar.

The hippest of all the town's eateries is **Mañanitas Beach Lounge** (tel. 5771-7768, 11 A.M.-I A.M., $4-8), fronting the beach along the pedestrian thoroughfare. Enjoy good smoothies, sandwiches, and cocktails from an airy, second-story patio while taking in gorgeous views of the sea.

Dining options are limited in Hawaii outside of the aforementioned hotels, though **Comedor Susy's** (open weekends) is a good bet for grilled chicken ($2), tacos, and refreshing *licuados*.

SERVICES

There is an ATM at Banrural, right in the heart of town. Monterrico's post office is on Calle Principal. You'll also find a nameless Internet communications center on this street.

Language Schools

If you want to learn Spanish at the beach, head to **Proyecto Lingüistico Monterrico** (Calle Principal, tel. 5619-8200, www.playademonterrico.com/proyling.htm), where 20 hours of one-on-one instruction per week cost $75. Accommodations with a local family are available for $50 per week for room and board.

GETTING THERE

There are two ways to get to Monterrico. The first of these is via the 25-kilometer road from Puerto Viejo (Iztapa). The other option is via the town of Taxisco, from which you continue south for 17 kilometers to La Avellana. At La Avellana you make a ferry crossing ($7 per vehicle), traveling for about 20 minutes through the mangrove swamps. Most people seem to prefer the route via Iztapa, as the road is smooth and fast and there are some new, enticing accommodations options along this route. Buses leave from Guatemala City's Zone 4 bus terminal every 30 minutes for Taxisco on their way to Chiquimulilla between 5 A.M. and 6 P.M. Connecting buses make the trip down to La Avellana. **Transportes Cubanita** leaves the

Zone 4 bus terminal directly for La Avellana at 10:30 A.M., 12:30 P.M., and 2:30 P.M. There are five buses a day from Puerto Viejo (Iztapa) to Monterrico leaving at 8 A.M., 10 A.M., noon, 1:30 P.M., and 4 P.M. As always, there's the occasional pickup truck heading this way. There are now also direct buses from Guatemala City ($5) and La Antigua ($6) a few times daily.

Increasingly popular are daily shuttle buses from Antigua costing about $25 on weekdays and $15 on weekends. Among the options is **Aventuras Vacacionales** (tel. 7832-6056, www.sailing-diving-guatemala.com/guatemala-tours/shuttles.php) and **Turansa** (tel. 7832-2928, info@turansa.com, www.turansa.com). Departure times are 8 A.M. and sometimes 1 P.M., depending on demand. They will continue to Hawaii (by request) for a few dollars more.

East to El Salvador

From Taxisco, the road continues east parallel to the coastline, passing near the town of Chiquimulilla before heading into higher elevations, from which there are fantastic panoramas of the ocean below.

CHIQUIMULA

Chiquimula is an adequate place to stop should you need to regroup after crossing the border from El Salvador or if you need a place to stay on the way there. If you need to hit an ATM, your best bet is the 5B ATM at Banrural (1a Calle and 1a Avenida Zona 3). There's also a Banco Industrial Visa ATM at 1a Avenida and 3a Calle Zona 2. Should you need to stay, try the **Hotel San Carlos** (Barrio Santiago, tel. 7885-0187, $13 d).

Outside of town at Km. 99 of the Pacific Coast Highway (CA-2) is **Erhco Park** (tel. 7885-0139), a fairly decent ecological park and working farm occupying almost 70 acres. There are nature trails, horseback riding, waterfalls, and farm animals. There's a small restaurant and you can camp or spend the night here in simple bungalows.

LAS LISAS

As you head east from Chiquimulilla close to the Salvadoran border, a turnoff from the Pacific Coast Highway (CA-2) at Km. 144 heads south to the small village of Las Lisas, which has some nice beaches on the other side of the Canal de Chiquimulilla in Barra El Jiote. The town itself is unremarkable and the tourism infrastructure virtually nonexistent, though there are a growing number of hotels in the area that merit mention. The only drawback is accessibility. To get to the beaches you must hire a boat from the main dock in Las Lisas at a cost of $13 each way, though you may be able to arrange pickup service from the area lodges if you call ahead. It's about a 20-minute ride to the Barra El Jiote from Las Lisas. As most of these lodges cater to sporadic visitors in these remote stretches of coastline, it's always a good idea to call ahead and reserve.

Accommodations and Food

One of Guatemala's most exotic hideaways, and the area's pioneering lodge, **Isleta de Gaia** (tel. 7885-0044, www.isleta-de-gaia.com, $77-84 d), is spectacularly set on a sandy spit between the Chiquimulilla Canal and the Pacific Ocean. There are 12 attractive bamboo bungalows of varying sizes facing the clean, sandy beach or the lagoon; all are built around a nice swimming pool. The restaurant is open for breakfast, lunch, and dinner, and serves excellent international fare in the $5-12 range. The service is second to none.

Divers will want to check out **Caleta Azul** (Barra del Jiote, tel. 5715-2849 or 5715-4101, www.caletaazul.net, $145 d all-inclusive), fronting a nice stretch of wide, sandy beach. In the waters just off the coast are the remains of two sunken vessels, one dating to the 1950s, which scuba divers can explore with the help of the lodge's diving outfit. The lodge itself features 10 rooms in comfortable thatched-roof cabanas, each with private bathroom, fan, a patio, and hammocks. There's also a two-bedroom furnished apartment with air-conditioning. Meals are included in the room rate and feature tasty Caribbean dishes, including seafood stews, served in an airy *palapa* structure with lovely sea views. A bar and swimming pool are also on the premises. Other recreational options include visits to the surrounding mangrove swamps and deep-sea fishing. If you call ahead, the lodge can help you out with transportation from the boat dock at Las Lisas.

Another wonderful addition to Guatemala's Pacific Coast is the lovely **Eco Hotel Playa Quilombo de Cucurumbé** (Barra El Jiote, tel. 5206-7984 or 2253-1228, www.playaquilombo.net), where room prices range from $20 in a ground-floor double room to $47 for a bungalow. The comfortable and tastefully decorated rooms are built around a swimming pool and front a gorgeous, wide, sandy beach. The restaurant serves bountiful portions of good food, including lasagna, barbecued steak, and chicken fajitas.

CIUDAD PEDRO DE ALVARADO

The border crossing to El Salvador is found at Ciudad Pedro de Alvarado, which is fairly quiet. Most traffic uses the crossing farther north at Valle Nuevo/Las Chinamas. There are frequent buses from here to Escuintla and onward to Guatemala City. There are basic accommodations and eateries on both sides of the border.

EL ORIENTE AND IZABAL

These two very different geographical regions comprise the part of Guatemala east of Guatemala City all the way to the Honduran border and the Caribbean Sea. Izabal is a sweltering jungle coastland with rainforests and beaches sharing some similarities with Belize to its north. The region known as El Oriente, meanwhile, is a mix of temperate mountains and semiarid plains. As you head east from Guatemala City on the Carretera al Atlántico (CA-9), the road descends into this region of dusty plains and cactus-studded hills. Farther along, in the department of Izabal, the terrain becomes lush and green before ending at Puerto Barrios, on the Caribbean Sea, just about 300 kilometers from the capital.

The Izabal region features a unique kind of Caribbean experience not at all like Cancún or the West Indies but nonetheless beautiful. Tourism promoters have labeled this, "A different Caribbean." Cruise ships regularly dock at Puerto Santo Tomás de Castilla, just across the bay from Puerto Barrios. Its new cruise-ship terminal is fast becoming a motor for the tourism development of this long-overlooked Caribbean coastal region. Cruise-ship day-trippers can explore a rainforest and pristine jungle river with waterfalls and pools in the lush green mountains looming over the port. From Puerto Barrios, it's just a quick hop to remote beaches on the peninsula of Punta de Manabique, the

HIGHLIGHTS

PETEN

BELIZE

The Zapotillo Cayes

Punta de Manabique Wildlife Refuge

GUATEMALA

Cerro San Gil and Río Las Escobas

Bocas del Polochic Wildlife Refuge

IZABAL

The Ruins of Quiriguá

ZACAPA

HONDURAS

The Ruins of Copán

CHIQUIMULA

0   25 mi

0   25 km

EL SALVADOR

© AVALON TRAVEL

LOOK FOR (TO FIND RECOMMENDED SIGHTS, ACTIVITIES, DINING, AND LODGING.

(The Ruins of Copán: This wonderful Mayan city just across the border in Honduras

is home to some of the finest carved stelae in the Mayan world and to an outstanding museum housing several original monuments (page 263).

(The Ruins of Quiriguá: Harboring beautifully carved stelae set amid luxuriant banana plantations and jungle, this small Mayan site is one of only three UNESCO World Heritage Sites in Guatemala (page 276).

(Cerro San Gil and Río Las Escobas: This fantastic rainforest preserve harboring a protected watershed with waterfalls and pristine pools is just minutes away from the cruise-ship terminal at Puerto Santo Tomás de Castilla (page 281).

(Punta de Manabique Wildlife Refuge: A remote peninsula abounding in wildlife and pristine nature, it also offers deserted beaches and the opportunity to explore adjoining wetland canals for excellent bird-watching (page 284).

(The Zapotillo Cayes: Sail or motorboat to the picture-postcard beaches of this remote island chain on the southern fringes of the Belize Barrier Reef for scuba diving, swimming, or just plain relaxation (page 295).

(Bocas del Polochic Wildlife Refuge: An excellent spot for bird-watching, this seldom-visited park has excellent visitor facilities from where you can explore jungle trails, wetland canals, caves, and sinkholes (page 306).

intriguing Caribbean town of Lívingston, or the exotic jungle canyon of the Río Dulce.

The seldom-explored beaches and wetlands of Punta de Manabique are protected as a wildlife refuge and offer some unique opportunities for ecotourism, wildlife-viewing, and beachcombing. Lívingston is a standout for its unique Garífuna culture brought to coastal Guatemala from the Caribbean island of St. Vincent by way of Roatán, Honduras. This Black Carib influence provides a fascinating contrast to Guatemala's largely Mayan heritage

with rhythmic dancing and musical customs that complete the Caribbean experience. The Río Dulce canyon connects Lívingston (and the Caribbean Sea) to Lake Izabal, Guatemala's largest lake. Along the Río Dulce, you'll find lush jungle canyons, hot springs, and side streams offering unique options for jungle accommodations. In the town of Río Dulce, at the mouth of Lake Izabal, you'll find a variety of tourist services and boat marinas, as it's become a popular shelter for boats sailing the Western Caribbean. The homes of wealthy Guatemalans

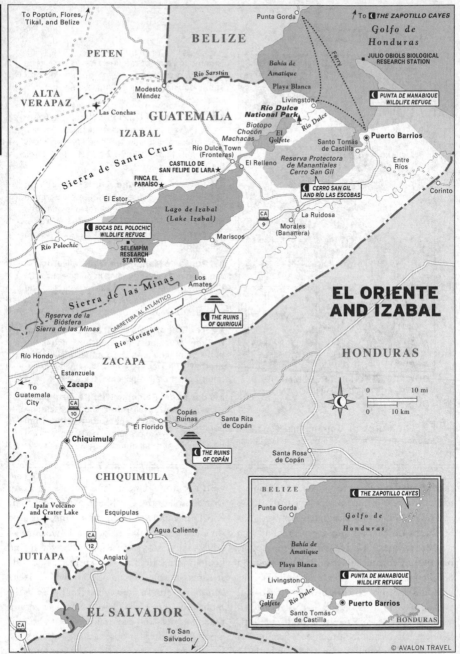

To Poptún, Flores,
Tikal, and Belize

PETEN

ALTA
VERAPAZ

Las Conchas

Modesto
Méndez

Río Sarstún

GUATEMALA

IZABAL

Sierra de Santa Cruz

Río Dulce Town
(Fronteras)

CASTILLO DE
SAN FELIPE DE LARA ★

FINCA EL
PARAÍSO ★

El Estor

Lago de Izabal
(Lake Izabal)

BOCAS DEL POLOCHIC
WILDLIFE REFUGE

Río Polochic

SELEMPÍM
RESEARCH
STATION

Mariscos

Los
Amates

Sierra de las Minas

Reserva de la
Biósfera
Sierra de las Minas

CARRETERA AL ATLÁNTICO

Río Motagua

Río Hondo

Estanzuela

To
Guatemala
City

Zacapa

ZACAPA

CA 10

Chiquimula

El Florido

Copán
Ruinas

Santa Rita
de Copán

THE RUINS
OF COPÁN

CHIQUIMULA

Ipala Volcano
and Crater Lake

Esquipulas

Agua Caliente

JUTIAPA

CA 12

Angiatú

EL SALVADOR

CA 1

To San
Salvador

Punta Gorda

BELIZE

Bahía de
Amatique

Playa Blanca

Livingston

Río Dulce
National Park

Biotopo
Chocón
Machacas

El
Golfete

El Relleno

Santo Tomás
de Castilla

Reserva Protectora
de Manantiales
Cerro San Gil

CERRO SAN GIL
AND RÍO LAS ESCOBAS

La Ruidosa

Morales
(Bananera)

CA 9

THE RUINS
OF QUIRIGUÁ

To THE ZAPOTILLO CAYES

Golfo de
Honduras

JULIO OBIOLS BIOLOGICAL
RESEARCH STATION

Ferry

PUNTA DE MANABIQUE
WILDLIFE REFUGE

Río Dulce

Puerto Barrios

Entre
Ríos

Corinto

HONDURAS

EL ORIENTE
AND IZABAL

0   10 mi
0   10 km

Santa Rosa
de Copán

BELIZE

Punta Gorda

THE ZAPOTILLO CAYES

Golfo de
Honduras

Bahía de
Amatique

Playa Blanca

Livingston

El
Golfete

Río Dulce

PUNTA DE MANABIQUE
WILDLIFE REFUGE

Puerto Barrios

Santo Tomás
de Castilla

HONDURAS

© AVALON TRAVEL

also dot the river's banks. Lake Izabal harbors some intriguing natural attractions of its own, including a vast, seldom-explored wetland preserve of astounding biological diversity and a funky Spanish castle built to repel the attacks of 17th-century pirates.

Back on Highway CA-9 closer to Guatemala City, a branch road heads southeast to El Oriente, partially occupied by Guatemala's Eastern Highlands. The road continues east to Honduras, where you can visit the incredible ruins of Copán, just 12 kilometers across the border. Along with the nearby Mayan site of Quiriguá (Guatemala), Copán showcases some of the Mayan world's finest stelae, carved monuments depicting historical events in the life of Mayan dynasties. Copán's museum is among the finest attractions in the Mayan world, along with its restored temple pyramids, palaces, hieroglyphic stairway, and ball court. The surrounding mountainous countryside is also becoming increasingly popular with travelers exploring coffee farms, a jungle bird park, and hot springs. Also near the border, on the Guatemalan side, is the town of Esquipulas, a popular pilgrimage site with Central American tourists for its Black Christ, believed to have miraculous healing powers.

Radically different from the department of Izabal, Guatemala's other eastern departments comprising the region of El Oriente are semiarid and populated by ladino cowboys, attracting few international travelers. A standout in this area is the odd crater lake atop the Ipala Volcano, near the town of Chiquimula.

CLIMATE

The overall climate in these parts is warm, even in the Eastern Highlands, which lack the dramatic altitude of their western counterparts. The Motagua Valley is arid, whereas the Izabal region is warm and humid year-round. During the warmest months of April and May, the temperature and humidity can seem unbearable,

though coastal regions get a lightly refreshing sea breeze that helps alleviate some of the tropical swelter. Temperatures can hover round 100°F during this time of year. At other times, it hovers somewhere between 85°F and 95°F. Izabal is particularly rainy and is sometimes battered by storms or the occasional hurricane.

PLANNING YOUR TIME

Copán can be done in a day or two, while Quiriguá requires only a couple of hours at most. It makes a good stop on the way to Puerto Barrios. If you really want to see Ipala Volcano and crater lake, you can probably do it as a day trip from Chiquimula or Esquipulas. I would recommend most foreign visitors give the latter town a miss, unless you really want to see the Black Christ statue housed in the town's basilica. There is plenty to see and do on the Caribbean Coast. Puerto Barrios is not the most pleasant town, but there's no need to stay here as there are now better alternatives for exploring the Cerro San Gil Reserve and Río Las Escobas across Bahía de Amatique in Santo Tomás de Castilla. It's worth at least a half day for exploring, though you could easily spend the night in a comfortable lodge or take a few days to cross the rugged Montañas del Mico to Río Dulce for the ultimate jungle adventure. Puerto Barrios merits an hour or two at best as a transit point to Lívingston or Río Dulce.

A few days in Lívingston will allow you time to explore nearby waterfalls, beaches, and rainforests. For a real treat, sail the Caribbean to the outlying Belize cayes for a week or explore the remote peninsula of Punta de Manabique. The latter requires at least one night's stay because of its remote location. From Lívingston, you can also explore the Río Dulce canyon in a few hours while traveling to Río Dulce town, but it's also possible to stop over midway and spend a night or two at some comfortable lodgings on the Río Tatín tributary. Río Dulce will probably captivate you with its tropical charm and location at the mouth of Lake Izabal. It makes a great place to chill out for a few days before heading north to Petén or before or after some exploring on the lake.

ORIENTATION

The eastern department of El Progreso is dominated by the presence of the Motagua River Valley, a region of cactus-studded plains lying between the rain-soaked Sierra de las Minas to the north and the Sierra del Espíritu Santo, along the Honduran border to the east. The Carretera al Atlántico passes through much of this terrain. South of here, the low-lying departments of Jalapa and Jutiapa have some green hills and a volcano or two, though they are not of the dramatic, conical kind found in the Western Highlands. The Ipala Volcano and crater lake is this region's best-known geographical feature. East of here, the areas along the Honduran border near Copán and Esquipulas have some pretty mountain scenery where coffee is grown.

The department of Izabal is one of Guatemala's most attractive for those who enjoy coastal environments. There are still large expanses of tropical rainforests, which receive ample rainfall when warm, moist air from the Caribbean Sea rises on mountain slopes. The Montañas del Mico stand as silent sentinels dominating a biological corridor between the Bahía de Amatique and the lazy Río Dulce to the north, which empties into the Caribbean. Guatemala's Caribbean coastline lacks the aquamarine beaches of Cancún and Belize, but the peninsula of Punta de Manabique stands out for its wild and scenic white-sand coastline. Farther out to sea is the tail end of the Belize Barrier Reef and some easily accessible cayes. Inland, Lake Izabal is a huge body of water with some nice beaches of its own and some impressive wetlands.

Río Hondo to Esquipulas

The town of Río Hondo is an oasis of fun, featuring excellent restaurants, refreshing swimming pools, and even a water park. Many travelers heading between Guatemala and Puerto Barrios like to break up their journey here. Heading south from the Río Hondo Junction, the road passes through the hot lowland towns of Zacapa and Chiquimula before climbing into the mountains and into a bowl-shaped valley dominated by Esquipulas. There's really not much here for international travelers, so the towns along this corridor won't be covered in depth, aside from a few hotel and restaurant listings, should you need to stop while passing through en route to other attractions. The Ipala Volcano and crater lake make a worthy side trip.

RÍO HONDO JUNCTION

The hotels and restaurants lining highway CA-9 (the road to the Atlantic Coast) at Río Hondo are popular places to stop and eat for travelers heading to or from faraway Puerto Barrios or Esquipulas. The dry, warm climate lends itself marvelously to swimming and other water-centered activities.

Accommodations and Food

All of the options listed here are found at Km. 126 and offer comfortable air-conditioned rooms with private bathroom and cable TV. All have swimming pools. Among the options is old standby **Hotel Longarone** (tel. 7934-7126, $45 d). Its large swimming pool has diving boards and a water slide. Some of the rooms are more dimly lit than others. The restaurant and bar serves international food ($6-12) with excellent service and cleanliness. In addition to a large, attractive palm-trimmed swimming pool, **Hotel El Atlantico** (tel. 7934-7160, $45 d) boasts lovely gardens, a gym, and children's play areas. The indoor and outdoor restaurants and bars serve international cuisine. **Hotel Santa Cruz** (tel. 7934-7075, $50 d) has beautifully landscaped, flower-filled gardens around its swimming pool, spotless rooms, and an excellent restaurant serving (you guessed it) international dishes.

Valle Dorado Water Park
Another 23 kilometers east from Río Hondo along highway CA-9 is Valle Dorado Water Park (Km. 149, tel. 7943-6666, www.hotelvalledorado.com, 6 A.M.-6 P.M. Tues.-Sun., $7 adults, $5 children), well worth the wait if you can curb your appetite, as there are a variety of food options inside the park and tons of fun stuff for the kids (or the kid in you). The large theme park has a variety of pools and water slides as well as a very comfortable hotel with room rates starting at $70 (d).

ESTANZUELA
Continuing southeast about six kilometers from Río Hondo along Highway CA-10 (the junction is at Km. 135), the first town you'll come across is Estanzuela. The terrain here is decidedly dry, resembling parts of Arizona, making for an excellent environment for the preservation of fossils. Sure enough, you can see some dinosaur bones, including the skeleton of a 50,000-year-old mastodon and that of a prehistoric whale at **Museo de Paleontología Bryan Patterson** (tel. 7941-4981, 9 A.M.-5 P.M. daily, free admission). To get here, go through the town and follow the blue signs to the *museo*.

ZACAPA
The next stop along Highway CA-10 is the departmental capital of Zacapa. Its redeeming quality is the award-winning **Ron Zacapa**

Centenario, sold in a festive woven-straw bottle holder. You don't have to go all the way to Zacapa to pick up a bottle, as it's available from its own duty-free shop at Guatemala City's international airport. You can pick up a bottle before your flight home.

CHIQUIMULA
Chiquimula is a hot, dry town and also a departmental capital. Like Zacapa, there is very little here for the international traveler. It does, however, serve as a transit point for southwest travel to the Ipala Lagoon or east to Copán, Honduras.

Accommodations and Food
Should you need to stay here, your best bet is **Hotel Hernandez** (3a Calle 7-41 Zona 1, tel. 7942-0708), with various types of rooms ranging from $6-20 d. The most expensive rooms overlook the swimming pool and have air-conditioning. A backup plan is **Hotel Posada Perla de Oriente** (2a Calle and 12 Avenida, tel. 7942-0014, $25-45 d), with tropical gardens, a swimming pool, and large, clean rooms with fans, hot-water bathrooms, and cable TV. There are also rooms with air-conditioning. The restaurant serves decent food.

Other options for food include **Pollo Campero,** on the corner of 7a Avenida and 4a Calle, serving the fried chicken so beloved by Guatemalans in an air-conditioned environment. A fancier option is **Restaurante Chiquimulja** (3a Calle 6-51 Zona 1), part of its namesake hotel, serving pasta dishes, grilled meats, and other international fare ($5-8) in an attractive two-story palm-roofed building. It overlooks the central plaza. Guatemala's best-known supermarket chain, **Paiz** (recently acquired by Walmart), is next door on the corner of 7a Avenida and 3a Calle.

Services
Among the services you'll find here are a bank, Banco G&T Continental (half a block south

of the plaza at 7a Avenida 4-75 Zona 1). The post office is on 10a Avenida between 1a and 2a Calle. For phone calls, Telgua is on 3a Calle east of the central plaza. Internet is available at Email Center (6a Avenida 4-51, 9 A.M.-9 P.M. daily).

Getting There

The town bus terminal is midway between the plaza and the highway on 1a Calle between 10a and 11a Avenidas. There are hourly buses to Guatemala City (3.5 hours) and Puerto Barrios (four hours), half-hourly minibuses to Esquipulas (one hour), hourly buses and minibuses to Ipala (one hour) and the Salvadoran border at Anguiatú (one hour). Buses to the El Florido border (1.5 hours, for Copán, Honduras) leave from a separate terminal one block north every 45 minutes until 4:30 P.M.

NEAR CHIQUIMULA
Ipala Volcano and Crater Lake

It's a pleasant drive southwest of Chiquimula to the wonderful crater lake of the 1,650-meter-high Ipala Volcano. The summit is most easily accessible from the village of Agua Blanca (you'll see blue INGUAT signs leading the way), from which a paved road continues to an area near the top. Once at the crater lake, you'll see a visitors center, where the park rangers collect a modest park fee of $1.50.

A series of nature trails wind their way around the lagoon. You'll pass a lookout with an excellent view of the 3.5-kilometer-wide lake as well as the entrance to the **Cueva de la Leona** (Cave of the Lioness). The volcanic crater and its lake were designated as national parks in 1998. Water for four local villages continued to be extracted until very recently, meaning that the lake has lost much of its original water volume. The lake is filled entirely with rainwater.

There are hourly buses and pickups from the village of Ipala, on the north side of the volcano, to Agua Blanca. Minibuses run between Chiquimula and Ipala every half hour. You can camp at the lake or stay in a basic *hospedaje* in Ipala.

Esquipulas

The town of Esquipulas is popular with travelers from other parts of Central America who come here on a pilgrimage to see the miraculous Black Christ. Although the large white basilica is somewhat impressive, there is really little else of interest for the non-Central American traveler. If you really wish to see the Black Christ, by all means do so, but your time in Guatemala is probably best spent elsewhere. Nearby, there are a few natural attractions, but little that's been developed for tourism as in the Verapaces or Izabal regions. Esquipulas's other main claim to fame is the 1987 signing of an accord between area leaders outlining the establishment of peace processes to end the civil wars in El Salvador and Guatemala.

SIGHTS
Basilica

You'll see the large white church as soon as you enter the proximity of Esquipulas, as it dominates the view of town as you approach it from the road. Once you're in town, the basilica can be reached by crossing a large, pleasant palm-lined park leading to a flight of steps. A side entrance leads to the **Black Christ** (http://basilicadeesquipulas.org/, 6 A.M.-8 P.M. daily), where you can shuffle into the line and follow pilgrims to a glass case behind the church altar for a brief glimpse. The height of veneration occurs during an annual festival on January 15, with weekends and religious holidays also popular. You may have the place all to yourself during the week, contrasting sharply with the melee seen on weekends. Inside the church is the usual atmosphere of hushed reverence and incense found throughout Guatemala's churches. For a real treat, check out the vending stalls near the church where you'll find a motley assortment of religious kitsch.

Cueva de las Minas

This cave complex lies about 300 meters south of the turnoff into town along the road heading to Honduras. It's a further 500 meters from the entrance gate to the complex (6:30 A.M.-4 P.M. daily). There are a 50-meter-deep cave and the Río El Milagro, which folks say holds miraculous healing powers. Bring your own flashlight.

RECREATION
Chatun

After a visit to the Black Christ, many pilgrims feel the need to unwind for the rest of their stay. Among the recreational options for devotees and their families is Chatun (tel. 7943-0498, 9 A.M.-6 P.M. Wed.-Sun., $8 adults, $4 children), a very pleasant nature park three kilometers outside of town in the direction of Honduras. Among the many attractions are a nine-station canopy tour, a petting zoo, duck pond, inviting swimming pools, camping area, climbing wall, horseback riding, and nature trails. You'll probably work up an appetite with all there is to do, for which there are a restaurant and several snack bars. If you're traveling with kids, this would most certainly be an obligatory stop.

ACCOMMODATIONS

Avoid staying in Esquipulas's low-budget accommodations, as they are the hideout of large groups of men from elsewhere in Central America, including gang members, who hang out in these parts seeking to make their way north. Esquipulas is somewhat close to the Honduran border and so has become a transit point for illegal immigration.

$10-25

The first option in this category is the **Hotel y Restaurante Aposento Alto** (3a Avenida 10-66 Zona 1, tel. 7943-1115, $20 d), where the rooms have hot water, cable TV, fans, and fluorescent lighting. The restaurant downstairs serves inexpensive Guatemalan and international dishes for breakfast, lunch, and dinner. Among several options facing the park from the southwest is **Hotel Posada Santiago** (2a Avenida 11-58 Zona 1, tel. 7943-2023, $20 d), with comfortable rooms with hot-water baths, cable TV, and fans. One double room has a view of the basilica and there is a good restaurant serving Guatemalan and international fare in the lobby. At the upper end of this price category is **Hotel Villa Zonia** (10a Calle 1-84 Zona 1, tel. 7943-1143, $25 d), very close to the bus terminal and surrounded by budget accommodations. The smallish rooms have cable TV and private baths with hot water, but there are better values elsewhere. The single room prices, in particular, are a rip-off.

$25-50

An excellent value in this price category is **❰ Hotel Portal de la Fe** (tel. 7943-4124, www.portaldelafe.com, $40 d), with 29 attractive, spotless rooms with comfortable beds with wrought-iron headboard, ceiling fan, and private hot-water bath. Rooms are distributed on three floors around a pretty courtyard fountain lit from above by an opaque roof opening. Nightly rates include free half-hour use of Internet. It's on the main street heading into town (11a Calle) on the right. Another good value is **IV Centenario** (tel. 7943-1751, info@ ivcentenariohotel.com, www.ivcentenariohotel. com, $34 d), also along 11a Calle toward the park, in a colorful building painted in shades of yellow and blue with rooms built around the swimming pool. All have cable TV and hot-water private bathroom.

Facing the park from its southwest side is

popular **Hotel Payaquí** (tel. 7943-1143, $50 d), where there are two restaurants, one by the swimming pool, the other with a big-screen TV. They serve Guatemalan and international dishes including sandwiches and steaks. Meals are in the $5-8 range. Rooms are comfortable and spacious and include a fully stocked mini-fridge, fan, and private bath. Next door is the also-popular **Hotel El Peregrino** (tel. 7943-1054, $30 d), featuring cheerful rooms with fan, cable TV, and private bath. In-room furniture includes a plastic table and chairs. Directly behind, on 1a Avenida, is **Hotel Vistana al Señor** (tel. 5958-8426, $40 d), in a modern colonial-style building with comfortable beds and an upstairs sitting area with chairs and umbrellas.

$50-100

The attractive **☚ Porta Hotel Legendario** (9a Calle y 3a Avenida Zona 1, tel. 7943-1022 or 7943-1825, http://hotellegendario.com/, $75 d) has 42 rooms, including standard and deluxe rooms as well as suites, in a large building centered around the swimming pool. All are comfortable and spacious. There are a restaurant and bar. Online rates are substantially higher. Try to book by calling directly if you can. The other option in this category is **Hotel El Gran Chortí** (tel. 7943-1148, Km. 222 on the road into town, $85 d), where the rooms have all the usual comforts you'd expect to find in this price category. There are a nice restaurant and swimming pool.

FOOD

The restaurant at the **Porta Hotel Legendario** (9a Calle y 3a Avenida Zona 1, tel. 7943-1022, 7 A.M.-9 P.M.) serves international fare including decent breakfasts, steaks, pasta, and salads. Some of the best light fare in town can be found at **☚ Eco Moda Spa and Eco-Café** (Calle Real 3-48, tel. 7943-2764, 8 A.M.-9 P.M. Mon.-Sat.), set in a wonderful 250-year-old home. Delicious sandwiches, salads, coffee,

and pastries are served in a delightful garden courtyard. Before your meal, you can enjoy a relaxing massage in a quaint adobe parlor or opt for a sauna or hot-water whirlpool bath. The owners also arrange visits to their working coffee farm, **Finca Las Nubes** ($17 per person for accommodations), about an hour away via a rugged dirt road into the mountains, where you can sleep in a rustic but comfortable cabin and enjoy rappelling, taking walks to the nearby Río Frío, mountain biking, or simply doing nothing at all.

Other culinary options closer to the center of town include **La Rotonda** (11 Calle, opposite Rutas Orientales, tel. 7943-2038, 7 A.M.-10 P.M. daily), where the pleasant circular dining area is arranged under a large awning. The menu includes pizza ($10 for a large pie), pasta, and burgers. Breakfasts ($2-4) are also quite good. **La Hacienda** (corner of 2a Avenida and 10a Calle, 8 A.M.-10 P.M.) is your best bet for grilled steaks, chicken, and seafood with prices in the $10-20 range. The perennial favorite with Guatemalans is **Pollo Campero,** just off 2a Avenida southwest of the park, where you can get your fried-chicken fix.

SERVICES
Communications

The **post office** is a bit far from the town center (about 10 blocks north) at 6a Avenida 2-15. Telgua is on the corner of 5a Avenida and 9a Calle with plenty of card-operated telephones. For Internet, try **Global.com** on 3a Avenida across from Banco Internacional.

Money

Banco Industrial (3a Avenida and 9a Calle) has a Visa ATM and can exchange currency and cash travelers checks. Banco G&T Continental, across the street, will do the same. Banco Internacional (3a Avenida 8-87 Zona 1) has a Visa ATM and is the local American Express agent.

GETTING THERE

The most comfortable bus service is via **Rutas Orientales** (11 Calle and 1a Avenida), with service to Guatemala City every half hour. Minibuses for the Honduran border post at Agua Caliente ($2) leave from across the street every half hour 6 A.M.-5 P.M. Taxis also leave from here. Minibuses to the Salvadoran border at Anguiatú ($2) and Chiquimula ($1.50) leave from an area farther east along 11 Calle, near the market, with similar frequency. If traveling to Copán via the El Florido border post, you'll have to take a minibus to Chiquimula and then connect onward.

Copán Archaeological Site (Honduras)

The Mayan site of Copán, just 13 kilometers across the border in Honduras, features some of the Mayan world's greatest artistic treasures, including numerous stelae and a hieroglyphic stairway that is the longest known Mayan inscription. Whereas Tikal has been likened to the Manhattan of Mayan cities for its grand scale and a population once thought to have numbered 100,000, Copán is likened to Paris for the exquisite quality of its artwork, unmatched in the Mayan world. It is thought to have harbored 25,000 inhabitants in its heyday.

Archaeologists are still busy excavating and restoring this site in addition to deciphering the jumbled mess of a hieroglyphic stairway (found tumbled and out of order). In recent years, they have undertaken the ambitious enterprise of digging tunnels beneath existing structures to uncover previous constructions. Among the magnificent finds are the well-preserved Rosalila (Rose-lilac) Temple and the tombs of several of Copán's rulers. You can see a wonderful reconstruction of the temple in all its Technicolor glory at Copán's excellent Sculpture Museum, in addition to several of the original finely carved stelae and monuments found *in situ*.

In addition to the ruins, the nearby town of **Copán Ruinas** has become increasingly popular as a destination unto itself for its excellent restaurants and accommodations. From here, you can explore the ruins and the surrounding countryside with ease.

CROSSING THE BORDER

The bare-bones border crossing at **El Florido** (open 6 A.M.-6 P.M.) includes some basic services but little else. There are some snack and soda stands and a Banrural which changes dollars and travelers checks. Ubiquitous money changers are also on hand to help you change your quetzales for Honduran lempiras. However, note that many tourist places in Copán take quetzales.

Crossing the border is fairly straightforward. If you're driving a rental car, you'll need to present a written letter from your rental-car agency allowing you to take the vehicle into Honduras. Otherwise, you'll have to leave it at the border. Most Western nationalities, including U.S. citizens, need only a passport to get into Honduras; no visas are required. You can either get a three-day permit to enter and visit Copán and vicinity only or request a 30-day or 90-day entry permit by filling out an official request form. It all depends on your nationality what length of stay you're allowed. If on a three-day permit, you can still use your original entry stamp into Guatemala upon your return to continue traveling for the rest of your stay in the country. On the Guatemalan side, there is a $1.25 (Q10) exit tax. There is a $3 customs fee on the Honduran side (for entry only).

Once in Honduras, there are onward buses from the border to Copán Ruinas every 30 minutes or so ($2). Heading back, the last bus from El Florido to Chiquimula leaves at

THE RUINS OF COPÁN

STRUCTURE 2

STELA D

STELA C

STELA E   STELA B   STELA F

STRUCTURE 1   STELA 4   STRUCTURE 3

ALTAR G

STELA A   STELA H

STELA J

STRUCTURE 4

Great Plaza

To Visitors Center
and Museum

STELA 3

ALTAR K   ALTAR L

STRUCTURE 6

STELA 2

STELA 1   BALL   STRUCTURE 10

COURT

STRUCTURE 9

STRUCTURE 7

HIEROGLYPHIC
STAIRWAY

STRUCTURE 11,   STELA M   STRUCTURE 26
TEMPLE OF THE
INSCRIPTIONS   STELA N

TEMPLE 22

STRUCTURE 8   STRUCTURE 21

STRUCTURE 22A,   Los Jaguares Tunnel
THE MAT HOUSE

East   STRUCTURE 20
Court

West Court   Rosalila
Tunnel   STRUCTURE 19

STELA P

STRUCTURE 13   ALTAR Q   STRUCTURE 17   Archeological Cut

STRUCTURE 14   STRUCTURE 16
(ROSALILA TEMPLE)   STRUCTURE 18

STRUCTURE 29

CEMETERY

0   50 yds
0   50 m

© AVALON TRAVEL

© AL ARGUETA

one of Copán's magnificently carved stelae

4:30 P.M., but you are exhorted to cross the border much earlier in the day. To call Honduras, the country code is 504. Phone numbers are eight digits long. As in Guatemala, there are no area codes or city codes.

HISTORY
Early Copán

Although the fertile Copán Valley is thought to have been inhabited as early as 1,400 B.C., archaeological evidence points to its not having been occupied by the Mayans until around A.D. 100. Recorded history at the site does not begin until A.D. 426 with the establishment of Copán's royal dynasty. The site's early history was unearthed as recently as 1989, when excavations under the hieroglyphic stairway revealed a chamber subsequently nicknamed the **Founder's Room.** The chamber is thought to have been built by Copán's second ruler, **Mat Head** (after the odd-looking headdress with which he is depicted on stelae) in honor of his

father, Copán's first ruler, in power A.D. 426-435. Subsequent kings appear to have revered this king, **Yax K'uk'Mo',** and thought him to be semidivine. Archaeological evidence has found that he was indeed a great shaman. The tomb of Yax K'uk'Mo' was discovered in 1993 under the East Court of the Acropolis and the findings have yet to be fully revealed.

Little is known about the next several leaders in the dynastic line established by Yax K'uk'Mo', which ruled Copán throughout the entirety of its Classic Mayan history. It appears this dynasty was consolidating its rule at this time and establishing trade routes within the Mayan world and farther afield to powerful cities such as Teotihuacán. We know some of the names of Copán's leaders before A.D. 628: Cu Ix, the fourth king; Waterlily Jaguar, the seventh; Moon Jaguar, the 10th; and Butz' Chan, the 11th.

The Height of Power

The height of Copán's power came with the ascension to the throne of **Moon Jaguar** on May 26, 553. Moon Jaguar is credited with the construction of the **Rosalila Temple,** found buried beneath Structure 16 in 1993. Ruling A.D. 628-695 was one of Copán's greatest kings, **Smoke Imix,** the city's 12th ruler, who consolidated Copán into a regional commercial and military power. A stela at the nearby site of Quiriguá bears his name and image, attesting to his probable takeover of the site. A prolific monument builder, Smoke Imix left behind the most inscribed monuments and temples out of all of Copán's rulers. His successor, **18 Rabbit** (A.D. 695-738), was also a prolific builder and pursued further military conquest. He came to a very unfortunate end, however, being captured and beheaded in a war with Quiriguá by its ruler, Cauac Sky.

Decline

Next in line was **Smoke Monkey** (A.D. 738-749), the 14th ruler of Copán, who built only

© AL ARGUETA

the Hieroglyphic Stairway at Copán

one temple and erected no self-promoting stelae. The crushing blow suffered against Quiriguá may have resulted in the king's sharing power with a council composed of the city's nobility. Smoke Monkey's successor, **Smoke Shell** (A.D. 749-763), commissioned the creation of Copán's magnificent **Hieroglyphic Stairway,** containing 2,500 glyphs narrating the city's glorious past in an attempt to recapture the brilliance of the dynasty's heyday. By this time, however, it was evident that the city was in decline, a fact attested to by the subpar construction of the monument, which was later found collapsed, its narrative left scattered and out of order like a messy game of Jenga.

Yax Pac (A.D. 763-820) was Copán's 16th ruler, who continued along the same lines of beautifying the city. He left behind a fantastic monument known as **Altar Q,** depicting the city's 16 kings carved around a four-sided square monument with Copán's first king, Yax

K'uk'Mo', passing the baton of leadership on to Yax Pac, thus legitimating his rule.

Copán's 17th and final leader was **U Cit Tok',** assuming the throne in A.D. 822. His only legacy is the unfinished Altar L, of rather lackluster quality. Some believe this to be evidence of a sudden abandonment of Copán rather than a gradual collapse. As elsewhere in the Mayan world, Copán's collapse is thought to have been at least partially the result of exhausting the local ecosystem's carrying capacity, with a population thought to have reached 25,000 at its zenith. Agricultural areas were forced from the central part of the valley by urban expansion and the surrounding, less fertile hillsides eventually came under heavy cultivation. Soil erosion, droughts, deforestation, and rainy season flooding became the inevitable result. Though the city's core was abandoned, the valley was still somewhat heavily populated after this time. Archaeological evidence suggests another drop in population around 1200, after which the settlement patterns reverted to the small villages found by the Spanish in 1524. The ruins were left to be reclaimed by the jungle.

Rediscovery

The first known European to lay eyes on the ruined city was Diego García de Palacios, a representative of Spanish King Felipe II living in Guatemala and traveling through the Copán Valley. He described the ruins in a letter written to the king on March 8, 1576, and related that there were only five families living in the valley at the time, knowing nothing of the ruins' history or the people who built them. A Spanish colonel by the name of Juan Galindo would be the first to map the ruins almost 300 years later. Inspired by Galindo's report, John L. Stephens and Frederick Catherwood included a stop in Copán in 1839 during their famous journey to Mayan lands chronicled in *Incidents of Travel in Central America, Chiapas and Yucatán,* published two years later. Inspired by this book,

British archaeologist Alfred P. Maudsley would make his way down to Copán in 1881. He returned four years later to fully map, excavate, photograph, and reconstruct the site off and on until 1902. Other scholars, among them Sylvanus Morley and J. Eric Thompson, would follow on his heels.

Present Day

In 1975, Harvard's Peabody Museum continued the investigations it had previously supported through Maudsley. Among its goals was the excavation of temples lying beneath existing structures, a product of the customary manner in which the Mayans built atop existing temples and pyramids. They embarked on a project to tunnel through Copán's numerous layers of construction and so have a glimpse into the city's history. Among the fascinating discoveries was the 1989 unearthing of the Rosalila Temple by Honduran archaeologist Ricardo Agurcia. An even earlier temple, Margarita, lies beneath it. Rosalila was found with its vivid ochre paint still visible. You can visit the excavation tunnel nowadays and see a replica of Rosalila in the Sculpture Museum.

Tunneling farther into the East Court, archaeologists came across a glyph panel paying homage to Copán's original ruler, Yax K'uk'Mo'. His tomb was found buried far below the East Court in 1993 by a team led by Robert Sharer of the University of Pennsylvania. This area remains closed to the public. Teams from Harvard, Tulane, and the University of Pennsylvania continue to work in different areas of the site.

EXPLORING THE PARK

The ruins of Copán lie about 1.5 kilometers from the town of Copán Ruinas, a 20-minute walk along a footpath running parallel to the highway. The **visitors center** houses the ticket office, where you pay a $15 admission fee for entry to the park (8 A.M.-4 P.M. daily),

including entry to the neighboring site of Las Sepulturas. Another $15 gets you admission to two underground tunnels where, among other attractions, you can see the Rosalila Temple in its original context. The tunnels are recommended for serious Mayan archaeology buffs, but not so much for the casual visitor. You can also buy your $7 ticket for admission to Copán's excellent Sculpture Museum. There's a small exhibit placing Copán's importance in the context of the larger Mayan world at the visitors center.

Also at the visitors center are registered **guides** for hire, costing about $35 for a two-hour tour. There are English-speaking guides, though their skill levels vary, so be sure to assess their mastery of the English language before sealing the deal. Across the parking lot in front of the visitors center is a small **eatery** serving drinks and basic meals. There's also a small gift shop.

It's a few hundred meters' walk from the visitors center to the ticket checkpoint where you enter the ruins. A short **nature trail** winding its way through the surrounding forest diverts from the main path just before this checkpoint. A few semi-domesticated scarlet macaws sometimes hang out in this area. Try to visit the site right at opening time, as the crowds tend to get larger as the day goes on, especially on weekends. You'll also have better-angled light for photography.

◖ THE RUINS OF COPÁN

Enthusiasts of Mayan archaeology will find some of the best hieroglyphic carvings in the whole of the Mayan world along with well-restored structures, including palaces, temple pyramids, and a ball court. The hieroglyphic stairway alone is worth the price of admission, not to mention the chance to see the buried section of temple pyramids from tunnels (Rosalila and Los Jaguares) originally used by archaeologists excavating the ruins.

Great Plaza

The first place you'll come to as you walk along the forest path from the main entrance to the park is the Great Plaza. You'll see a variety of stelae in a spacious grassy area, which was once paved. Traces of red paint (created by mixing mercury sulfate and tree resins) can still be seen on **Stela C,** which dates to A.D. 730. Most of the stelae date to the rule of Smoke Imix (A.D. 628-695) and 18 Rabbit (A.D. 695-738). The latter ruler is depicted on Stelae 1, 2, 3, 10, 12, 13, and 19. The plaza's standout is **Stela A** (A.D. 731). Among its 52 glyphs are the emblem glyphs of Palenque, Tikal, Calakmul, and Copán, establishing Copán's position as one of the great cities of the Mayan world. As with many other important monuments, the original now resides in the Sculpture Museum. Another beautifully carved monument is **Stela H,** depicting what looks to be a woman wearing a skirt with a leopard skin underneath, wrists weighed down with jewelry, and an intricate headdress. This may be an image of 18 Rabbit's wife.

Copán's **ball court** is south of the Great Plaza after you cross what is known as the Central Plaza (Plaza Central). Completed in A.D. 738, it was the third ball court to have been erected at the site. There are three elaborate macaw heads on each side. It is one of the most often-photographed buildings in Copán.

Hieroglyphic Stairway

Farther south from the Great Plaza is the Hieroglyphic Stairway, which rises up the southeast corner of the plaza up the side of the neighboring Acropolis. The impressive structure, now covered with a roof for protection from the elements, contains 2,500 glyphs on its 72 steps and is the longest known hieroglyphic inscription found anywhere in the Mayan world. Commissioned in A.D. 753 by Smoke Shell, its substandard construction was evident in that it collapsed and was found by archaeologists as a jumbled mess, which they

reassembled in 1940. Only about 15 steps, primarily on the bottom section, are thought to be in the correct order. Archaeologists are working on getting the correct order and deciphering the long message encoded on the steps. Its construction came at a time when Copán's rulers were attempting to once again instill confidence in their city's power and glorious history after the gruesome death of 18 Rabbit at the hands of neighboring Quiriguá.

At the base of the Hieroglyphic Stairway is **Stela M** (A.D. 756), with a figure presumed to be Smoke Shell dressed in a feathered cloak along with glyphs telling of a solar eclipse in that year. An altar in front depicts a feathered serpent with a human head emanating from its jaws.

A tomb thought to belong to a royal scribe and possibly one of the sons of Smoke Imix was discovered underneath the Hieroglyphic Stairway in 1989. It was laden with painted pottery and well-carved jade objects. Digging ever deeper below the stairway, in 1993 archaeologists uncovered an earlier temple called **Papagayo,** erected by Mat Head. Farther below was a chamber dedicated to Yax K'uk'Mo', the city's original king. Archaeologists called it the **Founder's Room** and believe it was used as a place of reverence for the shaman king believed by subsequent kings to have been semidivine.

The Acropolis

Copán's dominating architectural feature is the massive Acropolis, which rises about 30 meters above the ground south of the Great Plaza. It is here that some of the more interesting archaeological finds have been unearthed in recent years by digging tunnels under existing structures to reveal what was originally beneath them.

South of the Hieroglyphic Stairway is a flight of steps running along the **Temple of the Inscriptions.** Walls atop the stairway are carved with various glyphs. Toward the top of the hieroglyphic stairway is a temple curiously adorned with engravings resembling woven mats and appropriately named the **Mat House,** also known as Structure 22A. It was built in A.D. 746 by Smoke Monkey shortly after the death of his predecessor, 18 Rabbit, and provides further evidence of the new power-sharing arrangement with the city's nobility after the shocking defeat at the hands of Quiriguá. It was thought to have operated as a council house, the mats being a symbol for authority and community. South of here is the **East Court,** the city's original plaza, underneath which were found the tombs of Yax K'uk'Mo' and his wife. It is also known as the "Patio de los Jaguares." Also buried in the East Court, below **Structure 18,** was Yax Pac, though it was unfortunately discovered and looted long before the arrival of archaeologists.

Between the East Court and nearby West Court lies **Structure 16,** which was dedicated to the themes of death, war, and veneration of past rulers. The well-preserved **Rosalila Temple** was found buried here in 1989.

In the **West Court** at the base of Structure 16 is a replica of the magnificently carved square monument known as **Altar Q,** depicting Yax Pac receiving the baton of rulership from Yax K'uk'Mo' himself. The altar is adorned with four kings on each side, giving us a complete line of succession for Copán's ruling dynasty of 16 kings from Yax K'uk'Mo' to Yax Pac, who commissioned its carving in A.D. 776. It was once thought to have portrayed a gathering of astronomers, but recent advances in glyph decipherment have shed light on its true meaning. The original can be seen in the Sculpture Museum. Behind the altar is a sacrificial vault, which contained the remains of 15 jaguars and several macaws sacrificed in honor of Yax Pac and his royal lineage.

Túnel Rosalila and Túnel de los Jaguares

Opened in 1999 to much fanfare, the original excavation tunnels used by archaeologists to discover the hidden gems of Copán are available for visitors to explore. The first of these, Túnel Rosalila, brings you to the Rosalila Temple found buried under Structure 16, still with some of its original brilliant hues. Only about 25 meters of the tunnel are open to visitors. Sheltered behind windows to protect it from the elements and human touch, you'll find small patches of the temple peeking out from underneath the outer layers of newer structures. Considered by some to be the best-preserved stucco structure in the Mayan world, the carvings are surprisingly crisp. To fully appreciate the scale, magnificence, and brilliant hue of this temple, you'll have to go to the Sculpture Museum, where it dominates the edifice and is beautifully lit from above by opaque sunlight.

The second tunnel, Túnel de los Jaguares, brings you to the Tumba Galindo beneath Structure 17 in the southern part of the East Plaza. About 95 meters of this tunnel, fully comprising 700 meters, are open to visitors. It is somewhat less dramatic than the Rosalila Tunnel, comprising burial tombs and niches for offerings, though there is also a nice macaw mask to be seen. The tomb's discovery dates to 1834.

At $15, admission to the tunnels is a bit on the pricey side and is recommended for serious enthusiasts of archaeology but less so for the casual visitor.

Las Sepulturas

This smaller residential complex is connected to the main group by a *sacbe,* or elevated causeway, running through the forest. This path is closed to visitors and so you must exit the archaeological site and head up the main road for two kilometers toward San Pedro Sula. You'll see a sign on the right (bring your admission ticket, as you'll need it to get in).

Las Sepulturas was ignored by archaeologists earlier in Copán's history but recent work here has revealed some information about the daily lives of the city's ancient inhabitants. Meaning "the tombs," the complex was named by local farmers who uncovered the remains of long-departed Mayan nobles who had been buried here.

This area is not of much interest to the casual visitor, though you might like walking along the quiet forest trails. Little remains of the original structures. An exception is the Hieroglyphic Wall found on Structure 83, comprising a group of 16 glyphs telling about events in the rule of Yax Pac and dating to A.D. 786. This site contains the remains of the **Palacio de los Bacabs** (Palace of the Officials), which is thought to have once housed 250 nobles. Only 18 of about 40 residential compounds have been excavated. In Las Sepulturas's Plaza A, archaeologists uncovered the tomb of a shaman from about A.D. 450, which can be seen in the town's Museo Regional de Arqueología. Traces of human settlement have been found here dating to 1000 B.C., long before the Copán dynasty's rise to power.

Los Sapos

An outlying part of Copán even farther away is Los Sapos, in the hills opposite the main site. A rock outcrop carved in the form of a frog gives it its name, though the years have worn it down considerably. An even more badly degraded carving is thought to depict a woman with her legs spread and possibly giving birth. The site is believed to have been a birthing center. The hillside setting overlooking the valley is more dramatic than the carvings, which are set on the grounds of the fabulous **Hacienda San Lucas.** The property harbors a fantastic upscale farmhouse lodge and the owner has built a network of trails through the farm leading to the site. Admission is $2. If you're worn out from the walk, stop in for a drink or lunch at the friendly hacienda or, better yet, spend the night.

THE SCULPTURE MUSEUM

Copán's on-site museum (8 A.M.-3:45 P.M. daily, $7) is surely the best museum of its kind in the Mayan world. Other sites would do well to follow its lead for the sheer variety of original monuments well presented in a spacious and airy environment. Dominating the large, two-story building is a full-scale replica of the outrageously colorful Rosalila Temple, decorated in hues of red, green, and yellow, and offering the visitor a rare opportunity to admire the full grandeur of what the ancient Mayan temples may have looked like during the fullness of the civilization's splendor.

Entrance to the museum is via the mouth of a serpent. Winding through a dark cavelike tunnel, you are greeted at once as you emerge from the darkness by the arresting view of the Rosalila Temple lit from above by a giant opaque skylight. On the first floor are various sculptures of skulls, bats, and assorted images of death and violence. Also found here is the

© AL ARGUETA

the Sculpture Museum

splendidly carved **Altar Q,** showing Yax Pac receiving the ceremonial ruler's baton from the highly revered first king of the Copán dynasty Yax K'uk'Mo'. The second floor contains original building facades, stelae, and other carved monuments. A reconstruction of Structure 22A, with its curious woven mat facade, should be open by the time you read this.

Copán Ruinas Town (Honduras)

Set amid the lush hills of the Río Copán Valley, this pleasant town of cobblestone streets serves as the perfect gateway for exploring the nearby archaeological site and some natural attractions, which include hot springs, a bird park, and coffee farms. The range of accommodations and places to eat here is excellent.

The Copán Valley is also the site of tobacco plantations, some of which supply the well-known Flor de Copán factory in Santa Rosa de Copán, east of here. The hillsides surrounding the Copán Valley grow good-quality coffee and cardamom. If you're visiting the ruins of Copán, try to spend at least one night in Copán Ruinas.

SIGHTS

As elsewhere in Central America, the town is built around its *parque central,* recently remodeled in questionable pseudo-Maya architectural style, but with a pretty colonial church. **Museo Casa K'inich** (up the hill north of town in the old fort, 8 A.M.-noon and 1-5 P.M. Mon.-Sat., adults $1) is an interactive children's museum on Mayan subjects such as music and the Mayan number system. Few museums in the Mayan world live up to Copán's on-site museum, though the **Museo Regional de Arqueología** (tel. 651-4437, 8 A.M.-noon and 1-4 P.M. daily, $2), on the southwest corner of the plaza, is worth a look. There are exhibits of carved jade, painted pottery, and figurines. The museum's highlight is the Tumba del Brujo, the tomb of a Mayan shaman said to have died around A.D. 700 and found buried under the Plaza de los Jaguares.

The town hall is the site of a wonderful photographic exhibit, titled "Fragile Memories," gleaned from a series of 19th-century glass plate negatives belonging to the Peabody Museum archives. The photos show the early days of Copan's excavation and restoration and provide new insights into Copan's history. The exhibit is open during normal business hours. Ask to see the exhibit (usually locked) at the information center.

ENTERTAINMENT

Two of the most popular watering holes include **Twisted Tanya's,** with its happy hour 4-6 P.M., and **Carnitas Nia Lola,** where you can find happiness 6:30-8 P.M. A popular after-dark option is **Café Via Via,** where you'll find plenty of fellow travelers.

For weekend movies, head to **Hacienda El Jaral,** a few kilometers outside of town on the road to San Pedro Sula. You'll see signs around town with current shows and schedules.

GUIDE COMPANIES

Locally owned **Yaragua Tours** (inside Hotel Yaragua, tel. 2651-4147, www.yaragua.com), under the same ownership of its namesake hotel, offers a variety of active tours, including caving, visits to hot springs, horseback riding, river tubing, waterfall hikes, and coffee farm visits at prices ranging $15-45 per person with a two-person minimum. Another option is **Basecamp Outdoor Adventures** (tel. 2651-4695, www.basecamphonduras.com), which is under the same management as the Via Via across the street and offers a variety

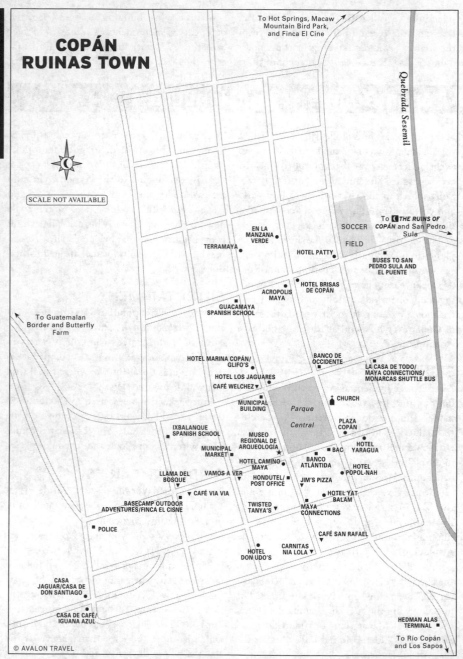

COPÁN RUINAS TOWN

SCALE NOT AVAILABLE

To Hot Springs, Macaw Mountain Bird Park, and Finca El Cine

Quebrada Sesemil

To Guatemalan Border and Butterfly Farm

EN LA MANZANA VERDE

TERRAMAYA

SOCCER FIELD

To **C** *THE RUINS OF COPÁN* and San Pedro Sula

HOTEL PATTY

BUSES TO SAN PEDRO SULA AND EL PUENTE

HOTEL BRISAS DE COPÁN

ACROPOLIS MAYA

GUACAMAYA SPANISH SCHOOL

HOTEL MARINA COPÁN/ GLIFO'S

BANCO DE OCCIDENTE

LA CASA DE TODO/ MAYA CONNECTIONS/ MONARCAS SHUTTLE BUS

HOTEL LOS JAGUARES

CAFÉ WELCHEZ

MUNICIPAL BUILDING

Parque Central

CHURCH

PLAZA COPÁN

IXBALANQUE SPANISH SCHOOL

MUSEO REGIONAL DE ARQUEOLOGÍA

HOTEL YARAGUA

MUNICIPAL MARKET

BAC

HOTEL CAMINO MAYA

BANCO ATLÁNTIDA

HOTEL POPOL-NAH

LLAMA DEL BOSQUE

VAMOS A VER

HONDUTEL/ POST OFFICE

JIM'S PIZZA

CAFÉ VIA VIA

HOTEL YAT B'ALAM

BASECAMP OUTDOOR ADVENTURES/FINCA EL CISNE

TWISTED TANYA'S

MAYA CONNECTIONS

POLICE

CAFÉ SAN RAFAEL

CARNITAS NIA LOLA

HOTEL DON UDO'S

CASA JAGUAR/CASA DE DON SANTIAGO

CASA DE CAFÉ/ IGUANA AZUL

HEDMAN ALAS TERMINAL

To Río Copán and Los Sapos

of alternative recreational options, including 2- to 6-hour hikes in and around the hills surrounding Copán Ruinas, motorcycle riding, and three- or five-hour horseback rides. It also runs daily shuttle buses to Antigua ($12) and Río Dulce ($20) with a 40-minute stop in Quiriguá along the way to the latter.

ACCOMMODATIONS
Under $10
Copán Ruinas's hippest budget accommodations are at **En la Manzana Verde** (tel. 2651-4652, www.enlamanzanaverde.com, $4 dorm bed), a clean hostel two blocks north of the park, where you'll find 18 beds in dorms named after personalities the likes of Fred Flintstone, 18 Rabbit, and Al Bundy, each with its own footlocker. There are two shared hot-water bathrooms. Guests have use of the kitchen (with fridge) as well as a TV lounge and hammocks. There are daily shuttles to Antigua and Guatemala City ($20) and you can book tours to Finca El Cisne with its nearby hot springs and mountain trails for horseback riding. The hostel is run by the same Belgian owners as the Café Via Via. You'll have to walk a few blocks southwest of the plaza to find the ❰ **Iguana Azul** (tel. 2651-4620, www.iguanaazulcopan.com, $7.50 dorm bed, $16 d), but it will be well worth it. There are excellent-value dorm beds and private rooms sharing a hot-water bathroom. The same Honduran-American owners run the beautiful La Casa de Café next door.

$10-25
Among the options in this category is **Hotel Via Via** (tel. 2651-4652, www.viaviacafe.com, $14 d), two blocks southwest of the park. Housed in the café of the same name, the hotel has spotless rooms with private hot-water baths and fans. There's a thatched-roof lounge on the second floor where movies are shown amid tropical foliage. On the southeast corner of the plaza, **Hotel Yaragua** (tel. 2641-4147, info@yaragua.

com, www.yaragua.com, $25 d) has guest rooms with private bathrooms, tile floors, and cable TV. Be aware that some beds have concrete slabs beneath them. There's a restaurant and bar in the lobby and Internet access. On the edge of town on the street leading off to the ruins is **Hotel Brisas de Copán** (tel. 2651-4566, $18-32 d) with 22 large rooms, orthopedic beds, fans, hot-water bathrooms, and cable TV. The cheaper rooms have smaller twin-sized beds.

$25-50
A block north of the plaza across from the Hotel Brisas de Copán is the **Acropolis Maya** (tel. 2651-4634, acropolis@copanhonduras.org, $50 d), with well-decorated rooms featuring nice, firm beds, tile floors, ceiling fans, reading lamps, air-conditioning, cable TV, and private hot-water baths. There's a small courtyard on the ground floor, along with a small living room in the lobby. A block south of the park, **Hotel Popol-Nah** (tel. 2651-4095) is a comfortable and modern 12-room hotel that has double rooms with fans and cable TV for $25 or double upstairs rooms with balcony views and air-conditioning for $45. All rooms have good mattresses and private hot-water bathrooms. **Hotel Los Jaguares** (tel. 2651-4451), on the plaza's northwest corner, has rooms with air-conditioning, private baths, firm beds, and cable TV.

$50-100
My favorite new discovery in Copán is ❰ **Terramaya** (two-and-a-half blocks north of the park, tel. 2651-4623, www.terramayacopan.com, $85-105 d). It's stylish and contemporary, with a beautiful outdoor patio and tables to enjoy the free breakfast and excellent coffee. A nice garden overlooks a wonderful view of the Copán valley. There are six rooms, all beautifully decorated. Rooms on the ground floor are slightly noisier on account of their fronting a busy street. The four upstairs rooms feature high ceilings that make the rooms feel even

more spacious. They also have ceiling fans, air-conditioning, cable TV, and DVD player. All rooms have private patios or balconies; the two most expensive rooms have balconies overlooking the rear of the property and the best view.

The enchanting 🔹 **La Casa de Café** (tel. 2651-4620, www.casadecafecopan.com, $55 d, breakfast included) is Copan Ruinas's premiere bed-and-breakfast inn, set in a quiet neighborhood a few blocks southwest of the plaza. The rooms are well furnished and tastefully decorated. You can enjoy fantastic views of the Copán Valley and Guatemala, farther west, from your patio hammock in a wonderful garden setting. The friendly Honduran-American owners also rent out fully furnished private villas across the street, including the **Casa Jaguar** (www.casajaguarcopan.com, $90 per night) and **Casa de Don Santiago** (www.casadedonsantiagocopan.com, $110 per night).

Lovely **Yat B'alam Boutique Hotel** (tel. 2651-4338, www.yatbalam.com, $75 d) is housed on the second floor of a small shopping complex. The ground floor features a coffee shop and handicrafts store. Rooms are on the second floor, some with pleasant street views, and feature nice extras like DVD players, mini-fridges, and high ceilings in addition to ceiling fans, air-conditioning, cable TV, and plenty of hot water. There's also a nice little sitting area fronting the street from the second floor. Decorative knick-knacks give it that boutique hotel feel. **Hotel Camino Maya** (tel. 2651-4518, info@caminomayahotel.com, www.caminomayahotel.com, $65 d) has comfortable rooms with all the usual amenities, including air-conditioning and telephone. There's also a small lobby with wicker furniture. In a large building on the southeast corner of the plaza is the similarly priced **Plaza Copán** (tel. 651-4508, www.plazacopanhotel.com, $67-73 d), where well-furnished rooms have tile floors, air-conditioning, mini-fridges, TVs, and private hot-water bathrooms. A restaurant and a

small swimming pool are also on the premises. The town's fanciest accommodations are found at **Hotel Marina Copán** (tel. 2651-4070/71, 877/893-9131 toll-free U.S., www.hotelmarinacopan.com, $92-145 d, including breakfast), built in the old family home of Doña Marina Welchez about 60 years ago. There are standard rooms and suites; all rooms have cable TV, ceiling fans, air-conditioning, and telephones. Amenities include a sauna, gym, swimming pool, bar, and the excellent Glifo's restaurant. 🔹**Hotel Don Udo's** (tel. 2651-4533, www.donudos.com, $55-90 d) scores major points for atmosphere with comfortable tiled-floor rooms tastefully decorated with Guatemalan furnishings and accents centered around a delightful garden courtyard. There are rooms with or without air-conditioning and TV; all have fans and private hot-water baths. Some bathrooms have a tub. There's a lobby lounge where you can watch DVDs. Alternatively, you can relax in a sauna or the whirlpool tub. There's also a decent restaurant.

Outside of Town

On the outskirts of Copán Ruinas are a variety of excellent lodging options. On a pleasant hilltop setting overlooking town is the resort-style **Clarion Hotel Copán Ruinas** (tel. 2651-4480, www.clarionhotel.com, $90 d), with 80 rooms equipped with purified tap water, air-conditioning, and cable TV, and with a swimming pool, two bars, and a restaurant. You may hear about 🔹 **Hacienda San Lucas** (tel. 2651-4106, www.haciendasanlucas.com, $100 d) even before your arrival in town, as it has a well-earned reputation for excellent service. The beautiful accommodations are set on a renovated 100-year-old hacienda oozing with atmosphere, the brainchild of Honduran Flavia Cueva. The lodge's eight rooms, spread about the beautifully landscaped grounds, manage to be comfortable and yet stylishly rustic at the same time, with adobe walls, wooden furniture,

© AL ARGUETA

the view from Hacienda San Lucas

and Guatemalan fabrics. At night, candles provide additional atmosphere. Enjoy a drink and watch the sunset over the Copán Valley before settling down to a delicious five-course dinner ($33) served in a gorgeous garden patio. Another wonderful old farm-turned-chic-hotel can be found along the road to San Pedro Sula near the village of Santa Rita at **Hacienda El Jaral** (tel. 2656-7091 or 2656-7147, $100 d), where you can stay in cozy wooden cabins near a lagoon. The rooms have ceiling fans, TVs, private hot-water bathrooms, and hammocks on a small porch. There's also a swimming pool. Choose from activities including hiking, mountain biking, horseback riding, or tubing on the Río Copán. Its owners also run a small shopping center, water park, and movie theater just down the road.

FOOD
Cafés and Light Meals
Avoid drinking beverages with ice cubes while in Copán's restaurants, as they seem to be of dubious origin.

◖ **Café San Rafael** (Avenida Centroamerica, across from Carnitas Nia Lola, tel. 2651-4546, 7:30 A.M.-8 P.M. daily) is more a delicatessen than a simple café, with a fine selection of artisanal cheeses, coffee from the family farm, and tasty food you can wash down with beer and wine. It enjoys a pleasant garden setting with nice mountain views. **La Casa de Todo** (tel. 2651-4185, www.casadetodo.com, 7 A.M.-9 P.M. daily) serves delicious snacks all day, including delicious *baleadas,* flour tortillas filled with beans and cheese, or scrumptious homemade yogurt with granola and fruit ($3.50). The breakfasts here are excellent ($2-4) with good, potent coffee. Enjoy your meal in the sunny garden courtyard. Right on the plaza next to the Hotel Marina Copán, **Café Welchez** (7 A.M.-9 P.M. daily) is Copán's best coffee shop, with espresso drinks and delicious cakes, pastries, and assorted other baked goods.

Italian

Jim's Pizza (tel. 2651-4381, 11 A.M.-9 P.M. daily), a block south of the plaza, makes tasty pizzas ($6-10) and pasta.

Honduran

Carnitas Nia Lola (tel. 2651-4196, 7 A.M.-10 P.M. daily), two blocks south of the Museo Regional de Arqueología, is a popular gathering spot for its scrumptious quesadillas, nachos, large *baleadas,* and savory *carnitas* served in a funky restaurant and bar. Stop in for happy hour 6:30-8 P.M. and stay to satiate your beer munchies. Popular with locals is **Restaurant Llama del Bosque** (tel. 2651-4431, 6 A.M.-10 P.M.), across from the Via Via, where the varied menu includes steak and seafood entrées for around $7. Go here for traditional breakfasts of eggs and beans or fondue cooked in a clay pot with beans and sausage ($5). Honduran cigars are also sold here.

International

There are a variety of good choices for international fare. **☾ Twisted Tanya's** (tel. 2651-4182, www.twistedtanyas.com, 3-10 P.M. Mon.-Sat.) manages to be classy yet casual in a pleasant, second-story balcony setting overlooking the street. For $20, you get a soup or salad starter, main course, and dessert. Typical dishes include such creations as curry shrimp, Chinese dumplings with wasabi, fish fillet with sautéed vegetables, and seafood pasta with crab. The desserts are equally creative and appetizing. It's a block west and then half a block south of the plaza. Stop in for happy hour 4-6 P.M.

Café Via Via (tel. 2651-4652, 7 A.M.-midnight daily) is a popular watering hole with travelers that doubles as a hip and trendy café. You can substitute vegetarian options for many of its dishes, including veggie burgers ($6). It also makes a good stab at Thai curry ($8). There are tables overlooking the street where you can enjoy the wonderful organically grown coffee.

Fine Dining

One of the finest restaurants in town can be found inside the Hotel Marina Copán. **☾ Glifo's** (tel. 2651-4070/71, 877/893-9131 toll-free U.S., www.hotelmarinacopan.com, 6:30 A.M.-9:30 P.M. daily, $8-14) serves a variety of international dishes with a distinctly Mayan slant in a pleasing blue and yellow dining room. For a local treat, try the Pollo al Loroco, cooked in a savory sauce of pungent edible flowers. The house specialty is Glifo's Traditional Chicken, cooked in a sauce of roasted, ground sesame and squash seeds flavorfully seasoned with Mayan herbs. International dishes include curry chicken, steak in mushroom wine sauce, and tarragon fish. **Don Udo's** (tel. 2651-4533, www.donudos.com, $6-10) has a stylish restaurant to accompany the hotel's tasteful atmosphere. Among the excellent dishes are steak and seafood dishes, homemade pastas, and Mayan cuisine. Outside of town, the delightful restaurant at **☾ Hacienda San Lucas** (tel. 2651-4106, www.haciendasanlucas.com) is the perfect place to catch the sunset from a perch overlooking the Copán Valley before digging into a scrumptious five-course dinner ($33). Much of the produce used in preparing the meals comes right from the farm. Typical dishes include cream of corn soup, tamales, chicken in adobo sauce, and flan for dessert. Reservations are required for dinner, though you can drop in for breakfast or lunch anytime. Even if you're not staying here, you should aim to eat at least one meal (preferably dinner) at Hacienda San Lucas during your visit to Copán. It's THAT good.

INFORMATION AND SERVICES

Copán Ruinas's tourist office (tel. 2651-4394, 8 A.M.-7 P.M. daily) is just east of the plaza on the same street as La Casa de Todo.

Communications

The post office (8 A.M.-noon and 1-5 P.M. Mon.-Fri., 8 A.M.-noon Sat.) is half a block west of the plaza.

Laundry

For laundry, head to Casa de Todo (tel. 2651-4185, www.casadetodo.com), where a load costs about $1.

Language Schools

Spanish instruction is slightly more expensive here than in Guatemala, with two schools to choose from. **Ixbalanque Spanish School** (tel. 2651-4432, www.ixbalanque.com) offers five days of one-on-one instruction for $125 or $185 including homestay with a local family. The other option is **Guacamaya Spanish Academy** (tel. 651-4360, www.guacamaya.com), where a week's worth of instruction costs $130 alone or $200 including room and board with a local family.

GETTING THERE

Minibuses to the El Florido border leave town from the corner next to the market about every half hour for the 20-minute, 12-kilometer trip. There are hourly onward buses from there to Chiquimula, taking about an hour. A much more comfortable and increasingly popular option is to book a shuttle bus. **Hedman-Alas** (tel. 2651-4037, www.hedmanalas.com) operates twice daily direct first-class bus service to Guatemala City ($35, four hours) and Antigua ($41, five hours) from its terminal on the road south of town heading toward the river. There are also onward buses to Tegucigalpa and San Pedro Sula. Shuttle buses to Guatemala City ($20), La Antigua ($20), and further into Honduras can be booked from **Café Via Via** (tel. 2651-4652).

If driving a rental car to Copán from Guatemala, be aware that you'll need written permission from your car-rental agency.

NEAR COPÁN RUINAS
Enchanted Wings Butterfly House

On the road from Guatemala, just before the turnoff into town, Enchanted Wings Butterfly House (tel. 2651-4133, http://

Hacienda San Lucas

© AL ARGUETA

For Internet, the most popular spot is Maya Connections (tel. 2651-4077, 8 A.M.-8 P.M. daily, $1.75 for one hour) at La Casa de Todo a block east of the park and near Jim's Pizza a block south of the park. Another option is Copán Net (one block south and one block west of the park, tel. 2651-4460, 9 A.M.-9 P.M.), where a lightning-fast connection costs $1.50 an hour.

For phone calls, Hondutel (7 A.M.-9 P.M. Mon.-Fri., 7 A.M.-noon and 2-5 P.M. weekends) can be found just south of the square but you can also make phone calls from the Internet hot spots.

Money

On the south side of the park, Banco Atlántida and BAC both have Visa ATMs and cash travelers checks, dollars, and quetzales. Banco de Occidente, on the park's northeast corner, exchanges dollars and quetzales as well as cashing travelers checks and issuing cash advances on Visa cards.

hondurasbutterflyfar.tripod.com/copan.htm, 8 A.M.-5 P.M. daily, $6 adults, $2.60 children under 12) is run by former Peace Corps volunteer Robert Gallardo and his wife. There are between 30 and 35 species of butterflies being bred here in a screened-in facility beside a river. Included in the admission price are a tour (you'll get a laminated placard with various pictures of butterflies to help you follow along) and a visit to an orchid nursery on the other side of the river. There are snacks and drinks available for purchase. It's best visited in the morning, when butterfly hatchings are frequent. There are reports that this attraction may be closing shop soon, so call ahead.

Macaw Mountain Bird Park

A few kilometers outside of town in the surrounding hillsides, Macaw Mountain Bird Park (tel. 2651-4245, www.macawmountain.com, 9 A.M.-5 P.M. daily, $10 adults, $5 children) has a collection of birds, including macaws, parrots, and toucans, housed mostly in cages found along a trail and wooden walkways winding through the park's splendidly sylvan riverside setting. In one area, you can interact freely with domesticated birds outside of their cages. There's a restaurant at the main entrance serving mostly meat and seafood dishes ($5-8) as well as a café along the trail. There's also a gift shop.

Hot Springs

About 22 kilometers from town along this same road are a series of pleasant hot springs ($1.50), where you can soak in a synthetic pool or take a series of trails to several hot springs that get cooler as you go downhill. A nice mix of cool river water blends with boiling hot water from the springs to make the water perfect for a soak. The jungle setting is also very relaxing. It's not quite as nice as Costa Rica's Tabacon hot springs, but it's certainly worth a visit. You

Finca El Cisne

© AL ARGUETA

can catch a pickup here from town, but a better way to get here is to combine a visit to the springs with a trip out to Finca El Cisne, preferably overnight, when you can use the springs after they have closed to other visitors.

Finca El Cisne

Farther along this same road and a 45-minute drive from Copán Ruinas is Finca El Cisne (www.fincaelcisne.com), a century-old, 1,000-hectare coffee farm where you can ride horseback, tour the coffee and cardamom plantations, and bathe in warm jungle hot springs. Cowboy Carlos Castejón, whose family owns the farm, leads most trips and speaks good English. He can show you around the farm and

show you everything you ever wanted to know about coffee cultivation. The farm also produces breadfruit, beans, avocados, corn, plantains, and oranges, among other crops. Riding on horseback through the extensive plantation affords the opportunity to really appreciate the surrounding countryside.

Day trips (leaving at 8 A.M. and returning at 6 P.M., $70) include horseback riding, visits to the cardamom and coffee fields, a home-cooked lunch, and a visit to the nearby hot springs. You can also stay overnight in a cozy solar-powered cabin with all of the above plus breakfast and dinner for $90. The booking and information office is inside the Via Via in a shared office with Basecamp Outdoor Adventures.

Quiriguá to Puerto Barrios

Quiriguá, a Mayan site that once rivaled Copán as the regional center of power, is still home to the region's tallest stelae. It makes a good excursion on the way to Puerto Barrios when traveling along highway CA-9.

QUIRIGUÁ

Set amid banana plantations, the Mayan site of Quiriguá is smaller but somewhat similar to Copán, particularly in regard to its inhabitants' skill and propensity in the carving of stelae. It's just 50 kilometers from Copán as the macaw flies, back on the Guatemalan side, though getting here from Copán is a bit more complicated than it looks on a map because the roads are structured so as to make you loop west, north, and then finally east on the highway leading to the Caribbean Coast (CA-9). Coming from Guatemala City, it's just a few kilometers down a dirt road turnoff from the main highway (CA-9), making it a worthy side trip along the road to Puerto Barrios or Río Dulce. Restoration of the site was conducted by

the University of Pennsylvania in the 1930s and in 1981 Quiriguá was declared a UNESCO World Heritage Site. The only other sites of this kind in Guatemala are Tikal and Antigua. It boasts the tallest known Mayan stela.

History

Quiriguá's history largely mirrors that of Copán, of which it was a vassal state for much of its history. In A.D. 653, for example, Copán's very own king Smoke Jaguar erected Altar L in Quiriguá's Great Plaza in his own honor after installing the city's new ruler. Quiriguá's stelae were carved with help from Copán's artisans using beds of brown sandstone brought from the nearby Río Motagua. The sandstone was soft when first cut, allowing the artisans to create the excellent-quality carvings, which hardened through time and can still be seen today.

Quiriguá's subservient status changed dramatically under the leadership of its king Cauac Sky with the capture and subsequent beheading of Copán's ruler 18 Rabbit in A.D. 737, an event which would mark the beginning of Copán's gradual downward slide. Cauac Sky quickly embarked on his own plan to expand the greatness of Quiriguá, carving most of the stelae in evidence there today. He can be seen on Stelae A, C, D, E, F, H, and J. Cauac Sky was succeeded by his son, Sky Xul (784-800), who lost his throne to Jade Sky, Quiriguá's last great king, who embarked on his own grand-scale reconstruction of the city's Acropolis. Quiriguá managed to remain independent of Copán for the remainder of its history until its own silent and mysterious demise in the middle of the 9th century.

Like Copán, Quiriguá captured the attention and fascination of John L. Stephens, who compared it to "the rock-built city of Edom, unvisited, unsought and utterly unknown." Stephens even attempted to buy the site in 1840 and cart it off to New York City via the Río Motagua and out to sea. Assuming that Stephens was negotiating on behalf of the U.S. government, the landowner quoted an exorbitant price and the deal was never made. The noted archaeologist Alfred Maudsley followed up with his own visit and excavations between 1881 and 1894, making some fine illustrations of the site's stelae and zoomorphic rock figures. In the early 1900s, the site and surrounding lands became the property of the United Fruit Company, which preserved the ruins and the area in its vicinity. The rest of the land was converted to banana plantations, miles and miles of them.

◖ The Ruins of Quiriguá

What is left of Quiriguá is limited to its ceremonial center. As you enter the park from the main entrance, you'll see the **Acropolis** straight ahead and the various stelae and zoomorphs (stone sculptures depicting animals and hybrid human-animal forms) in the **Great Plaza** to your left. The stelae are housed under thatched-roof structures to protect them from further deterioration from the elements. It can be somewhat difficult to view the carvings and even more difficult to get a good photograph. The most impressive is **Stela E,** standing almost 11 meters high, making it the tallest known Mayan stela. Noteworthy features in the carvings include their bearded subjects with elaborate headdresses, the staffs of authority clutched in their hands, and glyphs running up and down the monuments' sides. The various zoomorphs can also be seen here, depicting turtles, jaguars, frogs, and serpents. Near the Acropolis, **Altar P** depicts a figure seated in a strange, Buddhalike pose. The Acropolis itself is rather unimpressive, failing to rise in height above the treetops of the surrounding jungle, though it is somewhat spread out. There's a small ball court on its western side.

Practicalities

The park is open 7:30 A.M.-5 P.M. daily. Admission is $4. There's a small museum housing displays on the site's significance in relation to Mayan history and geopolitics along with a model showing the extent of the site's boundaries and unexcavated sections.

The site lies four kilometers from the main road with frequent transport heading up and down thanks to the activities of the nearby banana plantations. At the entrance to the site are a ticket office, the museum, and a few simple soda stands as well as some folks selling coconuts. The turnoff to the park from the main road (CA-9) is between Km. 204 and Km. 205, about 70 kilometers northeast of the Río Hondo Junction. The village of Quiriguá lies two kilometers back along the road toward Guatemala City and has some basic accommodations, though a better option is the town of Los Amates, at Km. 200 of Highway CA-9, if you should need to spend the night in these parts. Any bus heading along Highway CA-9 can drop you off at the junction to the road leading to the park.

MORALES (BANANERA) AND ENTRE RÍOS

Just north of this roadside town is the **La Ruidosa Junction,** where those heading to Río Dulce will have to change buses. Morales was formerly known as Bananera when it was the United Fruit Company town. Farther down, at about Km. 280, is the Entre Ríos Junction, from where the road heads east to Honduras.

JARDÍN BOTÁNICO Y RESTAURANTE ECOLÓGICO EL HIBISCUS

Near Puerto Barrios, at Km. 284 of Highway CA-9, is the Jardín Botánico y Restaurante

Ecológico El Hibiscus (tel. 7294-0397 or 5514-9525, www.hibiscusprojectizabal.com, 6 A.M.-5:30 P.M. Mon.-Sat.), a pleasant restaurant tastefully furnished with tropical wicker furniture and Mayan textiles that serves excellent breakfasts ($3-4), seafood, steaks, sandwiches, salads, and Guatemalan dishes. A tasty *caldo de gallina criolla* (chicken soup) is served on Saturdays. You can enjoy your meal in a pleasant wooden dining room or outside on one of two patios. Visitors can also enjoy a stroll through the botanical gardens housing a wide variety of flowers and tropical plants. It makes a pleasant stop on the way to Puerto Barrios or a good place to eat outside of town if you're staying there. The restaurant also serves as an information center for the Cerro San Gil and Punta de Manabique protected areas.

Puerto Barrios and Vicinity

This hot, humid port city holds little of interest for travelers except as a jumping-off point to surrounding attractions such as Punta de Manabique, Livingston, and resorts across the Bahía de Amatique. It was once Guatemala's main Caribbean shipping port but has been replaced by Puerto Santo Tomás de Castilla across the bay. It may be one of the main beneficiaries of a new $7 billion "dry canal" due to begin construction in 2012. The project is a joint venture between the public and private sectors and encompasses the construction of two new ports, a railroad, a four-lane highway, and a gas pipeline that will link Guatemala's Caribbean and Pacific coasts. It is meant to compete with none other than the Panama Canal, providing an alternative means of transportation for shipping containers traveling between the two oceans.

Construction of the port that now bears his name was initiated by reformist President Justo

Rufino Barrios in the 1880s and was linked to Guatemala City via a railroad completed in 1908. Puerto Barrios was important during the long-past glory days of the United Fruit Company. The company financed much of the railroad's completion and linked its banana plantations to Puerto Barrios, which served as the company-controlled shipping center for produce bound for New Orleans and New York. United Fruit was sold to Del Monte in the 1970s and Puerto Barrios sank into a tropical slumber.

NIGHTLIFE

The bars at the **Hotel del Norte** or **Safari** (northern end of 5a Avenida, tel. 7948-0563, 10 A.M.-9 P.M.) make good places for a drink while enjoying the bay views. Across from Hotel del Norte, **Jeffrey's Place** (weekends only) is a simple snack and beer stand. If you really want to get a feel for Puerto Barrios's sleazy, after-dark honky-tonk bars, head to the area around 8a Avenida between 6a and 7a Calle west of the post office, where you'll find a collection of a dozen or so bars and other "establishments."

EXCURSIONS

Social Travel (based out of Amatique Bay Resort, tel. 7948-1836 or 4172-2104, www.socialtravel.com.gt) provides recommended tours using local community guides to attractions just across the bay, including Cerro San Gil and Rio Las Escobas. Far-flung adventures include trips to Punta de Manabique.

ACCOMMODATIONS

Many of the ultra-low-budget accommodations in this town are used for prostitution, which is rampant in this sweltering coastal town, so backpackers beware. For Caribbean atmosphere and antique charm, you can't beat the 100-year-old **Hotel del Norte** (7a Calle and 1a Avenida, tel. 7948-2116, $20-33 d). Its quaint, crooked wooden floors evoke another time and have a certain dilapidated charm. Double-occupancy rooms in the original building cost $20 and have cold water, fans, and fluorescent lighting. Newer double rooms in a separate building cost $33 and have hot water, ceiling fans, warmer tungsten lighting, air-conditioning, and hot water. The restaurant, housed in a pleasant open-air thatched-roof building overlooking the hotel pool and sea, serves seafood, grilled meats, pasta, and other international dishes for $5-10. Just 1.5 blocks from the municipal docks, **Hotel Europa 2** (3a Avenida and 12 Calle, tel. 7948-1292, $13 d) is friendly and family run with clean rooms with bathrooms around a parking lot and courtyard. Next door is the friendly and family-run **Hotel Miami** (tel. 7948-0537, $12-20 d), containing clean rooms with or without air-conditioning. Another budget option is **Hotel La**

Caribeña (4a Avenida between 10 and 11 Calles, tel. 7948-0384, $11-20 d), with bare-bones but clean rooms with bathrooms and fans or air-conditioning.

On the outskirts of town are some pricier options that are conveniently near the main highway should you not want to stay in the heart of town. **(Hotel Marbrissa** (25 Calle y 20 Avenida, Colonia Virginia, tel. 7948-0940, http://hotelmarbrissa.com, $85-140 d) has comfortable rooms centered around the hotel's large swimming pool with all the amenities you would expect in this price range, including air-conditioning and minifridge. There are also larger suites with kitchenettes and living and dining rooms. The open-air *palapa*-style restaurant here is one of the nicest in town for its tranquil atmosphere overlooking the swimming pool.

On the main road into town at the junction leading to Puerto Santo Tomás de Castilla, **Hotel Puerto Libre** (tel. 7948-3064/65, www.hotelpuertolibre.com, $28-40 d) has rooms with air-conditioning, private hot-water bath, and TV. There's a lively swimming pool and the hotel restaurant serves mainly seafood dishes but also does delicious *parrilladas*. Entrees are priced $5-12.

Outside of town just past the airstrip on tropical grounds bordering the sea is the sprawling **(Amatique Bay Resort and Marina** (tel. 7931-0000, www.amatiquebay.net, $120-250 per room), where comfortable accommodations are housed in neocolonial villas. There are standard rooms and larger suites with full kitchens; the largest of these have additional sofa beds and a living room. All have air-conditioning and the usual amenities. There's an artificially constructed white-sand beach on the tranquil waters of the Bahía de Amatique and a swimming pool complete with a Spanish galleon. Three restaurants keep vacationers happy, including one that's right beside the swimming

PUERTO BARRIOS

Bahía de
Amatique

▼ SAFARI

1A CALLE

2A CALLE

3A CALLE

4A CALLE

POST
OFFICE

5A CALLE

Parque
Tecún
Umán

HOTEL
DEL
NORTE

CYBERNET DEL
ATLÁNTICO

JEFFREY'S
PLACE

BANCO G&T

8A CALLE

BANCO AGRÍCOLA
MERCANTIL

7A CALLE

BANCO
INDUSTRIAL

8A CALLE

Mercado
Municipal

9A CALLE

TRANSPORTES
LITEGUA

BANRURAL

10A CALLE

TRANSPORTES
EL CHATO

HOTEL
CARIBEÑA

TELGUA

CATEDRAL DE LA
INMACULADA CONCEPCIÓN

11 CALLE

MIGRACIÓN

HOTEL MIAMI

HOTEL EUROPA 2

LA FONDA
DE QUIQUE

MUELLE
MUNICIPAL

To Lívingston and
Punta Gorda (Belize)

12 CALLE

CENTRO
DE SALUD

13 CALLE

LA HAVANA VIEJA ▼

C@FÉ INTERNET

Bahía de
Gálvez

Río Escondido

14 CALLE

BANCO INMOBILIARIO

CALZADA JUSTO RUFINO BARRIOS

UNIVERSIDAD DE
SAN CARLOS

0   200 yds

0   200 m

RINCÓN ▼
URUGUAYO

16 CALLE

FUNDARY

17 CALLE

To Carretera al Atlántico
and Guatemala City

PEPÍN BURGER ▼

© AVALON TRAVEL

pool, serving lighter fare and sandwiches. The other two are more formal and serve a variety of international dishes. All in all, this complex is a self-contained leisure city built in colonial style somewhat resembling a seaside version of Antigua, complete with a whitewashed church. It is a popular day trip amongst cruise-ship passengers docking at nearby Puerto Santo Tomás de Castilla. The hotel is affiliated with Interval International.

FOOD

Local dishes include *tapado,* a seafood stew made from prawns, fish, and shellfish, seasoned with plantains, yucca, and coriander, and cooked in coconut milk. *Tortillas de harina* are flour tortillas stuffed with cheese, or anything else for that matter.

As for restaurants, **C Safari** (northern end of 5a Avenida, tel. 7948-0563, 10 A.M.-9 P.M.) is popular with locals for its large portions of excellent seafood dishes ($7-10) served in style on an open air, thatched-roofed platform over the sea. It also does excellent chicken and meat dishes ($4-6). Another good seafood option is the restaurant at **Hotel La Caribeña** (4a Avenida between 10 and 11 Calles, tel. 7948-0384), known for its *caldo de mariscos* and *tapado.* For lighter fare, try the rice and beans. For burgers, *tortillas de harina* and delicious fajitas, head to **Pepín Burger** (17 Calle between 8a and 9a Avenida, closed Tues.) in a second-floor terrace where you can catch the tropical breezes.

You'll find delicious Cuban food at lively **La Havana Vieja** (13 Calle between 6a and 7a Avenidas). A stylish option for seafood and international dishes is **La Fonda de Quique** (corner 12 Calle and 5a Avenida), in a pleasant air-conditioned dining room with formal tablecloths. The best steak house in town is the **Rincón Uruguayo** (7a Avenida and 16 Calle, closed Mon.), serving excellent *parrilladas* (grilled meats South American-style),

papas asadas, and *cebollines* (grilled spring onions).

If you're staying at the **Hotel Marbrissa** (25 Calle y 20 Avenida, Colonia Virginia, tel. 7948-0940, www.marbrissa.com) or nearby, try its excellent restaurant and bar set on the second floor of a large *palapa*-style building above the hotel lobby and overlooking the swimming pool. Parrots roam the premises while you dine on excellent seafood, grilled steaks, pasta, and other international dishes. You can also enjoy use of a pool table and a large flat-screen TV.

SERVICES

A useful website for checking out area attractions, restaurants, and accommodations is www.izabalonline.com.

Communications

The post office is on the corner of 8a Avenida and 6a Calle. Telgua is at 8a Avenida and 10a Calle.

Internet costs about $1.50 an hour at most places. Options for Internet use include Café Internet (13 Calle and 6a Avenida, 9 A.M.-9 P.M. daily), Cybernet del Atlántico (7a Calle, east of Hotel del Norte), and Red Virtu@l (17 Calle and Calzada Justo Rufino Barrios, 8 A.M.-9:30 P.M. daily).

Money

Banco Industrial (7a Avenida Norte #73) has a Visa ATM and changes U.S. cash dollars and travelers checks. Banrural (8a Avenida and 9a Calle) has a MasterCard ATM and also changes dollars and travelers checks. Just outside of town at the junction of the roads leading to Guatemala City and Puerto Santo Tomas is La Pradera Puerto Barrios shopping mall, with various ATMs.

Immigration

The offices of *migración* are on the corner of 12 Calle and 3a Avenida, a block from the municipal docks. This is where you get your entry or exit stamp when arriving from or heading to Belize. There is a $10 departure tax. The offices are open 7 A.M.-8 P.M.

GETTING THERE
Air
Puerto Barrios's long, paved runway has been inaugurated several times and even supported frequent flights to Guatemala City at one time. That service is suspended for the moment, but the airport remains one of the main landing strips in a nascent network of domestic airports. The runway is equipped to receive jet aircraft, including Boeing 737s.

Bus
Most of the transport in and out of Puerto Barrios is via the excellent **Transportes Litegua** (6a Avenida and 9a Calle, tel. 7948-1172, www.litegua.com), which operates comfortable, modern buses departing every half hour to and from Guatemala City. Some buses stop in Morales en route, where you get off for Río Dulce.

It's also possible to travel overland to Honduras by bus. Minibuses depart from the marketplace every half hour between 6:30 A.M. and 4:30 P.M. heading to the town of **Entre Ríos,** where there's an immigration post, and then continue to the border (one hour). Once in Honduras, take an awaiting pickup or minibus for the town of **Corinto,** four kilometers away. From Corinto there are buses every 90 minutes to Puerto Cortés (2.5 hours), stopping in Omoa along the way. There are frequent departures from Puerto Cortés to San Pedro Sula and onward in Honduras.

Boat
Boats leave from the municipal dock at the end of 12 Calle. There is **ferry** service to Lívingston ($1.50, 1.5 hours) Monday-Saturday at 10 A.M. and 5 P.M. Try to get there at least 30 minutes prior to departure time to secure your seat.

Lanchas, taking 30 minutes to make the journey, depart when they have a dozen people or so and cost about $5 one-way. Most of the traffic heading to Lívingston is in the morning hours.

There are also departures to Punta Gorda, Belize ($20 one-way), via **Transportes El Chato** (1a Avenida between 10a and 11a Calles, tel. 7948-5525 or 7948-8787, www.transporteselchato.com) leaving Puerto Barrios at 10 A.M. daily and taking about an hour. You'll need to stop by the immigration office to get your passport stamped prior to getting on the boat.

PUERTO SANTO TOMÁS DE CASTILLA
Cruise ships dock in Santo Tomás de Castilla, just across the bay from Puerto Barrios, where those wishing to go ashore will find some of the country's best bird-watching, lush tropical rainforests, and refreshing jungle rivers. Local tourism authorities in nearby Lívingston and Río Dulce are improving the quality of their services to cater to arriving visitors.

The history of Santo Tomás de Castilla actually dates to 1604, when it was founded as the coast's original colonial port. It was abandoned within a few years but later became the site of an ill-fated Belgian colony in 1843 after Guatemala's independence from Spain.

A paved road from Puerto Barrios leads to the main shipping center. From there, a dirt road continues along the coast to some of the area's natural attractions.

C Cerro San Gil and Río Las Escobas
This idyllic park, centered around the Cerro San Gil mountain, comprises more than 7,700 hectares (19,000 acres) of lush rainforest. Bathed in rainfall throughout most of the year (averaging 255 inches) as warm, humid air rises over the mountains from the sea to elevations in excess of 1,100 meters (3,900 feet), the preserve

THE GUATEMALA-BELIZE BORDER DISPUTE

During your travels, you might be surprised to find the neighboring country of Belize included as part of Guatemala on many maps produced in-country. It would seem that Belize is just another Guatemalan *departamento* despite its status as an independent nation since 1981. Guatemala did not in fact recognize its neighbor's independence until 10 years later in a highly criticized and unconstitutional move by then-president Jorge Serrano Elías. Guatemala's constitution clearly states that any decision regarding the independence or territorial integrity of Belize must be submitted to a public referendum. And so the debate continues over the "Belize question." It seems to be one of those issues that just won't go away, with succeeding governments always promising a final solution to this centuries-old problem.

Several governments have used the issue as a diversionary tactic during times of civil unrest, particularly during the military regimes of the 1970s. Matters came to a head in 1977 when Great Britain sent 6,000 troops to the border in anticipation of an invasion by Guatemalan troops during the presidency of military strongman Romeo Lucas García. Today, there are occasional reports of incidents along the northern Petén region's eastern border with Belize when Guatemalan peasants are forcefully evicted from the "no-man's land" along the border in clashes with Belizean security forces. The border is often referred to as a *zona de adyacencia,* or "imaginary border" area. Guatemalan newspapers love to publicize these incidents of supposed injustice against unarmed peasants, calling for a final solution to the long-standing problem.

The dispute dates to colonial times, when Spain officially claimed all of the Central American coast but was unable in practice to enforce its claim. English privateers and traders established a beachhead along the southern coast of Belize and extracted valuable timber products, including mahogany. The English presence was officially recognized by Spain in 1763, granting the British the right to extract forest products but refusing them the right of permanent settlement. The first permanent settlements came soon after Central American independence from Spain, the British clearly taking advantage of the power vacuum created in the aftermath of Spanish rule. The weakness of Guatemala's early governments was evident in an 1859 treaty, which officially recognized the British presence and "lent" the Belize territory to them for further resource extraction in exchange for a payment of £50,000 and the construction of a road from Belize to Guatemala City. Great Britain never held up its end of the bargain on either point and so the treaty was rendered null and void. British occupation of the lands continued, however, and the land eventually became known as the colony of British Honduras, which was granted its independence from England in 1981.

In recent years, Guatemala has limited its claims to the southern half of Belize, from the Río Sibún to the Río Sarstún, arguing that historical documents support its claims and include this territory as part of the region of "Las Verapaces." Some Guatemalan analysts believe there might be a case here, though the reasons for Guatemala's insistence in this matter remain a mystery. The current government has expressed its interest in getting its case settled once and for all by international arbitration, which would mean bringing it to the International Court in The Hague if all other avenues fail. Belize has tried to get the matter resolved in the Organization of American States (OAS), so far unsuccessfully, and has repeatedly stated that it will not cede "a single inch of its territory."

It's doubtful Guatemala will ever be able to recover its full claim, though the possibility for comanagement of the Sapodilla Cayes Marine Park (also claimed by Honduras) as a trinational park might be the most realistic outcome of any internationally mediated settlement on this matter. It would give Guatemala the one thing its geography and tourist offerings lack: white-sand Caribbean beaches with clear, turquoise waters. A referendum to decide whether the case goes to arbitration at the International Court in The Hague will be celebrated simultaneously in both countries on October 6, 2013.

© AL ARGUETA

Río Las Escobas

harbors an astounding level of biodiversity. Among the wildlife protected here are 56 species of mammals, including tapir and jaguars, 50 species of reptiles and amphibians, and more than 350 species of birds, including toucans, black and white hawk eagles, and keel-billed motmots. More than 90 neotropical migrants winter in the area and include the blue-winged warbler and wood thrush.

The park also protects the important watershed of the Río Las Escobas, which supplies water to Puerto Barrios. Part of the watershed is open to visitors ($8, including guided tour), who can bathe in Las Escobas's cool, clear waters and hike a series of nature trails winding through the park. The park is administered by the private conservation group **FUNDAECO** (tel. 7948-4404, www.fundaeco.org.gt), which in partnership with The Nature Conservancy has been able to buy large tracts of this rainforest ecosystem for preservation.

Facilities for visitors are found at **Las Pozas**

(tel. 5708-0744 and 5004-1143, http://riolasescobasizabal.com/travel.htm, 9 A.M.-6 P.M. daily) and include a visitors center, tropical gardens, a snack bar (open on weekends and when cruise ships are in town), and picnic areas. An excellent system of **trails** winds through the river and waterfalls and includes wooden bridges with stops along the way for swimming in stunning turquoise pools. More adventurous types can explore areas deeper into the reserve beginning at a trailhead just up the mountain and going from there to the Río Las Escobas through a dense stretch of forest (one hour) or to Cumbre Las Torres (four hours there and back), or encompassing multiple days of strenuous jungle hiking to the village of Carboneras (where there is a basic eco-lodge) and down the mountain to Río Dulce. Contact FUNDAECO if you wish to explore these options, as you will need prior authorization. A guided trek of either of the first two options costs $30 per person. Rates for the longer trip are negotiable.

The park is an increasingly popular day trip with cruise-ship passengers, many of whom reportedly state this to be their favorite stop after the crass commercialism of places such as Cancún and beaches that all pretty much look the same. The park lies just off the road, hugging the coastline from Puerto Santo Tomás de Castilla to the beach of Punta de Palma. **Social Travel** (based out of Amatique Bay Resort, tel. 7948-1836 or 4172-2104, www.socialtravel.com.gt) provides trips to Cerro San Gil and Río Las Escobas departing from Puerto Barrios, Lívingston, or Río Dulce. Prices range from $60 per person (two-person minimum) for a half-day tour to $150 per person for a trip including a stay of two nights. They can also arrange day trips and overnight stays at the eco-lodge in Carboneras (from Río Dulce) for about the same price.

Green Bay Hotel

Farther along this same road is the 50-room

Green Bay Hotel (tel. 7948-2361, $60 d room-only or $130 d all-inclusive), which was built far ahead of its time in the early 1990s but now seems perfectly situated to cater to cruise-ship day-trippers. The comfortable thatched-roof duplex bungalows are built into the side of a beautifully forested hillside near the water's edge and have all the comforts, including air-conditioning, TV, private hot-water bathroom, and bay windows that look out to the jungle. Although the exteriors are thatched-roof, it's really only for show, as the room interiors pretty much look like any standard modern hotel room. There is an airy, thatched-roof restaurant and bar overlooking the swimming pool and Bahía de Amatique. In addition to seafood, the restaurant serves international dishes including pasta, sandwiches, and grilled steaks. It's a bit overpriced at about $8 for a basic pasta dish.

Out front is a dock from where you can book a tour of the bay or a motorboat transfer to Punta

© AL ARGUETA

Villa Weyu in Punta de Palma

de Palma, Punta de Manabique, Lívingston, or Río Dulce. Otherwise, you can catch some rays on the lagoon-front beach or explore the waters in a kayak. Two small mangrove islets, known as the Cayos del Diablo, lie just off the coast. Mountain bikes are also available for rent and there's a sandy beach volleyball court. As at most of Guatemala's Caribbean beaches, the water here is not clear like that along the Yucatán Peninsula, but more emerald in color. It's what the tourism promoters have called "a different Caribbean."

Punta de Palma Beach

The road continues north from here to the beaches of Punta de Palma, a popular weekend getaway for folks from Puerto Barrios and where a sliver of sand meets the Caribbean Sea. There are some refreshment stands but little else here. Although locals might try to talk it up, you'll probably be very disappointed, as the Riviera Maya this is not. If you really want to hit the beach, there are some better options near Lívingston and across the bay at Punta de Manabique.

On the up side, there is at least one pleasant villa available for rent fronting its own private beach in Punta de Palma. **Villa Weyu** (www.realadventures.com, $750 for three nights) has 4 bedrooms, all with private bathroom, and sleeps eight. It's got a full kitchen and open-air living room fronting the house's infinity-edge swimming pool. It makes a nice secluded getaway or a good base for area explorations. The rental fee includes a cook and maid service.

◖ PUNTA DE MANABIQUE WILDLIFE REFUGE

Some day the white-sand Caribbean beaches along this remote peninsula on the northeast extreme of Bahía de Amatique may be home to resort hotels, but for now they remain largely uninhabited and lovely. The seas on the outer extreme of the peninsula can be particularly rough, as the land mass takes a bashing from the Atlantic Ocean while sheltering the waters of Bahía de Amatique, keeping them comparatively calm. In addition to the white sandy beaches where four species of sea turtles lay their eggs, there are mangrove swamps inhabited by manatees and more than 300 bird species, including the endangered yellow-headed parrot *(Amazona oratrix)*. Savannahs and flooded swamp forests harbor jaguars, tapir, and howler monkeys. Also protected are coral reef outcrops, the only ones of their kind in Guatemala, at the tip of the peninsula. All in all, it's one of Guatemala's most wonderful and least-visited wild places.

The reserve is managed by the conservation organization Fundary, which is working with some of the approximately 2,000 people inhabiting this area in an effort to involve them in the conservation of the wonderful marine ecosystem. Locals live mostly from fishing, particularly *manjua*, a type of small sardine. The waters off the coast of Honduras, Belize, and Guatemala have been somewhat overfished and so economic alternatives, including ecotourism, are being sought to provide a livelihood for the local population.

As fishing continues to be an important part of the local economy, new ways to make existing fishing operations more efficient have come into play. Together with USAID, Fundary has recently been able to bring solar power to the area, allowing locals access to heretofore uneasily obtained luxuries, such as ice, in a sweltering coastland. The availability of ice and refrigeration, in turn, makes it easier to cater to visitors and keep food for their consumption. The community of San Francisco del Mar, about halfway down the peninsula, now has its own solar-powered freezer and fish-processing plant. The women are making some extra cash producing and selling ice cream. It's all a bit reminiscent of Paul Theroux's *The Mosquito Coast*.

Recreation

Now is a great time to explore this area, as it's clear tourism is still in its infancy. That all might change soon, however, with the new cruise-ship terminal just a few miles away in Puerto Santo Tomás de Castilla. For now, your best bet is to contact **Fundary** (tel. 7948-0435, Puerto Barrios or 2232-3230, Guatemala City, www.guate.net/fundarymanabique), which is working with local communities to promote ecotourism. Among the activities are visits to the mangrove-lined canals of **Bahía La Graciosa, Laguna Santa Isabel,** and adjacent **Canal Inglés** for bird-watching and manatee-spotting. The canal is named after British loggers who dug the 10-kilometer trench connecting Laguna Santa Isabel to the Río Piteros. Along this canal is the small community of **Santa Isabel,** with a solar-powered visitors center, where you can fish with the locals or sit in on a demonstration of the local charcoal-making process. You can also kayak in the mangrove swamps and canals near the small community of **Estero Lagarto,** farther north and closer to the Punta de Manabique outcrop. Farther east, the Río Motagua marks the border with Honduras. Near the mouth of this river is the small settlement of **El Quetzalito,** where you can also do some bird-watching or crocodile-spotting. It's reached by road one hour from Puerto Barrios and then by traveling for half an hour downstream on the Motagua.

Accommodations and Food

Fundary runs a small basic lodge, **El Saraguate,** in the community of Punta de Manabique, just before you round the tip of the peninsula. Accommodations are in dorm-style bedrooms and cost $8 per person. It also offers package deals costing $75/95/120 (double, per person) for 1/2/3 nights' accommodations, food, and transport from Puerto Barrios. Food is heavily centered on seafood and is prepared by local families. Nearby is a fantastic trail with wooden bridges giving you a glimpse of the peninsula's largely flooded forest environment. A large dock goes out over the emerald-green waters fronting the lodge; from there you can snorkel in the clear, shallow waters. There's not much sand here and the locale feels very lagoonlike.

It's also possible to stay at the **Julio Obiols Biological Research Station,** run by Fundary, on the north end of the cape at Cabo Tres Puntas, where there's also a lighthouse. It has recently installed solar-powered electricity at the station and now hosts research teams with greater frequency. Accommodations ($100 for two nights per person, double occupancy, including transport from Puerto Barrios and meals) are in basic but clean rooms with 2-4 beds and mosquito netting. The ambience here is somewhat more typical of a Caribbean seaside setting, with a nice stretch of white, sandy beach against which the waves come crashing from the Atlantic Ocean. The months of March-May offer somewhat calmer seas.

The community of Estero Lagarto has a very basic, three-bedroom lodge for accommodating guests. Santa Isabel is putting together a community-run lodging of its own and may be in operation by the time you visit.

Getting There
There is no regularly scheduled service to Punta de Manabique, though you might get lucky and hitch a ride with a group going out on any given day. A better option is to book a package trip with Fundary with food, lodging, and transport included. Your money helps support conservation efforts. If you want to explore the area on your own, you can hire a boat to take you there from the municipal dock in Puerto Barrios. It's about an hour's ride. **Transportes El Chato** (1a Avenida between 10a and 11a Calles, tel. 7948-5525 or 7948-8787, www.transporteselchato.com) charges $180 for the trip. It's also possible to make the trip from Lívingston and it might be slightly cheaper.

Lívingston

A bit of an anomaly in Mayan and ladino Guatemala, Lívingston is an interesting Caribbean enclave of Garífuna culture and completes Guatemala's list of offerings with the authentic feel of a West Indian coastal town. This characteristic is made even more poignant by the fact that it's accessible only by boat. The town's setting is as exotic as its culture, splendidly situated at the mouth of the Río Dulce on the shores of the Bahía de Amatique. It makes a great base for upstream explorations of the Río Dulce canyon as well as nearby beaches, waterfalls, and pools, or the outlying Zapotillo cayes. The sounds of *punta* rock and reggae drifting out from the town's numerous restaurants and bars complete the Caribbean atmosphere. You can find some useful information on the town at www.livingston.com.gt.

SIGHTS
Museo Multicultural de Lívingston
The Museo Multicultural de Lívingston (tel. 7947-0944, 9 A.M.-5 P.M. daily, $0.70 admission) is just to the left of the municipal docks and features displays on the local Garífuna, Kekchí, and Cagey cultures in addition to the local flora and fauna. There are some interesting old fishing nets as well as some old and new photographs on display. It's worth a quick stop and the friendly staff will be happy to answer your questions.

Los Siete Altares
A side stream forms this series of seven waterfalls and emerald-green pools known as Los Siete Altares (Seven Altars, $1.50 admission) lying five kilometers northwest of town. You

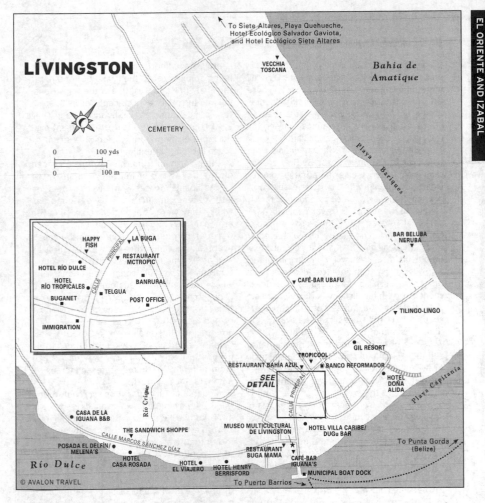

LÍVINGSTON

To Siete Altares, Playa Quehueche,
Hotel Ecológico Salvador Gaviota,
and Hotel Ecológico Siete Altares

VECCHIA
TOSCANA

*Bahía de
Amatique*

CEMETERY

Playa Bariques

0   100 yds
0   100 m

HAPPY
FISH

LA BUGA

RESTAURANT
MCTROPIC

HOTEL RÍO DULCE

HOTEL
RÍO TROPICALES

BANRURAL

TELGUA

BUGANET

POST OFFICE

IMMIGRATION

BAR BELUBA
NERUBA

CAFÉ-BAR UBAFU

TILINGO-LINGO

GIL RESORT

TROPICOOL

RESTAURANT BAHÍA AZUL

BANCO REFORMADOR

SEE
DETAIL

HOTEL
DOÑA
ALIDA

Playa Capitanía

Río Crique

CASA DE LA
IGUANA B&B

THE SANDWICH SHOPPE

MUSEO MULTICULTURAL
DE LÍVINGSTON

HOTEL VILLA CARIBE/
DUGu BAR

To Punta Gorda
(Belize)

CALLE MARCOS SÁNCHEZ DÍAZ

POSADA EL DELFÍN/
MELENA'S

Río Dulce

HOTEL
CASA ROSADA

HOTEL
EL VIAJERO

RESTAURANT
BUGA MAMA

HOTEL HENRY
BERRISFORD

CAFÉ-BAR
IGUANA'S

MUNICIPAL BOAT DOCK

© AVALON TRAVEL

To Puerto Barrios

may be disappointed if you visit here after visiting Río Las Escobas, as the waterflow at Siete Altares has declined in recent years due to increased consumption upstream. There's now very little water actually making it into the pools. Robberies have also been reported here in the past, so it's safest to go as part of a group. Any of the recommended guide companies can get you there, though Exotic Travel runs an adventurous option on mountain bikes. The river falls can be reached by walking along the shore northwest of Playa Quehueche for a few kilometers and then wading across a side stream before turning left onto a path leading to the first of the falls. The seventh waterfall and pool is the nicest. You'll have to clamber up the slippery rocks to get there.

Beaches

Lívingston has some acceptable beaches nearby, though the ones adjacent to town are generally not the cleanest and have had some security

LÍVINGSTON'S GARÍFUNA CULTURE

Lívingston is one of Guatemala's most culturally diverse regions, with Garífuna, Hindu, Q'eqchi', and ladino cultures peacefully coexisting here. Of these, the Garífuna and Hindu influences are particularly interesting because they are not found elsewhere in Guatemala, giving this region a unique flavor. Guatemalans are often surprised to see Afro-Caribbean people when they visit the Atlantic Coast, as they are not readily in evidence elsewhere in the country, looking upon them with a certain sense of wonder simultaneously fueled by a form of racism familiar to the country's Mayan people. A number of far-fetched myths have been affixed to Garífunas, including the belief that seeing an Afro-Caribbean person on the street (outside of Lívingston) means you will soon come in contact with a long-lost acquaintance. Also common is the general suspicion of widespread practice of voodoo and cannibalism by Garífuna peoples.

Guatemala's Garífuna population numbers about 4,000 and traces its history to the Caribbean island of St. Vincent. Ethnically, they are a mix of Amerindian and African peoples and their language comes from the Brazilian Arawakan language family. These Arawak-speaking peoples migrated from northern Brazil long before the arrival of Europeans in the New World and lived peacefully on the island until they were subdued by Carib speakers from the South American mainland. The African element of their bloodline came about after intermingling with the survivors from the wreck of a Spanish ship carrying Nigerian slaves just off the coast of St. Vincent. These people eventually became known to the British as Black Caribs—in their own language, Garinagu. Garífuna is the Spanish translation of this word. In the 1760s, the British tried to take St. Vincent but were driven off by the Caribs with help from the French. The Caribs would continue to oppose the British on and off for several years until finally being defeated in 1796, when they surrendered. The Garífuna were subsequently captured and imprisoned by the British before being shipped off to the island of Roatán, off the coast of Honduras. One of the ships transporting the prisoners was captured by Spanish forces and sent to the Honduran mainland. Only 2,000 Garífuna made it to Roatán, as many died during their imprisonment on St. Vincent or along the subsequent journey.

Pleas for help from the Garífuna stranded on the tiny island of Roatán were answered by the Spanish forces who arrived some time later to take survivors to Trujillo (Honduras), where they were conscripted to serve in the armed forces or work in agricultural fields. The Garífuna continued to move along the coast, eventually settling other parts of Honduras as well as Nicaragua. Some were taken to southern Belize to work in logging operations, from where they spread to Guatemala, establishing Lívingston in 1806. Today, the largest population of Garífuna can be found along the coast of Honduras (100,000), but there are also sizable populations in New York (50,000), New Orleans, and Los Angeles. Like other ethnic groups in Central America, they have been emigrating to the United States in increasing numbers since the 1970s.

Modern Garífuna speak Spanish, English, and the Garífuna language, which melds French, Arawak, Yuroba, Swahili, and Banti. Central to their culture are music and dance, namely *punta,* a form of musical expression with obvious West African influences incorporating ritual chanting, mesmerizing drumbeats, and rhythmic dancing. A traditional Garífuna band consists of three large drums, a turtle shell, a large conch shell, and maracas. You will probably hear live *punta* music at least once during your visit to Lívingston. Also common is *punta* rock, a more modern version of popular Garífuna music. Another fascinating traditional dance is the *yancunu* New Year's dance, similar to those of indigenous South American rainforest peoples with distinctly West African musical origins.

© AL ARGUETA

Playa Capitanía

issues in the past. Locals insist the group perpetrating past robberies has been caught, with at least one of them having met an unfortunate end. The nicest beach close to town is that of **Playa Quehueche,** about two kilometers northwest along Bahía de Amatique. There are a couple of comfortable hotels here, allowing you the opportunity to stay right on the beach. Both have nice wooden docks for swimming in the placid Caribbean waters. Playa Quehueche becomes **Playa Bariques** as you get closer to town. A standout among the beaches bordering Lívingston is **Playa Capitanía,** on the town's southeast fringes.

The beaches in and around Lívingston are of white or grayish brown sand, unlike the volcanic sands on the Pacific Coast. It's not the talcum-powder white typically found on Caribbean shores elsewhere and the water is not turquoise as in the Belize cayes, mostly because silt from the surrounding jungle rivers flowing into the bay conspires to keep the

waters a greenish-brown color. But they're still perfectly nice for swimming. A boat ride from Lívingston to Playa Quehueche costs about $4.

Another 12 kilometers or so northwest is my favorite Guatemalan beach, **Playa Blanca** (entrance $1.50), with a pretty stretch of white sand and palm trees on the tranquil Caribbean Sea. The private beach is under the same ownership as the Villa Caribe and it wouldn't be surprising to see a hotel here within the next five years. For now, it remains pleasantly quiet, though it's becoming increasingly popular as a day trip from Lívingston. There are bathrooms and showers here, along with beverages for purchase, but little else.

Several outfitters including La Casa Rosada, Happy Fish, and Exotic Travel do trips to Playa Blanca for $13 per person with a six-person minimum and including a box lunch. The Exotic Travel tour stops at the waterfalls of **Siete Altares** and the **Río Cocolí** along the way. The river is a pleasant side stream suitable

© AL ARGUETA

Playa Blanca

for swimming with a small sliver of beach along the bay. Trips leave around 9 A.M. and return in the afternoon around 5 P.M. If you're looking to hook up with a group, try Exotic Travel first, as it seems to be the popular favorite and might have a group already going out.

NIGHTLIFE

If you're the kind of person who likes to spike the punch at the party, you might want to try a *coco loco,* a rather fun concoction consisting of a coconut with the top chopped off and enhanced with a generous helping of rum. The bars along Calle Principal as you come up the street from the municipal docks, including **La Buga** and **McTropic,** can usually satiate your thirst should the fancy take you.

Lívingston has a fairly vibrant nightlife scene befitting of its tropical location by the sea. Down by the beach on the northern end of town (Playa Bariques) is **Bar Beluba Neruba** with a small dance floor and tables right on the

sand. It can be reached by heading west along the beach at the end of Calle Principal.

Along a side street also heading west from Calle Principal, **Café-bar Ubafu** is usually hopping, with live music on weekends. On Calle Principal, **Tropicool** is a disco that opens at 8 P.M. on weekends.

The classiest place in town is part of the Villa Caribe hotel. **Dugu Bar** (5 P.M.-midnight daily) is housed in a cheerful, yellow wooden house on the town's main street opposite the Immigration office. The interior is decorated with tons of old pictures and there's a full bar. The poolside bar at **Vecchia Toscana** (Barrio París, tel. 7947-0883 or 7947-0884, www.vecchiatoscana-livingston.com) is also a good bet.

EXCURSIONS

Social Travel (tel. 7948-1836 or 4172-2104, www.socialtravel.com.gt) provides recommended tours using local community guides to nearby attractions, including **Tiger Cave** and the community of Plan Grande Tatin, the forest reserve near Plan Grande Quehueche and Lagunita Creek (on the Río Sarstún). The tours are reasonably priced and provide unique opportunities for socially and ecologically responsible tourism allowing close interaction with the local populace. Tourism dollars directly benefit the host communities and are partly reinvested into maintaining and improving their tourism infrastructure. A full-day tour to either of the two local communities runs about $30 per person (two-person minimum).

Another new and original option is that of **Reggae on the River** (tel. 7947-0064, $16), a full-day adventure exploring Río Dulce aboard a 28-foot pontoon boat fitted with sofas and a good selection of tunes. Not your usual booze cruise, the tour makes frequent stops along the river for swimming and taking in the natural surroundings. Additional stops include the river hot springs (and its adjoining caves) as well as Ak' Tenamit for a short jungle hike and waterfall swim. Cocktails cost $2 but you can also do the trip on an all-you-can-drink rum-and-coke basis for $29. The trip leaves daily from La Casa de la Iguana at 10 A.M., returning at 5 P.M. Maximum occupancy is 15 passengers and you must book it by the night before.

Hotel Casa Rosada (tel. 7947-0303, www.hotelcasarosada.com), **Happy Fish** (tel. 7947-0661 or 7947-0268, www.happyfishresort.com, $5-25), and **Hotel Río Dulce** (tel. 7947-0764) do trips to Siete Altares ($13) and Playa Blanca ($15) with a minimum of six people. Hotel Río Dulce's Playa Blanca trip also stops at Siete Altares and Río Cocolí along the way.

Hotel Posada El Delfín (tel. 7947-0056, www.turcios.com/eldelfin) offers a number of adventurous itineraries, including a full day of deep-sea fishing, an overnight scuba-diving trip to San Nicolás caye (in the Belize cayes), and a hike up a nearby mountain for an overnight stay in a jungle villa.

ACCOMMODATIONS

Despite its location right on the Caribbean Sea, Lívingston lacks beachside resort properties, as the beaches in the immediate vicinity are somewhat lacking. There are, however, some mid-range accommodations on a serviceable beach just north of town. Most of the listed accommodations are found in the heart of town.

Under $10

The most pleasant budget accommodations are found at the rustically charming █ **Casa de la Iguana B&B** (tel. 7947-0064, www.casadelaiguana.com, $5-8 per person), about one kilometer from the center of town along Calle Marcos Sánchez Díaz, where fan-cooled rooms housed in thatched-roof bungalows with private bath and hot water go for $8 per person or $5 per person in a shared-bath dormitory. Breakfast ($3) is served 7-10 A.M. in a thatched-roof dining room overlooking a pleasant tropical garden and includes a choice of scrambled

eggs, pancakes, or cereal. There's also a book exchange. If you're in a pinch, head to the no-frills **Hotel El Viajero** (tel. 5718-9544), closer to the center of town along the same street where rooms sharing a bathroom cost $2 per person or $6 d with private (cold-water) bathroom. Continuing toward town the next place you'll come across is **Hotel Henry Berrisford** (tel. 7947-0471/72), offering basic rooms spread out among several floors with ceiling fan, spongy foam mattresses, TV, and private cold-water shower for $10 per person or $7 minus the TV.

On Calle Principal, **Hotel Río Dulce** (tel. 7947-0764) has good-value rooms with shared bath for $5 or with private cold-water bath for $6. The shared-bath rooms are upstairs, are somewhat more cheerful, have balconies with street views, and get more ventilation than rooms with private bathroom, which are all on the first floor. All rooms have fan and spongy mattresses.

$10-25

On Calle Principal, **Hotel Ríos Tropicales** (tel. 7947-0158, www.mctropic.com) has basic shared-bath accommodations for $8 per person as well as nicer rooms with private bathroom for $18 d. There is hot water and an attractive courtyard with hammocks. The more expensive rooms have ceiling fan and some nice furniture. There's a small café serving breakfasts. Along the waterfront is **Hotel Doña Alida** (tel. 7947-0027, $25 d), with 10 large, modern rooms with private bath on a quiet street overlooking a beach. Rooms 10 and 11 are worth requesting for the sea views. To get here, turn right on the street just behind the Villa Caribe and walk north 2.5 blocks.

Along Calle Marcos Sánchez Díaz, about 400 meters west of the boat docks, is █ **Hotel Casa Rosada** (tel. 7947-0303, www.hotelcasarosada.com, $20 s/d), a delightful place to stay with 10 rooms, all with shared bath, centered around a pretty pink wooden house on the shores of the Río Dulce. The rooms are housed in attractive wood-and-thatch cabins with nice furnishings and hand-painted accents. Amenities include ceiling fans and mosquito netting. Some rooms are brighter than others. There is a dock leading out to the river where you can get dropped off. The restaurant here is excellent.

Out of town northwest toward Siete Altares is Playa Quehueche, a sliver of a beach that holds a few comfortable lodgings. The first of these is **Hotel Ecológico Salvador Gaviota** (tel. 5514-3275 or 5514-7933, www.hotelsalvadorgaviota.com), which has simple rooms in thatched-roof cabins, including shared-bath doubles ($20), rooms with private bath ($13 p/p), and bungalows sleeping up to five for $60. There is a simple seaside café serving local fare and there's a pier out front over the ocean where you can swim or lounge in a hammock. A boat ride into town costs about $5. Also in this neck of the woods and farther west is **Hotel Ecológico Siete Altares** (tel. 5514-3339 or 5205-7864, www.geocities.com/sietealtares, $15 p/p), where thatched-roof beachfront bungalows sleeping 2-6 people have ceiling fan and private bathroom. A restaurant serves a variety of menu items from hot dogs and barbecue chicken wings to grilled meat and seafood dishes, along with cocktails to enjoy by the beach.

$50-100

Right at the entrance to town near the main dock, the **Hotel Villa Caribe** (tel. 7947-0072, www.villasdeguatemala.com, $79-110 d) is a large white building with a commanding presence over the waterfront. Standard rooms have tile floors, fan, and private hot-water bath, while three attractively furnished suites housed in separate bungalows come with air-conditioning, TV, minibar, and lovely sea views. There's a large swimming pool and a restaurant that serves bland international fare. Splurge for the suite.

About 500 meters west of town along Calle Marcos Sánchez Díaz is the **℄ Posada El Delfín** (tel. 7947-0694 or 7947-0056, www.turcios.com/eldelfin, $75-150 d), where the modern, comfortable rooms have air-conditioning, private bath, ceiling fan, phone, and wooden furniture. All upstairs rooms have carpeting. There are also larger suites, including the wonderful honeymoon suite on the end of the two-story dock with a balcony overlooking the river below. It comes equipped with fridge, TV, and a CD player. Guests can relax in a lounge on the second floor, in the small swimming pool, or in hammocks on the dock over the river. For overall comfort and relaxing riverside ambience amid refreshing breezes, this place can't be beat.

On the street parallel to Playa Capitanía is **Gil Resort** (tel. 7947-0039, www.gilresorthotel.com/english/index.html, $50 d), housed in an airy, two-floor wooden building. The comfortable rooms have wood paneling, TV, and a/c. There's a nice sitting area with sea views and a Jacuzzi hot tub. The nicest of the town's accommodations is **℄ Vecchia Toscana** (Barrio París, tel. 7947-0883 or 7947-0884, www.vecchiatoscana-livingston.com, $40-150). The tastefully decorated rooms feature mosquito netting and a fan or a/c and are built on well-manicured grounds surrounding a swimming pool. The star attraction is the beachfront bungalow, with a private roof terrace, Jacuzzi tub, minibar, and comfortable lounge chairs.

On the other bank of the Río Dulce and at its mouth, **Sierramar Eco-Lodge** (tel. 5590-0789 or 7832-3885, www.sierramar.com, $25 d) is a comfortable eight-room lodge with bungalows fronting a pretty beach on Bahía de Amatique.

FOOD

The specialty here and elsewhere in Izabal is a dish known as *tapado,* a seafood stew prepared using coconut milk and bananas.

On par with the wonderful accommodations

at **(Hotel Casa Rosada** (tel. 7947-0303, www.hotelcasarosada.com, 6:30 A.M.-9 P.M. daily) is its excellent restaurant, where delicious meals are served on charming hand-painted tables in a thatched-roof covered patio overlooking the Río Dulce. Dinner is a three-course set menu, including fresh salad and coconut bread, main course, and dessert costing about $13. Typical entrées include lobster, shrimp, filet mignon, Thai curry, and fish. Lunch and breakfast are served à la carte and include sandwiches, fruit salads, and quesadillas. Try the banana pancakes for breakfast. Excellent coffee and espresso drinks are also served here.

A few doors down Calle Marcos Sánchez Díaz, heading west, **(Malena's** (inside the Hotel Posada El Delfín, tel. 7947-0694, www. turcios.com/eldelfin, 6 A.M.-9:30 P.M. daily) is one of Lívingston's finest restaurants, serving a varied menu of international dishes at reasonable prices, including vegetarian nachos with Provençal sauce, chicken, burgers, and veggie burgers. Seafood entrées include *tapado,* ceviche, fish chowder, and sea bass. There are delicious homemade desserts, coffee, and espresso beverages to top off your meal. The restaurant is on the second floor of a two-story dock jutting over the Río Dulce with pleasant modern decor, sea breezes, and the unmistakable feel of the tropics.

Along this same street close to the municipal dock, **(Restaurant Buga Mama** (tel. 7947-0891, www.bugamama.org/, 10 A.M.-10 P.M. Tues.-Sun., noon-10 P.M. Mon., $5-25) is a good place for reasonably priced fish, shrimp, and pasta dishes. The restaurant, housed in a bright-blue wooden building, is wonderfully staffed by tourism industry students from a local school run by grassroots development organization Ak' Tenamit.

Calle Principal has a number of eateries. One of the first places you'll see as you come up the hill from the main dock is **Happy Fish** (tel. 7947-0661 or 7947-0268, 7 A.M.-10 P.M.

daily), serving reliable seafood and salads in a pleasant patio setting just off the street. It's a good bet for breakfast. Across the street is Restaurante McTropic (7 A.M.-10 P.M. daily), under the same ownership as the Hotel Ríos Tropicales, where the specialty is Cantonese food, including chop suey and fried rice. A few doors down and across the street is the popular **Restaurante Bahía Azul** (tel. 7947-0151, 7 A.M.-10 P.M. daily), where meals are also served on a patio overlooking the street. The creative menu includes curry, sweet and sour or soy sauce chicken. There is live music some nights. It's also a good bet for breakfast. Try the "Gangster" breakfast sandwich with ham, cheese, hot cakes, and honey—a bit like a McGriddle. Farther up the same street toward Playa Bariques, **Tilingo-Lingo** (7 A.M.-11 P.M. daily) serves good nachos, curries, fish, and *tapado.*

If you crave authentic Italian cuisine, head to **(Vecchia Toscana** (tel. 7947-0883/84, www.vecchiatoscana-livingston.com/, 8 A.M.-1 A.M. daily), in Barrio París on the beach north of town toward Playa Quehueche. There are delicious pastas and wood-fired-oven pizzas with prices in the $4-9 range.

For the town's best sandwiches, check out **The Sandwich Shoppe** (Calle Marcos Sánchez Díaz across from Casa Rosada, lunch and dinner Sun.-Thurs., until 6 P.M. Fri., 6 P.M.-close Sat., $5-8), where you'll find some of your favorite subs including meatball, Philly cheese steak, BLT, and even Cuban sandwiches.

SERVICES

For money, Banrural is on Calle Principal, just past Villa Caribe, with an ATM. Farther up the street is Banco Reformador, also with an ATM.

The immigration office (6 A.M.-7 P.M. daily) is also on Calle Principal across the street from the Villa Caribe. You'll need to stop here first if heading out to or arriving from Belize. Telgua and the post office are right next to each other just up the street on the right side.

For Internet access, try La Buganet (8:30 A.M.-9 P.M. Mon.-Sat.) or Happy Fish (7 A.M.-10 P.M. daily), both on Calle Principal and costing about $2 an hour. La Casa Rosada does laundry for about $0.35 an item.

GETTING THERE

The only access to and from Lívingston is by water, either from the Caribbean Sea to Puerto Barrios, Belize, or Honduras or via the Río Dulce. There is Monday-Saturday ferry service to Puerto Barrios at 5 A.M. and 2 P.M. (1.5 hours, $1.50), along with motorboats ($5) leaving all day when they have a full load of people. From Puerto Barrios, there are departures to Lívingston Monday to Saturday at 11 A.M. and 5 P.M. There is also service to Punta Gorda, Belize, on Tuesdays and Fridays at 7 A.M. (one hour, $25). Any of the town's travel agencies can book tickets for you, but you must have the confirmed ticket the night before, along with your exit stamp from the immigration office. There's a $10 departure tax when leaving Guatemala by sea. From Punta Gorda to Lívingston, the boat leaves Tuesdays and Fridays at 12:30 P.M. **Exotic Travel** also runs shuttle transport directly to Placencia for $50 per person with a six-person minimum. If you're heading to Honduras and have at least four people, it can also take you to La Ceiba for $75 per person, including boat to Puerto Barrios and then a minibus for the rest of the way.

The water taxi association, ASOCOLMORAN, runs transfers to Río Dulce (2.5 hours, $13) leaving at 9 A.M. and 1:30 P.M. but these stop along the way at the Río Dulce hot springs. Boat transfers to Río Dulce are also available from **Ríos Tropicales** (tel. 7947-0158, www.mctropic.com, $16).

NEAR LÍVINGSTON
Río Sarstún

As you head northwest along the Caribbean coast past the beaches of Playa Blanca, the last stop along the Guatemalan Caribbean shores is the Río Sarstún, which forms the border between Belize and Guatemala. This beautiful jungle river has just recently become a viable option for exploration now that it is fully protected as a park administered by conservation group FUNDAECO (www.fundaeco.org. gt). The park ($20 admission) protects 2,000 hectares of tropical rainforest, flooded forest, wetlands, and mangroves. You can kayak and explore wetland canals, see the recently discovered Cerro Sarstún cenote, swim in the emerald-green waters of a small lagoon, or hike along well-maintained nature trails, all of which are included in the price of admission.

Accommodations are in the **Eco-Albergue Lagunita Creek** (tel. 2253-4991 and 5241-9342, www.fundaeco.org.gt), a modern facility with clean, shared-bath dormitories with bunk

© AL ARGUETA

dense rainforests along the Río Sarstún

beds for $10 and double rooms with private baths, queen-sized beds, and balconies overlooking the river for $35. You can buy meals from the local community for $7-10. There's also a biological station here. **Social Travel** (tel. 7948-1836 or 4172-2104, www.socialtravel. com.gt) provides trips to Lagunita Creek from Lívingston with a two-person minimum for $100 per person for a day trip, or $150 per person with an overnight stay at the lodge. Prices include roundtrip transportation, park entry fee, local guides and meals.

【 The Zapotillo Cayes

For the ultimate Caribbean adventure, cruise out to the Zapotillo Cayes, part of the famous Belize Barrier Reef. As you head out to sea from the mainland, the waters transfuse into gorgeous hues of emerald green. The talcum-powder beaches along the small cayes are the stuff of Caribbean postcards with inviting turquoise waters perfect for swimming. The cayes are protected as a nature preserve, meaning there are no hotels on these islands. Camping is allowed. The reef is particularly well preserved with excellent opportunities for scuba diving.

Several of the Lívingston travel agencies go out to the cayes with a minimum of four people. **Exotic Travel** (tel. 7497-0133 or 7497-0151, www.bluecaribbeanbay.com) runs a day trip to the cayes, taking two hours to get there from Lívingston by a fast boat and including a stop along the way for deep-sea fishing. A box lunch and snorkel gear are also included. The trip costs $40 per person with a five-person minimum, plus a $10 entry fee to the park. You'll have to check out with immigration and pay a $10 exit tax for your brief departure from Guatemala, something that has only recently begun to be enforced. Have your group together by 5 P.M. the night before, along with your immigration formalities.

Overnight stays are available by booking highly recommended sailing adventures starting in Río Dulce, taking you up the lush jungle river and out to the cayes for a memorable weeklong experience. Booking is available through **Aventuras Vacacionales** (tel. 7832-6056, www.sailing-diving-guatemala.com, $380 per person, double occupancy) and on *"That"* (tel. 5529-0829), a 62-foot trimaran.

Río Dulce National Park

One of Guatemala's oldest parks, the waterway connecting the Caribbean Sea with Lake Izabal is protected as Río Dulce National Park, covering 7,200 hectares along the river's 30 kilometer (19-mile) course. Much of the riverbank is shrouded in dense tropical forest punctuated at its most dramatic point by a large jungle canyon with hundred-meter rock faces known as **La Cueva de la Vaca.** The canyon is a 15-minute boat ride upstream from Lívingston. Along this route you'll also come across a graffiti-covered rock escarpment known as **La Pintada** with the earliest painting in evidence dating to the 1950s.

Just after the canyon (heading upstream from Lívingston), you'll come across the first of Río Dulce's many accommodations. **The Round House** (tel. 4294-9730, theround-house@live.ca, www.roundhouseguatemala. com, $5 p/p in dorm, $14 d in shared-bath private room) is a well-run, fun sort of place with dorms and private rooms. There's a swimming pool and a Sunday afternoon pool volleyball game that includes lunch and drink specials. Kayaks are available for rent. Meals are served family-style in the open-sided dining room. Bungalows are under construction.

SAILING TO THE BELIZE CAYES

One of the highlights of many visitors' travels in the Guatemalan Caribbean is the unique opportunity to sail down the Río Dulce canyon and out to the Belize cayes. Trips last about a week and there are stops en route to swim and enjoy the magical beauty of the jungle river and canyon before stopping in Lívingston for immigration formalities. From there, the trip rounds the cape at Punta de Manabique before continuing to the open seas, where the water morphs into luminescent shades of aquamarine. You can enjoy learning the ins and outs of sailing, lingering on the deck under the sun or stars, delicious meals of fresh-caught seafood, snorkeling, scuba diving ($35 per dive), and lounging on pretty white-sand beaches. Typical stays on the cayes are about three days, with the rest of the time spent sailing to and from these wonderful offshore islands.

The islands you'll sail to are part of Belize's Sapodilla Cayes Marine Park, also known as the Zapotillo Cayes, and consisting of Lime Caye, Hunting Caye, Nicholas Caye, Seal Caye, and French Caye. The islands form a hook shape and are the southern extreme of the world-famous Belize Barrier Reef, second in length and marine splendor only to Australia's Great Barrier Reef. Divers will be delighted to find a variety of beautiful coral gardens, double reefs, canyons, and steep drop-offs in these waters.

At least two companies operate the trip out of Río Dulce. **Aventuras Vacacionales** (tel. 7832-6056, www.sailing-diving-guatemala. com, $380 per person, double occupancy) has been sailing to the cayes since 1990. Its office is in Antigua. Sailing is on *Las Sirenas*, a 46-foot Polynesian catamaran captained by its owner, John Clark, and by Guatemalan captain Raúl Hernandez. This company also offers a shorter, four-day version of its sailing trips encompassing the Río Dulce canyon and Lake Izabal for $165 per person, double occupancy. Sailing adventures are also available on *That* (tel. 5529-0829), a 62-foot trimaran. Its office and meeting point in Río Dulce is at the Sundog Café.

RÍO TATÍN

This small tributary diverts north from the Río Dulce just upstream from the canyon. Along its course, you'll find some excellent accommodations built into the surrounding jungle and in complete harmony with their environment.

Finca Tatín

◖ **Finca Tatín** (tel. 5902-0831 or 5776-5156, www.fincatatin.centroamerica.com) is a wonderfully secluded jungle camp and backpackers' haven about half a kilometer up the river where you'll find a variety of accommodations, including shared-bath dormitory beds for $5 per person, shared-bath doubles for $15, and bungalows with charming stone showers in the private bath for $25. Couples might want to splurge for the bungalow, as the shared-bath double rooms have very thin walls. All rooms have mosquito netting and fan. The lodge gets

major props for ecological consciousness. Water for the showers comes from the river, while water for the bathroom sinks is collected rainwater. All the bungalows have their own septic tanks with all waste material being buried.

Excellent meals are served in the lodge's open-air restaurant housed under a thatched roof. Dinner is a family-style affair, allowing for opportunities to meet fellow travelers. Breakfast, lunch, and dinner cost $4, $5, and $7. The menu is a varied palette of creative vegetarian, Guatemalan, and international dishes.

Activities include bird-watching in the surrounding forests, hikes lasting from 30 minutes to four hours all the way to Lívingston, and kayaking in the Chocón Machacas Biotope or down the Río Dulce to Lívingston. A two-person kayak rental costs $6 per day plus gas for the return *lancha* pickup. The lodge is run by a friendly Argentine. Italian, English, and French are spoken.

Rancho Corozal

A little farther down the Río Tatín is **❰ Rancho Corozal** (tel. 5309-1423 in Guatemala, 866/621-4032 toll-free U.S., www.quintamaconda.com), an absolutely astounding private villa that can be yours for $250 per night for the entire villa for 2 people, or $82 per person per night for 9-10 people, including breakfast. The owners are quick to point out that it's not a hotel but rather a private hideaway. It can sleep up to 10 people in five double beds with stylish safari netting. The beautiful house, designed with soaring thatched roofs and attractive ceramic and stucco accents, is set right beside the river on its own 20-acre forest reserve. There are tastefully landscaped tropical gardens, a short nature trail, open-air living and dining rooms, and a hammock patio. The house is wonderfully watched over by its live-in caretaker, Sabino, who can show you around and take you to area attractions aboard the house skiff ($125 per day). At night, the villa is lit by the warm glow of gas lamps and torches. Food can be arranged at the house or at one of a few local eateries. Try the freshwater crab cooked in coconut milk at neighboring Doña Lola's.

Ak' Tenamit

Heading back downstream toward the Río Tatín's confluence with the Río Dulce, you'll find Ak' Tenamit (tel. 7908-3392 or 7908-4358, www.aktenamit.org), a grassroots health and development organization helping to provide a better living for the local Q'eqchi' Maya who inhabit the area in several villages. Thanks to this organization's efforts, these extremely impoverished communities now have access to health care and education, among other basic necessities. There is a women's handicraft cooperative, a 24-hour clinic, primary and secondary schools (including curricula in tourism and

the Río Dulce canyon

© AL ARGUETA

social welfare), and an ecotourism center. At the visitors center you can buy locally made crafts and enjoy light meals in a pleasant *palapa*-style café, which is open 7 A.M.-4:30 P.M. Volunteer doctors, dentists, and nurses who can commit for at least one month are always welcome.

RÍO LÁMPARA

Continuing upstream, on the south bank of the Río Dulce, is another tributary known as the Río Lámpara. You'll see a small island known as Cayo Quemado at the mouth of this small river. This area is seldom explored, though a new jungle camp has put this remote area on the map.

Accommodations

The exquisite little jungle lodge, **El Hotelito Perdido** (tel. 5725-1576 or 5785-5022, www.hotelitoperdido.com, dorm beds $4, bungalows $13-20 d), lies on the quiet banks of the Río Lámpara hidden away (as its name implies) from civilization. If you're looking for

© AL ARGUETA

Rancho Corozal, a private hideaway in Izabal

an exotic, affordable escape to the outer limits of civilization, El Hotelito Perdido might just do the trick. The accommodations are built in typical thatched-roof jungle style and include a dorm and shared or private bath bungalows with typical Guatemalan fabric accents. Solar panels provide electricity, while rainwater is collected for showers. Breakfast, lunch, and dinner ($1.50-5.50) are available at the hotel's restaurant and include a variety of dishes including vegetarian fare. There's a nearby waterfall for exploring in addition to gorgeous views of the Río Dulce canyon from the grounds, kayaks for rent, hammocks for lounging and a swimming dock. Other activities include full-moon kayaking trips to nearby hot springs, jungle hikes, and bird-watching.

To get here, hitch a ride on any of the boats heading in either direction between Río Dulce town and Lívingston. They should have no problem dropping you off here. The lodge also offers a pick-up service for $5 per person from the Lívingston municipal dock.

EL GOLFETE

Back along the Río Dulce, another kilometer or so upstream, is a spot where warm sulfurous waters bubble from the base of a cliff, providing a pleasant place to swim. The local community has banded together to provide quality tourism infrastructure for visitors in the form of **Centro Turístico Agua Caliente** (tel. 5375-0496, www.turismocomunitarioguatemala.com, $1.50 admission). Among the facilities are a thatched-roof bar and snack stand, a gift shop selling locally made handicrafts, and a dock from which to swim in the river or soak in the warm waters. Heading inland, you'll find a series of caves with an interesting array of rock formations and even a large central chamber.

Shortly after the hot springs, the river widens into a lake known as El Golfete. The lake is home to a dwindling population of manatees protected on its northern shore by the **Chocón Machacas Biotope** (7 A.M.-4 P.M. daily, $5). The large, slow-moving aquatic mammals (also known as sea cows) are extremely elusive creatures and fewer than 100 are thought to inhabit these waters. The walrus-like animals are threatened throughout their range by long reproductive cycles (they reach sexual maturity late in life) and collisions with motorboats. The 186-square-kilometer (72-square-mile) park is run by CECON and there are aquatic routes through several jungle lagoons as well as a nature trail running through the park and its protected forests.

A comfortable base for exploring the area is the community tourism project at **Lagunita Salvador** (tel. 5992-1843 or 5363-0018, www.lagunitasalvador.com). There are rustic but clean and comfortable accommodations in thatched-roof structures fronting jungle wetlands. There are dormitory-style rooms with shared bathrooms ($10 p/p) or bungalows with private bathrooms ($37 for up to six people). The restaurant serves tasty seafood dishes, fried chicken, fruit plates, and cold beer and soda. There are guided tours to the reserve and surrounding areas (including several lush, little-known lagoons) in addition to kayaks for rent.

You can even witness a traditional Dance of the Deer performance.

Heading west from here, the river continues its course upstream past the expensive villas of Guatemala's oligarchy to the town of Río Dulce, at the confluence of the river and Lake Izabal. A long bridge connects both shores along Highway CA-13, which continues north to Petén.

Río Dulce Town (Fronteras)

The town of Río Dulce is the community centered around a long bridge crossing over the river near its meeting point with Lake Izabal. You'll find most of the town's accommodations on the north side of the bridge, also known as Fronteras.

RECREATION

Although the river and jungle are all around you, exploring this area may not be so easy on your own. It's always possible to hire a *lanchero* to take you around. Bargain hard. A more viable alternative is to stay at one of the more ecologically oriented lodges, which usually offer a full range of options for exploring. The two best places to stay in this regard are **Hacienda Tijax** (tel. 7930-5505, 7930-5506, or 7930-5507, VHF channel 09, www.tijax.com) and **Tortugal** (tel. 5306-6432 or 7742-8847, VHF channel 68, www.tortugal.com), which both do an excellent job of providing engaging nature hikes as well as supplying equipment (kayaks, for example) to explore on your own.

Sailing to the Belize Cayes

Aventuras Vacacionales (tel. 7832-6056, www.sailing-diving-guatemala.com, $200-440 per person) offers sailing trips up the Río Dulce and out to the Belize cayes on *Las Sirenas,* a 46-foot Polynesian catamaran. Sailing adventures are also available on *"That"* (tel. 5529-0829), a 62-foot trimaran.

ACCOMMODATIONS

Most of Río Dulce's accommodations can be found on the north side of the bridge, starting from there and spreading east and west a few kilometers along the riverbank. Directly underneath the bridge is **Bruno's Hotel and Marina** (tel. 7930-5175, www.mayaparadise.com), a popular establishment with the sailing set containing rooms in shared-bathroom dormitories for $5 per bed, double rooms with shared bath for $20; or double rooms with air-conditioning, hot-water private baths, and porches overlooking the gardens and river for $40. There's a small swimming pool next to the river, which makes a great place to hang out. A few doors down along the busy road leading out of town, the **Riverside Hotel** (tel. 7930-5668) makes an acceptable budget choice with shared-bath double rooms on the first floor going for $5 or upstairs with private bathroom for $10. All rooms are bare-bones but clean enough.

About one kilometer farther east along the river is ◖ **Hacienda Tijax** (tel. 7930-5505, 7930-5506, or 7930-5507, VHF channel 09, www.tijax.com), one of Guatemala's most enjoyable places to stay. The quaint little A-frame cabins on the riverfront are what this place is all about. Double-occupancy cabins with shared baths go for $29, or $60 with private bathroom. There are six double private-bath cabins with air-conditioning available for $73. Spacious

© AL ARGUETA

one of the hanging bridges at Hacienda Tijax

bungalows cost $84. All rooms have comfortable beds with mosquito netting and fan. There is an excellent restaurant housed under a large *palapa* structure, an inviting swimming pool, and Internet access. Activities include a guided tour around the hacienda's working rubber plantation to a lookout tower with gorgeous views of the river and El Golfete, passing a hanging bridge over the forest along the way, two-hour horseback riding tours around the farm, kayaking, and sailing. Tours cost $10-25 per person. There's a boat marina here.

Farther east along the river, the next place over is the fancier, 35-room ◖ **Catamaran Island Hotel** (tel. 7930-5494, www.catamaranisland.com), set on a splendid private island. Rooms are housed in comfortable wooden cabins with ceiling fan, air-conditioning, and private bath. There are double rooms on land for $85 including breakfast or set over the water for $91 d, also including breakfast. There's a fancy restaurant serving seafood and international

dishes, a tennis court, and a poolside bar with a happy hour 4-7 P.M. There are sports on its DirecTV-equipped units. There's also a marina here.

Casa Perico (tel. 7930-5666 or 7909-0721, VHF channel 68), lies another few kilometers farther east. Situated beside the Río Bravo, a small tributary of the Río Dulce, the lodge offers rooms in a dormitory above the restaurant and bar for $7 per person or double-occupancy wooden cabins with private baths for $25. It's a bit out of the way, which is precisely what brings most guests here. The Swiss owners cook good meals (dinner is about $5-6) and will pick you up from Río Dulce for free and drop you off at the end of your stay.

Back near the bridge, on its south side, is **Hotel Backpackers** (tel. 7930-5480, www.hotelbackpackers.com). Another budget travelers' hideout, it has rooms in shared-bath dorms for $3 per person, double rooms with shared bath for $8, or doubles with private bath for $16-20. It's run by Casa Guatemala, a nonprofit that manages a center on El Golfete for abandoned and malnourished children. There's a restaurant and bar here serving inexpensive international dishes, beers, sodas, and cocktails. Services include laundry, phone, fax, and email. You can inquire here about volunteer opportunities with Casa Guatemala. If arriving on the bus from Guatemala City, get off before crossing the bridge so as to avoid a long walk back from its other end.

On the right side of the bridge, southwest about one kilometer from the bridge toward the Castillo de San Felipe is ◖ **Tortugal** (tel. 5306-6432 or 7742-8847, VHF channel 68, www.tortugal.com, $10 p/p to $50 d), where a splendid setting, beautiful accommodations, and attention to details make this one of the best places to stay in Río Dulce. You'll fall in love with this place as soon as you step off the boat and onto its private dock. Jefe, the friendly resident watchdog and an adorable dalmatian/

boxer/bull terrier mix, will greet you. Enjoy staying in rustically comfortable, tastefully decorated, thatched-roof cabins (with adjoining sun deck or on raised platforms). Some cabins come with tables and chairs, a couch, and hammocks. There are also two dormitories with beds for $10 per person, one of which is directly over the water on a raised platform over a dock. All beds have reading lamps. The filtered tap water here is drinkable. There's an excellent restaurant serving vegetarian fare and Guatemalan takes on international dishes in a lovely soaring thatched-roof structure built on a platform over the water. Above the restaurant is a clubhouse where there's a big-screen TV with satellite connection, pool table, and computers with Internet access. Activities include catching some rays on the docks, kayaking (free for guests), sailing, and Rover tours to the jungle hot springs of nearby Finca El Paraíso.

FOOD

Bruno's Hotel and Marina (tel. 7930-5175, www.mayaparadise.com, 7 A.M.-10 P.M. daily) is especially popular with boaters for its varied menu of International dishes and snacks in the $5-10 range as well as its TV news and sports in an open-air dining room right beside the water. There are pancakes, omelets, and hash browns for breakfast; burgers and ribs for lunch and dinner. Just up the street, **C Restaurante Río Bravo** (tel. 7930-5167, 7 A.M.-10 P.M. daily) serves a similar menu, including good seafood, pasta dishes, and pizzas ($11) on an open-air deck over the water. There's a full bar and it's a popular place for meeting fellow travelers. Along the same side street, **Sundog Café** (tel. 5529-0829, $3-6) has delicious hot sandwiches, including an avocado melt, baguettes, and pastrami sandwiches. There's a 5:20 happy hour. The café is the local booking agent for sailing trips aboard *That*, a 62-foot trimaran.

Just west of the bridge at Marina Xalaja and serving authentic Mexican food is **Las Mexicanas** (tel. 5726-5043, noon-8 P.M. daily, $5-8), which has quickly become a town favorite thanks to the culinary prowess of the Mexican sisters who run it.

Whether or not you're staying at **Hacienda Tijax** (tel. 7930-5505, 7930-5506, or 7930-5507, VHF channel 09, www.tijax.com), it makes a great place to eat for its rugged jungle ambience and delicious sandwiches, seafood, salads, pasta, and steak dishes in the $5-13 range served in an airy high-ceilinged *palapa* structure. It brews excellent coffee and has a full bar. Farther out this way, about two kilometers downstream from Río Dulce, is **Mario's Marina** (tel. 7930-5569/70, www.mariosmarina.com), which has a restaurant and bar that is popular with the sailing crowd and serves a variety of seafood and international dishes. Bar patrons can browse the book exchange or enjoy a game of darts.

West from the Río Dulce bridge toward the Castillo de San Felipe, the restaurant at **C Tortugal** (tel. 5306-6432 or 7742-8847, VHF channel 68, www.tortugal.com, 7 A.M.-10 P.M.) is worth a stop for its deliciously prepared, creative menu options and superb location right on the water away from the noise and traffic closer to town. Prepared using fresh ingredients, the menu harmoniously blends authentic Guatemalan cuisine with American and European flourishes. Dinner options range $5-12 for items varying from a quarter-pound barbecue burger to seafood stew. It's also a great place for breakfast ($2.50-6) or lunch ($4-6). The bar here serves some excellent cocktails that you can enjoy along with the gorgeous jungle river scenery. There's always something on special for $2.50, served in a large cocktail glass.

For Tex Mex and Southern-style home cooking, check out **Texan Bay Restaurant** (tel. 5890-4330, texanbaymarina.com/restaurant.html), located at its eponymous marina. There's a well-stocked bar and indoor or outdoor seating overlooking the water.

INFORMATION AND SERVICES

An excellent source of information on all things Río Dulce is the *Río Dulce Chisme-Vindicator* (http://riodulcechisme.com).

Communications

Restaurante Río Bravo and Bruno's, on the north end of the bridge, both have Internet access. Next door to Bruno's, Captain Nemo's Communications (tel. 7930-5174) offers phone, fax, and Internet services. Several local hotels, including Hacienda Tijax, Backpackers, and Tortugal, are all wired.

Money

All of the banks are on the main road on the north side of the bridge. Banco Industrial has a visa ATM and Banrural has Visa and MasterCard ATMs.

Travel Agencies

You can book shuttle buses, sailing trips, and boat transfers from three very similar travel agencies on a small alleyway just north of Bruno's along the main road. These are Otitours (tel. 7930-7674), Atitrans (tel. 7832-0644 or 5218-5950), and Tijax Express/Gray Line Tours (tel. 7930-5196/97, www.grayline-guatemala.com).

GETTING THERE

Bus

The north end of the bridge, also known as Fronteras, is a hub for transport heading out in several directions from here. Buses heading north to Petén all stop here before continuing to Poptún and Flores ($7, four hours). The same is true for the return trip south from Flores to Guatemala City ($6, six hours). Bus lines covering this route include Línea Dorada and Fuente del Norte. Both companies also have some more expensive luxury coaches plying this route. **Litegua** buses can take you to and from Puerto Barrios directly or by changing buses at La Ruidosa Junction near Morales. From there you can catch a westbound bus to Guatemala City or east to Puerto Barrios. All of these companies have offices in Río Dulce. There are shuttle buses to Guatemala City ($30), Antigua ($37), and Copán Ruinas ($37) that can be booked through the local travel agencies. Buses to El Estor (1.75 hours) leave from here about every 90 minutes.

Boat

Boats to Lívingston leave from underneath the north side of the bridge via **ASOCOLMORAN** (tel. 5561-9657), the local water taxi association, at 9 A.M. and 1:30 P.M., taking about 90 minutes and costing $13 one-way.

MARINAS

Several of the aforementioned hotels and restaurants also operate full-service marinas. Among these are Tijax, Tortugal, Bruno's, Catamaran Island Hotel, and Mario's Marina. Other options include **Monkey Bay Marina** (www.monkeybaymarina.com), **Mar Marine** (www.marmarine.com.gt), and **Texan Bay Marina** (www.texanbaymarina.com). The latter is situated near El Golfete and is the closest full-service marina to the Caribbean. A full listing of other available options can be found online at http://riodulcechisme.com.

SAFETY

Sailing vessels should take care to anchor in protected private marinas and not out in the middle of the open water where they may fall prey to local pirates. In June 2008, an American citizen was murdered while attempting to resist an armed robbery aboard his yacht anchored in the waters near Río Dulce town. In the aftermath, several of the town's marinas and local tourism authorities contracted the services of an overnight boat patrol to make the rounds at several of the better-known marinas. These include Hacienda Tijax, Bruno's, and Tortugal, among others.

Lake Izabal

Guatemala's largest lake is a mostly undiscovered region. Of particular note are the Bocas del Polochic Wildlife Preserve, centered around the Río Polochic's delta, and the 17th-century fortress of Castillo de San Felipe de Lara.

CASTILLO DE SAN FELIPE DE LARA

More commonly known as "El Castillo de San Felipe" (8 A.M.-5 P.M., $1.50), the fortress also gives its name to a small community on the northern shores of Lake Izabal. The castle was originally built by the Spanish in 1652 in an attempt to deter the activities of pirates, who would come up the Río Dulce to raid supplies. It would later serve as a prison but was finally abandoned and left to deteriorate. The present fortress was reconstructed in 1956. It's worth a look around for its thick walls enclosing a maze of small rooms as well as its old cannons. There are some nice lake views, a picnic area, and green grounds.

Accommodations and Food

One of the fancier options along the shores of the lake near the Castillo de San Felipe is **Mansión del Río** (tel. 7930-5020, www.mansiondelrio.com.gt, $109-133 d), a large, 95-room resort-style property popular with vacationing Guatemalans. Large and attractive rooms have air-conditioning, ceiling fan, cable TV, minifridges, gorgeous bay views, and nice decorative touches, including marble counters in the private bathrooms. Also included are a large swimming pool, a restaurant, two bars, a fairly well-equipped gym,

© AL ARGUETA

Castillo de San Felipe de Lara

and well-cared-for gardens. Paddle boats and a playground will keep the kids busy. The Cocodrilo Creek restaurant serves international dishes and has both an indoor, air-conditioned section, or a breezy outdoor dining room under a thatched roof with beautiful bay views. The Bonito River Bar has a nice lounge for relaxing as well as foosball and Ping-Pong tables. A similar property, **Banana Palms Resort and Marina** (tel. 7930-5023 or 2331-2815, www.bananapalms.com.gt), can be found just down the road to the west. Here you'll find modern rooms housed in attractive units with two rooms on the ground floor and one deluxe suite on the top floor. Rates range from $92 for a standard double room to $129 for a deluxe suite. Junior suites ($116 d) have ceiling fan, large bathroom, living room, small kitchen, and a deck with lake views. The deluxe suite has all of the above plus a whirlpool bath with lake views. All rooms have DirecTV and air-conditioning. The pleasant thatched-roof lobby leads out to a thatched-roof bar next to a swimming pool with foosball and pool tables and DirecTV. There are a nice dock and marina, game areas, a fitness center, and a large, airy restaurant housed under a high-roofed *palapa* structure. The restaurant/bar serves seafood, Guatemalan, and international dishes.

From the castle, a road heads northwest to its juncture with the road back to Río Dulce. Along this road you'll find **Hotel Chang-Gri-La** (tel. 7930-5467, hotelchangrila@yahoo.com, $39 d), with modern rooms and bungalows (sleep six, $152), including hot-water private baths, air-conditioning, and cable TV. There is a swimming pool, and a restaurant serves simple international fare. A few paces away to the west, **La Cabaña del Viajero** (tel. 7930-5412) has charming tin-roofed cabins centered around a swimming pool. There are simple rooms with shared bath ($12) and much nicer double rooms with private baths, air-conditioning, and TV

for $22; all have mosquito netting and fans. There's a restaurant here.

Getting There

Castillo de San Felipe is three kilometers along the lakeshore from Río Dulce or four kilometers by road, which you can walk in about 45 minutes. Heading north out of town on the main road, turn left after the Banco Industrial. After a few kilometers, you'll pass the turnoff for El Estor on the right. Continue straight on the main road for another kilometer or so from here to the castle. Minivans ($0.50) leave every 30 minutes from the north end of the bridge, or you can hire a water taxi ($5).

EL ESTOR

El Estor is a pleasant, friendly lakeside town on the western shores that is becoming a gateway to some natural attractions in its vicinity. The town supposedly gets its name from a corruption of the English word "store," as it was referred to in the days of old when British pirates sailing up the Río Dulce and across the lake would come here to buy supplies.

The town is also home to a nickel mine, which functioned here in the 1970s but was later closed. Under the current government's push to exploit Guatemala's mineral wealth, the mine has been revived and debate ensued on whether or not to allow minerals and heavy equipment to be transported up the Río Dulce between Lake Izabal and the port of Santo Tomás de Castilla. It's all rather reminiscent of a similar push some years back to log the Río Dulce and float the wood downstream on large boats. The loggers failed in their attempt to gain approval for their plans, and at last check the Ministry of Agriculture and Natural Resources (MARN) had not decided what approach to take in this latest case based on the National Protected Areas Council's (CONAP) assessment of the activities as not in compliance with the park's management plan. It remains to be seen what effect the renewal of strip mining will have on the environment in the region surrounding El Estor.

In any case, locals have spent some time working to make El Estor a viable ecotourism destination. A website (www.senderonatural.com/elestor) showcases the nearby natural attractions, which include an impressive canyon, the **Bocas del Polochic Wildlife Refuge,** and the eastern end of the **Sierra de las Minas Biosphere Reserve.** There is also a tourism information office (tel. 5415-1516 or 5818-0843) right on the main plaza.

Accommodations

El Estor has a variety of comfortable accommodations, all in the budget category. **Hotel Vista al Lago** (6a Avenida 1-13, tel. 7949-7205, vistalago@intelnett.com, $20 d) is an attractive, clean lodging overlooking the lake. Housed in an old wooden building dating to 1815 and originally owned by an English-Dutch business partnership, it is supposedly the original "store" that gives El Estor its name. All rooms have fan and private bath, but the best ones are those on the second floor fronting the lake. **Cabañas Chaabil** (west end of 3a Calle, tel. 7949-7272 or 5544-1066, $20 d) has four attractive wooden guest rooms with private bathrooms, mosquito netting, and fans.

Under the same ownership as Hugo's Restaurant, (**Hotel Ecológico Cabañas del Lago** (tel. 7949-7245, $30 d) is peacefully set aside on its own lakeside oasis one kilometer east of town in Barrio La Corroza. Its seven guest rooms housed in large, attractive bungalows have ceiling fans and private baths. There's a private beach and a dock for swimming and sunbathing. A small restaurant serves local food and cocktails, which you can enjoy in its pleasant lakeside setting. The owners can bring you here from Restaurante Hugo's in the center of town.

Right on the town's central park, **Posada de Don Juan** (5a Avenida 3-08, tel. 7949-7296)

has simple, clean rooms housed in a cheerfully painted concrete building built around a parking lot courtyard. Rooms with private bath cost $9 d and rooms with shared bath cost $7 d. All rooms have fan. From the central park 1.5 blocks toward the lake is the motel-style **Hotel La Playa** (2a Calle 4-23, tel. 7949-7407), housed in a neocolonial concrete building (or a pink and green wooden annex) with simple, clean rooms with shared bath ($5) or private bath ($8) and fan.

Four blocks from the park on the road heading out to Lanquín and right on the lakeshore, **Posada Valle Verde** (tel. 5901-8907, www.posadalasmarias.com) has rooms housed in large, wooden A-frame cabins, including dorm beds ($4), shared-bath doubles ($10), and doubles with private bathrooms ($20). The restaurant/bar serves Guatemalan and international dishes. Trips to the Bocas del Polochic Wildlife Refuge can be arranged through the hotel, which is under the same ownership as the Posada Las Marías in Lanquín.

Food

Chaabil (west end of 3a Calle, tel. 7949-7272 or 5544-1066, all meals daily, lunch and dinner $4-9) means "good" in Q'eqchi' and the food here lives up to its name with family recipes specializing in seafood served in a pleasant thatched-roof dining room with quaint handmade wooden furniture and right on the lake. On the plaza, **Café Portal** (5a Avenida 2-65, tel. 7818-0843, 6:30 A.M.-10 P.M. daily) and **Restaurante Hugo's** (tel. 7949-7245, all meals daily) serve a wide range of Guatemalan and international dishes, including vegetarian dishes and fast-food munchies such as burgers and sandwiches.

Information and Services

Banrural (3a Calle and 6a Avenida) can exchange currency and cash travelers checks. In addition to the tourism information office on the central plaza, some folks at Hugo's Restaurant (Hugo Fajardo) and Hotel Vista al Lago (Oscar Paz) can answer your questions on local attractions and getting around.

Getting There

There are buses from Río Dulce to El Estor leaving every 90 minutes or so from the north end of the bridge. The buses leave hourly from El Estor for the return trip 6 A.M.-4 P.M. The dirt road continues west from here to Panzós, Tucurú, and Tactic, just south of Cobán, though it is not recommended because it's notorious for highway holdups. Check on the situation if you choose this route by inquiring at Hugo's Restaurant. If driving your own vehicle, you'll need four-wheel-drive for this road.

A better option for getting to Las Verapaces is to take a truck leaving the town's central plaza at 9 A.M. daily for the village of Cahabón ($2, five hours). From there, you can take a pickup or bus to Lanquín, all the while being careful not to get stranded in Cahabón because it's not the safest place after dark. Coming back east to El Estor though here, the bus leaves at 4 A.M., so unless there's a later bus running at the time of your visit it would be ill-advised to take this route, as you'd have to spend the night in Cahabón. You'll also need four-wheel-drive on this road if you've got your own set of wheels.

A direct bus leaves for Guatemala City daily at 1 A.M., taking six hours and costing $7. The same bus leaves Guatemala City's bus terminal at 10 A.M.

There are no public boat routes between El Estor and any other of the lakeside settlements, but local *lancheros* would be happy to take you anywhere you like. Bargain hard.

NEAR EL ESTOR
Finca El Paraíso

On Lake Izabal's northern shore, between El Estor and Río Dulce, is the wonderful waterfall hot springs of Finca El Paraíso (tel. 7949-7122), a working farm easily accessible from either town. Here a wide, 12-meter-high warmwater fall plunges into a clear pool cooled by flows from surrounding streams. If you think soaking in warm water in a tropical climate wouldn't be inviting, think again. Above the falls are some caves worth exploring, for which you'll need to bring a flashlight. Two kilometers west from the falls is a comfortable lodge and restaurant. The wooden bungalows have private bathrooms and you can catch the cool lake breezes from a hammock on your very own patio. The restaurant is housed in a bamboo-and-thatch open-air structure with a menu that includes pasta and meat dishes.

The farm lies along the Río Dulce-El Estor bus route, about an hour from Río Dulce and 40 minutes from El Estor. Buses and pickups go by about every hour in both directions, with the last of these around 4:30 P.M. Hacienda Tijax and Tortugal, in Río Dulce, can also bring you here on a tour.

El Boquerón

Roughly six kilometers east of El Estor, the dramatic limestone canyon of El Boquerón lies 500 meters off the road to Río Dulce. For about $3, locals can take you up the Río Sauce in a wooden canoe to explore the canyon and admire its 250-meter-high rock faces. There's a small beach in the canyon not too far from where the trip begins. They can leave you here and pick you up at an agreed upon time. The canyon extends for another five kilometers or so from here, should you want to do some more exploring.

◖ Bocas del Polochic Wildlife Refuge

This park encompasses the Río Polochic delta and includes wetlands, flooded forests, and savannas harboring a wide range of resident and migratory bird species as well as Lake Izabal's remaining manatee and crocodile populations. There are abundant populations of freshwater turtles and green iguanas. Larger mammals include tapir, howler monkeys, and three species of cats, including jaguars. The park is managed by **Defensores de la Naturaleza** (office in El Estor at 5a Avenida and 2a Calle, tel. 7949-7237 or 7949-7130, www.defensores.org.gt), which also manages the Sierra de las Minas Biosphere Reserve beginning just south of Bocas del Polochic and running west all the way to Baja Verapaz. Together, both parks account for about 80 percent of Guatemala's biodiversity. Their management by a private conservation group translates into more-than-adequate facilities for tourism and scientific investigation. They afford great opportunities to explore some of Guatemala's most remote expanses with relative ease from a comfortable base.

If you want to explore either of these remote wilderness parks from here, call or stop by Defensores's office in El Estor, one block from the park. Defensores runs the highly recommended **Selempím Biological Station,** near its namesake community and river midway between both parks, where there are comfortable accommodations in screened-in private wooden cabins or dorms ($15 per person), shared bathrooms with showers, a hammock lounge, research facilities, and solar power. Meals can be arranged through the local community ($3-5) or you can bring your own food and use the station's cooking facilities ($2). Guides ($7 per group) can take you around by canoe or kayak through various canals for wildlife-viewing or land-based explorations along two nature trails. One of these offers a fantastic lookout point from where you can see the river's delta and fully appreciate the scale of the surrounding wilderness. Hidden in the pockmarked karst landscape of this rugged terrain are a number of sinkholes in addition to a cave near the biological station, where you can view some interesting stalactites and stalagmites.

To get here, your best option is to take one of the community-run boat transfer services ($8, 1.25 hours) leaving from El Estor at 11 A.M. on Mondays, Wednesdays, and Saturdays. The return trip leaves Selempím at 7 A.M. on the same days. Or you could hire a private boat transfer by inquiring in El Estor at Defensores's office. The typical rate is about $100 round-trip. The folks at Hugo's Restaurant or Hotel Vista del Lago might be able to hook you up with a local boatman for a little less. Admission to the park is $5.

MARISCOS

Things have gotten substantially quieter at the lake's main south-shore town, which once provided access to El Estor by way of a ferry boat but which has taken a backseat now that there's a road to El Estor from Río Dulce. The main attraction here is the fantastic 🄲 **Denny's Beach** (tel. 5171-7477, www.dennysbeach. com), a lakeside resort four kilometers east of town, which has grown substantially from its humble beginnings as a restaurant and a few simple cabanas. A wide range of accommodations includes dorms ($7 per person), rustic cabanas ($16-20 d, with shared or private bathrooms), beach-house rooms ($20-27 d, with shared or private baths and air-conditioning), beachfront cabanas ($40-67 d, with private baths, air-conditioning, and hot-water showers) or newly added luxurious villas with their own patios and lovely lakeside views ($80-100 d). The restaurant here has a varied menu in the $3-11 range for breakfast, lunch, and dinner, including excellent seafood, pastas, sandwiches, nachos, quesadillas, and creative shrimp burritos. There's a fully stocked beachside bar where you can hang out and meet other travelers. The available activities are as varied as the lodging options and include wakeboarding, horseback riding, beach volleyball, basketball, horseshoes, and Ping Pong. There are trips to the Sierra de las Minas, Finca Paraíso, Quiriguá, Río Obscuro, Río Dulce canyon, and Lívingston, or you can explore a nature trail meandering through the surrounding forests.

The easiest way to get here is by taking a daily water taxi leaving from Bruno's in Río Dulce between 4 and 4:30 P.M. (call ahead to confirm). By bus, travel along the Caribbean-bound highway (CA-9) and get off at the Las Trincheras Junction (Km. 221), from where you take a connecting minibus for the remaining 15 kilometers northwest to Mariscos. Once there, look for the **Ferretería de Doña Judith,** on the road leading out of town toward Playa Dorada. A hotel-owned water taxi can take you from there to the hotel. If you've driven your own car, you can also leave it here. The lodge can be reached on VHF channel 63. Many businesses in Mariscos use radios and can contact the lodge for you to arrange a pickup if you get lost along the way or if the water taxi isn't there.

LAS VERAPACES

Collectively known as "Las Verapaces," the departments of Alta and Baja Verapaz are mostly mountainous, remote, and clothed largely in verdant forests. Guatemala's national bird, the resplendent quetzal, and its national flower, a rare orchid known as the *monja Blanca*, inhabit the cool cloud forests of this region. This is probably Guatemala's most overlooked area in terms of tourism potential, as it sees surprisingly few visitors. The recreational opportunities and natural attractions are boundless and include spectacular waterfalls, cool mountain forests, mysterious caves, Mayan ruins, turquoise lagoons, and white-water rivers. Perhaps because Guatemala has always had more fame as a cultural destination, its equally splendid natural attractions have been overlooked. This tendency seems to be changing.

Although it might seem the Verapaz Highlands are a continuation of the rugged Western Highlands, they are unique in a number of ways, including their settlement patterns, history, climate, geology, and population. You won't find much traditional attire being worn in these parts, particularly among the men. The women tend to wear traditional skirts with white blouses not nearly as colorful or intriguing as those worn elsewhere in the highlands. Still, Mayan culture is very much alive and well in the mountain towns and villages of the Verapaz Highlands. The stunning mountain scenery is on par with that found in the Western Highlands.

HIGHLIGHTS

MEXICO
PETÉN

GUATEMALA

C Cancuén

C Laguna Lachuá National Park

C Candelaria Caves National Park

Parque Ecológico Hun Nal Ye **C**

Rafting the Río Cahabón **C**

Semuc Champey **C** Natural Monument

ALTA VERAPAZ

Biotopo Mario **C** Dary Rivera

El Salto de Chilascó **C**

BAJA VERAPAZ

EL PROGRESO

0   15 mi

0   15 km

JALAPA

© AVALON TRAVEL

LOOK FOR **C** TO FIND RECOMMENDED SIGHTS, ACTIVITIES, DINING, AND LODGING.

C El Salto de Chilascó: This waterfall, among Central America's highest, can be reached with moderate effort from a nearby community on the fringes of the Sierra de las Minas Biosphere Reserve (page 318).

C Biotopo Mario Dary Rivera: Also known as the Quetzal Biotope, this beautiful mountain park conveniently situated along the road to Cobán is the easiest way to explore the region's cloud forests and try your luck at glimpsing Guatemala's national bird, the resplendent quetzal (page 320).

C Rafting the Río Cahabón: Adventurers won't soon forget a white-water rafting trip down the Class III-IV Río Cahabón, where you can battle rapids with names such as Rock and Roll, Sex Machine, and Corkscrew Falls between more peaceful stretches. You can also explore caves and thermal hot springs along the forested riverbanks (page 334).

C Semuc Champey Natural Monument: The turquoise limestone pools and waterfalls of Semuc Champey are among Guatemala's most exquisite natural attractions. Don't miss a somewhat difficult trail up the side of a mountain for a fantastic view of the pools from above (page 337).

C Cancuén: This Mayan site, still being excavated and restored, has yielded new insights into the last days of the Classic Mayans and lies in the remote jungles straddling the border between Alta Verapaz and Petén (page 339).

C Candelaria Caves National Park: This large cave complex is among the most impressive in all of Latin America. Don't miss the chance to explore underground rivers by cave tubing or rafting into its depths (page 340).

C Parque Ecológico Hun Nal Ye: One of Guatemala's best-kept secrets is this private 135-hectare nature reserve where you can swim in pristine rivers, visit a limestone sinkhole, ride horses, and zip across the forest canopy. It's also the site of one of the Maya world's rarest finds—a carved stone box now housed in a Guatemala City museum (page 344).

C Laguna Lachuá National Park: This exquisitely beautiful and remote lagoon lies in the northwest corner of Alta Verapaz surrounded by dense rainforest and is thought to have been the site of a prehistoric meteor impact. The surrounding forests and the azure jungle river known as Río Ikbolay are worth some exploration (page 344).

Perhaps most exciting for the visitor is the palpable sense of the Verapaces's being a well-kept secret just waiting to be told. It's easy to fall in love with all that this wonderful area has to offer. New and increasingly comfortable accommodations with greater sophistication in services make this Guatemala's ecotourism frontier.

CLIMATE

As elsewhere in Guatemala, the main determinant of climate is the altitude. As both Alta and Baja Verapaz are largely dominated by the presence of mountain chains, you can expect to find some chilly weather at high altitudes. The Sierra de las Minas reaches altitudes of 2,375 meters (7,800 feet), while Cobán displays similar temperatures to those in Guatemala City, which sits at the same altitude. It is considerably damper in these parts, as much of the year sees the *chipi chipi,* a misty drizzle that often dampens the atmosphere for entire days. The Baja Verapaz capital of Salamá is in a valley at about 1,065 meters (3,500 feet) and so is slightly warmer. Its climate is among the most agreeable in the country. Farther north, toward Chisec and the jungle flatlands extending northward, the temperature is substantially warmer and it can be extremely humid. All of these conditions are further influenced by the seasons (rainy and dry) dominating the entire country, though this area tends to see much more rainfall throughout the year with a shorter dry season (Dec.-Apr.) than elsewhere in Guatemala.

HISTORY

The history of the Verapaces is also quite different from elsewhere in Guatemala. The region was populated by the fierce Achi' Mayans, who were historically at war with the K'iche' of the Western Highlands before the Spanish conquest. The Spanish themselves were unable to conquer the Achi' and eventually gave up on this task, declaring the area a *tierra de guerra,* or

"land of war." The church eventually succeeded where the conquerors had failed. Convinced by Fray Bartolomé de las Casas, the Spanish military forces agreed to leave the region for five years to give de las Casas and his men a chance to pacify and convert the Indians. De las Casas and three friars set out for the Verapaz Highlands in 1537, quickly befriending the Achi' chiefs and learning the local dialects. New converts were made and the Mayans living in scattered hamlets were convinced to move into Spanish-style settlements. After this five-year term, the Achi' were officially recognized as subjects of the Spanish crown, partially as a result of the passing of the New Laws in 1542 granting Indians basic rights and prohibiting their enslavement. The Spanish crown renamed the region Verapaz, or "true peace."

The region began to grow and develop with the arrival of coffee cultivation in Guatemala, aided by its proximity to the Caribbean port via the Río Polochic and across Lake Izabal. A railroad would eventually be built along this corridor. In the early 1900s, a flood of German immigrants snapped up large pieces of land and began cultivating coffee and cardamom, thus further altering the regional demographics. By 1915, half of all Guatemalan coffee was grown on land owned by these German immigrants, who sold a large percentage of the harvest to their fatherland. Cobán in particular was greatly altered by this demographic shift, as it took on the appearance of a German mountain town. The vestiges of this Old World influence can still be seen here and there. German economic and cultural dominion over the region was abruptly put to an end during World War II, when the United States prevailed upon Guatemala to deport the German farm owners, many of whom were unabashed in their support for the Nazis.

Today, the Achi' still inhabit Baja Verapaz in the area around Rabinal, with a largely Q'eqchi' and Poqomchi' population inhabiting the lands

MEXICO

To Sayaxché
and Flores

PETÉN

RN
5

GUATEMALA

CANCUÉN

Playa Grande
(Cantabal)

CRUCE DEL PATO

San Antonio
Las Cuevas

LAGUNA LACHUÁ
NATIONAL PARK

CANDELARIA CAVES
NATIONAL PARK

Raxrujá

Fray Bartolomé
de las Casas

Chisec

Sebol

Lagunas de
Sepalau

ALTA VERAPAZ

Río Negro (Chixoy)

PARQUE ECOLÓGICO
HUN NAL YE

Lanquín Caves
National Park

Sachichaj
Waterfall

Lanquín

QUICHÉ

SEMUC CHAMPEY
NATURAL MONUMENT

Parque Nacional
Las Victorias

San Pedro
Carchá

RAFTING THE
RÍO CAHABÓN

Cobán

San Juan
Chamelco

To Sacapulas and
Huehuetenango

San Cristóbal
Verapaz

Chelemhá Cloud
Forest Preserve

Tactic

CHIXOY DAM

Tucurú

Peña de Ángel

Purulhá

0   5 mi

0   5 km

BIOTOPO MARIO
DARY RIVERA

CA
14

EL SALTO
DE CHILASCÓ

BAJA
VERAPAZ

Cubulco

San Miguel Chicaj

Salamá

Sierra de las Minas
Biosphere Reserve

Rabinal

San Rafael
Chilascó

To Joyabaj

San Jerónimo

EL
PROGRESO

Sierra de Chuacús

MIXCO
VIEJO

Pachalum

El Rancho

CA
9

CHIMAL-
TENANGO

To Poptún, Flores, Tikal, and Belize

LAS VERAPACES

Las Conchas

Cahabón

Río Cahabón

Sierra de Santa Cruz

IZABAL

El Estor

Lago de Izabal

Refugio de Vida Silvestre Bocas de Polochic

Río Polochic

Sierra de las Minas

CA 9

ZACAPA

Río Hondo

Río Motagua

CARRETERA AL ATLÁNTICO

Estanzuela

Zacapa

CA 10

© AVALON TRAVEL

of Alta Verapaz. The region is still very much rural, much like the rest of Guatemala. Coffee and cardamom cultivation are still at the heart of the economy, with tourism beginning to make some significant inroads.

PLANNING YOUR TIME

You could easily spend your entire Guatemalan holiday in Las Verapaces and it would be entirely worth it. But, time being the finite entity that it is, you'll probably have to narrow your stay to your particular interests. If you're entering the region from the south along Highway CA-14, you might want to take a detour west to **Salamá** if your visit coincides with its annual fiesta during September. The nearby town of **San Jerónimo** is certainly worth a stop for its pleasant atmosphere and an excellent museum dedicated to the history of sugar production, of which it was the first center in Central America. North along Highway CA-14, the newly established **Cloud Forest Biological Corridor** is shaping up as a wonderful spot to explore a variety of natural attractions along the road to Cobán. Among these are some of the highest waterfalls in Central America at **El Salto de Chilascó,** on the border of the well-preserved cloud forests of the **Sierra de las Minas Biosphere Reserve.** Cobán still serves as the most convenient base for exploring all that the region has to offer and has some wonderful restaurants and hotels in addition to a pleasing mountain atmosphere. East of Cobán are the must-see turquoise pools and waterfalls of **Semuc Champey** and the nearby caves of Lanquín.

Lovers of cave exploration will want to spend some time in the area around Chisec, north of Cobán, where there are numerous cave formations, including the sinkhole of B'omb'il Pek and the spectacular **Candelaria Caves National Park** just a little farther north. Archaeology buffs will not be left wanting for attractions here, as the Mayan site of **Cancuén,** still being excavated and restored, lies north of here just across the border of Petén.

Last but certainly not least is the almost perfectly circular **Laguna Lachuá,** a magnificent azure lagoon in the flat jungles of northwestern Alta Verapaz.

ORIENTATION

Baja (Lower) Verapaz is the name given to the southernmost of the two departments. It is fringed by semiarid plains at its southern extremes before mountains, most notably the impressive **Sierra de las Minas,** rise and give way to lush cloud forests. The department is bisected by a number of flat valleys, the most important being the lush river valley that is home to its departmental capital of Salamá. A number of other interesting towns can be found along this corridor extending west toward the department of El Quiché. To the east, the Sierra de las Minas extends into Alta (Upper) Verapaz before descending into the neighboring flatlands of Izabal department. The two regions' unique ecosystems together comprise the bulk of all biodiversity found in Guatemala.

To the north, Baja Verapaz again meets the department of Alta Verapaz. Its departmental capital, Cobán, lies north of this boundary in a lush valley flanked by green hills and coffee farms at a comfortable altitude of 1,500 meters (5,000 feet). To the north, the mountains give way to smaller limestone hills and flatlands pockmarked by a variety of caves and sinkholes. The jungle flatlands extend west into the Ixcán region of Quiché and northward into Petén.

The entry point for most travelers making their way into this region is from the south via highway CA-14, which branches off from the semiarid plains west of Guatemala City at El Rancho Junction and climbs its way northward into the mountains of Baja Verapaz. An excellent paved highway also leads south from Petén into Alta Verapaz, from where you can see the rugged limestone peaks off in the distance. It is one of Guatemala's most wonderfully scenic stretches of highway.

Salamá and Vicinity

The road from the El Rancho Junction (CA-14) winds its way through the dry hill country, eventually making its way into the lush Baja Verapaz hillsides. Along Km. 132 is a turnoff known as "La Cumbre," from where the road branches west (CA-17) and begins its descent into the lush Río Salamá Valley. Fifteen kilometers down this road is the departmental capital of Salamá. There are some absorbing villages in these parts, and the town fiestas are among Guatemala's finest.

SALAMÁ

Salamá is mostly a ladino town, which really comes alive during its annual fiesta (Sept. 17-21). Other than that, there's really not much going on here. The old crumbling pedestrian

bridge on the edge of town is worth a look, as is the ornate church of **San Mateo Apóstol,** on the east side of the plaza.

Guide Companies

For exploring the areas of Baja Verapaz, a good bet is **Eco-Verapaz** (8a Avenida 7-12 Zona 1, tel. 7940-0146). It offers mountain biking, caving, horseback riding, guided hikes, and cultural tours with prices somewhere around $40 per day for most itineraries.

Accommodations and Food

The best place to stay in town is the **Hotel Real Legendario** (8a Avenida 3-57, tel. 7940-0501, hotelreallegendario.com, $30 d), with clean rooms, all with private baths, firm beds, and cable TV. There is a small café on the premises. Another good choice is **Hotel Argentina** (Diagonal 4, 2-57 Zona 2, Barrio San José, tel. 7940-1004, $15 d), featuring fan-cooled rooms with private hot-water baths and cable TV. An acceptable backup plan is **Hotel Tezulutlán** (Ruta 4 4-99 Zona 1, Barrio El Centro, tel. 7940-0141, $8-12 d), with 13 rooms set around a courtyard full of greenery, some with private bath. Just across the street is **Hotel San Ignacio** (4a Calle "A" 7-09 Zona 1, tel. 7940-0186, $5-9 d), with 18 bright, airy rooms with or without private hot-water bathrooms. There's a pleasant *palapa* sitting area overlooking the street.

There are several places to eat near the plaza. For coffee, cakes, and snacks try **Café Deli-Donas** (15 Calle 6-61). **Cafetería Central** (corner of 15 Calle and 9a Avenida) is another good choice, particularly for lunch. A fancier option is **El Balcón de los Recuerdos** (8a Avenida 6-28, 8 A.M.-8:30 P.M. Mon.-Sat., $5-7), half a block west of the plaza on the way out of town, serving grilled meats and seafood in a fan-cooled dining room. Though its name evokes images of fast food, **Pollo to Go** (on the north side of the plaza) serves pretty decent burgers, chicken, and good breakfasts.

Information and Services

For banking, there's a Banrural on the south side of the plaza with a MasterCard ATM. The police station is one block west of the plaza. Telgua, just east of the plaza, has Internet access for $1.50 an hour. Lavandería 2000, next door to Hotel San Ignacio, does reasonably priced laundry.

Getting There

There are hourly buses leaving for Guatemala City from in front of Deli-Donas between 3 A.M. and 8 P.M. The 4 A.M. bus is a nicer, more expensive Pullman. Buses coming from Guatemala City continue west to Rabinal and Cubulco. Buses and minibuses for San Jerónimo leave from in front

of the town hall every half hour 6 A.M.-5:30 P.M. There are also departures for the La Cumbre Junction with onward connections to Cobán departing from this same location about every half hour from early morning until 4 P.M.

SAN JERÓNIMO

About 10 kilometers from Salamá, back toward the La Cumbre Junction, is the wonderfully atmospheric town of San Jerónimo. This is about as clean and pleasant as highland Guatemalan towns get. The weather, at a comfortable altitude around 1,100 meters (3,600 feet), is just warm enough. San Jerónimo has an interesting history, as it was here that sugarcane cultivation first made inroads into the local economy with the establishment of Central America's first sugar mill by Dominican friars in 1601. The new crop came from Jamaica, along with new technology and 700 slaves from the island nation.

During the 17th century, the friars built a Roman-style aqueduct with **124 archways** to bring water to the sugar mill and town as production continued to increase. Wine and moonshine were also eventually produced in addition to sugar. The growth of these industries would be checked in 1829 with the expulsion from Guatemala of various religious orders under the liberal government of the time. You can still see the old remains of the archways scattered throughout town, giving San Jerónimo a unique feel.

Among the town's most interesting attractions is its beautiful 17th-century baroque **church,** set on the plaza. Inside, there's an altar brought from France and crafted with sheets of 18-karat gold. The plaza also harbors some ancient carved stones.

There are minibuses every half hour from Salamá to San Jerónimo between 6 A.M. and 7:30 P.M.

Museo del Trapiche

The town's most interesting attraction is the Museo del Trapiche (tel. 5514-6959, 8 A.M.-4 P.M.

LAS VERAPACES

Mon.-Fri., 10 A.M.-4 P.M. Sat. and Sun., donation), set on the grounds of the old Hacienda San Geronimo, Central America's first sugar mill. It once housed 1,000 workers and boasted a production of 90 tons of processed sugar per year, a figure matched only by the great sugar mills of Mexico and Brazil. Among the relics you'll find here are a giant press and metallic waterwheel measuring seven meters in diameter and weighing a ton. There are displays on popular art and handicrafts, including old costumes, baskets, and woven items as well as archaeological relics, including pre-Columbian pottery.

With the expulsion of the Dominican friars, San Geronimo became state property and was later auctioned off. It was eventually abandoned in 1893 but has now regained some of its former splendor.

Accommodations and Food

Complementing the town's lovely provincial atmosphere are some nice hotels, should you wish to stay here. **Hotel Hacienda Real del Trapiche** (tel. 5649-3479, hotelhaciendareal.galeon.com, $20 d) is right at the entrance to town and has 10 pleasant rooms with good beds, private hot-water baths, and cable TV. There is a restaurant with excellent home-cooked meals. Another excellent option is the ☾ **Hotel Posada de los Frayles** (Barrio Arriba, tel. 7723-5733, $28 d), with 10 comfortable rooms in a beautiful colonial-style building set among nicely landscaped gardens with tropical flowers and plants. Rooms have private hot-water bathrooms, comfortable beds, and cable TV. There's a swimming pool and the restaurant serves decent meals for breakfast, lunch, and dinner.

SALAMÁ TO CUBULCO

West from Salamá are some interesting villages known for their weavings and annual fiestas. The first of these is **San Miguel Chicaj,** where the annual fiesta is held September 25-29.

To the west along a wonderfully scenic road, the next town over is **Rabinal,** founded in

1537 by Fray Bartolomé de las Casas. Rabinal is known for the quality of its pottery and its citrus products as well as for its observance of pre-Columbian traditions, dance, and folklore. The annual fiesta is held January 19-25 and it is by all means dramatic. The highlight is a dance performed on January 23 known as the **Rabinal Achi',** which reenacts a battle between the Achi' and Quiché tribes.

The small **Museo Comunitario Rabinal Achi'** (4a Avenida and 2a Calle Zona 3, 8:30 A.M.-5 P.M. Mon.-Sat.) features exhibits on the history and culture of the Achi' Mayans living in this area. The most interesting exhibit pertains to the effects of the civil war, as the region was particularly hard-hit during the violence. Several mass graves dot the hillsides around Rabinal and about 4,400 victims have been exhumed and reburied in the past few years.

There are a few basic accommodations here. Try **Posada San Pablo** (3a Avenida 1-50 Zona 1, tel. 7940-0211, $7-12 d), where some of the clean rooms have private baths. The **Hospedaje Caballeros** (1a Calle 4-02) is another good alternative. Also on 1a Calle is the **Gran Hotel Rabinal Achi,** harboring large rooms with private bath and a small eatery.

As for services, there is a Banrural on 1a Calle and 3a Avenida, which can exchange your cash dollars. There are hourly buses to Salamá and five daily frequencies to Guatemala City via La Cumbre.

West from Rabinal the road continues up a high mountain pass along some uninhabited territory before plunging into yet another valley to the isolated Achi' Mayan and ladino town of **Cubulco.** The main attraction here is (you guessed it) the annual fiesta, with the peak of the action on July 25. This is one of the few places in Guatemala where you can witness the *palo volador,* a rather dodgy ritual in which dancers spin around a pole with a rope tied around their legs, eventually making it to the ground (most of the time, alive).

Along the Cloud Forest Biological Corridor

The Cloud Forest Biological Corridor (Corredor Biológico del Bosque Nuboso) is a relatively new creation that encompasses a forested area bisecting the Quetzal Biotope and Sierra de las Minas Biosphere Reserve. Its purpose is to provide an uninterrupted biological corridor for many species of animals living in these protected cloud forests. The area along the road to Cobán (CA-14) between Km. 144 and Km. 170 is part of this corridor, and it is clearly marked at its beginning and end. The corridor covers 28,640 hectares and includes nine communities and eight private reserves. A number of these private reserves are part of local hotels and restaurants that have begun catering to visitors interested in exploring all that this exuberant highland forest ecosystem has to offer. The result is an emerging ecotourism development area, which may serve as a model for other areas in Guatemala with roads adjacent to protected areas.

The initiative is managed by an association based at Restaurante Montebello, at Km. 164 in the vicinity of Purulhá, which can provide additional resources and information. It can be contacted at tel. 7953-9234. Ask for Marlen de Moino.

ACCOMMODATIONS

The first stop along this ecotourism corridor is ◖Hacienda Río Escondido (Km. 144, tel. 5308-2440 or 5208-1407, ecorioescondido@ yahoo.com, $25 per person), where you'll find pleasant wooden cabins on a private nature reserve bisected by the cool, clear waters of the Río San Isidro. There are several kilometers of nature trails, horseback riding, and inner tubing to keep you busy should you not want to just relax and unwind. The best of the cabins are set along the creek. The restaurant here does barbecued meats and has

some delicious smoothies you can enjoy in an open-air patio.

SIERRA DE LAS MINAS BIOSPHERE RESERVE

The Sierra de las Minas is a vast, 242,642-hectare mountain park harboring an astounding diversity of plant and animal life and encompassing a motley assortment of ecosystems, including cloud forests harboring several species of endemic conifers, as well as tropical moist forests and rainforests. The park extends 130 kilometers eastward (it's 30 kilometers wide) into the neighboring department of Izabal, where it meets with the lowland forests and grasslands of the Río Polochic delta. The biosphere reserve ranges in elevation from 400 to 2,400 meters and is composed mainly of cloud forests throughout its mountainous core in Baja Verapaz. Sixty-two permanent streams have their source in the upper slopes of the biosphere reserve, making it an important watershed supplying the Motagua and Polochic Rivers. It is home to healthy populations of quetzals and jaguars, among other exotic species. Together with the adjacent Bocas del Polochic Wildlife Refuge, the parks account for 80 percent of Guatemala's biodiversity.

The biosphere reserve is privately administered by **Defensores de la Naturaleza,** a well-known local conservation group with ties to The Nature Conservancy, among others. Although you may contact this organization for trips to the reserve, your best bet is to go via one of the local **community tourism cooperatives** in the villages near the park, which have trained guides who can take you on trips of a few hours or several days. Contacting this NGO proved virtually impossible despite repeated attempts and some

WHAT IS A CLOUD FOREST?

Cloud forests are essentially high-altitude rainforests, though the biological characteristics and corresponding classification are much more complicated than a matter of mere altitude. In Guatemala, cloud forests average an annual precipitation of between 2,000 and 6,000 millimeters and are found at altitudes between 1,000 and 2,500 meters. The forests essentially serve as a large sponge, retaining water that is later distributed to surrounding areas by means of evaporation or the formation of small streams. More than 60 small streams originate in Guatemala's Sierra de las Minas, for example.

A distinct characteristic of these forests is the presence of low-lying cloud banks forming on the mountains, under which the forest is immersed for much of the time. Large amounts of water are deposited directly onto vegetation from the clouds and mist, with the leaves of trees at higher elevations often dripping water.

Cloud forests serve as the habitat for many species of plants and animals, including epiphytes, which grow on other plants. You'll see tree branches thick with bromeliads, orchids, and tree ferns. As for wildlife, the forests support an abundance of rare and endangered species, including quetzal birds, howler monkeys, jaguars, and wild boars.

The Verapaz Highlands still contain many of these forests, including the largest protected cloud forest in Central America, the Sierra de las Minas Biosphere Reserve. The cloud forests that once covered much of the Western Highlands have been largely lost to subsistence agriculture by indigenous peasants who seek to make a living by clearing the forests and cultivating crops on steep hillsides. Outside of the Verapaces, there are still some patches of cloud forest left in the Sierra de los Cuchumatanes as well as on the slopes of Guatemala's volcanoes.

help from the folks at INGUAT. A newer option is to contact Guatemala City-based **Extremo a Extremo** (tel. 2369-5735, www. extremoaextremo.com), which runs regular trips to the Chilascó waterfall.

San Rafael Chilascó

San Rafael Chilascó is a small agricultural settlement that serves as the rallying point for visits to nearby waterfalls and into the biosphere reserve. The town's well-organized, friendly, and professional Chilascó Community Tourism Organization has stepped in to cater to visitors' recreational needs where NGOs have fallen short. It runs the local Tourist Information Office (tel. 5301-8928 or 5776-1683, elsaltodechilasco@ yahoo.es, 7 A.M.-7 P.M. daily) at the entrance to town. The visitors center charges the $2 admission fee for entry to the falls, rents horses, can set you up with a guide, and provide you with comfortable accommodations

with a local family or in its own basic lodge ($5 per person). Meals are available at local *comedores.*

San Rafael Chilascó is reached via a 12-kilometer dirt road branching east from the main highway heading northward toward Cobán (CA-14). The turnoff is at Km. 146. There are daily buses to Salamá leaving at 5:45 A.M., 8:30 A.M., 12:30 P.M., and 3 P.M., all of which pass by the Highway CA-14 turnoff ($0.50). You can flag down a northbound bus to Cobán or southbound to Guatemala City from the turnoff.

◖ El Salto de Chilascó

Among the places local guides can take you is the spectacular El Salto de Chilascó, which they claim is the highest waterfall in Central America, at 130 meters. Other sources, however, place the falls at 70 meters and claim the highest waterfall in Guatemala is Tzuul Tak'a, recently discovered in a remote corner of the Sierra de las Minas, with a height of 115

El Salto de Chilascó

Lomo del Macho

If you wish to go farther into the reserve, guides can take you on single- or multiday hikes to such places as Lomo del Macho, eight kilometers down a trail crisscrossing the mountains on the fringes of the biosphere reserve. There are two smaller waterfalls along the way, one of which forms a pleasant swimming hole. The trail continues to the trail's namesake mountain ridge, where you have a breathtaking view of the forested slopes of the rugged mountain chain at the heart of this biosphere reserve. Horses are available for rent at about $4 for both of these hikes, but they can take you only part of the way, as the trail eventually gets quite steep and narrow.

Albores

A five-hour hike from San Rafael Chilascó deep into the heart of the reserve brings you to the farming community of Albores, on the southeastern side of the mountain range. Defensores has built comfortable **cabins** ($30 per person) to house visitors at its **biological research station** nearby. You can also stay in the community with a local family for $5 per person. There are about 70 families living in Albores, most of which have traditionally made a living from cultivating coffee, cardamom, and vegetables. Ecotourism is a relatively new source of income for these families and they welcome visitors with open arms. They can provide you with meals for about $5.

A park admission fee of $5 applies for exploring this part of the reserve. From Albores, there are two trails into the surrounding cloud forest. The first trail takes you to the magnificent **Peña del Angel,** an igneous rock formation at an altitude of 2,400 meters, from where you have an incredible view of the surrounding cloud forest and the Polochic and Motagua River Valleys. The rock gets its name from its appearance, like that of two extended angelic wings, thanks to the 1976 earthquake, which

meters. To the best of my knowledge, the highest waterfall in Central America is still Belize's Hidden Valley Falls, at more than 450 meters.

In any case, the Chilascó falls are certainly one of the region's highest and are well worth a visit. They can be reached via a well-maintained trail in about 1.25 hours. From the tourist information center in town (where you pay a $2 admission fee), it's two kilometers to a parking lot and the trailhead. It's another three kilometers from there to the falls. You'll first come to a smaller waterfall known as El Saltito before reaching the point where you descend to the larger waterfall via a separate trail. You'll be treated to wonderful vistas along the way and to an opportunity to see the gradual progression from agricultural fields dotted with potato, broccoli, and cabbage patches to dense cloud forest with wonderful bromeliads, orchids, and ferns. There are two lookout points from where there are fantastic views of the spectacular waterfall. A guide is recommended and costs about $4.

broke the rock in two. The second trail takes you to a lookout point built by Defensores to monitor forest fires, from which there are also fabulous views.

For visits to this part of the reserve, you should technically contact **Defensores de la Naturaleza** (tel. 7936-0566 or 7959-5341, sminas@defensores.org.gt or info@defensores.org.gt, www.defensores.org), though you may never hear back. A better option is to contact **Ecotourism and Adventure Specialists** (tel. 2337-0009 Guatemala, 415/762-3996 U.S., info@ecotourism-adventure.com, www.ecotourism-adventure.com). Another option is Guatemala City-based **Extremo a Extremo** (tel. 2369-5735, www.extremoaextremo.com). If you don't mind making arrangements until you are in Guatemala, try planning a visit with the **Chilascó Community Tourism Organization** (tel. 5301-8928 or 5776-1683, elsaltodechilasco@yahoo.es).

◖ BIOTOPO MARIO DARY RIVERA

Also known as the Quetzal Biotope ($3.50, 7 A.M.-4 P.M. daily), this 1,044-hectare protected area is one of several biotopes administered by University of San Carlos's Center for Conservation Studies (CECON) and is conveniently situated along Highway CA-14 at Km. 160.5, about an hour from Cobán. Though quetzal birds are easier to spot in Sierra de Las Minas, the elusive creatures are said to frequent the yard of some local eating establishments (Biotopín Restaurant and Ranchitos del Quetzal), where they like to feast on the fruits of the *aguacatillo* tree. The Quetzal Biotope's convenient roadside location means that if you're on your way to or from Cobán, you should at least stop in for a look. You might just get lucky and see one of Guatemala's most beloved national symbols, with its exotic green plumage, long tail feathers, and bright red breast. Your best chances are between February

and September. Plan on being up early if you want to see them.

Exploring the Park

Only a small part of the reserve is open to visitors, though there is plenty to keep you busy. There are two trails beginning at the visitors center, winding their way through the exuberant vegetation. The shorter Los Helechos (The Ferns) trail is two kilometers long, while Los Musgos (The Mosses) trail is twice as long. While you may or may not see a quetzal bird, you'll certainly see a dense growth of epiphytes, mosses, ferns, and orchids along the well-maintained trails. Both trails pass by some nice waterfalls where you can swim.

Trail maps are available for $1 at the visitors center, where there is also an exhibit. A small shop sells snacks and drinks and there are camping and barbecue areas. Check with the guards before camping, as it may or may not be allowed at the time of your visit.

Accommodations and Food

A number of comfortable lodgings are alongside the road in the vicinity of the biotope. The first place you'll find, coming from Cobán, is **Ranchitos del Quetzal** (tel. 2434-5919), where eight basic rooms in thatched-roof huts or concrete structures with electric hot-water heater cost $10 per person. The restaurant here serves basic, inexpensive meals ($3-6) and there is a trail to a waterfall and swimming hole 40 minutes away. Quetzals are sometimes seen here. Across the street from the biotope is **Restaurante Biotopín** (tel. 5202-0528 or 2473-9017, 7 A.M.-5 P.M. Fri.-Sun.), serving snacks, barbecued meats, burgers, hot dogs, and other picnic fare in an open-air dining room facing the woods. Farther along the highway at Km. 158.5 is ◖ **Hotel y Restaurante Ram Tzul** (tel. 5908-4066, ramtzul@intelnet.net.gt, www.m-y-c.com.ar/ramtzul, $40 d), with comfortable accommodations in wooden

MARIO DARY RIVERA

Considered by many to be the patriarch of Guatemala's environmental movement, Mario Dary Rivera was a biologist who served as rector of the University of San Carlos in 1981, the same year in which he was assassinated. Dary succeeded in getting the municipality of Salamá to donate part of the land for the creation of the Quetzal Biotope, which was subsequently named after him; he served as the new park's director from 1977 to 1981. Dary also founded the University's Center for Conservation Studies (CECON) in 1981, along with its system of protected areas known as biotopes, set aside for the protection and scientific study of endangered plants and animals.

Today there are at least half a dozen of these biotopes throughout Guatemala. Among the animals being protected and studied are the quetzal bird, sea turtles, jaguars, bats, deer, and Petén turkey.

Although the urban militant wing of the leftist Guatemalan Workers Party (PGT) has been attributed with Dary's assassination, some believe his conservation activities stirred the waters with local logging interests, who may have also played a part in his assassination. Unlike most political killings at the height of the violent civil war, Dary's stands out because he was generally perceived to be right of center in his political inclinations.

cabins, all with private bath. A large restaurant tastefully constructed using 3,500 bamboo shoots serves good food three meals a day. The lodge is on a private 150-hectare forest preserve. A 45-minute hike leads to a pretty waterfall. Another lodge on a private forest reserve is **Posada Montaña del Quetzal** (Km. 156.5 on the road to Cobán, tel. 6620-0709 or 2332-4969, reservaciones@hposadaquetzal.com, www.hposadaquetzal.com, $36-46 d), where you have a choice of staying in standard rooms or family-size bungalows. There are firm beds and an on-demand hot-water heater. The rooms can be moldy, which is common in these cold, humid parts. There are two swimming pools, table tennis, and a trail leading to a waterfall 30 minutes away.

Getting There

Any bus heading along the Cobán-Guatemala Highway can let you off at the biotope, though be sure to let the driver know you're getting off here. The entrance is at Km. 160.5.

PURULHÁ AND VICINITY

As you continue along the road toward Cobán, the next sizable town is Purulhá. Though the town itself is unremarkable, there are several important stops on the biological corridor along the road in the vicinity of town and farther east from the town itself.

Reserva Natural Privada Montebello

This private nature reserve and restaurant (tel. 7953-9234 or 7953-9215) sits along Km. 164 of Highway CA-14. The specialties are a tasty chicken stew and traditional pastries. A small shop sells locally made handicrafts and there are nature trails for hiking amid several pleasant streams crisscrossing the property.

Accommodations

At Km. 166.5, **Reserva Natural Privada Country Delight** (tel. 5514-0955, countrydelight@hotmail.com, 7 A.M.-7 P.M. daily) is a quaint family-run inn and café. The delicious homemade food includes sandwiches, breads, cookies, and cakes. There are also smoked meats for sale. Double rooms in the main house with tiled floor, cable TV, large, firm beds, tasteful decor, and private hot-water bath go for $45. Bungalows range from $30 for a unit accommodating two people to $100 for

comfortable cabins at Reserva Natural
Privada Country Delight

a large, six-bed cabin. Camping in a covered
area with cooking facilities, shower, bathroom,
and a common area with table tennis, foosball,
and a swimming pool is a great value at $7 per
person. Bonfires and nighttime lightning bug
shows between April and June are among the
fun activities available.

The restaurant and lodge are on Country
Delight's own private reserve, but there are
also other reserves adjacent to the property:
Reserva Natural Privada Llano Largo and
Reserva Privada Santa Rosa. Combined,
they are roughly the same size as the Quetzal
Biotope. The lodge can arrange visits to both.

East from Purulhá

A number of beautiful natural attractions in the
vicinity of Purulhá have begun making their
way onto travelers' radar screens with the establishment of the biological corridor. A turnoff at Km. 166 heads east to Purulhá and then

continues for 32 kilometers to **Peña del Ángel,**
a dramatic limestone canyon surrounded by
tropical moist forest and bisected by the **Río
Panimá.** To get to Peña del Ángel, contact the
local *comité de turismo* (tel. 5317-6344), which
operates a restaurant and some simple cabanas
at the site. You can also get there by foot via an
11-kilometer trail starting just off the road at
Km. 164. (Note that this is not the same Peña
del Ángel mentioned under *Sierra de las Minas
Biosphere Reserve.*)

Another option is to arrange a visit via the
Reserva Natural Privada San Rafael (tel.
5475-1236, ask for Beatriz Thomae), one hour
away from Purulhá along a 27-kilometer stretch
of road descending into lower elevations. It offers trips to local coffee and cardamom plantations in addition to inner tubing on the Río
Panimá and hikes to Peña del Ángel along
hanging bridges used by villagers to cross the
river. Lodging and food are also available here.

Chicoy Cave

As you head toward Tactic at Km. 167.5 of
Highway CA-14 you'll reach the Chicoy Cave
($2.50), with a depth of 70 meters and some
large stalagmites. Locals still come to this
place to perform Mayan rituals dedicated to
the earth, seeking blessings upon their harvest.

CHELEMHÁ CLOUD FOREST PRESERVE

A turnoff at Highway CA-14's Km. 180 heads
east for 22 kilometers to the town of Tucurú,
from where it's another 26 kilometers via a
rugged dirt road passable only in a four-wheel-
drive vehicle to the fantastic Chelemhá Cloud
Forest Preserve. This privately managed protected area comprises 500 hectares of primary
cloud forest and is part of the **Sierra Yalijux
mountain range,** said to harbor Guatemala's
highest density of quetzal populations. The
reserve forms part of an important migratory
corridor to and from the Sierra de las Minas.

© AL ARGUETA

LAS VERAPACES

a cloud forest in Sierra Yalljux

On the outskirts of the reserve, the ◖**Maya Cloud Forest Lodge** (tel. 7941-7674, www.chelemha.org, $50 per person) is a comfortable, well-equipped wooden cabin built right into the side of the mountain in an environmentally friendly manner. Each of its four rooms comes with private hot-water bath and two beds. There are a lounge, dining area, and an observation deck with outrageous views of the forest-clad mountains in the vicinity. Its Swiss-born manager serves delicious European and international dishes for breakfast ($7), lunch ($10), and dinner ($12). Activities include hikes through the reserve along trails with local Kekchí guides, visits to a local village, wildlife-viewing and, of course, bird-watching. This is one of the best places in the country to spot a quetzal.

Volunteer opportunities in the reserve are available through Unión Para Proteger el Bosque Nuboso (UPROBON, tel. 7941-7674, uprobon@chelemha.org), which manages the park. It also offers opportunities for scientific study and research.

TACTIC

Back on Highway CA-14 northbound, the next town over is Tactic, 32 kilometers south of Cobán. The turnoff into town is at Km. 183. The town's best-known attraction is the so-called **Pozo Vivo** (Living Well), named as such because its muddy waters supposedly bubble up when there are people nearby. It has unfortunately become very polluted, as it's a popular destination for locals, who aren't always environmentally conscious. It also may be dry depending on the time of year. It's just off the highway directly opposite Gasolinera Tactic, at Km. 184, should you want to take a gander.

A far more interesting attraction is the **Chi-ixim church,** which overlooks the town from a high hill reached by a steep staircase. The main attraction for pilgrims here is a visit to the black saint of Chi-ixim, also known as **El Dios del Maíz** (Maize God), to give thanks for ascribed miracles.

On the town plaza, the **Cooperativa de**

© AL ARGUETA

The rooms are comfortable at the Maya Cloud Forest Lodge.

Tejedores sells its wares and demonstrates weaving techniques. The plaza's ornate colonial-era church is decorated on its facade with jaguars and mermaids.

Accommodations and Food

For a place to stay, you could do far worse than **Chi'ixim Eco Hotel** (Km. 182.5 on Highway CA-14, tel. 7953-9198, $20 d), where there are eight cozy bungalows complete with fireplace, dining room, and private hot-water bath. There's a good restaurant at the lodge serving sandwiches and local dishes. Delicious food is also served at the log cabin-style **Café La Granja,** at Km. 187. Among the menu options you'll find salads, sandwiches, and Guatemalan specialties.

Cobán and Vicinity

Pleasant Cobán sits amid evergreen forests and coffee-studded mountains, making an excellent gateway for exploring nearby natural attractions. It has good hotels and food, as well as a tranquil country atmosphere. A small national park lies square in the middle of town. Though it is no stranger to urban sprawl and noise, the tranquility of this small town quickly reveals itself to you as you walk down its quieter side streets away from the noisy central area.

Cobán can sometimes feel a bit dreary, as much of the year sees the presence of a rainy mist known as *chipi chipi,* though it's not nearly as prominent nowadays because of local climate change from deforestation. Still, there's something upbeat about this place and the abundance of nearby natural wonders gives it an entirely different feel from towns in the Western Highlands.

The town and its surroundings are an important gourmet coffee-growing center and also produce cardamom and allspice for export. The town is often referred to as the "Imperial

City," owing to its charter by Emperor Charles V in 1538. More recently, in the 19th century Cobán saw an influx of German families, who came to dominate the local culture and economy owing to their fortunes made growing coffee for export. The United States pressured the Guatemalan government to remove the Germans from the country during World War II. There are still bits of German influence here and there, giving the city its distinctive air.

Cobán is home to a yearly folklore festival taking place in late July or early August known as **Rabin Ajau,** in which a Mayan beauty queen is selected from among various hopefuls. Another important event is the annual **orchid show** held here in December.

A number of excellent outfitters have regular departures for the Lanquín caves and Semuc Champey as well as the Quetzal Biotope and points farther afield. Cobán makes a great place to regroup and get information before heading out on deeper explorations of all that Las Verapaces have to offer.

COBÁN

SCALE NOT AVAILABLE

© AVALON TRAVEL

Parque Nacional
Las Victorias

ZONA 1

ZONA 2

ZONA 3

ZONA 4

To San Pedro Carchá, Lanquín, and SEMUC CHAMPEY NATURAL MONUMENT

To Chisec and Playa Grande

To Airport, Tactic, Plaza Magdalena Shopping Mall and Guatemala City

To Vivero Verapaz

Río Cahabón

9A AVENIDA
8A AVENIDA
7A AVENIDA
6A AVENIDA
5A AVENIDA
4A AVENIDA
3A AVENIDA
2A AVENIDA
1A AVENIDA

1A CALLE
2A CALLE
3A CALLE
4A CALLE
5A CALLE
6A CALLE
7A CALLE
8A CALLE
9A CALLE
10A AVENIDA

DIAGONAL 1

SAFARI RENTA DE AUTOS
ALCAZAR DE DOÑA VICTORIA
BUS TERMINAL
POSADA DE CARLOS V
TRANSPORTES ESCOBAR MONJA BLANCA
POSADA DE DON ANTONIO
BAR MILENIO
CYBERCOBÁN
CASA DURANTA
MUSEO EL PRINCIPE MAYA
OXFORD LANGUAGE CENTER
HOSTAL DE DOÑA VICTORIA
INQUE RENTAUTOS
POSADA DON JUAN MATALBATZ
BUSES TO CHISEC
MINIBUSES TO PLAYA GRANDE
HOTEL CENTRAL
PALACIO MUNICIPAL
TELGUA
CATEDRAL SANTO DOMINGO DE COBÁN
Mercado Central
POST OFFICE
HOTEL LAS TERRAZAS
CAFETO
BANCO G&T
Parque Central
PALACIO DEPARTAMENTAL
CYBERNET
POSADA DE DON PEDRO
BOK'ATAS
LAVANDERÍA PROVIDENCIA
CHIPI CHIPI HOSTEL
MAYA'CH EXPEDITIONS
CAFÉ EL TIROL
BANCO G&T CONTINENTAL
HOTEL LA POSADA / CAFÉ AND RESTAURANT
RESTAURANTE CANTONES
CASA D'ACUÑA / EL BISTRO
HOTEL RABIN AJAU
ACTIVE SPANISH SCHOOL
HOTEL LA PAZ
HOTEL COBÁN IMPERIAL
BANCO INDUSTRIAL
PENSIÓN MONJA BLANCA
FINCA SANTA MARGARITA
HOTEL MANSIÓN ARMENIA
KAM MUN
TABARINI RENTA AUTOS
CAPILLA EL CALVARIO
ESTADIO VERAPAZ
CAPILLA DE LA ERMITA DE SANTO DOMINGO GUZMAN

An excellent resource for planning a trip can be found online at www.cobanav.net.

SIGHTS
Parque Central
Cobán's triangular central park is interesting in that it is on a hilltop from which the rest of the town drops off in all directions. The cathedral contains the remains of a large, cracked church bell. A block behind the cathedral is the town's market.

Templo El Calvario
For many, this whitewashed church dating to 1810 holds greater significance than the town's cathedral because of its prominence as a site for Kekchí religious rituals on altars lining the long staircase leading up to it. Among the themes represented at its different altars are the granting of wishes for love and health, among others. The inside of the temple is virtually covered with votive candles, while hundreds of corncobs hang from the roof. Outside, there are fantastic views of Cobán and the rolling green hillsides all around. To the southeast is Mount Xucaneb, the highest point in Alta Verapaz. To get there, head west from the main plaza up 1a Calle and then north two blocks on 7a Avenida. You'll see the long, winding staircase heading up to the temple.

Parque Nacional Las Victorias
Next door to the church is Parque Nacional Las Victorias (11 Avenida and 3a Calle Zona 1, 8 A.M.-4:30 P.M. daily, $0.75), an 84-hectarenational park right in the middle of town where you can take a walk on nice paths through mostly evergreen forests, passing a lagoon along the way. Try not to visit alone, as there have been isolated incidents involving muggings at the hands of local gangs.

Museo El Príncipe Maya
This excellent private museum (6a Avenida 4-26 Zona 3, tel. 7952-2809, museoprincipemaya@yahoo.es, 9 A.M.-6 P.M. Mon.-Sat., $2) harbors an impressive collection of artifacts, including carvings in mother-of-pearl and jade, polychromatic pottery, ceremonial objects, tools, and weapons. Among the highlights is a Classic-period hieroglyphic panel from Cancuén and an Olmec crystal figurine with decidedly Asian features. The museum gets its name from a figurine of a Mayan prince dressed in full regalia, including a quetzal-feather headdress.

Finca Santa Margarita
Cobán has some of Guatemala's best coffee, so it's only fitting that you might have the opportunity to go behind the scenes and see the process of how the morning elixir makes it from a bush to your Bodum. The Dieseldorff family's Finca Santa Margarita (3a Calle 4-12 Zona 2, tel. 7951-3067, 8 A.M.-12:30 P.M. and 1:30-5 P.M. Mon.-Fri., 8 A.M.-noon Sat., $5) is a working coffee farm where excellent, 45-minute guided tours are available in English or Spanish, thanks to a knowledgeable Guatemalan guide who once lived in New York. You will get up-close and personal with the process governing the planting, picking, roasting, packaging, and exporting of these wonderful beans. At the end of the tour, you're treated to a cup (or two) of coffee fresh from the roaster and can buy a bag (or several) of the farm's excellent coffee. The more exclusive "special" selection is a steal at just $5 per pound.

Vivero Verapaz
Lovers of orchids will find nirvana at Vivero Verapaz (Carretera Antigua de Entrada a Cobán, tel. 7952-1133, 9 A.M.-noon and 2-4 P.M. daily, $1.50). This wonderful nursery is just outside of town and has several hundred species of orchids on display. The best time of year to visit is between October and February,

when many of the flowers are in bloom. The national orchid show is held here in December and is reportedly magnificent. A guide is on hand to show you around and will lend you a magnifying glass for viewing miniature orchids. Guatemala's national flower, the rare *monja blanca*, can be seen here in season. Otto Mittelstaedt, the original collector of the nursery's orchids, has died but the nursery lives on. Vivero Verapaz is about a 40-minute walk from the central plaza, two kilometers southwest. A taxi costs about $4.

Chixim Church

Much like the better-known church at Esquipulas, the church at Chixim attracts pilgrims from all over Guatemala thanks to the presence of its supposedly miraculous Christ figure. January 1st and 15th are the days of greatest visitor affluence, the latter being the day of the Black Saint of Chixim. The walls of the room immediately left of the main altar are chock-full of plaques in thanksgiving for miracles ascribed to El Señor de Chixim. Outside, the patio fronting the church affords a lovely panoramic vista of the Tactic valley.

NIGHTLIFE

A good place for a drink and some decent music is **Bok'atas** (4a Calle 3-34 Zona 2, tel. 5204-1353, www.bokatas.net, 4 P.M.-1 A.M. Mon.-Fri., noon-1 A.M. Fri.-Sat.), an open-air tapas bar. There is live music some weekends and it serves Mediterranean (Spanish) food. **Bar Milenio** (3a Avenida 1-11 Zona 4, no cover charge) caters mostly to an older crowd, serves food, and has pool tables and TV screens to watch sports. The fanciest place to go after dark is **Keops** (3a Calle 4-71 Zona 3, $5 cover charge, open Fri. and Sat. nights), where the music is a mix of mostly Latin tunes catering to a high-class clientele.

If you're in the mood for a movie, the complex at **Plaza Magdalena Shopping Mall** (1a Calle 15-20 Zona 2) west of the town center on the road out to Guatemala City screens new releases.

SHOPPING

Plaza Magdalena Shopping Mall (1a Calle 15-20 Zona 2) is where you can go to find First World goods you might need while on the road or indulge in a fast-food binge at McDonald's. Run by a handicrafts cooperative, **Aj K'uubanel** (Diagonal 4, 5-13 Zona 2, tel. 7951-4152) has a variety of textiles, maize and wax art, and silver jewelry for sale.

RECREATION

Cobán has a variety of nearby attractions that can be visited in one day as well as numerous outfitters that can get you there. Popular day trips include the **Semuc Champey** pools and the **Lanquín caves.** Although these can certainly be done in a day, they are worth a stay of at least one night, as there are comfortable accommodations and plenty to see and do. If you have the time, stay overnight in Lanquín.

Other day-trip options include the **Quetzal Biotope, Chicoy cave,** and **Chixim church,** all south of Cobán.

North of town, along Km. 24 on the road heading to Chisec, is the **Sachichaj waterfall,** another increasingly popular attraction. Most of the following tour operators can get you there.

Guide Companies

Housed inside the Hostal de Doña Victoria, **Aventuras Turísticas** (3a Calle 2-38 Zona 3, tel. 7951-4213/14, www.aventurasturisticas.com) does the usual day trips to the nearby sites and adventurous options in destinations farther afield, including rappelling in the Bombil Pek caves near Chisec, backdoor treks to Semuc Champey, and trips to Lagunas de Sepalau. This is *the* place to contact for caving, trekking, inner tubing, and kayaking, among other exciting options. It also does the usual daily tour of Semuc Champey ($35 p/p), leaving at 7:30 A.M. and returning by nightfall.

Recommended is **Maya'ch Expeditions** (1a Calle 3-25 Zona 1, across from Hotel La Posada, tel. 7951-4335), offering one- and two-day trips to Semuc Champey in comfortable vans with breakfast and lunch included. Overnight visitors stay at the outfitter's lodge, Casa El Zapote, 2.5 kilometers from Semuc Champey. You can also book transport-only to Semuc Champey or a package including round-trip transport and lodging at Casa El Zapote.

Casa D'Acuña (4a Calle 3-11 Zona 2, tel. 7951-0482 or 7951-0484, casadeacuna@yahoo.com) also does trips to Semuc Champey and has some excellent guides. It has daily shuttles to Tikal and Antigua leaving at 6 A.M. and costing $28 one-way. Unlike on other shuttles, however, you can get off at intermediate points such as Chisec, Candelaria, Sayaxché, and Flores on the trip north, or at the Quetzal Biotope heading to Antigua.

Proyecto EcoQuetzal (2a Calle 14-36 Zona 1, tel. 7952-1047, bidaspeq@hotmail.com, www.ecoquetzal.org) is a local NGO working with indigenous people in two communities near well-preserved areas of cloud and rainforest in Chicacnab (southeastern Alta Verapaz) and Rokjá Pomtilá (near Laguna Lachuá) to offer economic alternatives to deforestation via sustainable tourism. Guides are rural Kekchí Mayans who know the forest intimately and have received thorough training as nature guides. Trekkers to these remote parts stay in the guides' homes, which have been fitted with beds, toilets, and boiled drinking water, among other basic comforts. It allows for a true cross-cultural experience as well as a means for providing locals with a viable alternative to the destruction of the fragile ecosystem they call home. Your chances of spotting a rare quetzal bird are also fairly good. A two-night trip to Chicacnab costs about $45 per person, including guide, food, and accommodations with

additional nights available for about $15 apiece. A two-night stay at Rokjá Pomtilá also costs $45.

ACCOMMODATIONS
Under $10
In the budget range is one of the best values you'll find anywhere in Guatemala. ☪ **Casa D'Acuña** (4a Calle 3-11 Zona 2, tel. 7951-0482 or 7951-0484, www.casadeacuna.com) lies at the bottom of a steep hill south of the main plaza and has four comfortable dormitories with four beds apiece ($7 per person) as well as two private double rooms ($20 d). All rooms have shared baths. There is also an excellent restaurant built around the main courtyard of the colonial building in which the lodge is housed. On the next street over toward the park is **Posada de Don Pedro** (3a Calle 3-12 Zona 2, tel. 7951-0562), with acceptably comfortable beds and five rooms with shared bath at $7 per person along with two rooms with private baths for $10 per person. The main entrance doubles as a small corner store. **Hostal de Doña Victoria** (3a Calle 2-38 Zona 3, tel. 7951-4213/14) has a shared-bath, bunk-bed dormitory where you can stay for $7 per person. North of the main plaza and conveniently situated near the bus terminals (though not in the best part of town) is **Posada Don Juan Matalbatz** (3a Calle 1-46 Zona 1, tel. 7951-0811). It has rooms around a pretty courtyard in a neocolonial building with somewhat saggy beds, cable TV, reading lamps, and ancient hot-water heaters. There are rooms with shared baths for $8 per person and some with private bath going for $26 (d). There's also a café downstairs with a pool table. It doesn't get any cheaper or more basic than **Chipi Chipi Hostel** (1a Calle 3-25 Zona 1, tel. 5226-0235), just off the main plaza, where a bed in a shared-bath dormitory can be had for $3.50. It has an Internet lounge and hammock area.

A few blocks west of the plaza is **Pensión Monja Blanca** (2a Calle 6-30 Zona 2, tel.

7952-1712), run by a charming elderly couple who keep the place spotless. Centered round a lovely garden are comfortable tiled-floor rooms with shared bath ($7 per person) or private bath ($26 d). Also featured are a balcony with a sitting area, a pay phone, and a pleasant tea room where you can have breakfast. Friendly **Hotel La Paz** (6a Avenida 2-19 Zona 1, tel. 7952-1358) is another good budget option with basic but clean, cheerful rooms with electric hot-water heater for $10 (d). **Hotel Cobán Imperial** (6a Avenida 1-12 Zona 1, tel. 7952-1131) is an old standby popular with Guatemalan families and has double rooms with TV and shared bath for $8 or doubles with private baths with electric hot-water heaters for $17.

$10-25

Hostal de Doña Victoria (3a Calle 2-38 Zona 3, tel. 7951-4213/14, $25 d), is housed in a rather atmospheric 400-year-old colonial home. Its eight rooms centered round a pretty courtyard and café are looking somewhat worn these days but have TV, desks, and private hot-water bathrooms. A better, newer option in this price range is ◖ **Guatefriends Coban** (Aldea Chicuxab, tel. 2261-3460, $15 p/p in dorm to $40 d). You're essentially staying in someone's home, but the location ten minutes outside of town overlooking forested mountains, and the host family itself, couldn't be friendlier. The house is made entirely of wood and stone and feels quite cozy. You'll feel right at home. In a green building occupying the corner of 2a Avenida and 4a Calle, **Hotel Las Terrazas** (tel. 7951-2763, $25 d) has 22 rooms with private baths and electric hot-water heaters. West of the plaza, the **Hotel Rabin Ajau** (1a Calle 5-37 Zona 1, tel. 7951-4296, $20 d) has rooms with private bath and ancient electric hot-water heaters, firm beds, and cable TV. The rooms are lit by a single fluorescent bulb and tend to feel dark. Just off the plaza

and centrally situated, as its name would indicate, is **Hotel Central** (1a Calle 1-79 Zona 1, tel. 7952-1442, www.hotelcentralcoban. com, $25), with clean rooms built around a garden courtyard. All rooms have private hot-water bathroom and cable TV.

$25-50

Cobán has several excellent choices in this category. West of the central plaza is **Hotel La Posada** (1a Calle 4-12 Zona 2, tel. 7951-3516, www.laposadacoban.com, $50 d), in a 400-year-old colonial mansion with tiled floors, Guatemalan accents, and attractively tiled private hot-water bathrooms. The main drawback here is its location right in between the town's two busiest roads. Under the same management as the Hostal de Doña Victoria, the **Alcazar de Doña Victoria** (1a Avenida 5-34 Zona 1, tel. 7952-1388, www.hotelescoban.com/alcazar.htm, $38 d) is a much larger, 50-room operation. The spacious, tastefully decorated rooms centered around a courtyard have firm beds and cheerful private hot-water bathroom, though rooms on the first floor can be a bit damp. All have tile floors and cable TV. There are a café and bar as well as banquet halls. Near the bus terminal is **Posada de Carlos V** (1 Avenida 3-44 Zona 1, tel. 7951-3501 or 7951-3502, www.hotelcarlosvgt.com, $30 d), which has homey rooms housed in a large wooden house reminiscent of a rural Swiss chalet, all with firm beds, private hot-water bath, and cable TV. Downstairs there are a lounge with a big-screen TV and a restaurant serving three meals daily. A newer section of 10 additional rooms housed in a separate concrete building is equally comfortable though not as quaint.

Just a block from the Iglesia El Calvario, **Hotel Mansión Armenia** (7a Avenida 2-18 Zona 1, tel. 7951-4244, $30 d) is housed in a modern concrete-block building and is clean and neat throughout. Rooms have firm beds, private hot-water bathrooms, cable TV, and in-room phones. Hot water is available 5 P.M.-8 A.M. Under the same ownership as Transportes Monja Blanca, the pleasant **Posada de Don Antonio** (5a Avenida 1-51 Zona 4, tel. 7951-4287, www.hotelposadadedonantonio.com, $42 d including breakfast) has 21 rooms in a two-story colonial building centered around a beautiful garden with a pretty fountain. There are nice tiled floors and decorative tiled stairs throughout. Rooms have firm beds, cable TV, and hot-water private baths. There's also a restaurant open daily for breakfast and dinner. This hotel is a good value.

In a class all by itself on the road into Cobán from Guatemala City, Italian-owned **◖ Park Hotel** (Km. 196.5 Carretera a Cobán, Santa Cruz Verapaz, tel. 7952-0807, www.parkhotelresort.com) is situated on its own 15-acre forest preserve and has many excellent amenities, including a gym, tennis courts, nature trails, and even a small zoo. Its 96 comfortable and well-decorated rooms are an excellent value starting at $35 for a standard double room with all the usual amenities, though they are near the road and tend to be noisy. A better option is a junior suite ($50 d). Try to book one in the Firenze building, where odd-numbered rooms have a view of sprawling gardens and a fishpond under a quaint wooden bridge. Suites with a living room and chimney are also available ($60 d), but these tend to feel smaller than the junior suites. Italian food is the specialty at one of its restaurants, while the other is a Uruguayan steakhouse. The gift shop sells orchids.

Over $50

Beautiful **◖ Casa Duranta** (3a Calle 4-46 Zona 3, tel. 7951-4188, info@casaduranta.com, www.casaduranta.com, $54 d) has 10 tastefully decorated, well-appointed rooms—all with private baths—with Guatemalan indigenous blankets, tiled floors, and wrought-ironworks inside and outside the rooms. There are a TV lounge, a reading area, and wireless Internet throughout the colonial house centered round an appealing courtyard. An on-site café is open for three meals daily.

FOOD

On the road to Cobán from Guatemala City, **Hotel y Restaurante la Lupa di Roma** (Km. 200 on the road to Cobán, tel. 7951-4444, www.otupactours.com) serves authentic Italian cuisine in an attractive country setting. Arguably the best food in town, Casa D'Acuña's peaceful courtyard restaurant, **◖ El Bistro** (4a Calle 3-11 Zona 2, tel. 7951-0482 or 7951-0484, www.casadeacuna.com, 6:30 A.M.-10 P.M. daily), serves a variety of excellent international dishes, including great pasta ($5-6), pizzas, meat dishes, homemade breads and pastries, salads, and sandwiches. Another excellent place to eat is the café inside **Hostal de Doña Victoria** (3a Calle 2-38 Zona 3, tel. 7951-4213/14), though the menu is not as intricate as that at El Bistro and leans more toward Guatemalan dishes. It's always a good bet for breakfast. A good option for fine dining can be found at **◖ Café and Restaurant La Posada** (1a Calle 4-12 Zona 2, tel. 7952-1495, www.laposadacoban.com), inside the Hotel La Posada. The café (1-8:30 P.M. Wed.-Mon.) is at the far end of the building and looks out onto the plaza. The fancier restaurant (7 A.M.-9:30 P.M. Mon.-Sat., 7-11 A.M. Sun.) is set in an attractive dining room with a fireplace and two terraces facing a garden. The food at both is excellent, though the service is notoriously slow. It's a good place to relax and unwind if you have a few hours to kill or aren't in a hurry. The menu includes Guatemalan and international dishes.

A newer dining option enjoying favorable early reviews is Venezuelan-owned **◖ La Abadia** (Calle Belice 3-98 Zona 3, tel. 7952-1782, www.abadiacafe.com/gt/, $7-13). Set in a cozy colonial-style house, the restaurant serves a unique fusion of Guatemalan and Venezuelan flavors. There's a good selection of wines to pair with your meal. **El Peñascal** (5a Avenida 2-61 Zona 1, tel. 7951-2102, 7 A.M.-11 P.M. daily, $7-13) is the place to go for regional specialties, including tasty *kaq-ik,* but the more original cardamom steak steals the show.

For paella and other Spanish and Mediterranean specialties, head to **Bok'atas** (4a Calle 3-34 Zona 2, tel. 5204-1353, www.bokatas. net, 4 P.M.-1 A.M. Mon.-Fri., noon-1 A.M. Fri. and Sat.). There's also a lively bar playing good tunes.

There are a variety of decent cafés in Cobán, among them the café at **Casa Duranta** (3a Calle 4-46 Zona 3, tel. 7951-4188, www.casaduranta.com, 7-10 A.M. and 3-8 P.M. daily), where the specialty is crêpes (sweet and salty) as well as sandwiches and pastas. West of the plaza, (**Café El Tirol** (1a Calle 3-13 Zona 1, tel. 7951-4042, 7:30 A.M.-9 P.M. Mon.-Sat.) is a great place for breakfast or a light meal and coffee enjoyed in a pleasant terrace. The smoothies and sandwiches are particularly tasty. On the south side of the plaza, Cafeto (tel. 7951-2850, 9 A.M.-9 P.M. daily) is a pleasant wine and coffee shop serving an affordable daily set lunch menu, including soup, half a sandwich, and salad, as well as European dishes such as bratwurst with mustard and sauerkraut. **Xkape Kob'an** (Diagonal 4, 5-13 Zona 2, tel. 7951-4152) does a variety of coffee drinks but specializes in local dishes such as chicken stew, tamales, and *kaq-ik* in addition to pastries in a pleasant atmosphere with rustic wooden tables in a garden setting. There is artwork for sale and the café is managed by the Artisans' Association of Verapaz.

For Asian food, try the clean and tidy **Restaurante Kam Mun** (1a Calle 8-12 Zona 2), where heaping portions of Chinese dishes ($5-10) are served in a pleasant atmosphere. Another alternative is **Restaurante Cantonés** (behind Hotel La Posada at Diagonal 4, 4-24 Zona 2, tel. 7952-1592, 11:30 A.M.-10 P.M.

daily), where a tasty large plate of fried rice can be had for $5.

There are several cheap eats lining the central plaza, the best (and safest) of which is **Empanadas Argentinas,** on the north end next to Telgua, where you can savor a tasty chicken empanada for just $0.85.

INFORMATION AND SERVICES

Tourist Information

Cobán doesn't have an INGUAT office but you can find out everything you might need to know from the friendly staff at Casa D'Acuña (4a Calle 3-11 Zona 2, tel. 7951-0482) and Hostal de Doña Victoria (3a Calle 2-38 Zona 3, tel. 7951-4213/14), which act as the de facto tourism information offices.

Communications

The post office is on the corner of 2a Avenida and 3a Calle one block southeast of the main plaza. Telgua is right on the plaza, on the north side, with card phones outside.

You'll find several options for access to the Internet in Cobán, with the going rate at about $1.75 an hour. Among the options are Access Computación (1a Calle 3-13 Zona 1, tel. 7951-4040, 9 A.M.-7 P.M. Mon.-Fri., 8 A.M.-6 P.M. Sat.), Hostal de Doña Victoria (3a Calle 2-38 Zona 3, tel. 7951-4213/14), CyberCoban (3a Avenida, 1-11 Zona 4, tel. 7951-1777, 8:30 A.M.-7 P.M. daily), and Cybernet (on the south side of the plaza at Diagonal 4, 3-12 Zona 2, tel. 7951-4390). Navega.com. (8 A.M.-8 P.M.) is right next door to Café Tirol and has lightning-fast connection speeds. Mayan Internet (6a Avenida 2-28 Zona 1, tel. 5694-7696, 8:30 A.M.-8 P.M. Mon.-Sat., 2:30-9 P.M. Sun.) is another option.

Money

Banco Industrial has a Visa ATM at 1a Calle and 7a Avenida, Zona 1. Banco G&T Continental has a branch at 1a Calle and

4a Avenida, across the street from Hotel La Posada, with a versatile 5B ATM. There's another branch at 1a Calle and 2a Avenida, Zona 3. You can change travelers checks and dollars at all of these.

Laundry

Lavandería La Providencia (8 A.M.-noon and 2-5 P.M. Mon.-Sat.) is on the south side of the plaza. It costs about $3.50 to wash and dry a load. Otherwise, it's about $5 to wash and dry a load at Casa D'Acuña (4a Calle 3-11 Zona 2, tel. 7951-0482).

Language Schools

Though Spanish-language instruction isn't nearly as prolific in Cobán as elsewhere in Guatemala, the increasing number of visitors to these parts has translated into the opening of a number of schools in the past few years. Among the options are **Active Spanish School** (3a Calle 6-12 Zona 1, tel. 7952-1432, $120 per week including room and board with host family), known for its instructor who is an invaluable source on the local nightlife scene and organizes day trips to outdoor attractions. **Oxford Language Center** (4a Av 2-16 Zona 3, tel. 7951-4042, www.olcenglish.com) charges $170 for 20 hours of language instruction per week. Another option is **School of Arts and Language** (16 Avenida 2-50 Zona 1, tel. 7953-9062, alftujab@intelnett.com, $150 per week with local host family). Outside of town on a tranquil farm is **Eco Cabaña Spanish School** (Km. 6 Carretera a Chamil, San Juan Chamelco, tel. 7951-5898, ecocabana@yahoo.com), where four hours of daily instruction cost $100 per week. An additional $70 gets you a home stay with a local family or on-site.

GETTING THERE
Bus

The situation with public bus transport in Cobán is rather chaotic, as different buses heading for different places leave from various parts of town despite the presence of (in theory) a central bus terminal. You can find complete bus schedules for virtually any place you might want to go from Cobán at www.cobanav.net/bus.php. Check the Cobán map in this book for pickup locations for the various destinations. That being said, buses to Guatemala City via **Transportes Escobar Monja Blanca** (tel. 7951-3571) depart from a pleasant bus station at 2a Calle 3-77 Zona 4 every 30 minutes between 2 A.M. and 5 P.M. Departures from the so-called "Terminal Nueva" (New Terminal) near the soccer stadium are limited to Tactic (every 30 minutes), the Quetzal Biotope (every 30 minutes), El Estor (six buses daily), and Fray Bartolomé de las Casas via Pajal (five buses daily).

Microbuses to Lanquín leave from 3a Calle near the Posada de Don Juan Matalbatz. Buses for San Juan Chamelco (4a Calle and 4a Avenida Zona 3) and San Pedro Carchá (2a Calle and 4a Avenida Zona 4) leave every 20 minutes. Buses to San Juan Chamelco also reputedly leave from the Wasen Bridge, Diagonal 15, Zona 7, every half hour.

Shuttle Bus

Casa D'Acuña (4a Calle 3-11 Zona 2, tel. 7951-0482 or 7951-0484, casadeacuna@yahoo.com) runs daily shuttles to Tikal and Antigua leaving at 6 A.M. and costing $30 one-way. You can get off at intermediate points such as Chisec, Candelaria, Sayaxché, and Flores on the trip north, or at the Quetzal Biotope heading to Antigua.

Car Rental

Several car-rental companies (though none of international stature) have offices in Cobán: **Inque Renta Autos** (3a Avenida and 2a Calle Zona 4, tel. 7952-1994 or 7952-1431), **Tabarini Rent A Car** (8a Avenida 2-27 Zona 2, tel. 7952-1504, www.tabarini.com), and **Safari Renta Autos** (3a Avenida 8-47 Zona 11, tel. 7952-1175).

NEAR COBÁN
San Pedro Carchá

This small town lies six kilometers east of Cobán, though the urban sprawl around both towns means they are gradually merging into a single agglomeration. In the center of town, you'll find the small, recently renovated **Museo Regional** (9 A.M.-noon and 2-5 P.M. Mon.-Fri., $1) beside the church. There are stuffed birds and animals as well as Mayan artifacts and dolls in traditional costume. The town's other main attraction is the **Balneario Las Islas,** a 10-minute walk from the center of town, where a river runs down into a natural pool.

There are some decent places to stay on the outskirts of town that make a nice alternative to staying in Cobán proper, if you seek a more natural environment. Along Km. 216 of the road from Cobán to San Pedro Carchá is **Hotel Mansión Santo Domingo de Guzman** (tel. 7950-0777, www.mansionsantodomingodeguzman.com, $40 d), a wonderful colonial hacienda-style property set on forested grounds. The rooms and common areas are tastefully decorated with antiques. Each room has a private hot-water bath, comfortable beds, cable TV, and a desk. There is also a good restaurant with outdoor patio seating overlooking well-manicured lawns. Also out this way near the *arco* bridge at the entrance to town along Km. 217.5 is **Hotel Posada de Don Francisco** (tel. 7951-3356, $44 d), also featuring comfortable rooms in a similar setting, some with river views.

Access to the cloud forests of **Chicacnab** is from San Pedro Carchá via bus to the village of Caquipec and then on to San Lucas. There are buses every 20 minutes from Cobán to Carchá.

San Juan Chamelco

Seven kilometers southeast of Cobán, San Juan Chamelco is a Q'eqchi' town whose women are known for their traditional attire, which includes earrings made from a layered series of old coins. The church here sits on a small hill and provides wonderful views of surrounding areas. There are paintings inside depicting the arrival of the Spanish conquerors. Outside, it is interestingly decorated with Mayan adaptations of the Hapsburg double eagle, providing further evidence of the historic German influence in this region. The church's bell was a gift to local villager Juan Matalbatz from the Holy Roman Emperor Charles V. Mass here is held in Spanish and Q'eqchi'.

In nearby Aldea Chajaneb, five kilometers outside of Chamelco, are the **Grutas del Rey Marcos** (tel. 7951-2756, 8 A.M.-5 P.M. weekends or by appointment weekdays, $3 including guide and hard-hat and boot rental). They're worth a look for some interesting stalagmites reached by wading across an underground river. Though the caves are a kilometer long, you'll see only a small part of the complex on the tour. Also in this neck of the woods is **Balneario Cecilinda** (tel. 5308-9307, $1.50, open weekends), a series of natural pools and waterfalls that are just perfect on a hot day. The easy way to get here is to take a cab ($7) but you can also take a Chamil-bound bus from San Juan Chamelco and ask to be let off near the caves or the *balneario.* Don Jeronimo's, a pleasant riverside lodge run by a friendly American, has closed.

San Cristóbal Verapaz

Nineteen kilometers west of Cobán is the Poqomchi' Mayan town of San Cristóbal Verapaz, set beside Lake Chicoj. The Holy Week festivities here are similar to those in La Antigua, with processions and the making of colorful sawdust-and-flower petal carpets. The **Museo Kitanamit** (tel. 7950-4039, cecep@intelnet.net.gt, $1), run by the local Centro Comunitario Educativo Pokomchi' (CECEP), features exhibits on the Poqomchi' way of life, including art, textiles, and tools used in everyday life. The organization also runs the **Aj Chi Cho Language Center** (www.ajchicho.50g.com), which teaches Spanish and Poqomchi'.

If you need a place to stay, try the Poqomchi'-owned **El Portón Real** hostel (tel. 7950-4604).

Sachichaj Waterfall

From Cobán, as you head north on the road to Chisecis, is the Sachichaj waterfall at Km. 24. This beautiful, 15-meter-high cataract spills from the mouth of a cave into a gorgeous cobalt lagoon. You can get here via a tour booked with Casa D'Acuña or Hostal de Doña Victoria. To get here on your own, drive to the point where the Río Sachichaj crosses the road at Km. 24 of the road to Chisec. Just past this point on the left-hand side is Tienda y Comedor Reina, where you can hire a guide, which is highly recommended as it's easy to get lost in the twisting maze of paths. It's a 40-minute walk from here to the falls.

Lanquín and Semuc Champey

Lanquín and its caves, along with the turquoise pools of Semuc Champey, are quickly becoming requisite stops for travelers making their way through Guatemala. Recreational opportunities abound and you may find yourself spending more time here than you had originally planned. Whether it's exploring caves, whitewater rafting, river tubing, or swimming that suits your fancy, you'll find plenty to see and do in these parts.

LANQUÍN

From San Pedro Carchá, a paved road diverts northeast through coffee and cardamom plantations to El Pajal, where there is a turnoff for a dirt road that twists and turns for another 12 kilometers to the small town of Lanquín. Lanquín is home to some interesting caves and has some comfortable accommodations to use as a base for exploring the nearby countryside.

Lanquín Caves National Park

The Lanquín caves (8 A.M.-6 P.M. daily, $4) lie one kilometer northwest of town. They are several kilometers long, though only a small part is open to visitors. Although there are diesel generator-powered lights, these sometimes fail, so bring a flashlight and good shoes for navigating the slippery, guano-laden surfaces inside. The entire cave system has yet to be fully explored or mapped, so don't wander too far into the cavern's core. There are some interesting stalactites to be found here.

Another highlight of a visit to these caves is the thousands of bats flying out from the cavern at dusk. The Río Lanquín also flows out of this cave and forms a turquoise ribbon meandering through the surrounding jungle. It's perfect for a refreshing swim.

Rafting the Río Cahabón

In addition to the caves, Lanquín serves as a departure point for white-water rafting trips down the Class III-IV Río Cahabón. **Maya Expeditions** (tel. 2363-4955, www.mayaexpeditions.com) pioneered white-water rafting in Guatemala starting in 1987 and was named one of the "Top 20 Eco-Outfitters in the World" by *Condé Nast Traveler*. The outfit takes groups to both the upper and lower gorges as day trips ($115/155), but it also has various options for 3-6-day adventures ($210-678). The complete six-day adventure begins in Guatemala City and includes stops at the Quetzal Biotope, Cobán, Lanquín, Semuc Champey, and the Candelaria caves in addition to rafting both the upper and lower gorges of the Cahabón. A newer option is **Guatemala Rafting** (tel. 7983-3056, www.guatemalarafting.com), offering one- and two-day trips on the river ($50/140). It is based at El Retiro lodge. Bring your own tent if you're going on the overnight trip with

LAS VERAPACES

© AL ARGUETA

corkscrew rapids on the Río Cahabón

this one. Both outfitters provide other basics such as food, transport, and equipment.

Accommodations and Food

One of the hippest backpacker hotels in all of Central America lies 500 meters along the road from Lanquín toward the village of Cahabón. El Retiro (tel. 7832-4446 or 4513-6396, el-retirolanquin.com) offers a variety of accommodations for all budgets in a splendid setting beside the Río Lanquín. The so-called "posh block" has tastefully decorated rooms with private baths and electric hot-water heater ($24 d). There are hammocks out front for taking in the wonderful vistas toward the river and surrounding hillsides. A bed in one of the four-person dormitories costs $4. Rooms with shared baths are also available, and range $10-13 for a double. You can camp here or sleep in a hammock for $2. The *palapa*-style bar plays great music and is lined with rope-swing bar seats. The restaurant serves excellent food, with dinner being

a nightly communal experience. There are barbecues on Wednesday nights; Saturday night's theme is Mexican. The lodge can arrange a variety of activities for you, including inner tubing on the river for $2.50 and horseback riding ($5-16). Also in this neck of the woods is the newest arrival to Lanquín's backpacker scene, Zephyr Lodge (tel. 5168-2441, zephyrlodgelanquin@gmail.com, $8-20 d). The beautiful lodge is housed in several thatched-roof structures and has a fun, feel-good atmosphere along with some amazing views of the surrounding countryside. Shared-bath dorm rooms start at just $4 per person but there are also rooms with private bathroom and cabins set away from the main building. There's great food, including delicious pizza made in a wood-fired oven, and a well-stocked bar. The prices are a little on the high side when compared to other properties in this locale, but consider your location on a remote hillside overlooking the river. To get to Zephyr (and El Retiro), turn left at the junction

THE RAGING RAPIDS OF THE RÍO CAHABÓN

Guatemala's best white-water river is the Class III-IV Río Cahabón. In addition to the exhilarating rapids, the traverse downstream on its emerald waters is interspersed with more tranquil stretches that afford opportunities to view several species of birds and explore caves, waterfalls, and hot springs along its forested banks.

The Cahabón is the same river that flows into a cave under the limestone pools of Semuc Champey, reemerging several hundred meters downstream. Most river trips begin at a put-in point near Lanquín. There are some rather menacing rapids along this stretch of the Upper Cahabón, including Rock and Roll, Entonces, and Las Tres Hermanas, making for an adrenaline-filled ride. The Middle Gorge has some nice jungle scenery and continuous Class III rapids. There are a few more challenging rapids after passing the bridge at a place called Oxec before reaching an obligatory takeout point at Takinkó to portage the Class VI (not possible to run) Chulac Falls. A dam was once planned here, but dam builders seem to have gone cold on the idea after discovering a fault line running right beneath the proposed dam site. The two-day river trip camps here.

The Lower Gorge is a boatload of fun with titillating rapids such as Saca Corchos (Corkscrew) and Saca Caca. There are stops along the way to explore caves and enjoy lunch at "El Pequeño Paraíso," a small sidestream with delightful waterfalls and hot springs flowing into the Cahabón. The next rapid is appropriately named Lose Your Lunch, shortly after which the river widens and you are treated to a serene stretch of river with mountainous jungle-clad banks. The takeout is at Cahaboncito, where the intrepid can take a plunge into the river from a 30-foot bridge.

Rafting the Cahabón affords the opportunity to see some remote natural attractions and come in contact with the local people inhabiting the area. As is often the case in Guatemala, the beauty coexists with a sobering reality. In addition to still-forested areas you will see some steep, badly deforested slopes given over to corn cultivation, shedding light on the desperate plight of peasants willing to live and grow their crops anywhere they can.

---

in town heading up the hill, opposite the way to Semuc Champey.

In town, **Hotel Rabin Itzam** (tel. 7983-0076) has 14 clean rooms with somewhat hard beds and shared baths for $4 per person. On the other end of town as you come in to Lanquín from the El Pajal Junction is **Hotel El Recreo** (tel. 7983-0056), with rooms in a wooden main house or in an adjacent concrete structure. The main house has a lower-level section with shared-bath rooms for $20 (d). The lighting is fluorescent. Nicer rooms with private bath are $31 (d). This lodge is usually empty unless there's a tour group in town. There's a restaurant here, too.

Other options for food include **Comedor Shalom,** near the Hotel Rabin Itzam, with set-menu lunches and dinners comprised of mostly meat and rice dishes for around $2.

Cuevas de K'an Ba

Along the road from Lanquín to Semuc Champey, in the vicinity of Posada Las Marías (tel. 7861-2209, www.posadalasmarias.com), you'll find these rather interesting caves found on the lodge's private property. There are wonderful opportunities for exploring the caves by floating through on inner tubes ($5 for hotel guests, $7.50 for non-guests). You'll see several formations and underground waterfalls before emerging onto the clear, turquoise waters of the Río Cahabón. The trek through the caves involves climbing waterfalls with the aid of a rope or ladder and jumping into pools in virtual darkness. It's not for the faint of heart. El Retiro and Zephyr Lodge also organize trips to the caves.

■ SEMUC CHAMPEY NATURAL MONUMENT

These gorgeous limestone pools (6 A.M.-6 P.M. daily, $7) lie at the end of a rough dirt road nine kilometers from Lanquín. Although they were once considered a remote attraction far off the beaten path, they are now one of Las Verapaces's top tourist draws. Accordingly, infrastructure has improved to keep up with the rising numbers of visitors. Try not to visit on a weekend, as there are day-trippers in droves from Cobán and vicinity.

A giant, 300-meter-long limestone bridge forms the backbone for the descending series of pools and small waterfalls that make up Semuc Champey. The water that fills the pools is the product of runoff from the Río Cahabón, churning as it plunges into an underground chasm from where it reemerges downstream at the end of this massive limestone overpass.

Recreation

In addition to **swimming** in the perfectly placid pools, you can travel a series of **trails** and hanging wooden bridges to the sites where the river makes its underground plunge and where it re-emerges downstream. It is truly awe inspiring to see the force of nature as the raging river is crammed into an underground cavern. A longer, 1.2-kilometer trail heads straight up the side of a mountain to a fantastic **lookout point,** where you can see the pools from above. It's worth the substantial effort required to climb on the steep mountainside, sometimes with the help of vines and tree roots. Closer to the park entrance is a walkway that will take you to an **observation platform** where you can see a pretty waterfall gushing into the Río Cahabón over the point where it re-emerges from its cave.

Across from the parking lot and park entry booth, you'll find a visitors center where you can buy drinks and food. The latter is a set menu ($3-6) consisting mainly of local dishes and grilled meats. Vehicle parking costs $1.30.

Guides are available here to take you around. As always, tipping is a good idea.

Accommodations and Food

There are now at least two hotels just minutes away from the park entrance. Coming from Semuc Champey, the first place you'll come across is **Hostal El Portal de Champey** (tel. 7983-0046, $5 p/p to $26 d) where there are pleasant A-frame cottages set on a hillside overlooking the Río Cahabón. Service at the on-site restaurant may be spotty when one of the caretaker's frequent parties is being held. (You might have better luck if you bring a cooler full of beer with you.)

Another option lies about one kilometer from Semuc Champey. **Posada Las Marías** (tel. 7861-2209, www.posadalasmarias.com) enjoys a wonderful riverside location and offers accommodations in dorms with shared bath ($5 p/p), rooms with shared bath ($10 d), or rooms with private bath ($20 d). The restaurant serves three meals a day ($4-7) and the menu includes sandwiches, nachos, and barbecued steak. Activities include inner tubing on the Río Cahabón and visits to the nearby caves of K'an Ba ($5 for guests), where you can explore an underwater river.

Also near Semuc Champey (if all else fails) is **Jam Bamboo** (tel. 4549-9735, cabralmariano@ hotmail.com). There are private rooms ($7 p/p shared bath, $12 p/p with private bath and fan) along with six-bed and twelve-bed dorm rooms ($4 p/p, shared bath). The dorm beds consist of a small mattress on a wooden floor and are set above the restaurant/bar. The beds are firm and there is hot water. Breakfast here costs $4 and lunch or dinner cost $5; all are set-menu options. The hotel staff likes to jam on their drums, lending credence to the lodge's peculiar name.

The newest offering in this neck of the woods is **Utopia Eco Hotel** (tel. 4096-4653, www.uto-piaecohotel.com, $1.50 in hammock to $20 d in room with private bathroom). Located three

LAS VERAPACES

kilometers from Semuc Champey, the lodge enjoys a splendid location on the banks of the Río Cahabón. Accommodations run the gamut from a hammock to rooms with private bathrooms, and include camping or dorm rooms in between. It's a good place for outdoor adventures, including overnight hikes and camping trips ($25) and extreme inner-tubing on the river ($7). More serene options include 700 feet of riverside to enjoy, along with a rope swing and sun deck. There's a full restaurant and bar. Spanish lessons start at $75 per week.

Getting There

There are several tour companies in Cobán operating day and overnight trips to Lanquín and Semuc Champey. Shuttle-only options are available and are highly recommended as the best way to get here. From Antigua, **Old Town Outfitters** (tel. 5399-0440, info@adventureguatemala.com, www.bikeguatemala.com) runs a four-day trip to Lanquín, Semuc Champey, and the cave of K'an Ba for $295 per person with a two-passenger minimum, including transport, meals, and accommodations. There are stops in Cobán and the Quetzal Biotope along the way.

If you're driving, you'll need a four-wheel-drive vehicle for the road from El Pajal to Lanquín. Schedules change frequently so check current schedules. Hourly buses (5 A.M.-5 P.M.) from Lanquín to Cobán cost $3.75. There are six microbuses and at least two shuttles a day to Cobán.

Northern Alta Verapaz

Northern Alta Verapaz is quickly gaining momentum as the site for a varied assortment of ecotourism options thanks to the presence of some well-organized community tourism initiatives and its location along the corridor connecting Alta Verapaz and Petén on a good paved road. Among the highlights in this neck of the woods are the Candelaria Caves National Park, Lagunas de Sepalau, Cuevas B'omb'il Pek, and Laguna Lachuá National Park. It will be interesting to see how this area grows and develops during the next several years with the ever-increasing presence of international tourism. For now, the scene here is very low-key, but it won't be that way forever. Get out and explore this part of Guatemala, where there are relatively few visitors, while you can.

EL PAJAL TO FRAY BARTOLOMÉ DE LAS CASAS

From the El Pajal Junction, the road winds through the mountainous Alta Verapaz terrain north to the small village of **Sebol** (about two hours), which is attractively set on the banks of the Río La Pasión with waterfalls flowing into it. It might make an attractive stopover someday, though there is no infrastructure to accommodate visitors as of yet. Here the road branches east to Fray Bartolomé de las Casas, referred to simply as "Fray" or "Las Casas." This nondescript town has a few basic accommodations, should you need to stay here. The best of these are **Hotel Diamelas** ($13 d) and **Hotel y Restaurante Bartolo** ($8 d).

You'll find the town is fairly spread out, with the plaza and most visitor services on one end of town and the bus terminal and market on the other, a 10-minute walk away. On or near the plaza, you'll find a post office, police station, Banrural, and the local town hall (*municipalidad*). There are at least three ATMs near the town entrance.

There is a bus departing daily for Poptún at 3 A.M. ($4), and hourly buses for Cobán between 4 A.M. and 4 P.M.

Las Conchas Pools

Las Casas's sole nearby attraction is Las Conchas, a series of limestone pools and waterfalls on the Río Chiyú, 50 kilometers east toward Izabal. The pools are rather large and great for swimming, though the water is not of the sweet emerald color found at Semuc Champey. There is a small picnic area.

The falls' remote location means you may find yourself needing to spend the night in the area. Thanks to a recent addition to the local hotel offerings, you can combine a trip to the waterfalls with a stay at a nearby jungle camp. **Oasis Chiyú** (www.naturetoursguatemala. com), a 10-hectare (25-acre) working farm and lodge owned by a transplanted American, is beautifully situated at the confluence of two jungle rivers. The lodge runs on an all-inclusive plan ($30 per person per day with a two-night minimum) and includes three square meals daily, accommodations in the main house or in nearby bungalows, guided hikes, and transportation. The gorgeous views of the surrounding jungle, rivers, and waterfalls alone are worth the price of admission. Meals are prepared on a wood-burning stove using fresh ingredients and include vegetarian specialties such as fried rice, pastas, curries, hummus, sandwiches, and salads. Bikes and kayaks are available to explore the surroundings, and guided hikes can take you to nearby waterfalls, mysterious caves, sultry jungles, and cool rivers. This is your chance to really become one with nature: no phones, fax, email, or electricity—truly an oasis of tranquility.

Chahal

The closest settlement near Las Conchas is Chahal, which is fairly unremarkable but nonetheless offers at least one hotel worthy of mention. **Hotel Villa Santa Elena** (Franja Transversal del Norte Km. 365, tel. 7983-2355, www.hotelvse. com, $20 d) offers basic, clean rooms with hot water, plastic furniture, and good beds housed in a neocolonial building built around a patio. Some of the rooms have air-conditioning. Cabins were recently added on the neighboring grounds. The restaurant here serves very good food.

Raxrujá

An alternative base for exploring the Candelaria caves and the nearby ruins of Cancuén is the small town of Raxrujá, a few kilometers east of the "Cruce del Pato" Junction. Among the basic accommodations found here are **Hotel Cancuén** (tel. 7983-0720, www.cuevaslosnacimientos.com), on the edge of town, with basic rooms for $10 d or more modern tiled-floor rooms with TV, air-conditioning, and private bath for $15 d. The **Restaurante Tu Casa** next door serves good meals and is well staffed.

Another dining option is found just outside of town. **El Bistro Francés** (tel. 5352-9276, noon-4 P.M. Sat.-Sun. and holidays, $7-12) is run by the same French owners as Candelaria Lodge. It's a good place for grilled meat dishes. Though they close at 4 P.M., you can have dinner here if you call ahead.

Minibuses leave every hour for Chisec with continuing service to Cobán until 4 P.M. Buses and minibuses head north to Sayaxché with similar frequency.

◖ CANCUÉN

The Mayan site of Cancuén (8 A.M.-5 P.M. daily, $8) lies north of Raxrujá, just across the border of the northern Petén department. It is treated in this section because it is actually more accessible from Alta Verapaz. Cancuén's rediscovery dates to the early 1900s, but it was only recently that archaeologists began piecing together its rich past and the full extent of its power, along with its corresponding significance in the place of Mayan history. Cancuén was largely overlooked by archaeologists for much of the 20th century because it lacked large temple pyramids and defensive structures like those found elsewhere in the Mayan world. It is thought that Cancuén existed as a mostly secular trading center, which gained much of its prosperity from its enviable position on the Río La Pasión at a strategic geographic transition zone between the southern highlands and the northern lowlands. Its importance as a trade center is substantiated by large amounts of pyrite (for making mirrors), jade, obsidian, and fine ceramics found here. It has been speculated that the absence of large temple pyramids may be a product of the site's proximity to the Candelaria caves, which certainly held spiritual significance for the Mayans living here in those times, as they still do today.

Adding to Cancuén's splendor is a paved plaza covering two square kilometers. It may have doubled as a marketplace. The largest known Mayan palace is among the incredible finds uncovered in recent years by a U.S.-Guatemalan team working under the direction of Vanderbilt University's Arthur Demarest. Built in A.D. 770 during the reign of Taj Chan Ahk, the three-story palace covers about 23,000 square meters and has 200 rooms built around 11 courtyards. The archaeologists working here have also recently uncovered the third and final marker from a royal ball court, which has been gradually excavated during the last century. The markers served as goalposts. The first of these markers was unearthed in 1915 and can be seen in Guatemala City's archaeology museum. The second marker was looted from the site in 2001 but recovered two years later thanks to unprecedented collaboration between Guatemalan undercover agents, local villagers, and archaeologists. The third marker is an elaborately carved stone altar uncovered from the stucco surface of the ball court.

A separate, 100-pound stone panel with hieroglyphics and carved images was also found at the ball court, the second such panel to be unearthed here. It depicts Taj Chan Ahk installing a subordinate ruler at the smaller state of Machaquilá. The panel is interesting in that

it confirms Taj Chan Ahk's status as a great Mayan king who was able to maintain power over a large area through politics and economic clout, rather than warfare, at a time when most Mayan city-states had begun their decline.

The peaceful prosperity would be short-lived, however, as recent finds reveal a wide-scale massacre of at least 31 nobles and several others at the hands of invading armies from Machaquilá and Ceibal sometime around A.D. 800. This marked the beginning of the end for Cancuén, and the city was abandoned shortly thereafter.

Excavations and restoration work at the site are ongoing, and it is certainly thrilling to walk around the site and see the work in progress. The jungle around the site is thick with vegetation and mosquitoes descend in droves. Bring plenty of bug spray and wear long pants. There is a recently opened visitors center with informative displays and a campground, as well as restrooms and showers.

Accommodations and Food
You can camp at La Unión for $3.50. Meals are available from local families with prior notice ($3.50-5.50). At the Cancuén visitors center, camping and tent rental for two costs $7, or you can camp in your own tent for $3. Meals are also available ($3-5). Book in advance.

Getting There
Pickups leave about every hour from Raxrujá to the village of La Unién, 16 kilometers to the north, where there is a visitors center. From there, boatmen take you on the 30-minute boat ride up the Río La Pasión ($40 for 1-12 people) to the site. You can also book a tour via one of the Cobán travel outfitters.

◀ CANDELARIA CAVES NATIONAL PARK
From Sebol, the dirt road branches west to Raxrujá, from where a paved road continues west to San Antonio Las Cuevas. The road

from Petén also connects to San Antonio Las Cuevas from the "Cruce del Pato" Junction. The main attraction along this corridor is a visit to the fantastic Candelaria caves, recently awarded national park status. The cave system, discovered in 1974 by Frenchman Daniel Dreux, is composed of seven separate caves interconnected by the Río Candelaria and spanning about 22 kilometers. The caves are 20-30 meters wide in places with ceilings typically 10-60 meters high.

Caves were sacred to the Mayans and it is thought that nearby cities such as Cancuén lacked the substantial temple pyramids found elsewhere in the Mayan world because of the proximity of the Candelaria caves, which were used as a center for worship. In Mayan lore, caves are thought to be entrances to the underworld, known as Xibalba. The Candelaria caves are one possible location for the mythical Xibalba; the Chiquibul caves running east-west from the northern Petén department into Belize are another.

In 2002, the Guatemalan government awarded management of the caves to local villagers, though Dreux continues to operate a lodge he built adjacent to one of the cave's entrances. The lodge is staffed by local villagers working for Dreux and there are at least two other options for visiting the caves operated by local tourism initiatives. Among the recreational highlights is the chance to explore the caves via underground rivers on an inner tube or inflatable raft.

Complejo Cultural y Ecoturístico Cuevas de Candelaria

The most convenient gateway to one of Central America's largest cave systems is via the Complejo Cultural y Ecoturístico Cuevas de Candelaria (tel. 4035-0566, www.cuevasdecandelaria.com), at Km. 316.5 of the paved road (RN-5), near San Antonio Las Cuevas. The complex is the brainchild of Daniel Dreux, who quickly set out to map

the extensive cave system shortly after discovering it. His growing concern over the long-term survival of this unique natural area led him to establish Tierra Maya, a conservation and sustainable development organization that aims to protect the forests surrounding the cave system while improving living conditions for local residents.

Entrance to the complex costs $3.50 (two-person minimum), including a guide and two-hour tour of the Cueva del Mico section of the caves, featuring large chambers that in places are 20-30 meters wide with ceilings 10-60 meters high. The impressive 200-meter-long Tzul Tacca chamber is a standout, with ethereal shafts of light shining from the ceiling onto the rocks below.

For more in-depth explorations, **Maya Expeditions** (tel. 2363-4955, www.mayaexpeditions.com) runs a fantastic three-day/two-night trip to the Candelaria caves ($398) from Guatemala City, allowing the opportunity to journey on inflatable rafts through rarely seen sections of this incredible cavern and its underground rivers.

The Complejo Cultural y Ecoturístico also includes the wonderful ◖ **Candelaria Lodge** (tel. 4035-0566, reservaciones@cuevasdecandelaria.com, $15-20 per person), which serves as the perfect base for exploring the caves and several other local attractions. The comfortable, stylishly decorated cabins (all with shared baths) are set amid the tropical forest. Delectable French and international dishes (including crêpes that are to die for) are served in the lodge's main dining room and your gracious host, Arnoldo, will cater to your every need. There are packages, including one night's accommodations and three meals for $50 per person per night. Otherwise, meals range from $5 for breakfast to $15 for lunch or dinner.

If arriving by car, you'll have to park your vehicle at a parking lot across the road from the entrance to the complex. From there, it's a 15-minute walk to the main entrance and

© AL ARGUETA

view from the lodge at Complejo Cultural y Ecoturístico Cuevas de Candelaria

another five minutes to the lodge. If staying at the lodge, bring a clean pair of flip-flops, as you'll be required to remove muddy shoes and leave them at the lodge's main door so as not to muddy the wooden walkways crisscrossing the property.

Candelaria Muq'b'il Ha'

Another alternative for visiting the Candelaria caves is via one of the local community tourism organizations at Candelaria Muq'b'il Ha', which you'll find farther west along the Raxrujá-Chisec road (RN-5) at Km. 315. You'll find a marked entrance indicating the turnoff for a two-kilometer dirt road to the parking lot. A 30-minute walk down a trail leads to the visitors center. From here you can take a guided tour of the Venado Seco cave (1.5 hours, $5.50), take a guided cave-tubing tour (1.5 hours, $7), or do both for $10. Food is available and you can stay at the rustic ecolodge **Peña del Tigre**

for $7 per person or camp for $3.50 per person. Overnight parking costs $5, $1.50 for the day.

Candelaria Camposanto

Yet another option is found at Km. 309 along the same road, where there are two dry caves and one river-tubing section available for exploration. The visitors center is right beside the highway. The caves are a 20-minute walk away. You can tour the Ventana de Seguridad and Cúpula de los Murciélagos caves for $5.50, go cave tubing for $7, or combine all three for $10. Camping costs $3 and there is meal service with prior arrangement ($3-5). Parking is $1.50.

CHISEC AND VICINITY

Chisec lies along the highway (RN-5) connecting Petén and Cobán about 26 kilometers southwest of Raxrujá. The town has grown in the past few years thanks to a ubiquitous infusion of land-hungry peasants eking out a living on parcels of land in the surrounding wilderness areas. Seeking to provide locals with more ecofriendly economic alternatives, development agencies have masterminded a fairly successful sustainable tourism project to ensure locals benefit from the use of the area's substantial natural and cultural attractions. The community ecotourism projects were developed with financial support from USAID and the help of Guatemala's Ministry of Culture and Sports, the Guatemala Tourist Commission (INGUAT), CONAP, the National Geographic Society, and Vanderbilt University, among others. Local guides can take you to several area attractions, including the Lagunas de Sepalau and Cuevas de B'omb'il Pek. You can find more information online at www.puertamundomaya.com.

Sights

About two kilometers north of town are the "painted caves" of **B'omb'il Pek** ($5.50-8, including equipment rental and guided tour). A community-run guide service (8 A.M.-3:30 P.M.

daily) can be found right beside the highway. You can pay your entrance fee here and grab a flashlight and helmet. Inner tubes are also available for rent ($3) for inner tubing on the cool waters of the **Río San Simón,** another fun nearby activity.

The trip to B'omb'il Pek begins with a 40-minute hike through forest and cornfields. A steep wooden staircase leads you down into the sinkhole. Inside the cave, there are ceramics, and the caves are still used for Mayan religious ceremonies. There is a second, much smaller chamber where there are some faded cave paintings of two monkeys and a jaguar. The community tourism organization offers the option to do the tour with rappelling into the cave for $8. Cobán-based **Aventuras Turísticas** (3a Calle 2-38 Zona 3, tel. 7951-4213/14, www.aventurasturisticas.com) also does rappelling into the sinkhole as well as visits to the Sepalau Lagoons.

The **Lagunas de Sepalau** ($5.50) is a

sublime assortment of four turquoise, jungle-shrouded lagoons found nine kilometers east of town. The gateway to these fantastic swimming holes is the small Q'eqchi' village of Sepalau Cataltzul, where another community-run tourism initiative will lead you to the lagoons, a further one kilometer away. The first lagoon you'll find is **Laguna Paraíso,** surrounded by thick jungle. Unfortunately, you can't swim here, as it serves as the source of drinking water for nearby communities. There are, however, boats for rent if you want to paddle across its peaceful waters. The next lagoon is right next to it and is smaller, but swimming is permitted. Walking through a jungle path for another kilometer will bring you to the third and fourth lagoons, which are the most spectacular, framed by a background of high limestone cliffs. Swimming is not allowed in the third and fourth lagoons.

At the park entrance, there are showers and restrooms. Camping and tent rental for two costs $7 or you can camp in your own tent for $3. Parking is $1.50. Meals are also available from the local community ($3-5) with prior notice.

Accommodations and Food

Among Chisec's basic accommodations you'll find **Hotel La Estancia de la Virgen** (tel. 7979-7748, $12 d), along the road heading north out of town. Clean, basic rooms with air-conditioning and private bathrooms are spread out over two floors. There's a good eatery and a small swimming pool. The other option is the no-frills **Hotel Nopales** ($10 d), on the east end of the plaza. It's clean. One block north of the plaza is the pleasant **Restaurante Mi Casita.** Decent food (and Internet access) can be found in the center of town at **La Huella Café Internet,** serving burgers, Guatemalan favorites, cakes, and coffee. Next to the *municipalidad* (town hall) is **Cafetería El Manantial,** which is a good bet for breakfast. On the southern end of town as you head toward Cobán is the pricier **Restaurant Bombil Pek.**

© AL ARGUETA

Lagunas de Sepalau

Services

There is a Banrural on the plaza where you can exchange currency or cash travelers checks. On the north end of the plaza, Banco Agrícola Mercantil has an ATM.

Getting There

Minibuses make the 1.5-hour trip to Cobán every half hour. Heading north, there are hourly minibuses to Candelaria and Raxrujá.

(Parque Ecológico Hun Nal Ye

This eco-amusement park and museum lies along a dirt road turn-off from Km. 259.5 along the road from Chisec to Cobán (RD-09). Hun Nal Ye (tel. 7951-5921, www.parquehunnalye. com, Wed.-Sun. 8 A.M.-6 P.M., $10 adults, $4 children) is a private reserve sprawling across 135 hectares of tropical rainforest with an abundance of plant and animal life and bisected by emerald green rivers and lagoons. Activities include bird-watching (over 200 species of birds have been recorded), fishing, tubing, kayaking, snorkeling, and scuba diving. There's a cave, an eight-meter (26-foot) waterfall, a limestone sinkhole *(cenote)*, observation towers, a canopy zipline, and trails for horseback riding, all-terrain vehicles, and mountain bikes. Facilities include a restaurant, archaeology museum, picnic areas, changing rooms, and a swimming pool. You can stay at the comfortable on-site accommodations consisting of five neocolonial tile-roofed cabins ($25 d) with private baths. A family-sized cabana sleeping eight goes for $135 a night. You can camp here for $3.50.

Lest Hun Nal Ye strike you as just another theme park, you should know that it lays claim to the very important discovery of an ancient Mayan box engraved with exquisite hieroglyphs and dating to Early Classic times. It was discovered in 2005 by landowner Leonidas Javier and is thought to have once harbored a Maya codex, or book. The box made headlines when it was stolen by looters in 2006 and returned anonymously about a month after it was reported missing from the cave. The item had been purchased on the black market by a collector who, in an apparent attack of conscience, shipped the item to the Ministry of Culture in Guatemala City after realizing the priceless value of his purchase from widespread publicity of the heist. A replica of the box is housed in the park's museum; the original is now in Guatemala City's Museo Nacional de Arqueología in Zona 13.

To get to the park, take the dirt road turnoff heading east from RD-09 at Km. 259.5. From there, it's about six kilometers to the village of Samanzana, where you'll head south for one kilometer and then continue east another five kilometers to San Vicente Chicatal. From there, follow the signs another 500 meters to the park entrance. If you don't have a car, there are buses and pick-up trucks heading from the Cobán-Chisec road to San Vicente Chicatal.

PLAYA GRANDE (CANTABAL)

This remote outpost in the northwest corner of Alta Verapaz was once the scene of intense fighting during the civil war, with regular military operations in the neighboring Ixcán jungles, where URNG rebels hid out. All that is now in the past, opening some wonderful attractions that were once off-limits. Heading northwest from Chisec, it's a 62-mile journey down a rough dirt road to the town of Playa Grande, also known as Cantabal or Ixcán. There is little to see or do here, but nearby is a remarkable natural attraction.

(Laguna Lachuá National Park

This almost perfectly circular turquoise lagoon is its own ecological island, like a square patch of forest floating on a surrounding sea of deforestation. To see it from the air is to get a crash course in tropical forest management and the significance of ecological islands. The razor-sharp park boundaries stand out from the quiltlike fields all around this giant mirror in the middle of nowhere. You'll probably arrive by land, but this description at least gives you some appreciation for the natural beauty of this park and the need to protect it from those who might further encroach upon its boundaries. Already, logging operations have unscrupulously harvested some of the forest's giant mahoganies with reckless disregard for what is, on paper at least, a national park. But I digress.

The 14,500-hectare Laguna Lachuá National Park (tel. 4084-1706, $6.50 admission) is still one of the most beautiful places on earth, despite its challenges. Here you can enjoy the refreshing waters and the dense forest all around in an atmosphere of utter tranquility. From the banks of the lagoon, you can see the forested peak of La Sultana. There are more than 300 species of birds found here, including mealy parrots and keel-billed toucans. Jaguars still roam the park and you can sometimes see their footprints. The lagoon's Caribbean-like waters contain calcium deposits and high levels of sulphur, indicating the probable presence of petroleum beneath its waters. The lake lies partially below sea level, at an altitude of 173 meters above sea level but also 222 meters deep. One of the more exciting theories concerning the lake's formation contends the lakebed is an old meteor crater, with the rest of the meteor that created it having fallen near Cobán in an area known as the Nim Tak'a depression.

There's a visitors center where you'll find cooking facilities, a campground, a shelter with bunk beds ($4 p/p), showers, hiking trails, and canoes for rent ($1). You can string a hammock up for $0.75.

The park's main entrance is a few kilometers before Playa Grande as you come along the road from the east. From there it's a four-kilometer

© AL ARGUETA

Laguna Lachuá

walk to the lakeside through some very nice forest trails.

Río Ikbolay

This stunning azure river flows through the jungle near Laguna Lachuá. Situated on the banks of this river in the middle of a 600-square-kilometer forest reserve is the community of Rokj'á Pomtilá (tel. 5381-1970 or 4621-6508). From this fantastic riverside setting, you can enjoy guided hikes into the surrounding rainforest to view abundant plant and animal life as well as explore lagoons, caves, and waterfalls. **Proyecto Eco-Quetzal** (2a Calle 14-36 Zona 1, tel. 7952-1047, bidaspeq@hotmail.com, www.ecoquetzal.org) can arrange homestays with local villagers. A two-night stay at Rokj'á Pomtilá costs $45 per person, not including transportation.

PETÉN

Guatemala's northernmost department has always conjured images of a remote wilderness characterized by dense forests and lost Mayan cities inhabited only by loggers and chicle harvesters. Today, that image is only partly true, as much of the Ohio-sized Petén has been cleared by settlers for subsistence agriculture and cattle ranching. In an attempt to save the remaining forest and the still unexcavated Mayan ruins they harbor, roughly a third of Petén has been protected since 1990 in the form of several national parks collectively known as the Maya Biosphere Reserve. It is one of the largest remaining continuous tracts of tropical forest in Central America. Recreational opportunities inside and outside the reserve are boundless and the region is slowly becoming a magnet for adventure and ecotourism, thanks in large part to the filming of *Survivor Guatemala* here in 2005.

Among the attractions are the enigmatic Mayan ruins of Tikal, one of the largest cities ever populated by the Mayans and certainly a must-see for any visitor to the area. Not only are the restored ruins impressive, to say the least, but the abundant wildlife found in the lush rainforests protected within the adjacent national park make this a prime spot for birders and wildlife enthusiasts. Along the paved road to Tikal, you'll pass the spectacular Lake Petén Itzá, one of Guatemala's largest, surrounded by jungles and characterized by its luminescent turquoise-blue waters. The village of El Remate

© AL ARGUETA

HIGHLIGHTS

LOOK FOR ◖ TO FIND RECOMMENDED SIGHTS, ACTIVITIES, DINING, AND LODGING.

◖ **Parque Natural Ixpanpajul:** The hanging bridges and nature trail here provide a toucan's-eye view of the Petén forests. There are other fun activities in this private nature reserve just minutes from Flores (page 372).

◖ **El Remate:** Once a sleepy lakeside fishing village, El Remate's strategic location along the road to Tikal has caused it to grow up and become a destination in its own right. It offers a convenient alternative to staying in Tikal's limited hotel offerings while providing access to beautiful Lake Petén Itzá and a variety of recreational opportunities such as kayaking, swimming, bird-watching, and horseback riding (page 376).

◖ **The Ruins of Tikal:** No trip to Petén, or Guatemala for that matter, would be complete without a visit to the enigmatic ruins of one of the largest cities ever built and inhabited by the Mayans (page 389).

◖ **Yaxhá:** Featured in *Survivor Guatemala*, the ruins of Yaxhá enjoy a spectacular location beside the site's namesake lagoon and provide commanding views of the surrounding forests (page 402).

◖ **El Mirador:** Deep in the northern recesses of the Maya Biosphere Reserve, the ruins of El Mirador offer the opportunity for a world-class adventure encompassing an arduous two-day journey through swampy forests. Marvel at the highest known Mayan structure with a base the size of three football fields (page 404).

◖ **Las Guacamayas Biological Research Station:** Observe nesting scarlet macaws from observation platforms or forest trails with the knowledge that the money you spend is going directly toward giving them a fighting chance at survival (page 411).

has sprung up along the highway and is quickly becoming a destination unto itself with a number of very comfortable accommodations and plenty of activities for the outdoor enthusiast. Many travelers now spend an extra day here after exploring the ruins.

Southeast of Tikal, the remote ruins of Yaxhá, overlooking the site's namesake lagoon, remain a remote jungle outpost despite their prime-time TV fame and you can still have the place all to yourself on a typical afternoon. But that probably won't last too much longer.

Petén is without a doubt the cradle of Mayan civilization, as it lays claim to some of the oldest known Mayan sites along with the earliest evidence of the writing and royal dynastic rule characterizing the civilization that flourished here. At the remote site of El Mirador, on the northern fringes of Petén near the Mexican border, you can gaze in awe at the massive temple pyramids of El Tigre and La Danta, which were erected centuries earlier than most other well-known Mayan sites but nonetheless show much the same level of sophistication. All of these sites are harbored within the Maya Biosphere Reserve and its seemingly interminable expanses of mostly undisturbed tropical forests. Hikers will appreciate the numerous opportunities for trekking to remote Mayan ruins along jungle paths, creating the potential for adventures not unlike those of the early explorers.

HISTORY

During colonial times, Petén remained a backwater, the only Spanish settlement being the island city of Flores, a pleasant town of pastel-colored houses that remains the region's main tourist services hub. In 1840, Guatemalan President Rafael Carrera dispatched a small platoon of soldiers to officially claim the Petén region as part of the country. Mexico decided the territory was not worth the trouble of contesting. The region has been a backwater ever since, officially the poorest of Guatemala's departments, which is especially evident to travelers coming in from Belize along an unpaved highway lined with cattle ranches and simple thatched-roof huts.

Petén harbors 550,000 of Guatemala's inhabitants, making it the country's most sparsely populated region, though its rate of population increase from immigration is the highest in the country. Much of this unprecedented growth is the product of an ill-conceived 1960s government program to colonize Petén, meant as a safety valve to relieve pressures for land reform. A battle is being waged to save this valuable natural and cultural heritage, and visitors to Guatemala's northern parks can derive some satisfaction from the knowledge that their visit lends importance, justification, and the financial means for the continued preservation of what remains.

PLANNING YOUR TIME

Petén is one of Guatemala's most fascinating regions, particularly for lovers of archaeology and outdoor activities. The parks encompassing the **Maya Biosphere Reserve** could keep you busy for weeks, in addition to the requisite visit to **Tikal National Park.** Some people make day trips to Tikal, coming across the border from Belize or flying in from Guatemala City. This will certainly serve only to whet your appetite for more Petén explorations. Visitors on one of these short stints should at least consider spending the night at Tikal or nearby **Lake Petén Itzá.** Another increasingly popular destination is the archaeological site of **Yaxhá,** site of *Survivor Guatemala*. There is a comfortable jungle lodge right on the shores of Yaxhá Lagoon where you can spend the night, a good idea if you want to take in all that this site has to offer, given its remote location.

El Mirador, deep in the jungle near the Mexican border, involves an arduous journey of two days from the nearest village but is well worth it for the opportunity to visit one of the largest and earliest Mayan cities in existence. The tallest, and some of the largest, manufactured pre-Columbian structures can also be found here in the form of the massive La Danta and El Tigre pyramids, with bases the size of three football fields. A typical round-trip itinerary to El Mirador takes 5-7 days, depending on how long you want to stay at the ruins and if you want to stop at other nearby sites on the way back.

The most natural starting point and hub for any in-depth Petén explorations is the island city of **Flores,** with its pretty pastel-colored houses and quiet streets; it's unlike any other town in Guatemala. Its sister city of Santa Elena, on the mainland shores of Lake Petén Itzá, is an equally logical choice for a base, though it's not nearly as attractive. Many conservation organizations and adventure travel outfitters are based in Flores/Santa Elena. Air and ground service connects Flores/Santa Elena to most of Petén, other parts of Guatemala, and Belize.

In southern Petén, the **Petexbatún** region harbors many fascinating archaeological sites set alongside the Petexbatún Lagoon. If you have an extra few days after checking out Tikal, Yaxhá, and Lake Petén Itzá, and if you're a big fan of Mayan ruins, by all means continue south and check out the Petexbatún region. Farther east, the area surrounding the town of **Poptún,** along the road connecting Petén and Izabal, lies at a comfortably higher elevation and is an excellent destination for cave tubing, spelunking, hiking, and hanging out at area lodges. A requisite stop along the Petén-Izabal Highway is **Finca Ixobel,** the most popular of the Poptún lodges, and with good reason. If you're heading north into Petén from Izabal, you'll want to spend a night or two in Poptún, assuming you have enough time to visit Tikal.

Some of Petén's attractions, Tikal National Park for example, can easily be explored on your own. The remote location and rugged topography characterizing the great majority of Petén's parks and ruins, however, means you will probably find yourself needing the services of an experienced guide sooner or later. Another issue to consider is that hiring a guide provides locals with tangible evidence that the local environment and the Petén forests are worth more standing than cut down for cattle ranching or timber. It also provides a much-needed source of income and broadens cultural horizons. There are several outfitters, based mainly in the city of Flores, offering excellent guided trips to some of Petén's more exotic offerings and all of these work with local communities to ensure the sustainability of their tourism practices. While there is certainly a glut of tour companies in and around Flores, not all of them are reliable, and many of their owners are not in the least socially or environmentally conscious. Try to stick to one of the recommended outfitters.

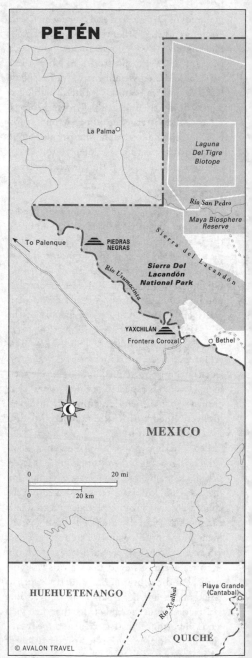

PETÉN

La Palma

Laguna Del Tigre Biotope

Río San Pedro

Maya Biosphere Reserve

To Palenque

PIEDRAS NEGRAS

Sierra del Lacandón

Río Usumacinta

Sierra Del Lacandón National Park

YAXCHILÁN

Frontera Corozal   Bethel

MEXICO

0   20 mi
0   20 km

HUEHUETENANGO

Río Xalbal

Playa Grande (Cantabal)

QUICHÉ

© AVALON TRAVEL

Poptún and Vicinity

The small town of Poptún is unremarkable in and of itself, but there are a number of good recreational opportunities in the vicinity. Travelers coming from Guatemala City often break up their journey with a stay in Poptún's landmark Finca Ixobel. In the vicinity of Poptún are numerous caves, jungle rivers, and forests easily explored with help from area lodges.

POPTÚN

Halfway between Río Dulce and Flores, Poptún has always been a favorite stopping point, particularly before the road to Flores was paved and travelers needed to split up the grueling journey on a rutted dirt road. Nestled in the foothills of the Maya Mountains, which extend into neighboring Belize, the area is unlike the rest of Petén in that it is cooler by virtue of its altitude at more than 600 meters (2,000 feet) and features a largely pine-forested, karst landscape. There are many relatively unexplored Mayan sites here as well as some small expanses of tropical forest, which have survived the expansion of the agricultural frontier to which most of southern Petén has succumbed. A military base once operated in this area, but it has been closed down since the 1996 peace accords, as elsewhere in Guatemala.

Recreation

Poptún's wonderful setting at a comfortably higher altitude and its pine-studded, karst landscape make exploring this part of Guatemala a delight. You can choose from, among others, treks to remote Mayan sites, jungle hikes, caving, or tubing down lazy stretches of jungle river. All of these activities can be arranged at area lodges, particularly Finca Ixobel (on the road from Río Dulce, tel. 5892-3188, www.fincaixobel.com), which pioneered ecotourism in this neck of the woods and is always interested in new offerings. You can choose from a number of **caves,** which can take two hours, a half day, or a full day of exploring. The full-day trip takes you to **Cueva del Río** ($10), an underground river with rapids and waterfalls where you can swim and leap into the river in total darkness. There are also trips twice a day to **Ixobel Cave** ($5), with its rim stone walls, stalactites, and stalagmites a 45-minute walk from the farm. Just 25 minutes' walk from Finca Ixobel, **Echoing Cave** ($5) offers a fun adventure exploring the cave's hidden chambers and caverns, and it is a good option if you have only two hours' time.

Horseback riding is also available at the Finca Ixobel with trips lasting as little as two hours or as much as two days ($53). A full day of horseback riding costs $23.

Finca Ixobel also runs a number of excellent multiday jungle adventures lasting a minimum of three days and costing $30 per person per day, with a two-person minimum. The treks take you to remote Mayan sites such as **Ixcún,** a replica of the caves of **Naj Tunich,** and waterfalls on the **Río Mopán.** All trips are on horseback.

Inner tubing on the **Machaquilá River** from Finca Ixobel ($20, including lunch and transportation) is possible in June and July, when the water is high enough but before the summer rains are in full swing.

Villa de los Castellanos (tel. 7927-7541), another local lodge, is set right beside the river and also offers inner tubing. Trips to the remote ruins and forest reserve of **Machaquilá** are also available from here, as well as to the **Chiquibul Forest Reserve,** farther north.

Accommodations and Food

There is at least one good place to stay in Poptún proper, though you are probably better off staying at one of the local, highly recommended

NAJ TUNICH

The Naj Tunich caves have long been a local attraction and were even featured in the August 1981 issue of *National Geographic*. The caves, which are more than one kilometer long, are famous for their intricate murals and hieroglyphic text. Naj Tunich appears to have been one of the most highly revered sites in the Mayan world, and it is known that several of the glyphs were painted by scribes from such faraway cities as Calakmul, in present-day Mexico.

The caves were defaced some years ago and the site was closed to visitors. A replica of the caves showcasing some of the best of the Naj Tunich cave paintings is located just 400 meters from the original caves. Check with the staff at Finca Ixobel (tel. 5892-3188, www.fincaixobel.com) for details.

jungle lodges. Should you get stuck in town, **Hotel Posada de los Castellanos** (tel. 7927-7222, corner of 4a Calle and 7a Avenida, $10 d) is your best bet with basic, clean rooms with fan and private hot-water bath. For eating, **La Fonda Ixobel** has tasty baked goods and snacks.

Services
Banrural (5a Calle, 8:30 A.M.-5 P.M. Mon.-Fri., 9 A.M.-1 P.M. Sat.) has a MasterCard ATM and changes U.S. dollars and American Express travelers checks.

Getting There
The Poptún area is accessible via several buses and minivans leaving Flores daily at half-hour intervals during daylight hours. **Línea Dorada** (tel. 7926-1788, www.tikalmayanworld.com, $15-30 one-way) has buses from Guatemala City (10 A.M. and 9 P.M. daily), stopping in Río Dulce and Poptún along the way. Buses arrive and depart on Playa Sur in Flores.

Buses heading north from Guatemala City

via Río Dulce also come this way and stop at Finca Ixobel, Poptún, and Machaquilá.

NEAR POPTÚN
Finca Ixobel
Just south of Poptún, on the road from Río Dulce, ◖**Finca Ixobel** (tel. 5892-3188, www.fincaixobel.com) has long drawn travelers coming overland to Petén for its wonderful accommodations and excellent food at moderate prices in an attractive jungle setting. Its wide-ranging activities allow guests the chance to explore myriad attractions nestled in the surrounding cool pine forests and rolling green hills. There are accommodations to suit every taste and budget, including hammocks ($3), clean, comfortable dorms for $4 per person, double rooms with shared bath for $13, and double rooms with private bath for $26. There are more luxurious bungalows and a suite for $30 and $36 (d). The latest addition to Finca Ixobel's offerings is a series of tree houses set amid spacious grounds. Some have electricity; others are candlelit. Prices range from $11 (d) with candlelight to $17 (d) with electricity. Only one of the so-called tree houses is actually in a tree, but all are attractive, quite comfortable, and set above the ground. A deluxe tree house with its own bath and electricity is popular with honeymooners and goes for $23 (d).

The restaurant here serves delicious, inexpensive meals, largely using ingredients grown in the finca's vegetable garden. Breakfast and lunch are à la carte, while dinner is served buffet style ($4-8). Breakfast items include homemade yogurt and granola, pancakes, and eggs, with plenty of vegetarian options for lunch and dinner. There is also a bar set beside a swimming pond where you can chill out in a hammock or play a game of "Twister" with your new friends and fellow travelers.

Any bus traveling the Río Dulce-Flores Highway will drop you off at the turnoff to Finca Ixobel. From there, it's just a short

PETÉN

sculpture at Museo Regional del Sureste de Petén

15-minute walk to the lodge. You can arrange minibus transport to Flores and book bus tickets to Guatemala City from Finca Ixobel. Minibuses go by every half hour 8 A.M.-5 P.M. and cost $5.50 one-way. Transport to Guatemala City on Linea Dorada bus lines ranges $12.50-20 one-way. If you are arriving at Finca Ixobel after nightfall, your best bet is to go to La Fonda Ixobel in Poptún town and get a cab from there to the farm.

Villa de los Castellanos

In the town of Machaquilá, seven kilometers north of Poptún, Villa de los Castellanos (Aldea Machaquilá, tel. 7927-7541, $25-40 d) is just off the road in a peaceful riverside setting overlooking the Río Machaquilá and set on 12 acres of land encompassing forest and a medicinal plant garden. Its 14 comfortable cabanas all have private baths. There is also a good restaurant. The friendly Guatemalan

owners, who live on-site, organize trips to local caves, ruins, and forest preserves. One of the owners is a beekeeper and uses traditional techniques involving hollowed-out logs to care for the surprisingly docile honeybees. There's also a small display of ancient Mayan artifacts (registered with the Institute of Anthropology and History) found while living on the property.

Cocay Camping

Back toward Poptún is Cocay Camping (tel. 7927-7024, $5 per person), set in splendid isolation on the banks of the Río Machaquilá just past the town proper. There are camping spaces, very basic cabins, and a café serving vegetarian fare.

DOLORES

At first glance, Dolores, north of Poptún, appears to be just another roadside town in rural Petén. But closer inspection reveals it harbors a decent archaeology museum and several lesser-known Maya sites in its vicinity. Located on a hill in the heart of town, **Museo Regional del Sureste de Petén** (museodolores@mcd.gob. gt, 8 A.M.-5 P.M. daily, $4) holds an impressive collection of artifacts and stone sculptures excavated from sites in the southeastern portion of the Petén lowlands. The displays are well presented and include descriptions in Spanish and English. Most of the items on display are ceramic pottery. There are wonderful views of the town and its jungle surroundings from the museum's courtyard.

Ixcun and Ixtonton

Ixcun is a large Maya site showing signs of occupation from Preclassic times on through the Postclassic period. It is believed to have been the most important of four cities located in the upper Mopan valley and subservient to the larger kingdom of Caracol, lying 22 miles northeast in present-day Belize. Ixcun is located just 4 miles north of Dolores via a rough dirt road.

The site itself occupies about 16 square kilometers and includes a ball court, palaces, stepped pyramids, and several stelae. Most of the site remains unexcavated, consisting of overgrown temple mounds, and was most recently excavated by the *Altas Arqueologico de Guatemala,* which runs the *Museo Regional.* It enjoys a peaceful park-like setting, with a splendid jungle location. The Mopan river flows just two-and-a-half miles from here. There are ranger facilities and a covered pavilion for camping.

Ixtonton is a smaller Maya site that once rivaled Ixcun located 2 kilometers east of Dolores. Although it wasn't officially discovered until 1985, it had already been looted of artifacts prior to that. Only two of its stelae survived and are on display in the *Museo Regional.*

Sayaxché and Vicinity

Sayaxché is the departure point to a number of nearby Mayan ruins, though it also has a reputation as fast becoming a narco hideaway. The remote stretches of river still harbor some semblance of wildlife, though ongoing deforestation in these parts makes it feel somewhat less wild than other, better-preserved parts of Petén department.

impressive and the jungle scenery in these parts alluring, you may want to inquire with travel agencies in Flores before heading out here. Robberies were reported for some time at Ceibal, though locals say the group responsible was caught long ago, and there are no recent robberies to report. If you have plenty of time in Petén, it's certainly worth exploring.

SAYAXCHÉ

Sayaxché, on the southern shore of Río La Pasión, is the natural gateway for trips to the Mayan sites of **Ceibal** and the archaeological wonders hidden amid the lagoons and forests of the **Petexbatún Wildlife Refuge.** It is a rough-and-tumble kind of town, though security forces are reported to have gotten at least a partial hold on the situation. Still, you may want to limit your time here to that required to cross the Río La Pasión on your way south to the Verapaces or to organize a trip to one of the nearby attractions. In addition to serving as an important waterway for trade in Mayan times, the river and surrounding town nowadays serve as a transshipment point for the local cocaine cartels said to operate in this region for some time now. Although they don't tend to get involved with tourists, it certainly adds to the remote lawless frontier atmosphere that seems to permeate this town.

While the Petexbatún region's sites are

Accommodations and Food

On the north bank of the river, before crossing on the ferry when coming from Flores, is **Café del Río** (tel. 6620-1742, all meals daily). With sweeping views from its perch above the river, it is a great choice for its location away from the considerably busier atmosphere on the other side. Should you need to stay here, your best bet is **Hotel Guayacán** (tel. 7928-6111, hotelguayacan1@hotmail.com), on the southern bank of the river. It has decent rooms with wooden beds and tiled floors going for $20 (d) with fan on the first floor or $25 (d) with air-conditioning on the second floor. One block up the street and three blocks to the right is **Hotel Petexbatún** (tel. 7928-6166), where rooms with fan and TV cost $10, or $15 with private bath. On the second street to the left as you come from the docks, **El Botanero** features a varied menu including shrimp, fish, chicken, and beef in addition to cocktails and has a pleasant atmosphere with decent music.

PETÉN

Getting There

The paved, 62-kilometer road from Flores to Sayaxché continues south all the way to Cobán. Minibuses from Flores leave every half hour between 5 A.M. and 6 P.M., with three daily Pinita buses leaving Flores at 11 A.M., 2 P.M., and 2:30 P.M.

A ferry shuttles passengers and vehicles across the river. A number of boatmen are on hand for trips down the river to Ceibal or up the Arroyo Petexbatún to the other sites. Recommended is **Lanchas Don Pedro** (tel. 7928-6109), on the riverbank, run by the amiable Pedro Méndez. Don Julián Mariona, owner of Posada Caribe, can also help you with boat trips.

If you are going south, there are two daily minibuses to Cobán (3.5 hours) via Chisec at 10 A.M. and 3:30 P.M. You can also catch one of several minibuses to Raxrujá, leaving about every 90 minutes until 4 P.M. Several buses leave from there for Cobán and other Alta Verapaz destinations.

CEIBAL NATURAL MONUMENT

The Mayan site of Ceibal blossomed in the twilight years of the Classic period after being infused with new life from the invading Putún Mayans' merchant warrior culture from Mexico's Tabasco region. It grew quickly between A.D. 830 and 910, harboring an estimated 10,000 inhabitants at its peak.

There are four main clusters of structures connected via causeways and the ruins here have a distinctly non-Mayan feel to them. Round platforms dot the site and several of the inscribed monuments feature unusual items such as waist-length hair, speech scrolls, and straight noses. There are 57 stelae here, many of them huge and in fairly good condition. Several of these are in the **Central Plaza,** along with its unrestored temples, and in the neighboring **South Plaza.** Another of the site's curiosities is **Structure 79,** a large round stone platform set in a forest clearing used for religious ceremonies and maybe even serving as a platform for astronomical observation.

The protected forest around Ceibal is particularly striking, as it is home to several of the large ceiba trees giving the area its name. It is among the few stands of well-preserved forest remaining in this area.

Getting There

The site is accessible both from land and by river. **Boat trips** from Sayaxché can be arranged by negotiating with the local *lancheros.* A round-trip boat ride to the ruins with a two-hour wait should cost about $50. The hour-long ride from Sayaxché is a pleasant journey down the Río La Pasión. A short walk up a hill from the river brings you to the site.

Ceibal is only 17 kilometers by road from Sayaxchá and any transport heading south out of town can drop you off at the turnoff for the ruins. From there it's an eight-kilometer walk to the site, but you may get lucky and hitch a ride from someone heading that way. Or you can

the ruins of Ceibal

© AL ARGUETA

Take a boat on the Río La Pasión to Ceibal.

book a taxi ride from Sayaxché. Pickup trucks carrying several people might be making the run on any given day and you can inquire at one of the local recommended restaurants or hotels about this possibility.

Several of the Flores tour operators offer Ceibal on their list of itineraries. **Explore** (4a Calle and 7a Avenida Zona 1 in Santa Elena, tel. 7926-2375, www.exploreguate.com) is a safe bet.

PETEXBATÚN WILDLIFE REFUGE

This protected area is set beside the placid waters of Petexbatún Lagoon and harbors the remains of several small Mayan cities along with some nice stretches of forest. Wildlife is abundant and includes several species of fish, freshwater turtles, howler monkeys, crocodiles, and several kinds of birds, including egrets, kingfishers, and herons.

History

The history of this region is fascinating, as it portrays violent struggles between neighboring states concurrent with the widespread abandonment of Petén's Classic Mayan sites, giving us a glimpse into the local state of affairs in various Mayan city-states before the Classic Mayan collapse. The area's largest site, Dos Pilas, was founded sometime around A.D. 640 by a renegade prince from Tikal who fled after Tikal's defeat by Calakmul. Later Dos Pilas defeated Tikal in two wars culminating in the capture of Tikal's ruler Shield Skull in A.D. 679. The event was duly recorded in the stelae at Dos Pilas and launched a reconstruction of the site's plaza.

Subsequent rulers would carry out building programs, including the construction of three hieroglyphic staircases, and wage wars of conquest. Ceibal was defeated in A.D. 735 and several lords from other Mayan cities were captured. Dos Pilas eventually came to dominate most of the lands between the Chixoy and Pasión Rivers.

The same Putún Mayans who came to dominate Ceibal eventually made their way over to Dos Pilas, and in A.D. 761, allied with the vassal state of Tamarindito, they captured and killed the site's fourth ruler. The remaining nobility fled to Aguateca, naturally fortified on a bluff, which had already begun functioning as a second capital. Some of the peasantry stayed behind and continued to farm the area around Dos Pilas, attempting to fortify it against their enemies, but it succumbed to the continuing onslaught of these invaders from the north and was completely abandoned by the 9th century.

Aguateca would suffer a similar fate and was abandoned sometime around A.D. 790, after three defensive moats were built along Petexbatún Lagoon across Punta de Chimino in a vain attempt to keep the invaders at bay.

Aguateca Cultural Monument

This cultural monument protects the site of Aguateca, situated on the banks of the Petexbatún Lagoon, as well as the wonderfully isolated peninsula of **Punta de Chimino.**

© AL ARGUETA

PETÉN

Aguateca sits at the southern edge of the lake on a high outcrop. The site is being excavated and restored after its rediscovery in 1957. A dramatic natural chasm splits the site in two and features exuberant vegetation. Two lookout points with wonderful lake views contribute to the site's sublime atmosphere. The two main groups of ruins being restored include the **Palace Group** and the **Main Plaza,** connected to one another by a causeway. You'll find some wonderful replicas beside the original, fallen over stelae in the Main Plaza.

The rangers here will let you camp for free. It's always a good idea to bring in some extra food as a token of your appreciation. They can also provide walking sticks for the potentially hazardous, slippery trails found throughout the site. **Explore** (4a Calle and 7a Avenida Zona 1 in Santa Elena, tel. 7926-2375, www.exploreguate.com), **Martsam** (Calle 30 de Junio, tel. 7926-0346, www.martsam.com), and **Tikal Connection** (Calle 15 de Septiembre, tel. 7924-8664, www.tikalcnx.com) all offer trips to Aguateca and you can camp here with them upon request. **Posada Caribe** (tel. 5304-1745, www.posadacaribe.com) and **Chiminos Island Lodge** (tel. 2335-3506 or 5750-8628, www.chiminosisland.com) also offer guided trips.

Farther north about four kilometers is **Punta de Chimino,** the peninsula that served as the last stand for the local Mayan population in its attempt to repel its northern invaders. A citadel complete with ramparts and trenches once crossed the peninsula's narrow neck. You won't see any of this in evidence today, but the vegetation and lakeside setting make this a very special place, as Spanish moss graces large trees in a jungle unlike any in Petén. Today, it is the site of the highly recommended Chiminos Island Lodge.

Dos Pilas Cultural Monument

In addition to the site of Dos Pilas, you'll find the smaller neighboring sites of **Tamarindito** and **Arroyo de Piedra** within the confines of this protected area. Though the site's well-documented history is almost epic in proportion, its remains are much less astounding, mostly because of the circumstances under which its reign came to an end. Still, there are some well-carved stelae and some rare hieroglyphic staircases surrounding the main plaza. A palace and a temple can also be seen here, with a tomb having been discovered underneath the latter. The jungle vegetation here is also well preserved.

Dos Pilas is accessible by boat from Sayaxché via the Arroyo Petexbatún. A trailhead lies just before the Posada Caribe at a place known as **Paso Caribe,** from where it's a three-hour hike down the 12-kilometer trail to the site. You can do the trip for about $26 per person per day including horses and mule skinner. Contact the **Posada Caribe** (tel. 5304-1745, www.posadacaribe.com) to arrange this option. Along the way, you'll pass the smaller sites of **Arroyo de Piedra,** with a plaza and two stelae, and Tamarindito, the site of another hieroglyphic stairway. Camping is permitted at Dos Pilas and is free. There is also a trail from here to Aguateca, which is about 12 kilometers away.

Thanks to the Guatemalan government's efforts to make remote Mayan sites more accessible, a road also leads to the vicinity of Dos Pilas. Heading south from Sayaxché, the road is paved for the first 34 kilometers to the small community of Las Pozas. From there it's a 21-kilometer dirt road west to El Nacimiento and a further three-kilometer foot trail to Dos Pilas to round out the journey.

Accommodations and Food

All of the area's accommodations are in the vicinity of the Petexbatún Lagoon. Family-owned and operated by the very helpful and friendly Julián Mariona, **Posada Caribe** (tel. 5304-1745, www.posadacaribe.com, $60 d) is the first place you'll come across as you navigate the river network leading from Sayaxché to Petexbatún Lagoon. Comfortable thatched-roof cabanas with private bath are set among tropical landscaping at the river's edge. There are packages for $45 per person including one night's stay and three meals, but you must arrange your own transportation. Packages including transfers from Sayaxché start at $150 and include a guide and one night at the lodge with meals. Whether or not you stay at the lodge, Don Julián can help you with planning and logistics in the Petexbatún area, which he knows quite well. Farther toward the Petexbatún Lagoon, the next place you'll come across is **Petexbatún Lodge** (tel. 7926-0501 or 5806-5860), where the rooms in stucco and wood cottages are slightly nicer and include ceiling fans, mosquito netting, and large private bathrooms with semioutdoor showers. Rates are $44 (d) in cabins or $12 per person

in shared-bath dormitory. Breakfast in an attractive open-air dining room costs $5 and lunch/dinner are $12. The Petexbatún area's finest accommodations are at the gorgeous **❰ Chiminos Island Lodge** (tel. 2335-3506 or 5750-8628, www.chiminosisland.com), where you'll find six comfortable thatched-roof bungalows with lovely views, firm beds, colorful Guatemalan blankets, and wood and tile accents in your private hot-water bathroom. The rooms are made from tropical hardwoods and have beautiful wooden decks overlooking Petexbatún Lagoon. The elegant open-air restaurant serves delicious set meals and is adjacent to a pleasant hammock area overlooking the fantastic lakeside setting. Rates are $110 per person, including one night's accommodations and three meals. Children under 12 are $55 each.

Flores

In the heart of Petén, the twin towns of Flores and Santa Elena are often referred to simply and collectively as "Flores." The latter is actually limited to a small island on Lake Petén Itzá connected to Santa Elena, on the mainland, by a causeway. Flores is a pleasant island town unlike any other in Guatemala with pastel houses and quiet streets. Santa Elena is a bit noisier and more chaotic because of its prominence as Petén's main commercial center. Farther west, Santa Elena runs into the downright ugly town of San Benito.

Flores is the natural starting point for a visit to Petén's wild interior, as it is the region's transportation and services hub. Many NGOs are based here and the quiet streets are lined with a variety of shops, restaurants, and comfortable lodgings. While Flores is excellent from a logistical standpoint and entirely attractive, it has been somewhat displaced in recent years by the emergence of El Remate, a lakeside town on

the road to Tikal that is convenient for travelers to and from Belize. Still, there are a number of local attractions that make spending at least one day in the Flores area worthwhile.

History

Flores started out as the Mayan site of **Tayasal,** home to the Itzá people and one of the last Mayan strongholds. It is thought that Tayasal was founded by a group of displaced Mayans from Chichen Itzá, in present-day Mexico, sometime between the 13th and 15th centuries. The Itzá held out for quite a while in their remote island outpost deep in the Petén jungle. Spain's relative lack of interest in the hot, steamy lowlands of Petén inevitably allowed them to continue life largely unhindered by the Spanish. In 1525, Hernán Cortés stopped by on his way to Honduras and had a peaceful meeting with the Itzá King Canek, also leaving behind a lame horse. A statue of it was made

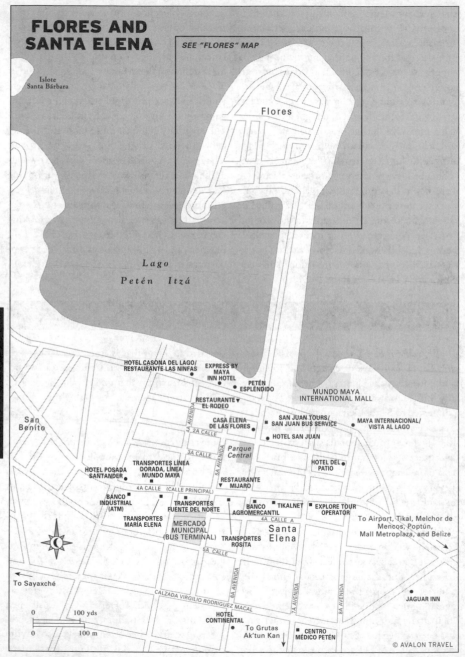

FLORES AND SANTA ELENA

SEE "FLORES" MAP

Islote
Santa Bárbara

Flores

Lago
Petén Itzá

San
Benito

HOTEL CASONA DEL LAGO/
RESTAURANTE LAS NINFAS

EXPRESS BY MAYA INN HOTEL

PETÉN ESPLÉNDIDO

MUNDO MAYA INTERNATIONAL MALL

RESTAURANTE EL RODEO

CASA ELENA DE LAS FLORES

SAN JUAN TOURS/ SAN JUAN BUS SERVICE

MAYA INTERNACIONAL/ VISTA AL LAGO

HOTEL SAN JUAN

2A AVENIDA

2A CALLE

3A CALLE

Parque Central

5A AVENIDA

HOTEL DEL PATIO

HOTEL POSADA SANTANDER

TRANSPORTES LÍNEA DORADA, LÍNEA MUNDO MAYA

RESTAURANTE MIJARO

4A CALLE (CALLE PRINCIPAL)

BANCO INDUSTRIAL (ATM)

TRANSPORTES FUENTE DEL NORTE

BANCO AGROMERCANTIL

TIKALNET

EXPLORE TOUR OPERATOR

4A CALLE A

TRANSPORTES MARÍA ELENA

MERCADO MUNICIPAL (BUS TERMINAL)

TRANSPORTES ROSITA

Santa Elena

To Airport, Tikal, Melchor de Mencos, Poptún, Mall Metroplaza, and Belize

5A CALLE

6A AVENIDA

7A AVENIDA

8A AVENIDA

To Sayaxché

CALZADA VIRGILIO RODRIGUEZ MACAL

JAGUAR INN

0   100 yds
0   100 m

HOTEL CONTINENTAL

To Grutas Ak'tun Kan

CENTRO MÉDICO PETÉN

© AVALON TRAVEL

PETÉN

when it died, and Spanish friars visiting the region in 1618 would find it being worshipped by the Itzá. The friars destroyed the idol, which probably explains why the next round of visitors, a military expedition in 1622, was captured and sacrificed.

Tayasal finally came under Spanish rule in 1697 at the command of Martín de Ursúa. As was the custom, the Spanish conquerors destroyed the city's temples, pyramids, and artwork, leaving no trace behind. Today, the small

Flores town plaza, church, and government buildings sit on the highest point in the city atop what was once Tayasal's ceremonial plaza.

To the north, across the small finger of Lake Petén Itzá in which Flores lies, are the remains of the Mayan site of Tayazal. It dates to the Classic Period, long before the arrival of the Itzá.

SIGHTS
As nothing remains of the original settlement, there is very little to see in terms of historical

© AL ARGUETA

Flores's new *malecón*

sights on the island. The quaint plaza contains a small church and government buildings flanked on one side by a basketball court. Flores itself is very different from any other town in Guatemala and a leisurely stroll around the island will allow you enough time to take in the funky pastel architecture and the quiet streets. One addition to Flores's infrastructure is the *malecón,* or waterfront walkway, spanning the entire island. The town's main street has also been re-paved.

CINCAP (10 A.M.-noon and 2 P.M.-8 P.M. Mon.-Fri.), housed in the Castillo de Arismendi on the north side of the park, once served as an information center on Petén's culture and natural history but now holds only a small gift shop.

If you're really into caves and won't have time to explore the areas of southern Petén or Las Verapaces, you might want to check out **Ak'tun Kan** (8 A.M.-5 P.M. daily, $1.50), also known as the *cueva de la serpiente* for the large snake said to inhabit it. To get there, follow 7a

Avenida south out of Santa Elena until you get to the power plant. Turn left to get to its east side, and continue south another kilometer.

ENTERTAINMENT

Like many small towns in Guatemala, Flores tends to shut down after dark. Though the restaurants mentioned here are perfectly fine for stopping in for a drink, you may find yourself drinking alone. Depending on the season, it can get very quiet here and some places may even shut their doors well before their posted 1 A.M. closing time. On weekends, locals like to party and if you are up for it you can certainly mingle with them at any of a number of establishments. Just follow the sound of music.

Aside from being a fine restaurant, **La Luna** (corner of Calle 30 de Junio and Calle 10 de Noviembre, tel. 7926-3346, Mon.-Sat. until 1 A.M.) has a pretty swanky bar where you can enjoy the very atmospheric old building in which it's housed under a whirring ceiling fan.

Café-Bar Las Puertas (corner of Calle Central and Avenida Santa Ana, tel. 7926-1061, 11 A.M.-midnight Mon.-Sat.) is popular with travelers for its margaritas, funky atmosphere, and live music on weekends. A house across the street screens movies. Another favorite haunt for movie-watchers is the **Mayan Princess Café** (corner of Calle 10 de Noviembre and Avenida Reforma), showing movies at 4 P.M. and 9 P.M. daily.

Right on the lake, **Raíces Bar and Grill** (tel. 5521-1843, 2 P.M.-10 P.M. Sun.-Thurs., 2 P.M.-1 A.M. Fri.-Sat.) is a great place to catch the sunset while you enjoy your favorite cocktail. You'll find the locals in the cantinas on the Playa Sur strip facing the Gran Hotel de la Isla.

SHOPPING

There are several handicrafts stores lining Calle Centroamérica, on the south side of the island. For more modern needs, there are two shopping malls nearby. **Mundo Maya International Mall,** just across the way in Santa Elena and immediately east of the causeway, has a modern selection of shops, a large grocery store and a movie theater. Burger King and Pollo Campero outlets are adjacent.

Metroplaza (9 A.M.-8 P.M. daily) lies across the road from Mundo Maya International Airport and has a Pizza Hut, electronics stores, a travel agency, and a pharmacy among its stores.

RECREATION

Although Flores's location by the lake would make water sports a logical recreational option, most recreation is outside of town and curiously lacks the water-borne focus you would expect to find. Still, you can rent **kayaks** and **mountain bikes** at La Villa del Chef (tel. 7926-0296, 8 A.M.-11 P.M. Mon.-Sun., 1 P.M.-11 P.M. Tues.-Sun.) for $7 a day.

The other main recreational option involves **lake tours** offered by various boatmen congregating at the embarcaderos opposite Hotel Santana and on Playa Sur. Direct *colectivo* boats ($0.50) can take you across the lake to the town of San Miguel and leave from a dock next to Posada de Don José. The lake tours can be had for $15-20 and include a trip to the lakeshore opposite the island's northwest corner to **Petencito Zoo,** the Mayan ruins of **Tayazal,** and **ARCAS,** a wildlife rescue center.

Guide Companies

Flores makes a natural starting point for trips into the wilderness because of its central location within Petén and its proximity to roads leading from here in all directions. The following recommended outfitters can hook you up with one day or multiday adventures to Petén's increasingly popular parks and archaeological sites.

Highly recommended, **The Mayan Adventure** (www.the-mayan-adventure.com/go/index.html) is run by the owners of Café Yaxhá, who are very knowledgeable about the region. Trip options include the usual sites such as Tikal and Yaxhá, but also some lesser-known communities they work with. They can also organize trips to El Mirador, which is no easy task. **Tikal Connection** (Calle 15 de Septiembre, tel. 7924-8664, www.tikalcnx.com) works with local communities to involve them in the business of sustainable tourism in and around several of Petén's protected areas. Tikal Connection offers multiday treks from the site of El Zotz to Tikal, rigorous journeys to El Mirador, and the "Scarlet Macaw Trail," in Laguna del Tigre National Park near the Mayan site of Waka'-Perú.

Martsam Tours and Travel (Calle 30 de Junio in the lobby of Capitán Tortuga restaurant, tel. 7926-0346, www.martsam.com) has an excellent reputation and offers a variety of trips throughout Petén. In addition to El Zotz-Tikal, Waka'-Perú, and El Mirador, it offers day trips to Tikal and multiday adventures involving hikes from Tikal to Yaxhá, stopping in Nakum along the way. There are also daily departures from Flores to Yaxhá for $20 per person (minimum of two).

PETÉN

Conservation Tours Tikal (Calle 15 de Septiembre, inside Hotel Mirador del Lago, tel. 7926-0670 or 5592-9509, www.cct@intel-nett.com) is run by locals Nery Medrano and Héctor Aldana. A spinoff of the environmental group Rare (www.rareconservation.org), the company offers some unique options, including a jungle survival course, kayaking on Lake Petén Itzá, and mountain biking from Tikal to Uaxactún. Five percent of proceeds go directly toward the protection of the parks they work in.

ACCOMMODATIONS
Under $10
Among the first places you'll come upon after crossing the causeway leading into Flores is **Hotel La Canoa** (tel. 7926-0853), where 10 rooms, all but one with private bath, go for $11 (d). The room with shared bath goes for $4 per person. All rooms have firm beds, though the fluorescent lighting can be somewhat dreary. A bar directly underneath the rooms can make things noisy. Farther down the same street is **Hotel Playa Sur** (tel. 7926-0351, $7 d). Its 10 clean rooms feature firm beds, fan, and make a stab at decor. Another option in this part of town is **Hotel El Faisán** (tel. 7926-3438, $11 d), with ceiling fans, cable TV, and acceptably firm beds. The electric hot-water heaters, however, look a bit scary.

Hotel Mirador del Lago (Calle 15 de Septiembre south of Avenida Flores, tel. 7926-4363) is a good value at $11 d in somewhat plain rooms with firm beds and fan. Its 32 rooms are spread between two buildings on opposite sides of the street. Two rooms on the top floor with lake views go for $16. The eight rooms at **Posada de Don José** (Calle Fraternidad, tel. 7926-1371, laposadadonjose@hotmail.com) offer firm beds, cable TV, air-conditioning ($20 d) or fan ($11 d), electric hot water, and some attempt at decor in a nice family atmosphere. In-room lighting is fluorescent. Guests have free use of the kitchen and there is

a tranquil hammock area on the second floor overlooking the lake.

Calle Unión holds a high concentration of lodgings in this budget category. A popular option is **Hospedaje Doña Goya** (tel. 7926-3538), where rooms with shared bath and fan go for $11 and those with private bath cost $13 (d). Guests gather at the rooftop terrace with lake views at sunset. An annex just a few houses down, **Doña Goya the 2nd** (tel. 7926-3540), features rooms with slightly more comfortable beds and fan starting at $11 (d). Rooms with private baths, air-conditioning, cable TV, and lake views rent for $25 (d).

For the best value in town head to Flores's hostel, ■ **Los Amigos** (Calle Central next to ProPetén, tel. 5584-8795 or 5521-2873, www.amigoshostel.com). This backpacker's paradise features a restaurant/bar, security lockers, broadband Internet, and laundry service among its well-rounded list of amenities. The friendly Guatemalan and Dutch owners can also help you plan your travels to other parts of Guatemala. For the ultimate in affordable lodging, you can sleep in a hammock for under $5 or in dorm beds costing $6. Private rooms with shared bath cost $13 (d) or $19 (d) with private bath.

Readers have informed me to beware of Hotel Casablanca (formerly known as Los Peches), on Playa Sur fronting the lakeshore. It appears there have been alleged instances of bag pilfering while guests are away on day trips.

$10-25
There are several good options in this category, including **Hotel La Mesa de Los Mayas** (Avenida La Reforma, tel. 7926-1240, mesamayas@hotmail.com), where clean double rooms with reading lamp, cable TV, hot water, and fan cost $20. Rooms with air-conditioning are $25. Across the street is the new **Villa Margarita** (tel. 7926-3240, $13 d). Its nine clean but rather plain rooms have firm beds, air-conditioning,

cable TV, and private baths with hot water. Another good choice on Avenida La Reforma, to the south, is **Hotel El Peregrino** (Calle Reforma Casa #3, tel. 7926-0477, h_peregrino@hotmail.com), a family-run operation in a three-story building where rooms have cable TV and ceiling fan. Rooms with private bath are $17 (d); two rooms with shared bath go for $13. **Hotel Posada de la Jungla** (corner of Calle 30 de Junio and Calle Centroamerica, tel. 7926-0634, www.travelpeten.com) offers fan-cooled double rooms for $13 or air-conditioned rooms for $30. All have private baths and basic furnishings, including a bedside table and chairs. Internet service is also available.

On Calle 30 de Junio, a good choice in this category is the friendly ☾ **Green World Hotel** (tel. 7867-5662, $13 d), offering cable TV, hot water, ceiling fan, comfortable beds, and some nice decorative touches. The spotless rooms are painted a pleasant light green, evoking tranquility and space. The reflected fluorescent accent lighting is surprisingly pleasant. Some upstairs rooms have balconies with lake views for the same price. Across the street is the simpler **Hotel Santa Rita** (tel. 7926-3224, hotelsantarita_flores@yahoo.es), where slightly less attractive rooms with ceiling fans, hot water, and stiffer mattresses cost $11 (d). Rounding out the list of possibilities is **La Casa del Lacandón** (Calle Unión, tel. 7926-4359), where pleasant enough rooms with fan and private bathroom (some with lake view and terrace) rent for $13 (d).

$25-50

Several Flores hotels fall into this price range. Among them are three belonging to **Corpetur** (www.hotelesdepeten.com), a local hotel chain of excellent repute. The first of these properties is **Casazul** (Calle Unión, tel. 7867-5451 or 2366-2841, $48 d), where pleasant rooms with air-conditioning, cable TV, private baths, and minibars are housed in a pretty blue house, as its name would indicate. It has a nice balcony with wonderful lake views.

An excellent value in this price range is ☾ **Hotel Casa Amelia** (Calle Unión, tel. 7926-3328, www.hotelcasamelia.com). Its attractive, spotless double rooms with original decor incorporating burlap bags for curtains, wooden furnishings, firm beds, ceiling fans, air-conditioning, and large hot-water bathrooms go for $49. Some of the 10 rooms have nice lake views. All have large cable TVs. **Hotel Sabana** (Calle Fraternidad, tel. 7926-1248, www.hotelsabana.com, $45 d) is painted in pretty pastel greens and offers comfortable rooms with air-conditioning, cable TV, in-room phone, reading lamps, and hot water. Some rooms have ceiling fans. There are a swimming pool with deck chairs for lounging and a restaurant, which may or may not be open depending on whether the hotel is hosting tour groups, which fill this usually quiet hotel to capacity. Under the same management as Tikal's Jungle Lodge, the **Hotel Isla de Flores** (corner of Avenida La Reforma and Calle 10 de Noviembre, tel. 2477-0570, $50 d) is a modern three-story building housing 18 comfortable rooms with ceiling fans, cable TV, firm beds, and air-conditioning. On Calle 30 de Junio, **Hotel Santana** (tel. 7926-0662, informacion@santanapeten.com, $45 d) has 35 rooms with the usual amenities of its price category as well as firm beds, large mirror, and in-room safe-deposit box. Some rooms have very pleasant balconies with chairs and a hanging lamp. A swimming pool, colonial restaurant, and ice-cream shop are on the ground floor. The hotel caters periodically to large tour groups on package itineraries.

On Playa Sur, facing Santa Elena and the lake, is **Hotel El Itzá** (tel. 7926-3666), where large double rooms with cable TV, ceiling fan, air-conditioning, and private bath with on-demand hot water can be had for $40.

$50-100

Hotel Petén (Calle 30 de Junio, tel. 7867-5203

or 2366-2841, www.hotelesdepeten.com, $54 d) is said to be the island's oldest hotel, dating to 1960. You have a choice of air-conditioning and/or ceiling fan in its smallish but comfortable rooms with private bath and cable TV, some of which have balconies overlooking the lake. A small swimming pool and a dining room are on the ground floor just opposite the lobby. Probably the nicest of the three Flores Corpetur properties is the lively ◖**La Casona de la Isla** (Calle 30 de Junio, tel. 7867-5200 or 2366-2841, www.hotelesdepeten.com, $59 d), an attractive lakeside house painted in bright yellow and orange hues housing 26 rooms with air-conditioning, cable TV, and private bath. There is a nice outdoor swimming pool, around which the rooms are centered, as well as a whirlpool. The hotel's Isla Bonita restaurant and bar serves three delicious meals a day at reasonable prices. The island's most expensive hotel is near the causeway as you come into town on the shore facing Santa Elena. The multistory **Gran Hotel de la Isla** (tel. 7926-0686, ventas@hoteldelaisla.com, www.hoteldelaisla.com, $80) is a large yellow building that seems somewhat out of place in mostly low-rise Flores. Rooms include all the usual comforts of its price range such as private bath, air-conditioning, cable TV, and attractive furnishings. There is a good restaurant and bar and a swimming pool dominated by a wall mural depicting Tikal's Gran Jaguar temple. Internet access is available in the lobby. It's nice enough, but unless you have your heart set on staying on the island, you may want to stay across the lake in Santa Elena in one of several comparable hotels in this price category.

FOOD

Flores has a small grocery store. **La Colmena** (corner Calle 30 de Junio and Avenida 10 de Septiembre, tel. 7926-1268) has a variety of local and imported favorites. It also takes credit cards. There is also a 24-hour mini-mart across the street from Capitán Tortuga restaurant on Calle 30 de Junio. The larger La Torre grocery store is across the causeway in Santa Elena's Mundo Maya Mall.

Cafés and Light Meals

Flores has no shortage of coffee shops and cafés, most of which offer something different and equally pleasing, depending on what you're in the mood for. The **Mayan Sunset Café** (Calle 30 de Junio, tel. 7926-4726, 11 A.M.-11 P.M.) has a varied menu, including Thai chicken or beef, pasta, sandwiches, and quesadillas served on an airy deck overlooking the lake's western shore. There are a full bar and good music to chill out to. It also shows movies. Check the daily program to find out what's playing. ◖ **Café-Bar Las Puertas** (corner of Calle Central and Avenida Santa Ana, tel. 7926-1061, 11 A.M.-midnight Mon.-Sat.) serves good espresso beverages and is a popular place, partially on account of its lively atmosphere as a bar with funky decor involving paint-splattered walls. Try one of the many pasta dishes, or if just here for a drink, go with a margarita.

El Café Chilero (Cool Beans Café) (Calle 15 de Septiembre, tel. 5571-9240, 8 A.M.-10 P.M. daily except Tues.) has a wide assortment of hot and cold coffee beverages using gourmet beans from a very well-known coffee farm in Alta Verapaz. It also serves smoothies and light meals in a relaxing jungle garden atmosphere and makes a great place for breakfast.

If you're looking for inspiration before an adventure to one of Petén's numerous archaeological sites, head to ◖**Café Arqueológico Yaxhá** (Calle 15 de Septiembre, tel. 7926-0367, www.cafeyaxha.com, 7 A.M.-10 P.M. daily), where you can dine in a pleasant atmosphere featuring colorful Guatemalan tablecloths and photo montages of various Mayan sites, including Tikal, Yaxhá, and Nakum. Although it does a variety of dishes, including steak, chicken, seafood, pasta, and even curry, it specializes in what it calls "pre-Columbian" fare (a variety of Petén-Yucatec dishes), which come highly recommended. It is also the local representative for La Casa del Jade, a jade shop based in Antigua, and has a small assortment of jade jewelry on display. A separate dock on the island's western shore is open 5 P.M. to 11 P.M. and is a great place to go for an evening swim or watch the sunset from a hammock while enjoying your favorite drink.

Also on Calle 15 de Septiembre, **La Galería del Zot'z** (tel. 7926-1257, 6 A.M.-10 P.M. daily) serves decent sandwiches, pizzas, and pastas as well as good coffee and espresso drinks in a quaint atmosphere next to the quiet street.

Cheap Eats
On the street facing Playa Sur (South Beach), across from the Gran Hotel de la Isla, is **Inka Ti Jesh Maâch** (tel. 7926-3259, all meals daily), serving quality deli sandwiches and smoothies. It opens early and closes late. Also on Playa Sur and a safe bet for cheap eats is **Los Peches** (5 A.M.-midnight daily), just off the causeway as you enter town, where you can eat from a set menu of chicken, fried fish, burgers, and steaks for about $3.50. It's open early for those crack-of-dawn bus rides to Belize and Tikal. Next door is **Restaurante La Canoa** (tel. 7926-0853) in the hotel of the same name. There are cheap eats here and a decent bar where it is purportedly always happy hour.

Steakhouses
La Hacienda del Rey (corner of Calle Playa Sur and Calle 30 de Junio, tel. 7926-3647, all meals daily) is a South American steakhouse in the $10 range set in a wooden building with open sides that allow breezes to flow. It serves tacos in addition to sizable *parrilladas* (South American-style barbecued meats). A bar on the second floor, **La Taberna del Rey,** is set in an open-air deck overlooking the street below. Down the street on the island's western shore is

Raíces Bar and Grill (tel. 5521-1843, 2 P.M.-10 P.M. Sun.-Thurs., 2 P.M.-1 A.M. Fri.-Sat.), serving large portions of grilled steak, chicken, and fish with scrumptious side dishes in a hip semioutdoor setting featuring a deck built over the lake. If you're lucky, you might catch a thunderstorm here during the rainy season for a spectacular lakeside lightning show. Prices are in the $10 range. Order the kebabs and share with a friend. If you're into exotic meats or just want to give them a try, check out **Restaurante El Gran Jacal** (Calle Centroamerica, tel. 7926-3578, 7 A.M.-10 P.M. daily), where the specialty is farm-raised venison, Petén turkey, and *tepescuintle*. For a touch of authentic Petén cuisine, try the Pollo a la Jacal, tasty chicken in a somewhat sweet sauce.

European
Housed in a tastefully decorated old building festooned with overhanging bougainvillea blossoms and painted in bright shades of green and blue, the finest restaurant in Flores is undoubtedly **La Luna** (corner of Calle 30 de Junio and Calle 10 de Noviembre, tel. 7926-3346, lunch and dinner Mon.-Sat., $6-12). Culinary highlights include stuffed peppers, steak in a black pepper cream sauce, boneless chicken breast in wine sauce, pastas, and vegetarian dishes, including falafel. Also on Calle 30 de Junio is **Capitán Tortuga** (tel. 7926-0247, 7 A.M.-10 P.M. daily). There is a spacious dining room housed under a large *palapa* structure and a two-story terrace with lake views where you can enjoy pasta, tacos, sandwiches, chicken quesadillas, grilled meats, and tasty pizzas in addition to a fully stocked bar. For snacks, try the burritos for about $5. Across the street is **La Albahaca** (tel. 7926-3354 or 7926-0505, 6 P.M.-11 P.M. Tues.-Sun.), a cozy little place with a quiet atmosphere serving delicious beef and chicken recipes as well as scrumptious homemade pasta at reasonable prices. There is a nice assortment of Chilean wines.

PETÉN

© AL ARGUETA

Pizzería Picasso

For pizza and Italian food, try **Pizzería Picasso** (Calle 15 de Septiembre, tel. 7926-0673, 10:30 A.M.-10:30 P.M. Tues.-Sun.), serving reliable pastas and very good pizzas for around $10 for a large pie.

There are a number of good choices along Calle Unión, on the island's northwest corner. **La Villa del Chef** (tel. 7926-0296, 8 A.M.-11 P.M. Mon.-Sun., 1-11 P.M. Tues.-Sun., $4-15), theoretically specializes in Arab and Mediterranean food, but serves a wide variety of sandwiches, pasta, chicken, and seafood dishes in an attractive lakeside atmosphere atop a small wooden deck. The *parrillada petenera* ($13) is a good option for sharing. Just down the street, **◖Il Terrazo** (tel. 7867-5479, jpzeas@gmail.com, 7:30 A.M.-10 P.M. Mon.-Sat., $5-12) is a welcome addition to Flores's restaurant offerings. The owners have plenty of restaurant experience, having worked as chefs in some of the country's best restaurants. There are delicious paninis, pastas,

tagliatella, oven-baked fish fillet in potato, as well as smoothies and a full bar. The ambiance is also quite pleasant, set in an airy second-floor thatch roof terrace overlooking the lake. Chill music plays on the stereo.

INFORMATION AND SERVICES
Tourist Information
INGUAT has a desk at the airport, where staff can answer your questions and help you get your bearings. With the departure of CINCAP as a regional information center, your best bet for getting tourist information is **Café Arqueológico Yaxhá** (Avenida 15 de Septiembre, tel. 5830-2060, www.cafeyaxha. com, 7 A.M.-10 P.M. daily). Its German owner knows a lot about the local Mayan sites and has even authored a guidebook to the Mayan region in his native tongue. It's a great place to learn about Petén's archaeological sites and is often a meeting place for folks working on archaeological digs or environmental projects.

Communications
Flores's post office is about a block south of the plaza on Avenida Barrios. Calle Centroamerica has several places for access to the Internet. Among the options are Tikal Net and Petén Net, next door to each other and open 8 A.M.-10 P.M. daily. Another option is Flores Net, just up the way on Avenida Barrios across from the post office. On the north end of town, try Tayazal Net (Calle Unión next to Doña Goya the 2nd, tel. 7926-2052, 8 A.M.-10 P.M. daily). Internet access costs about $1.40 per hour in most places.

Money
The only bank in Flores is Banrural, about a block east of the plaza. There's an ATM next to Hotel Petén on Calle 30 de Junio, but it's sometimes out of cash. You might find yourself crossing the causeway into Santa Elena to get cash at one of the ATMs there.

Laundry

The Mayan Princess Travel Agency on Calle 30 de Junio does laundry for about $4 a load (wash and dry). There's also Lavandería Petenchel, on Calle Centroamerica, and Lavandería Amelia, behind CINCAP.

Emergency and Medical Services

For the police, dial 7926-1365. The closest hospital is Hospital San Benito (tel. 7926-1459).

Volunteer Work

Volunteer opportunities are available with several of the NGOs working in town. Among the options is the opportunity to volunteer at the Las Guacamayas Biological Research Station (tel. 7926-1370, www.propeten.org) in Laguna del Tigre National Park. Another option is working with the local Wildlife Rescue and Conservation Association, or ARCAS (www.arcasguatemala.com), at its site on the other end of the lake opposite Flores's north shore. San Andrés-based Nueva Juventud Language School has set up a website for volunteers looking to work with it on various projects benefiting the local community. Check out www.volunteerpeten.com or send email at volunteerpeten@hotmail.com.

Spanish School

Dos Mundos Spanish School (Calle Fraternidad, tel. 5830-2060, www.flores-spanish.com) offers 30 hours of language instruction for $150 per week, plus a $25 enrollment fee. Accommodations options with host family, including meals, start at $90 per week.

SANTA ELENA
Accommodations

Santa Elena has several pleasant accommodations along the lakeshore with wonderful views of Flores as well as a variety of less expensive options in the town center. Among the budget accommodations is **Hotel San Juan** (2a Calle between 6a and 7a Avenida, tel. 7924-8358), where you'll find rather plain rooms with saggy mattresses in a large concrete building. Double-occupancy rooms with and without air-conditioning are $20 and $10, respectively. A better choice is the **Jaguar Inn** (Calzada Virgilio Rodriguez Macal 8-79, tel. 7926-0002, www.jaguarinn.com, $25), where tastefully decorated rooms are centered around a courtyard and the helpful staff can help you plan your onward travel. Air-conditioning is an extra $5 and there is a small pizzeria on-site. The owners also have a hotel at Tikal National Park by the same name. Another good budget choice is the **Hotel Posada Santander** (4a Calle, tel. 7926-0574), where spotless double rooms with TV and shared bath go for $10. Rooms without TV but with private baths go for the same price. There is no hot water but there is a small restaurant on-site.

Hotel Continental (6a Avenida, south of Calzada Virgilio Rodriguez Macal, tel. 7926-0095, $13-25 d) offers a variety of prices and corresponding levels of comfort in its 51 rooms. The owners and staff are friendly.

Moving up in price range and correspondingly closer to the lakeshore is **Casa Elena de las Flores** (Calle Principal, Ingreso a Isla de Flores, tel. 7926-2239, www.hotelcasaelenadelasflores.com, $40 d), where 26 comfortable rooms are set in a pleasant colonial building around a nice swimming pool with palm trees and a garden. A popular repository for tour groups, the **Hotel del Patio** (8a Calle, tel. 7926-0104, www.hoteldelpatio.com.gt, $65) is comfortable and offers many services and amenities but has seen better days. Rooms are in a neocolonial building. Those on the first floor are particularly susceptible to mold. There are better deals elsewhere in this price range.

Along the lakeshore, as you approach town from the airport, is the **◖ Maya Internacional** (Calle Litoral del lago, Zona 1, tel. 2223-5000 central reservations or 7926-2083 direct, www.

villasdeguatemala.com), with 24 standard rooms and two junior suites ranging in price $70-100. One of the area's first accommodations, the recently remodeled property features tastefully decorated rooms with balconies overlooking the lake, tiled floors, ceiling fans, air-conditioning, and cable TV. The lodge's Vista al Lago Restaurant offers gorgeous lake views and a varied menu, including a Sunday brunch. A swimming pool, great service, wireless Internet, and lovely open-air *palapa* lobby round out the list of features making the Maya Internacional an excellent choice.

Farther along the lakeshore near the causeway connecting Santa Elena to Flores are a number of newer options, including the 62-room **Petén Espléndido** (tel. 2360-8140, www.petenesplendido.com), where doubles cost $90 and the feel is that of a U.S. chain hotel with all the usual amenities. Next door is the curiously named **Express by Maya Inn Hotel** (tel. 7926-1817), where 20 comfortable if bland double rooms go for $40 and include air-conditioning, cable TV, and somewhat cheerful furnishings. The in-room lighting is fluorescent.

The standout in this part of town is the **Hotel Casona del Lago** (tel. 7952-8700 or 2366-2841, www.hotelesdepeten.com, $90-100 d), a beautiful blue house that could just as easily fit in to the seaside landscape of Cape May, New Jersey. The large, bright rooms have spacious bathrooms, tasteful decor and the usual comforts, including cable TV. Some have lake views; all are centered around a pretty swimming pool with a whirlpool. The hotel's Restaurante Las Ninfas serves varied international cuisine for breakfast, lunch, and dinner in a pleasant dining room overlooking the pool and lake. The lobby is decorated with classic photos from Petén's past dating to the 1920s, 1930s, and 1940s, along with some more modern scenes.

Food

Although Flores is really where most of the action is, Santa Elena does have a few eateries worthy of mention. A perennial favorite is **Restaurante Mijaro** (Calle Principal, across from the Catholic church, tel. 7926-1615, 7 A.M.-10 P.M. daily), with a varied menu including fish, meats, pastas, and burgers at very reasonable prices. Locals like **Restaurante El Rodeo** (tel. 7924-8045, 10 A.M.-10 P.M. daily), conveniently situated across from Santa Elena's nicer lakefront resorts, for its Western-style decor meshed with tropical architecture and its good chicken, fish, steak, and pasta, mostly under $10. There is also a fully stocked bar. The nicer hotels, including Petén Espléndido and La Casona del Lago, have their own decent restaurants next to swimming pools with lake views. Of these, the best option is La Casona del Lago's **Restaurante Las Ninfas,** with a varied menu, including pastas and grilled meats. The outdoor restaurant at the Hotel Maya Internacional, **Vista al Lago** (tel. 7926-2083, 7 A.M.-9 P.M. daily), serves international dishes and is a fine choice for its Sunday brunch. It offers lovely lake views from its covered wooden deck.

Money

Three blocks up 6a Avenida from the Flores causeway on the corner of 4a Calle is Banco Agromercantil with a MasterCard ATM. Three blocks west, also on 4a Calle, is Banco Industrial, with a Visa ATM.

GETTING THERE
Air

Flights arrive at **Mundo Maya International Airport** (FRS), a few kilometers outside of Santa Elena east on the road to Tikal. In 2008, the airport underwent a substantial renovation and the facilities are vastly improved (including badly needed air-conditioning). Most flights to the Flores/Santa Elena airport arrive from Guatemala City, with two daily on **TACA** (800/400-8222, www.taca.com) and a handful of smaller local carriers, among them **TAG** (www.tag.com.gt). From Belize City, **Tropic Air** (800/422-3435, www.tropicair.com) flies to Flores twice daily.

The only direct service to FRS from the United States, a Saturday-only flight via Houston on Continental Express, was dropped in November 2006 after 18 months in operation. Flights to Cancún, Mexico were rather inexplicably dropped by TACA, leaving a potentially large market without air service. Flights between Guatemala City and Flores are usually in the $250 range for a round-trip flight.

Bus

Linea Dorada (tel. 7926-1788, lineadorada.info, $15-30 one-way) has buses from Guatemala City at 10 A.M. and 9 P.M. daily, stopping in Río Dulce and Poptún along the way. There are also daily buses to and from Belize City ($24 one-way), leaving at 7 A.M. Buses arrive and depart from the main bus terminal along 4a Calle in Santa Elena as well as from another office on Playa Sur in Flores (tel. 7926-3649).

You'll find minibuses to Melchor de Mencos, Poptún, and Sayaxché west of the market in Santa Elena on 4a Calle. Buses and minibuses to San José and San Andrés ($1, 40 minutes) leave from 5a Calle, west of the market.

San Juan Travel (2a Calle, Santa Elena, and Playa Sur, Flores, tel. 7926-0041 or 7926-0042) operates service to Belize City ($27), continuing to Chetumal, Mexico, leaving daily at 5 A.M. and 7:30 A.M. from its office on 2a Calle in Santa Elena. The shuttle also picks up passengers at the hotels in Flores and Santa Elena with prior arrangement. Return trips are at 9:30 A.M. and 4:30 P.M.

Fuente del Norte (grupofuentedelnorte.com) buses make the trip to Belize City daily at 5 A.M. There are 15 daily departures to Guatemala City.

GETTING AROUND
Taxis and *Tuk-Tuks*

You'll find taxis at the larger hotels in Santa Elena and at the Mundo Maya International Airport. A taxi from the airport to Flores should cost no more than $3. More popular and much less expensive are the *tuk-tuks* (Asian-style motorized rickshaws) you'll find seemingly everywhere. Short trips of about a kilometer or two within the Flores and Santa Elena area on *tuk-tuks* are usually in the range of $0.75.

Shuttle Buses

Shuttle buses and minivans ply the road between Flores and Tikal. **San Juan Travel** (2a Calle, Santa Elena, and Playa Sur, Flores, tel. 7926-0041 or 7926-0042) shuttles leave hourly between 5 A.M. and 10 A.M. with a final bus at 2 P.M. *Colectivo* buses also ply the road between Flores and Tikal. If arriving at the airport, your best bet is to negotiate a ride with a bus taking a tour group (if not booked in advance) or go across the street to the shopping mall, where roadside pickup on cheap *colectivo* buses is facilitated. Once-frequent *colectivo* buses leaving straight for Tikal from the airport seem to have disappeared with fewer flights flying in to FRS utilizing smaller aircraft.

Car Rentals

You'll find several options at the airport upon your arrival. Among them are a few local operations I can't bring myself to recommend. Stick with **Hertz** (tel. 2470-3700 Guatemala City or 800/654-3001 U.S., www.hertz.com) or **Alamo** (tel. 800/462-5266 U.S., www.alamoguatemala.com), both of which have offices in or near the airport.

NEAR FLORES AND SANTA ELENA

There are a variety of attractions in and around Flores and Santa Elena that work well if you have a day or half a day while awaiting connecting flights or onward travel. Several of these attractions—**ARCAS, Petencito Zoo,** and **Tayazal**—are a five-minute boat ride across the lake from Flores's north shore near the village of San Miguel. A road also goes this way along the shoreline and is useful in this discussion for orientation only, as most visitors find themselves catching a boat when heading out in this direction. You can take in 2-3 of these destinations as part of a lake tour leaving from Flores, which should cost between $15 and $20. *Colectivo* boats ($0.50) leave from a dock beside Restaurante La Guacamaya, on the north shore of Flores, as they fill up.

◖ Parque Natural Ixpanpajul

Covering an area of nine square kilometers and conveniently just off the highway toward Guatemala City, the main attraction at Parque Natural Ixpanpajul (tel. 5619-0513 or 7863-1317, www.ixpanpajul.com, 7 A.M.-6 P.M. daily) is a series of six suspension bridges built over the forest canopy, giving you a toucan's-eye view of the forest. The trip along the forest trail takes a little more than an hour and includes a stop at a lookout point to take in the astounding view from the top of the mountain. Other activities include a Tarzan Canopy Tour (zip line), Spot Lighting (nighttime wildlife-viewing), horseback riding, mountain biking, tractor rides, and ATV rentals. You can tour the hanging bridges (Skyway) for $30 per adult or $22 per child. You also have a choice of mountain biking, tractor rides, or horseback riding, ranging from $5 to $25. Packages allow you to combine the Skyway with the Tarzan Canopy Tour and/or the Spot Lighting tour for a full day of adventure. You can combine two activities for $55 or all three for $75.

There is a campsite on the premises ($5) and you can rent tents ($10) and other equipment, but you have to book at least one of the main activities at a cost of $30. There are now also accommodations consisting of comfortable cabins with bunk beds and private bathrooms sleeping up to 5 people.

The park can provide transportation from Flores or Tikal if you call in advance. A taxi from Flores should cost about $5.

Cooperativa Nuevo Horizonte

Seventeen kilometers south of Santa Elena on the road to Guatemala City lies Cooperativa Nuevo Horizonte (http://cooperativenewhorizon.blogspot.com), a community of returned refugees and former combatants from the Guatemalan civil war. The cooperative was formed in 1998, when the community was resettled near the town of Santa Ana following the 1996 peace accords.

Nuevo Horizonte offers a fascinating glimpse into Guatemala's sociopolitics. Although each family retains individual ownership of their house and farm plot, the pasturelands, a 250-acre forest preserve, a lake, and plantations of pineapple, pine, and lime trees are collectively owned. The co-op provides free day care, primary and secondary education, adult vocational

skyway at Parque Natural Ixpanpajul

training, and operates a pharmacy and clinic. The community also keeps two pickups and a minivan for anyone's use. Additional infrastructure includes a welding shop and two corn mills. In an effort to minimize dependence on outside sources, the community maintains its own seed bank.

Many of the community's residents lived in the Petén rainforests during the war years, on the run from Guatemalan government forces. In time, the jungle became a source of food, shelter, and safety and these experiences provided insights into uses for medicinal plants and food.

Among the cooperative's initiatives is community-based tourism. They are happy to show you around the village and share their stories, and also take great pride in their forest preserve and reforestation program. Rustic cabins and meals from the community are available for visitors.

Hotel Villa Maya

As you head east along the road to Tikal, an unpaved road cuts north toward the Petenchel Lagoon for about four kilometers to the excellent **C Hotel Villa Maya** (tel. 2223-5000, www.villasdeguatemala.com, $85 d), with its 56 comfortable, tastefully decorated rooms equipped with air-conditioning, hot water, and balconies overlooking the placid lagoon. There are also a swimming pool and an excellent restaurant. It's a bit out of the way, but the exclusive feel of this jungle outpost only adds to its allure.

Petencito Zoo

Farther west along this same road leading to the village of San Miguel is Petencito Zoo (8 A.M.-5 P.M., $3), housing a collection of local wildlife, including jaguars, monkeys, and macaws. The intrepid can ride the concrete water slides here, though their safety is questionable and at least one death has been reported.

ARCAS

Continuing west, the road again connects to the larger Lake Petén Itzá to ARCAS (tel. 7926-0946, www.arcasguatemala. com), the Wildlife Rescue and Conservation Association, where an animal rehabilitation center harbors animals captured from poachers, including jaguars, macaws, monkeys, and coatis. Although the animal rehabilitation area is not open to outsiders, an **Environmental Education and Interpretation Center** caters to the casual visitor. There is a nature trail showcasing a variety of medicinal plants, a beach, a bird observation platform, and an area for observing animals that cannot be reintroduced to the wild. During turtle season there are public hatchling releases with informative lectures (tel. 4144-9762, 8 P.M. daily, $1.50).

Although the site is perfectly accessible by road, most visitors come by boat. Tours leave Flores on weekdays at 8:30 A.M. (Spanish) and 3:30 P.M. (English) from the boat dock next to Restaurante La Guacamaya on the north end of the island. A tour costs $7 per person for a group of 1-2 people. Call ahead to confirm availability. You can also take a tour 9 A.M.-3 P.M. for $1.25 but you'll have to arrange your own transportation. Confirmation is not required if you choose to go this route.

Tayazal

Not to be confused with Tayasal, which once occupied the same territory as present-day Flores, the remains of this small site can be found up a hill near the village of San Miguel. Although the ruins themselves are not overly impressive, there is a wonderful lookout, known as a mirador, built into a tree atop a temple mound from where you have an exceptional view of Flores. The lookout is about two kilometers outside of town. Follow the signs for the "mirador."

PETÉN

Lake Petén Itzá

Once a pit stop for travel between Flores and Tikal, Lake Petén Itzá is quickly becoming a destination in its own right. The area around El Remate is home to Petén's fanciest accommodations, the 72-room Camino Real Tikal and the smaller, more exclusive La Lancha. There are also simpler accommodations, allowing you to take in the serene beauty of this large lake without busting your budget.

On the western shores of the lake, the towns of San Andrés and San José offer pleasant lakeside atmosphere and are an excellent place to learn Spanish. Language instruction here is combined with the opportunity to experience Petén's rich ecology and even contribute to its preservation while helping to meet the needs of local people. The Itzá culture has largely survived the onslaught of modernity and its people are more than willing to share their proud heritage with visitors.

SAN ANDRÉS AND SAN JOSÉ

The road from Flores heads west before cutting north along the lakeside to the small town of San Andés on its shores. You'll find the people here and in neighboring San José extremely friendly and laid-back. Many of the villagers still make their living from harvesting forest products such as chicle, allspice, and *xate* palm. The NGOs have been particularly active here since the creation of the Maya Biosphere Reserve and have found the communities very amenable to their conservation goals. The creation of a Spanish school was done in partnership with Conservation International several years ago, providing a viable alternative for income along the lines of sustainable development. The successful model has been emulated elsewhere, and there are now four Spanish schools operating in this area. They offer a unique alternative to more typical language-school destinations, where a large presence of foreigners sometimes works against the language-immersion experience.

Although the towns are accessible from Flores by boat, the high cost of motorboat fuel and the ease of access from the road have made this a less popular option for getting here. Still, boats sometimes leave from the boat dock near Hotel Santana and this is still the best option if you're staying at the wonderful Ni'tun Lodge near San Andrés.

San Andrés

Most travelers in these parts are almost certainly studying Spanish or helping out with one of the local NGOs in conservation or community development projects. Rates at all the area schools are comparable, somewhere between $150 and $175 per week, including 20 hours of one-on-one instruction and room and board with a local host family. The original San Adrés language school, **Eco-Escuela de Español** (tel. 5498-4539 or 5490-1235, www.ecoescuelaespanol.org), is still going strong and is the area's largest. Also in San Andrés is the newer **Nueva Juventud Spanish School** (tel. 5711-0040, www.volunteerpeten.org), set on a medicinal plant reserve where the focus is largely on volunteer opportunities with various projects benefiting the local community. Recent projects have included the construction of a local library and schools.

For budget accommodations in San Andrés, try the **Hotel Corina,** set atop a hill to the left as you come into town.

A more luxurious option is found three kilometers east of San Andrés along the road from Flores and then a few kilometers down a rugged dirt road accessible only by four-wheel-drive vehicles. Charmingly rustic ◖ **Ni'tun Lodge** (tel. 5201-0759 or 5414-5780, www.nitun.com,

© AL ARGUETA

a room at Ni'tun Lodge

$160 d) is set on the lakeshore with comfortable cabins made from stone, stick, and mortar. Inside you'll find wooden tree-trunk floors and typically Guatemalan accents, including Mayan blankets, rugs, and wooden furniture. All rooms have private hot-water bathroom. Room rates include breakfast. Gourmet meals, including a choice between 2-3 main courses, cost $25-30 for lunch or dinner. Most of the lodge's high-end clientele arrives by boat from Flores on all-inclusive packages, which you can book directly through the lodge. The lodge's creator and live-in manager, Bernie, has explored Petén extensively and is also the inspiration behind **Monkey Eco Tours,** which can take you to many of Petén's more remote sites in relative comfort and style with accordingly expensive prices. A five-day trek to El Mirador, for example, costs $250 per person per day.

San José

San José is a surprisingly pleasant town complete with a municipal recreation area on the lakeshore. Its somewhat steep streets meander into the surrounding hillside, affording stunning views of the pretty bay below. Adding to the town's intrigue is a Mayan cultural revival of the Itzá people. You'll see signs in this Mayan dialect around town. A community organization, the **Bio Itzá,** has its own language school and also manages a private forest preserve north of town along the fringes of El Zotz-San Miguel La Palotada Biotope.

According to local lore, the Itzá people came to San José from the Yucatán site of Chichén Itzá, led by the mythical figure Taitzá along a pathway known as the Camino Real 100 years before the arrival of the Spanish in the New World. Another unique aspect of the local culture are the town's two main annual **fiestas.** The first of these takes place between March 10 and 19 and includes a parade and fireworks, capped off by an unusual costumed dance in which a young girl and a horse skip together through the town streets. The second annual festival takes place on October 31 and November 1. It begins with a solemn Mass in the town's Catholic church, which houses three skulls in a glass case thought to belong to Spanish missionaries or the town's founders, depending on whom you believe. One of these skulls is removed from its resting place and is put on the church altar during the service; it is then carried through town on a velvet pillow by black-clad devotees, followed closely by children in traditional village costume and townsfolk. The procession stops along the way in several homes, where cane liquor, along with traditional food, are consumed and prayers and chants are offered. At the end, the skull is returned to its glass case in the town church, where it remains on display throughout the year.

The first of the town's two Spanish schools, **Escuela Bio Itzá** (tel. 7926-1363, bioitza@guate.net), works with the Bio Itzá's women's cooperative, which runs a botanical

PETÉN

garden for the production of natural products such as soap. San José's other language school is the more recently established **Mundo Maya Ecological Spanish School** (tel. 7928-8321, www.mundomayaguatemala.com). For food, there's pleasant **El Búngalo** serving reasonably priced Guatemalan fare right at the lakeside.

For accommodations, there's splendid ⟨ **Bahía Taitzá** (along the road into town in Barrio El Porvenir, tel. 7928-8125 or 5402-1961, www.taitza.com, $55 d), set along the lakeshore on one of Lake Petén Itzá's prettiest beaches. Its eight comfortable rooms are housed in a large building. All have high wooden ceilings and come equipped with fans, tiled floors, comfortable beds, and private hot-water baths. A patio out front offers nice views of the manicured lawns toward the lake. There are lakeside hammocks and a restaurant and bar serving good food and wonderful cocktails.

⟨ EL REMATE

El Remate starts about one kilometer past the turnoff to Yaxhá and the Belize border on the road from Santa Elena to Tikal. Once considered a stopping point along this road, El Remate has come into its own in recent years and has begun to pull its fair share of the Petén travel market. Its proximity to Tikal, fabulous lakeside setting, and variety of accommodations makes it a wonderful alternative to staying at Tikal or Flores, or better yet, a destination unto itself worthy of at least one night's stay.

Sights

The turnoff for the road heading west toward Belize, about two kilometers south of El Remate, was once known as "El Cruce," though the small settlement here is now known as **Ixlú**. Just off the road, about 200 meters down a signed path, are the ruins of **Ixlú** on the shores of **Laguna Salpetén**. There is a basic

campsite where you can rent canoes to take on the lake, but there is otherwise little else to do. A small information center can be found under a thatched-roof shelter by the road, with toilets and a map of the site.

Along the shores of Lake Petén Itzá, three kilometers down a dirt road heading west from the main Tikal-bound branch, is the **Biotopo Cerro Cahuí** (7 A.M.-5 P.M. daily, $4). This 650-hectare mountainside park is particularly good for **bird-watching** and was initially set aside for the protection of Petén's oscillated turkey. It encompasses part of the lake's watershed and ranges in elevation 100-360 meters above sea level. You'll find several lowland rainforest species of birds, including toucans, parrots, and trogons. Two trails (2.75 miles or 3.75 miles long) take you up the hill into the surrounding forest to lookout points where there are wonderful views of the lake below. Maps and information are available at the entrance kiosk. A swimming dock near the entrance juts to a splendidly clear expanse of turquoise water and is a great place for a swim.

Shopping

El Remate is also a great place to pick up local crafts, consisting of some very attractive wood carvings made from fallen logs and providing a sustainable alternative to wide-scale forest destruction for agriculture. You'll find several handicrafts shops on the main strip along the road to Tikal.

Recreation

Bird-watching tours with knowledgeable, English-speaking local guides can be arranged from La Casa de Don David (tel. 7928-8469 or 5306-2190, www.lacasadedondavid.com) and cost between $40 and $75 for a 3-6 hour tour. In addition to Biotopo Cerro Cahuí, trips are available across the lake to roosting sites and other birding areas up the Río Ixpop and Río Ixlú.

Most of the area lodges can arrange

© AL ARGUETA

Lake Petén Itza beckons for a swim.

horseback riding to Ixlú and Laguna Salpetén for about $20 per person. Casa Mobego (tel. 5909-6999) does **walking tours** to Laguna Salpetén for $10 per person and rents double **kayaks** for about $4 for one hour or $8 for four. Casa de Doña Tonita (tel. 5701-7114) also rents kayaks for about $2 an hour and **mountain bikes** for $5 a day. Alternatively, La Casa de Don David can arrange almost anything you can think of and also sells discount tickets to area **canopy tours.**

There are some wonderful **swimming** docks around the lake, the best of these at Restaurante El Muelle along the main road, in front of the Cerro Cahui Biotope, and in front of Casa Mobego.

Accommodations

You'll find plenty of accommodations along the town's main drag beside the northbound Tikal road as well as along the dirt road diverting west that hugs the lakeshore.

UNDER $10

From the northbound Tikal road, the first place you'll come across (on the right) is the **Hostal y Camping El Paraíso** (tel. 4077-8538, elparaisodejuan@hotmail.com), where you can camp for $2 or stay in a rustic dorm room overlooking the lake for $4. Bathrooms and showers are shared, but there is mosquito netting and hammocks for lounging. Guests have use of the kitchen. Just down the road is the offbeat **Hotel Sak Luk** (tel. 5494-5925, tikalsakluk@ hotmail.com), where four- or five-person dorms with lake views and mosquito netting start at $4 per person. Double-occupancy rooms with private baths, mosquito netting, and lake views are available for $13. Hammocks go for $2 and you can camp here for the same price. There is a restaurant serving Italian food and you can have your laundry done here. As one guest put it, though, "It seems like the guy just gave up on it at some point." Another cheapie along the Tikal road is **Bruno's Place** (tel. 7928-8080,

$8 d), with seven shared-bath guest rooms of acceptable cleanliness with fans and splashes of decor. Entrance is through the host family's living room.

On the dirt road running alongside the Lake Petén Itzá shore toward Cerro Cahuí Biotope are a number of very pleasant budget accommodations set far off from the noise of the main highway. **Hostal Casa Mobego** (tel. 5909-6999) is a popular place, also known as Casa Roja. Rooms with shared bath are housed in attractive stone and wood cottages; beds on a concrete base with squishy foam mattress and mosquito netting cost $5 per person. There is a nicely decorated main house where breakfast is served ($5) and dinner ($7) can be arranged with a bit of notice. There's also a book exchange, kayaks for rent, and the staff can arrange minibus transportation anywhere you may need to go. As you continue along the road, a few steps away is **Casa de Doña Tonita** (tel. 5701-7114), offering five simple wooden cabins, all with shared bath and hammocks on balconies affording lovely lake views for $6 per person. A night in the five-bed dorm will set you back a mere $5. There is a nice dock out front over the lake with hammocks. **Hotel Don Ernesto** (tel. 5750-8375) is another budget option in this neck of the woods where you have a choice of rooms with shared bath for $4 per person or slightly nicer double rooms with private baths, ceiling fans, and decks with hammocks for $27. A restaurant serves breakfast, lunch, and dinner.

Farther down the road as you approach the entrance to Cerro Cahuí is **Hotel y Restaurante Mom Ami** (tel. 7928-8413 or 7928-8480, www.hotelmonami.com), with a variety of accommodations from a six-bed dormitory with shared bath at $7 per person to bungalows with private hot-water bath costing $20-26 d. The lodge is owned by ecologist Santiago Billy, a pioneer of Petén's environmental movement who has fought for many years for the preservation of the Maya Biosphere Reserve.

$10-25

There are several good values in this price range. Along the main street is the friendly **Hotel y Restaurant Sun Breeze** (tel. 7928-8044 or 5898-2665, www.sunbreezehotelytransportation.blogspot.com), where clean, simple double rooms with mosquito netting and fans go for $20 with shared-bath accommodations or $25 with private bathrooms. The helpful staff can do your laundry and also arrange reasonably priced transport or guided tours to area attractions such as Tikal and Yaxhá. Another solid choice is **Posada Ixchel** (tel. 7928-8475, www.posadaixchel.es.tl), where simple but clean rooms in wooden cabins go for $11 (d) with shared bath or $17 (d) with private bathroom. All rooms have fans; most have mosquito netting and porches with chairs for lounging. **(Hotel Las Gardenias** (www.hotelasgardenias.com, $20 d) has comfortable, wood-paneled rooms with nice extras like purified drinking water and reading lamps. Some of the rooms have air-conditioning. Outside are patios with hammocks for lounging. There's a decent on-site restaurant serving three meals a day.

$25-50

On the main Flores-Tikal highway, midway through town you'll find **El Muelle** (Km. 30, tel. 5514-9785, www.hotelyrestauranteelmuelle.com, $40-50 d) along with its namesake dock on the lake. The comfortable rooms are housed in an airy wooden building and there's a nice swimming pool to cool off in. More rooms (with better lake views) are being added.

Along the lakeside road toward Cerro Cahuí, at the junction with the road leading to Tikal, is **(La Casa de Don David** (tel. 7928-8469 or 5306-2190, www.lacasadedondavid.com), a highly recommended establishment owned by a native Floridian transplanted to Guatemala in the late 1970s. His friendly wife and daughter help run the lodge, consisting of 15 rooms with private hot-water bathrooms set amid nicely landscaped grounds that include a ceiba tree. Eleven of the rooms have air-conditioning; all have fans. Rates range from $46 for slightly noisier double rooms with fans under the restaurant to $70 for quieter double rooms with air-conditioning set farther back from the main house. All prices include one free meal per day. The restaurant serves delicious international dishes ranging $5-10 for lunch or dinner. The friendly staff can help you book transportation to virtually anywhere and can answer your travel questions. You can also snag discounted tickets for area canopy tours at the attractive gift shop in the main lobby. The hotel's very informative website is well worth checking out before visiting Petén.

Near the entrance to the Biotopo Cerro Cahui preserve, my favorite of El Remate's hotels is **Posada del Cerro** (tel. 5376-8722, www.posadadelcerro.com, $13 p/p in dorm; $40-64 d). It's an excellent value and a great place to get away from it all. The comfortably rustic rooms lack nothing in style; some feature cool stonework, while others have angled thatched-roof ceilings. There are also more modern apartments with full kitchens available. There's a small restaurant where guests can enjoy meals or simply hang out under the *palapa* roof. The lake is right in front of the property and there's a nice swimming area.

Charming **La Mansión del Pájaro Serpiente** (tel. 5702-9434 or 7928-8498, www.30minutesfromtikal.com, $44-55 d) is another fine choice. Owned by a Guatemalan-American family, the lodge sits along the main road to Tikal at the southbound entrance to El Remate. Set on a hillside overlooking the lake are 11 stylish guest rooms housed in stone and thatched-roof exteriors with Guatemalan furnishings and stone, tile, and hardwood accents; they have fans or air-conditioning and private hot-water bathrooms inside. It has a restaurant serving three meals a day and a swimming pool amid the tropical landscape.

$50-100

Straight out of a West Texas cowboy's dream is **Palomino Ranch Hotel** (tel. 7928-8419 or 2474-0758, www.hotelpalominoranch.com, $50 d), with quirky antiques and cool Western-inspired decor that's tastefully done. There's even an old jukebox. Rooms are housed in a large hacienda-style building centered round a swimming pool and have hot water and air-conditioning. The lodge organizes horseback-riding trips to area attractions and there is a daily horse show in the large horse pen. The lodge is on the Cerro Cahui road about 500 meters from the junction with the main Tikal-bound highway.

Also in this price range is the **Hotel Gringo Perdido** (tel. 2334-2305, www.hotelgringo-perdido.com, $70-90 d), which started several years ago as a budget accommodation but has gradually worked its way into pricier domains. Rates include a tasty four-course dinner and breakfast. The lodge's setting is right on the lakeshore within the boundaries of the Cerro Cahui preserve. The pricier rooms have private baths; all rooms are semi-open with roll-up blinds. A newer concept is its **Piramide Paraiso** boutique hotel, on the adjacent grounds, where stylish and spacious villas housed in more modern concrete constructions with hardwood and Maya textile accents go for $100 per person, breakfast and dinner included. The rooms also have ceiling fans, air-conditioning, and plasma TVs.

$100-200

Lake Petén Itzá is not without a large resort. The **Camino Real Tikal** (tel. 7926-0204/09, www.caminoreal.com.gt, $120 d) is a 72-room complex that has been in operation for over 20 years. A planned expansion may soon make it twice as large. The Camino Real has all the comforts you would expect from an international resort chain. The modern rooms are housed in concrete structures topped with thatched-roof exteriors. There are two restaurants, a bar, a coffee shop, and a swimming pool. Recreational activities available to guests include sailing, kayaking, and sailboarding. A large ship does lake tours on weekends and transfers from the Mundo Maya International Airport can be arranged before arrival via a free shuttle service. Discounted accommodation packages are often available by calling directly or booking via a travel agency.

For Petén's ultimate in style and luxury, head to fabulous **(La Lancha** (tel. 7928-8331, www.coppolaresorts.com), farther west along the lakeshore in the village of Jobompiche. Part of movie director Francis Ford Coppola's impressive portfolio of properties, including two other hotels in Belize, La Lancha is Petén's best-kept secret. Its 10 comfortable rooms are housed in lake-view casitas ($175-280 d) or rainforest casitas ($110-210 d, depending on season). All rooms have exquisite Guatemalan fabrics and Balinese hardwood furniture. The rooms' wooden decks are graced with hammocks in which you can lounge the day away watching the sky's reflection on placid Lake Petén Itzá or order drinks from the bar via your in-room "shell phone." Rates include a continental breakfast and the restaurant serves gourmet Guatemalan dishes for lunch and dinner for about $25 per person.

There is a swimming pool, but if you wish to cool off in the lake, a short downhill walk leads to the water's edge. Kayaks and mountain bikes are available for exploring at your leisure and you can book day trips to Tikal. Other activities include sightseeing in El Remate and Flores, fishing on the lake, and bird-watching at Cerro Cahuí.

Food

There are a number of more-than-adequate restaurants in El Remate. Along the road to Tikal, the first place you'll come to is **(El Muelle** (tel. 5514-9785, all meals daily), serving daily specials for about $10. The menu is heavy on meat dishes and lake fish, but it also serves pasta, vegetarian fare, and a wide assortment of desserts. The atmosphere is quite pleasant with views of the lake and the establishment's attractive namesake dock from which you can take a refreshing plunge into the turquoise waters. Upstairs, five rooms with air-conditioning and private baths were nearing completion. Expect prices to be in the $50 d range. There is also a small gift shop selling books, woodcarvings, and other knick-knacks.

Back on the road toward Tikal, the next place you'll come across is **Restaurante Cahuí** (noon-8:30 P.M. daily), a well-established place overlooking the lake under an airy *palapa* roof, where a varied menu of inexpensive dishes is served. Another good option in this neck of the woods, **Restaurante Nakun's** (tel. 4014-2324 or 7823-9174, 9 A.M.-10 P.M. daily) specializes in tasty pizza and burgers; a large pie costs about $14. They also rent motorcycles for $16 per day.

Along the road fringing the lake shore, you'll come across **Las Orquídeas** (tel. 5701-9022, lasorquideasremate@yahoo.com, 6 A.M.-10 P.M. Tues.-Sun.), serving decent pizza, pasta, and sandwiches. Just down the road, **Mon Ami** (tel. 7928-8413, all meals daily) serves tasty French and Guatemalan fare. In accordance with the Western-inspired digs at **Palomino Ranch Hotel** (tel. 7928-8419 or 2474-0758, www.hotelpalominoranch.com, $4-16) is a menu that includes decent fajitas, chicken wings, and grilled steaks.

For a splurge, head to **(La Lancha** (tel. 7928-8331, all meals daily) for gourmet Guatemalan cuisine for about $20 per person for lunch and dinner. You can enjoy an assortment of flavors from the Francis Ford Coppola wineries or your favorite drink from the bar while dining in an airy *palapa*-style building high above the lake. It's housed in its namesake lodge west of El Remate in Jobompiche.

© AL ARGUETA

the dining room at La Lancha

Getting There and Around

El Remate is extremely easy to get to and from, as there is plenty of traffic heading up and down the road between Tikal and Flores. A local transport cooperative also operates minivans for trips to local attractions. Check with **Hotel y Restaurant Sun Breeze** (tel. 7928-8044 or 5898-2665) for availability and prices.

East to Belize

The road heading east to Belize is paved only about halfway despite repeated government announcements to the contrary. It seems the completed, paved road has been inaugurated by several presidents but the truth is that local authorities have inexplicably dragged their heels in getting one of the most important roads in Petén up to snuff.

There are some interesting sites along the way, the most important being the ruins of Yaxhá, 11 kilometers north from the main road. (The ruins are covered in the section on the *Maya Biosphere Reserve,* of which the site is a part.) Encouragingly, some of the lagoons and surrounding forest just north of this road are being opened to ecotourism by forward-thinking entrepreneurs, thus providing an alternative to the ecological destruction that has characterized the traditional northward advance of the agricultural frontier into protected lands.

LAGUNA SALPETÉN

Just one kilometer from the Ixlu turnoff (where there is a small settlement by the same name) on the road heading east to Belize is Laguna Salpetén. Although most of the forest around this beautiful emerald-colored lagoon was cleared for agriculture long ago, a small patch of forest remains on a spit of land jutting into the body of water. This is also the well-chosen location of **Maya Zacpetén Lodge** (tel. 5597-1111 or 7823-5843, mayazacpetenjunglelodge.com, $140 d). The rooms are housed in comfortable concrete cottages with thatched-roof exteriors. Activities include bird-watching, hiking the jungle trails, horseback riding, boat tours of the lagoon and nighttime crocodile sighting. Access is via a lake-bound turnoff from the main road heading east to Belize and then a short boat ride across the lagoon or directly to the lodge on a rough dirt road from El Remate (4.5 kilometers).

LAGUNA MACANCHÉ

This lovely lagoon lies seven kilometers east of Ixlú. A northbound, signed turnoff leads another two kilometers to **El Retiro Lakeside Sanctuary and Eco-Lodge** (tel. 5932-0644, www.retiro-guatemala.com, $20 p/p camping to $60 d), a private nature preserve set on the spectacularly wild north shore of the turquoise lagoon. Accommodations are in comfortable thatched-roof bungalows with private hot-water bath and porch or in tents on raised wooden platforms. You can also camp here in your own tent. The lodge features a good restaurant and a dock for swimming as well as a **serpentarium,** featuring 20 species of snakes found in Guatemala; all are professionally housed in secure glass tanks.

The lodge offers guided hikes on jungle trails to remote, jungle-lined lagoons and cenotes (limestone sinkholes) or nighttime crocodile scouting starting at $30 per person.

HOLTÚN

This small, unrestored Maya site lies 30 kilometers from Ixlú and then a 20-minute walk south from the main road. It features small temple mounds and is really suitable only for the die-hard fan of Mayan ruins.

MELCHOR DE MENCOS

This small border town sits on the edge of the Río Mopán and is fairly pleasant as far as border towns go. The border crossing with Belize is fairly straightforward, though you'll probably be asked to pay the local equivalent of about $1.50 to exit or arrive in Guatemala, which is technically illegal. Some travelers have asked for a receipt in an attempt to dissuade the collection of the token bribe, but border officials sometimes issue you a deposit stub stamped with an official-looking immigration seal. The account most likely belongs to the bribe's collector.

Many people cross the border from Belize on day trips to Tikal or Yaxhá from one of the Belize jungle lodges. Daily shuttle vans make the trip to the border from Flores continuing to Belize City and there is also public transport to the border from the bus depot in Santa Elena.

On the Belize side, there are buses leaving from the border every half hour. You can also take a taxi ride three kilometers to **Benque Viejo del Carmen,** the first sizable settlement, from where there are more frequent services. Another 13 kilometers east is **San Ignacio,** a pleasant town with much to see and do.

Accommodations and Food

There is little reason to linger here, as at most border crossings in Guatemala, but there are at least two serviceable hotels should you need to spend the night here. Right at the border overlooking the Río Mopán is the aptly named **Río Mopán Lodge** (tel. 7926-5196, www.tikaltravel.com, $20 d). Its Swiss owner organizes various nature tours to local attractions—including remote archaeological sites such as Holmul—and is a great source for local information. Other activities include canoeing or tubing on the river. The lodge has a restaurant specializing in Mediterranean food. Another option is **Hotel La Cabaña** (Barrio El Centro, tel. 7926-5205, $40 d), with comfortable rooms including air-conditioning, private hot-water bathrooms, and cable TV. There are also a swimming pool and a restaurant serving local and international dishes. Aside from a few snack and drink stands on the road leading to the border crossing, these two hotels are your best (and really, your only) options for food.

MAYA MOUNTAINS-CHIQUIBUL BIOSPHERE RESERVE

South of Melchor de Mencos and skirting the border between Belize and Guatemala is the Maya Mountains-Chiquibul Biosphere Reserve. Although its name makes it sound rather official, it is really the epitome of a "paper park," as it lacks any real protection and is being lost due to the advance of the agricultural frontier originating around populated areas in southern Petén. Still, there remain some beautiful areas of intact forest and the park is certainly worth saving for the ruggedness of the terrain and its corresponding ecological and biological diversity.

Recreation

National Geographic has put the word out concerning the existence of Central America's longest cave network, the **Chiquibul caves,** which originate in Guatemala but continue for most of their expanse in Belize. The Zactun entrance (Guatemala) is the passageway to the westernmost **Xibalba** cave, harboring one of the cave system's largest chambers, averaging about 80 meters (260 feet) in width and accentuated by spectacular vaulted rooms. The caves are extremely remote and have been explored only by hard-core spelunkers. They are probably more

easily accessible from Belize, which is where most scientists studying the caves have focused their efforts. It will be interesting to see if any work is done on the Guatemalan side during the next few years.

Access to the caves begins from the town of Dolores, 24 kilometers north of Poptún. From there, a gravel road leads to the settlement of Sacul Abajo. A rough dirt road continues to the village of Las Brisas, which is the final jumping-off point for the remaining 3-4-hour hike to the Zactun entrance. Dr. Ric Finch, a retired geology professor, has been leading trips to Guatemala since 1987. In April 2007, together with Antigua resident caver/explorer Mike Shawcross, Finch led a cavers' trip to various sites in Guatemala, including the Chiquibul caves. Finch and Shawcross scouted the access routes and contacted local guides in the village of Las Brisas. The trip may be replicated in the coming years. For more information, contact **Rutahsa Adventures** (299 Allen Hollow Rd., Cookeville, TN 38501, 931/520-7047 U.S., www.rutahsa.com).

The **Río Chiquibul** originates in the hills of Belize and flows westward into Guatemala, going underground in many places through the Chiquibul cave system. It's a cool jungle river perfectly suited for rafting trips. **Maya Expeditions** (tel. 2363-4955, www.mayaexpeditions.com) offers 1-3-day river trips ($85-130) via raft or kayak combining a visit to some little-explored caves along the river's course. Longer trips, including horseback riding to Mayan sites, are also available.

Tikal National Park

Tikal National Park, the oldest and best known of Guatemala's national parks, was created in 1956. It encompasses 575 square kilometers (222 square miles) of primary tropical forest and protects a vast array of wildlife, as well as harboring the remains of one of the Mayan civilization's greatest cities. Tikal is understandably high on the list of priorities for any visitor to Guatemala and shouldn't be missed, as it affords the unique opportunity to combine a visit to a site of mammoth historical importance both in terms of natural and human heritage. Owing to its singular importance in the spheres of natural and human history, UNESCO declared Tikal National Park a World Heritage Site in 1979.

Tikal's towering Temple I dominates the city's Great Plaza and is an icon for Guatemala itself, much like the Eiffel Tower and Paris. Perhaps not as readily apparent, Tikal National Park also represents the ongoing effort to protect what remains of Petén's tropical forest ecosystem. The park is at the edge, geographically speaking, of the Maya Biosphere Reserve, but at the very heart and soul of what conservationists and archaeologists are trying to protect. The conservation of Petén's rich archaeological and natural treasures has the potential to provide a livelihood to a growing population of *Peteneros* long after any perceived benefits from clearing the forests for short-term gain. The lessons learned from Tikal's 50-plus-year existence can help conservationists better manage newer parks deeper inside the forest reserve, which will eventually be open to increasing numbers of visitors. Whatever the approach to managing these newer parks, what is certain is that Petén's vast wealth as the heartland of the Mayan civilization remains largely untapped.

If you are fortunate enough to visit Tikal, go home with the knowledge that you have been afforded a glimpse into the vast wilderness that remains mostly untouched north of this complex. In the forests beyond Tikal are countless other sites, some still undiscovered, which deserve as much protection and require the vigilance of international travelers and activists to ensure their continued preservation.

HISTORY

Tikal was settled somewhere between 900 and 700 B.C. on a site undoubtedly selected because of its position above seasonal swamps that characterize much of the terrain in this part of Petén, as well as the availability of flint for trade and the manufacture of tools and weapons. It remained little more than a small settlement for at least 200 years. By 500 B.C. the first stone temple was erected and later used as the basis for the large Preclassic pyramid dominating the complex now known as El Mundo Perdido. Tikal continued its steady progress during the late Preclassic period, sometime around 200 B.C., with the construction of ceremonial buildings found in the North Acropolis and the completion of the pyramid at El Mundo Perdido.

Classic Period

By the time of Christ, Tikal's Great Plaza had begun to take shape and by the Early Classic period, around A.D. 250, Tikal was an important religious, commercial, and cultural center with a sprawling population. King Yax Ehb' Xoc established his dynasty at this time, one which was recognized by the 33 subsequent rulers of Tikal until recorded history at the site goes silent in A.D. 869.

The history of Tikal is closely tied to the emergence of Teotihuacán, a powerful city-state to the north in Central Mexico, which it should be noted was completely non-Mayan

Tikal's Great Plaza

in origin. Its influence began to be felt during the middle of the 4th century A.D., when Teotihuacán dispatched a warrior by the name of Siyak K'ak' (Born of Fire) to aid Tikal in its war against the neighboring city of Uaxactún. Siyak K'ak' introduced the use of the atlatl, a wooden sling that allowed Tikal's warriors to defeat their enemy by firing arrows without having to engage in hand-to-hand combat. The aid from the north, according to recorded texts chronicling the execution of Tikal's Jaguar Paw I, amounted to a military takeover with the installation of Yax Nuun Ayin I (Curl Nose or First Crocodile), of Teotihuacán royalty, who later married into Tikal's dynasty.

With Teotihuacán hegemony now firmly established, Tikal dominated central Petén for most of the next 500 years. It grew to become one of the richest and most powerful Mayan city-states, aided by its dominance of strategic lowland trade routes. Tikal's influence

reached as far south as Copán and as far west as Yaxchilán.

At the same time, the city-state of Calakmul, just north of the Guatemalan border in present-day Mexico, began its assent toward regional dominance. As the power and influence of Teotihuacán waned in the 5th century A.D., Calakmul emerged as a geopolitical force to be reckoned with, incorporating a number of vassal states surrounding Tikal and contesting its dominion over the Mayan lowlands. A key alliance was forged between Calakmul and Caracol, in present-day Belize. Tikal launched a preemptive strike against Caracol in A.D. 556. With backing from Calakmul, Caracol launched a counterattack on Tikal in A.D. 562; the latter suffered a crushing defeat. Desecration of Tikal's stelae and ritual burials, in addition to the destruction of many of its written records, followed.

After this defeat, Tikal underwent a 130-year hiatus from erecting inscribed monuments, though it has recently been discovered that Temple V was constructed during this period. Mayanists now believe Tikal was never completely broken, despite defeat at the hands of its bitter rival.

Height of Power and Decline

Tikal reemerged as a dominant power beginning in A.D. 682 under the new leadership of Hasaw Chan K'awil (Heavenly Standard Bearer), whose 52-year reign was marked by the definitive defeat of Calakmul in A.D. 695 with reassertion of control over regional satellite cities such as Río Azul and Waka' as well as a frenzy of new temple construction. The six great temples dominating Tikal's ceremonial center were reconstructed between A.D. 670 and 810 by Hasaw Chan K'awil and his successors.

At the height of the Classic period, Tikal covered an area of about 30 square kilometers and had a population of at least 100,000,

PETÉN

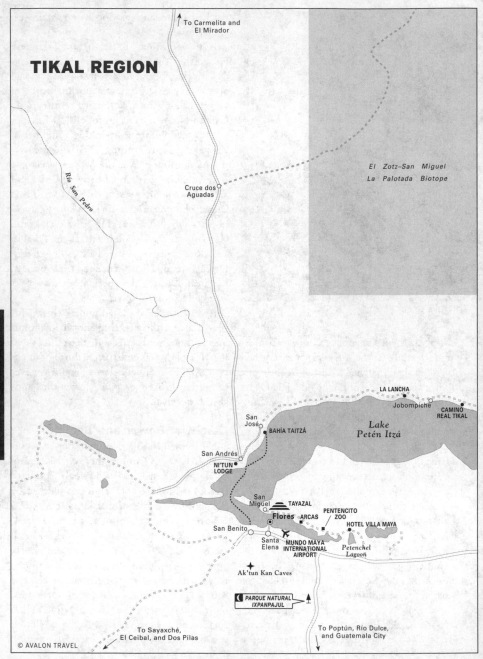

TIKAL REGION

To Carmelita and
El Mirador

Río San Pedro

Cruce dos
Aguadas

*El   Zotz–San   Miguel
La   Palotada   Biotope*

LA LANCHA

Jobompiche

CAMINO
REAL TIKAL

San
José

BAHÍA TAITZÁ

*Lake
Petén Itzá*

San Andrés

NI'TUN
LODGE

San
Miguel

TAYAZAL

Flores

ARCAS

PENTENCITO
ZOO

HOTEL VILLA MAYA

San Benito

Santa
Elena

MUNDO MAYA
INTERNATIONAL
AIRPORT

*Petenchel
Lagoon*

Ak'tun Kan Caves

*PARQUE NATURAL
IXPANPAJUL*

To Sayaxché,
El Ceibal, and Dos Pilas

To Poptún, Río Dulce,
and Guatemala City

© AVALON TRAVEL

To Uaxactún

THE RUINS OF TIKAL

Tikal

Tikal National Park

Cerro Cahui Biotope

MAYA ZACPETÉN LODGE

EL REMATE

POSADA DEL CERRO

IXLÚ

Salpetén Lagoon

SANTUARIO ECOLÓGICO EL RETRIO

Macanché Lagoon

Ixiú

To Melchor de Mencos and Belizean border

Río Ixpop

Río Ixlú

0   10 mi

0   10 km

though some Mayanists believe it may have been much greater.

By the beginning of the 9th century A.D., conditions worsened for many city-states across the Mayan lowlands with the Classic Maya collapse in full swing. Tikal was no exception. The city-state's last inscription is recorded on Stela 24, which dates to A.D. 869. Tikal, like Petén's other Mayan cities, was completely abandoned by the late 10th century A.D. The city would be reclaimed by the jungle and largely forgotten until its rediscovery in the late 17th century.

Rediscovery

The Itzá who occupied the present-day island of Flores probably knew about Tikal and may have worshipped here. Spanish missionary friars passing through Petén after the conquest mention the existence of cities buried beneath the jungle, but it wasn't until 1848 that the Guatemalan government commissioned explorers Modesto Méndez and Ambrosio Tut to visit the site. The pair brought along an artist, Euseblo Lara, to record their discoveries. In 1877, Swiss explorer Dr. Gustav Bernoulli visited Tikal and removed the carved wooden lintels from Temples I and IV. He shipped them to Basel, where they remain on display at the Museum für Völkerkunde.

Scientific study of the site would begin in 1881 with the arrival of British archaeologist Alfred P. Maudslay. His work was subsequently continued by Teobert Maler, Alfred M. Tozzer, and R. E. Merwin, among others. The inscriptions at Tikal owe their decipherment to the work of Sylvanis G. Morley. In the mid-1950s, an airstrip was built, making access to the site much easier. The University of Pennsylvania carried out excavations between 1956 and 1969, along with Guatemala's Institute of Anthropology and History. With help from Spanish Cooperation, Temples I and V have been restored as part of a project begun in 1991.

A relatively small part of Tikal has been

© AL ARGUETA

Coatimundis are a common sight in Tikal National Park.

the air. The roof combs of the Great Plaza pyramids pop out from the jungle canopy as toucans dart from tree to tree with their curious yellow beaks, like bananas with big black wings. More than 400 species of birds have been recorded at Tikal. *The Birds of Tikal,* by Frank Smythe, is a useful guide in this regard.

Other animals you may come across during your visit include coatis, which you should refrain from feeding. If you spend the night here, don't be afraid if you awake to the raucous of a howling roar emanating from the forest. Sometimes confused with wild cats by first-time visitors, the sounds come from the locally abundant howler monkeys. During your explorations in Tikal, you will probably come across the smaller and ever-more-playful spider monkeys, which swing from tree to tree in the forest surrounding the ruins.

Among the park's most fascinating creatures are jaguars. Recent studies done over a two-month span have revealed the confirmed existence of seven of these large spotted cats within the national park's boundaries and it is thought that at least nine roam its 575-square-kilometer (222-square-mile) confines.

EXPLORING THE PARK

Many visitors come to Tikal on day trips from Belize, Flores, and Guatemala City. While a day at the ruins is adequate for seeing some of the archaeological highlights, staying at the park allows you to enjoy its equally splendid natural setting. After the crowds have departed, you'll be free to wander about the ruins unhurried, and at times you may feel as if you have the site all to yourself. The sunset from the top of Temple IV is truly inspiring, but is now only an option in the winter months when the sun sets earlier as park rangers make sure everyone is out by 6 p.m. For movie buffs, the view from Tikal's Temple IV can be appreciated in *Star Wars: Episode IV,* as the site of the rebels' secret base. The Great Plaza also made an appearance in the movie *2012.*

officially discovered and excavated. New discoveries await, along with new information that will undoubtedly continue to shed light on the turbulent history of the Mayan civilization. Among the more recent discoveries are the 1996 unearthing of a stela from A.D. 468 in the Great Plaza and the location of Temple V inscriptions challenging the notion of Tikal's 130-year hiatus after its defeat against Calakmul.

FLORA AND FAUNA

Tikal's abundant wildlife is most active early and late in the day, with birds and forest creatures more easily seen at these times. The summit of Temple IV, Tikal's highest structure, is a particularly popular place at sunrise and sunset. From your position high above the forest canopy, you can watch the sun dip below (or rise above) the horizon of unbroken tropical forest as far as the eye can see, while the chatter of myriad birds and forest creatures permeates

© AL ARGUETA

Watch out for wildlife on the road Into Tikal National Park.

The park's main gate is found along the road from Flores and El Remate, where there's a checkpoint. From here, it's another 17 kilometers to the main entrance, parking lot, and visitors center. Entrance to the park costs $19 ($3 for Guatemalan nationals) and is collected at the booth just opposite the parking lot. The park is open 6 A.M.-6 P.M. daily. If you arrive after 3 P.M., your ticket should be stamped with the next day's date, allowing you to enter the ruins the next day at no additional cost. Tickets are checked at a second booth on the trail between the first gate and the entrance to the ruins proper, opposite an oft-photographed ceiba tree gracing the side of the road. Sunrise tours, once a popular activity, are no longer an option, as no one is allowed inside the park before 6 A.M.

The visitors center is at the main entrance to the park on your left. There are a scale model of the site, the Museo Lítico, an overpriced eatery,

and a few small shops selling books, souvenirs, snacks, and sundries, including color print film, bug spray, and sunscreen. Nearby are the park campsite, police substation, and a post office. The other museum is farther along, near the airstrip next to the hotels. You can book licensed guides at the visitors center for $40 for up to four people, plus $5 for each additional person.

The park website is www.tikalpark.com and has lots of very useful information for planning your visit. A modern archaeological research facility, with a donation from Japan, was being built opposite the visitors center.

Guided Tours

Guided tours of Tikal are best arranged with one of the recommended Flores travel agencies, though you can also hire the services of a certified freelance guide at the visitors center near the park entrance for $40 for up to four people.

◖ THE RUINS OF TIKAL

There is plenty to explore in this vast Mayan city that once harbored thousands of people and you could easily spend several days here taking it all in. The ruins in evidence today are representative of the latter years of Tikal's existence, as the Mayans built on top of existing temples and palaces. Most of the major structures you'll see were built after the time of Tikal's resurgence in the late 7th century A.D.

The Great Plaza

Most visitors to Tikal head straight from the park entrance to the Great Plaza, and if you are crunched for time this is probably the best approach. A path from the ticket control booth leads you to the plaza in about 20 minutes. You'll gain an appreciation for the site's elevated setting as you walk uphill toward the heart of the ceremonial center. The view from the back of Temple I as you approach the Great Plaza is always impressive at first sight, as it gives

PETÉN

a ceiba tree in Tikal National Park

you an idea of the sheer size of the monuments erected by the Mayans. Tourist brochures and posters can never adequately convey just how large and impressive Tikal's temples are.

The path continues alongside the temple and you are at once greeted by the magnificent Temple II, which faces Temple I, as you enter the large, grassy plaza. Also known as "El Gran Jaguar" (The Great Jaguar), Temple I rises to a height of 44 meters (144 feet). The imposing structure was erected to honor Hasaw Chan K'awil (Heavenly Standard Bearer), the ruler who successfully led Tikal to victory against Calakmul. It was built to harbor his remains and was completed shortly after his death in A.D. 721 by son and successor Yik'in Chan K'awil, probably with instructions from his father.

The tomb was situated at the temple's core and contained the ruler's remains surrounded by jade, stingray spines, seashells, and pearls, which were typical of Mayan burials. It was believed the instruments would aid the person

in his journey into the underworld. This journey is depicted on a bone fragment, also found in the tomb, showing a royal figure in a canoe rowed by mythical animal figures. Tikal's museum harbors a reconstruction of the tomb, known as Tumba 116. Carried off to a museum in Basel, Switzerland, is the door lintel found at the top of the pyramid depicting a jaguar from which the temple gets its name.

It was once possible to climb Temple I, but this has not been allowed for several years now. The view from the top was truly spectacular, with Temple II in the foreground and the roof combs of Temples III and IV protruding from the jungle behind it. The structure was closed to climbers partly because of damage caused by a chain aiding in this activity, though the death of at least two visitors after tumbling down its steep steps certainly put the final nail in the coffin. The view from the top was popular in tourism posters and brochures from the early 1980s and you can still sometimes see them in unexpected places.

Across the plaza stands the slightly smaller **Temple II,** built to honor Hasaw Chan K'awil's wife, Lady 12 Macaw. Also known as the Temple of the Masks for the large, severely eroded masks flanking its central staircase, it is thought to predate Temple I by a few years. About 10 years ago, a staircase was constructed on its side to allow access to the top, though you could once climb directly up its central staircase. The view from the top is still as good as ever, with a frontal view of Temple I and the North Acropolis off to the side. Temple II probably once stood at the same height as its counterpart when its roof comb was intact, though its restored height is 38 meters (125 feet).

The North Acropolis

Occupying the Great Plaza's northern end is the aptly named North Acropolis, its foundations dating as far back as 100 B.C., though the 12 temples sitting atop this large structure

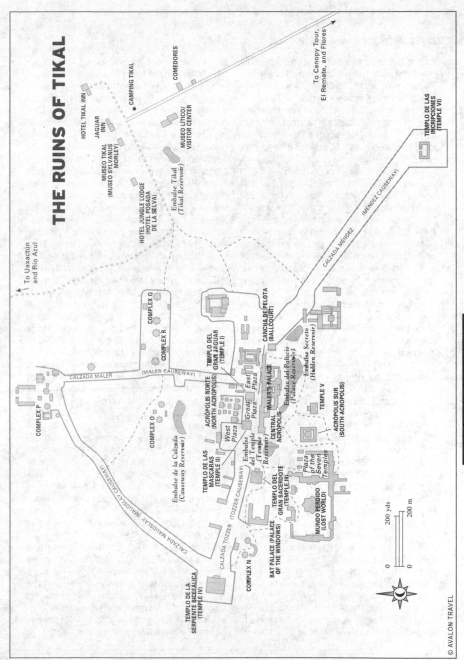

THE RUINS OF TIKAL

To Uaxactún and Río Azul

To Canopy Tour, El Remate, and Flores

HOTEL TIKAL INN

JAGUAR INN

MUSEO TIKAL (MUSEO SYLVANUS MORLEY)

CAMPING TIKAL

COMEDORES

HOTEL JUNGLE LODGE (HOTEL POSADA DE LA SELVA)

MUSEO LÍTICO/ VISITOR CENTER

Embalse Tikal (Tikal Reservoir)

CALZADA MÉNDEZ

(MÉNDEZ CAUSEWAY)

TEMPLO DE LAS INSCRIPCIONES (TEMPLE VI)

COMPLEX Q

COMPLEX R

CALZADA MALER   (MALER CAUSEWAY)

COMPLEX P

COMPLEX O

Embalse de la Calzada (Causeway Reservoir)

CALZADA MAUDSLAY (MAUDSLAY CAUSEWAY)

ACRÓPOLIS NORTE (NORTH ACROPOLIS)

TEMPLO DEL GRAN JAGUAR (TEMPLE I)

CANCHA DE PELOTA (BALLCOURT)

Great Plaza

East Plaza

West Plaza

MALER'S PALACE

Embalse del Palacio (Palace Reservoir)

Embalse Secreto (Hidden Reservoir)

TEMPLO DE LAS MASCARAS (TEMPLE II)

Embalse del Templo (Temple Reservoir)

CENTRAL ACROPOLIS

CALZADA TOZZER   (TOZZER CAUSEWAY)

TEMPLO DEL GRAN SACERDOTE (TEMPLE III)

TEMPLE V

ACROPOLIS SUR (SOUTH ACROPOLIS)

Plaza of the Seven Temples

CALZADA TOZZER

TEMPLO DE LA SERPIENTE BICEFÁLICA (TEMPLE IV)

CALZADA MAUDSLAY (MAUDSLAY CAUSEWAY)

COMPLEX N

BAT PALACE (PALACE OF THE WINDOWS)

MUNDO PERDIDO (LOST WORLD)

0   200 yds

0   200 m

PETÉN

BALAM

Among the most beautiful and highly revered rainforest animals both in ancient and modern times is the jaguar (Panthera onca), which inhabits Mexico, Central America, and parts of South America. It is one of the big cats, along with the leopard, lion, and tiger, and is the third largest of these. Jaguars are similar to leopards, though their spots present different arrangements (jaguars have spots within spots, or rosettes, and are larger). Jaguars are also stockier in build. They inhabit mostly forested lands but will also range across grasslands and open terrain. Also notable is their love of water and ability to swim. These gorgeous jungle cats are largely solitary and known for their hunting skills. They will attack cattle in areas fringing jungle zones and have been known to attack jungle camps to stalk human prey, usually children. Their powerful jaws are capable of puncturing tortoise shells.

Perhaps for these reasons, the Mayans had great respect and reverence for the jaguar, which they called balam. Jaguars were a symbol of power and strength and were believed to act as mediums for communication between the living and the dead. Kings were often given names incorporating the word balam, which they viewed as their companions in the spiritual world and protectors of the royal household. Rulers wearing jaguar pelts and man-jaguar figures frequently appear in pre-Columbian art. The jaguar was the patron deity of Tikal and is featured in a royal burial scene depicted on a human bone fragment found in the burial tomb of Hasaw Chan K'awil (Heavenly Standard Bearer) in which the ruler travels to the underworld in a canoe rowed by mythical animal figures.

Ranges for female jaguars are in the vicinity of 25–40 square kilometers, with the range of males being roughly twice as much and encompassing that of 2–3 females. Male jaguars' ranges do not overlap. For this reason, attempts to conserve existing numbers of jaguars require large expanses of territory such as that found in Guatemala's Maya Biosphere Reserve. The reserve also adjoins reserves in neighboring Mexico and Belize as part of a vast biological corridor. An estimated 550–650 jaguars remain in the Maya Biosphere Reserve.

Scientists have been studying jaguars in the Maya Biosphere Reserve and are trying to get a more accurate estimate of their remaining numbers in addition to a greater understanding of their behavioral patterns. Within the Laguna del Tigre National Park, biologists have been using radio collars to track five jaguars and a puma in the area surrounding the site of Waka'-Perú in an effort to determine migration patterns along an important biological corridor connecting this area with Mirador Río Azul National Park. It is not uncommon to see jaguar prints on the muddy trails in the vicinity of Waka'-Perú. Ironically, in 2006, a camera crew visiting the park to film a program on scarlet macaws for Guatemalan TV channel Guatevisión was unable to find any macaws but did manage to get a jaguar sighting on tape. Recent video monitoring along 15 stations in the central core of Tikal National Park detected seven jaguars during a two-month period. The Sierra del Lacandón National Park is also believed to harbor large numbers of these jungle cats.

Luckily, you don't need to go traipsing through the jungle with a saucer of milk if you want to see a jaguar, though chances are it will see you first. Guatemala City's excellent zoo has jaguars, as does Petén's ARCAS wildlife-rescue center. A jaguar cub was born in Guatemala City's zoo as recently as 2003. Several zoos in the United States have partnered with facilities in Central America to breed jaguars in captivity. In California, Sacramento's zoo welcomed the arrival of Tina, a Guatemalan jaguar, and Mulac, a male jaguar from Belize, in 2002.

As part of a larger regional initiative along with Mexico and Belize known as Selva Maya, local conservation group Defensores de la Naturaleza and Fundación Monte Carlo Verde launched the **SalvaBalam** campaign in 2006 aimed at increasing public awareness of the jaguar's plight and raising funds for continued study of these fascinating creatures. The project is still active, but is now part of Defensores de la Naturaleza (http://defensores.org.gt).

are part of a later rebuilding effort dating to A.D. 250. Some of these earlier structures can be seen today thanks to a tunnel excavated by archaeologists that provides a glimpse of two giant masks from Early Classic times guarding the entrance to a still-buried temple. The remains of Yax Nuun Ayin I, the first of Tikal's rulers under Teotihuacán hegemony, were found buried here in 1959 and revealed many details of Teotihuacán influence, including ceramics and the dreaded atlatl.

Some much-eroded stelae line the front of the North Acropolis. These depicted Tikal's ruling elite and many have been subjected to ritual defacement at the hands of invaders from neighboring states such as Calakmul.

The Central Acropolis

Commonly referred to as palaces, this complex of interconnecting rooms and stairways built around courtyards probably housed administrative offices and residences for Tikal's elite, though their exact use is uncertain. The Central Acropolis occupies the south end of the Great Plaza. It is known that the configuration of the various rooms was altered frequently, lending credence to the idea that it served as a royal dwelling place for the ruling elite. One part of the acropolis housed archaeologist Teobert Maler in 1895 and 1904, subsequently coming to be known as **Maler's Palace.**

The West Plaza and Temple III

The West Plaza, or Plaza Oeste, lies north of Temple II. Its main features include the presence of a large Late Classic temple on its north end and the unrestored **Temple III,** across the Tozzer Causeway, to the southwest. Temple III, which is 60 meters high, gives you a good idea of what Tikal's temples looked like to the early explorers when they were still covered in jungle vegetation. That's about all you'll be able to admire of it, as it is closed to visitors.

Some believe Temple III was built to honor the last of Tikal's great rulers, Dark Sun, and he may in fact be the figure depicted in the structure's badly eroded lintels. Behind the temple is a large palace complex. One of them, known as the **Bat Palace,** has been restored. It is also known as Palacio de las Ventanas.

Temple IV and Complex N

Continuing along the Tozzer Causeway, which is one of the original elevated walkways connecting various parts of the city, you'll come across Complex N on the left. Complex N is a twin-temple complex of the variety frequently constructed by Tikal's Late Classic rulers, supposedly to commemorate the passing of a *katun,* or 20-year cycle in the Mayan calendar. Found here is the beautifully carved **Stela 16,** showing Hasaw Chan K'awil in a plumed headdress. The complex was built in A.D. 711 to mark the 14th *katun* of *baktun* 9, a *baktun* being 400 years. **Altar 5,** also found here, depicts Hasaw victoriously presiding over sacrificial skull and bones with a lord from one of Calakmul's former vassal states. The corresponding text also mentions the death of Lady 12 Macaw, Hasaw's wife.

Farther along, you'll come to the colossal Temple IV, the tallest of Tikal's temples at 65 meters (212 feet). Like the Great Plaza's temples, it was completed in A.D. 741 by Yik'in Chan K'awil and may have served as his burial monument, though there is no concrete evidence as of yet. In addition to offering the best views of the site from its summit, it is also known as the origin of some excellent lintels depicting a victorious king surrounded by glyphs. As in the case of the lintels from Temple I, you'll now have to travel to Basel if you want to see the originals. A replica of Lintel 3 is in Guatemala City's archaeology museum.

The climb to the top of the temple up a series of wooden ladders attached to its side can be described as simply breathtaking, both for the effort required and for the spectacular views of

Tikal's Temple IV

the forest on all sides. The base of the temple is currently being restored and affords the opportunity to more fully appreciate the massive scale of these impressive constructions.

Temple V and the South Acropolis

The South Acropolis, due south of the Great Plaza, is the site of some excavations that are just beginning to unravel its significance. Its top layers are from Late Classic times, much like elsewhere in Tikal. Temple V lies just east of the South Acropolis. Standing to a height of 58 meters, it may be the original of Tikal's six temples dating to A.D. 600. A wooden staircase providing access to the somewhat cramped area below the roof comb and an interesting side view of the Great Plaza was closed during my last visit.

Plaza of the Seven Temples

This small plaza can be found to the west of the South Acropolis and contains a series of seven temples arranged in a straight line dating to Preclassic times. There is a triple ball court on the plaza's north side similar to a larger one just south of Temple I. It's one of the least visited areas and yet one of the most visually interesting.

The Lost World Complex

Known in Spanish as El Mundo Perdido, this complex is strikingly different from the rest of the site owing to its Preclassic origins, which may help to shed light on Tikal's early history. The area is dominated by the presence of a 32-meter pyramid, its foundation dating as far back as 500 B.C., when it served as an astronomical observatory similar to the one found at Uaxactún. The structure now in evidence marks the top of four layers of construction. There are fabulous views of the Great Plaza and Temple IV from the top, though the stone central staircase on the temple's steep face can be slippery after it rains. Exercise due caution.

Temple of the Inscriptions (Temple VI)

The most remote of Tikal's temples, Temple VI lies about one kilometer southeast of the Central Acropolis along the **Mendez Causeway,** where it stands all by itself. Rediscovered in 1957, this temple is unique because it contains inscriptions much like the temples found at Quiriguá and Copán but unlike Tikal's other temples. On the back side of the temple's 12-meter roof comb are a series of 180 glyphs, barely visible today, charting the history of Tikal's ruling dynasty A.D. 200-766. They also chart Tikal's early history as far back as 1139 B.C., which the Mayans probably guessed at. Still, ceramic evidence at Tikal has corroborated other dates found at the site. The temple is most likely the work of Yik'in Chan K'awil. Stela 21 and Altar 9 adorn the front of the temple at its base and date to A.D. 736.

The temple's relative isolation makes it an excellent location for spotting wildlife. Robberies, none of them recent, have been reported here. That said, you should probably not wander off to these parts unaccompanied.

Complexes Q and R

Two other areas deserve mention in this discussion of Tikal's archaeological highlights. You'll find them shortly after entering the park, on a path bearing right after passing the ticket control booth. Complex Q and Complex R comprise two sets of Tikal's twin-temple complexes built by Yax Ain II to commemorate the passing of a *katun*. One of the pyramids at Complex Q has been restored with its corresponding stelae repositioned in front of it. The best of these, **Stela 22,** can be seen at the **Museo Lítico** and depicts Yax Ain II's ascension to the throne. The temple here dates to A.D. 771.

Farther west, as you approach the Maler Causeway, is Complex R, another twin-pyramid complex dating to A.D. 790.

MUSEUMS

Tikal's two museums are oddly in different parts of the park. The first of these is the **Museo Lítico** (9 A.M.-noon and 1 P.M.-4:30 P.M. Mon.-Fri., 9 A.M.-4 P.M. Sat. and Sun., $2.50 for both museums), housing stelae and carved stones from the archaeological site with a scale model outside showing what the city probably looked like around A.D. 800. There are some interesting photos taken by explorers Alfred Maudslay and Teobert Maler showing Tikal's temples overgrown by a tangle of jungle vines and branches as they looked when they were first discovered.

The **Museo Tikal** (9 A.M.-5 P.M. Mon.-Fri., 9 A.M.-4 P.M. Sat. and Sun., $2.50), across the way next to the Jaguar Inn, has some interesting exhibits, including the burial tomb of Hasaw Chan K'awil found inside Temple I.

RECREATION

In addition to exploring the ruins, there are a variety of recreational opportunities in and around Tikal National Park.

Canopy Tour

You have a choice of two zip-line trajectories between raised platforms in the jungle at **Tikal Canopy Tour** (tel. 5819-7766, www. canopytikal.com, 7 A.M.-5 P.M. daily, $30, at the national park entrance). The first of these includes 11 platforms with zip lines ranging in length 75-150 meters while you dangle 25 meters over the forest floor. The second, more adrenaline-inducing option, includes zip lines up to 200 meters long hovering 40 meters above the safety of ground level. Pick your poison.

Bird-Watching

Specialty tours for bird-watchers can be arranged by contacting **La Casa de Don David** (tel. 7928-8469 or 5306-2190, www.lacasadedondavid.com) in El Remate. The lodge's

PETÉN

knowledgeable staff can connect you with good English-speaking local guides who know the park and its birds. Another recommended outfitter is Guatemala City-based **Cayaya Birding** (tel. 5308-5160, www.cayaya-birding.com).

ACCOMMODATIONS

Lodging at Tikal National Park is limited by law to three lodges and a campground. An increasing amount of competition from accommodations at nearby El Remate has spurred the Tikal hotels toward higher standards while keeping prices relatively reasonable. There are few places in the world where you can stay in a comfortable jungle lodge inside a national park just minutes away from a UNESCO World Heritage Site. That being said, the Tikal hotels do feel somewhat overpriced in terms of what you get for your money.

Electricity at the park is sporadic, with accommodations and other facilities having to limit the hours during which this convenience is available. Power is usually turned on in the morning for 2-3 hours and then again in the evening shortly after sunset for another three hours. If you need to use a computer provided by one of these facilities for checking email or need to recharge camera batteries or cell phones, you should plan accordingly. If you absolutely need a fan to cool your room while you sleep overnight in the humid Petén jungle, you may want to stay outside the park, as ceiling fans go silent once the electricity turns off. It can get very hot here, even at night. None of the lodges have air-conditioning. More recently, the Jaguar Inn has begun providing electricity round-the-clock and this seals the deal for many a traveler.

Beware if booking online, as at least two of the three lodges have lower-priced accommodations mysteriously missing from their online price lists. If you call the hotels looking for one of the less expensive shared-bath rooms, you'll most likely need to ask for one specifically, as they'll automatically try to sell you one of their premium rooms.

Coming from the ruins, the first place you'll come across is the **Jungle Lodge** (tel. 2476-8775, www.junglelodge.guate.com, $65-100 d), offering decent bungalows with private hot-water baths, ceiling fans, and two double beds as well as a few very basic, less expensive rooms with shared bathrooms. All are set amid a pleasant tropical garden atmosphere and there is a swimming pool. The restaurant here serves breakfast ($7), lunch, and dinner ($8-12). Be advised the lodge is closed every year during September. As you head toward the old airstrip just past the museums, you'll reach the friendly **Jaguar Inn** (tel. 7926-0002, www.jaguartikal.com), where you can choose from nine comfortable bungalows with small front patios with hammock ($70 d), a dormitory ($10 p/p), hammocks with mosquito netting ($5), or camping ($3.50). You can rent a tent for $7. The restaurant here is a safe bet, serving adequate portions of good food (though the service can be very slow). Dinner is about $9. There are laptops available for Internet surfing and checking email ($5/hour). The electricity here stays on round-the-clock, thanks to a generator. Next door, **Tikal Inn** (tel. 7926-1917 or 7926-0065, www.tikalinn.com, $45-100 d) gets consistent praise for its good service and large, comfortable rooms centered round the swimming pool just behind the hotel's restaurant. You can choose from standard rooms or pricier, more private bungalows; all have ceiling fan and private bath. The restaurant serves three meals a day.

Tikal's **campground** is opposite the visitors center with a spacious grassy area for tents as well as *palapa* structures for stringing hammocks. There are showering stalls among the bathroom facilities. Hammocks and mosquito netting are available for rent and there are tiny, two-person basic cabanas for $7 per person. It costs $4 per person to camp here.

FOOD

Your best bet for food is at one of the three on-site lodges, but there are a number of *comedores* here serving basic yet passable fare in adequate portions for about $7 for a full meal and a drink. The menus are virtually indistinguishable from one another and are heavy on local staples such as beans, eggs, and tortillas. The restaurant at the visitors center, **Restaurant Café Tikal**, is fancier but a bit overpriced and you are probably better off eating at one of the lodges if you're not on a small budget. It serves pasta, steaks, chicken, and sandwiches and is open until 6 P.M. daily. The other *comedores* are across from the visitors center on the right-hand side as you enter the park from the main road. They include **Comedor Tikal, Restaurant Imperio Maya**, and **Comedor Ixim K'ua**, all of which open early for breakfast and close at 9 P.M. daily. **El Meson** (tel. 7952-8700, open for lunch only) is a simple, open-air, thatched-roof eatery that serves tasty set menus that include soup, chicken or beef, rice, vegetables, and fruit. It's located at the end of a short trail to the right of the main entrance to the park (if you're coming from the parking lot). The trail is a few meters past the oft-photographed ceiba tree at the junction with the road leading to Uaxactún.

As for the hotel restaurants, the large dining room at the **Jungle Lodge** is a popular stop for lunch with tour groups. As such, it tends to offer dependable set-menu lunches of meat or chicken dishes accompanied by rice and salad for about $8. Dinner options include a varied assortment of meat dishes, pasta, and sandwiches. The **Jaguar Inn** caters largely to the international backpacker crowd and makes a particularly decent place for good-value dinners, including tasty pastas and desserts. The **Tikal Inn** gets props for its hearty breakfasts with good, strong coffee.

GETTING THERE

Most people arrive here from Flores, El Remate, or Belize. See the corresponding sections for information on how to get here. Minibuses leave Tikal from the airstrip fairly frequently, particularly after about noon, heading south toward El Remate, Ixlú, and Flores. Change buses at Ixlú if you're heading east to Belize. If all else fails, a taxi to Flores should cost about $40.

PETÉN

The Maya Biosphere Reserve

The largest protected tropical forest in North America, this 1.7 million-hectare (4.3 million-acre) reserve is Guatemala's last chance for preserving a significant part of the forests that once covered all of Petén. It is gradually gaining notoriety among international travelers for its vast expanses of tropical forest and the remote Mayan ruins that lie buried within. It is hoped that ecotourism here will take hold as a major industry, providing jobs and a viable alternative to ecological destruction, as in neighboring protected areas in Belize and Costa Rica. A cursory glance at a map of Guatemala reveals that the northern third of Petén is a sparsely populated region harboring an unusually high concentration of Mayan sites, remote jungle wetlands, rivers, and lagoons. Those with a strong sense of adventure will find plenty to see and do in one of Central America's last ecological frontiers.

Although the biosphere reserve has been in existence since 1990, many of the parks that compose it remain little more than "paper parks," as the government entities charged with enforcing protection of these areas are woefully underfunded and understaffed. Several of the parks are now being administered jointly between Guatemala's National Protected Areas

Council (CONAP) and local conservation organizations. Foreign NGOs have also joined the battle to preserve the Maya Biosphere for future generations against seemingly insurmountable odds. Threatening the continued existence of this unique area are traditional factors common to tropical forests in Third World countries, including the expansion of the agricultural frontier by land-hungry peasants and changes in land use such as cattle grazing. But there are also more sinister forces at work here, and the reserve is under serious assault by wildlife and timber poachers, both from within Guatemala and neighboring Mexico, as well as from the activities of drug smugglers occupying large extensions of the park to move their product.

Guatemalan authorities have stepped up their efforts to regain control of this vast wilderness area and it should be noted that not all of the above-mentioned forces are in operation throughout the park. There are many areas within this vast biosphere reserve that are easily and safely explored, combining the splendors of some of the Mayan civilization's most spectacular ruins with the wonders of a largely intact tropical forest all around. In some cases, these are not so easily accessible, but the rewards for those putting forth the effort to reach some of Guatemala's least-visited attractions are well worth it.

Among the highlights of the reserve are the **Mirador-Rio Azul National Park,** which is home to the largest manufactured pre-Columbian structures in the Americas, found at **El Mirador,** and at least 25 other smaller Mayan sites. Some, such as Wakná, have been discovered only as recently as 1998 and many more undoubtedly await discovery. At the site of **San Bartolo,** archaeologists uncovered the earliest evidence of Mayan writing in a wall mural discovered in 2001. The area is also home to the last remaining undisturbed tropical forests in Guatemala and is being considered for special protection as the **Mirador Basin National Park.**

Much of the western part of the reserve, particularly **Laguna del Tigre National Park,** has unfortunately been lost due to population pressures. Still, the area around the Mayan site of **Waka'** (also known as El Perú or Waka'-Perú), remains well preserved and is the home of a biological research station and a project to help conserve Petén's last remaining populations of scarlet macaws.

In 2006, The Nature Conservancy helped local conservation organization Defensores de la Naturaleza secure the purchase of 31,000 hectares (77,000 acres) of privately held land to help ensure the preservation of **Sierra del Lacandón National Park,** an area of incredible biological diversity due to the ruggedness of the terrain, which includes mountains, freshwater lakes, savannas, and rainforests running along the magnificent Usumacinta River. Squatters were evicted from the park soon after (not without much difficulty), and how this area will be managed and opened to low-impact tourism is yet unknown. Nestled in the jungles of Sierra del Lacandón are at least two sites worthy of mention and exploration—Piedras Negras and, across the Usumacinta and upstream in Mexico, Yaxchilán.

The Maya Biosphere was also featured on U.S. television with the filming of *Survivor Guatemala* at the Mayan ruins of Yaxhá. The spectacular ruined city is rivaled in magnificence only by Tikal and El Mirador, and its splendid setting next to a tropical lagoon complete with hungry crocodiles is second to none.

Survivor Guatemala certainly catapulted Guatemala and Yaxhá into the collective consciousness, and many people believe it is just a matter of time before the treasures hidden in the Petén forest gain greater notoriety and become an engine for the preservation of this incredible but often-overlooked adventure-travel destination.

© AL ARGUETA

ruins of Yaxhá

UAXACTÚN

The remote site of Uaxactún lies just 23 kilometers north of Tikal on an unpaved road through the jungle passable by four-wheel-drive vehicle. The Wrigley Company once had a busy chicle extraction operation here, complete with an airstrip. Today the airstrip lies in disuse, with the ruins and small community built around it. Many of Uaxactún's residents make their living from gathering forest products such as chicle, allspice, and *xate* palm leaves. In 2000, Guatemala's Protected Areas Council (CONAP) granted the community a sustainable forestry concession to selectively harvest timber from surrounding multiple-use zones of the Maya Biosphere Reserve. While it's yet to be seen how sustainable it is in practice, the logging concession has already been partially nullified in areas approaching the subsequently created Mirador Basin archaeological zone and could be completely eliminated with the eventual creation of a proposed Mirador

Basin National Park. Locals also guide visits from here to remote sites such as Río Azul and El Zotz, which may be their best hope for earning income without harming the fragile tropical forest ecosystem they inhabit.

The ruins themselves might seem a bit unimpressive after a visit to their better-known neighbor to the south, as they are smaller and not nearly as well preserved, though Uaxactún's main claim to fame is the presence of a fairly elaborate astronomical observatory. Sylvanus G. Morley is credited with rediscovering Uaxactún in 1916. Its original name has subsequently been deciphered as Siaan K'aan (Born in Heaven), though Morley is said to have chosen the name Uaxatún (Eight Stone) as a reference to a stone dating to the 8th *baktun* in the Mayan calendar, then the earliest-known Mayan inscription. It is also speculated that his choice of name was a play on words for "Washington," the U.S. capital and home of the Carnegie Institute that funded his explorations. Morley's initial investigations focused on the site's inscriptions. Uaxatún's structures would have to await being mapped and more closely inspected until the arrival of Frans Blom in 1924. The Carnegie Institute excavated the site between 1926 and 1937.

History

Uaxactún is a Middle Preclassic site dating to about 600 B.C. that came into its own in the Late Preclassic sometime between 350 B.C. and A.D. 250 with the appearance of its first ceremonial plazas in the areas now known as Groups A and E. Its earliest stelae date to around A.D. 328. More complex architecture and several other plazas also make their appearance at this time.

After the decline of El Mirador in the 2nd century A.D., Uaxactún and Tikal became embroiled in a great political and military rivalry for local supremacy until the site was conquered by Tikal in A.D. 378. Tikal was aided in its

THE MURALS OF SAN BARTOLO

Fascinating discoveries at the newly famous site of San Bartolo have rocked the world of Mayan scholars, completely shattering long-held beliefs about the origin of elaborate Mayan art and writing that narrates the stories of ruling monarchies. It is now clear that Preclassic Mayan societies had achieved a degree of sophistication in art, writing, and government once thought to have been attained only several centuries later. San Bartolo, deep in the jungle near Río Azul, has yielded the earliest known Mayan mural and the oldest known Mayan burial tomb. The murals are impressive not only for their early date (A.D. 100-200), but also for their quality. The best-known Mayan murals, at the site of Bonampak (Mexico), date to the late 8th century A.D. San Bartolo's location, while no longer secret, is known only to a few in the archaeological community. Visitors are not welcome, but there are plans to make a replica of the murals available to tourists in the future. The Mayan site of San Bartolo encompasses more than 100 structures, among them temple pyramids (at least two of which are more than 25 meters high), a palace, and ball court, and is still being excavated.

The mural was discovered in 2001 by Harvard University's William Saturno when, in search of shade from the midday sun, he ducked into a trench hacked by looters under an unexcavated pyramid. What followed were two years of planning the painstaking excavation, and the mural depicting creation mythology was reclaimed from the soil beneath the temple structure. It is similar to one found in the *Dresden Codex*, one of three Mayan books to survive the wide-scale destruction of ancient Mayan texts by Spanish priests in the 16th century (the other two are the Madrid Codex and the Paris Codex).

Among the themes depicted are the establishment of order to the world, the latter portrayed as upheld by trees with roots leading to the underworld and branches holding up the sky. Stationed at each tree are four deities providing a blood sacrifice and an offering.

In another section, the mural shows the maize god setting up the tree at the center of the world and crowning himself king. This section of the panel traces the maize god's birth, death, and resurrection. In the final scene, a historic coronation of an actual Mayan king is depicted with his name and title written in hieroglyphics.

Project iconographer Karl Taube believes the writing style differs from that evidenced in later periods of Mayan history, but it is nonetheless sophisticated. He also points to the appearance of similar scenes in the *Dresden Codex*. Saturno speculates the king depicted in the mural likely claimed the right to rule from the gods themselves and not merely from lineage, as did kings in later times.

The second major discovery is the tomb of an early Mayan king dating to 150 B.C. found in 2005 by Guatemalan archaeologist Mónica Pellecer Alecio about a mile away from the mural, also under a small temple pyramid. The find provides further evidence of early monarchic rule.

A full-length feature on these amazing discoveries can be found in the January 2006 edition of *National Geographic* magazine and online at www.sanbartolo.org.

takeover of Uaxactún by its newly formed alliance with Teotihuacán and the introduction of a spear-throwing apparatus imported from the Central Mexican city-state. Uaxactún remained a subordinate state for the remainder of its history.

The Ruins

The most impressive set of ruins lies a 15-minute walk southeast of the airstrip and is called **Group E.** A series of small, partially restored temples, Structures E-I, E-II, and E-III, are arranged side by side, going north to south, and designed as an astronomical observatory. The structures are arranged in such a manner as to coincide with the sunrise on key dates. When viewed from the top of nearby Temple E-VII-Sub, the sun rises over E-1 on the summer solstice and over the southernmost E-III on the winter solstice. Temple E-VII-Sub's foundations date to about 2000 B.C. and there are some much-deteriorated jaguar and snake heads flanking the temple's side.

Northeast of the airstrip are Groups A and B, which were less carefully excavated but include several altars and stelae found mostly fallen among the remains of the larger temple palaces.

Accommodations and Food

Lodging and dining options in Uaxactún are extremely basic, as it is a remote forest community literally in the middle of nowhere. The settlement's best accommodations are at **Campamento El Chiclero** (tel. 7926-1095) on the north end of the airstrip with 10 basic rooms with shared bath and mosquito-netted windows for $7 per person. You can also camp or string a hammock here for $3. The restaurant here serves large portions of good, basic food ($5 per meal) and there is a small on-site museum (free admission) with local artifacts. The friendly owners can arrange trips to some of the more remote places in the biosphere reserve, including El Zotz, Río Azul, Naachtun, and El Mirador. A less expensive alternative is **Aldana's Lodge,** just off the street leading to Groups A and B, where simple thatched-roof cabanas are $4 per person, or you can camp for $2 per person. Aldana's can also arrange visits to area sites.

You can eat at your choice of three simple *comedores* in town: **Comedor Uaxactún, Comedor La Bendición,** and **Comedor Imperial Okanarin.**

Getting There

A Pinita bus leaves Santa Elena at 1 P.M. daily, stopping in Tikal at about 3 P.M. From there it's about 1.5 hours to Uaxactún. These times are not set in stone, as with most schedules in Guatemala, and the bus can arrive in Uaxactún as late as 6 P.M. sometimes. The return trip to Santa Elena leaves Uaxactún at 6 A.M. (There is sometimes a minivan leaving Uaxactún for Tikal at 8 A.M. with the inbound minivan from Tikal arriving at 6 P.M., but it's sporadic and doesn't always operate.)

If you're driving, be aware that the road is passable only in a 4WD vehicle at any time of year. If you're unable to fill your gas tank in Flores, the last gas station en route is at Ixlú, south of El Remate.

BIOTOPO EL ZOTZ-SAN MIGUEL LA PALOTADA

"Zotz" means "bat" in Mayan, and this CECON biotope, predictably, is set up for the protection of the thousands of bats that emerge from the mouth of a large cave at dusk. It's quite an impressive sight to see, the sky darkening with myriad winged creatures making their way out in search of insects and fruit. The biotope also protects an archaeological site that has been severely plundered and remains unexcavated. You can climb to the top of the tallest mound, the **El Diablo Temple,** from which you can make out the roof combs of Tikal's pyramids 23 kilometers to the west. The forest here remains well preserved and there is a small biological station with guards patrolling the park stationed here. You can camp for free and there is no park admission fee, as in most of the remote jungle parks of the Maya Biosphere Reserve. The biotope abuts Tikal National Park to the east, which partially explains why it remains mostly intact. It is part of an important biological corridor ensuring the survival of many of Petén's most threatened species.

Several Flores travel agencies arrange trips to the biotope. Highly recommended is **Martsam Tours and Travel,** offering an excellent three-day and two-night trek from El Zotz to Tikal for about $175 per person for two people. It begins in Flores with a private vehicle transfer to the village of Cruce dos Aguadas, west of the park. From there, you hike five hours to

PETÉN

El Zotz, see the bat cave, and spend the night. The second day is spent exploring the site's temple mounds before hiking to a campsite midway between El Zotz and Tikal, where you bed down for the night before the final 18-kilometer march to Tikal the next day. You explore Tikal on the last day, and the trip concludes with a chance to see the sunset from Temple IV. **Tikal Connection** also runs a similar trip for the same price. Both use local community guides.

Another option is to book a trip from Uaxactún. **Campamento El Chiclero** can arrange pack horses, guides, and equipment. The trip from Uaxactún affords the opportunity to see a little more of the forest, as the forests along the western approach from Paso Caballos have been somewhat disturbed.

YAXHÁ-NAKUM-NARANJO NATURAL MONUMENT

This park encompasses the Mayan sites of Yaxhá, Topoxté, Nakum, and El Naranjo. Most prominent of these is Yaxhá, which gained international fame in 2005 with the filming of *Survivor Guatemala*. The park was closed for two months, during which time contestants lived among the ruins eating corn, plotting ways not to get voted off, and fighting off mosquitoes. Only El Mirador and Tikal are bigger than Yaxhá (8 A.M.-5 P.M. daily, $10 admission includes entrance to Nakum), and its isolated setting on a limestone ridge overlooking the lagoons of Yaxhá and Sacnab is simply splendid. Despite its TV fame, you can still wander the site with nary another visitor in sight. Don't even think of swimming in the lakes here, as they have a healthy population of rather large crocodiles.

◖ Yaxhá

The relative lack of inscribed monuments found at Yaxhá has made tracking its history a bit of a challenge, though it appears it was a major player during the Classic period. It is believed Yaxhá was locked into an ongoing power struggle during much of this time with its smaller neighbor, Naranjo, about 20 kilometers northeast. Yaxhá's sphere of influence was almost certainly limited by the proximity of Tikal and the architecture here shows many similarities to that of the latter site. Naranjo eventually overran Yaxhá in A.D. 799. Spanish friars passed through here in 1618, and Austrian explorer Teobert Maler visited in 1904. Much of the site remained unexcavated until recently. A German-Guatemalan effort is conducting the site's ongoing excavation and restoration.

Yaxhá's highest structure is **Structure 216,** offering wonderful views of the lagoons and forests from its summit. Watchers of *Survivor Guatemala* will probably recognize the temple from numerous aerial shots shown during the program's run. It features a broad central staircase and rises to a height of about 100 feet. Access is via a wooden staircase built into the temple's side.

The temples at Yaxhá appear constructed from a very light-colored limestone markedly different from the stones used elsewhere in the Mayan world, giving the ruins a very different feel. You'll find the ruins spread out over nine plazas with 500 mapped structures, including temples, ball courts, and palaces. Other highlights include the recently restored **North Acropolis,** surrounded by three temples, two of which are fairly large. A path known as **Calzada Blom** leads almost one kilometer north from here to the **Maler Group,** a complex featuring twin temples facing each other across a plaza similar to the setup at Tikal. A number of weathered stelae and the broken remains of a large circular altar further adorn the complex. Another great location affording wonderful views closer to the heart of the ruined city is the top of an unnamed astronomical observation pyramid between Plaza F and Structure 116.

view of Yaxhá from atop Structure 216

The parking lot and restrooms are on the east side of the park near Plaza C, along with a small museum. There are two boat docks here, one below the parking lot and one at the western end of the site.

You can camp for free at **Campamento Yaxhá,** a designated lakeside campsite below the ruins proper. A more comfortable option is the friendly **Campamento Ecológico El Sombrero** (tel. 7861-1687 or 7861-1688, www.ecosombrero.com), about 200 meters from the main road before you come to the park entry post. Its 13 comfortable rooms are housed in thatched-roof bungalows fronting the lake. There's a dock, but it's not recommended for swimming because of the crocodiles. A restaurant serves adequate food, with the variety of menu items on offer heavily dependent on whether or not there's a group staying at the lodge. If you're just stopping by, you'll probably end up eating pasta, which actually seems a delicacy when you're in the middle of the jungle.

The lodge arranges boat trips to **Topoxté** and guided tours of Yaxhá.

A series of roads leads to Yaxhá. About 31 kilometers east of Ixlú, on the road toward the Belize border, a well-marked turnoff leads a further 11 kilometers north to the Yaxhá guardpost, where you pay admission and sign in to the park. It's another three kilometers from here to the actual ruins of Yaxhá. The road is in good condition, even during the rainy season. If traveling by bus, you can get off at the junction to Yaxhá and hitch a ride with an occasional passing pickup truck or fellow travelers. There is some traffic along this route because of the presence of the small village of La Máquina, about two kilometers from the park guardpost.

Several of the Flores tour operators now do Yaxhá with certain frequency. You can also get a minivan from El Remate to the site, but expect to pay about $60 round-trip. Try to find people to share the ride.

Topoxté

This smaller site is situated on an island close to the southwest shore of Yaxhá Lagoon near the Reserva Natural Privada Yaxhá and dates to Preclassic times, though the structures in evidence are mostly from the Late Postclassic period. Plazas and temples are being restored, though nothing is of the scale found at Yaxhá. Topoxté was one of the last strongholds of the Itzá people.

The site was surveyed on several different occasions throughout the 20th century starting in 1904, though restoration and preservation would have to wait until the early 1990s. The most notable structure here is **Temple Pyramid C,** the only Postclassic building remaining in Petén. Similar to structures in the Yucatán and Guatemala's highlands, it has three levels crowned by a portal supported by two pillars.

The only feasible way of getting here is to catch a boat ride from Campamento Ecologico El Sombrero.

Nakum

North of Yaxhá on a road suitable only for dry-season driving is the Late Classic site of Nakum, now being excavated. Near the site lies the marshy swampland of **Bajo La Justa,** which was under intense cultivation during Mayan times. You'll pass through it on your way there. Nakum features the usual assortment of pyramids, plazas, and temples, though there are some unique arches found here along with stelae dating from A.D. 771-849. Noted archaeologist Alfred Tozzer passed though here in 1909-1910, working for the Peabody Museum; he recorded his findings in a work titled, *A Preliminary Study of the Prehistoric Ruins of Nakum, Guatemala.*

MIRADOR-RÍO AZUL NATIONAL PARK

This vast wilderness area encompasses the ruins of El Mirador, one of the earliest and largest Mayan cities to emerge from Petén's jungles, as well as several other Preclassic Mayan sites. It abuts Mexico's Calakmul Biosphere Reserve to the north, which protects another important archaeological site and a large tract of forest in its vicinity. The protected status along the southern border of Guatemala's northern neighbor, and the lack of road access, have allowed this park to remain a largely untrammeled wilderness. Access is difficult and best attempted during the dry season, as seasonal flooding of swamps known as *bajos* turns forest paths into knee-deep mud for much of the year. The other major Mayan site giving its name to this park is Río Azul, which lies deep in the jungle near the western border with Belize.

Archaeologists and environmentalists are lobbying for the creation of the Mirador Basin National Park and the Guatemalan government has shown interest in preserving this wilderness area harboring Mayan ruins of at least equal importance to that of Tikal.

◖ El Mirador

This massive city, rediscovered in 1926 and photographed from the air in 1930, but only recently the focus of ongoing excavations, holds great promise both as a tourism destination rivaling the magnitude of Tikal and as an important piece in the puzzle concerning the advancements of Preclassic Maya society. El Mirador flourished between 200 B.C. and A.D. 150 (about 1,000 years before Tikal), and has revealed a greater level of sophistication than once thought concerning early Mayan society. It is thought to have been home to 80,000 people at the height of its occupation. Its sheer size and the earliness of its development have earned it accolades, such as the "Cradle of Mayan Civilization."

The site sits on a series of limestone hills at an altitude of just over 240 meters (800 feet) and occupies about 16 square kilometers. El Mirador's dominating feature is the presence

La Danta Complex, El Mirador

of two large pyramid complexes, El Tigre and La Danta, running east to west and facing each other. The architecture is characterized by triadic structures composed of one large temple pyramid flanked on either side by two smaller pyramids, a pattern that is repeated elsewhere in the Preclassic sites of the Mirador basin.

The base of the **El Tigre Complex** is as large as three football fields, while the large temple dominating the structure reaches 55 meters (180 feet) in height. The lower flanking pyramids contain gigantic stucco jaguar masks.

The city's **Central Acropolis** takes the form of a narrow plaza bordered on one side by a series of small buildings. Moving south from the El Tigre Complex, you come to the **Monos Complex,** another triadic structure named after the howler monkeys tending to congregate in this area.

The colossal **La Danta Complex** lies to the east of the main plaza and Central Acropolis. Although technically lower than El Tigre, it rises to a height of 70 meters (230 feet) thanks to its elevated location on a hillside, making it the tallest structure in the Mayan world. Its base is equally impressive. There are jaguar and vulture heads built into the sides of the smaller temples here and the spectacular views from the top of the pyramid afford views of nearby Mayan sites, including Nakbé and Calakmul.

Other interesting site features include the León Pyramid, at the northern edge of the city, and Structure 34—a Preclassic building with the oldest known Mayan standing wall.

Excavations are being done under the direction of UCLA's Dr. Richard Hansen, who has led a larger project aiming to protect the entire Mirador basin as an ecoarchaeological preserve. The preservation of its delicate monuments is being aided by technological advances, including housing structures under polycarbonate roofs designed by Hansen and his associates, so as to protect them from rain and ultraviolet light.

In 2009, Hansen and Guatemalan authorities unveiled the discovery of a frieze at El

THE MIRADOR BASIN PROJECT

Deep in the untouched forests of northern Petén in what archaeologists call the Mirador Basin, far from the throngs of tourists at other Mayan sites, lie the overgrown remains of the most fascinating cities ever built in Preclassic times. The Mirador Basin, as defined by its geographical characteristics, is an elevated basin dominated by low-lying swamps known as *bajos* surrounded by karst limestone hills to the south, east, and west, forming a triangular trench covering roughly 2,100 square kilometers. Some of its sites, including El Mirador and Nakbé, are being excavated and have yielded many clues concerning the advanced nature of early Mayan civilization. As the excavations continue to bring fascinating new discoveries, archaeologists, conservationists, and local residents remain at odds about how best to preserve the remaining Petén forests and the important monuments they harbor.

At the heart of the controversy is the proposal for a Mirador Basin National Park, spearheaded by UCLA's Dr. Richard Hansen, who heads the excavation project at El Mirador. The park would stretch clear to the Mexican border at its northernmost points, encompassing parts of Mirador-Río Azul National Park. At its southern tip, it would stretch all the way down to El Zotz-San Miguel La Palotada Biotope. The area is home to Petén's last remaining expanses of well-preserved forests.

Hansen envisions a large national park guarded by armed rangers similar to those of the U.S. National Park Service. There would be several luxurious ecolodges, visitors centers, an airstrip, a narrow-gauge railroad, and hiking trails linking the various restored Mayan sites within the basin. The proposed park would be roughly four times the size of Tikal National Park and would be largely based upon the same management model. Hansen sees the potential to accommodate up to 80,000 visitors per year.

Hansen's plans, though well-intentioned, have met substantial opposition from local communities and Petén's powerful environmental groups, who have spent many years and millions of dollars developing relationships with local communities to encourage the sustainable extraction of forest products. The sustainable forestry programs have received support from The Nature Conservancy and the U.S. Agency for International Development, among others.

Some believe the communities could receive greater economic benefit from sustainable forestry than from working as staff in tourist hotels and restaurants. The community of Uaxactún, for example, was awarded a sustainable forestry concession in 2000 by CONAP, and villagers there have made a living from collecting forest products for decades.

Although the park itself will supposedly be without roads, new infrastructure would have to be built to make the region more accessible to visitors, raising the specter of a much-talked-about road connecting Tikal to Mexico's Calakmul. Along these lines, Mexico has been insisting on the construction of a road from Chetumal to Tikal in an attempt to integrate the two countries' archaeological sites as part of the Plan Puebla-Panama, an idea vehemently opposed by local conservationists because it would bisect some of the best-conserved areas of the Maya Biosphere Reserve.

For more information on the Mirador Basin project, check out the FARES website at www.miradorbasin.com.

Mirador depicting a scene from a Mayan sacred book, the *Popol Vuh,* in which the mythical "Hero Twins" visit the underworld. According to Hansen, the frieze lends further credence to the *Popol Vuh*'s creation myth and its authenticity as a Mayan document, despite its first translation well into the Christian era in the 1700s. The frieze took three months to excavate and was found while archaeologists were looking for water reservoirs at the site.

GETTING TO EL MIRADOR

Getting to El Mirador is not an easy task, though you wouldn't know it judging by the readiness of certain Flores tour operators to book you on a trip even at the height of the rainy season. The trek to El Mirador is not for the faint of heart and should not be attempted July-November, when the mud is knee-deep throughout most of the trail. In the worst of places, a rope is tied to the end of a tree and trekkers must pull themselves through shoulder-deep mud. This is, after all, a tropical forest and the terrain is characterized by swamplands. Add to this the incessant buzz of hungry mosquitoes, extreme heat and humidity, and you start to realize why so few people make it to this remote site. Your best bet is to attempt the trek at the height of the dry season between February and April. Mel Gibson has visited on several occasions. He arrives by helicopter.

Treks begin in the village of **Carmelita,** inside the biosphere reserve at the end of the line for the road from Flores. Carmelita consists of a small cluster of houses grouped alongside the road with a few basic services such as a *comedor,* a small general store, and simple accommodations. The journey usually lasts five days. The first night is spent at El Tintal and the next day is a grueling hike that puts you at El Mirador close to nightfall. You spend two nights at the ruins before the two-day hike back to Carmelita. Trip prices vary, but expect to pay about $250 per person for two people. Some outfitters do the trip in seven days, allowing more time at El Mirador and stopping en route at Nakbé and Wakná. Mules carry the supplies, but you can also rent additional mules or horses for riding. This is particularly recommended if you make the journey in the wet season. Expect to pay an extra $10 per day for riding horses.

Be very careful in your selection of an outfitter to get you to El Mirador. The community of Carmelita, with help from NGOs, has trained and licensed guides to take visitors on the hike as part of a sustainable tourism initiative contributing to the ecologically friendly livelihood of local residents. While it's a nice idea in theory, it may not always be the best way to go. Not all of the local guides have the same skills or experience in running the trek and you run the risk of getting one of these lesser-experienced guides if you book your trip directly through the community. The task invariably falls on whoever is available to take you at that particular time. Further complicating the scenario is the presence of "gypsy" guides falsely claiming to be part of the local tourism committee.

That being said, you can save some money by taking public transport to Carmelita and then hooking up with the local **Comité de Turismo** (tel. 7861-1809, Spanish-only, ask for Brenda Zapata). The trip should cost about $235 per person for two people. Book at least a few days in advance, as the supplies and food must be brought in from Flores and the guides must go into town to get them. If you do go this route, make sure the guide buys adequate amounts of food for the duration of the trip. A common complaint is that food runs low halfway through the trek. You should also verify that there is enough water. Have the guide unpack all the supplies and show you exactly what you're taking. Don't hesitate to tell the guide if the food supply is inadequate for the trip's duration. In the worst of cases, you might buy a chicken to eat from the guards at the site, though it won't be cheap and there's no guarantee they'll have one to sell to you.

A final consideration if booking directly through the community is that the guide will want the money up front so as to buy food and supplies. This may or may not be an inconvenience to you, but it bears mentioning nonetheless. The more established Flores tour operators take credit cards and arrange everything for you in advance.

This leads us to your second option, that of booking the trip from Flores through one of several recommended outfitters. Although any Flores travel agency will claim to offer the trip, the quality of the service is not the same and you run the risk of getting set up with an inferior guide at premium prices. These

PETÉN

outfitters may or may not contract the services of the local Carmelita guides. Matthias, one of the friendly owners of **Los Amigos Hostel** (tel. 5584-8795 or 5521-2873, www.amigoshostel.com) in Flores, organizes trips using local guides for $200 per person for two people and says he is happy with his current selection of guides after much trial and error. Another guide recommended by readers is **Henry Sánchez** (tel. 7821-0115 or 5751-3241, sanchezhenry5@hotmail.com).

Part of the current administration's plan to bring more visitors to El Mirador under the banner of *Plan Cuatro Balam* involves the construction of visitor facilities. These include two new tent platforms, a kitchen, eating area, hammock lounge, showers, and toilets. Facilities at Carmelita have likewise been improved with a visitor information center, a gift shop selling maps and souvenirs, and toilets.

Nakbé, El Tintal, and Wakná

Part of the proposed Mirador Basin park, the smaller sites of Nakbé, El Tintal, and Wakná are important links in the chain unveiling the mysteries of early Mayan civilization. **Nakbé** is thought to be the earliest of Petén's Mayan cities with settlement as early as 1000 B.C. and several thousand inhabitants by 400 B.C. Its layout is much like that of El Mirador, with triadic temple structures in two groups separated by a causeway. Its tallest structure, the Western Temple, reaches a height of just under 46 meters (150 feet), making it about as tall as Tikal's Temple I. It was completed in 500 B.C. A large stucco mask has also been unearthed here, on the side of one of the temples, much like at El Mirador. The excavations here, under the direction of Richard Hansen, are still in their early stages but more finds are sure to follow.

On the trek to El Mirador, 21 kilometers south, you'll pass by the site of **El Tintal,** which is also similar in construction to the larger city to the north. It has been badly looted and the temples here remain unrestored. There are excellent views of the surrounding forest from the top of its highest temple, including a glimpse of El Mirador far off in the distance. It's sure to motivate you to continue the second leg of the journey. Trekkers usually camp here the first night en route to El Mirador.

Rediscovered by Landsat imagery as recently as 1998, **Wakná** is another Preclassic site buried under the forest cover of the Mirador Basin. A ground crew led by Dr. Hansen confirmed the site's existence but unfortunately also found evidence of looting. A deep trench had been dug into a tomb allowing looters to cart off the priceless artifacts found therein. Richard Hansen's plans to restore and protect the Mirador Basin's sites may prevent further plunder of Wakná and other sites within the proposed park.

Río Azul

Occupying a remote corner of Guatemala near a border shared with Mexico and Belize, the Middle Preclassic site of Río Azul was rediscovered in 1962. The population reached its zenith sometime between A.D. 410 and 530, coinciding with the installation of the new Teotihuacán rulership at Tikal, with which it also shares a similar city layout. The population is believed to have reached 5,000 inhabitants occupying an area of about 300 hectares (750 acres).

Río Azul played an important part in the expansion of Tikal's dominance of the Petén area, likely as a vital trading post linking Tikal to sites on the Caribbean coast and farther north to Central Mexico. It also served as an important ally against Tikal's archrival, Calakmul. By A.D. 530, however, the tables had turned and Calakmul invaded Río Azul, forcibly allying it. After Tikal regained its former splendor in the Late Classic period, Río Azul's population once again soared and new monuments were built, further reflecting the city's status as a subservient outpost to the area's more powerful cities. It rounded out the Classic period invaded by Puuc Mayans from the Yucatán in A.D. 830.

Río Azul's claim to fame is the discovery of several tombs with bright red paintings on white plaster. Many of the burial scenes contain elements of Teotihuacán culture, providing further evidence of strong influence on Tikal and its satellite cities. Unfortunately, Río Azul fell prey to some of the most severe looting ever seen in the Mayan world in the 1960s and '70s. A minor section of these murals lining royal burial tombs remains intact, as most were chiseled out and taken away. There are some more recent discoveries, though not nearly as elaborate, pertaining to burial chambers of noblemen. It is hoped Petén's newer discoveries can avoid the same fate through better protection. Many of Río Azul's treasures are in private collections, though you can see several pieces on display in Guatemala City's archaeology museum.

GETTING TO RÍO AZUL

Río Azul is connected by road to Uaxactún at a distance of about 95 kilometers. The road is passable only in the dry season via four-wheel-drive. About halfway, you'll pass the **Naachtun-Dos Lagunas Biotope.** It is also possible to hike or ride horseback to this remote outpost, taking about five days each way. Trips can be arranged at **Campamento El Chiclero** in Uaxactún. Once at the site, you'll need to cross the Río Ixcán to the guards' campsite on the other side, where you can stay the night. The archaeological site proper is another six kilometers away, along a good road.

The road continues north another 12 kilometers to the intersection of the Belize, Guatemala, and Mexico borders, a place known as **Tres Banderas.** There are plans to improve the road from Uaxactún clear to the border at Tres Banderas under the auspices of a regional initiative known as *Plan Puebla Panamá.* So far,

conservationists have been able to get the project shelved, arguing that the new road would bring in settlers, much as in Laguna del Tigre to the west, with devastating consequences for this well-preserved swath of forest.

NAACHTUN-DOS LAGUNAS BIOTOPE

This biotope is managed by Guatemala's University of San Carlos Center for Conservation Studies (CECON) and was established for the protection of white-tailed deer. The biotope forms a corridor connecting the area around El Mirador to that surrounding Río Azul within the larger **Mirador-Río Azul National Park.** It also protects the Mayan ruins of Naachtun.

Naachtun lies 25 kilometers east of El Mirador and about one kilometer from the Mexican border in a remote pocket of jungle. A Late Classic site, its architecture bears strong influence from Tikal and Calakmul, probably owing to its being caught in the tug-of-war between these two great rivals. At least 45 stelae have been found here.

The biotope is in fairly good shape because of its remote location and the absence of roads, with abundant wildlife, including many of Guatemala's endangered species—jaguars and other jungle cats, such as margays and ocelots, brocket deer, crocodiles, river turtles, monkeys, tapirs, peregrine falcons, and mealy parrots. The plant diversity here and within the Mirador-Río Azul National Park is said to be the highest in the Maya Biosphere Reserve with a particularly high concentration of mahogany trees. Little has been done to promote tourism to the reserve and it remains a delightfully remote natural oasis off the beaten tourist trail.

Access to the biotope is along the road connecting Uaxactún to Río Azul, a little more than halfway. The road is passable only in the dry season, and then only via four-wheel-drive. You can also hike or ride on horseback

PETÉN

to the site from Uaxactún in about two days. Trips can be arranged through **Campamento El Chiclero.**

Park facilities are rudimentary and only about 40 visitors make it here every year, mostly foreigners. The park rangers have an encampment on the shore of one of the lagoons and will allow you to stay and cook there. Basic shelters for setting up a tent or stringing up a hammock are available, as are showers.

LAGUNA DEL TIGRE NATIONAL PARK

This vast park on the northwestern corner of Petén encompasses important wetlands, the largest in Central America. It also contains the only remaining populations of scarlet macaws in Guatemala, which are being protected via ongoing conservation efforts at a biological research station. Oil drilling, present before the park's creation, continues in the western part of the reserve, despite protests from environmental groups and their having been declared a violation of the park's intended use. In 2006, the Guatemalan government granted further oil exploration concessions in the park's multiple-use zone.

Visitors to this park should limit their activities to those centered around the Scarlet Macaw Biological Research Station and the site of Waka'-Perú, as the security conditions and the loss of much of the local habitat prevent me from recommending more in-depth explorations of this wild frontier.

Within the larger national park is the **Biotopo Laguna del Tigre Río-Escondido,** which has two biological stations open to researchers. It has been badly fragmented by seasonal forest fires and the encroachment of communities illegally settled inside park boundaries.

Sights

Unlike other parts of Petén, Laguna del Tigre has not been widely explored for the presence of archaeological sites or in terms of its biological diversity. Among the few archaeological discoveries is the site of **Waka'-Perú,** now being excavated by archaeologists from Southern Methodist University under the direction of David Freidel and Héctor Escobedo. Waka'-Perú has yielded some amazing finds, including the 2004 discovery of the royal burial tomb of a queen dating to about A.D. 620. The find is especially significant because there are only a handful of known tombs pertaining to women in the entire Mayan World. The location of yet another royal tomb was announced in May 2006.

Waka'-Perú is thought to have been an important commercial and political center because of its location on a tributary of the Río San Pedro, giving it direct access to the sites of Central Petén, the Southern Highlands, and Mexico. It flourished between A.D. 400 and 800, apparently coming under the dominion of Calakmul in its protracted power struggle with Tikal. It was later invaded by a resurgent Tikal in A.D. 743. There are several well-preserved stelae here, including Stela 16, which tells of the visit of a Tikal-bound Teotihuacán warrior in A.D. 378.

Nearby, the rediscovery of **La Corona** has solved the decades-old mystery of the location of a long-sought Mayan city. The limited amount of exploration in this part of Petén inevitably leads you to wonder what else may be lying undiscovered in this vast park of wetlands and jungle.

The park enjoys on-site protection by armed guards that are part of a joint task force involving the Civilian National Police (PNC) and SEPRONA, a specially trained unit of the military created to guard and protect nature preserves. You will see the guards at the site's ranger station, about a 25-minute walk from the riverbank. You are welcome to camp here.

LOST AND FOUND: THE MYSTERY OF SITE Q

For much of the 20th century, looters worked Petén's remote sites undisturbed, raiding tombs and extracting precious artifacts before archaeologists had a chance to study and document them. At the height of the looting, in the 1960s, archaeologists marveled at a series of magnificent glyphs making their way into a number of private collections and museums from an unknown site. Archaeologists dubbed the pieces' origin "Site Q" and the search to find the mysterious producer of the wonderful glyphs was on.

The glyphs made repeated references to a place deciphered as *kan*, or "snake head," which was eventually deduced to be Calakmul, and recorded several events in its history. It was once thought that this might be Site Q, but the badly eroded stelae at Calakmul were not of the same high-quality limestone.

The identity of Site Q would remain a mystery for more than four decades. The mystery first began to unravel in 1997 when an expedition headed by Ian Graham of Harvard University and David Stuart, now at the University of Texas at Austin, found evidence at remote La Corona leading them to suggest the possibility that it was Site Q. Then, in 2005, a one- by one-half-meter limestone panel containing 144 hieroglyphs was unearthed when an anthropologist working at the site followed a looter's trench into a small chamber.

Marcello A. Canuto, of Yale University, made the amazing discovery, which matches the Site Q pieces geologically. The translated text of the La Corona glyph panel, meanwhile, is consistent with the writings on the other Site Q pieces.

Although archaeologists are satisfied with finally putting to rest one of the longest-running searches for a lost Mayan city, they still have some unanswered questions. Among the Site Q glyph panels in private collections is one known as the "Dallas panel," which archaeologists believe was cut from a throne room. No such room has yet been found at La Corona.

❰ Las Guacamayas Biological Research Station

Las Guacamayas Biological Research Station (tel. 7926-1370, www.propeten.org) is owned by ProPetén and welcomes visitors. The biological station sits amid verdant jungle on the shores of the Río San Pedro, a 20-minute boat ride from the village of Paso Caballos. It is one of the best places in Petén to combine wildlife-viewing and rainforest trekking while staying in relative comfort, offering easy access to the ruins of Waka'-Perú and the surrounding forests. The current facility is the second incarnation of the biological station; the first was burned to the ground by angry villagers from Paso Caballos in the 1990s. ProPetén has since worked on strengthening ties to local communities and educating them about conservation.

You may contact ProPetén directly if you wish to stay here, as you don't need to be on an organized trip (Scarlet Macaw Trail) to book a room. It's recommended that you stay at least one night, as the station's remote location doesn't make for a reasonable day trip. A stay here can be arranged with or without meals, and you are free to use the kitchen to cook your own. There are basic dorm rooms with stiff mattresses, shared bath, mosquito netting, and screened-in rooms accommodating up to 20 people. For extended stays, try packing a sleeping pad for extra cushioning.

Nice views of the river and a series of nature trails round out the list of amenities. The shortest trail leads to an observation tower, where you have a sweeping view of the Río San Pedro and the wetlands of Laguna del Tigre National Park west to the foothills of the Sierra del Lacandón. There is a six-kilometer-long network of trails.

In the evening, you can go out on the river in search of crocodiles with the station's staff. Bird-watching is available in the mornings.

PETÉN

There are observation platforms inside the site of Waka'-Perú where the scarlet macaw project operates. The staff may offer photo safaris whereby you can watch and photograph macaws from a platform sometime in the near future. The best time to visit for a glimpse at nesting macaws is during February and March, though the macaws can usually be seen between November and April.

A two-day, three-night package including meals, accommodation, round-trip transport from Flores, bird-watching, and a tour of El Perú costs $300 each for two people, but better deals can probably be found through one of the Flores travel agencies.

Volunteers are also welcome at the biological station. During one of my last visits, two Spanish women were busy on a two-week tour of duty recollecting animal droppings for scientific investigation as to the health of local populations of certain species. Volunteers provide their own food and pay an average of $7 per day. The station prefers a two-week minimum commitment. Other activities you may be asked to assist with include wildlife monitoring and trail building and maintenance.

Recreation

Many travelers visit Waka'-Perú as part of a tour known as the **Scarlet Macaw Trail,** which can be booked from a number of travel agencies in Flores and costs anywhere between $200 and $300 per person. The duration of the trip, as well as the places to visit, can be adjusted to suit your preferences. Most visitors combine the site of Waka'-Perú with hikes into the surrounding pristine forests to see the nesting sites of scarlet macaws, which local scientists here are working to protect. A nearby biological station offers comfortable accommodations on a nice stretch of jungle river. Some travelers extend their stay to include a hike to the impressive cliffs of **Buena Vista,** which stand out from the surrounding jungle and afford wonderful views from the top.

Getting There

Access to the park and, more specifically, Waka'-Perú, is via a dirt road heading northwest from Flores to the village of Paso Caballos (two hours). From there, it's a 20-minute motorboat ride up the Río Sacluc to the biological station and another five minutes to the entrance to Waka'-Perú.

SIERRA DEL LACANDÓN NATIONAL PARK

Ironically, Guatemala's civil war helped protect many pristine areas from invasion and environmental degradation. This was especially the case in Sierra del Lacandón, a mountain chain in the western part of Petén along the Usumacinta River, where guerrillas and so-called Permanent Communities in Resistance (CPR) hid out in the jungle along the Guatemalan shore. Their presence discouraged illegal logging, poaching, and looting, as well as the surveying activities of dam engineers. The subsequent absence of the expelled CPRs after the end of the civil war left the area open to invasion, illegal logging, and smuggling of immigrants, arms, Mayan relics, and drugs.

The 1996 Guatemala peace accords and the Zapatista Rebellion across the border in Mexico reshaped the nature of things in the Usumacinta watershed. Bandits began robbing rafting trips, including the author and eight others while camping on the Mexican bank in April 2004. Wilderness travel on the river north of Yaxchilán (Mexican bank) has pretty much ended since then, putting a monkey wrench into one option for low-impact, economically beneficial activities contributing to the conservation of this beautiful area.

That said, the park is extremely important as a biological corridor and is believed to hold one of the largest populations of jaguars in all of Central America as well as an incredible degree of biodiversity, qualities enhanced by the rugged terrain of this jungle mountain park.

Hidden in the forests are the remains of several Mayan sites, the most important of which is Piedras Negras, deep inside the park along the Usumacinta River. The only other way to reach the site is by air.

The park is privately administered by Fundación Defensores de la Naturaleza. In June 2006, together with The Nature Conservancy, it completed the purchase of 77,000 acres of privately owned land in the core zone of Sierra del Lacandón. Soon thereafter, a number of ranger stations inside the park were burned to the ground by squatters invading parklands. As in other cases, the squatters are said to have ties to drug traffickers and smugglers of illegal immigrants who find these remote areas very attractive. An attempt to evict squatters from an area known as Arroyo Macabilero in June 2006 ended with a gunfight between heavily armed men and park rangers. Four park rangers were taken captive but were released a few days later unharmed.

In the summer of 2006, authorities were attempting to regain control of the area in a joint venture between Defensores de la Naturaleza and governmental security forces. Shortly thereafter, in October 2006, the press widely reported the retaking of Sierra del Lacanón by large numbers of Guatemalan security forces, who ousted about 80 families living at Arroyo Macabilero in a peaceful expropriation overseen and verified by human rights organizations. It remains to be seen if control of this wild frontier can be retained and if ranger stations or other tourist infrastructure will be rebuilt. For now, it is advisable to stay out of this park, with the possible exception of visits to Yaxchilán, across the Usumacinta River in Mexico, or via motorboat to Piedras Negras. In any case, check on the situation with one of the recommended Flores outfitters before heading out to these parts, as the situation can vastly improve or degenerate in a matter of weeks. **Tours Guatemala** (www.toursguatemala.com,

tel. 7926-0398) runs three-day tours to Piedras Negras and Yaxchilan camping at a secure campsite in Piedras Negras.

If the security situation is ever cleared up, Sierra del Lacandón promises to be one of the Maya Biosphere's most exquisite offerings because of the diversity of the terrain and corresponding biological significance. It is an absolutely beautiful park despite its current woes. Piedras Negras is a fascinating Mayan city and the jungle-lined banks of the Usumacinta offer an incredible river adventure. Having flown over much of the reserve, I can personally attest to the relatively well-preserved state of its mountain rainforests.

El Naranjo

This rough-and-tumble frontier town, accessible by bus from Santa Elena, is a jumping-off point for those heading west to Mexico via an unreliable boat transport down the Río San Pedro to La Palma. A better option into Mexico is to cross the Río Usumacinta via Bethel, arriving in Frontera Corozal.

Bethel

This small, pleasant settlement serves as a much better option for onward travel to Mexico or down the Río Usumacinta. There is an immigration office here, lodging, and several simple *comedores*. The best place to stay is at the community-run **Posada Maya** (tel. 7861-1799 or 7861-1800, $20 d) with simple rooms in thatched-roof bungalows. The restaurant here serves decent meals in a pleasant *palapa* building.

There is a small Mayan site here about 1.5 kilometers from the village, though its most impressive feature is probably the view of the river from a lookout about 20 minutes' walk from the site's core.

Boats leave Bethel downstream for Frontera Corozal, Yaxchilán, and Piedras Negras. Five daily buses and three daily minibuses leave the Santa Elena bus depot for the 3-4 hour ride to Bethel. The last of these departs at 1:30 P.M.

SAVING GUATEMALA'S SCARLET MACAWS

Among Petén's most beautiful creatures are the brightly colored scarlet macaws that once roamed freely throughout Petén. You'll probably run into these large parrots throughout your travels in Guatemala; they are popular pets in hotel courtyards on account of their colorful red, blue, and yellow plumage—including two beautiful red tail feathers—in addition to their boisterous squawking and ability to mimic human speech. Unfortunately, their populations have been decimated by habitat loss and wildlife poaching for the international pet trade. Still, there remain pockets where macaws continue to nest, and local scientists have taken it upon themselves to help protect what's left of Guatemala's dwindling numbers of these exotic birds.

In the dense forests that still surround the site of Waka'-Perú, biologists from several agencies working in Petén, including ProPetén (www.propeten.org) and Wildlife Conservation Society (www.wcs.org), have established protected nesting grounds. There are 21 nests in hollow forest trees and additional "artificial" nests are being created. The latter involve creating hollowed-out tree trunks, which are then placed high in the treetops. Biologists report success with this new method. Like most parrots, scarlet macaws lay 2-4 white eggs in a tree cavity, with their young hatching after about 25 days. The hatchlings fly about 105 days later and leave their parents as late as one year.

The nests at Waka'-Perú enjoy year-round protection by a joint military-police force charged with safeguarding Guatemala's natural resources.

Volunteers are welcome at the site, giving visitors an exciting opportunity to help out in the conservation of Guatemala's exotic creatures while helping to fund the biological station's efforts.

Río Usumacinta

This mighty river is Central America's longest and harbors the remains of at least two important Mayan cities along its banks. Ten-day rafting trips once made their way down this waterway starting at Yaxchilán and putting out at the Mexican town of Tenosique, but these have been suspended for the time being because of robberies. The robberies seem to occur downstream from Yaxchilán on a very remote stretch of the river on the way to Piedras Negras. It's really a shame, as the stretch harbors some truly spectacular banks of riverside rainforest on the Guatemalan side protected as the Sierra del Lacandón National Park. On the Mexican side, there are a variety of communities and some bad deforestation, though there are some beautiful waterfalls downstream from Piedras Negras. All is not lost, however, as you can still reach **Busiljá Falls** from Mexico. Willy Fonseca, the friendly owner of **Restaurante Vallescondido** (Km. 61 on the Palenque-Comitán Road, tel.

916/348-0721), can get you there and also offers trips to Piedras Negras.

Farther downstream, the river leaves Guatemala behind and narrows into the impressive **Cañón de San José,** where there are Class III rapids flanked by 1,000-foot canyons.

While it is entirely possible to do part of the trip by motorboat, as opposed to slow-moving inflatable rafts, it seems even these vessels are occasionally shot at from the riverbank in an attempt to make them stop. Much of the boat traffic here pertains to the transport of illegal immigrants crossing international borders on their way north, and thieves are only too eager to rid them of their money. Drug smugglers also use the river as a highway for transporting their merchandise. It really makes you long for the "good old days" when the Guatemalan ORPA guerrillas patrolled the banks, at worst flagging you down from the shore for a lecture on the justice of their cause. If the Mexicans can get their security issues straightened out, white-water rafting trips may once again be a viable recreational option here.

© AL ARGUETA

Busiljá Falls

Yaxchilán

This beautiful Mayan site enjoys a spectacular setting on the Mexican shore of the Río Usumacinta, on a densely forested horseshoe-shaped bend on the river. It was unquestionably the most important Usumacinta site in Mayan times. At the height of its power, in the late 7th century A.D., it came to dominate much of the river's trade and formed powerful alliances with neighboring sites as far away as Tikal and Palenque. Sprawled throughout the site's raised banks are several temples, plazas, and ball courts. Several palaces can be found along lower parts of the city.

Among the site's most impressive features is the presence of superb artwork adorning several structures, including door lintels and stucco carvings on roof combs. Many of these have been removed to museums around the world. A long staircase leads from the plaza to **Temple 33,** Yaxchilán's most impressive structure, featuring impressive carved lintels under its doorways.

The ruins are open 8 A.M. to 5 P.M. daily. Admission costs $3. You can pitch a tent at a campground overlooking the river if you wish to spend the night. The easiest way to get here is from the community of Bethel. The **Posada Maya Bethel** can arrange trips to Yaxchilán for about $100 round-trip. A cheaper option is to book a trip on one of several boats heading downstream to **Frontera Corozal.** You can hire a boat from Frontera Corozal to the ruins for about $60 round-trip for up to four people. It's about a 45-minute trip downstream to the site and an hour upstream on the return.

Piedras Negras

About 40 kilometers downstream amid the dense rainforests of Sierra del Lacandón lie the exotic ruins of Piedras Negras. The site is exquisite both because of its location on a lonely stretch of river and for the quality of its carved monuments, which are considered some of the best in the Mayan world.

© AL ARGUETA

superbly carved glyphs from Piedras Negras

Its remoteness gives you the privileged sensation of being one of a very select number of visitors and, along with El Mirador, most closely mirrors what the early explorers must have felt upon first rediscovering some of the great Mayan cities.

Piedras Negras was founded sometime around A.D. 300 and fought Yaxchilán for much of its history in a struggle for supreme control over the Usumacinta's trade routes. It would form strategic alliances both with Tikal and Calakmul in this pursuit. This large city is thought to have housed 10,000 inhabitants at its peak population.

Among Piedras Negras's excellent carvings are several stelae, hieroglyphic panels, and even a royal hieroglyphic throne. Several of these are on display in Guatemala City's archaeology museum.

The site gets its Spanish name from the black rocks lining the riverbank here. Among them is a giant stone near the entrance to the site with several eroded hieroglyphs and a depiction of two seated figures. From here, you head up the hill to the ruins. Several structures remain well preserved, among them the **Acropolis,** containing a large twin-palace complex, as well as several Mayan saunas used by the elite and scattered throughout the site. The remains of a giant **stairway** reaching down to the riverbank can also be found here.

Famed Russian epigrapher Tatiana Proskouriakoff, who deciphered many of the Mayan glyphs here and at Yaxchilán, is buried among the ruins. Proskouriakoff first postulated the idea that many of the events described in Mayan hieroglyphs corresponded to events in a ruler's life span, a theory initially discarded by Mayanists but subsequently proven correct.

Since 1997, after the departure of the guerrillas formerly occupying Piedras Negras, excavations have once again been carried out under the leadership of Héctor Escobedo. The site is among the World Monuments Fund's list of "100 Most Threatened Places" because of a hydroelectric project tossed around by the Mexican government for decades, threatening to flood Piedras Negras and several smaller, recently discovered nearby sites. Only about 200 visitors make the trip to Piedras Negras every year.

The best way to visit Piedras Negras is on an organized tour. **Maya Expeditions** (www.mayaexpeditions.com), which pioneered rafting trips on the Usumacinta, has updated its itineraries to reflect the security situation on the river. By the same token, folks at the **Posada Maya** (tel. 7861-1799 or 7861-1800) in Bethel can help arrange transport if you choose to go. The most feasible

© AL ARGUETA

Usumacinta River

option at this time is to do the trip from the Mexican side of the river via Willy Fonseca's **Restaurante Vallescondido** (Km. 61 on the Palenque-Comitán Road, tel. 916/348-0721 or 916/100-0399, busil_h@hotmail.com). Trips go out with a minimum of four people, with each person paying $125 for an overnight camping trip.

There is an excellent riverside campsite with a wide sandy beach a few hundred meters downstream from Piedras Negras at El Porvenir, where there is a CONAP guard station.

BACKGROUND

The Land

GEOGRAPHY

Guatemala is the third-largest country in Central America. It occupies 42,042 square miles, making it about the size of Tennessee. The country shares borders with Mexico, Belize, Honduras, and El Salvador. Within Guatemala's relatively small area are 14 distinct ecosystems found at elevations varying from sea level to higher than 4,200 meters (14,000 feet). Many people think of Guatemala as a sweltering tropical country, which is only partially true. While it does feature warm tropical coastal environments and hot lowland jungles, a rugged spine of mountains and volcanoes runs through the country's center. In the tropics, elevation mostly determines climate and this is certainly the case in Guatemala. Temperatures drop dramatically the higher you go in elevation and precipitation varies greatly depending on what side of a mountain chain you're on. All of this translates into a dizzying array of landscapes, making Guatemala a delight to explore.

The country divides rather neatly into various geographical zones. The volcanic highlands run through the country's center going west to east from Mexico to El Salvador. Elevation

© AL ARGUETA

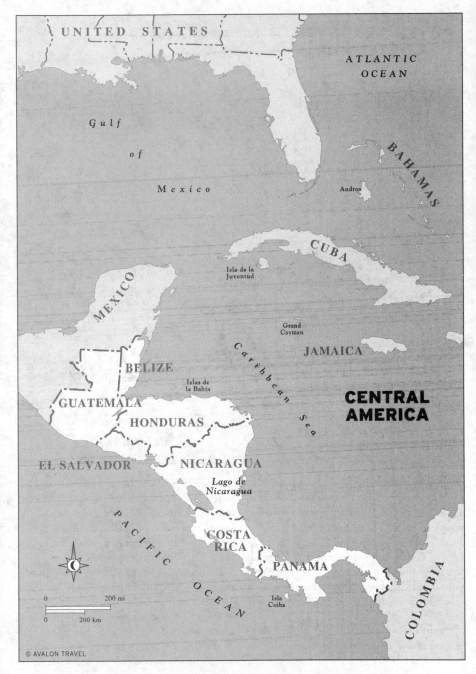

UNITED STATES

ATLANTIC OCEAN

Gulf

of

Mexico

BAHAMAS

Andros

CUBA

Isla de la Juventud

MEXICO

Grand Cayman

JAMAICA

BELIZE

Caribbean Sea

Islas de la Bahía

GUATEMALA

HONDURAS

CENTRAL AMERICA

EL SALVADOR

NICARAGUA

Lago de Nicaragua

PACIFIC

COSTA RICA

PANAMA

COLOMBIA

Isla Coiba

OCEAN

0   200 mi

0   200 km

© AVALON TRAVEL

PHYSIOGRAPHY
OF GUATEMALA

MEXICO

Tierra Fría (Cold Lands)
Tierra Templada (Temperate Lands)
Tierra Caliente (Hot Lands)

Lago
Petén Itzá

Flores

BELIZE

Río Usumacinta

Golfo de

Honduras

CARIBBEAN & NORTHERN
TROPICAL LOWLANDS

Río Negro
(Río Chixoy)

Cobán

Lago de
Izabal

Puerto
Barrios

Río Polochic

HIGHLANDS

HONDURAS

Quetzaltenango

Lago de
Atitlán

Río Motagua

Zacapa

Volcanic Axis

Guatemala City

Retalhuleu

Antigua Guatemala

BOCA COSTA

PACIFIC

PACIFIC SEABOARD

Jutiapa

OCEAN

Monterrico

EL SALVADOR

© AVALON TRAVEL

0   20 mi
0   20 km

tends to get lower closer to the Salvadoran border. The eastern areas of Alta and Baja Verapaz are largely mountainous but also largely composed of limestone. A curious feature of this area, found in its northern limits, is the presence of small, forested limestone hills much like those found in parts of China. East from Guatemala City toward Honduras, the terrain is largely dominated by semiarid flatlands covered in cactus.

Closer to the Caribbean coast in the department of Izabal, the terrain once again becomes lush and largely filled with banana plantations.

A small sliver of Caribbean coastline runs between the Honduran border and Belize but features white-sand beaches, swamplands, and some impressive tropical rainforests. Small mountains are interspersed throughout parts of the Caribbean coastal region.

Running roughly parallel to the highlands, to the south, are the Pacific Coast flatlands. This is a rich agricultural area once covered in tropical forest but now home to vast sugarcane and coffee plantations, the latter being on the slopes of the highland zones as they descend into the coastal plain. The Pacific Coast is also home to wetlands, mangrove swamps, and beaches of curiously dark color because of their proximity to the country's volcanic chain.

The northern third of Guatemala is a vast Ohio-sized limestone flatland known as Petén. Once covered entirely in tropical forests, it has increasingly become deforested in its southern parts with only the northern third retaining large unbroken swaths of forest.

Here is a brief discussion of some of Guatemala's outstanding geographic features and why they might be of interest to the visitor.

Mountains

The highest of Guatemala's mountains are actually volcanic peaks. There are 33 of them in total with a handful now active. Volcán Tajumulco, at 4,220 meters (13,845 feet), is the highest point in all of Central America, followed closely by nearby Volcán Tacaná, at 4,110 meters (13,484 feet). The most frequently climbed volcanoes include the active Pacaya, near Guatemala City, the three volcanoes on the shores of Lake Atitlán, Agua, and Acatenango near Antigua. Some volcanoes, such as Chicabal and Ipala, feature turquoise lagoons, which fill their craters. Other active volcanoes include Fuego and Santiaguito.

Among the nonvolcanic mountains, the Sierra de los Cuchumatanes, near the border with Mexico, is Guatemala's, and Central America's, highest mountain chain. It stands 3,837 meters (12,588 feet) at its highest point. Its smooth, rounded peaks attest to years of erosion from being glaciated thousands of years ago. Other noteworthy mountain chains include the Sierra de Las Minas, in the eastern part of the country. Protected as a private forest reserve, it still contains large stands of virgin cloud forest. Farther east near the Caribbean Coast are the Cerro San Gil and Montañas del Mico, which are still covered in dense tropical

San Pedro Volcano and Lake Atitlán

rainforest. Petén has relatively few mountains, but the foothills of the Maya Mountains of neighboring Belize run into the department's southeastern corner with an elevation of over 1,000 meters (3,300 feet) at Petén's highest point. Petén's other noteworthy mountain range is the remote and mostly forested Sierra del Lacandón, at the far western edge of the department bordering Mexico and exceeding 600 meters (2,000 feet) at its highest point.

Guatemala's mountain scenery comes largely as a product of its geographic location at the intersection of the North American, Cocos, and Caribbean plates, making it one of the most seismically and volcanically active places in the world. Indeed, Guatemala is no stranger to earthquakes. Among the many fault lines running through the country are the parallel Chixoy-Polochic and Motagua faults. The latter is responsible for the most recent major earthquake to rock Guatemala, a magnitude-7.5 whopper in February 1976 killing thousands and wiping entire villages off the face of the map. A series of massive earthquakes in 1776 resulted in the relocation of the Guatemalan capital from the Panchoy Valley (Antigua Guatemala) to the Valley of the Hermitage, where it remains today, better known as Guatemala City.

Rivers

Guatemala has several rivers worthy of mention. The greatest of these is the Usumacinta, which is formed by the confluence of the Chixoy and Pasión Rivers, making it Central America's most voluminous river. Guatemalan author Virgilio Rodríguez Macal, in his novel *Guayacán,* calls it the "father and lord of the Central American rivers." The Usumacinta forms much of Guatemala's border with Mexico and continues its northwesterly flow all the way to the Gulf of Mexico. On the Guatemalan side, the Usumacinta borders the relatively untouched Sierra del Lacandón

National Park, which harbors dense tropical rainforests. Rafting trips once made their way down the Usumacinta, visiting Yaxchilán (Mexico) and the Guatemalan site of Piedras Negras, but an increase in violent armed robberies has meant their indefinite suspension. The Usumacinta is indeed a wild frontier and is an active waterway for drug smuggling, contraband logging, and boats carrying illegal immigrants on their journey north. An on-again, off-again Mexican dam project has been vehemently opposed by environmentalists and, until 1996, Guatemalan rebels camped out in the jungle. The project would reportedly flood Piedras Negras, Yaxchilán, and several smaller sites along the Usumacinta. The project appears to have been called off, for the time being.

The Pasión, an Usumacinta tributary, meanders through southern Petén. Much like the larger Usumacinta, its watershed was extremely important in Mayan times. Several Mayan sites lie near the river. In the arid southeastern part of the country, the Río Motagua connects the highlands to the Caribbean Sea and forms a dry river valley of agricultural importance since Mayan times. Other notable rivers include the Río San Pedro, also in Petén; the Verapaces-area Río Cahabón, which has excellent whitewater runs year-round; and the Río Dulce, a lazy tropical river connecting Lake Izabal to the Caribbean.

Lakes and Lagoons

Guatemala has several lakes noteworthy for their size, recreational opportunities, and sheer natural beauty. Foremost among these is highland Lake Atitlán, called "the most beautiful lake in the world" by author Aldous Huxley during his travels through the region. The lake's spectacular mountain scenery is punctuated by the sentinel presence of three towering volcanoes along its southern shores. Near Guatemala City, Lake Amatitlán has been a weekend getaway for city dwellers since time immemorial

© AL ARGUETA

Guatemala's mountain terrain

but industrial pollution has spoiled the once-clear waters. Still, Guatemalans have taken on the ominous task of rescuing its waters with foreign help and the lake may soon be safe again for swimming. An aerial tram operating on surrounding hillsides has recently reopened the area to visitors, making a side trip to this tranquil spot increasingly alluring for wonderful views of the rugged mountain terrain. The largest of Guatemala's lakes, Lake Izabal, is a tropical lake connected to the Caribbean by the Río Dulce. The Río Polochic delta, on Izabal's southwestern shore, is becoming increasingly popular as a bird-watcher's paradise. Petén's Lake Petén Itzá is also a tropical flatland lake with the added bonus of tropical forests, crystal-clear waters, and a variety of accommodations from which to enjoy all of these. As much of Petén is limestone, the lake's waters have a distinct turquoise color near the lakeshores and from the air look very much like those of the Mexican Caribbean. Farther east toward

Belize is Yaxhá Lagoon, near the ruins of the same name. The lagoon, and its aggressive crocodiles, was made famous by the *Survivor Guatemala* television series filmed here in the summer of 2005.

There are many beautiful lagoons in the Guatemalan highlands. Some, atop volcanoes such as Ipala and Chicabal, are believed by the Mayans to harbor mystical powers and are the site of rituals. Laguna Lachuá is a beautiful, almost perfectly round lagoon in the Ixcán jungle region just north of the highlands. The surrounding rainforest has been preserved, but unfortunately it is an ecological island, a green square in a surrounding sea of deforestation.

The Coasts

Guatemala has a significant amount of coastline along the Pacific Ocean, though there are few beaches to speak of. Still, there are a few places with surf-worthy waves and the Pacific Coast beaches are exotic because of their dark sands, which are due to the proximity of active volcanoes. Among the best places to hit the beach are Monterrico and Las Lisas. Guatemala is gaining international fame among anglers for the quality of its deep-sea fishing. On the Caribbean side, there are a few pleasant white-sand beaches on the remote peninsula of Punta de Manabique as well as closer to the towns of Puerto Barrios and Lívingston. There is excellent scuba diving in the outlying Belize cayes and around Punta de Manabique.

CLIMATE

Guatemala has a tropical climate, though temperatures vary greatly between regions because of differences in altitude. The coastal plains and lowlands have an average yearly temperature of about 27°C (80°F), with little seasonal change. Mountain valleys 1,200-1,800 meters (4,000-6,000 feet) high are usually comfortably mild. Major cities such as Guatemala City, Antigua, and Quetzaltenango all lie at these altitudes, meaning they have mostly pleasant year-round springlike temperatures of 16°C-21°C (60°F-70°F). Higher mountain peaks and valleys sometimes have frost and average 4°C (40°F). Keep in mind that these are averages and certain times of year are markedly warmer than others. The North American winter solstice often brings the arrival of cold fronts, which make temperatures in the highlands dip below freezing on mountain summits but also in highland cities such as Quetzaltenango. If you're traveling to Guatemala November-February, bring a warm sweater or two for the chilly highlands and a heavy jacket if you plan to climb some volcanoes. At the other extreme, March and April, coinciding with the spring equinox, is the warmest time of year. Temperatures in the Petén lowlands, Izabal, and Pacific Coast plain routinely hover around 38°C (100°F) during these months. Guatemala City and Antigua hover at around 29°C (85°F).

There are distinct dry and rainy seasons in Guatemala. The dry season runs from November to the beginning of May. If you are a photographer interested in capturing images of Guatemala's fantastic mountain scenery, you may want to avoid visiting during March and April, when haze from dust and agricultural burning tends to obliterate any views of surrounding scenery. The volcanoes around Antigua and Lake Atitlán become extremely difficult to spot during this time of year.

The rainy season generally lasts May-November with daily showers during most of this period, usually in the afternoon. Mornings are usually sunny and clear, with a gradual buildup of giant rain clouds throughout the day, culminating in a torrential downpour. The latter months tend to be the rainiest with deluges sometimes lasting entire days. The rainy season is sometimes referred to as *invierno*, meaning winter, though it is officially summer in the Northern Hemisphere, where Guatemala lies. *Verano*, or summer, refers to the tail end of the dry season.

The Pacific Coastal plain and Western Highlands receive 76-150 centimeters (30-60 inches) of rain a year, and the Eastern Highlands average 51-76 centimeters (20-30 inches). Again, these figures vary greatly from place to place depending on factors such as altitude and what side of the mountain chain you're on. An example of this is the presence of ample rainfall and lush cloud forests on the forested slopes of the Sierra de las Minas in contrast to semiarid plains in the mountain's rain shadow along the neighboring Motagua Valley. Petén receives 200-381 centimeters (80-150 inches) of rain annually, which falls throughout most of the year. The rainiest place in Guatemala is said to be the Cerro San Gil rainforest, on the Caribbean Coast, where warm, moist air rises from the ocean and dumps precipitation on this small mountain chain. There is really no dry season to speak of in this area.

There are sometimes breaks in the rainfall, known as *canícula*, for a week or two in July and/or August. Rainfall can vary substantially from year to year, which is due to factors such as the presence of El Niño or La Niña. El Niño often means a prolonged dry season, which can lead to intense wildfires in forested areas such as Petén.

Hurricanes and tropical storms sometimes hit Guatemala during the latter months of the rainy season, causing widespread damage. Much of this is due to soil saturation on deforested and waterlogged hillsides, which give way to devastating mudslides, as occurred in parts of the Lake Atitlán basin after Hurricane Stan in 2005. Hurricane Mitch also left a trail of devastation along the Caribbean Coast in 1998, obliterating much of the banana harvest and destroying thousands of homes.

ENVIRONMENTAL ISSUES

Guatemala's environmental issues, particularly in regard to tropical deforestation, can seem daunting at times. The country and its people seem to be caught in a vicious cycle that will end only when the environmental degradation reaches its peak and the consequences are fully reaped. It seems greed, apathy, poverty, corruption, ignorance, and neglect have all conspired against Guatemala's precious natural resources. I do not mean to sound pessimistic in my introduction to this subject. I just think I've had the opportunity to see what's at stake, having explored much of Guatemala during my teenage years and seeing firsthand the gradual encroachment of the agricultural frontier into what was once virgin forest. It is hoped that visitors to Guatemala, much like those to Belize and Costa Rica, will play a pivotal role in raising awareness of the abundant natural heritage with which Guatemalans been blessed, enabling the conservation of these resources to become a source of economic and moral value.

There is a long way to go to make environmental awareness a matter of national consciousness, as demonstrated by how frequently one sees garbage by the roadside or car and bus passengers casually throwing refuse out their windows. The problem of raising this consciousness is exacerbated when one takes into account the overwhelming lack of education of the general populace, with its alarming levels of illiteracy, and the fact that environmental protection always takes a back seat when it comes down to a question of preserving the forest or cutting it down to plant subsistence crops.

At the same time, there is much to be hopeful about, particularly in the three decades since Guatemala established its democracy, during which time the country has been governed by civilian presidents interested in environmental matters. In addition to establishing the Maya Biosphere Reserve, Vinicio Cerezo Arévalo pushed through congress much of the legislation serving as a basis for the protection of Guatemala's natural heritage. Many valiant Guatemalans have likewise done their part to establish a genuine environmental movement in their country. Their courage is underscored by the fact that, in Guatemala, environmental activism necessarily entails standing firm in the face of death threats and intimidations. Environmental protection often conflicts with the interests of the still-powerful agricultural elites, among these: lumber barons; drug cartels using remote parks for illicit activities; cattle ranchers, some of whom have military ties; and land-hungry peasants. Environmental martyrs are many in Guatemala, much the same as the legacy of those campaigning for greater respect for human rights and better socioeconomic conditions. In these ways, environmental issues in Guatemala are largely circumscribed within the larger social issues of endemic poverty, power politics, and the rule of law.

Deforestation

In 2005, about 37 percent of Guatemala was still forested, down from 40 percent in 2001. Most of the country was at one time covered by forests, a fact attested to by Guatemala's ancient Mayan-Toltec name meaning "land of the trees." The once-forested Pacific plains have given way largely to sugarcane and coffee plantations while the forests of the Caribbean slope have been turned largely over to banana plantations. The highlands, for their part, have been under intense cultivation since preconquest times, though there are still substantial forests left in remote corners of Quiche and Huehuetenango. Most of the loss of forest cover in the past 40 years has been due to government incentives aimed at colonizing the northern department of Petén in an attempt to ease pressure for land by an ever-increasing population. The Petén thus became an escape valve from pressures for land reform historically thwarted by Guatemala's agricultural elites. It is here that a modern-day battle is being waged over Guatemala's remaining forests.

It is hoped that history will not repeat itself,

as the ancient Mayans have a valuable lesson to teach about what happens when the forests are cut down. It is speculated that among the reasons for the Classic Mayan collapse is widespread drought caused by the overwhelming deforestation of the tropical lowlands the Mayans inhabited. This may have, in turn, led to widespread warfare among Mayan city-states as populations scrambled to assert dominance over dwindling resources. The southern and central sections of Petén have been almost completely deforested, leading to local declines in annual rainfall marked by prolonged and warmer dry seasons. The northern third of Petén remains mostly intact, for now, protected as the Maya Biosphere Reserve. Pressures against the reserve continue to mount, however, with illegal land grabs and clandestine logging continuing to make inroads. There is no guarantee that the reserve's borders will remain inviolate or that they will stave off the advance of the agricultural frontier.

It bears discussing here the process by which seemingly endless tracts of forest become tropical wastelands resembling the dustbowl-era plains of Kansas. While the lowland Mayans practiced advanced farming techniques, including terracing and irrigation canals, what survives today is a simplified form of subsistence farming known as slash-and-burn agriculture. An area of forest will be felled and burned to the ground, with nutrient-rich ashes allowing crops to grow, though generally for a period of only two years. After that, a new plot of forest must be destroyed to grow crops again. The problem lies in that the soil of tropical forests is notoriously lacking in nutrients; the vast part of the ecosystem's biomass is in the trees themselves, with forest topsoil only reaching about two inches in depth. The old plot is abandoned, with the soil having been compacted, and sold to cattle ranchers. And so, each year more and more land is deforested and turned into a jungle wasteland. The forests are particularly at risk at the tail end of the dry season, when slash-and-burn agriculture can get out of hand and burn uncontrolled into protected areas. Many times fires are set purposely inside park lands.

In addition to the activities of peasant farmers steadily encroaching on virgin forests, the activities of contraband loggers, looters of unexcavated archaeological sites, and wildlife poachers inside park boundaries constitute an additional threat to the forests. Adding insult to injury, contraband loggers, wildlife poachers, and peasants from neighboring Mexico have been scuttling the border separating their country from Guatemala to burn forest, kill wildlife, and plant crops in cleared lands. A now-famous Landsat image appearing in the October 1989 issue of *National Geographic* shows the once razor-sharp border between Mexico and Guatemala's Laguna del Tigre National Park. The border is now dotted with burned-out land parcels along much of this boundary marker as a curious extension of the wide-scale deforestation in Mexico.

A recent development is the clearing of forest to build clandestine landing strips for drug-laden aircraft coming in from South America. With the virtual absence of local law enforcement and the aid of poor peasants eager for extra income, drug lords have found a haven for their illicit activities in Guatemala's remote parks. They have even gone so far as to acquire property by buying lands from settlers and then registering them illegally in their own names. Whether through bribes or the falsification of documents, *narcos* have infiltrated Guatemala's protected lands to suit their illicit operations. The existence of these "narco-farms" was brought to the attention of Guatemalan authorities after eight park guards were kidnapped and held hostage by armed men in June 2005 in Sierra del Lacandón National Park. The guards and members of a conservation group had decided to verify reports of clandestine logging inside the park. They were later released unharmed. The Public Ministry began a long process of expropriating the illegally titled lands while lawyers and land surveyors working the case faced intimidations and death threats. Meanwhile, the narcos reportedly moved their operations south to the Petexbatún region after a new military-trained environmental protection unit was created to destroy many of the clandestine landing strips and prevent further illicit activity.

Water Resources

Access to safe drinking water is a widespread problem throughout most of Guatemala. According to figures from the United Nations Development Program, roughly a quarter of Guatemalans still lack this basic necessity. This figure becomes even more dramatic in rural areas, where it is actually closer to 50 percent. The lack of potable water in turn leads to many illnesses, including intestinal parasites and amoebic dysentery, among others. Although most cities have sewer systems, wastewater treatment is virtually nonexistent—raw sewage often flows into rivers, lakes, and oceans. Guatemala City's sewage, for example, is responsible for polluting the nearby Motagua River with human excrement, solvents, and metallic waste. Adding to Guatemala's water woes is pollution from petroleum-based fertilizers used in commercial coffee, banana, and sugar plantations, which openly dump wastewater into nearby rivers and streams.

Air Quality

Guatemala City is notoriously polluted by old, recycled U.S. school buses, the basis of its public transportation network, which belch out diesel fumes in the form of black clouds. A promising recent development is a revamping of the city's public transportation system to include newer vehicles and stop older buses from circulating in the city center. In addition to auto exhaust, pollution from industrial facilities and burning garbage from the city dump combine to form a thick haze often hanging over the city. The worst days occur when thermal inversions cause the haze to hang in a low-altitude pollution gulag, much like a pineapple-upside-down cake. Concentrations of particulates, ozone, and nitrogen dioxide often exceed World Health Organization safety standards, particularly on these days. During the rainy season, the haze is washed away by the afternoon rains, after which the atmosphere is amazingly free of pollutants.

Elsewhere, smoke and ash from occasional volcanic eruptions can make the atmosphere somewhat hazy, though the worst pollution comes from dry-season agricultural burning and forest fires. When one considers that more than half of all energy consumption comes from burning firewood, the reasons behind the thick haze hanging over much of the country during March and April begin to emerge.

Resource Extraction

Mining activities have made Guatemalan newspaper headlines in recent years, as mining interests have cast an interested eye upon Guatemalan lands. Although environmental-impact studies are required by law, these often fall prey to government corruption in the form of payoffs in exchange for a favorable assessment. Threats and intimidation against environmental groups often attempt to quell any opposition to these projects.

Residents of the Western Highlands town of Sipacapa have demonstrated vehement opposition to the opening of a strip mine in the vicinity of their town, bringing the case directly to the president of the World Bank and officials of the International Finance Corporation (IFC), the World Bank's private-sector lending arm. Among the arguments against the installation of mining activities is the conflict of an open-pit mine with Mayan belief in the sacredness of the Earth.

Residents of Sipacapa held a referendum overwhelmingly rejecting the presence of a mine on community lands. In early 2005, protests against the mine's establishment, including roadblocks, were broken up by military forces, resulting in 11 people being injured and one killed.

More than 550 mining concessions now cover 10 percent of the country. Almost 20 percent of these are for open-pit mining of minerals such as gold, silver, nickel, and copper.

Petroleum extraction continues in the northern Petén lowlands and parts of Alta Verapaz, including the Laguna del Tigre National Park, although ecological organizations have long denounced its negative effects upon the environment. Oil exploration and extraction were present before the creation of the Maya Biosphere Reserve and have thus been allowed to continue, mostly in parts of the buffer and multiple-use zones. During the civil war, oil pipelines became a frequent target for guerrillas sabotaging the activities of multinationals involved in resource extraction. Occupations of oil-drilling facilities were also frequent. In addition to creating roads through sparsely populated areas, the oil extraction activities have come under fire because of oil spills in protected lands.

In 2005, the Guatemalan government opened new concessions in an area along the Petén-Alta Verapaz border said to harbor an estimated 200 million barrels of oil. Guatemala's total estimated reserves amount to about 2 billion barrels. Guatemalan oil's high sulfur content prevents it from being used in the production of diesel or gasoline, relegating it to use in the production of asphalt.

Soil Erosion

Unbridled deforestation on steep hillsides is responsible for much of the erosion of Guatemala's soil. Already about one-third of all land cover is considered eroded or seriously degraded, a significant amount when one considers the high degree of susceptibility to erosion of Guatemala's soil, which is composed largely of unconsolidated volcanic ash. Deforestation and soil erosion work hand in hand and are responsible for many of the tragic mudslides in the aftermath of tropical storms such as Hurricanes Mitch and Stan. Soil erosion has also contributed to greatly shortening the useful life of Chixoy Dam, which supplies about 15 percent of Guatemala's electricity, through siltation of the dam's reservoir.

Conservation Groups

Many grassroots environmental organizations operate in Guatemala in partnership with international conservation organizations. Among the best-known groups is **Fundación Defensores de la Naturaleza** (7a Avenida 7-09 Zona 13, Guatemala City, tel. 2440-8138 or 2471-7942, www.defensores.org.gt), which administers Sierra del Lacandón National Park, Sierra de Las Minas Biosphere Reserve, Bocas del Polochic Wildlife Refuge, and the United Nations National Park just outside of Guatemala City. Through private land purchases, Defensores has been able to acquire large tracts of land in Sierra de las Minas and Sierra del Lacandón with help from The Nature Conservancy.

The Nature Conservancy also works locally with the Fundación para el Desarrollo y la Conservación (Foundation for Development and Conservation), or **FUNDAECO** (7a Calle "A" 20-53 Zona 11, Colonia Mirador, Guatemala City, tel. 2474-3645). Together, they have bought more than 9,000 acres of tropical rainforest in the Caribbean coastal mountain chain of Cerro San Gil.

Another organization working to protect local ecosystems is **FUNDARY** (Diagonal 6, 17-19 Zona 10, Guatemala City, tel. 2333-4957, 2366-7539, or 2367-0171, www.guate.net/fundarymanabique/index.htm), named after the late Mario Dary Rivera, creator of the CECON biotopes. FUNDARY has centered its efforts on the protection of coastal environments, particularly the Punta de Manabique peninsula, on Guatemala's Caribbean Coast.

The forests of Petén are understandably the center of much attention from local and international organizations. **ProPetén** (Calle Central, Flores, Petén, tel. 7926-1370, www.propeten. org), an offshoot of Conservation International, began operating shortly after the creation of the Maya Biosphere Reserve and is credited with implementing innovative approaches to bridge the gap between the need for environmental conservation and the needs of communities living in or near the reserve. Among its successful programs are the establishment of a research station for the protection of scarlet macaws, forestry concessions with local communities in the Maya Biosphere Reserve's buffer zone, and two Spanish-language schools owned and operated by local villagers.

Alianza Verde (Parque Central, Flores, Petén, www.alianzaverde.org), for its part, has done an excellent job of promoting low-impact tourism in Petén as part of its mandate to aid in the protection and conservation of the region's precious natural resources. In addition to marketing efforts, Alianza Verde certifies ecotourism operations and aids in the training of tourism staff to improve Petén's tourism offerings and visitor experience. It functions as an association of businesses, organizations, and individuals who make their livelihood from Petén's valuable tourism industry.

Another important organization is the Asociacion de Rescate y Conservacion de Vida Silvestre (Wildlife Rescue and Conservation Association), or **ARCAS** (4 Ave. 2-47, Sector B5, Zona 8 Mixco, San Cristóbal, Guatemala, tel. 2476-6001, www.arcasguatemala.com). It works to protect and rehabilitate wildlife, including sea turtles on the Pacific Coast and animals falling prey to poaching for the lucrative pet trade in Petén, including cats, monkeys, and birds.

Several organizations operate in Guatemala's eastern Verapaces and Izabal regions. Working to preserve the endangered quetzal, **Proyecto Ecoquetzal** (2a Calle 14-36 Zona 1, Coban, Alta Verapaz, tel. 7952-1047, www.ecoquetzal.org) works with local communities to provide alternative income sources such as ecotourism and promote sustainable agriculture in the remaining cloud forests of northern Alta Verapaz. **Asociacion Ak' Tenamit** (11 Avenida "A" 9-39 Zona 2, Guatemala City, tel. 2254-1560 Guatemala City, tel. 7908-3392 Lívingston, www.aktenamit.org) is a grassroots, Mayan-run development organization focusing its efforts on education, health care, the creation of alternative income sources and sustainable agriculture.

Finally, **Tropico Verde** (Vía 6 4-25 Zona 4, Edificio Castañeda, Oficina 41, Guatemala City, tel. 2339-4225, www.tropicoverde.org) is a watchdog organization monitoring the state of Guatemala's parks via field studies. In addition to local monitoring, it helps bring awareness of local repercussions of international environmental issues such as Guatemala's participation in international conventions on whaling, to name just one example.

Flora and Fauna

Guatemala harbors an astounding degree of biodiversity due greatly to the variety of ecosystems found within its borders. Its location in the Central American land bridge between North and South America means it is the southernmost range for certain North American species as well as the northernmost range for certain Southern Hemisphere species. Fourteen of the 38 Holdridge Life Zones are represented in Guatemala.

FLORA

Among the cornucopia of plant life are 8,000 varieties of plants, including more than 600 types of orchids. Of these, nearly 200 are unique to Guatemala. The rugged cloud forests of Sierra de las Minas, meanwhile, boast the presence of 17 distinct species of pine trees

© AEIGUANA/123RF.COM

The ceiba tree was sacred to the ancient Mayans.

found nowhere else on earth. Endemic orchid species include Guatemala's national flower, the rare *monja blanca,* or "white nun." It is found in the cloud forests of the Verapaces region.

Guatemala means "land of the trees" in the ancient Mayan-Toltec language. According to 2005 figures, 37 percent of Guatemala remained covered in forest in 2005, down from 40 percent in 2001. Among the different types of forests present in Guatemala's varied climate zones are tropical rainforest, tropical dry forests, evergreen forests, and cloud forests. In some cold, mountainous parts of Guatemala there are temperate forests whose broadleaf trees' leaves briefly change color before falling to the ground, though not at all to the extent of the displays of fall foliage present in parts of North America.

The forests of Petén are officially classified mostly as tropical moist and tropical wet forests. Guatemala's only true rainforests, strictly speaking, are found in the Cerro San Gil along the Caribbean Coast.

Most of Guatemala's remaining forest cover is found in Petén, especially the northern third of the department in a huge park known as the Maya Biosphere Reserve. The Verapaces, Izabal, Quiché, and Huehuetenango also have significant amounts of forest cover remaining. Many of these forests are on remote mountains that have remained inaccessible and have therefore escaped the ravages of the advance of the agricultural frontier. Significant wetlands, including four of international importance, are found in Petén, Izabal, and the western section of the Pacific Coast plains near the Mexican border. Mangrove forests are found on the Pacific and Caribbean Coasts.

Among the plants you'll find in Guatemala's tropical forests is the towering ceiba *(Ceiba pentandra),* which is Guatemala's national tree and was considered sacred by the Mayans. It has a wide trunk and buttressed roots with branches found only at the very top. The ceiba can reach heights of 60 meters. You will often find them in cleared fields—one of only a few trees left standing amid grazing cattle. The most famous example is along the footpath at the entrance to Tikal National Park, where visitors are often photographed standing next to the tree's colossal trunk.

Another common tropical forest tree is the *chicozapote,* from which chicle is extracted for use in the manufacture of chewing gum. *Chicleros* cut V-shaped notches in the tree's trunk, allowing the sap to drip down the tree to a receptacle placed there for its collection. These days chicle goes to Japan, which still favors the traditional base for making gum. During the early 20th century, most of Guatemala's chicle went to the Wrigley Company.

The *ramón,* or breadnut tree, is found throughout the tropical flatlands and was widely used during Mayan times for making tortillas and drinks, among other things. Archaeologists have linked the increasing consumption of ramón seeds to decreasing food-production cycles during Mayan times, speculating that it served as a replacement to more traditional staples during periods of drought.

One of the most curious plants found in the tropical forests is the strangler fig, or *mata palo (Ficus obtusifolia),* which wraps itself around its host, eventually killing it. It has thick roots and looks much like a wooden rope wrapped around a tree. It's easy to spot; you'll recognize it when you see it.

Guatemala's forests contain excellent hardwoods, the most prominent of these being cedar *(Cedrela angustifolia)* and mahogany *(Swientenia alicastrum).* Much of the Petén forest has been logged, legally and illegally. Peasant forestry cooperatives operate in the multiple-use zone of the Maya Biosphere Reserve sustainably harvesting ecocertified hardwoods. Guatemalan mahogany is highly prized in the making of furniture. The cabinets of the Four Seasons resort on Costa Rica's Pacific Coast, for example, are made from Guatemalan mahogany. Also important as a forest product is *xate* palm *(Chamaedorea spp.),* which is harvested in the forests using sustainable methods, though overcutting is entirely possible. The bright green palm leaves are used in floral arrangements throughout the United States and Europe.

FAUNA
Birds

Guatemala's abundant birdlife includes more than 700 different species. Although not nearly as popular a bird-watching destination as Belize or Costa Rica, Guatemala has become increasingly well known among birders now that pristine areas conducive to the activity are no longer the site of skirmishes between army and

© AL ARGUETA

Numerous species of parrots dwell in Guatemala's forests.

guerrilla forces, as was the case during the civil war. This has opened new areas to bird-watching and Guatemalans are quickly taking steps to gain some ground in catering to this very lucrative tourism market.

Among the highlights of a visit to Guatemala is the opportunity to spot its rare, endangered national emblem, the resplendent quetzal *(Pharomacrus mocino)*. The quetzal gives its name to the national currency and was revered by the Mayans for its long green tail feathers used in ceremonial headdresses. Quetzals have become increasingly rare because of the loss of their cloud forest habitat, but they still survive on the slopes of the Lake Atitlán volcanoes, parts of the Sierra de los Cuchumatanes, and particularly in the Sierra de las Minas. A forest preserve in Baja Verapaz, known as the Quetzal Biotope, has been set aside specifically to protect the quetzal. It can often be seen on the grounds of one of the area lodges feeding on the *aguacatillo* trees. The larger, nearby Sierra de Las Minas Biosphere Reserve is also a safe bet. Some grassroots organizations such as Proyecto Eco-Quetzal are working with local communities in Alta Verapaz to promote sustainable tourism in the hopes they will see the economic value of preserving the forest instead of destroying it for slash-and-burn agriculture.

Among endemic species is the flightless Atitlán grebe *(Podilymbus gigas)*, commonly known as *poc,* which was officially declared extinct in 1989. The introduction of nonnative large- and smallmouth bass into the lake seems to have precipitated its drastic decline in numbers from about 200 in 1960 to only 32 in 1983. The bass ate the young grebes as well as the crabs and fish species on which *poc* fed.

Endemic to the northern Petén region is the Petén ocellated turkey *(Meleagris ocellata),* readily seen strutting around Tikal. It is smaller but much more colorful than its northern relatives, somewhat resembling a peacock. Other interesting birds found in Guatemala's

tropical forests include the keel-billed toucan *(Ramphastos sulfuratus),* a perennial jungle favorite because of its large, colorful, banana-like beak. Many of these can be seen at Tikal around sunrise and sunset flying among the temples peeking from the forest canopy. A large variety of parrots also inhabit the Petén forests. The most impressive of these is the scarlet macaw *(Ara macao),* which once inhabited large parts of Petén as well as the Pacific Coastal plain. It now inhabits only very remote parts of the Petén forests. Conservationists are fighting to save the birds from local extinction and protected nesting sites have been established in the Maya Biosphere Reserve, specifically in Laguna del Tigre National Park. Rounding out the list of noteworthy birds is the harpy eagle *(Harpia harpyja),* a large, powerful raptor that also enjoys healthy populations at Tikal National Park.

Land Mammals

Guatemala's list of native land mammals is impressive, with a large variety of exotic cats, primates, and other furry creatures. The largest of Guatemala's cats is the jaguar *(Felis onca),* found in lowland parts of Petén, Izabal, and the Verapaces. Referred to as *tigre* by locals, it is known to sometimes wander into *chiclero* camps as well as kill livestock in remote cattle ranches that have encroached on remote areas. Sightings of this beautiful spotted cat are rare, so consider yourself lucky if you are able to glimpse one in the wild. Its tracks are more likely to be seen on travels to the remote forests of the Maya Biosphere Reserve, which can be exciting enough. Other cats include the jaguarundi *(Herpailurus yaguarondi),* puma *(Puma concolor),* and their smaller relatives the margay *(Leopardus wiedii)* and ocelot *(Leopardus pardalis).*

Among the most widely seen mammals are monkeys. You are likely to hear the roar of howler monkeys *(Alouatta pigra)* during the early morning hours if camping overnight in

© AL ARGUETA

Howler monkeys inhabit many of Guatemala's tropical forests.

Petén. Less aggressive, smaller, and ever more playful, are spider monkeys *(Ateles geoffroyi).*

The gray fox *(Urocyon cinereoargenteus)* can often be seen in the early morning and evening among Tikal's temples. More exotic forest dwellers include the piglike collared peccary *(Tayassu tajacu)* and white-lipped peccary *(Tayasu pecari)* as well as the hefty Baird's tapir *(Tapirus bairdii),* and the tamandua anteater *(Tamandua mexicana).*

Also easy to spot are some of the smaller mammals, particularly in parks such as Tikal and Yaxhá. Among these are the raccoonlike white-nosed coati *(Nasua narica),* which practically walk up to you at Tikal; mouselike agoutis *(Dasyprocta punctata),* and kinkajous *(Potos flavus).*

If you happen to like bats, you'll be pleased to know Guatemala harbors more than 100 species of the flying critters. Many of these are found in the limestone caves of Petén and the Verapaces. Most of these are harmless to humans, feeding on fruits and insects. There are blood-sucking vampire bats *(Desmodus rotundus)* flying about, though these feed mostly on cattle.

Sealife

Five species of sea turtles can be seen on Guatemala's Atlantic and Pacific Coasts, where they also come ashore to lay their eggs. These are olive ridley, hawksbill, leatherback, green, and loggerhead. Of these, olive ridley, leatherback, and hawksbill turtles nest on the Pacific shores and can be seen at the Monterrico-Hawaii Biotope. Between September and January, visitors to this park have the rare opportunity to hold baby sea turtles in their hands before releasing them to begin their mad dash across the sand and a lifetime at sea. If they survive to adulthood, the females will return to very same beach to lay their eggs and begin a new life cycle. All of these turtle species are endangered because of the harvesting of their eggs by poor coastal dwellers in search of food and a means to supplement their incomes.

Guatemala's Pacific sailfish have become the object of widespread praise in the angling circuit with blue marlin, Pacific sailfish, and yellowfin tuna just waiting to be caught. Humpback whales can also be seen breaching in the Pacific waters. As for the Caribbean Coast, Guatemala just missed out on the Belize Barrier Reef, as it ends right at the doorstep of the Punta de Manabique peninsula. The barrier reef is easily accessible, however, along with the wonders of its corals and exotic fish. Although lacking the barrier reef per se, the waters off Guatemala's Atlantic Coast are certainly not devoid of exotic sea life. Bottlenose dolphins readily follow motorboats as they make their way along the Caribbean coast. The endangered manatee *(Trichechus manatus),* or sea cow, has become increasingly rare as the large, slow, sea grass-eating mammal has fallen prey to hunting, motorboats, and drowning in fishing nets. A small reserve in Izabal's El Golfete is attempting to protect the few that remain in Guatemalan waters.

Amphibians

There are 112 species of amphibians represented in Guatemala. Guatemala is out of range for some of the colorful miniature frogs, such as poison arrow frogs, found farther south in Costa Rica and Panama, but there are still some interesting frogs to be found in Guatemala's tropical forests; among these are the red-eyed tree frog *(Agalychnis callidryas)* and the similar Morelet's tree frog *(Agalychnis moreletti).* Fleischmann's glass frog *(Hyalinobatrachium fleischmanni)* is translucent and lime green with small yellow spots and yellowish hands. Its organs and bones are visible through the abdominal skin. All three of these prefer vegetation near rivers and streams.

Reptiles

With 214 species of reptiles, Guatemala has no shortage of snakes. Among the little critters

to watch out for are the fer-de-lance *(Bothrops asper),* known locally as *barba amarilla.* The aggressive pit viper is found in abundant quantities in the tropical forests of Petén, Izabal, and the Verapaces, though you are not likely to see one. Baby fer-de-lance can be especially dangerous as they are yet unable to control the amount of poison they inject into a bite.

Other snakes include tropical rattlesnakes *(Crotalus durissus),* several species of colorful coral snakes, and nonvenomous boa constrictors.

If you watched the *Survivor* TV series, you probably noticed there are crocodiles in Guatemala, particularly in and around Lake Yaxhá. The crocodiles seen on *Survivor* are Morelet's crocodiles *(crocodylus moreleti).* The larger American crocodile *(crocodylus acutus)* can be found in coastal areas, swamps, and larger rivers in Petén and Izabal. Many species of river turtles inhabit the tropical lowlands. Basilisk lizards and at least two species of iguana round out the highlighted list of Guatemala's reptiles.

Insects

This subject might give some readers "the itchies" but in addition to the myriad species of arachnids, such as tarantulas and scorpions, or plentiful amounts of mosquitoes in some places, Guatemalan lands are host to many other and more beautiful creatures. Among these are thousands of species of butterflies, including the beautiful blue morpho, which you might see flitting about the forest in an iridescent flash of blue. While hiking Guatemala's forests, keep an eye out for the industrious leaf-cutter ants, which cut pathways through the forest and carry small pieces of bright green leaves to their nests, where they are used as compost for underground fungus farms. Butterflies and leaf-cutters are virtually guaranteed favorites among the youngest of travelers to these parts.

History

Guatemala's history is complicated and fascinating, though it often reads like a tragic novel. An understanding of its history is a crucial element for the well-informed traveler hoping to get the most out of a visit to this mystifying land of culture and contrasts. This section will familiarize you with the basics of Guatemala's past and what it means in relation to its present, with an emphasis on Guatemalan history in the years since the end of its civil war.

PREHISTORY

It is generally accepted that the first inhabitants of the American continent came in waves by way of a land bridge across the Bering Strait connecting Siberia to Alaska, some 25,000 years ago. The migrants continued to make their way southward, possibly using boats to assist them, and eventually came to populate, albeit thinly, large portions of the Americas occupying a diverse range of climates. It is believed passage via the Bering Strait was intermittently open until about 10,000 years ago when the last Ice Age ended, submerging the land bridge with rising sea levels.

MAYAN CIVILIZATION

The people that settled the New World eventually grew in population and transitioned from hunter-gatherers to nascent agricultural societies. The developing civilizations then made a clear transition from hillside swidden agriculture to more intensive forms of cultivation, including terrace farming, the construction of drainage ditches, and the development of fertilizers, which in turn produced large food surpluses. With greater food security, the population gradually became more specialized in its individual occupations, paving the way for advances in writing, art, architecture, and mathematics. A common language and universal belief system are thought to have existed throughout the Mayan region, providing a necessary social cohesion that served as a catalyst for the development of a larger civilization.

Today, the remains of this civilization can be seen throughout northern Guatemala's Petén region at sites such as Tikal, Uaxactún, Yaxhá, Piedras Negras, and El Mirador. The inhabitants of these Mayan cities, now lying in ruins, spent their time trading, stargazing, and fighting wars before abandoning their cities, which were later reclaimed by the surrounding jungle.

Our knowledge of the Maya comes largely from the edification of large carved monuments, or stelae, which document the lives of the individual city-states' rulers and include historical events associated with their reign, such as battles, marriage alliances, and successions. The Maya built their temples and palaces atop previous constructions; what we see today is literally the pinnacle of their progress.

Of particular note is what is sometimes referred to as the Classic Maya collapse, giving the impression that the civilization collapsed and vanished into thin air. This is certainly not the case. The Mayan civilization proper indeed came crashing down for reasons that are becoming increasingly evident, and the Maya simply dispersed into other parts of present-day Mexico, Guatemala, Belize, and Honduras while falling prey to increasing cultural and military dominance from invading central Mexican Toltecs.

The site of modern-day Guatemala City was originally occupied by Kaminaljuyú, whose commercial dominance was established largely on the strength of its strategic location for the trading of obsidian and jade.

© AL ARGUETA

a finely carved hieroglyphic bench from Piedras Negras

THE PRECONQUEST PICTURE

Toltec-Maya Yucatán cities, such as Chichén Itzá and Uxmal, finally gave out sometime in the late 13th century and were abruptly abandoned. At about the same time, the Guatemalan highlands were invaded by groups of Toltec-Maya, though it is uncertain whether they are the product of a mass exodus from the Yucatán cities or a new group from the Toltec heartland in the Gulf of Mexico. In any case, their arrival in the Guatemalan highlands signaled a transition from the existence of relatively peaceful, religious village societies to ones increasingly secular and warlike.

Quickly establishing themselves as a ruling elite, the Toltec invaders founded a series of competing empires including the K'iche', Kaqchikel, Tzutujíl, Mam, Ixil, Achi', and Q'eqchi', among others. Interestingly, these and other tribes encompassing the highland indigenous groups continue to form the basis for today's cultural landscape, with differentiation based on their individual dialects.

Among these tribes, the K'iche' and Kaqchikel emerged as dominant forces, a rivalry the conquering Spanish would later use to their advantage. Prior to the arrival of the Spanish, the highland region was engulfed in a widespread power struggle between rival groups for cultivable land to feed an increasing population.

THE SPANISH CONQUEST

After the Spanish conquered the Aztec empire and captured its capital at Tenochtitlán in 1521, the K'iche' sent ambassadors north to Mexico informing Hernán Cortés of their desire to be vassals of the newly established power structure. In 1523 Cortés dispatched Pedro de Alvarado to Guatemala on a fact-finding mission meant to verify the veracity of the tribe's claim. If indeed Cortés's intentions were limited to fact-finding, he could have done better than to choose Alvarado for the job. Alvarado is described as handsome, athletic, distinguished, eloquent, and graceful, among other things, from Spanish accounts of the conquest. He was also extremely cruel.

Alvarado arrived in Guatemala along the Pacific Coast flatlands accompanied by 120 horsemen, 173 horses, 300 soldiers, and 200 Mexican warriors from the allied Tlaxcalan armies. He made his way up to the highlands, where he met the K'iche' in battle near present-day Quetzaltenango, also known as Xelajú. An estimated 30,000 K'iche' were unable to forge alliances with neighboring tribes to repel the Spanish invasion and faced the Spanish alone. Legend has it Alvarado met Tecún Umán, grandson of the K'iche' ruler, in hand-to-hand combat, cutting him down.

Following these events, the K'iche' invited the Spanish to their capital at Utatlán for the signing of a formal surrender but secretly planned to ambush them from the safety of their mountain fortress. Alvarado knew an ambush when he saw one and so he withdrew to the city's outskirts, followed by the K'iche' rulers, whom he seized and later had burned at the stake. Eight days of fighting followed, with the Spanish enlisting the help of the rival Kaqchikels to finally gain the upper hand against the K'iche'. Utatlán was then burned to the ground.

The Kaqchikel alliance with the Spanish stuck for a time, with the Spanish establishing the first capital of Guatemala alongside the Kaqchikel capital of Iximché, from which they launched raids to conquer Guatemala's remaining highland tribal groups. The campaign would last several years and was made increasingly difficult when the Kaqchikel severed their alliance with the Spanish in 1526 in response to demands for tribute. They abandoned their capital at Iximché and took refuge in the mountains, launching a guerrilla war. The Spanish then moved the Guatemalan capital, establishing the city of Santiago de Los Caballeros on November 22, 1527. Now known as Ciudad Vieja, it lies near present-day Antigua.

Indigenous uprisings and resistance would continue throughout Guatemala's history into the present day, as various groups respond to repressive policies imposed by those in power. The recent civil war has been likened by scholars, human rights activists, and journalists to a kind of "second conquest" aimed at eliminating the indigenous population through genocidal extermination attempts.

A final aspect of the conquest that bears mentioning is the work of European diseases and their hand in greatly reducing the population of the indigenous peoples who had no resistance to smallpox, plague, typhus, and measles. These diseases were responsible for the loss of more than three-quarters of Guatemala's two million inhabitants in the first 30 years following contact with the Spanish. It is thought that a third of the population died before Alvarado's invading army even set foot in the indigenous peoples' Guatemalan homeland.

COLONIAL GUATEMALA

The Guatemalan capital required 10 years from its founding to complete and included a cathedral, town hall, and Alvarado's palace. Alvarado died in 1541 while in Mexico attempting to subdue an uprising. The city was destroyed shortly thereafter by a mudslide that rolled down Agua Volcano after an earthquake and heavy rains combined to unleash the contents of the flooded crater.

Guatemala's capital was then moved a few miles away to present-day Antigua. It would serve as the administrative headquarters of the newly established Audiencia de Guatemala, which included the provinces of San Salvador, Nicaragua, Honduras, Costa Rica, Chiapas, and Guatemala. The city of Santiago de los Caballeros, as it was officially known, would grow to become the third-largest city in Spanish colonial America, surpassed only by Mexico City and Lima. In 1776, a series of devastating earthquakes destroyed most of the city's buildings and churches, leading to a final move of the Guatemalan capital to the Valley of the Hermitage, just over a mountain to the east, where it has resided ever since.

The colonial period is significant in that it completely transformed Guatemala's physical and cultural landscape, establishing new cities and institutionalizing new economic and religious systems that would come to form the basis for a racist hierarchy persisting largely unaltered to this day. Guatemala's history displays a striking symmetry throughout the years. The key to understanding many of the more recent tragedies to befall its people lies in understanding the significance of earlier events dating back to just before the conquest.

At the center of Guatemala's new power structure was the Catholic Church, which arrived with the conquistadors and included various sects such as Franciscans, Mercedarians, Dominicans, and Jesuits. These were granted large concessions of land and indigenous people, allowing them to amass huge fortunes from the cultivation of cash crops including sugar, indigo, and wheat. This power structure was held in place by institutions established by the Spanish crown, namely the *encomienda* and *repartimiento.*

The *encomienda* was a grant of Indian labor and tribute, though not necessarily of land, over a geographical area. The *encomenderos* holding such a grant were allowed to tax the indigenous peoples under their care and to conscript them for labor in exchange for their promise to maintain order and educate the indigenous populace in the Spanish language and Catholicism.

The *repartimiento,* which is essentially indistinguishable from its predecessor, is a reformed version of the *encomienda* system, at least on paper. It put control of the distribution of workers into the hands of local magistrates and called for the donation of a percentage of laborers from populations close to Spanish settlements, between 2 and 4 percent of the indigenous population.

Further adding to the transformation of community organization in the conquered territories was the establishment of *reducciones,* part of the larger process of *congregación,* consisting of towns founded in the Spanish vein with the purpose of congregating indigenous populations into manageable settlements and assimilating them into the dominant culture and religion. They would also serve as a handy nearby source from which to pool labor.

INDEPENDENCE

Guatemalan, and indeed Central American, independence came more as a result of pressures from without than from a genuine internal uprising demanding freedom from Spanish rule. This is not to say that all was well with Spanish colonial rule, as there were policies and social stratifications in place contributing to unrest among the lower strata of society. Spanish policies kept wealth and power in the hands of Spanish-born elites, or *chapetones. Criollos,* or those born in the New World of Spanish descent, were the next rung down the ladder, with the lowest standings reserved for mixed-blood *mestizos* and full-blooded Indians.

Napoleon's invasion of Spain in 1808 led to the imposition of a liberal constitution on Spain in 1812. When Mexican general Agustán Iturbide declared his own country's independence from Spain, Guatemala followed suit. The reigning Captain General Gabino Gaínza bowed to demands for independence but hoped to maintain the existent power structure with the support of the Church and landowning elites. The declaration of independence essentially maintained the old power structure under new management. Mexico quickly dispatched troops to annex Guatemala, and all of Central America, to Iturbide's new empire.

Iturbide was dethroned in 1823, and Central America, minus the state of Chiapas, declared its independence from Mexico. This second declaration joined the remaining states in a loose federation and adopted many U.S.-modeled liberal reforms, such as the abolition of slavery. A protracted power struggle between liberals advocating a secular, more egalitarian state and conservatives wanting to maintain the Church-dominated political and economic structures marked the early years of independence. The Central American Federation was weakened not only by inner power struggles within individual member states, but also by a struggle to determine regional leadership over neighboring states.

JUSTO RUFINO BARRIOS AND THE LIBERAL REFORMS

The liberals would finally succeed in 1871 under the leadership of General Justo Rufino Barrios, who, along with Miguel García Granados, set out from Mexico with a force of just 45 men, gaining numbers as their approach to the capital grew closer. The capital was taken on June 30, 1871, and Granados was installed as the leader of the new liberal government. Granados made only limited reforms and by 1872 a frustrated Barrios marched to the capital with his troops and demanded elections, which he won overwhelmingly.

Among the reforms quickly instituted by Barrios, who would go down in Guatemalan history as "The Reformer," were educational reform and separation of church and state. Barrios was the first of the *caudillos,* military strongmen who ruled the country with an iron fist and sense of absolute omnipotence, mostly uninterrupted, until the revolution of 1944. He masterfully strengthened his power over the entire country with links to local strongmen in rural areas wielding power on his behalf but unable to challenge his hold because of the restricted development of secondary market centers and the overwhelming economic dominance of Guatemala City.

To further exercise his dominion, Barrios professionalized the military, creating a new military academy, the Escuela Politecnica, still in existence today. The addition of rural militia further strengthened national control over the rural hinterlands. Barrios was decidedly pro-Western and sought to impose a European worldview to suppress what he saw as a vastly inferior Indian culture. Liberal economic policies ensured minimal protection of village lands, Indian culture, or the welfare of peasant villages.

During this time, coffee came to dominate the Guatemalan economy and Barrios's economic policies ensured the availability of a peasant workforce to supply the labor-intensive coffee harvest with its share of needed workers. Furthermore, the increasingly racist attitudes of Guatemala's coffee elites toward the Indians served to justify the coercive means used to secure this labor force. The Indians were seen as lazy, making forced labor and the submission of the indigenous masses both necessary and morally justified. In this regard, the *mandamiento,* which came to replace the *repartimiento,* was increasingly enforced in the last two decades of the 19th century, requiring villages to supply a specified number of laborers per year.

Increasingly, however, elites found more coercive ways to exact labor from the Indians by way of debt peonage. Rural workers were required to carry a *libreto,* a record containing an individual's labor and debt figures. *Habilitadores,* or labor contractors, were charged with advancing money to peasants in exchange for labor contracts. The contractors often used alcohol as an added incentive and took advantage of widespread peasant illiteracy to ensure many of them contracted debts they would never be able to repay. In this way, depressed rural wages from debt peonage and low-cost labor increased the wealth of agricultural elites while making the rural peasantry even poorer.

MANUEL ESTRADA CABRERA

Justo Rufino Barrios died in battle in 1885 while fighting to create a re-unified Central America under Guatemalan leadership. He was succeeded by a string of short-lived *caudillo* presidents. The next to hold power for any significant time was Manuel Estrada Cabrera, whose legacy included undivided support for big business and crackdowns on labor organization. He ruled from 1898 until his overthrow in 1920, having been declared mentally insane. Among Cabrera's many peculiarities was the construction of several temples to honor Minerva, the Roman goddess of wisdom. Cabrera's legacy includes gross corruption, a beefed-up military, and a neglected educational system.

Export agriculture continued its unprecedented growth under Cabrera, thus paving the way for the dominance of two foreign groups that would come to control much of Guatemala's economy in later years. The first of these were German coffee planters who settled in the region of Las Verapaces. By 1913 this German enclave owned 170 of the country's coffee plantations, with about half of them in the vicinity of Cobán. The other significant foreign presence in Guatemala during this time was the U.S.-owned United Fruit Company (UFCo), aptly nicknamed "El Pulpo" (The Octopus), and its tentacles consisting of International Railways of Central America (IRCA) and the UFCo Steamship Lines. Its vast control of land, rail, and steamship transportation, in addition to Guatemala's sole Caribbean port, Puerto Barrios, made it a political and economic powerhouse. Its political clout would be seen in the mid-20th century when, together with the CIA, it would be directly responsible for ousting Guatemala's president, Jacobo Árbenz Guzmán, from power when land reform policies interfered with the company's vast land holdings.

JORGE UBICO

After the overthrow of Estrada Cabrera in 1920, the country entered a period of instability and power struggles culminating in the rise to power of Jorge Ubico. Continuing in the now well-established pattern of megalomaniacal, heavy-handed leadership that would come to characterize many of Guatemala's presidents, Ubico continued the unconditional support for U.S. agribusiness and the local oligarchy. By 1940, 90 percent of Guatemala's exports were sold to the United States. Ubico caved in to U.S demands for the expulsion of the German coffee planters from Guatemala during World War II, evidencing the increasing U.S. hold on Guatemalan domestic policy.

Within Guatemala, Ubico embarked on various reforms, including ambitious road-building projects, as well as improvements in health care and social welfare. Debt peonage was also outlawed but was replaced by a vagrancy law enforcing compulsory labor contributions of

Manuel Estrada Cabrera

150 days upon landless peasants in either rural plantations or in the government road-building programs. Ubico's reforms always had in mind the modernization of the state economy. Far from an attempt to free the indigenous peoples from coercive labor practices, the vagrancy law asserted centralized control over the national labor force while keeping the political power of the oligarchy firmly in check.

Ubico was also obsessed with internal security. He saw himself as a reincarnated Napoleon and became increasingly paranoid, creating a network of spies and informers used to repress opposition to his increasingly tyrannical rule. Much of this opposition came from the indigenous peasant population, whom Ubico ignored and regarded as retrograde and inferior. This led to numerous revolts in the late 1930s and early 1940s. The discovery of an assassination plot in 1934 led to the execution of 300 suspected conspirators within 48 hours.

THE OCTOBER REVOLUTION OF 1944

Opposition finally reached a head in June 1944 when widespread discontent erupted in violent street protests by large portions of the urban middle class demanding democratic opportunities and new economic policies. Ubico was forced to resign after 14 years in office. When his interim replacement signaled to be more of the same, young students, professionals, and forward-thinking military officers orchestrated a widespread social movement culminating in his overthrow in what has been dubbed "The October Revolution." Elections were called for in December of that same year. In a radio address, then front-running presidential candidate Juan José Arévalo, an exiled professor living in Argentina, described the transcendental nature of the recent events: "What has occurred in Guatemala is not a *golpe de estado* (coup d'etat); it is something more profound and beneficial; it is a revolution.... It is a revolution that will go to the roots of the political system.... In a word: It is a revolution called to wash, to purify our political life, to quiet everyone, and to honor Guatemala."

Arévalo would go on to win the election with an overwhelming majority and take office on March 1, 1945.

A DECADE OF "SPIRITUAL SOCIALISM"

Guatemala made much progress under Arévalo, who quickly set out on the road to badly needed structural reform. Prominence was given to education and health care with the construction of new schools and hospitals, immunization programs, and literacy campaigns. A new national budget allowed for a third of government spending to go into these programs, which were further facilitated by a new constitution drafted prior to Arévalo's taking office. Ubico's hated vagrancy laws were abolished and in their place a labor code was instituted establishing union representation and granting workers the right to strike. Many of the farms expropriated from German planters during World War II, now in state hands, were transformed into peasant cooperatives. Government policies provided technical assistance and credit for peasant farmers and protected their lands from usurpation by agricultural elites and foreign agribusiness.

The gains in social justice ruffled the feathers of many of Guatemala's traditional power elites, including the Church, urban business elites, the landed aristocracy, and the politicians who defended their interests. They increasingly opposed much of the reformist legislation passed by Arévalo in congress. A divided military also became the source of much opposition, with Arévalo surviving 25 coup attempts originating from conservative sectors of the armed forces. Meanwhile, U.S. business interests became increasingly unsettled by the reforms. At the top of this list was the United Fruit Company. As opposition stiffened, Arévalo was unable to fully implement the social transformation of the country he had intended and passed on to his successor an increasingly polarized political landscape.

His successor, Jacobo Árbenz Guzmán, continued along the path of reform, concentrating on fomenting economic development and independence from foreign intervention in politics and the economy. At the core of his economic development program was the Agrarian Reform Law of 1952, intended to redistribute land ownership by breaking up large plantations and promoting high productivity on smaller, individually owned farms. The urgent need for land reform was historically evident in the nature and function of institutions that, over time, placed Guatemalan land in the hands of a wealthy few to the detriment of indigenous peasants. It is estimated that 2 percent of the country's population controlled 72 percent of all arable land in 1945, but only 12 percent of it was being utilized.

Central to the law were stipulations limiting expropriation to lands lying fallow. Arbenz himself was not immune to land expropriation, giving up 1,700 acres of his own land in the process. Also among the lands to be expropriated were extensive holdings by United Fruit ceded to the company under Estrada Cabrera and Ubico, which had made United Fruit Guatemala's largest landowner. Fully 85 percent of its holdings remained uncultivated. The Agrarian Reform Law allowed for the compensation of expropriated lands based on values declared for tax purposes, which United Fruit had, of course, grossly underreported.

Unfortunately for Arbenz and his reformist policies, UFCo had strong ties to the U.S. government and, more specifically, the CIA. Among United Fruit's shareholders were U.S. Secretary of State John Foster Dulles and his brother, CIA Director Allen Dulles.

On the home front, it was clear that Arbenz had incurred the wrath of the oligarchy and conservative military sectors. He faced increasing political fragmentation despite attempts to forge a functional revolutionary coalition of political parties to further his goals, and he looked to several dedicated, competent individuals for support in implementing the agrarian reform and labor organization. Many inside and outside of Guatemala conveniently labeled Arbenz and his supporters Communist, though how much influence the Communists actually had in Guatemala is still hotly debated. In 1952 Guatemala's official Communist party, the Partido Guatemalteco de los Trabajadores (PGT, the Guatemalan Labor Party), was legalized. Communists subsequently gained considerable minority influence over important peasant organizations and labor unions, but not over the governing political body, winning only 4 of 58 seats.

In any case, the country became increasingly unstable. This instability, combined with Arbenz's tolerance of the PGT and other Communist and labor influences, caused Washington to grow increasingly alarmed. The CIA finally orchestrated the overthrow of Arbenz in 1954 in the form of a military invasion from Honduras dubbed "Operation Success," led by two exiled Guatemalan military officers. The invading forces established Colonel Carlos Castillo Armas, who had previously led a failed coup against Arbenz, as chief of state. A series of military governments supported by the nascent military oligarchy partnership and conservative elements of Guatemalan society followed. Thus began one of the most tragic chapters in Guatemala's already turbulent history.

THE CIVIL WAR (1960-1996)

With the professionalization of Guatemala's army now in place thanks to the policies of Barrios and Ubico, the military was now poised to become the country's dominating political force and would do so for the next 30 years. Further paving the way for military dominance over Guatemalan politics was the Cold War climate and the fight against Communism. U.S. policy and military aid would assist the dictators' rise to power and facilitate their increasingly repressive nature, all in the name of defeating Communist insurrection.

Among the new regime's first move was the revocation of the 1945 constitution, with the consequent reversal of the reforms of the previous years. The rule of the oligarchy was firmly reestablished and a wave of repression against peasants, labor unions, and agrarian reformers was unleashed.

Castillo Armas would only be in power until 1957, when he was shot by one of his own palace guards. Political turmoil ensued, followed by the rise to power of Miguel Ydígoras Fuentes, an army officer from the Ubico years now representing the National Democratic Renovation Party. His five years in office were characterized by incompetence, corruption, nepotism, patronage, and economic decline. Opposition to Ydígoras grew, with young army officers led by Marco Yon Sosa and Turcios Lima attempting an unsuccessful coup in 1960. Ydígoras was finally ousted by a military coup in 1963 with approval from Washington after Arévalo threatened to return to Guatemala to run in the next election, firmly putting the establishment in both Guatemala and Washington on edge.

During the subsequent military government of Alfredo Enrique Peralta Azurdia, Turcios Lima and Yon Sosa launched a guerrilla offensive from the eastern highlands, marking the beginning of a protracted armed conflict between leftist rebels and the Guatemalan government. Ironically, both had received U.S. military training while serving in the Guatemalan forces and now used their skills to attack local army garrisons. The battle was soon joined by another armed rebel group, the Fuerzas Armadas Rebeldes (FAR, Rebel Armed Forces). The PGT, meanwhile, formed an alliance with the rebels while advocating the return of Arévalo.

A self-proclaimed "third government of the revolution" came to power in 1966 under Julio Cesar Montenegro of the center-left Partido Revolucionario, who tried to continue in the vein of Arévalo and Arbenz. It was clear, however, that his hands were tied and power was in the hands of the military. Political violence escalated during his administration, with death squads killing hundreds of students, unionists, academics, and peasant leaders.

By the end of the decade the guerrilla movement had been virtually eliminated from the eastern highlands. FAR shifted its focus to Guatemala City, where it kidnapped and murdered the U.S. ambassador in 1968.

Electoral fraud and political violence, accompanied by economic decline, would mark much of Guatemala's history between 1970 and 1990. A reign of terror became firmly entrenched, with successive governments each going to greater lengths to contain the guerrilla threat and repress an increasingly unsatisfied populace from which the movement drew its support. At the heart of the matter was a system of government that ensured the continued prosperity of a wealthy minority to the detriment of a poor, landless, illiterate peasant class forced to work the elites' land. The demands of a growing urban middle class, meanwhile, were repressed with the help of the armed forces and right-wing death squads.

The United States, meanwhile, continued to pour money and logistical support into the increasingly bloody repression. Three years after the election of Carlos Arana Osorio in 1970, who was nicknamed "the butcher of Zacapa," 15,000 Guatemalans had been killed or disappeared. The United States did its share by training 32,000 Guatemalan policemen through the Agency for International Development (AID) via its public safety program. Guatemala's

Policía Nacional was notoriously linked to the paramilitary death squads operating with impunity in the cities and countryside. Many off-duty policemen filled the ranks of these right-wing extremist groups working parallel to, but with unofficial sanction from, the more traditional forms of counterinsurgency.

In 1971, another guerrilla unit, the Organización Revolucionario del Pueblo en Armas (ORPA, Revolutionary Organization of the People in Arms), was formed. The unit was led by Rodrigo Asturias, the son of Nobel Prize novelist Miguel Ángel Asturias. It operated in the vicinity of Lake Atitlán, Quetzaltenango, San Marcos, and Suchitepéquez, setting up operations in a strategically important corridor between the highlands and the agriculturally rich coastal lowlands. ORPA spent eight years recruiting local combatants, then training and indoctrinating them into its ranks. Believed to be the most disciplined of the rebel organizations, it launched its first offensive in 1979 with the occupation of a coffee farm near Quetzaltenango.

Yet another guerrilla organization, the Ejército Guerrillero de los Pobres (EGP, Guerrilla Army of the Poor), exploded onto the scene in 1975 with the much-publicized execution of a notoriously ruthless Ixcán landlord. It had spent three years developing political consciousness among the peasantry in the remote Ixcán jungle where it operated prior to launching its first assault. The Guatemalan military began increasingly violent reprisals against the peasantry living in remote jungle outposts, some of whom kept the guerrillas fed and supplied. In Ixcán, as well as throughout Guatemala, peasants would become increasingly caught in the cross fire between the military and the rebel groups often serving as a scapegoat for the army's wrath.

On February 4, 1976, a massive earthquake struck the Guatemalan highlands, leaving 23,000 dead, 77,000 injured, and about a million homeless. The reconstruction efforts saw a renewed push to reform the inherent injustices of Guatemalan society with increased activity on behalf of the trade unions. In 1977, President Jimmy Carter, citing increasingly gross human rights violations, cut off military aid to Guatemala.

The 1978 elections were rigged to the benefit of Romeo Lucas García, who unleashed a fresh wave of repression against the usual victims, as well as academics, journalists, and trade unionists now. The guerrilla war grew increasingly strong in rural Guatemala at this time, with the number of total combatants estimated at 6,000 distributed among the four guerrilla groups, along with some 250,000 collaborators. The guerrillas actively recruited from a historically disenfranchised peasant base, particularly in the Ixil and Ixcán regions, which only strengthened the army's resolve to do away with the insurgency and intensified punitive measures against real and perceived collaborators. Peasants, priests, politicians, and anyone perceived to have ties to the guerrillas were massacred in the thousands. It is estimated that 25,000 Guatemalans were killed during the four-year Lucas regime.

Many atrocities were committed by the Lucas regime in a spiral of violence—making the Spanish conquest look increasingly benign by comparison—including an army massacre in the village of Panzós, Alta Verapaz, and the firebombing of the Spanish embassy in Guatemala City during a peaceful occupation by peasant leaders. In Panzós, at least 35 peasants, including some children, lay murdered in the town square with dozens more injured or killed as they tried to make their escape. The occupation of Guatemala City's Spanish Embassy was carried out by the Guatemalan military and eventually led to all-out genocide by Ixil peasants on January 31, 1980. Without regard for embassy staff or the Spanish ambassador, Policía Nacional forces stormed the

FORCED DISAPPEARANCE

Among the most horrific aspects of Guatemala's civil war was the kidnapping, torture, and murder of at least 50,000 citizens by an army bent on brutal counterinsurgency and the elimination of any and all political opposition, whether real or imagined. Parallel to the oppression at the hands of the military, death squads such as "White Hand" and "Eye for Eye" began operating independently of government forces but with their full knowledge and acquiescence. The kidnappings targeted people from all walks of life but especially journalists, union leaders, intellectuals, opposition party leaders, university students, laborers, teachers, and clergy.

In the 1970s the Inter-American Commission on Human Rights (IACHR), a branch of the Organization of American States, began issuing a series of annual human-rights reports on countries around the world. In 1985, it issued a scathing report on the human-rights situation in Guatemala, just before the country's return to democratic rule. As the stories of the tortured and disappeared are probably best told by the victims themselves, the 1985 report is significant in that it includes testimony from an actual kidnapping victim and torture survivor.

In addition to shedding light on the heinous crimes perpetrated against thousands of Guatemalans, the testimony is significant in that it demonstrates that the kidnappings and torture were carried out with surgical precision using methods undeniably linked to the training of counterinsurgency forces throughout Latin America by the United States's very own CIA. This and other documented cases of abuse by military and paramilitary forces, some involving U.S. citizens, offer irrefutable evidence of U.S. involvement in perpetuating widespread oppression and human-rights abuses via military aid and training to repressive regimes. This fact was acknowledged during President Clinton's visit to Guatemala in 1999, when he officially apologized for U.S. involvement in Guatemala's civil war.

Clinton's apology came shortly before the official release of a secret Guatemalan military document smuggled out by human-rights organizations that revealed the fate of more than 180 victims of forced disappearance between August 1983 and March 1985. The document's release provided the first news many of the victims' families had concerning the fate of their loved ones. After years of getting nowhere with Guatemalan authorities in the pursuit of justice against perpetrators of torture, murder, and forced disappearance, the relatives of 20 of the victims filed a suit against the Guatemalan government for denial of justice with the Inter-American Commission on Human Rights.

embassy and firebombed it. The sole survivor was the Spanish ambassador. The victims included the father of Nobel Peace Prize winner Rigoberta Menchú, who recounts this and other atrocities in her book, *I, Rigoberta Menchú*. Spain severed diplomatic relations with Guatemala in the aftermath of the massacre, not restoring them until several years later.

In addition to the ambassador's survival, it should be noted that one of the peasant activists also survived the tragedy, only to be murdered a few days later by a paramilitary death squad while recovering in a local hospital.

In 1982, Guatemala's armed rebel groups—FAR, EGP, ORPA, and PGT-FA—consolidated to form the Unidad Revolucionaria Nacional Guatemalteca (URNG, Guatemalan National Revolutionary Unity), which would go on to fight for its ideals as a political force, while continuing armed resistance, and negotiate a peace treaty with the government in 1996.

Efraín Ríos Montt

The 1982 elections were again manipulated by the extreme right, this time to the benefit of Aníbal Guevara, but a coup on March 23 orchestrated by young military officers installed General Efraín Ríos Montt as the head of a three-member junta. The coup leaders cited the rigging of elections three times in eight years as justification for their actions, which were supported by most of the opposition parties. It was hoped Guatemala could be somehow steered once again on the path of peace, law, and order and that the terror would stop.

Ríos Montt was an evangelical Christian with ties to Iglesia del Verbo, one of several U.S.-based churches gaining ground in Guatemala after the 1976 earthquake. Among his many eccentricities was the delivery of weekly Sunday night sermons in which he expressed his desire to restore law and order, eliminate corruption, and defeat the guerrilla insurgency, allowing for the establishment of a true democracy.

On the surface things did seem to get better, particularly in the cities, thanks to an odd mix of heavy-handed discipline and strict moral guidelines governing all facets of government operations. Montt, for example, made a regular show of executions of alleged criminals before firing squads. He also offered amnesty to the guerrillas during the month of June 1982, but only a handful of these accepted. Some later accounts of the Guatemalan civil war attribute this to communities' being either held hostage by guerrilla occupation and unable to make the trip down from the mountains or simply too frightened and distrustful of the military.

Whatever the reason, the cool response to Montt's amnesty offer unleashed a new wave of counterinsurgency terror against the guerrillas and the indigenous peoples believed to be aiding and abetting them. Under a scorched-earth campaign, entire villages were destroyed, with survivors being resettled into a series of so-called "model villages," allowing the army to keep a close watch on the peasantry while indoctrinating them with anti-Communist rhetoric. The repression was made worse by a new system of conscripted labor in the form of civil defense patrols (PACs) composed of rural peasants controlled by the army. PACs were forced to make routine night patrols and report any suspicious activities. Failure to do so would result in their own suspicion in the army's eyes, meaning further reprisals on their villages. In this way, two modern-day variants of important colonial structures survived well into Guatemala's recent history, the *congregación* and the *encomienda*.

An estimated 100,000 of Guatemala's indigenous Mayan descendants fled the violence, flooding refugee camps in neighboring Mexico or migrating farther north to the United States during the reign of Lucas García and Ríos Montt.

Cerezo and the Democratic Opening

Ríos Montt was eventually overthrown in August 1983 after just over a year in power by a military coup with U.S. backing. The underlying ideal was to get Guatemala firmly on the road back to democracy. Elections were called to take place in 1985 and General Mejía Víctores was installed as an interim chief-of-state. Repression in the countryside continued to escalate under the military's tireless scorched earth campaign. The Ixil Triangle alone saw the displacement of 72 percent of its population and the destruction of 49 villages. Totals for Guatemala at this time included the destruction of 440 villages and more than 100,000 dead. In this context, the first free election in more than three decades took place. A new constitution was also drawn up.

Vinicio Cerezo Arévalo, a Christian Democrat, won the election with an overwhelming majority of the vote and widespread hope for change in Guatemala with the country firmly on the road to democracy. It was clear that the military still held the cards, however, and kept Cerezo under a tight leash via the Estado Mayor Presidencial, a notorious military security force officially charged with presidential protection but in reality designed to keep presidential power in check. Cerezo candidly admitted that the military still held 75 percent of the power.

Cerezo sought to give the democratic opening a chance, knowing that the military's power could not be broken in the five years his term in office would last, by taking a nonconfrontational approach to the demands of Guatemala's various societal sectors. He kept a happy courtship with the powerful business interests, landowners, and generals. Among the latter was his defense minister, General Héctor Alejandro Gramajo, who curtailed much of the violence in the countryside and allowed Cerezo to survive numerous coup attempts.

In September of 1987 the Central American heads of state convened in the eastern highland town of Esquipulas, where they signed a treaty aimed at bringing the pacification and democratization of the region. Costa Rica's Oscar Arias Sánchez would later win the Nobel Peace Prize for his role in bringing the peace plan to fruition. Esquipulas II, as it was called, would open the doors for peace negotiations between the Guatemalan government and the URNG.

Although the levels of repression and violence dropped, they by no means disappeared. The armed struggle continued in remote corners of the highlands and Petén while death squads continued their reign of terror. Formal labor organization was once again given the official go-ahead, and widespread protests marked much of Cerezo's later years as the average Guatemalan saw little economic improvement.

Jorge Serrano Elías

Barred from running for a second term under the 1985 Constitution, Cerezo yielded power to his successor, Jorge Serrano Elías, in 1991. Also barred from running under the new constitution was Efraín Ríos Montt, though there was much speculation as to his role behind the scenes because Serrano had served in his government. The new constitution specifically prohibited anyone rising to power as the result of a military coup from running for president, a decision Montt has repeatedly tried unsuccessfully to have rescinded.

Indigenous-rights advocates, already enjoying greater freedom since the democratic opening, received a huge bolster from the awarding of the Nobel Peace Prize in 1992 to activist Rigoberta Menchú Tum for her efforts in bringing worldwide attention to the genocidal civil war still raging on in the countryside. The Guatemalan military issued an official protest to what it saw as disgraceful approval for an advocate of Communist insurrection but removed its opposition on the wave of worldwide fanfare for the awarding of the prize to Menchú.

Guatemala's historical problems continued to plague the nation, and Serrano's incompetence at the helm soon became evident. The peace process stalled with the Catholic Church's mediator accusing both sides of intransigence. Popular protests against Serrano's government, bolstered by corruption charges involving his suspected links with Colombian drug cartels, forced him to declare an autocoup in May 1993. He assumed dictatorial powers, citing the country's purported spiral into anarchy, and also dissolved congress, citing the gross corruption of the legislative body while calling for the election of a new one.

Widespread protests and the withdrawal of U.S. support for Serrano's government resulted in his removal from office just two days later. Congress met and voted on the appointment of Ramiro de León Carpio, the country's human-rights ombudsman, to succeed Serrano and finish out his term.

De León quickly set about rearranging the military high command in an attempt to purge some of the more radical elements and achieve a measure of political stability, though it was clear his powers over the military were limited. The URNG declared a cease-fire as a measure

CASE 9303: ALVARO RENÉ SOSA RAMOS

On Sunday March 11, 1985, Alvaro René Sosa Ramos was captured while walking near Avenida Roosevelt on a soccer field in Guatemala City's Zone 11. At the time, his capture was denied by security forces in the government of General Oscar Humberto Mejía Víctores; the victim was classified as "missing." Following is an excerpt from the testimony Sosa gave after his escape:

As I walked that way, a man off to the side called me and, as I turned around to see who it was, aimed a gun at me. I thought about running, but I saw eight men getting out of three vehicles with dark polarized windows. They captured me and put a jacket over my face, violently pushing me into a van. They then took me to a house. The men left me seated for more than two hours, during which time I could hear the screams of people coming from other rooms.

With my hands in cuffs, they forced me to take off my clothes, then tied my feet and hung me upside-down. Moments later, they beat me with the butt of a machete, accusing me of being a member of the Guatemalan Revolutionary Organization. I remember that a kaibil (special forces) struck my face with the butt of his rifle. One of these blows opened my eyebrow completely. When they weren't beating me, I could hear the beatings and screams of the other victims. I lost all track of time while being tortured. Afterwards, they lowered me and threw me to the ground. A few hours later they hung me upside-down by my feet again and a kaibil would arrive periodically just to kick me in the face. After receiving these blows, they would lower me so that I could see them doing the same thing to another man.

They asked me if I knew that man, who was very deformed from the tortures he had endured. I recognized him as Silvio Matricardi Salam. I knew him when he was President of the National Front of Professors and I was a union leader of the Diana Products factory. I was impressed upon seeing his body so deformed by the many blows he received. I immediately told them that I did not know the man. When we returned to the first room, they hung me up again, this time applying electrical currents to my body....

After the application of electrical shocks, they always asked me if I would talk and identify people.... On one occasion when they asked me, I said that perhaps there would be people I knew on Montúfar Street in Zone 9. I had remembered there was an embassy on that street. I told the torturers that if they continued striking me, I would have no energy left to walk. In addition, it became nearly impossible for me to see because my eyes were very swollen from all of the blows. After that, the kidnappers stopped hitting me.

Sosa escaped the next day while his captors were temporarily distracted with another kidnapping operation. He opened the door of the van he was in and flung himself onto the pavement. Running straight to the Belgian embassy, he somehow jumped over the main gate and ran across the grounds to the entrance. Without any regard for innocent staffers inside the compound, his kidnappers shot into the embassy, inflicting multiple gunshot wounds upon Sosa. He reached safety and was taken to a nearby hospital, where he received surgery. The Belgian and Venezuelan embassies provided protective custody, and Canada agreed to grant him asylum.

of goodwill toward the new administration. The guerrillas made some progress with the new administration, eventually signing an accord on indigenous rights and identity as well as a human rights accord establishing the creation of U.N.-mandated MINUGUA to oversee the implementation of the peace accords once the final agreement was reached. Although optimistic at first, Guatemalans soon lost hope in the De León administration when they saw he was incapable of addressing crime, constitutional reform, and land and tax issues.

Alvaro Arzú Irigoyen

Former Guatemala City mayor Alvaro Arzú Irigoyen won the 1996 presidential elections thanks to a strong showing in the capital despite widespread electoral abstention elsewhere. Arzú, a businessman, represented the Partido de Avanzada Nacional (PAN, National Advancement Party), with deep roots in the oligarchy and a commitment to economic growth fostered by the development of the private sector under a free market. He quickly appointed new defense, foreign, and economic ministers and set out to sign a final peace accord with the URNG.

The agreement for a "Firm and Lasting Peace" was signed on December 29, 1996, in the Palacio Nacional de la Cultura, which once served as the presidential palace. After years of bloodshed, the final death toll stood at 200,000 with about 50,000 being cases of forced disappearance. A subsequent U.N. report by the Historical Clarification Commission (CEH) squarely placed blame for most of the violence in the hands of the military and the civil-defense patrols, with 80 percent of the victims said to be of Mayan origin. "The majority of human rights violations occurred with the knowledge or by order of the highest authorities of the state," the report declared. It further stated: "State terror was applied to make it clear that those who attempted to assert their rights, and even their relatives, ran the risk of death

by the most hideous means. The objective was to intimidate and silence society as a whole, in order to destroy the will for transformation, both in the short and long term."

The ambitious peace accords marked the culmination of years of negotiations between the government and guerrillas; if properly implemented, they would serve as the basis for the construction of a completely different Guatemala. Unfortunately, the provisions set forth in the accord have yet to be fully adopted. One example of this disappointing trend was the failure to amend the Constitution via a May 1999 referendum to officially redefine the country as "multiethnic, pluricultural, and multilingual," as stipulated in the accord on indigenous rights and identity. Voters stayed away from the polls in droves and the few who did vote decided against the reforms.

The Catholic Church issued its own report on the violence during the country's civil war, which also placed the blame for the majority of the atrocities in the hands of the military. Two days after issuing his report, Bishop Juan Gerardi Conedera was murdered in his garage, much to the outrage of the general populace. By this time, most political killings had all but ceased and the murder sent shock waves of indignation throughout Guatemalan society, which was clamoring for justice against Gerardi's killers. It soon became clear the act was a reprisal from military factions intent on demonstrating their continued hold on the country's power structure.

Subsequent investigations and attempts to bring the guilty parties to justice ended in frustration as key witnesses, prosecutors, and judges fled the country in the face of death threats. While political kidnappings and disappearances became mostly a thing of the past, the country's security situation drastically worsened in the aftermath of the civil war. Bank robberies, murders, extortionary kidnappings, and armed robbery were at an all-time high. Using many of the same methods as in the "disappearance" of thousands of Guatemalans, kidnappers unleashed a wave of terror in which 1,000 people were abducted in 1997 alone. The country, at the time, had the fourth-highest kidnapping rate in the world.

U.S. President Bill Clinton visited Guatemala in March 1999 for a summit meeting with the Central American presidents. In a surprising declaration, he expressed regret on behalf of the United States government for its role in the atrocities committed during the country's civil war, saying that U.S. support for military forces that "engaged in violent and widespread repression" in Guatemala "was wrong."

The crime spree was largely blamed on a power vacuum created during the departure of Guatemala's Policía Nacional and its subsequent replacement by the new Policía Nacional Civil, in accordance with the peace accords. The new police force was trained by experts from Spain, Chile, and the United States. It was hoped that a more professional police force would help bring greater security once fully established, but it quickly became evident that this was not the case. Meanwhile, political murders such as the Gerardi and Myrna Mack murders remained unresolved, shedding light on the lackluster state of Guatemala's judicial system, a situation exacerbated by widespread lynching of supposed criminals in remote areas where the rule of law was merely a vague concept.

Security issues aside, Arzú was a gifted administrator and government corruption remained at low levels, for Guatemala. Arzú's strengths as Guatemala City's mayor had always been infrastructure and public works. His time as president was no different in this regard, with various infrastructure projects being completed during his term in office. Guatemalans widely recognize his hard work backed by a concrete list of accomplishments, and he is still popular in opinion polls. If Guatemala were to

ever allow former presidents to run in elections, it is speculated that Arzú might give opponents a run for their money.

Arzú also privatized many state entities, including the notoriously inefficient telephone company, as part of a neoliberal economic approach to state participation in the economy. Guatemala's telecommunications laws have subsequently been heralded for their contributions to vast improvements in service coverage, increased competition, and lowered prices. At the end of Arzú's presidency, however, many critics pointed to a perceived affinity for serving the interests of Guatemala's wealthy elite, a criticism his successor would play largely to his advantage at the polls in the 1999 election campaign.

THE 1996 PEACE ACCORDS

In addition to officially marking the end of hostilities between leftist insurgents and the Guatemalan government, the UN-brokered 1996 peace accords established a starting point from which to address historical grievances leading to the conflict and begin the construction of a more equitable society. From the start, the agreements established a fact-finding mission known as the Historical Clarification Commission (CEH) to investigate culpability for wartime atrocities committed largely against the country's Mayan population. The CEH and an independent wartime inquiries body created by Guatemala's Catholic Church, the Recuperation of the Historical Memory Project (REMHI), blamed the vast majority of atrocities on the army, with some violations also committed on the part of the guerrillas. Since the findings, many family members of victims of the civil war have sought to bring to justice those responsible for crimes against humanity, including genocide, torture, and illegal arrest. Because of the inadequacies of the Guatemalan judiciary, many have been forced to seek recourse in international courts, as in the case of the suit filed in a Spanish court under universal jurisdiction by the Rigoberta Menchú Foundation against eight government officials accused of crimes against humanity.

The accords also created an ambitious framework for reestablishing the rule of law as the country returned to peacetime while also seeking to address the war's underlying causes. In this regard, agreements were reached in the following areas: human rights, socioeconomic and agrarian issues, the strengthening of civil society and the role of the army in a democratic society, and rights and identity of indigenous peoples. Interestingly, these were negotiated by the establishment of a consensus among various sectors of society working with the Guatemalan government to have their interests and demands addressed at the negotiating table.

The first accord in the long process of negotiations dating to 1991 was the Human Rights Accord, signed in March 1994. While human rights were already guaranteed on paper in the 1986 Constitution, the accord was significant in that it created a new mechanism for ending their systematic violation via a UN verification mission known as MINUGUA.

The Accord on Socioeconomic and Agrarian Issues officially recognizes poverty as a problem and hints at government responsibility to ensure the well-being of the general populace. It committed the government to increasing the tax base as a percentage of GDP from 8 percent (the lowest in the hemisphere) to 12 percent within the next four years. A glaring omission was the ubiquitous issue of land reform. The government's conservative economic policies and the need to get Guatemala's wealthy elites to support the peace process were undoubtedly behind the relative weakness of this accord's reach.

In contrast, a relatively far-reaching accord, if fully implemented, is the Accord on Strengthening of Civilian Power and the Role of the Army in a Democratic Society, signed in September 1996. It covers the demilitarization

of Guatemalan society, in which the military has long had its tentacles, requiring far-reaching constitutional reforms to be fully implemented. The accord limits the role of the military to the defense of Guatemala's territorial integrity. It eliminated the much-hated Civil Defense Patrols and counterinsurgency security units while reducing the size and budget of the military by a third. It also created a new civilian police force to replace the notoriously corrupt Policia Nacional with a mandate to guarantee citizen safety. Last, it mandates necessary reforms of the judicial system to eliminate pervasive impunity. The importance of this last point cannot be understated, as the state of the judiciary serves as a type of barometer in the progress report for Guatemala's democratization. As the CEH described in its final report:

> The justice system, non-existent in large areas of the country before the armed confrontation, was further weakened when the judicial branch submitted to the requirements of the dominant national security model...by tolerating or participating directly in impunity, which concealed the most fundamental violations of human rights, the judiciary became functionally inoperative with respect to its role of protecting the individual from the State, and lost all credibility as guarantor of an effective legal system. This allowed impunity to become one of the most important mechanisms for generating and maintaining a climate of terror.

The 1995 Accord on Identity and Rights of Indigenous Peoples issues a groundbreaking call to amend the 1985 Constitution to redefine Guatemala as "multiethnic, multilingual and pluricultural." Its full implementation requires deep reforms in the country's educational, judicial, and political systems, laying the foundation for a new entitlement of Guatemala's indigenous majority to make claims upon the state and creating a new context for social interactions. It thus goes beyond mere antidiscrimination protections for Guatemala's indigenous majority.

The far-reaching accords offer hope for the construction of a brand-new Guatemala among more equitable lines. The implementation of the reforms called for in the accords, however, has been a daunting task. A major blow to the implementation of the peace accords came in 1999 after a constitutional referendum defeated 50 proposed reforms. Although the peace accords called for only 12 such changes, it is believed that many Guatemalans voted against the package of 50 reforms because they simply felt uninformed about what they were voting to approve. The government did little to explain the nature of the numerous complex reforms or to promote their approval. Voter apathy was widespread with just 18 percent of eligible voters participating in the referendum. In areas where voters were mostly in favor of the reforms, mainly the rural areas most affected by the civil war, voter turnout was generally less than in the capital, which voted overwhelmingly against them.

Whatever the reasons, failure to implement the key changes to Guatemala's legal framework to allow full implementation of the accords meant change would have to come via the legislature. In Guatemala, this is easier said than done. The Portillo administration, in office from 2001 to 2004, was particularly reluctant to implement the main elements of the accords or to use them as a basis for the elaboration of government policy. Observers pointed out that the peace process stalled, and in many cases receded, under Portillo. Among the most critical areas requiring immediate attention were human rights, justice, and security.

The peace accords were officially taken up again by the Berger administration as government policy with concrete plans for new legislation to address many of the pending elements of the agreements. Many laws associated with the accords had trouble making their way through Congress, however, in a legislative assembly that was notorious for its inability to reach consensus on many issues. On a positive note, the reduction of the military by one-third was completed, as stipulated in the accords, and a plan for its modernization is in the works. Its official mandate now includes protecting the country's borders and combating drug traffic, environmental depredation, and smuggling of illegal immigrants.

In the end it can be said that the peace accords have brought some degree of benefit to Guatemalan society. Some of the agreements have been fully complied with, state repression ended, and some opening for political participation has been opened up in recent years. There are still, however, many lingering issues, including lack of security, poverty, socioeconomic exclusion, and a high degree of confrontation between varying sectors of society. Structural problems also persist, a case in point being the glaring deficiencies in the judiciary, leaving it open to manipulation and corruption while preventing it from being truly at the service of the country's citizenry. In essence, what we are seeing is a reflection of the peace accords' intimate connection to the process of Guatemala's continued democratization. Ironically, it is this very process of democratization that opened the door for the ending of the civil war via negotiations in the first place and that will ensure that the spirit and the letter of the accords are eventually fulfilled.

POSTWAR GUATEMALA
Alfonso Portillo and the "Corporate Mafia State"

During the 1999 elections, Alfonso Portillo ran on a populist ticket, hoping to lure the lower classes away from his main opponent, who was fashioned after Arzú. He promised to cut poverty by ending corruption and tax evasion. His party, the Frente Republicano Guatemalteco (FRG, Guatemalan Republican Front), was actually the brainchild of Ríos Montt, the mastermind behind some of the worst atrocities against Guatemala's indigenous peoples during the army's scorched-earth campaign of the early 1980s. He was forbidden, once again, from running in the election. It never stopped him from trying.

Another important campaign issue, and one Portillo played masterfully to his advantage, was citizen safety in the face of skyrocketing crime rates. A long-past incident in Mexico, whereby Portillo killed two men in self-defense before fleeing the country, was dug up during the campaign but actually worked in his favor in machismo-dominated Guatemalan society. Portillo played off the incident as evidence that he was willing and able to take a hard stance on crime.

History has not been kind in its assessment of the Portillo administration. It can be confidently stated without fear of exaggeration that the Portillo administration was one of the worst, if not *the* worst, of Guatemala's governments to date. Among the elements of his atrocious legacy was the solidifying of what analysts have called the "Corporate Mafia State," defined in a February 2002 Amnesty International report as, "The 'unholy alliance' between traditional sectors of the oligarchy, some 'new entrepreneurs,' elements of the police and military, and common criminals."

Among the few achievements under the Portillo administration was the 2001 conviction of three persons involved in the Gerardi murder. Although two military officers and a priest were tried and convicted of the murder, the general consensus was that the intellectual authors of the crime were still at large. Progress was also made in the case of the long-running saga of the murder of anthropologist Myrna Mack. The material author of the crime, Noel de Jesús Beteta, is currently serving a 25-year prison sentence. The intellectual author, Colonel Juan Valencia Osorio, was sentenced to 30 years in prison in 2002, but an appeals court granted his release the following year. Shortly after an order for his re-arrest and return to prison, Valencia escaped while in military custody and under dubious circumstances.

Meanwhile, Efraín Ríos Montt, the dictator who presided over some of the worst atrocities during the army's scorched-earth campaign of the early 1980s, got himself elected president of congress. From his position, he and the military interests were said to run the show via the creation of a parallel power structure while Portillo remained a convenient government front man. Corruption, always a problem plaguing Guatemala's governments, ballooned to unparalleled proportions. Scandals involved embezzlement by the interior minister as well as a highly publicized cover-up involving Ríos Montt himself.

In an event subsequently labeled "Guategate" by the local press, Ríos Montt and 19 other FRG members of congress were accused of secretly altering a liquor tax law, which had already been passed by congress, at the behest of powerful liquor interests. The altered rate lowered the tariffs by as much as 50 percent. When opposition parties denounced the illegal changes to the law, congressional records from the meeting disappeared, while other documents were falsified. Although a popular outcry arose to have Montt and the other members of congress stripped of their diplomatic immunity to stand trial for their actions, the crime remained in impunity, as is so often the case in Guatemala.

In May 2003, the FRG nominated Ríos Montt as its presidential candidate in the elections to be held in November of that year. Once again, his candidacy was rejected by the electoral authorities and by two lower courts, in accordance with the constitutional ban on coup participants' running for presidential office. In July 2003 the Constitutional Court, with several judges appointed by the FRG, approved his candidacy for president, ignoring the constitutional ban that had prevented him from running in previous elections. Adding insult to injury, Ríos Montt had publicly (and correctly) predicted the margin by which he would win the decision prior to its announcement. Days later, the Supreme Court suspended his campaign for the presidency and agreed to hear a complaint presented by two opposition parties.

Ríos Montt denounced the ruling as tampering with the judicial hierarchy and issued veiled threats concerning possible agitation by supporters of his candidacy. Days later, on July 24, a day known as Black Thursday, thousands of ski-masked and hooded FRG supporters invaded the Guatemala City streets armed with machetes, guns, and clubs. They had been bused in from the interior by the FRG and were led in organized fashion by well-known FRG militants, including several members of congress, who were photographed by the press while coordinating the actions.

The demonstrators quickly targeted the offices of outspoken media opposing Ríos Montt's candidacy, holding an entire building hostage for several hours after trying to occupy it. They also marched on the courts and opposition party headquarters, shooting out windows and burning tires in city streets. Journalists were attacked, including a TV cameraman who died of a heart attack while running away from an angry mob. The rioters finally disbanded after the second day of riots when Ríos Montt publicly called on them to return to their homes.

Following the unrest, the Constitutional Court, laden with allies of Ríos Montt and Portillo, overturned the Supreme Court decision and cleared the way for Ríos Montt to run for president. A majority of Guatemalans were disgusted with his actions and the corrupt legacy of his party. They expressed their discontent at the polls, where Ríos Montt finished a distant third in the presidential race.

Óscar Berger Perdomo

The winner after a second, runoff election between the top two candidates was Óscar Berger Perdomo of GANA (Gran Alianza Nacional or Grand National Alliance), a former Guatemala City mayor who represented the interests of the economic elite but surrounded himself with a diverse cabinet. Among them was Rigoberta Menchú, who was named the governmental goodwill ambassador for the peace accords, which the government promised to take up again.

The new government's first priority quickly became cleaning up the mess left behind by the FRG. The national treasury had been ransacked of more than US$1 billion, with corruption on an unprecedented scale involving theft, money laundering, monetary transfers to the army, and creation of secret bank accounts in Panama, Mexico, and the United States by members of Portillo's staff. Berger promised to bring corrupt officials from the FRG government to justice. Remarkably, he was able to make good on his promises, and many corrupt officials are now behind bars awaiting trial, although some have managed to escape prosecution due to the inefficiency and corruption still rampant in the country's judicial system. As of February 2010, Portillo was in a Guatemalan prison cell awaiting extradition to the U.S. to face charges.

Crime and lack of security continued to be problems affecting a wide spectrum of the population. Gang violence plagued Guatemala City and numerous other cities and towns. The police force increasingly came under fire for corruption, initiating a long process of cleansing out its corrupt elements in the hopes of making it more effective. In the face of the police force's inability to abate the continuing upswing in violent crime, which included 16 daily homicides, Berger was forced to integrate joint police-military patrols. These came under fire as evidence of increasing militarization, contrary to the 1996 peace accords.

The economic picture was severely disrupted when thousands of rural peasant farmers had their crops annihilated and their villages destroyed by Hurricane Stan in October 2005. Government reconstruction efforts in the storm's aftermath were slow in making it to affected communities.

Despite some public opposition, Berger was able to implement many of his neoliberal economic policies, including laws governing the concession of government services and construction projects to private entities, securing mining rights for multinational mining conglomerates, and the ratification of DR-CAFTA, the Central American Free Trade Agreement.

The judicial and legislative branches continued to come under fire for gross inefficiency and corruption charges. The existence of clandestine groups, a legacy of the corporate mafia state with links to state agents and organized crime, continued to plague the government. Meanwhile, the creation of a UN-sponsored Commission for the Investigation of Illegal Groups and Clandestine Security Organizations (CICIACS) was blocked by Constitutional Court rulings. A second, reworked version of the proposal, known as the International Commission Against Impunity in Guatemala (CICIG), was the product of an agreement signed between the United Nations and Guatemalan government in December 2006, though it would need congressional approval. The United States and other foreign governments offered financial support for the program, which was to be composed of expert international detectives providing material support to the Public Ministry in its investigations of parallel power structures.

In February 2007, the urgent need to get CICIG up and running was demonstrated by a heinous crime perpetrated against three visiting Salvadoran diplomats and their chauffeur, who were found dead, shot execution-style and burned in their car on the outskirts of Guatemala City. Following an unprecedented investigation fueled by outrage from Salvadoran authorities, the perpetrators turned out to be high-ranking police officers from the Department of Criminal Investigations operating as contract killers. Things really came to a head when the captured policemen were executed by a death squad while awaiting questioning in a high-security prison just days later. Initial government statements and doublespeak had pinned the blame for the executions on fellow prison inmates, including gang members. The incident opened a can of worms in which high-ranking government officials have been implicated in the continued operation of death squads and ties to organized crime. The reconstruction of the Policía Nacional Civil, already a matter of national concern, came to the forefront following these incidents.

As Berger's presidency drew to a close, the general consensus was that his time as president was marked by mostly good intentions but also some modest gains, particularly in terms of a redress of Guatemala's historical ills. Among the glaring omissions was a long-term, inclusive strategy to develop rural areas, where the majority of Guatemala's indigenous peoples live. Delays in the reconstruction process after Hurricane Stan were continually cited as symptoms of weak leadership and an inability to coordinate efforts to reach a common goal.

Among the positive aspects of his presidency were infrastructural projects, or *megaproyectos,* including new roads and airports to make Guatemala more attractive to investors. The creation of so-called *gabinetes móviles* (mobile cabinets) was also a welcome aspect of Berger's administration, allowing those in rural areas the opportunity to have their demands personally addressed by the president and his cabinet members during visits to their towns and cities. Continued economic growth and a more favorable investment climate were duly recognized by international financial organizations. The full effect of DR-CAFTA, which officially took effect on July 1, 2006, remains to be seen. The creation of CICIG was approved by Guatemala's congress on August 1, 2007.

The top two candidates in the 2007 presidential election were Álvaro Colom, a self-proclaimed social democrat of the UNE party (Unidad Nacional de la Esperanza, or National Unity for Hope), and Otto Pérez Molina of the Partido Patriota (Patriot Party), an ex-military hardliner whose main campaign promise was to combat Guatemala's rapidly deteriorating security situation with a "strong hand." Persistent rumors of ties to organized crime continued to haunt the UNE party during the campaign, but in the end Colom's appeals to Guatemala's mostly poor indigenous majority won him the victory in the countryside, though he was decidedly the loser among better-educated Guatemala City voters. As is usually the case for Guatemalan voters, their choice for president came down to what (or who) they perceived to be the lesser of two evils.

Álvaro Colom

Shortly before taking office, Vice President Rafael Espada, a well-known former Houston heart surgeon, told MSNBC that, "Guatemala is sick, very sick, in intensive care." Colom chose Espada as a running mate in part because of his credibility with Guatemalan elites, though some had doubts regarding his limited political experience. The foreign press was generally kind in its assessment of Colom and was happy to back a social democrat with the U.S. government seal of approval. Colom told the Associated Press he was confident his government could make Guatemala more conciliatory and that he and Espada knew the country's problems inside and out.

As usual, however, campaign promises led to few tangible results during the early days of the administration, despite a much-touted "100 Day Plan" to combat nagging grievances such as spiraling crime rates and a generally somber economic outlook. It became clear early

on that the oft-quoted U.S. bumper sticker "If you're not outraged, you're not paying attention" might also be applied to Guatemala's new government. These early days were marked by a palpable lack of direction on the part of the Colom government, as it reacted (or failed to react) to one issue after another.

Colom and Espada frequently made contradictory statements to the press, especially concerning government officials who were to be removed from office. Colom was apparently bent on cleaning house and quickly requested the resignation of many government officials, some of whom had good service records, replacing them with some very questionable appointments. The removal of Civil Aviation Director José Manuel Moreno Botrán, in favor of a coffee farmer whose only connection to civil aviation was a private pilot's license (which later turned out to be expired), is a particular case in point. The official reason for removal was supposedly financial malfeasance during the construction of Guatemala City's new airport, though evidence to back these claims was never found. It should be noted that the highly respected International Civil Aviation Organization (ICAO) oversaw the funding and execution of the project in its entirety.

On at least two occasions, Colom completely butchered the names of his new appointees, as if he had no idea who he was talking about. Making matters worse, and a matter of national disdain, is Colom's marked speech impediment.

At about the same time, the press began reporting on a surprising element of power behind the scenes: First Lady Sandra Torres de Colom. It became a matter of public scrutiny that she was also, in fact, presiding over cabinet meetings. Torres de Colom was placed at the helm of the newly created Council for Social Cohesion, which oversees the health and education ministries, among others. The legal framework creating this mechanism granted her tremendous powers and complete control over a $282 million budget free from any third-party oversight. Torres de Colom, according to several analysts, in fact became Guatemala's co-president, usurping powers that would normally fall under the jurisdiction of government ministers and the vice president. The Council for Social Cohesion eventually implemented a program of *bolsas solidarias,* or rations of basic food items given to Guatemala's poor. Their continued distribution, however, was often conditioned by party support for UNE. The manipulated masses essentially became a platform for Sandra Torres's future presidential candidacy.

The greatest scandal in Colom's first three months in office involved the firing of Security Consultant Víctor Rivera, a naturalized Venezuelan who presided over investigations involving drug trafficking, kidnapping, bank robberies, and other important cases, including the murder of three Salvadoran diplomats in February 2007. Rivera had worked with three successive governments, but Colom abruptly terminated his contract in April 2008. Days later, just minutes after granting a candid interview to the daily newspaper *Prensa Libre,* Rivera and his secretary were intercepted in a drive-by shooting that left Rivera dead, his secretary injured, and 18 bullet holes in his white Toyota Starlet. The government remained silent for two days after the murder, adding to suspicions that they were probably behind it, though only human-rights champion Helen Mack would dare go on record saying so.

Other scandals during the first year in office included the uncovering of wiretaps and unauthorized surveillance in the Palacio Nacional and presidential offices by unknown sources. In October 2008, ex-President Alfonso Portillo returned to Guatemala from his Mexican exile after his visa expired. Although he should have faced numerous charges on counts of well-documented financial malfeasance during his administration, he was released on bail the same day. Many saw this as evidence that Colom and Portillo were in cahoots, an accusation Colom vehemently denied. As of 2012, Portillo was in a Guatemalan prison awaiting extradition to the U.S.

On May 10, 2009, prominent Guatemala City lawyer Rodrigo Rosenberg was assassinated while bicycling in Zona 14. The next day, a video surfaced in which he plainly accused the government of orchestrating his death. In the video, recorded just days before his death, Rosenberg states, "If you are hearing this message, it means that I, Rodrigo Rosenberg Marzano, was murdered by the president's private secretary, Gustave Alejos, and his associate Gregorio Valdez, with the approval of Mr. Alvaro Colom and Sandra de Colom." The alleged reason for the murder given by Rosenberg claimed it was a government plot to silence opposition to government corruption in Guatemala's Banrural, including claims of money laundering and using it as a front to fund campaign funds for a future run for office by Sandra Torres de Colom. Mr. Musa had been appointed to Banrural's board of directors, but his appointment was withheld by the government over a period of three months prior to his murder.

Rosenberg fought valiantly for the solving of the Musas' murder and had received death threats in the days leading up to his murder. In light of these allegations, an outraged Guatemalan populace took to the streets demanding Colom's resignation. Colom, meanwhile, denied any wrongdoing and ordered a full investigation. He also orchestrated counter-demonstrations with the UNE party affiliates, bussing in supporters to the capital from the provinces. The murders were investigated by CICIG, though many of the assertions made by Rosenberg in his video were corroborated through other sources, most importantly evidence of Musa's pending appointment to Banrural.

In January 2010, the results of CICIG's

investigation into the murder of Rodrigo Rosenberg were revealed. It was found that the lawyer orchestrated his own death with the unknowing help of friends and family members, who thought they were being recruited to arrange the execution of his would-be assassin. The truth in Guatemala is often harder to believe than lies.

In true Machiavellian fashion, Sandra Torres divorced Alvaro Colom in March 2011 with the intention of bypassing a Constitutional ban prohibiting family members of the sitting president from running for office. Her case would eventually make it to the highest court in the land after Guatemala's electoral authorities rejected her attempts to register her candidacy, citing the constitutional ban. In an Oscar-worthy performance Sandra Torres tearfully appealed to the magistrates of the *Corte de Constitucionalidad* for permission to run for office. The court unanimously rejected her candidacy in its final decision two days later.

The much-anticipated 2011 elections eventually came down to a runoff election between Manuel Baldizon, of the Lider party, and Otto Perez Molina. Baldizon's platform was very similar to UNE's and many believed he was a puppet of Sandra Torres. He made ridiculous campaign promises that could only appeal to the poor and uneducated masses, including bringing Guatemala's national soccer team to a World Cup showing and an extra yearly work bonus. A textbook narcissist, Baldizon had publicly (and unabashedly) stated he was a Clark Kent look-alike and seemed more concerned with his opponents' alleged copying of his fashion sense than in seriously debating any of the issues proposed during televised debates. Baldizon campaign posters in Guatemala City began morphing overnight with clown noses spray-painted on. Perez Molina, and his vice-presidential candidate Roxana Baldetti, offered a more serious strategy to combat the country's drug cartels and other forms of organized crime while continuing social aid programs initiated by Colom. Lider was quite evidently the loser in Guatemala City, where Perez Molina won overwhelmingly with over 70 percent majority. The national results revealed Perez Molina was the victor by a 54 percent majority. In the days following the election, Perez Molina and Baldetti quickly set to making strategic plans and new cabinet appointments (something never before seen in Guatemala) in preparation for their inauguration on January 14, 2012. The mood in Guatemala was particularly upbeat and hopeful going in to the new year.

Government

ORGANIZATION

Guatemala is a constitutional democracy. The president is the chief of state, assisted by a vice president, both of whom are elected to office for a single four-year term. The president is constitutionally barred from a second term, but the vice president may run for office after a four-year hiatus from office. The Congreso de la República is the national (unicameral) legislative body, consisting of 158 members. Congress members serve four-year terms running concurrently with the presidential term. Guatemala has 22 administrative subdivisions (departments) headed by governors appointed by the president. Popularly elected mayors or councils govern Guatemala City and 331 other municipalities.

JUDICIAL SYSTEM

The judicial branch is independent of the executive branch and the legislature and consists of a Constitutional Court and a Supreme

POLITICAL GEOGRAPHY OF GUATEMALA

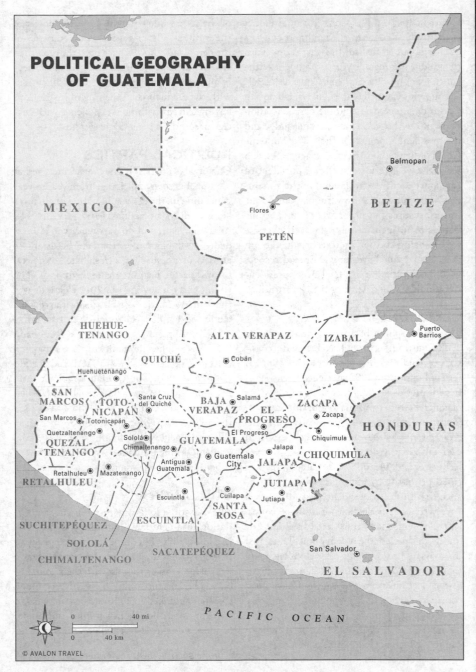

MEXICO

BELIZE

Belmopan ⊛

Flores ⊙

PETÉN

HUEHUE-
TENANGO

ALTA VERAPAZ

IZABAL

Puerto
Barrios ⊙

QUICHÉ

Cobán ⊙

Huehuetenango ⊙

SAN
MARCOS

TOTO-
NICAPÁN

Santa Cruz
del Quiché ⊙

BAJA
VERAPAZ

Salamá ⊙

ZACAPA

San Marcos ⊙

Totonicapán ⊙

EL
PROGRESO

Zacapa ⊙

HONDURAS

Quetzaltenango ⊙

QUEZAL-
TENANGO

Sololá ⊙

Chimaltenango ⊙

GUATEMALA

El Progreso ⊙

Chiquimula ⊙

Retalhuleu ⊙

Mazatenango ⊙

Antigua ⊙
Guatemala

Guatemala ⊛
City

Jalapa ⊙

JALAPA

CHIQUIMULA

RETALHULEU

Escuintla ⊙

Cuilapa ⊙

Jutiapa ⊙

JUTIAPA

SUCHITEPÉQUEZ

ESCUINTLA

SANTA
ROSA

SOLOLÁ

SACATEPÉQUEZ

San Salvador ⊛

CHIMALTENANGO

EL SALVADOR

0   40 mi

0   40 km

PACIFIC OCEAN

© AVALON TRAVEL

Court of Justice. The Constitutional Court is the highest court in the land and consists of five judges elected for five-year terms, with each judge serving one year as president of the court. Congress, the Supreme Court of Justice, the Superior Council of the Universidad de San Carlos de Guatemala, and the bar association (Colegio de Abogados) each elect one judge and the president appoints the fifth. The Supreme Court of Justice consists of 13 magistrates who serve five-year terms and elect a president of the court each year from among their members. The judiciary suffers from a poor public image because of suspicions that it has become porous to influence from drug traffickers as well as being corrupt and inefficient, though it recently gained greater widespread respect with the rejection of Sandra Torres's presidential candidacy, in defense of the Constitution.

ELECTIONS

The current power balance is a product of the 1985 Constitution, formulated before the country's official return to democracy in 1986. A series of reforms in 1993 shortened terms of office for president, vice president, and members of congress from five years to four; for Supreme Court justices from six years to five; and increased terms for mayors and city councils from two-and-a-half years to four.

Between 1954 and 1986, Guatemala was ruled primarily by a military-oligarchy alliance that installed presidents periodically via widely fraudulent elections or military coups. In the few elections considered free and fair during this period, the military quickly stepped in to assert its dominant role while ensuring that the president remained a figurehead. All of the elections from 1985 onward have been considered free and fair, though the military still holds much power in Guatemala, probably more so than in any other Latin American country. Much of Guatemala's democratic process has consisted of a gradual strengthening

of the state while trying to limit the power of the military. Other general characteristics of the democratic process have been the growth of citizen participation from all sectors of society in an atmosphere of greater freedom concurrent with the gradual strengthening of institutions having extremely limited experience with governance under a democratic system.

POLITICAL PARTIES

Guatemala's political parties constitute a veritable alphabet soup and change from year to year depending on the capricious nature of alliances between different factions. Parties are unstable, to say the least, and no party has won a presidential election on more than one occasion. As an election approaches, a fresh batch of newly-formed parties begin to make the rounds. The ruling party following the 2011 elections was the Partido Patriota (PP). Other parties include the Unidad Nacional de la Esperanza (UNE), Libertad Democratica Renovada (LIDER), Frente Republicano Guatemalteco (FRG), Vision con Valores (VIVA), and Partido Unionista (PU). The Unidad Revolucionaria Nacional Guatemalteca (Guatemalan National Revolutionary Unity, also URNG-MAIZ) is the political party formed by the former guerrilla movement, which fought against the government during the country's 36-year civil war. It holds three congressional seats.

BUREAUCRACY

There is still a long way to go in the consolidation of a genuine functioning democracy in Guatemala. The judiciary and legislative branches are badly in need of reform and have lost virtually all credibility with their constituents. The current situation is still very much like that described in 2000 by the Guatemalan Institute of Political, Economic, and Social Studies, a nongovernmental organization:

In our society, agents or former agents of

the state have woven a secret, behind-the-scenes network dedicated to obstructing justice. They have created a virtual alternative government that functions clandestinely with its own standardized and consistent modus operandi. In such a context, crimes are not clarified, and those responsible are not identified. Society finally forgets the cases and becomes resigned.

If the actual material authors left evidence at the scene of their crimes, they then decide who to implicate as scapegoats. If there are actually any inquiries and if these eventually lead to any arrests, these are always of low-ranking members of the army, or at best, an official not in active service.

When they can't pin the crime on some scapegoat, the scene of the crime is contaminated and legal proceedings are obstructed and proceed at a snail's pace. If, nonetheless, investigations still continue, these powerful forces hidden behind the scenes destroy the evidence. And of course it cannot be forgotten that pressure, threats, attacks, and corruption are all part of the efforts to undermine and demoralize the judiciary, who, knowing they are not able to count on a security apparatus that will guarantee that the law is enforced, feel obliged to cede in the face of this parallel power.

The powerlessness of the Guatemalan judiciary has forced some people to seek remedies for their grievances in international courts under universal jurisdiction established by the United Nations concerning crimes against humanity. One example is the suit filed before the Spanish National Court in 1999 by the Rigoberta Menchú Foundation against eight former Guatemalan officials, including General Efraín Ríos Montt, for murder, genocide, torture, terrorism, and illegal arrest. The case seeks to try those responsible for wartime abuses and centers around the 1980 attack on the Spanish Embassy in Guatemala City that claimed the lives of 37 peasant activists, among them Menchú's father, and embassy staff. The Spanish court has heard other cases involving genocide and established a precedent for universal jurisdiction in the 1998 arrest of Chile's General Augusto Pinochet in the United Kingdom. He remained in custody for 14 months until British authorities ruled Pinochet was unfit for trial and let him return to Chile.

In July 2006, a Spanish judge ordered the detention of all eight accused after an unfruitful visit to Guatemala with the intention of gathering testimonies from plaintiffs and questioning the accused. Ríos Montt and General Mejía Víctores effectively paralyzed the process with a series of appeals upheld by the Constitutional Court. Menchú admitted the difficulty of getting Guatemalan officials to execute the arrest orders, calling it "a test of the Guatemalan justice system."

As for the legislature, there is talk of reducing the number of members of congress, elected partly by proportional representation. The Guatemalan congress has suffered in recent years from a gradual erosion of confidence on the part of its constituents because of gross inefficiency, corruption, and growing suspicion of widespread links to drug trafficking. In essence, a majority of Guatemalans view their congressional body as practically useless and expensive to maintain.

Political parties, likewise, have suffered a gradual decline in credibility. The general pattern since 1986 has been one of great expectation for change prior to elections and the installation of a new government, followed by disappointment with the new government's failure to deliver on its promises, ending in frustration and renewed hope for change with the next round of elections. The government of Álvaro Colom appeared to be no exception to this pattern after its first year in power. Opinion polls point to a growing desire to see the emergence of better leadership and an authentic political class, something Guatemala still lacks.

Economy

Guatemala's gross domestic product in 2010 was $70.15 billion, an increase of 2.6 percent over the previous year, with a per capita GDP of about $5,200. Inflation was about 4 percent for the same year. Although it is the largest economy in Central America, large sectors of the population remain only marginally active in the economy. Guatemala is also the region's most populous country. The economy has been growing steadily since the 1996 peace accords and has demonstrated macroeconomic stability.

AGRICULTURE, TRADE, AND INDUSTRY

Agriculture accounts for 13 percent of GDP, with agricultural exports of coffee, sugar, bananas, cardamom, vegetables, flowers and plants, timber, rice, and rubber being the chief products. Guatemala exported $8 billion worth of goods in 2008, with 75 percent of these being agricultural products. Light industry contributes to 25 percent of the GDP and manufactures include prepared food, clothing and textiles, construction materials, tires, and pharmaceuticals. The service sector accounts for 61 percent of Guatemala's GDP. The United States is Guatemala's biggest trading partner, accounting for more than half of the country's exports and a third of its imports. Other important trading partners include the neighboring Central American countries, Mexico, South Korea, China, and Japan.

In terms of employment, agriculture is the largest employer, with half of the population employed by this sector. Services, bolstered by tourism, employ 35 percent of the population and industry employs the remaining 15 percent. Unemployment in 2005 was 3 percent.

After the signing of the 1996 peace accords, Guatemala appeared poised for rapid economic growth, but a financial crisis in 1998 disrupted the expected pace. Despite gains in industry, the country's economy still showed much of its historical susceptibility to world commodity prices, specifically coffee. A collapse in coffee prices severely affected rural incomes and brought the industry into a serious recession, though exports of this commodity have bounced back since then.

Foreign investment has remained weak, with Guatemala unable to capitalize on foreign investment to the same degree as its neighbors. A notable exception is the privatization of utilities. Potential investors cite corruption, crime and security issues, and the lack of sufficient skilled labor as the principal barriers to new business.

Guatemala's economy is dominated by the private sector, which generates about 85 percent of the GDP. The government's involvement is small, with its business activities limited to public utilities, many of which have been privatized under a neoliberal economic model, and the operation of ports, airports, and several development-oriented financial institutions. The Berger administration passed legislation allowing for more private sector concessions of services in 2006.

The U.S.-Dominican Republic-Central America Free Trade Agreement (DR-CAFTA) was ratified by Guatemala on March 10, 2005. Priorities within DR-CAFTA include the elimination of customs tariffs on as many categories of goods as possible, opening services sectors, and creating clear and easily enforceable rules in areas such as investment, customs procedures, government procurement, electronic commerce, intellectual property protection, the use of sanitary measures for the protection of public health, and resolution of business disputes. Import tariffs were lowered as part of Guatemala's membership in the Central American Common Market, with most now below 15 percent.

© AL ARGUETA

Guatemala's economy is still very much based on agriculture.

Other priorities include increasing transparency and accountability in Guatemala's public finances, broadening the tax base as part of the peace accords, and completing implementation of reforms of the finance sector. The implementation of these changes involved reforming Guatemalan laws and a long, involved process in the national legislature. The process finally ended in June 2006, with DR-CAFTA officially taking effect on July 1, 2006, after the U.S. Department of Commerce officially certified the country in compliance with the trade agreement.

The ratification of DR-CAFTA was met with protests in Guatemala City. Its detractors feared the loss of jobs, increased dependence on food imports, and a broadening of the deep gap between Guatemala's rich and poor. Peasant organizations and at least one NGO calculated the loss of up to 100,000 jobs in the agricultural sector. The government offered to counteract perceived imbalances through a series of credits supporting small and medium-sized businesses, which employ more than 70 percent of the population and are the engine of the rural economy. Nontraditional export sectors were quick to point out the treaty will create an estimated 50,000 new jobs in nontraditional agriculture in the first two years of its implementation. Whatever the result, the implementation of DR-CAFTA will certainly involve major adjustments requiring the strengthening of agro-industry, and small farms in particular, via expansion to new markets and the application of new technologies, among other things.

Another major contributor to Guatemala's economy is the money sent home by over 1.5 million expatriate Guatemalans living and working in the United States. In 2008, this amounted to $4.3 billion, which Guatemalans on the receiving end used to supplement their incomes, start businesses, and put into savings. This phenomenon has helped to widely ameliorate the country's endemic poverty and accounts for almost 12 percent of the GDP.

Although income sent from abroad showed continued growth in 2008, Guatemalans feared that an increase in deportations of Guatemalan nationals from the United States would negatively impact the local economy.

DISTRIBUTION OF WEALTH

It remains to be seen whether DR-CAFTA will aggravate or alleviate Guatemala's skewed wealth- and land-distribution patterns, which are already some of the most unequal in the world. The wealthiest 10 percent of the population receives almost half of all income, and the top 20 percent receives two-thirds. More than half of the population lives in poverty, with about 15 percent living in extreme poverty and surviving on less than $2 a day. Belying these patterns of wealth and income distribution are Guatemala's social-development indicators, such as infant mortality and illiteracy, which are among the worst in the hemisphere. Chronic malnutrition among the rural poor worsened with the onset of the late-1990s coffee crisis and devastation wrought by Hurricane Stan in 2005.

TOURISM

On a much more positive note, tourism has greatly impacted the economy in recent years, particularly since the end of the civil war in 1996. In 2004, Guatemala received one million visitors for the first time and increased visitor numbers have continued in the years since. In 2007, Guatemala registered 1.6 million foreign arrivals with a tourism expenditure totaling $1.2 billion. According to the World Tourism Organization, between 2003 and 2004 Guatemala had the largest increase of international arrivals of any country in the Americas, with a growth of 34.3 percent.

Guatemala's tourist arrivals doubled between 2003 and 2007. In Central America, only Costa Rica receives more visitors.

About 30 percent of Guatemala's visitor arrivals come from North America, with another 34 percent coming from Central America, particularly El Salvador. U.S. visitors may be closing the gap, however, as statistics from the peak Easter travel season of 2006 show more Americans arriving in Guatemala than Salvadorans. Approximately 18 percent of Guatemala's tourists come from Europe and another 18 percent come from various other countries.

Much of the money generated by tourism stays in local hands, as many communities have been able to capitalize on their proximity to area attractions by catering to the demands of an increasing number of visitors. Foreign tourism investment is limited mostly to main tourist areas, and local entrepreneurs have done an excellent job of filling in the void created by the lack of foreign investment.

The government, meanwhile, is actively promoting tourism abroad via ad campaigns sponsored by the state tourism agency, INGUAT (Instituto Guatemalteco de Turismo), and investing in much-needed infrastructural improvements to the country's airports. The industry also got a boost from the filming of the CBS television series *Survivor* in the rainforests of Petén, which aired in 2005.

The main obstacle to the continued growth of Guatemala's tourism industry is security, and the Guatemalan government is actively working to make travel safer for visitors to Guatemala. Among the improvements in visitor security is the establishment of tourism police (Politur) in the main tourist destinations. In many places, their presence has resulted in fewer occurrences of robbery and assault.

People and Culture

Guatemalans are a complex breed. First, there are the city-dwellers, who are as cosmopolitan as the residents of any North American city of comparable size. Social stratification, racism, and classicism also figure prominently into the makeup of many middle- and upper-class Guatemalans, in particular those living in urban areas. You may find some urban Guatemalans downright rude, though they are careful to put on their best appearances for foreigners.

Then there are Guatemala's rural poor and middle class. Most of them are warm and friendly; you may even be the object of their gracious hospitality. However, you may have to get past some cultural isolationism, as rural Guatemalans are naturally suspicious of outsiders once you are past the informal, superficial relationships of a passing traveler. This is not surprising given the country's penchant for violent social upheaval, class struggle, and an unfortunate more recent phenomenon, rising crime statistics.

Guatemala has its fair share of social problems. Perhaps the greatest challenges are the constant contradictions between wealth and poverty. It colors daily life in seemingly innocuous ways, such as traveling on a Guatemala City highway overlooking slums while driving to a fancy Zona 10 restaurant. It also colors day-to-day interactions with people and you'll see it in the myriad ways Guatemalans treat each other.

It's no secret that the country has a legacy of violence from which it is still trying to recover. Its governments and leaders, with few exceptions, have mostly stayed in power long enough to rape the country of its resources and contribute to the wealth of fellow cronies while turning a blind eye to crime, social inequality, and widespread violence. The general populace seems resigned to live in a country where things simply happen, where governments make promises and then fail to deliver, where the rich continue to live privileged lives while the poor continue to somehow survive. Perhaps this is all the legacy of Spanish colonial government and the clashing of two very distinct cultures from opposite ends of the earth. Maybe it's the legacy of 36 years of civil war. What is certain is that Guatemala's cultural and sociopolitical makeup is a subject of much academic speculation, and you will certainly come to form your own opinions after some time traveling here.

I realize I haven't painted a very pretty picture of my fellow Guatemalans. It's sometimes difficult to spend time in such a beautiful country with so many sad contradictions. Part of traveling in Guatemala involves finding a way to live with these contradictions. It's all part of the experience.

ETHNICITY AND CLASS
Demographics

Guatemala's population is one of the fastest-growing in Latin America, with 2004 census figures placing the population at just over 14 million. The annual growth rate is 2.61 percent and 43 percent of the population is under the age of 15. The country's population density is 116 people per square kilometer, with an urban-to-rural ratio of 38.7 percent to 61.3 percent. Population density is much less in the northern Petén department, comprising a third of Guatemala's total land area but harboring only about 5 percent of the population. Urbanization is greatest in the western highlands region centered around Guatemala City and Quetzaltenango.

Ethnic Diversity

Guatemala has an incredible wealth of ethnic

diversity, as attested to by the as-of-yet-unfulfilled push to amend the national constitution to officially describe the country as "pluricultural, multilingual, and multiethnic." The country is divided about evenly between descendants of indigenous Maya (comprising 21 different linguistic groups) and *ladinos,* who are of Mayan descent but have adopted European culture and dress in addition to the Spanish language. A sizable percentage of the population is a mixture of Mayan and European, also known as *mestizo.* A much smaller percentage of the population is of purely European descent, primarily from Spanish and German families, and they control a disproportionate fraction of the country's wealth. Many of these are direct descendants of the *criollo* (New World Spanish-born elite) families dominating the country's economy since colonial times. Indigenous Maya descendants are found in greatest numbers in the western highlands, with Guatemala City, the Pacific, Caribbean, and Petén lowlands being largely *ladino.*

Additionally, there are two non-Mayan ethnicities thrown into the mix, Xinca and Garífuna. Only about 100-250 Xinca-speakers remain, confined to a small area near the Salvadoran border. The Garinagu (plural of Garífuna), a mixture of Amerindian and African peoples, arrived from St. Vincent via Roatán, Honduras, in the early 1800s and settled in the Guatemalan Caribbean coastal town of Lívingston. Their culture is more similar to that of the Western Caribbean, with whom they identify more readily, than the rest of Guatemala.

Mayan Groups

Ethnicity and language are intertwined when it comes to Guatemala's principal Mayan groups, which include K'iche', Kaqchikel, Tz'utujil, Mam, Ixil, Q'eqchi', Poqomchi', Poqomam, and Q'anjob'al. By far the most numerous group is K'iche', with nearly one million speakers. A little more than 400,000 people speak Kaqchikel, and there are about 686,000 Mam speakers.

ECONOMIC CLASS STRUCTURES
The Oligarchy

The direct result of Guatemala's Spanish colonial legacy granting privileges to Spanish-born elites is the modern-day oligarchy. In many cases, families can trace their roots to these colonial-era *criollo* families. As in neighboring El Salvador, where there is frequent reference to "The Fourteen Families," the Guatemalan oligarchy has a strong history of intermingling to the exclusion of outer echelons of society. For the purpose of this discussion, the oligarchy will also encompass the "new rich" and the subsequent generations of landowning business elites who remain firmly in control of Guatemala's politics and economy.

Much has been written about the Guatemalan elite's support for right-wing governments and military policies aimed at eliminating the threat of Communist subversion during the country's civil war (1960-1996). Although the war had genocidal aspects, it was also very much related to the distribution of wealth and the 1950s-era reforms that threatened economic elites' hegemony. In essence, the oligarchy allied with the military in an attempt to maintain the status quo.

The oligarchy also found a willing ally in the Unites States, which was happy to support Guatemalan elites in their emulation of U.S. consumption patterns and the expansion of private enterprise. Stephen Connely Benz, in his book *Guatemalan Journey,* provides some interesting insights on Guatemala's oligarchy and the way in which U.S. government aid via the U.S. Agency for International Development (USAID) may have unknowingly exacerbated Guatemala's inequitable social structures. He argues that capitalism, prior to the arrival of USAID, already functioned in its most brutal form in Guatemala, and he points to the history of "the conservative oligarchy and the essentially feudalistic economic system that remained the principle obstacle to a more equitable distribution of wealth." He goes on to say that, "This oligarchy did not care for democracy, modernization, or even economic liberalism; what it cared for was the perpetuation of an extremely lucrative arrangement... It was, in short, a segment of society that had long gotten its way and was principally interested in maintaining its privileges—reform was the furthest thing from its interests, unless by economic reform one meant lower export taxes, privatization of services, and the liberalization of price controls." In essence, Benz argues, U.S. aid money given to support agro-industry and free enterprise went directly to the oligarchy and thus helped perpetuate the continuance of a "wildly unjust, cash-crop-driven economy that necessitated U.S. aid for the impoverished masses in the first place."

More recently, the Guatemalan elites' uncontested hold on the reins of power can be seen in the stalling of the 1996 peace accords. Although the accords contain many provisions that would contribute to make Guatemala a more just society, the vast majority of these reforms have fallen by the wayside. Ironically, the major economic reforms taking place since the signing of the peace accords largely involve the lower export taxes and privatization of services Benz speculated about.

On a practical level, you can see the Guatemalan elite at fancy restaurants, shopping malls, and hotel lobbies in Guatemala City. You'll recognize them by their entourage of bodyguards, nannies to mind the children, and chauffeur-driven late-model luxury cars. They'll greet each other in courteous fashion and it will seem like everyone in the restaurant knows each other and is part of the same tight-knit clan. On a positive note, absent large quantities of U.S. foreign investment in Guatemalan real estate and tourism infrastructure, the oligarchy's presence has given Guatemala the condos, office buildings, and five-star hotels it would otherwise lack.

The Upper and Middle Classes

Guatemala's upper class has close ties to the oligarchy, and there is a bit of a gray area where the two intersect. Social class in Guatemala is very much about putting on appearances in an attempt to gain favor with the upper echelons of society. Statistically, Guatemala has the third-highest per capita private aircraft ownership in the Americas, which gives you some idea of the purchasing power of wealthy Guatemalans. The country's wealth can also be seen in the fact that many homes that would be considered high-end in neighboring Central American countries such as Nicaragua and Honduras would be quite middle class in Guatemala. To give you an idea of how this is possible, keep in mind that the wealthiest 10 percent of the population receives almost half of all the income and the top 20 percent receives two-thirds.

Some might argue that Guatemala has no true middle class, but I would disagree. The middle class in Guatemala most certainly looks different than it does in the United States and even neighboring Central American countries. It's also proportionally smaller, but not altogether nonexistent. You'll find most of the country's middle class living in urban areas such as Guatemala City and Quetzaltenango.

Lower Classes

It's no surprise that, in a country where race and social standing go hand in hand, the vast majority of the country's poor are of Mayan descent. This applies to those living in poverty in highland villages and urban slums or trying to eke out a living in the Petén lowlands. About 80 percent of Guatemala's population lives in poverty, with about two-thirds of that number living in extreme poverty on less than $2 a day. Guatemala's social indicators, such as infant mortality and illiteracy, are among the worst in the hemisphere.

RELIGION

Religion in Guatemala is fairly complex, with traditional Mayan spirituality still very much a presence, particularly in the highlands, along with Catholicism and the more recent incursions of Evangelical Christianity. In much smaller numbers, Guatemala's Jewish population is centered in Guatemala City. There is also a small Muslim population with at least one mosque in Guatemala City.

Mayan Spirituality

Mayan spirituality has its origins in pre-Columbian religious practices and a cosmology that venerated natural phenomena, including rivers, mountains, and caves. The soaring temples built by the Mayan and other Mesoamerican civilizations were built to mimic mountains and were usually built in alignment with the cardinal directions. The solstices were very important in this regard and many of their temple pyramids and observatories were built in precise fashion so as to mark these events. Caves were also sacred to the Mayans and believed to be passages to the underworld, a belief that persists to this day. Archaeologists speculate that at least one powerful economic center, Cancuén, lacked buildings of strictly religious significance because of its proximity to the massive Candelaria cave network nearby.

The Mayan calendar is still in use in parts of Guatemala today, particularly in the Western Highlands, and is pegged closely to the agricultural cycle. Maize is a sacred crop and is believed to have been the basis for the modern formation of man by the gods, as told in the K'iche' book of myths and legends, the *Popol Vuh,* discovered by a Spanish priest in Chichicastenango in the 18th century. Although the vast majority of the Mayans' sacred writings were burned by Bishop Diego de Landa in a 16th-century Yucatán bonfire, three Mayan texts, known as codices, survive in European museums. The *Chilam Balam* is another sacred book based on partially salvaged Yucatecan documents from the 17th and 18th centuries.

Modern-day Mayan religious practices, also known as *costumbre,* often take place in caves, archaeological sites, and volcanic summits. They often include offerings of candles, flowers, and liquor with the sacrifice of a chicken or other small animal thrown in for good measure.

Another curiosity of the Western Highlands is the veneration of a folk saint known alternatively as Maximón or San Simón, with a particularly persistent following in Santiago Atitlán and Zunil. The cigar-smoking, liquor-drinking idol is a thorn in the side of many Catholic and Evangelical groups, whose followers sometimes profess conversion to Christianity but often still hold allegiance to Maximón, who is thought to represent Judas or Pedro de Alvarado. Syncretism, combining Mayan religious beliefs and Catholicism, is a major player in highland Mayan spirituality.

The cult following of folk saints is also tied to the presence of *cofradías,* a form of Mayan community leadership with roots in Catholic lay brotherhoods wielding religious and political influences. The *cofradías* are responsible for organizing religious festivities in relation to particular folk saints and a different member of the *cofradía* harbors the Maximón idol in his home every year.

The Catholic Church

Catholicism has played an important role in Guatemala ever since colonial times, though the state increasingly took measures to limit its power starting in the late 19th century, when liberal reformers confiscated church property and secularized education. More recently, the Church wrestled with its official mandate of saving souls and its moral obligation to alleviate the misery and injustice experienced by many of its subjects, particularly the Mayans. Many parish priests, faced with the atrocities and

MAYAN ETHNOLINGUISTIC GROUPS

Achi': Spoken in western Baja Verapaz, including Cubulco, Rabinal, San Miguel Chicaj, San Jerónimo, and Salamá.

Akateko: Spoken in San Miguel Acatán and San Rafael La Independencia (Huehuetenango).

Awakateko: Spoken in Aguacatán, Huehuetenango.

Ch'orti: Spoken in La Unión (Zacapa) and Jocotán, Camotán, Olopa, and Quetzaltepeque (Chiquimula).

Chuj: Spoken in San Mateo Ixtatán and parts of Nentón.

Itzá: Spoken in Flores, San José, San Andrés, San Benito, La Libertad, and Sayaxché.

Ixil: Spoken in Chajul, Cotzal, and Nebaj (El Quiché department).

Kaqchikel: Spoken in 47 municipalities in seven departments, including Guatemala, Sacatepéquez, Chimaltenango, Escuintla, Sololá (Panajachel, Santa Catarina Palopó, San Antonio Palopó, Santa Cruz La Laguna, and San Marcos La Laguna), Suchitepéquez, and Baja Verapaz.

K'iche': Guatemala's most widely spoken Mayan dialect, with speakers in 75 municipalities spanning six departments, including Sololá, Totonicapán, Quetzaltenango, El Quiché, Suchitepéquez, and Retalhuleu.

Mam: Spoken in 55 municipalities in three departments, including Quetzaltenango, San Marcos, and Huehuetenango (Todos Santos and San Juan Atitán, among others).

Mopán: Spoken in San Luis, Dolores, parts of Melchor de Mencos, and Poptún (Petén).

Popti (Jakalteko): Spoken in parts of western Huehuetenango, including Jacaltenango, La Democracia, Concepción Huista, San Antonio Huista, Santa Ana Huista, and Nentón.

Poqomam: Spoken in Mixco and Chinautla (Guatemala department), Palín (Escuintla), and Jalapa department.

Poqomchi': Widely spoken in Alta and Baja Verapaz, including San Cristóbal Verapaz, Tactic, Tamahú, Tucurú, and Purulhá.

Q'anjob'al: Spoken in Soloma, San Juan Ixcoy, Santa Eulalia, and Barillas (Huehuetenango).

Q'eqchi: Most widely spoken in Alta Verapaz, including Cobán, Panzós, Senahú, San Pedro Carchá, San Juan Chamelco, Lanquín, Chisec, and Cahabón. Other locales include Uspantán (El Quiché department) and parts of Petén and Izabal.

Sakapulteko: Spoken in parts of Sacapulas, El Quiché.

Sipakapense: Spoken in Sipacapa, San Marcos.

Tektiteko: Spoken in parts of Cuilco and Tectitán (Huehuetenango).

Tz'utujil: Spoken in several of the Lake Atitlán villages, including San Lucas Tolimán, San Pablo La Laguna, San Juan La Laguna, San Pedro La Laguna, and Santiago Atitlán.

Uspanteko: Spoken in Uspantán, El Quiché.

injustices of the civil war, adopted the tenets of Liberation Theology, seeking a more just life in the here and now and officially opposing the military's scorched-earth campaign throughout the highlands. Many clergy paid for their beliefs with their lives or were forced into exile. Even after the civil war ended, Bishop Juan Gerardi was murdered in the days after his issuance of a scathing report on civil war atrocities perpetrated mostly by the military. The Church remains a watchdog and defender of the poor, which is evident in the ongoing work of the Archbishop's Human Rights Office.

Although there are many churches throughout the country, the Catholic Church often has trouble finding priests to fill them, a factor that has contributed to the explosive growth of Evangelical Christianity. Pope John Paul II visited Guatemala three times during his term at the helm of the Vatican; the last visit was for the purpose of canonizing Antigua's beloved Hermano Pedro de San José Betancur.

Catholicism can still draw a big crowd, though, most noticeably during Holy Week, with its elaborate processions reenacting Christ's crucifixion, and the annual pilgrimage to Esquipulas on January 16 to pay homage to the Black Christ in the town's basilica.

© AL ARGUETA

The Catholic Church has played an important role in Guatemala since colonial times.

Evangelical Christianity

According to some estimates, a third of Guatemala now claims adherence to Protestantism and, more specifically, Evangelical Christianity. The growth of this sect will become obvious as you travel around the country and hear the sounds of loud evening worship services, known as *cultos,* emanating from numerous churches, particularly in the highlands. The trend toward Evangelical Christianity dates to the aftermath of the 1975 earthquake, which destroyed several villages throughout the highlands. International aid agencies, several of them overtly Christian, rushed in to Guatemala at a time of great need and gained many grateful converts in the process. During the worst of the civil war violence of the 1980s, many Guatemalans sought comfort in the belief of a better life despite the hardships of the present. Other factors making Evangelical Christianity attractive to Guatemalans include the tendency toward

vibrant expressions of faith, spontaneity, and the lack of a hierarchy, which makes spiritual leaders more accessible to common people.

A notorious legacy of Guatemala's trend toward Protestantism was the dictatorship of Efraín Ríos Montt, a prominent member of Guatemala City's Iglesia El Verbo (Church of the Word), who sermonized Guatemalans on subjects including morality, Christian virtues, and the evils of communism via weekly TV broadcasts. Meanwhile, a scorched-earth campaign aimed at exterminating the guerrilla presence raged in the highlands, though violence in the cities was widely curtailed and order somewhat restored. He faces charges of genocide in a Spanish court, though it's doubtful he will ever be brought to justice. Also disturbing was the brief presidency of Jorge Serrano Elías, another self-proclaimed Evangelical now exiled in Panama after he dissolved congress in a failed autocoup, which ended in his ouster a few days later. His government faced widespread corruption charges.

On a more promising note, it is a well-documented fact that some Guatemalan villages have converted to Evangelical Christianity almost in their entirety with astounding results. The town of Almolonga, near Quetzaltenango, is a particular case in point. Alcoholism, which once ran rampant (as in other parts of the highlands), is now virtually unheard of and the city jail has been closed for years. It is hailed as a "miracle city" by Evangelical leaders, who like to point out that it was once a hotbed of cult worship for the folk idol Maximón. The town exports its fantastic fruits and vegetables to El Salvador, including carrots the size of a human arm, making it very prosperous.

Evangelicals these days, while still adhering to the belief in a better afterlife, are also very much focused on making things better in the here and now. There is a growing movement toward producing a generation of morally grounded political leaders with a vision to develop the country along inclusive lines that address Guatemala's substantial needs and challenges, though it remains to be seen if they can overcome the unfortunate legacy handed to them by the substandard Christian leadership experienced by Guatemalans thus far.

LANGUAGE

Guatemala's official language is Spanish, though as mentioned there are 23 other ethnolinguistic groups in this very diverse nation. Guatemalan Spanish is fairly clean and tends to avoid the dropping off of the last syllables in words, a common occurrence in Caribbean Spanish-speaking countries. This makes Guatemalan Spanish particularly easy to learn and understand for foreigners, a fact attested to by the overwhelming number of Spanish-language schools present in many parts of the country, but especially in Antigua and Quetzaltenango. Spanish schools are also present in Cobán, Huehuetenango, Todos Santos, San Andrés, San José (Petén), and Panajachel, to name a few. It's also possible to learn Mayan languages in many of these schools.

ARTS
Literature

Guatemala's first literary figure was Jesuit priest and poet Rafael Landívar (1731-1793). A native of Antigua, his most well-known work is *Rusticatio Mexicano,* a poem describing rural customs of the times. Landívar was forced to leave Guatemala in 1767 when his order was expelled from the Americas by the Spanish Crown. The country's best-known writer is Miguel Ángel Asturias (1899-1974), winner of the 1967 Nobel Prize in literature. His most famous works include *El Señor Presidente* (1946), about the maniacal dictator Manuel Estrada Cabrera, and *Hombres de Maíz* (1949, translated as *Men of Maize*), about the Mayan peasantry. One of the characters in the latter is a guerrilla warrior by the name of Gaspar Ilom, a name that Asturias's son Rodrigo, influenced by his father's writings, would appropriate as a pseudonym while leading one of the guerrilla factions comprising the Guatemalan National Revolutionary Unity (URNG). His other well-known works include *El Papa Verde* (*The Green Pope,* 1954, about the United Fruit Company) and *Weekend en Guatemala* (1968, about the 1954 coup that ousted Jacobo Árbenz Guzmán).

Modern Guatemalan authors of note include Francisco Goldman, author of several novels, including *The Long Night of White Chickens,* which takes place mostly in Guatemala, *The Ordinary Seaman* (1997), and *The Divine Husband* (2004). Arturo Arias is another modern-day author known for having written the screenplay for the movie *El Norte* and the book *After the Bombs,* chronicling the Arbenz period and the aftermath of his overthrow. Víctor Perera has written several excellent books on Guatemalan culture and history, including *Unfinished Conquest* (1993) and *Rites: A Guatemalan Boyhood* (1986).

A FEW *CHAPINISMOS*

A full glossary is found at the end of this book. The following is a listing of a few more commonly used Guatemalan expressions and slang terms.

aguas!: watch out!

a todo mecate: full-speed ahead

babosadas: lies or nonsense

cachito: a little bit

canche: blond or fair-skinned; also was a term used of guerrilla fighters during the civil war

capearse: to play hooky

caquero: arrogant or stuck-up, usually someone of wealth

casaca: tall tales or embellishments

clavos: problems

(tener) conectes: to have influence because of important or powerful friends

cuates: buddies

chapparro: person of short stature

chupar: to drink alcoholic beverages

goma (estar de): to be hungover

güiro: a child

jalón: a lift or ride (in a vehicle)

mango: a handsome man

mordida: bribe

muco: a person of low social class, usually used disdainfully by upper-class Guatemalans in reference to lower classes

pisto: money

salsa: to (mistakenly) think oneself cool and hip

sho (hacer): to be quiet (shut up)

shuco: dirty

shute: nosy

vonós: "let's go," a shortened version of "vámonos"

Visual Arts

Guatemala's rich history in the visual arts dates to pre-Columbian times, with the painting of exquisite murals and the carving of stelae by the Mayans. The colonial period also left a substantial artistic legacy, mostly by anonymous artists. An exception is the work of Thomas de Merlo (1694-1739), whose paintings can still be seen in Antigua's Museo de Arte Colonial. Sculptor Quirio Cataño carved the Black Christ of Esquipulas in 1595, now an object of much veneration for pilgrims from all over Central America.

More recently, Kaqchikel painter Andrés Curruchich (1891-1969) pioneered the "primitivist" style of painting from his hometown in Comalapa, Chimaltenango. The currents of *indigenismo* ran strongly throughout the 20th century and were marked by an often-romanticized portrayal of indigenous culture, as evidenced by the murals found in Guatemala City's Palacio Nacional de la Cultura, which are the work of Alfredo Gálvez Suárez (1899-1946). Also in this vein was sculptor Ricardo Galeotti Torres (1912-1988), whose works include the giant marimba sculpture found in Quetzaltenango and the Tecún Umán statue in the plaza of Santa Cruz del Quiché.

Perhaps Guatemala's best-known visual artist, Carlos Mérida (1891-1984) was a contemporary of Pablo Picasso, whom he met while studying painting in Paris between 1908 and 1914. His *indigenista* art predates the work of Mexican muralists the likes of Diego Rivera by about seven years and sought to unify European modernism with themes more specific to the Americas. Mérida's work exhibits three major stylistic shifts throughout the years: a figurative period from 1907 to 1926, a surrealist phase from the late 1920s to the mid-1940s, and a geometric period from 1950 until his death in 1984. Many of his works can be seen in Guatemala City's Museum of Modern Art, which bears his name. Mérida's murals also grace the walls of several Guatemala City public buildings.

Another artist whose work adorns Guatemala City architecture is sculptor and engineer Efraín Recinos, designer of the city's Centro Cultural Miguel Ángel Asturias. A large Recinos mural composed of blue and green tiles was formerly housed inside La Aurora International Airport but was recently demolished as part of the airport renovation project. The large, white sculptures lining the airport's exterior facade were also created by Recinos and have been restored and incorporated into the terminal's new design.

In March 2007, Guatemala City hosted a sculpture festival with the participation of 12 internationally acclaimed artists working during a two-week period to create unique art pieces from blocks of marble. It was the first event of its kind held in Central America. The sculptures are now part of the city's artistic legacy and can be found along the boulevard connecting the international airport to Bulevar Liberación.

Architecture

In addition to the well-documented architectural legacy of the Mayans, Guatemala is also known for its baroque architecture, found mostly in Antigua and Guatemala City cathedrals and government buildings. This style of architecture is a Spanish adaptation to local conditions, marked by the prevalence of earthquakes, with squat, thick-walled structures designed to weather numerous tremors throughout the years. Architecture in rural towns and villages tends to be rather functional, with a recent trend toward grotesque multistory concrete buildings replacing more traditional construction. Classic forms of rural architecture consist (or consisted) largely of whitewashed adobe houses with red-tile roofs.

Guatemala City has its fair share of assembly-line high-rise condominiums, though it also has some noteworthy modern architecture. If you have an interest in this topic, a recommended book is *Six Architects* (Ange Bourda, 2002), filled with wonderful color photographs chronicling the work of six Guatemala City architects who merged into a single firm and are responsible for several of the city's nicest buildings.

In April 2007 the Parisian Grande Arche de la Défense played host to a fascinating 48-image exhibit by photographer Ange Bourda, which chronicled the rich history of Guatemalan architecture from pre-Columbian times to the present.

Music

Guatemala's national instrument is the marimba, a huge wooden xylophone with probable African origins. You'll often hear marimba in popular tourist regions such as Antigua, where its cheerful notes can be heard emanating from garden courtyards housed in the city's larger hotels. Pre-Columbian musical instruments consisted largely of drums, wooden flutes, whistles, and bone rasps. An excellent place to check out the history and origins of Guatemala's highland Mayan musical traditions is Casa K'ojom, just outside Antigua in Jocotenango.

It's also not uncommon to hear music with Mexican influence in Guatemala, with the occasional mariachi band contracted to liven up a birthday party. Tejano and *ranchera* music can often be heard. You'll also hear American rock bands here and there, sometimes on bus rides, though the sounds favored by bus drivers seem to have gotten stuck somewhere around 1984.

On the Caribbean Coast, the Garífuna population tends to favor the mesmerizing beats of *punta* and reggae, with variations including *punta rock* and *reggaeton,* English-Spanish rap laid over slowed-down Caribbean-style techno and reggae beats.

Grammy award-winning rock musician Ricardo Arjona is Guatemala's best-known international recording artist. He lives in Mexico City. Spanish-language pop and rock are, of course, also widely heard throughout Guatemala.

TV and Cinema

Guatemala has its very own cable TV

channel, Guatevisión, which can be seen in the United States. It features a morning show based in Guatemala City as well as some fairly humorous entertainment programs that provide a glimpse of the nightlife and outdoor recreation scene throughout the country. Guatemala even had a celebrity newscaster of sorts, CNN's former Mexico City bureau chief Harris Whitbeck, who reported events around the world in English and Spanish. One of his more recent projects is a local TV show, *Entrémosle a Guate* (Let's Get in on Guate), with profiles of everyday Guatemalans who make the country a special place. He now has his own production company based out of Miami and is the host of the Spanish version of *The Amazing Race.*

As for movies about Guatemala, *El Norte* (1983, directed by Gregory Nava) is a classic tale of Guatemalan immigrants fleeing the civil war during the 1980s. More recently, in the summer of 2006, Antigua was the scene of on-location shooting for *Looking for Palladin,* a film about a young Hollywood go-getter who finds himself in Guatemala. Many folks in Antigua are hoping the film will open doors for more movies to be filmed in Guatemala.

CRAFTS

Guatemala is world famous for the artistic quality and variety of its crafts, with weaving at the top of the list. Each village has its unique style and you can recognize villagers from a particular location based solely on their traditional attire. Among the most fascinating handwoven pieces are *huipiles,* embroidered blouses worn by highland Mayan women that feature colorful motifs that often include plants, animals, and lightning bolts in a dizzying array of colors. While you are certainly welcome to buy village attire, it's never a good idea to wear it around while in

detail of fine Guatemalan embroidery

Guatemala, as indigenous peoples will find this highly offensive (or downright hilarious, at best). Many people buy *huipiles* to frame and hang as home decor, laying the blouse flat with the large head opening at its center or hanging it from a wooden rod. You can see examples where this has been tastefully done in numerous Antigua boutique hotels.

Jade jewelry mined from local quarries is a popular item in upscale shops in Antigua.

"Primitivist" paintings are popular in the villages of San Pedro and Santiago, on the shores of Lake Atitlán. For wool blankets, check out Momostenango, though you can also find them in markets throughout the country. The best wood carvings are found in the village of El Remate, in the northern Petén department, though traditional wooden ceremonial masks are still an item found exclusively in the Western Highlands.

ESSENTIALS

Getting There

BY AIR

Most international travelers to Guatemala arrive by plane. Several factors work together to make Guatemala more easily, though not always cheaply, accessible in this regard. First, Guatemala has become increasingly popular as a travel destination. Tourism statistics show the country has welcomed more than a million visitors annually since 2004. The Guatemalan government has recognized this and has invested millions of dollars into remodeling the country's two international airports while developing local airports for the creation of a domestic route network. U.S. carriers have stepped up their presence in Guatemala in recent years and are expected to continue this trend, particularly with the vastly improved infrastructure at Guatemala City's La Aurora International Airport and the Mundo Maya Airport in Flores/Tikal.

In addition to increased tourism, more and more Guatemalans have family living in the United States, which means this is easily one of the fastest-growing markets on U.S. carriers' radar screens. As for cost, the market is very elastic. The arrival of a new carrier into

© AL ARGUETA

Guatemala often signals an all-out pricing war, as seen with service start-ups by Delta in 1998 and US Airways in 2005, when flights from the United States to Guatemala hovered around $300 round-trip. Demand quickly catches up with supply, however, and prices double as carriers see little reason to discount flights in a market where planes are already flying full.

The future looks uncertain, however, as airlines attempt to do business amid record-high oil prices. Rising fuel costs have forced airlines to charge for services such as baggage handling, meals, and even seat selection. Airline routes worldwide have been cut in an attempt to streamline operations and reduce operating costs. In 2008, new flights from Mexico City via Interjet and Aeromexico were cut almost as quickly as they were added. U.S. carrier ATA went defunct just days before it was set to begin service to Guatemala City from Miami. The year also saw the departure of U.S. Airways from the Guatemalan market. In 2010, Continental and United Airlines announced a merger, restoring service to Guatemala. The new airline retains the United name and maintains Continental's flight schedules (via Houston and Newark).

As for airfares, the price of an average plane ticket from the United States to Guatemala varies widely depending on route and season, but ranges from about $350 to $750 round-trip. Still, deals can be had if you know where to look and are willing to give up comforts like advance seat selection and ticket changeability. Internet sites offer discounted tickets and air ticket consolidators are worth checking out; a particularly useful tool for comparison shopping is www.kayak.com.

Guatemala has an open-skies agreement with the United States, meaning that any carrier from either country can fly to any point in the other. Guatemala once had an official flag-carrier, Aviateca, but Salvadoran-owned TACA has since absorbed it. Domestic flights between

Flores and Guatemala City are officially operated by Aviateca, but this appears to be a mere formality, as the aircraft livery, ticket jackets, and related travel documents all clearly make it known that you are flying TACA. TACA operates the majority of flights into and out of Guatemala, flying nonstop from a handful of gateway cities in the United States as well as via its hubs in San Salvador and San José, Costa Rica. The U.S. carriers also have a strong presence here. Several Latin American carriers, some of them noteworthy, operate here as well. The only European airline serving Guatemala at this time is Iberia, the Spanish flag-carrier.

When departing on a flight from either of Guatemala's international airports, you will pay a $2.75 security fee in cash prior to passing through the security checkpoint. A $30 departure tax is also collected, but is included in the taxes paid at the time of ticket purchase.

Airports

Most international travelers flying to Guatemala arrive via Guatemala City's **La Aurora International Airport (GUA).** La Aurora could not be more conveniently located for Guatemala City residents, lying in the heart of the city just minutes from the business and hotel district. A recent renovation and expansion brought the once-obsolete La Aurora into the 21st century. The spacious glass-and-steel north and central terminals are vast improvements over La Aurora's former facilities and feature a number of good restaurants and duty-free shops. There's even a club lounge for United and Copa Airlines (Star Alliance) passengers. The flight departure check-in lobby, with a high, angular ceiling somewhat resembling an egg carton, is actually part of the original construction dating back to the 1960s. It was given an updated look and restored to full functionality.

It can be a bit chaotic when exiting La Aurora, as families of arriving Guatemalans

Several airlines fly daily to Guatemala City's La Aurora International Airport.

© AL ARGUETA

tend to load up cars (and sometimes entire buses) to welcome a returning loved one. The same is true for departing family members. Making your way out of the terminal (before merging with the crowds outside), you'll see an INGUAT tourist information kiosk. The English-speaking agents can provide maps and answer basic questions about ground transportation. Taxis and shuttle buses also operate out of kiosks found in the arrival area. A taxi to Zona 10 or Zona 14 costs about $9; trips to Carretera a El Salvador or elsewhere beyond the city limits cost more. Most of the Zona 10 hotels have courtesy shuttles to and from the airport. A shuttle bus to Antigua costs between $12 and $15. Likewise, car rentals can be booked from kiosks inside the airport terminal, located just after clearing customs.

Flores/Tikal (FRS), officially known as **Mundo Maya International Airport,** serves the northern department of Petén and the ruins of Tikal. It now has air conditioning and is a much-improved facility. Flights arrive several times daily from Guatemala City, Cancún, and Belize City. The flight to Flores from the Guatemalan capital takes about 30 minutes. Most travelers arriving here head straight for the ruins of Tikal, about an hour away via numerous minivans, or to the city of Flores, just five minutes away by taxi. A *colectivo* van to Tikal costs about $4. A taxi to Flores costs about $2. Arrival procedures are fairly straightforward thanks to the airport's smaller size.

Flights to Guatemala City

The majority of nonstop flights come from a handful of North American hub cities including Atlanta, Chicago, Dallas/Ft. Worth, Fort Lauderdale, Houston, Los Angeles, Miami, and New York/Newark. San Salvador and Panama City are becoming increasingly important as connecting points for flights from South America on TACA and Copa Airlines, respectively. Madrid holds the distinction of being the sole European city with direct service to Guatemala City via a nonstop flight four times per week on Spanish flag-carrier Iberia.

Among U.S. carriers, **American Airlines** (tel. 800/433-7300 U.S., www.aa.com) flies nonstop three times daily to Guatemala City from Miami and daily nonstop from Dallas/ Ft. Worth. It code shares with British Airways on flights from the U.K. and has excellent European connections of its own.

United Airlines (tel. 800/231-0856 U.S., www.united.com) has three nonstops daily to Guatemala City from Houston Intercontinental (IAH) (with an extra flight on Saturdays) as well as a Saturday-only nonstop flight from New York/Newark which may be flying daily by the time you read this. First Class passengers and United Club members enjoy access to the *Copa Club* lounge, located next to gate 14.

Delta Air Lines (tel. 800/221-1212 U.S., www.delta.com) flies daily from Atlanta and Los Angeles to Guatemala City. Discount carrier **Spirit Airlines** (tel. 800/772-7117 U.S., www.spiritair.com) flies nonstop to Guatemala City from Fort Lauderdale.

Among foreign carriers, **Copa Airlines** (tel. 800/359-2672 U.S., www.copaair.com), the Panamanian flag-carrier, flies nonstop five times daily to Guatemala City from its hub in Panama City, with excellent connections to/from South America, the Caribbean, and Europe. The latter feed into KLM's daily Amsterdam-Panama City service and operate as a codeshare. There are additional flights between Guatemala and Panama stopping in Managua and San José. The airline operates a *Copa Club* lounge in conjunction with United at La Aurora airport and at Panama City's Tocumen airport.

The only nonstop service to Guatemala from Europe is on **Iberia** (www.iberia.com) four times per week (Mon., Tues., Thurs., Sat.) from its hub in Madrid with excellent connections to the rest of the continent. The return flight to Madrid stops in San Salvador, as nonstop flights to Europe from Guatemala City's short, high-altitude runway are a logistical impossibility.

Mexican flag carrier Mexicana went the way of the dodo bird in 2010 but competing carriers AeroMexico and Interjet have stepped in to fill the void in the Mexico City-Guatemala City market. **AeroMexico** (tel. 2278-9488, www.aeromexico.com) flies the route twice daily. Interjet (www.interjet.com) flies once a day.

Salvadoran conglomerate Transportes Aereos del Continente Americano, or **TACA** (tel. 800/400-8222 U.S., www.taca.com), flies daily nonstop to Guatemala City from Miami and Los Angeles with three or four weekly nonstops each from Chicago and Orlando (seasonal). Other nonstops include flights from Mexico City and San Pedro Sula. There are numerous daily flights from TACA's hubs in San Salvador and San José, Costa Rica, with onward connections to/from South America.

Flights to Flores/Tikal

Flights to Flores/Tikal arrive primarily from Guatemala City, Belize City, and Cancún. **TACA** (tel. 800/400-8222 U.S., www.taca.com) operates three daily flights between Guatemala City and Flores using 40-passenger ATR-42 aircraft. **TAG** (800/528-8216 toll-free U.S. or 2332-1897 Guatemala) has a daily flight to Flores from Guatemala City leaving at 6:30 A.M. The return trip from Flores is at 5 P.M. The flight is operated with a 15-seat turboprop.

Tropic Air (tel. 800/422-3435, www.tropic-air.com), a Belizean airline, flies to Flores/Tikal from Belize City twice daily.

BY SEA

Cruise ships dock at Puerto Quetzal, on the Pacific Coast, and Puerto Santo Tomás de Castilla, on the Caribbean side. Cruise lines offer a variety of activities for those wishing to disembark and explore Guatemalan shores, including visits to local resorts and beaches near Santo Tomás and inland trips to Antigua, Tikal, and Lake Atitlán or deep-sea fishing in the Pacific waters. For those wishing not to travel inland, there is not much to see and do in the immediate vicinity of either port of call, although the pier is usually packed with vendors selling everything from bags of Guatemalan coffee to colorful textiles and clothing. A land-based activity close to a port of call worth mentioning is hiking in the Cerro San Gil forest preserve near Santo Tomás de Castilla. Puerto Quetzal boasts a nearby ostrich farm.

Ferry and water-taxi services connect the Guatemalan town of Lívingston with Punta Gorda, Belize (2.5 hours, $35), and Omoa, Honduras (1.25 hours, $16), both offered by Exotic Travel on Tuesdays and Fridays. Transportes El Chato has a daily boat to and from Punta Gorda costing $16 and taking roughly an hour to make the trip. A $10 departure tax applies when leaving Guatemala by sea.

If traveling to Guatemala on your own boat, you will most likely arrive on the Caribbean side and will need to check in with immigration officials in Lívingston before sailing up the Río Dulce, the most popular route with boaters.

BY RIVER

The most popular route into Guatemala by river is via the Usumacinta River, which divides Mexico and Guatemala. Boats travel from the Mexican town of Frontera Corozal to La Técnica and Bethel, in Guatemala's northern Petén department. This is the route of choice for travelers wanting to combine visits to the Mexican sites of Palenque and Yaxchilán with trips to the various Petén ruins. Yaxchilán lies on the Mexican bank of the Usumacinta and is highly recommended. Buses from Palenque to the Mexican border are available via Transportes Montebello and Autotransportes Rio Chancala. From La Técnica, buses leave

for the Petén departmental capital of Flores at 4 A.M. and 11 A.M. ($4, five hours). Buses leave Bethel for Flores at 5 A.M., noon, 2 P.M., and 4 P.M., cost $4, and take four hours to make the trip. Package trips encompassing bus and boat transportation are available from various travel agencies in Palenque and Flores for travel in either direction for about $35.

It is also possible to travel from Benemérito, south of Frontera Corozal, up the Río La Pasión to Sayaxché, Guatemala, and via the Río San Pedro between La Palma and El Naranjo. These routes lack scheduled passenger service and are not recommended as they are increasingly being used as transshipment points by the growing drug and illegal immigrant trade between Petén and Mexico.

BY LAND

Many travelers enter Guatemala by bus, as part of larger explorations encompassing neighboring countries. If traveling by car or bus, try to make the border crossing as early in the day as possible, as there are few serviceable hotels and restaurants in border towns and they are notorious for their seedy atmosphere. Onward bus service tends to wind down further into the day, so try to get a move on while you can.

Driving from the United States

When I was 10 years old, my parents moved my family to Guatemala from New Jersey. A year later, we took a trip back north with the mission of driving our Toyota van, previously left in the care of friends, down to Guatemala. I don't remember much about the trip, quite honestly; just a lot of highways, countless hours in a van with my family, a diet of fast food, and nights spent in roadside motels. Once we crossed the border into Mexico, I do remember staying at some pleasant hotels where we would relax in swimming pools after a long day of driving.

The trip also served as a good lesson in geo-politics, as the wealth disparities between the United States and Mexico became read-ily apparent as soon as we crossed the bor-der. Another oddity was the unavailability of unleaded fuel in Mexico in 1986, which caused our van to make a loud clickety-clack noise during our entire run through Mexico. I remember Guatemala felt somewhat more civilized than our northern neighbor simply because we had gas stations other than Pemex and (gasp) unleaded fuel.

Many folks make the overland trip to Guatemala. The country's location in the northernmost reaches of Central America keeps border crossings to a minimum. Rest assured, unleaded fuel is now available in Mexico. The advent of the Internet has also made it easy to find information for planning your road trip.

Most people cross into Mexico from the United States via Brownsville and then take the route through Mexico along the Pacific Coast. You can also travel via Mexico City or along the Atlantic side, but the Mexican capital's traffic and the inferior roads on the Atlantic side make the route less desirable. You'll need a tourist visa ($25) or a *trans-migrante* visa to travel through Mexico, but many experienced road-trippers discourage getting the *transmigrante* visa, deeming it unnecessary and more difficult to process. For Mexican vehicle insurance, some travel-ers have recommended Sanborn's Insurance (www.sanbornsinsurance.com). More de-tailed information for planning the drive to Guatemala is available in the *Gringo's Guide to Driving Through Mexico and Central America* (www.drivemeloco.com).

In Guatemala, you will also find many peo-ple make a living from bringing used American cars into the country, known as *vehículos roda-dos,* and then selling them locally.

If you're just driving a car to Guatemala but don't plan to leave it or sell it there, you'll need to have the following documents with you to get the car into the country:

- Passport
- Driver's license
- Vehicle registration
- Vehicle title
- Photocopies of all the above

Be aware that you must leave the country with the vehicle you originally entered with. In terms of fees and paperwork for getting your vehicle into the country, you'll need to get a tourist per-mit ($1.50), a vehicle entry form (RP-131) and sticker ($5) and, sometimes, fumigation ($3). The vehicle entry sticker is valid for 30 days (no extensions) and will be marked "SAT," which stands for Superintendencia de Administración Tributaria. This is the Guatemalan equivalent of an IRS/customs hybrid. After you've presented all the necessary paperwork, SAT agents will look through your car and you may be required to wait a few hours while your vehicle awaits processing.

It is at this point where most foreigners have issues with the entry process, since you've al-ready presented all the necessary documents and are mentally ready to be on your way. While an opening exists for corrupt govern-ment officials to collect bribes in an attempt to expedite your claim, SAT has made seri-ous inroads in recent years to reduce waiting times for customs transactions and has gener-ally done quite well at cracking down on cor-rupt officials. In June 2008, 24 SAT officials at the El Carmen border were relieved of their duties after undercover *Siglo XXI* newspaper re-porters revealed they were collectively charging about $8,000 a day in illegal processing fees.

Be patient and you'll soon be on your way. Also be advised that, once in Guatemala, you may run into military checkpoints a few kilo-meters down the road from the border cross-ing. If you are flagged down to stop, present all the required documents and be courteous and friendly.

From Mexico

The main border crossings on the Pacific flatlands are Ciudad Hidalgo/Tecún Umán and Talismán/El Carmen, near Tapachula, Mexico. On the Pan-American Highway, the border crossing is at Ciudad Cuauhtemoc/La Mesilla between Comitán, Mexico, and Huehuetenango, Guatemala. Many travelers recommend this last route as the best entry point into Guatemala from Mexico when traveling in your own vehicle. All of these border towns have frequent bus service to nearby cities within both countries.

There is direct bus service to Flores from Chetumal on Linea Dorada (www.tikalmayanworld.com) and San Juan Travel (tel. 7926-0041 or 5461-6010). Both services stop in Belize City en route with a total trip duration of about eight hours.

There is now an official border crossing at El Ceibo and a road connecting Mexico and Guatemala. This border crossing has essentially replaced the water route via El Naranjo on the Rio San Pedro. Be advised: On the Mexican side, the vehicle import/export desk is closed on Mondays.

From Belize

The Belize border crossing into Guatemala is at Benque Viejo del Carmen/Melchor de Mencos. There is twice-daily bus service from Belize City to Flores via Linea Dorada (www.tikalmayanworld.com). The trip lasts 4-5 hours and costs $15. San Juan Travel (tel. 7926-0041 or 5461-6010) also has a daily bus covering the route.

A less expensive option is to take Novelo's or Batty's buses from Belize City to the border and make onward connections to other points in Guatemala on frequent buses and minibuses from Melchor de Mencos.

From Honduras

The main border crossings are at El Florido (between Copán Ruinas, Honduras, and Chiquimula, Guatemala), Agua Caliente (between Nueva Ocotepeque, Honduras, and Esquipulas, Guatemala), and Corinto (between Omoa, Honduras, and Puerto Barrios, Guatemala). There are shuttle mini-buses running between Copán, Guatemala City, and Antigua, as well as first-class bus service to Guatemala City from the main Honduran cities. Hedman Alas (www.hedmanalas.com) has daily service to Guatemala City via the El Florido border from Copán, San Pedro Sula, Tegucigalpa, and La Ceiba.

From El Salvador

El Salvador's numerous borders with Guatemala are at Las Chinamas/Valle Nuevo (Highway CA-8), La Hachadura/Ciudad Pedro de Alvarado on Pacific Coast Highway (CA-2), San Cristóbal/San Cristóbal on the Pan-American Highway (CA-1), and Anguiatu/Anguiatu (Highway CA-10). Several bus lines operate service between Guatemala City and San Salvador, mostly via Las Chinamas, including Pullmantur (www.pullmantur.com).

To and From Points South

Ticabus (www.ticabus.com) connects Guatemala City to San Salvador, Managua, San José, and Panama City, taking several days to make the trip and stopping in the listed capitals along the way. A one-way ticket from Guatemala City to San José, Costa Rica, costs about $50.

Getting Around

BY AIR

The only scheduled domestic service within Guatemala is between Guatemala City and Flores, although ongoing improvements to local infrastructure at many smaller airports may mean a small network of local flights may soon be up and running. Some of the flights to and from Flores operate using smaller aircraft, though the largest bird on this route nowadays is the 40-seat ATR-42. Airfares for this domestic service have recently skyrocketed and are surprisingly expensive, particularly when taking into account the short distance involved in flying within Guatemala.

All of the domestic carriers flying out of Guatemala City operate from their private hangars, located on the east side of the runway, opposite the main terminal building. The only airline operating its domestic service from the main terminal at La Aurora airport is TACA.

New domestic airports with passenger terminals are either complete or nearing completion in Huehuetenango, Quetzaltenango, Puerto San José, Coatepeque, and San Marcos. Plans call for terminals at the Pacific Coast leisure destination of Retalhuleu and the existing paved runway at Puerto Barrios. Cobán has a functional airstrip, though there is no scheduled service. Flights from Guatemala City to the above destinations may become a reality once the terminals are complete and investors make inroads into a market with certain potential. During the late 1990s, TACA subsidiary Inter operated domestic air service between Guatemala City and Cobán, Quetzaltenango, Huehuetenango, and Puerto Barrios.

BY LAND
Buses and Shuttle Buses

Most travelers get around Guatemala by bus or shuttle bus. The majority of inter- and intracity buses are "chicken buses," as travelers have dubbed them, recycled U.S. school buses painted in lively colors. Cargo and carry-on baggage often consists of live animals, hence the name. Please be aware that robberies, including pickpocketing and armed hijacking, are increasingly common on these inexpensive public buses serving the interior. The U.S. State Department Consular Information Sheet cites the death of over 100 bus drivers and passengers in armed robberies in 1996. Chicken buses are also poorly maintained and frequently involved in traffic accidents in which the bus plunges into a ravine or makes a blind pass into a head-on collision. For the intrepid, the chicken bus is still an easy way to see Guatemala and get to virtually any part of the country cheaply.

Tourist shuttle buses plying the main tourist routes, though more expensive, have become increasingly popular for safety reasons and are highly recommended. Additionally, shuttle buses sometimes offer door-to-door service. Recommended shuttle buses are ATITRANS, Turansa, and Grayline Tours.

Also reliable are first-class buses that run between Guatemala City and major cities such as Quetzaltenango, Huehuetenango, Puerto Barrios, Cobán, and Flores. Prices are comparable to shuttle buses, but service is aboard large luxury coaches, often with restrooms and onboard food service.

Pickups and Minivans

Another common form of getting around, particularly in remote rural areas with infrequent bus service is via (roughly) scheduled service aboard pickup trucks. Minivans have also replaced cumbersome chicken buses in many rural areas with poor roads.

Rental Cars

Rental cars are plentiful in Guatemala and can be rented in Guatemala City, Panajachel, Antigua, Quetzaltenango, Cobán, and Flores. Some local agencies are also available. There's nothing like the freedom of having your own wheels when exploring new surroundings. Renting a car allows you to go wherever Guatemala's roads will take you. With that in mind, it's probably best to rent a four-wheel-drive vehicle. The only exception is if you plan to stick to urban areas such as Guatemala City and Antigua or along the Pan-American Highway. A compact car will run you about $300 a week, while a four-wheel-drive vehicle can cost as much as $400-600 a week. You might find better deals online. It sometimes pays to reserve something through an online booking service and then call around locally to get the best rates and comparison shop. Most cars in Guatemala are stick shift, with automatic transmission often costing a bit more.

If your credit card company doesn't offer adequate insurance coverage, make sure to purchase additional insurance. Coverage provided by credit cards such as Visa and American Express usually doesn't apply if you go "off-road," which you likely will. Coverage varies from one company to the next, but usually excludes personal liability (damage to property or other vehicles) and theft. If you stick to the basic coverage offered by the car rental agency, your credit card will have to cover outrageous deductibles, often in the vicinity of $750-1,500. Purchasing full coverage from the rental agency can run $25 a day and really adds to the final bill, but some find it a small price to pay for peace of mind.

Before leaving the car rental lot, make sure to check the car over, paying attention to every minute detail. Rental agents will go over the car with you and document any scratches, dings, and dents. They'll inspect it again when you return the vehicle. Any new damage (or

RENTAL CARS

The following U.S. car-rental agencies are represented in Guatemala and have kiosks at La Aurora International Airport:

Advantage (tel. 2332-7525 Guatemala City or 800/777-5500 toll-free U.S., www.advantagerentacar.com)

Alamo (tel. 5219-7469 Guatemala City or 800/462-5266 toll-free U.S., www.alamo.com)

Avis (tel. 2331-0017 Guatemala City or 800/331-1212 toll-free U.S., www.avis.com)

Budget (tel. 2332-7744 Guatemala City or 800/472-3325 toll-free U.S., www.budget.com or www.budgetguatemala.com.gt)

Dollar (tel. 2331-7185 Guatemala City or 800/800-4000 toll-free U.S., www.dollar.com)

Hertz (tel. 2470-3800 Guatemala City or 800/654-3001 toll-free U.S., www.hertz.com)

Thrifty (tel. 2379-8747 Guatemala City or 800/847-4389 toll-free U.S., www.thrifty.com)

previously undocumented damage) might cost you dearly.

Never leave a vehicle parked on the street overnight and never leave personal belongings inside an unattended vehicle.

Taxis

Taxicabs are available in almost any town or city. In smaller towns, the best way to find a taxi is in the central square, or parque central. In Guatemala City, taxis are available at the Zona 10 hotels, shopping malls, or (as a last resort) can be hailed from street corners. It's always best to call a cab, as certain city zones get more taxi traffic and not all companies are reliable. Highly recommended is **Taxis Amarillo Express** (tel. 2332-1515); you must call for a cab and will need an exact address for pickup. They are one of the only companies to use taxi meters. As a final word of caution, the U.S. Embassy discourages travelers from hailing cabs off the street in Guatemala City.

© AL ARGUETA

There are many ways to get around Guatemala.

In smaller towns and villages, you'll also find the Asian-style *tuk-tuks,* or motorized rickshaws powered by a motorcycle engine. These offer a lower-cost alternative to standard taxicabs and are great if you're traveling without luggage over short distances.

If you need to get around for days at a time, it might be worth renting a taxi by the day or week. This is particularly the case in Guatemala City, where there are many neighborhoods tucked into the varied terrain and certainly some places you'll wish to avoid. Many taxi drivers are willing to negotiate a daily or hourly rate, somewhere in the vicinity of $10 an hour or $75 a day. You can often get a really good deal if you negotiate for multiple days. Most Guatemalan taxi drivers are friendly and helpful, making great sources of conversation to gauge opinions on issues of daily life for the average Guatemalan. It seems almost everyone has a friend or a friend of a friend

who is a taxi driver, and they may be able to recommend someone to you. I can personally vouch for the services of **Yosaray Ramírez** (tel. 4159-5152, yosarayramirez777@hotmail.com). Yosaray speaks some English and has lived in the U.S. He is also a great option for trips to Guatemala's interior.

Hitchhiking

Though hitchhiking in its traditional form is not widely practiced in Guatemala, a local adaptation exists in remote rural areas where there is limited or nonexistent bus service. People with pickup trucks will often give you a ride in the back of their trucks. The fee is usually nominal, if anything at all.

If you're driving a rental car, you may be tempted to pick up hitchhikers as local people always appreciate a ride. It's a catch-22, however, as hitchhikers often don't know how to exit a vehicle and will sometimes jump from the back of a pickup truck while it's still in motion. I've heard horror stories of villagers suddenly turning on the driver of the vehicle (as if it were his or her fault) for the injured person's predicament. It's up to you whether or not to pick up hitchhikers but at least now you know what to expect.

Boat

In some areas, getting around by boat is the most practical option. This is particularly the case on the shores of Lake Atitlán, where regular ferry service and small motorboats make their way across the lake from Panajachel to the outlying villages. Boat service is also a major form of transportation in coastal areas, particularly in Izabal department along the Río Dulce, on Lake Izabal, and in coastal areas such as Lívingston and Puerto Barrios. On the Pacific side, motorboats traverse the Canal de Chiquimulilla, which separates the Pacific seaboard from the Guatemalan mainland along much of the coast.

HIGHWAY OVERVIEW

Roads in Guatemala are surprisingly good in some places, particularly on well-trodden paths like the Pan-American Highway. They are much better, overall, than the roads in neighboring Belize and Costa Rica. Roads in and around tourist areas are generally well marked, some courtesy of the Guatemala state tourism agency, INGUAT (Instituto Guatemalteco de Turismo). If while driving, you come across a large tree branch in the middle of the road, be prepared to stop. This is Guatemalans' way of officially signaling that danger lies ahead, usually in the form of a car stopped near the side of the road. Whether it be by bus or by car, do not travel on rural highways in Guatemala after dark.

Guatemala has several main highways. The **Pan-American Highway** (CA-1), also known as the Interamericana, runs from the Mexican border at La Mesilla through much of the Western Highlands, to Guatemala City and east to El Salvador at San Cristóbal border. This is the road taken (at least for much of the journey) from Guatemala City to many of the main travel destinations, including La Antigua, Lake Atitlán, Quetzaltenango, and Huehuetenango. CA-1 has been expanded to four lanes from Guatemala City all the way to the Cuatro Caminos junction near Quetzaltenango.

The **Pacific Coast Highway** (CA-2) crosses the Pacific slope from the Mexican border at Tecún Umán all the way to Ciudad Pedro de Alvarado and El Salvador. A new, wider Pacific highway is in the planning stages.

Highway CA-9 runs from the Pacific Coast to Guatemala City, encompassing the country's only toll road: a good, fast *autopista,* or freeway. From Guatemala City, the highway heads east to Puerto Barrios and is being widened to four lanes from the capital to El Rancho Junction. CA-14 branches north from El Rancho into the departments of Baja and Alta Verapaz.

Continuing east along CA-9, the next junction is at Río Hondo, where CA-10 branches southeast to Zacapa and Chiquimula before linking up to eastbound CA-11 for Copán, Honduras. Back on the main branch of CA-9, CA-13 is the designation given to the road branching off at La Ruidosa junction, just before Puerto Barrios, heading north to Río Dulce and continuing to Petén. It arrives in Flores and then branches eastward to the Belize border at Melchor de Mencos.

A road crossing the country from Izabal department west all the way to Huehuetenango, called the *Franja Transversal del Norte,* was under construction at the time of publication. Also in the works is an *Anillo Departamental* allowing traffic between CA-1 and eastbound Highway CA-9 to bypass traffic-congested Guatemala City altogether.

TRAVEL COMPANIES

There is a relative absence of package tours from the United States to Guatemala, particularly as compared to Belize and Costa Rica. Still, there are a few good companies to recommend for travelers who want to visit Guatemala on a package tour or need the services of an established tour operator. This is certainly not an exhaustive list, but the following come highly recommended for the quality of service and established experience.

Cayaya Birding

Bird-watchers will want to contact German-owned Cayaya Birding (tel. 5308-5160, www.cayaya-birding.com) for information on Guatemala's birding hot spots and to arrange trip details, including full itineraries. Knut Eisermann, an ornithologist living in Guatemala since 1997, runs the company.

Clark Tours

Highly recommended is Clark Tours (tel. 800/707-5275 U.S., www.saca.com/guat/

intro.html), represented in the United States by Massachusetts-based SACA Tours. The company, established by an American living in Guatemala, has been around for 80 years. You will probably come across the company's large, luxurious tour buses more than once during your travels in Guatemala. Clark Tours has a variety of established itineraries and can also tailor custom itineraries to suit the needs of the most discriminating travelers. Clark Tours is also the local representative for American Express Travel Services and has offices in many Guatemala City luxury hotels, including the Barceló, Westin Camino Real, and Holiday Inn.

No Limit Expeditions

Based in La Antigua Guatemala, No Limit Expeditions (tel. 720/295-4880, www.nolimitx.com) runs recommended adventure four-wheel-drive expeditions to far-flung locales deep in the rainforests of northern Guatemala and Belize aboard Land Rovers. Accommodations include comfortable jungle camps and luxury eco-lodges. The "Ruins and Rainforests" expedition includes some of the greatest Maya cities (Tikal, Uaxactun, Caracol, Yaxha) and seldom-visited locales such as the murals at San Bartolo. They also run expeditions to El Mirador and the Maya Highlands.

George's Travel Club of Guatemala

George's Travel Club of Guatemala (tel. 202/436-9983 U.S., 502/5175-9974 Guatemala, www.georges-travelclub.com) is an Antigua-based travel company owned by a U.S. expat. Well-thought travel itineraries include luxurious accommodations, four-wheel-drive road trips, sea fishing, kayaking, volcano climbs, and exploring Mayan ruins.

Maya Expeditions

Rated one of the top eco-outfitters in the world by *Condé Nast Traveler,* Maya Expeditions (13 Avenida 14-70, Zona 10, tel. 2363-4955, www.mayaexpeditions.com) is a Guatemala-based adventure-travel outfitter that comes highly recommended for its adventurous itineraries, particularly white-water rafting. Company founder Tammy Ridenour, a Colorado native, started the company in 1987 and is credited with pioneering ecotourism in Guatemala. Among the company's various offerings, which also include archaeological and cultural tourism, is a trip retracing the steps of the wildly popular *Survivor Guatemala* television series.

Play It Forward Adventures

Combining elements of volunteer opportunities and adventure travel, Minneapolis-based PLAY it Forward Adventures (tel. 651/493-8817 U.S., www.pifadventures.com) offers rugged, fun-filled, 10-day itineraries that include mountain biking rural areas around Antigua, visiting a Mayan women's cooperative, kayaking the waters of Lake Atitlán, hiking a "City of Stairs," building homes for families, and relaxing at an avocado farm and ecolodge just outside La Antigua.

Visas and Officialdom

TOURIST REQUIREMENTS

Citizens of the United States traveling to Guatemala will need a U.S. passport valid for at least six months beyond their intended length of stay and ticket documents for onward or return travel. Stays of up to 90 days are permitted without a visa. The United States now requires passports as the sole travel document for all travelers returning to the United States by air.

Requirements for other countries, including Australia, Canada, The European Union, Israel, Japan, New Zealand, and Switzerland include a passport valid for at least three months beyond their intended length of stay and ticket documents for onward or return travel. Entry is limited to 30 days. Extensions are allowed by going through the local Migración (Immigration) office.

Foreigners are required to carry their passport (or a clear photocopy) with them at all times. If you are driving a rental car and happen to be stopped, the police officer will ask for your passport in addition to your driver's license.

In June 2006, Guatemala entered into an agreement with El Salvador, Honduras, and Nicaragua known as the **CA-4 Border Control Agreement.** Under its terms, citizens of these four countries may travel freely across each other's land borders without completing entry and exit formalities at Immigration checkpoints. United States citizens and other eligible foreign nationals who legally enter any of the four member countries may also travel within the CA-4 without obtaining additional visas or tourist entry permits for the other three countries. Immigration officials at the first port of entry determine the length of stay, up to a maximum of 90 days. Foreign tourists who wish to remain in the four-country region beyond the length of stay initially granted for their visit will need to request a one-time extension from local Immigration authorities or travel to a country outside the CA-4 region and then reenter.

For visa extensions, head to the Departamento de Extranjería (7a Avenida 1-17 Zona 4, INGUAT Building, Guatemala City, tel. 2361-8476, 8 A.M.-2 P.M. Mon.-Fri.). You'll need to show evidence of financial solvency as well as an onward ticket.

CUSTOMS

Foreign travelers to Guatemala may import the following items duty free: personal effects, including clothing, jewelry, medicine, photography and video equipment, sports equipment, a personal computer, a wheelchair if the traveler has disabilities, 500 grams of tobacco, and three liters of alcoholic beverages. INGUAT can provide assistance to professional photographers and videographers needing to bring in large amounts of equipment.

Recreation

PARKS AND PROTECTED AREAS

Guatemala has more than 90 protected areas encompassing about 28 percent of the country's total land area. Among the different types of protected areas are biosphere reserves, national parks, biotopes, natural monuments, wildlife refuges, and private nature reserves. Several of these are encompassed within larger areas, as is the case with the national parks and biotopes making up the larger Maya Biosphere Reserve. Most of Guatemala's protected areas, including the biosphere reserves, have been created since 1990. All of Guatemala's volcanoes are protected areas. There are also laws in effect to protect endangered wildlife species; among these are Guatemala's big cats and parrots.

The National Protected Areas Council (CONAP) is the entity charged with administering Guatemala's protected areas. It was created in 1990, along with the National Environmental Commission (CONAMA), which oversees broader environmental matters and was replaced in 2000 by the Ministry of the Environment and Natural Resources (MARN). CONAP has been historically underfunded and understaffed, leaving few resources with which to protect vast areas of land from invasion. Private conservation groups have stepped in to assist CONAP in its mandate and there are now several parks coadministered or primarily administered by private organizations. A specially trained police force began operating in Guatemala's protected areas in 2005, particularly in the Maya Biosphere Reserve, aided by M-16s and AK-47s to combat well-armed timber and wildlife poachers. All the parks have at least rudimentary ranger stations. In an ongoing effort to attract more park visitation, many have excellent facilities for guest accommodations and well-marked trails.

Biosphere Reserves

Privately managed by conservation group Defensores de la Naturaleza, **Sierra de las Minas Biosphere Reserve** is a vast, 583,000-acre mountain park encompassing a diverse variety of ecosystems, including cloud forests harboring several species of endemic conifers, as well as tropical moist and rainforests. The peaks of Sierra de las Minas surpass 3,000 meters (9,800 feet) in elevation and are home to healthy populations of quetzals and jaguars, among other exotic animals. Sixty-two permanent streams have their source in the upper slopes of the biosphere reserve, making it an important watershed supplying the Motagua and Polochic Rivers. Together with the adjacent Bocas del Polochic Wildlife Refuge, the parks account for 80 percent of Guatemala's biodiversity.

The four-million-acre **Maya Biosphere Reserve** is composed of Tikal National Park, Laguna del Tigre National Park, Mirador-Dos Lagunas-Rio Azul National Park, Sierra del Lacandón National Park, Biotopo El Zotz-San Miguel La Palotada, Yaxhá-Nakum-Naranjo Natural Monument, and multiple-use and buffer zones. This large swath of land encompasses roughly a third of the Petén department and is Guatemala's last hope for preserving a sizable part of the Petén forests. Contiguous with large parks in neighboring Mexico and Belize, it is part of the largest protected tropical forest in Mesoamerica. The various parks are protected, on paper at least, from all human activity, though a sizable multiple-use zone exists in large areas of the park, permitting sustainable extraction of forest products such as *xate* palm and chicle, oil drilling (present before the park's creation), and community forestry concessions. Standing between the core zones and the deforestation characterizing much of the

Birds abound in the wetlands of Bocas del Polochic Wildlife Refuge.

© AL ARGUETA

rest of Petén is an ever-shrinking buffer zone increasingly porous to the advance of the agricultural frontier. The individual parks making up the biosphere reserve are covered here in their respective sections.

National Parks

Tikal National Park, the oldest and best known of Guatemala's national parks, was created in 1956 and declared a UNESCO World Heritage Site in 1979. It encompasses 222 square miles of primary tropical forest and protects a vast array of wildlife, as well as harboring the remains of one of the Mayan civilization's greatest cities. Tikal is understandably high on the list of priorities for any visitor to Guatemala and shouldn't be missed.

Laguna del Tigre National Park is a vast park on the northwestern corner of Petén encompassing important wetlands, the largest in Central America. It also contains the only remaining populations of scarlet macaws in Guatemala, which are being protected via ongoing conservation efforts at a biological research station. Oil drilling, present before the park's creation, continues inside the reserve, despite protests from environmental groups and its having been declared a violation of the park's intended use. Also going on inside the park are the clandestine activities of loggers, wildlife poachers, drug traffickers, and smugglers of illegal immigrants across the border to Mexico. The western border with Mexico running along the park's boundaries has also become permeable to incursions from Mexican peasants, who have made a once razor-sharp border between the two countries look more like patchwork. Archaeologists working in these parts enter under the escort of heavily armed guards. Visitors to this park should limit their activities to those centered around the Scarlet Macaw Biological Research Station, as the current lawless conditions prevent my recommending more in-depth explorations of this wild frontier.

PROTECTED AREAS
OF GUATEMALA

MEXICO

BELIZE

HONDURAS

EL SALVADOR

Mirador-Río Azul
National Park

El Zotz–San Miguel
La Palotada
Biotope

**Laguna Del Tigre
National Park**

**Tikal
National
Park**

Yaxhá–Nakum–Naranjo
Natural Monument

⊕ Belmopan

**Sierra del Lacandón
National Park**

★ Cerro Cahuí
Biotope

Lake
Petén Itzá

**Maya
Mountains–Chiquibul
National Park**

**Parque Nacional
El Rosario**

Ceibal Natural
★ Monument

Dos Pilas Cultural Monument

Petexbatún
★ Wildlife Refuge

Aguateca Cultural Monument ★

**Laguna Lachuá
National Park**

Punta de Manabique
Wildlife
Refuge

**Lanquín Caves
National Park**

Biotopo Chocón
Machacas

**Parque Nacional
Las Victorias**

P.N. Río Dulce

Lake Izabal

Reserva Protectora
de Manantiales
Cerro San Gil

Semuc Champey
Natural Monument

Bocas del Polochic
Wildlife Refuge

Biotopo Mario
Dary Rivera

Sierra de las Minas
Biosphere Reserve

**Parque Nacional
Riscos De Momostenango**

★ Monumento
Cultural
Quiriguá

Zona de Usos Múltiples
Cuenca de Atitlán

Monumento
Cultural
★ Iximché

Parque Regional
Laguna de Chicabal ★

Lake
Atitlán

⊕ Guatemala City

Reserva Natural Privada
Manchón Guamuchal ★

**Parque Nacional
Naciones Unidas**

Área de Protección
Especial Takalik Abaj ★

**Pacaya Volcano
National Park**

Biotopo
Monterrico–Hawaii

San Salvador
⊕

PACIFIC OCEAN

0   40 mi
0   40 km

© AVALON TRAVEL

SAFETY IN THE MAYA BIOSPHERE RESERVE

Potential travelers to Guatemala's Maya Biosphere Reserve are urged to contact one of the conservation groups managing the individual parks before planning a visit, so as to ascertain current safety conditions. As conservationists and archaeologists working in the field can attest, there are too many illegal activities perpetrated by heavily armed men, and far too many stories of run-ins with them, to be out running around in these parts oblivious to the potential dangers. That said, some well-established parks such as Tikal and Yaxhá can be considered generally safe, along with some well-established ecotourism circuits in the Maya Biosphere Reserve, including the Scarlet Macaw Trail, trips to El Zotz-San Miguel La Palotada, and treks to El Mirador.

Sierra del Lacandón National Park is a densely forested, rugged mountain park said to harbor one of the largest populations of jaguars in all of Central America as well as an incredible degree of biodiversity. Hidden in the forests are the remains of several Mayan sites, the most important of which is Piedras Negras, deep inside the park along the Usumacinta River, which marks the western border with Mexico. The park is privately administered by Fundación Defensores de la Naturaleza. In June 2006, together with The Nature Conservancy, it completed the purchase of 31,000 hectares (77,000 acres) of privately owned land in the core zone of Sierra del Lacandón. There are a number of ranger stations inside the park, the most prominent of which is at Piedras Negras.

A large park in the northern section of the Maya Biosphere Reserve near the Mexican border, **Mirador-Dos Lagunas-Río Azul National Park** protects vast expanses of tropical forests and the remains of several Mayan cities.

Among the most impressive ruins are those at El Mirador, including El Tigre temple, which is 18 stories high with a base the size of three football fields. Other sites inside the park include Río Azul and Nakbé, visible from the top of El Mirador's massive temples. Access to the park is by foot, a full day's walk from the village of Carmelita, or helicopter.

Laguna Lachuá National Park consists of a circular lagoon in the Ixcán jungle west of Cobán surrounded by 14,500 hectares of tropical forest and several miles of hiking trails. The karst limestone nature of this placid pool makes it a very attractive turquoise. A high concentration of mahogany trees in the surrounding forests has made it vulnerable to clandestine logging.

One of Guatemala's oldest protected areas encompassing the watershed of its namesake river connecting Lake Izabal with the Caribbean Sea, **Río Dulce National Park** covers 7,200 hectares along its 30-kilometer-long course. In many places, the banks of the river are shrouded in dense tropical forest punctuated at one point by a large canyon with high rock faces.

Natural Monuments

Television reality-show aficionados might recall **Yaxhá-Nakum-Naranjo Natural Monument** as the setting for *Survivor Guatemala*, filmed here during the summer of 2005. The park encompasses the ruins of three Mayan cities set amid dense tropical forest adjacent to Tikal National Park. Also in the park is Yaxhá Lagoon, with its healthy numbers of crocodiles.

The site of **Semuc Champey Natural Monument** is high in the Alta Verapaz mountains, where the Rio Cahabón flows into a giant cave before reemerging a few hundred feet downstream. Atop the churning turmoil is a natural bridge holding a splendid series of turquoise limestone pools surrounded by tropical forest. It is probably Guatemala's finest swimming hole.

Biotopes

Guatemala's biotopes are administered by **CECON** (Avenida La Reforma 0-63 Zona 10, Guatemala City, tel. 2361-5450 or 2331-0904), the Center for Conservation Studies of Guatemala's San Carlos University (USAC). The biotopes are the brainchild of former USAC Dean Mario Dary Rivera, who was murdered when the establishment of the Quetzal Biotope in Alta Verapaz conflicted with local lumber interests. The biotopes were created with the protection and study of a particular animal species in mind. Biotopes protect sea turtles on the Pacific Coast, manatees in the Izabal region, and bats in the Petén forests, among others.

Biotopo Mario Dary Rivera, also known as the *Biotopo del Quetzal* (Quetzal Biotope), is a cloud forest preserve conveniently situated along the road to Cobán near the village of Purulhá, in Baja Verapaz department. It covers 1,022 hectares with ranges in elevation up to 2,300 meters (7,500 feet). In the early morning, it is easily one of the best places to see Guatemala's national bird, the resplendent quetzal. The cloud forest vegetation consists largely of conifers, broadleaf trees, orchids, mosses, ferns, and bromeliads. There is an excellent network of nature trails, some of which lead to waterfalls and excellent views of the surrounding areas. Other amenities include information and visitor centers, a store, a cafeteria, showers, and cooking facilities. A variety of accommodations are found nearby.

On Guatemala's Pacific Coast, **Biotopo Monterrico-Hawaii** was designated for the protection of Guatemala's endangered sea turtles, which come to lay their eggs on its black sandy beaches. Between May and September, local residents are actively involved in collecting eggs for hatching at a local nursery in exchange for being allowed to keep part of the booty. After incubation, the hatchlings are released with the help of tourists, who jump at the opportunity to hold one of the tiny hatchlings in hand before sending them on their journey across the sand and into the sea. Monterrico is a popular beach with Guatemalans and foreigners alike. Nearby Hawaii is substantially quieter. The park also protects important mangrove forests and marshes in addition to several species of plants and animals. There is also an iguana-breeding program at the site.

Chocón Machacas Biotope, within Río Dulce National Park, encompasses 7,600 hectares and was created with the protection of the manatee in mind, though studies suggest very few of these creatures remain anywhere in Guatemala. The park is in an area known as El Golfete and features old-growth forests, flooded forests, mangrove swamps, canals, and lagoons. In addition to manatees, the park also harbors important populations of crocodiles, otters, and jungle cats.

"Zotz" means "bat" in Mayan dialects, and the multitude of furry little creatures emanating from one of **El Zotz-San Miguel La Palotada Biotope**'s caves at sunset is a dead giveaway for the park's nomenclature. Adjacent to Tikal National Park, 34,934-hectare El Zotz covers substantial areas of tropical forest and wetlands with unexcavated Mayan temple mounds breaking the landscape here and there. It is possible to hike from the park to Tikal and vice versa. The Tikal temples, about 23 kilometers away, can be seen far off in the distance from Devil's Pyramid, the tallest of the unexcavated mounds at El Zotz.

Also in Petén, on the shores of Lake Petén Itzá, **Cerro Cahuí Biotope** covers 650 hectares and consists of a small hill varying in altitude 200-300 meters (650-985 feet). The preserve was created to protect the Petén oscillated turkey and consists mostly of secondary-growth forest. There are several lookouts with excellent views of the lake along the park's well-marked trails. It is a popular spot for bird-watching, with a good range of nearby accommodations.

Wildlife Refuges

Punta de Manabique Wildlife Refuge encompasses a remote peninsula on Guatemala's Caribbean Coast and is unique for its combination of aquatic, coastal, and terrestrial habitats. The coastline is sparsely populated and includes some very attractive white-sand beaches. Logging, wildlife poaching, and the activities of drug traffickers pose the greatest threats to the park. A small biological station at the peninsula's northwestern tip houses visitors and scientists.

Petexbatún Wildlife Refuge is a wetland and tropical forest park in southern Petén encompassing a variety of lakes abounding in flora, fauna, and Mayan sites. It is one of the few areas in southern Petén where dense forests are still found. The archaeological sites of Ceibal, Aguateca, Dos Pilas, and Tamarindito are also in this area.

The Río Polochic delta, protected as **Bocas del Polochic Wildlife Refuge,** harbors important Lake Izabal wetlands and offers some of Guatemala's finest bird-watching. The park's wetlands and freshwater rivers and lagoons are crucial to the lake's ecological balance and water quality. The ecosystem is also vital to many migratory bird species and provides refuge to a variety of animals, including crocodiles, howler monkeys, and manatees. Together with the adjacent Sierra de las Minas Biosphere Reserve, it accounts for about 80 percent of Guatemala's biodiversity.

HIKING

Guatemala's terrain, featuring mountains, volcanoes, and vast forested flatlands, is a hiker's dream. Adding to the allure of hiking in Guatemala is the opportunity to interact with locals along the way. Many hiking circuits in Guatemala, particularly in the Verapaz cloud forests and the plateaus of the Western Highlands region, are operated via local community tourism initiatives. In addition to providing the opportunity to see the environment and culture through the eyes of local inhabitants, hiring the services of community guides also provides locals with a much-needed source of income and instills a sense of pride in their home. It also speaks loudly to the value (both economic and moral) of conserving precious ecosystems when tourists come from faraway lands to enjoy them.

Among the most popular hikes are the summits of several of Guatemala's 33 volcanoes (some active), including Agua, Acatenango, Pacaya, San Pedro, Santa María, and Tajumulco.

Many tourism circuits operated by local community tourism initiatives include adequate visitors centers and there are often campsites. The same is true for the government-run system of parks and protected areas.

BIKING

Road biking is a fairly popular sport in Guatemala, particularly in the highlands, where mountain roads offer unique challenges to strength and endurance. The country even has its own version of the Tour de France, known as La Vuelta Ciclística a Guatemala (The Biking Circuit of Guatemala). The event takes place yearly sometime in August.

More popular with visitors, **mountain biking** is increasingly popular in the hills around Antigua and Lake Atitlán thanks in part to a number of excellent local outfitters.

ROCK CLIMBING

Rock climbing is a relatively new phenomenon in Guatemala, though there are now at least two outfitters specializing in this activity. The rock faces fronting Lake Amatitlán, near Guatemala City, and an area known as "La Muela" (The Molar, also known as "Cerro Quemado"), near Quetzaltenango, are the prime climbing spots. Difficulty ratings of the various routes range from 5.8 to 5.13. It's also possible to rappel inside a waterfall, also known as canyoning, in Jalapa and other areas.

BEACHES

While Guatemala is not as well known for its beaches as some of its Central American neighbors, it nonetheless boasts some nice stretches on both the Pacific and Caribbean Coasts. On the Pacific, the wild black-sand beaches found along the coast near the **Manchón Guamuchal** wetlands are one of the region's best-kept secrets. If you're escaping the chilly highlands from Quetzaltenango for some sand and surf, other good bets include **Tilapa, Tilapita,** and **Playa El Tulate.** The closest beach to Guatemala City is **Puerto San José,** reached in about 90 minutes by a four-lane highway, though it's certainly not the most pleasant of the country's beaches. Just west of San José is **Chulamar,** with at least one recommended resort hotel.

Farther east, there are also some lovely stretches between **Iztapa** and **Monterrico.** The 25-kilometer road connecting both towns is experiencing a modest construction boom of stylish resort hotels, with land speculators quickly snapping up the remaining parcels of oceanfront property. East of Monterrico, **Hawaii** also has pretty stretches of nearly deserted beaches, though there are increasing numbers of Guatemala's elite building vacation homes here. The end of the line is **Las Lisas,** another attractive, though very remote, beach close to the Salvadoran border.

On the Caribbean Coast, Guatemala has some fairly decent white-sand beaches on the **Punta de Manabique** promontory. Along the coastline between Lívingston and the Belize border, the nicest beaches are at palm-fringed **Playa Blanca.** For talcum-powder white-sand beaches lapped by turquoise waters, head off the coast to the Belize Barrier Reef, where you'll find the **Zapotillo cayes.**

FISHING
Sailfishing

The Pacific Ocean waters off the port of Iztapa are hailed as the "Sailfish Capital of the World," with world records for single-day catch-and-release firmly supporting these claims. Apparently, a unique pattern of swirling ocean currents between Mexico and El Salvador creates an eddy unusually rich in pelagic fish, such as herring and mackerel, right on Guatemala's doorstep. Sailfish and marlin gather to feed on this bait, along with large concentrations of dorado, yellowfin tuna, and wahoo. The result is some of the world's best sailfishing.

Numerous outfitters have set up shop in Iztapa offering sailfishing year-round, though the most active season is between November and May because of the colder weather prevalent in the North American region from which most anglers hail. The Presidential Challenge, a yearly sportfishing event that has been held since 1997, usually takes place here in January.

Lake Fishing

Thanks to grand plans for recreational options to be offered on behalf of now-absconded Pan American Airways, Lake Atitlán saw the introduction of largemouth bass in the late 1950s. The lake's extreme depths make catching the larger fish said to inhabit the deeper waters quite a challenge, which only adds to the allure of fishing these waters. Your best bet for catching "the big one" is during the annual spring spawning season, between March and May.

WATER SPORTS
White-Water Rafting and Kayaking

Guatemala has a number of white-water rivers with rapids ranging from Class II-VI (Class VI being unpassable waterfalls). The most popular river for rafting and kayaking is the **Río Cahabón,** found in the region of Las Verapaces. It features some of Central America's finest stretches of white water complemented by jungles, caves, hot springs, and waterfalls. Also in the Verapaces region, the **Río Candelaria** winds its way through its namesake cave system and is a great place for river tubing and kayaking, allowing the chance to explore these fascinating caves to their full potential. Another worthy white-water excursion is Petén's **Río Chiquibul,** at the eastern end of the department near the Belize border. Although the rapids are not quite as exhilarating as those on the Cahabón, it's highly attractive for its jungle-lined riverbanks and proximity to Mayan sites such as Tikal and Yaxhá.

For more sedate kayaking on ocean kayaks, Lakes Petén Itzá and Atitlán are good bets.

Scuba Diving and Snorkeling

It's possible to scuba dive off the Caribbean Coast near **Punta de Manabique,** though you're probably better off heading just a bit farther north to the exquisite **Zapotillo cayes,** part of the Belize Barrier Reef. Several outfitters arrange trips from Lívingston. Scuba diving is also a popular activity in **Lake Atitlán,** where you might even be able to feel the heat emanating from underwater lava flows in this still-active volcanic region. Another peculiarity of diving here is that the lake is at a rather high altitude just over 1,500 meters (5,000 feet), adding another variable to the mix.

Surfing

An emerging surfing scene is centered around the Pacific Coast village of **Sipacate,** which enjoys excellent breaks. **Iztapa** also reportedly has good breaks, as does **Monterrico.** A useful website for checking out Guatemala's surf scene is www.surfinguatemala.com.

Boating

Boaters will find marinas on both Guatemalan coasts. On the Pacific, a new marina was built with partial backing from Dutch interests near the aging port facilities of **Champerico.** Farther east, the **Marina Pez Vela** caters to sportfishing boats and is adjacent to the **Puerto Quetzal Cruise Ship Terminal.** It has restaurants and good tourism infrastructure. On the Caribbean Coast, you'll find many boats traveling up the **Río Dulce** from the Caribbean Coast and docking at any of a number of marinas in the river's namesake town.

GOLF

Guatemala has some excellent golf courses, all in or around Guatemala City, housed in private clubs open to foreign visitors. Some afford excellent views of the city and all enjoy spectacular locations in the mountains flanking the urban area. New golf courses were in the planning stages on the Pacific Coast adjacent to IRTRA's theme parks at Xocomil and Xetulul, near Retalhuleu, and along the coastal corridor between Iztapa and Monterrico.

SPECTATOR SPORTS
Fútbol

Guatemalans love their soccer, known as *fútbol*. It is by far the most widely played sport in the country, with every town or village having at least something that resembles a soccer field. Almost everywhere you go, you'll find games being played on Sunday afternoons. As for professional soccer playing, the two most popular teams in the country's four-team national soccer league, denoted by the colors of their jerseys, are the Rojos (Municipales) and Cremas (Comunicaciones). The two usually end up going head to head at the end of the season for the championship title.

Games can be seen at Guatemala City's Estadio Mateo Flores, but be advised that the crowds can get quite rowdy. In 1996, things got so out of hand that a stampede ensued when stands collapsed, killing 100 people. The soccer stadium has been remodeled in the aftermath. If you've always wanted to see a Latin American soccer match, you might want to check it out. Guatemala also has a few star players in U.S. Major League Soccer and on some European teams.

International games played by the national squad are a big event, as Guatemala has never been to a World Cup. Guatemala is part of CONCACAF, the Caribbean, North, and Central American Confederation. CONCACAF gets three slots for the World Cup, which usually end up going to the United States, Mexico, and Costa Rica. In 2004-2005, the national squad (also known as *la bicolor*) got closer than it's ever been, advancing into the Final Round of the World Cup qualifiers tied in points with Costa Rica after beating Honduras 1-0. Postgame celebrations spilled into the streets and lasted into the wee hours of the morning. Unfortunately, the high hopes ended in bitter disappointment. Things got off to a great start with a 5-1 routing of Trinidad and Tobago, but Guatemala then lost 2-0 to the United States and never fully recovered.

Baseball

Known locally as *béisbol,* games can be seen at Parque Minerva's ballpark. The game has become increasingly popular in recent years and you'll often see league games going on at area ballparks, usually on Saturday mornings.

Accommodations

Options for accommodations in Guatemala vary from the backpacker's basic $3-a-night room in cheap, blue-light hotels or hostels to ultraswanky boutique hotels and five-star international chain hotels and resorts. It's possible to tour the country entirely on either end of the budget spectrum. There are certainly plenty of options in between, as well as the more recent development of attractive ecolodges in areas adjacent to pristine natural areas. Camping is also another fairly common alternative, particularly at the national parks, though RV hookups are still virtually nonexistent. The government levies a 12 percent sales tax in addition to a 10 percent tax that goes to INGUAT (Guatemala Tourist Commission), bringing the total to a whopping 22 percent. Most of the budget and many of the midrange hotels include these taxes in the prices they'll quote you, but this is not the case in higher-end accommodations.

In popular tourist areas, you'll often be approached by *comisionistas* offering to find you a place to stay. These people work with local hotels and are paid commissions for each person they bring to a particular property. Usually, the places they work with aren't the best deals in town since they have to pay these people, an expense that simply gets added to the room rates. Also, more reputable hotels with good clientele and favorable word of mouth are rarely the kinds of places that would need the services of these freelancers.

HOSPEDAJES, HOSTELS, AND CHEAP HOTELS

Guatemala is a major stop along the Central American backpacking circuit, so it's no surprise that there are a plethora of low-budget hotels to choose from. Many of these are *hospedajes* or *pensiones* with very basic rooms run by local families. The rooms at the most basic places may all be on a shared-bath *(baño compartido)* basis. This is particularly the case in some of the very remote mountain villages in the Western Highlands region. The next-highest level in comfort consists of rooms with private bath *(baño privado).* A recent trend in areas with heavy tourist presence is the establishment of excellent *hostales* (hostels), where several travelers share dormitory-type bedrooms and bathrooms. Antigua, Copán, Guatemala City, Flores, and Cobán, to name a few, have some excellent hostels.

The key thing to look for when scoping out hotels with bargain-basement prices is cleanliness. All of the hotels recommended in this guidebook pass the cleanliness standard, as there are some budget hotels that are truly filthy. I'm all about making my dollar go as far as possible, but I draw the line here. If you do end up staying in a hotel room of questionable cleanliness, break out the sleeping bag. It's always a good idea to pack one along if you're traveling on a budget. Rooms in the highlands tend to suffer from mold problems, so keep this in mind if you're allergic. For rooms in tropical areas, make sure there is a fan, preferably a ceiling fan, as this will make for a much more restful night's sleep.

Another consideration in budget hotels is the quality of the mattresses. Definitely check this out, as the quality of beds varies widely. In some tropical areas, beds might consist of a thin mattress atop a concrete block. This peculiar arrangement has been called to attention in hotel descriptions where applicable.

The cheapest of the cheap hotels may not offer hot water or may not have it on during the whole day. Always inquire about this. In many budget hotels, the hot water comes from an electric hot-water heater attached to the showerhead. These can often look scary, with wires jutting out all over the place. It's a good idea to check out your water-heater situation before taking a room. Be very careful not to touch the showerhead while in the shower, unless, of course, you enjoy being mildly electrocuted. As a final note, bring flip-flops or some other type of shower shoe to avoid catching a nasty fungus in shared bathrooms.

MIDRANGE HOTELS

There are a number of good-value, moderately priced hotels throughout Guatemala charging somewhere in the vicinity of $25-50 per night. Spending $50-100 a night in Guatemala gets you a very nice spread indeed. Despite its newfound popularity, you can still get some very good travel deals in Guatemala. You'll certainly get more bang for your buck than in Belize or Costa Rica, but it's anyone's guess as to how much longer this will last. In the $25-50 range, you'll be surprised at what you'll find. Many rooms in this category come with a private bathroom and almost all moderately priced rooms have cable TV (with channels in English), so you can catch up on the news back home or keep up with your favorite sports team while on the road. Decent mattresses and air-conditioning are also available in some of the better-value accommodations in this category.

Spending $50-100 on a hotel room in Guatemala City will land you in the chic Zona Viva district very close to the airport and near the best restaurants and nightlife venues. In Antigua, you can book a decent boutique property or even stay in a resort. Ditto for the coasts, Petén, and Lake Atitlán.

HIGH-END HOTELS AND RESORTS
Luxury Hotels

Guatemala City boasts the presence of many luxury chains, including Crowne Plaza, Westin, and InterContinental, among others. You'll also find luxury hotels in Antigua, Lake Atitlán, and the vicinity of Tikal and Flores, in Petén. Antigua has some of the nicest boutique hotels anywhere in the world, and plenty of them. Rates at Guatemala's nicer hotels can range $100-900 a night. Many Guatemala City luxury hotels cater to business travelers and deals might be available for weekend stays. These are usually advertised on their websites. Near Retalhuleu, the Hostales del IRTRA seem like a bit of a misnomer, as the complex is less like a hostel and more like a large resort complex with some truly luxurious suites with all the look and feel of a Four Seasons. There are plans in the works for a convention center and golf resort.

Beach Resorts

This category has gained relevance only in

recent years as the Pacific Coast's long-neglected beaches have become the target of tourism development. Most of the Pacific Coast's resorts are along the Iztapa-Monterrico corridor or in either of these towns, including brand-new Cayman Suites and Dos Mundos Pacific Resort. West of Puerto San José, Chulamar features the sprawling Villas del Pacífico, a sizable all-inclusive resort fronting black-sand beaches. It's popular on weekends, but you may have the place all to yourself during the week if a cruise ship isn't docked at nearby Puerto Quetzal.

On the Caribbean Coast near Puerto Barrios, Amatique Bay Resort is a sizable complex fronting an artificial white-sand beach with its own marina and three restaurants. Across the bay near Puerto Santo Tomás de Castilla and its new cruise-ship terminal, Green Bay Hotel also fronts an artificial beach along a lagoon and provides easy access to nearby nature preserves. It is rumored that international hotel chains have expressed interest in developing the remote beaches on the Punta de Manabique promontory, though it seems to contradict its status as a wildlife refuge. But then again, that's never stopped tourism development before.

Ecolodges

Another recent trend is the development of ecolodges springing up seemingly everywhere. These vary from somewhat simple community-run ecolodges to downright stylish, with Francis Ford Coppola's La Lancha (on Lake Petén Itzá) at the forefront of the latter category. Most ecolodges are found in Petén department and in the regions of Izabal and Las Verapaces.

Food

WHAT TO EAT

Guatemalan food may at first seem a bit odd to gringo palates, though the freshness and pungency of local ingredients, including a bounty of tropical fruits and vegetables, soon has many people enticed by the local flavors. Guatemalan dishes are based largely on corn, a staple crop with Guatemala's indigenous population. Corn is ground and made into a dough, which in turn is used to make tortillas, cooked over an open fire on a *comal*. Tortillas are a staple with Indians and ladinos alike and the average Guatemalan family consumes several dozen tortillas per week. In the countryside, tortillas with a dash of lemon and salt, along with beans, form the basis of meals in many low-income households. Even in the cities, tortillas are bought from the local *tortillería* or, in many cases, delivered fresh daily. Unlike revenge, tortillas are not a dish best served cold. Guatemalans like them piping hot and they usually arrive in a basket wrapped in traditional cloth to keep them warm. Many restaurants will have a *tortillería* at the front of the restaurant, where you can watch the tortillas being made, attesting to their freshness.

Other Guatemalan dishes include *tamales*, made from corn meal, pork or turkey, tomato sauce, and olives wrapped in a banana leaf and boiled. Traditionally, Guatemalans will eat a *tamal* at midnight on Christmas morning. *Chuchitos* are a delicious combination of cornmeal with turkey and tomato sauce wrapped in a cornhusk. *Paches* are similar to *tamales*, but they are made from potato-based dough instead of corn. Guatemalans are no strangers to tacos, though the local version is a corn tortilla filled with pork or chicken, rolled up, fried, and covered with tomato sauce and traditional cheese bits. Tostadas are flat, fried corn tortillas topped with tomato sauce or bean paste, shredded parsley, and cheese bits.

Among Guatemala's dishes are also a variety of spicy stews found regionally. Found in the northern region of Las Verapaces, *kakik* is a turkey stew requiring 24 ingredients. Served along the Caribbean Coast of Izabal, *tapado* is a seafood stew made with plantains and coconut milk. Spicy meat dishes include *pollo en jocón* (chicken in a tomatillo-cilantro sauce) and *pollo en pepián* (chicken in a tomato-pumpkin seed sauce).

In addition to three meals a day, Guatemalans are also big fans of the *refacción*, a midafternoon snack consisting of a light sandwich or pastry and coffee. The prominence of bakeries and cake shops throughout the country attests to the popularity of this extra half-meal. Not all Guatemalans can afford to eat three square meals a day—a large part of the population subsists on less than $2 daily. In many places, meat is a luxury few can afford. Dinner is usually late for North American tastes and is usually eaten sometime around 8 P.M.

Besides traditional food, heavy European influences on Guatemalan culture throughout the years have resulted in a wide array of culinary tastes. You'll see plenty of evidence of this in Guatemala City and Antigua, where there are numerous options for dining in addition to some very interesting fusions of Guatemalan and international flavors. In food and culture, Guatemalans love to emulate the consumption patterns of their North American neighbors. You'll see plenty of fast-food franchises, mostly in Guatemala City, but also with surprising frequency in other urban areas. Guatemala City also has its fair share of U.S. casual dining franchises the likes of T.G.I. Friday's, Chili's, and Applebee's. But, since you didn't come all this way to eat the same food you'd have back home you'll need a few tips on where to eat locally.

WHERE TO EAT

You can expect to find table service and menus in *restaurantes*. *Comedores* are much simpler eateries, sometimes with a menu but other times with a set dish for the day. The best *comedores* are easy to spot: They'll have the greatest number of locals eating there. You'll find Guatemalans often eat at streetside stalls serving greasy tacos, fried chicken, and the like. These places are often referred to in jest as *shucos* (dirties) and are best avoided by international travelers unless you have a very strong stomach or have developed resistance to intestinal critters through continued exposure to food of questionable cleanliness south of the border.

ORDERING AND PAYING

The menu is known as *la carta* or *el menú*. To request the check, order *la cuenta* or ask, "*¿cuánto le debo?*" ("How much do I owe you?"). Tips are not required at simple eateries and may already be included on your bill in many midrange restaurants. Check to see. If not, an average tip in Guatemala is 10 percent.

BUYING GROCERIES

Corner stores known as *tiendas* carrying basic food items are common in cities and towns throughout the country. Larger grocery stores are found in Guatemala City and some of the larger cities. Major grocery chains include Paiz (recently acquired by Walmart) and La Torre. Every town and village has a *mercado* (market), where folks go to buy fruits and vegetables as well as meats. Try to avoid the butcher section if you don't take well to displays of raw flesh covered with flies. Inquire about the price per pound of any required items instead of just picking up an odd-numbered assortment and then asking how much it is, because that's the best way to get ripped off.

BEVERAGES
Non-Alcoholic Drinks

Although Guatemala produces some of the world's finest coffee, most of it is set aside for export. Still, you can find an excellent cup of java in Antigua, Guatemala City, Cobán, and other tourist places, though the coffee served at many less expensive restaurants is not usually the greatest. There's almost always at least one decent place in town for coffee.

With the wide variety of fruits available in Guatemala's myriad vegetation zones, fruit smoothies (often made with milk and called *licuados*) are common beverages. At simpler smoothie stands, you should always be careful to make sure the water used in making your drink is purified. Also, try to get fruit smoothies made from produce that requires peeling, rather than from fruits that are found on or close to the ground. Good, safe bets are pineapple or cantaloupe (or, even better, these mixed together). Strawberries sold locally are notorious for carrying amoebas and other parasites, so unless you plan on disinfecting them yourself or are in a place where you have assurance that this has been done, stick to fruits with peels. Orange juice served in Guatemala is often freshly squeezed and delicious, a delightful surprise for North American palates that have become all too accustomed to the taste of juice made from concentrate.

Sodas and carbonated beverages are widely available, as you'll guess from the ubiquitous advertising on town walls. Although plastic soda bottles and cans have become more widely available in recent years, you'll still see plenty of glass bottles in use. If you plan on buying a soda and taking the glass bottle with you, you'll have to fork over a few extra bills for the glass deposit. Otherwise, you can have it put in a sandwich bag with a straw, which is a bit unnerving for first-time visitors but perfectly normal and hygienic.

Alcoholic Beverages

Guatemala's eastern region produces Zacapa Centenario, a highly acclaimed rum that has won numerous international awards. It makes a great gift for folks back home. If you're not heading to the eastern lowlands of Zacapa or don't want to lug your purchase around the country during the rest of your travels, keep in mind the Guatemala City airport has a Zacapa Centenario Duty Free shop where you can buy a bottle or two on your way out of the country. In the Mayan highland towns and villages, the liquor of choice is *aguardiente,* locally made moonshine also known as *guaro.* Popular brands include *Quezalteca Especial* and *Venado. Rompopo* and *caldo de frutas* are two types of alcoholic beverages made in the town of Salcajá, near Quetzaltenango. The first is essentially a spiked eggnog and the latter is made from fermented fruits.

Cervecería Centroamericana produces most of Guatemala's beers from its brewery in Guatemala City, including Gallo, a lager that is Guatemala's national brew. You can find it in the United States under the name Famosa, as Ernest and Julio Gallo Wines holds the rights to the use of the Gallo name in North America. "Gallo" means rooster in Spanish and the beer is easily identifiable by the stylized cock on its label. Other beers brewed by Cervecería Centroamericana include Dorada Draft, smooth export pilsner Monte Carlo, and dark beer Moza. Brewed by Cervecería Nacional and available only in and around Quetzaltenango, Cabro is another good beer. Cervecería Centroamericana once enjoyed uncontested dominion of the Guatemalan beer market but has seen competition in recent years with the arrival of competing brands, most notably Brazilian Brahva.

Conduct and Customs

You'll find most Guatemalans are warm and friendly. In many instances, they will be very curious about you as a foreigner, particularly in areas that are still getting accustomed to a growing presence of gringo travelers. Urban and rural settings have varying degrees of formality, though politeness and good manners are appreciated by Guatemalans from all walks of life and will get you far.

As a further introduction to this discussion of Guatemalan cultural mores, I quote Stephen Connely Benz from his book, *Guatemalan Journey:*

Guatemala City does not fit the stereotypical image of an exotic tropical city where any pleasure can be readily satisfied. It isn't Bangkok or the Havana of old; it doesn't even measure up to San José, Costa Rica–Central America's mild version of a sin city. The Guatemalan demeanor is too formal and, to some extent, too prim for openly displayed vice. Compared with other Central Americans, Guatemalans are almost prudish. Though appreciative of off-color jokes, especially those involving double entendres, they dislike blunt vulgarity, and their strongest swearing is but common speech in, say, El Salvador and Mexico. Guatemalans, for example, deplore public use of the word *puta*–"whore"–a word so common in El Salvador it is practically a term of endearment. Even the excessive use of English vulgarities in American movies disturbs Guatemalans. In clothing, too, Guatemalans favor the conservative. American diplomats who have been stationed previously in other Central American countries are surprised at how often they have to dress up in Guatemala. Suits and ties are more common than the typical guayabera favored in more relaxed countries. And wanton displays of exposed flesh are far less common than in the rest of the isthmus.

DRESS AND APPEARANCE

Guatemala is in many ways a rather formal and conservative country, probably owing to its legacy of colonialism and its status as the main base of regional power for the Spanish colonial aristocracy. It's a very class-conscious society, with good grooming, neat dress, and cleanliness expected. In many instances, the way you look is the way you'll be treated. You'll notice this the first time you go to a Guatemala City shopping mall (especially on weekends) and see well-dressed urbanites going for a cup of coffee or heading out to see a movie. Sneakers and shorts are considered much too casual for many events foreigners would find perfectly acceptable. This is starting to change, however, and you'll also see younger Guatemalans wearing shorts, T-shirts, and flip-flops typical of the Abercrombie & Fitch look that is also wildly popular with Guatemalan youth from wealthy families. If you plan on going out to dance clubs, be sure to bring a good pair of shoes, as you won't make it past the front door wearing sneakers. Dress is much more relaxed at the beach or in the countryside.

For business travelers, suits are still very much the norm for men. Professional women tend to wear conservative dresses or two-piece suits. The less affluent will pay careful attention to dress as neatly as possible, especially for trips to the capital or other urban centers.

Backpackers, known as *mochileros,* often get a bum rap as an unkempt group who contribute very little to the economy and only cause trouble for hotel owners and tourist service operators. This is generally manifested as a form of marked distrust, though this is usually not the case in places that cater to these types of travelers as their main clientele, such as budget hostels.

ETIQUETTE

The formality of Guatemalan culture also extends to etiquette. Guatemalans take titles seriously (including *doctor* or *doctora* for doctors and *licenciado(a)* for an attorney or holder of a bachelor's degree). Whenever possible, they should be used when addressing the individual in person or via correspondence. Women usually greet men and each other with air kisses. Men will greet friends with a handshake different from the standard business handshake. Grips tend to be firm. When meeting someone for the first time, it's customary to say, *"mucho gusto"* (a shortened version of "nice to meet you"). Simply saying *"hola"* is considered too casual. Other greetings include *"buenos días"* (good morning), *"buenas tardes"* (good afternoon), and *"buenas noches"* (good evening). Particularly in rural areas, people will greet each other with one of these as they pass each other along the trail, road, or street. In urban settings, you'll often hear one of these greetings when someone walks into a place of business, such as a doctor's office, for example. Another formality is the use of *"buen provecho"* when walking into a restaurant where people are eating and *"muchas gracias"* upon getting up from the table after a meal.

PHOTOGRAPHIC ETIQUETTE

It's never a good idea to photograph Mayan people without their permission, as they consider it highly offensive and it intrudes upon their spiritual beliefs. The old photographers' rule contending that it's easier to apologize (for taking a candid photo) than to ask permission doesn't really apply in Guatemala. This is especially true concerning photographs of children, and you should be careful not to show them undue interest and attention, as persistent rumors of foreigners involved in child-snatching of Guatemalan children for organ transplant abroad have led to mob incidents on at least two occasions, with two people killed and one seriously injured. (The last incident was in 2000 in the village of Todos Santos.) In both cases, the foreigners were trying to photograph a child. This scenario is most plausible in the highlands, though not exclusively so.

It can be understandably difficult at times to refrain from taking photographs because Mayan children (and Mayan people in general) are especially photogenic and can provide some wonderful opportunities for portraiture or candid shots. On the up side, the situation forces you to interact with the locals and get to know them. You'll soon find that many are willing to let you photograph them (often for the promise of sending them a photo) and your photographs will be better because of the rapport you've established with the subject.

SMOKING

As of February 2009, it is no longer possible to smoke in public places in Guatemala, including bars, restaurants, office buildings, and airports. Some foreigners (especially European travelers) may not yet know about this law; you may have to kindly but firmly point this out, or ask the property manager do so on your behalf.

GUATEMALAN BEHAVIOR
Confianza and Saving Face

One of the main traits of Guatemalan behavior is what is known as being *en confianza*. Attaining this level in your interpersonal relationships means having a high level of openness, trust, and comfort with those you are *en confianza* (in confidence) with. Once you have reached this level in your relationship with someone, you will most likely be visiting their home and sharing a few meals. *Confianza* is just as important for making friends as it is for doing business and overall success in Guatemalan society. You can erode your *confianza* by displaying character flaws such as losing your temper in public or dressing inappropriately, but Guatemalans will never confront you directly. Instead they will do what is known as "saving face." There may be a perceptible chill in their demeanor toward you.

Another player in the Guatemalan social lingo is the concept of *pena,* directly linked to the concept of saving face. To have *pena* is to feel badly, as in the case of imposing on your host or needing to say something unpleasant or accusatory. North Americans are very direct and to the point, which is not at all how Guatemalans are. They will go to great lengths to avoid the *pena* of having to tell you something or ask something of you they are not comfortable with.

North Americans (or those who have spent extended periods of time there) often find this idiosyncrasy quite frustrating. Vice President Rafael Espada, who spent several years as a prominent surgeon in Houston prior to being elected to office, highlighted this characteristic during an interview with *Prensa Libre* following his first year back in Guatemala. He said this face-saving mechanism, whereby people will tell you what they think you want to hear, was one of his biggest frustrations. Espada said it was hard to get things done when people have given you assurances that the wheels are set in motion, when often they haven't even started what you asked them to do in the first place.

Conversation

Guatemalans tend to use the *vos* form of *tu* (you), a derivative of the archaic *vosotros* now used only in Spain. This is particularly the case with two men of the same age or similar social standing. It shouldn't be used to address a person of perceived lesser social stature, as it's somewhat demeaning when used in this way, though upper-class Guatemalans tend to do it anyway. Stick to the formal *usted* unless the person switches to the informal *tu* or *vos.*

Related to the above concept of *pena,* keep in mind what people are saying in between the lines. Guatemalans tend to beat around the bush, so to speak, and you must use a keen sensitivity to the subject at hand (and the speaker) to decipher what is being implied.

Personal Space and Privacy

Guatemalans might be a bit "touchy feely" by North American standards. It's not uncommon to see two heterosexual male friends walking with their arms around each other. This is more common with school-age children, however. Guatemalans generally greet each other with hugs and kisses (or air kisses if it's a stranger of the opposite gender). They may also grab your arm when trying to emphasize a point (I have a beloved uncle who does this quite frequently).

North Americans' love of privacy might at times seem strange to Guatemalans. This is something to keep in mind if you are staying with a host family. What might seem like a normal degree of privacy to you may seem like seclusion and isolation, on your part, to them. Most host families who have had a number of North American visitors have grown accustomed to this.

Tips for Travelers

OPPORTUNITIES FOR STUDY AND VOLUNTEER WORK
Language Study

Guatemala is a popular place for Spanish-language study, particularly Antigua and Quetzaltenango. Here are a few basic things to look out for when deciding where to study Spanish in Guatemala. First of all, you'll want to decide what sort of environment you're looking for to choose a location. Antigua and Quetzaltenango offer some fine institutions in addition to the chance to combine your language instruction with time spent in interesting urban locales. Both towns have a lively nightlife scene and a fairly substantial presence of foreign travelers. This might be a pro or a con, depending on how you look at it. If you're looking to make new friends and traveling companions after your courses are finished, then this will certainly suit you. But if you're looking for a total language-immersion experience, you might find yourself speaking English outside of classroom time more often than not.

There are a few highland towns and villages with language schools that offer good instruction with (for now) a relatively small foreign presence. These include the language schools in Nebaj, Cobán, and Huehuetenango. San Pedro La Laguna, on the shores of Lake Atitlán, also has decent language schools and a slightly less substantial gringo presence compared to Antigua and Quetzaltenango. It's certainly a winner for its location on the shores of this magnificent lake. Monterrico is the place to go if you want to combine fairly decent language instruction with some serious time at the beach. The northern Petén region's language schools are found in the Itzá Maya towns of San Andrés and San José, on the shores of Lake Petén Itzá, and they are a good place to learn Spanish with little foreigner presence and a more ecological focus thanks to the proximity of the Maya Biosphere Reserve.

For the altruistic, Quetzaltenango offers the chance for language instruction in an environment oozing with fellow travelers, volunteers, and NGO workers plugged into a variety of projects hoping to make life better for people in Guatemala's impoverished Western Highlands.

Virtually all of Guatemala's language schools offer one-on-one instruction, and your choice of an instructor is particularly important to your progress. You should never feel locked into a deal with a particular instructor. If you find that you and the instructor just aren't jiving, don't hesitate to ask for a new one. All of the recommended schools get their strength from the quality of their individual instructors, so finding one that's right for you shouldn't be too difficult if you know where to look.

In terms of cost, you'll find it fairly accessible. The bulk of Guatemala's schools charge somewhere between $150 and $225 per week, including at least 20 hours of instruction per week and room and board with a local host family. Some schools, particularly in Antigua and Quetzaltenango, provide the option of staying in on- or off-campus housing or apartments.

As a final note, Guatemalan Spanish is relatively clear of the accents found in Caribbean, Mexican, and even Costa Rican Spanish. Guatemalans also tend to speak more slowly than Caribbean Spanish speakers. It's actually a very melodic Spanish and you'll soon recognize its singsong sound. In terms of value for the money you spend and variety of locales in which to learn, you really can't beat Spanish-language instruction in Guatemala.

Volunteer Opportunities

The country is also the focus of many relief

and development projects on the part of NGOs, some of which are almost always looking for volunteers. Many of these are linked to local language schools. Areas with a particularly heavy concentration of NGOs include Quetzaltenango, the Ixil Triangle, and Petén.

Foreign Study Programs

For college students seeking a study-abroad opportunity, **The University of Arizona** (www.studyabroad.arizona.edu), in partnership with the Center for Mesoamerican Research (CIRMA), offers semester- and yearlong programs in Antigua focusing on intensive Spanish-language instruction in addition to Central American history, politics, and culture.

TRAVELING WITH CHILDREN

Guatemalans love children and traveling with them will often be all that you need to break the ice with locals. Guatemala's cultural and natural wealth can also form the basis for a very educational trip allowing children to see and experience what they might only read about in textbooks and classrooms.

Guatemala has also been a popular place for U.S. citizens to adopt Guatemalan children. The U.S. government discouraged adoptions from Guatemala because of deficient legal parameters ensuring the protection of adopting parents and adopted children in line with international standards. Adoptions in Guatemala are suspended at this time. However, legislation has been passed to be in compliance with the tenets of the Hague convention governing international adoption.

ACCESS FOR TRAVELERS WITH DISABILITIES

Guatemala is a somewhat challenging country for people with disabilities, as there is little in the way of public infrastructure specifically catering to the needs of travelers with disabilities. Antigua might be a bit cumbersome for

travelers in wheelchairs because of its cobblestone streets but nonetheless it has ramps for wheelchair access on every street corner. There are a few exceptions to the general lack of access for those with disabilities. Guatemala City's new public transportation system, the Transmetro, was said to offer wheelchair access as part of its innovative infrastructure. The international airport now also features several elevators as part of its recent renovation. Modern Guatemala City hotels housed in high-rise buildings also have these amenities. For intercity travel, the best option for travelers with disabilities is to take shuttle buses.

WOMEN TRAVELING ALONE

As elsewhere in Latin America, men in Guatemala tend to be chauvinistic, particularly the country's ladinos. Women traveling alone might find themselves the object of unwanted attention. Guatemalan women are accustomed to fairly constant harassment by men on the street, including catcalls, whistling, and horn honking, which they tend to ignore. This is usually the best tactic, though it's somewhat difficult to put into practice. Take a deep breath and count to 10. Your best bet as a preventive measure in this regard is to dress demurely, particularly in urban areas. Although much less likely, there's also the possibility of having your butt or breasts groped by a passing stranger. It usually happens in an instant, with nary a second glance from the perpetrator. If it should come to a case of a lingering pervert, some Guatemalan women will scream at the perpetrator, something along the lines of *"cerdo"* (pig), which usually scares them off. The last thing they want is to be confronted in public and they certainly wouldn't expect it. Blondes and brunettes tend to be the most common targets of dudes who just can't keep their hands to themselves.

Solo female travelers should try to stick to the main tourist destinations in Guatemala and

KID-FRIENDLY GUATEMALA

Kids love Guatemala.

Latin Americans are very family oriented and Guatemalans are no exception. There is plenty to see and do in Guatemala for families traveling with children of all ages. The following is a list of kid- and family-friendly attractions throughout the country.

GUATEMALA CITY

Among the city's museums, none is more kid friendly than the **Museo del Niño** (Children's Museum), in Zona 13 near the airport. There are a number of interactive displays as well as opportunities for play. Just across the street, you'll find the city's excellent **La Aurora Zoo,** harboring a good collection of animals from Guatemala and around the world. Cages are being gradually phased out. If you want to see the city's sights but have kids in tow who might not want to walk, opt for a **trolley tour.**

LAKE ATITLÁN

On the lake's beautiful shores, there are plenty of places to stay for families traveling with children. Among the best are the family-sized villas at **San Buenaventura de Atitlán,** equipped with a kitchen and several rooms. Nearby, kids (and outdoor-loving parents) will enjoy the **Reserva Natural Atitlán,** where they can see monkeys and coatimundis along the nature trails leading to waterfalls. There are also a butterfly farm and private lake beach in addition to an excellent visitors center.

PACIFIC COAST

The Pacific Coast is extremely family friendly, primarily thanks to the presence of the twin theme parks of **Xocomil and Xetulul,** near Retalhuleu. Xocomil is a water park on par with the finest in the United States and Xetulul includes re-creations of famous Spanish, French, Italian, and Guatemalan landmarks along with an exhilarating roller-coaster and assorted other rides. After the parks close, the fun continues across the street at the excellent accommodations of **Hostales del IRTRA,** with numerous swimming pools, restaurants, and activities. For some seaside fun, head to **Monterrico,** where (in season) you can participate in a race involving newly hatched sea turtles making their maiden voyage across the sandy beach to their ocean home. Kids will also get a kick out of the **Auto-Safari Chapín,** in Taxisco about 90 minutes from Guatemala City. It's a drive-through safari experience, in which you can see several of kids' favorite animals, including lions, zebras, and parrots.

PETÉN

Children will certainly be impressed by the Mayan ruins at **Tikal,** along with the abundant wildlife found along the various nature trails criss-crossing the park or swinging from the trees. At the entrance to Tikal, older kids and adults will enjoy the **Tikal Canopy Tour,** allowing them to zip across the forest canopy along metallic cables while strapped to a harness. If you want to see more of the forest canopy on slightly less adrenaline-inducing conditions, head to **Parque Natural Ixpanpajul,** where there are plenty of outdoor activities, including walks along hanging bridges connecting forested jungle canyons.

not venture too far off the beaten path. There's really no reason to travel alone for too long unless you really want to, as you'll probably make friends along the way thanks to an abundance of foreign visitors. After dark, take a cab, but try to find someone to share it with.

GAY AND LESBIAN TRAVELERS

The prevalence of *machismo* (male-dominated culture) can make things difficult, if not downright dangerous, for gay and lesbian couples choosing to express mutual affection publicly. Gay travelers and residents will want to keep a low profile while in public areas in Guatemala so as not to attract unwanted attention. Homosexuality is still not widely accepted in Guatemala, and many commonly used slurs and epithets apply directly to gays. Still, things may be starting to change, as Guatemalans are quick to emulate the cultural standards they see on international TV, specifically the greater

acceptance of gay men and lesbians portrayed in the U.S. media. Acceptance of homosexuality, in this way, appears directly linked to socioeconomic status—or at least access to cable television. Some openly gay Guatemalans live with their partners and are open about their relationships with friends and family, though financial and social independence figure prominently into this decision.

Religious beliefs and prejudices vary and affect how gay men and lesbian women are treated in any society. It all depends on the individual. I've witnessed innkeepers issue disparaging remarks about gay guests behind their backs, but I've also run into uncommon acceptance of homosexuality.

As in many international cities, there's a growing gay-rights movement in Guatemala City, and there are a number of gay bars and nightclubs, mostly in Zona 1. As with most venues, things are constantly changing, so log on to www.gayguatemala.com for the latest.

Health and Safety

Guatemala's status as a poor, developing nation translates into a variety of health and safety risks for the foreign traveler. Many of these are directly related to poor hygiene. When it comes to safety and law enforcement, the **Policía Nacional Civil** (created by the 1996 peace accords) has not lived up to its expectations as an efficient, incorruptible, and professional police force. On a positive note, the **Tourism Police** have demonstrated proficiency in helping travelers as well as making areas somewhat safer with patrols and group escorts. Private initiatives, as they almost always do in Guatemala, have stepped in to fill the gaps, also providing some measure of protection for foreign visitors.

Travelers might want to consider buying traveler's insurance before heading to

Guatemala. Several different types of insurance with varying degrees of coverage are available in the United States, Canada, and Europe. A relatively new Guatemalan initiative offering assistance to foreign travelers is **Asistur** (www.asisturcard.com), which provides services via the purchase of its Asistur Card. You can buy policies for one day, 15 days, 30 days, or one year costing just $1 per day. Included in the coverage is round-the-clock telephone assistance for issues including legal and medical situations. Security escorts, roadside assistance, helicopter evacuation from remote areas such as volcanic summits or jungles, and special assistance in case of robbery, including provision of hotel room and meals, are also provided to those insured by Asistur. Other coverage options (at extra cost) include life insurance, coverage of medical expenses, and theft insurance. The card is available at the INGUAT kiosks at the Guatemala City and Flores/Tikal Airports. Asistur can be reached from anywhere in Guatemala by dialing 1500 or 1-801-ASIST (1-8012-7478). As this is a new venture, you could probably call if you find yourself in a bind, even if you haven't bought coverage. An Asistur agent might be nearby. Crimes against tourists are a great concern to Guatemalans in general and their gracious hospitality dictates their desire to help out a traveler in need. That being said, for $1 a day, the coverage and peace of mind are certainly worth it.

BEFORE YOU GO

Officially, no vaccinations are required for entry into Guatemala, though it's a good idea to be up to date on rabies, typhoid, measles-mumps-rubella (MMR), yellow fever, and tetanus shots. A hepatitis vaccine is now widely available and is probably also a good idea. If you plan on taking preventive medications against malaria, you'll need to start taking them a few weeks before potential exposure to the disease. The Centers for Disease Control and Prevention (CDC) maintains an international travelers' hotline, which can be reached at 888/232-3228, and a travel health home page found at www.cdc.gov/travel.

PREVENTATIVE MAINTENANCE

As the saying goes, "An ounce of prevention is worth a pound of cure." This is certainly the case for travel in Guatemala, as there are certain measures you can take to avoid succumbing to many of the most common ailments. Washing hands frequently and drinking only bottled water will help keep you free of stomach ailments as will consuming only cooked foods or peeled fruits such as bananas and oranges. Lettuce and strawberries are two common culprits, often leading to severe gastrointestinal distress. Likewise, stay away from ice cubes unless you have complete assurance that they come from purified water. By law, all ice cubes served in Guatemalan restaurants must come from purified water, a good idea in theory but certainly not always the case. I've often had my doubts even about supposedly purified ice cubes in restaurants after falling ill. When in doubt, leave the ice out. Be careful not only with what you eat, but where you eat. Stay away from street stalls selling cheap food, referred to jokingly by locals as *shucos* (literally, "dirties"). While Guatemalan stomachs have developed immunity through the years to nasty food-borne bugs, the average gringo traveler's has not.

FOOD- OR WATER-BORNE DISEASES

Despite these precautions, many travelers to Guatemala might find themselves experiencing a classic case of "the runs" as their digestive tracts adjust to new flora. This usually lasts only a day or two. If the problem persists, it may be a sign of more serious issues. In some cases, it may be food poisoning, which can occur just as easily back home. If this is the case, drink plenty of water and get some rest. You'll probably end up just having to ride it out for a few days and may want to take an anti-diarrhea medicine such as Pepto Bismol or Lomotil.

Travelers' Diarrhea

In addition to diarrhea, symptoms of this often-acquired malady include nausea, vomiting, bloating, and weakness. The usual culprit is *E. coli* bacteria from contaminated food or water. It's important to stay hydrated. Drink plenty of water and clear fluids and keep your strength up by eating bland foods such as crackers or steamed rice. As with food poisoning, you may want to take some over-the-counter anti-diarrhea medication.

Dysentery

Characterized by many of the same symptoms as described above, along with the possibility of bloody stools and generally prolonged malaise, dysentery comes in two flavors: bacillic (bacterial) and amoebic (parasitic). The onset of bacillic dysentery is usually sudden, characterized by vomiting, diarrhea, and fever. Treatment is via antibiotics, to which it responds well. Amoebic dysentery, on the other hand, has an incubation period and symptoms may not show up for several days. It's also harder to get rid of. It is usually treated with a weeklong course of Flagyl (Metronidazole), an extremely potent drug that will wipe out all intestinal flora— good and bad. It also has some marked side effects, such as a bitter taste in the mouth, irritability, and dizziness. You should avoid alcohol while taking this drug, as the combination can make you violently ill.

As with all gastrointestinal issues, it's very important to stay hydrated. Also, see a doctor to get an exact diagnosis. Because of the prevalence of gastrointestinal diseases among Guatemalans, most cities have at least one clinic that can take a stool sample and diagnose the exact nature of the problem.

Cholera

Not entirely unheard of in Guatemala, cholera can be an issue in poorer neighborhoods lacking adequate sanitation, which are usually not visited by foreign travelers. Today's cholera strains are not nearly as deadly as those of the past, though there have been outbreaks in Guatemala in years past. It's best to avoid raw fish and ceviche, a marinated raw-seafood salad popular throughout Latin America.

INSECT-BORNE DISEASES

Mosquitoes are the main carriers of insect-borne illnesses common throughout tropical areas around the world. The best approach to avoiding malaria and other mosquito-borne illnesses is to avoid being bitten by mosquitoes in the first place. Mosquitoes are most abundant during the rainy season, so take special care to protect against mosquito bites during this time of year. Some travelers favor liberal application of bug spray with DEET as the active ingredient, which seems to be the most effective at keeping the critters at bay. Plant-based bug sprays seem to be less effective. It's also possible to buy clothing treated with permethrin, a bug-repellent chemical. It's also possible to buy it separately and treat your clothing with it. Treated garments are scentless in addition to being highly insect repellent. You can find these products in camping and outdoor stores.

Malaria

Malaria is transmitted by the female *Anopheles* mosquito and is prevalent in the Caribbean lowlands and Petén jungles, though not in the highlands. Anopheles mosquitoes tend to bite at night. Flulike symptoms of malaria include high fever, chills, headaches, muscle pain, and fatigue. It can be fatal if left untreated.

Some travelers also opt to take antimalarial drugs, available locally without a prescription (and quite cheaply). The most widely used is chloroquine, known by its brand name Aralen. Although chloroquine-resistant strains of malaria are found in other parts of the world, including South America, this is not the case in Guatemala. You'll need to start taking the drug (500 mg) a week before arriving in malarial zones, weekly while there, and continue to take it once a week for at least four weeks after you've left the malarial zone. Other travelers opt to take two 500 mg doses with them to use if and only if the disease strikes.

Some people experience marked side effects while taking chloroquine, including nausea, headaches, fever, rashes, and nightmares. A newer antimalarial drug, malarone, was approved by the FDA in 2000, supposedly with fewer side effects than traditional drugs and which does not need to be taken for as long. It is not yet widely available in Guatemala.

Dengue

Dengue is also transmitted by mosquitoes and is prevalent in lowland areas, though it is far less common than malaria and only rarely fatal. Although there is no treatment, most people recover from its debilitating symptoms, which include a fever that can last 5-7 days, headache, severe joint pain, and skin rashes. The disease may last up to another week after the fever has lifted. Tylenol can help reduce the fever and counteract the headaches. Dengue is transmitted by a mosquito that bites during the daytime, the *Aëdes aegypti*. A far less common, though potentially fatal, form of dengue is hemorrhagic dengue. It needs to be treated within a few days of the appearance of symptoms, which are a carbon copy of regular dengue symptoms until severe hemorrhaging sets in, making medical treatment well advised at the first sign of dengue.

Chagas' Disease

Spread by the bites of the conenose and assassin bugs living in adobe structures and feeding at night, Chagas' disease is most common in Brazil but also affects millions of people between Mexico and Argentina. Curiously, Panama and Costa Rica are Chagas-free, probably because of the absence in local construction styles of adobe structures. Chickens, dogs, and rodents are thought to carry the disease. Avoid sleeping near the walls of an adobe structure and wear DEET-containing bug spray to bed. The only time this may be a consideration for the average traveler is if trekking across areas of the Western Highlands and staying with local families, who tend to live in adobe structures. Chagas-carrying bugs also tend to be found in dried palm leaves, which makes mosquito netting a must for the traveler sleeping under thatched-roof structures that are not insulated by wire mesh.

The disease usually starts off as a swollen bite accompanied by fever, which eventually subsides. Chagas' disease may eventually cause heart damage leading to sudden death and there is no cure for this disease. Only about 2 percent of those bitten ever develop Chagas' disease.

BITES AND STINGS
Sand Fleas and Sand Flies

Among the more annoying *bichos* (bugs) are sand fleas, which are virtually imperceptible but can leave a trail of welts on feet and ankles. The best way to avoid bites is by washing off after walking on sandy areas. Annoying and also extremely painful are the bites of sand flies known as *tábanos* inhabiting coastal areas, mostly on the Caribbean Coast. They look like a cross between a bee and housefly. You may not feel them on you until it's too late, as they have a knack for landing gently on their victims. Tábano infestations are worst during the dry months, when breezes off the ocean are greatly reduced. If traveling to remote beaches, go prepared with pants, long sleeves, bandana, hat, and bug spray. It may seem silly going to the beach with pants and long sleeves, but it sure beats the very unpleasant experience of being bitten and pursued by these persistent critters (I speak from experience).

Snakes

Lowland Guatemala is home to some of the world's deadliest snakes, including the aggressive fer-de-lance, a pit viper also known as *barba amarilla* for the yellow coloring under its mouth. It's easily distinguishable by its diamond-shaped head and intricate diamond patterns on its skin. It is fairly common in Petén, Izabal, and the Verapaces. Bites are usually fatal unless the victim receives medical attention within a few hours. Other poisonous snakes include rattlesnakes, the red, black, and yellow-banded coral snake, and the eyelash viper, which you should be particularly wary of, as it tends to blend in to vegetation, especially palm trees.

Wear high boots and long pants for hiking in the jungle. Always watch where you step and be particularly careful of woodpiles and rocks. Snakes tend to hang out near jungle watering holes and gaps created by fallen trees. For extended trips into the jungle, it's a good idea to go with a guide. Let guides lead the way, as their eyes are keenly attuned to the presence of snakes and they are usually armed with a machete.

HIV/AIDS

AIDS is a growing concern in Guatemala, particularly because of the wide-spread use of prostitutes in a society ruled by *machismo*. Certainly not making things any better is the economic need of infected prostitutes who continue working after being infected. If you plan on sleeping with a stranger or friend met in your travels, be sure to use a condom, available almost anywhere and known as *preservativos* or *condones*.

MEDICAL ATTENTION
Doctors and Hospitals

Medical services in Guatemala City are generally top-notch, particularly in many private hospitals. Outside the capital, there are several private hospitals providing quality medical care in urban areas. Public facilities such as the Instituto Guatemalteco de Seguridad Social (IGSS) should be avoided, as they are set up to cater to low-income people with no other alternative and are notoriously understaffed and underfunded. Rural areas are extremely lacking in health care, which has resulted in the presence of Cuban doctors in parts of the highlands who have arrived to help bridge the health-care gap. Asistur can help you find excellent English-speaking doctors for those under its coverage.

Pharmacies

In many cases pharmacists sometimes serve as de facto doctors, as prescriptions are not necessary for medications in Guatemala. Patients will

often describe symptoms and take something on the pharmacist's recommendations. Still, it's always best to see a doctor. Many drugs can be found more cheaply in Guatemala, as they are produced locally by a handful of pharmaceutical companies.

In almost every town, at least one pharmacy will be open all night thanks to a system known as *farmacia de turno* (on-call pharmacy), in which the local pharmacies stay open on a rotating basis. Local newspapers publish a listing of these pharmacies and sometimes the outlets themselves have a neon sign stating as such.

SAFETY
Crime

Crime has been a problem throughout Guatemala in the aftermath of the civil war, though statistics show most foreign travelers enjoy their visit to the country without any problems. As many veteran travelers to Guatemala like to point out, you're still safer here than in many large U.S. cities.

Among Guatemala's urban areas, Guatemala City has by far the greatest prevalence of crime. Much of this consisted of groups perpetrating robberies against arriving passengers heading into the city from La Aurora International Airport. Private vehicles, taxis, and shuttle buses have been targeted indiscriminately. Authorities were investigating suspected groups while simultaneously opening security checkpoints and police kiosks to provide greater police presence along this route. It remains to be seen whether large-scale infrastructural improvements involving roads adjacent to the airport (as part of the airport renovation project) will make things safer for arriving passengers.

A related issue is that of highway holdups on rural roads, a very unpleasant topic that I must nonetheless cover here. Sometimes, groups will use bends in the road and speed bumps to their advantage, stopping vehicles as they slow down and robbing passengers of valuables. In the most spectacular cases of highway banditry, pickup trucks carrying armed men will pursue a vehicle and then pass it. Another car might come alongside the victim's vehicle while the car in front shoots at it in an attempt to make the driver stop the car. In addition to taking the passengers' possessions, perpetrators occasionally drag the car's occupants out of the vehicle, tie them up, and steal the car.

Guatemalans who sniff out an impending carjacking have been known to speed up as would-be perpetrators signal them to slow down, not without significant risk of being harmed by the bullets that are often landed on the car by frustrated assailants. If you are stopped and robbed, it's best to remain calm and give them what they want. Opposing a robbery will only make things worse, as the thieves will see this as an invitation to use greater force (I speak from a personal experience in Mexico). It's hard to predict where robberies may occur, though certain areas do seem more prone to this type of crime than others. Among these areas are RN-11, along the southeastern side of Lake Atitlán, the road to El Salvador outside the Guatemala City area (Salvadorans are a favorite target), and some rural Petén roads.

For more on this topic, read the U.S. government's Consular Information Sheet, found online at www.travel.state.gov. Another useful site is that concerning recent incidents of crime against foreigners in Guatemala, available at http://guatemala.usembassy.gov/recent_incidents.html. It will give you an idea of what can happen, but try not to let it alarm you.

Gang violence is also a growing concern. The groups, known as *maras,* operate in parts of Guatemala City not usually frequented by international travelers as well as in some urban areas throughout the country.

Kidnappings reached an all-time high after the civil war, usually involving prominent citizens held for ransom and sometimes returned to their families, depending on whether or not the ransom money was collected. They seem to have subsided in more recent years and rarely, if ever, involve foreigners.

During your trip to Guatemala, there are a number of common-sense measures you can take to avoid becoming the victim of street crime. Don't walk around wearing flashy jewelry and carry only the amount of cash you need for the day in a concealed place. Use safety-deposit boxes for important documents such as passports and plane tickets. In crowded cities, carry your backpack in front of you and be aware of your surroundings at all times. Always keep an eye on your luggage at the airport, bus terminals, and hotels. At night, take a cab and don't go walking out and about after dark. At the beach, be sure not to bring too many things that might tempt thieves while you're in the water. Also, be careful not to walk along isolated stretches of beach, particularly around the Caribbean city of Lívingston. It's never a good idea to climb volcanic summits without a guide, particularly those around Antigua and Lake Atitlán, as these are especially prone to robberies.

That being said, there are still many areas of the country that are beautiful for backcountry hiking and remain crime-free, particularly the Western Highlands region of the Ixil Triangle, where you can explore freely. Before embarking on a backcountry hike or volcano climb, always inform someone who is not going with you of your plans and when you plan to return.

Police

The Policía Nacional Civil (PNC) was created after the civil war with help from Chilean and Spanish security forces but has not been the efficient security force it was hoped it would be. In addition to widespread allegations of corruption, it is perceived as being grossly inefficient. Corrupt agents are suspected of involvement with drug trafficking and the highway holdups, as many robberies occur shortly after travelers are stopped at police checkpoints and perpetrators are often described as wearing police uniforms. Despite these conditions, if you are stopped by police it is best not to offer a bribe, as straight cops will not hesitate to throw you in jail. It's best to go through the usual mechanisms and pay the fine (if applicable). After being stopped, be particularly mindful of your surroundings and especially on the lookout for vehicles that might be following you a little too closely. If you have hired the services of Asistur, you may want to call and see if there is an agent in the vicinity to accompany you the rest of the way to your destination.

The Guatemalan military sometimes jointly patrols areas with police forces because of the latter's demonstrated inability to provide a security presence that dissuades criminal activity. This has led to criticism because the joint patrols (as they're called) run counter to the peace accords allowing for the creation of a professional civilian security force. The involvement of high-ranking police officers in the assassination of three Salvadoran diplomats and their driver in February 2007, in addition to denunciations that police forces harbor death squads within their ranks, may have served as the needed impetus for a systematic purge and revamping of the police forces (once again) from the ground up. It was a hot topic leading up to the 2011 election campaign.

In contrast, Tourist Police (Politur) are generally helpful and have been dispatched to patrol tourist areas. They have been particularly effective at curbing robberies in areas where criminal activity was once getting out of hand, including Tikal National Park and areas in the vicinity of Antigua.

Drugs

Guatemala is a major transshipment point for cocaine coming into the United States from South America, as evidenced by the many clandestine landing strips found in isolated areas of Petén department. Marijuana is grown in remote lowland areas of Guatemala and poppy (the basis for heroin) is grown in the Western Highlands, particularly in the department of San Marcos.

High-ranking military officials have been implicated in drug smuggling, working with local cartels linked to Colombia's powerful Cali cartel. United States drug officials have begun referring to Guatemala as *la bodega* (the warehouse), as it houses a large share of the cocaine continuing north to Mexico, from where it makes its final entry into the United States. Among the local cartels, the most prominent are based in the eastern lowlands near Zacapa (not an area frequented by foreign tourists), Izabal department, and the southern part of Petén department near Sayaxché. Some travelers have reported run-ins with local drug traffickers on private lands, but you're unlikely to be harmed as long as you adopt a live-and-let-live attitude.

Cocaine consumption is an increasing problem among affluent Guatemalans, particularly in Guatemala City night clubs. Drug use is strictly forbidden by law and you will be thrown in jail without hesitation for violations. If you are arriving in Guatemala by air from elsewhere in Latin America, drug-sniffing dogs will probably be on hand to greet your flight and you may be questioned by authorities after clearing immigration procedures.

Information and Services

MONEY

Prices throughout this book are quoted in U.S. dollars unless otherwise noted. Guatemala's currency is the quetzal, which is pegged to the U.S. dollar and denoted by Q. The exchange rate was about Q7.68 to US$1 and it has remained at about the same rate for several years now. Bills come in denominations of 5, 10, 20, 50, and 100 quetzales, though the new polymer Q1, Q5 and Q200 bills are now in circulation. The Q500 bills might surface soon. Coins come in denominations of 1, 5, 10, 25, 50 *centavos* (Q0.01, Q0.05, Q0.10, Q0.25, Q.50) and Q1, though other than the one-quetzal coin they are more of a nuisance than anything else. Often, if your change is a few centavos, the merchant will keep it.

In smaller towns and villages, you might have trouble breaking Q100 (or larger) notes, so bring smaller bills with you if possible.

Exchange

Travelers have the option of getting around with cash U.S. dollars (which you will need to at least partially exchange for local currency), travelers checks (American Express being the most widely recognized and accepted), wire transfers (most expensive option), Visa or MasterCard cash advances (watch those interest rates), or through ATMs linked to international networks (recommended).

Banks

Banks in Guatemala tend to keep long hours, typically 9 A.M.-6 P.M. Monday-Friday and 9 A.M.-1 P.M. on Saturday. Changing money and travelers checks at banks is relatively painless and routine, though you'll probably be asked to show your passport or at least a photocopy of it for identification. You'll also notice that banks,

like convenience stores and other businesses, are heavily guarded by armed watchmen.

In border areas, you'll typically be approached by money changers offering slightly better rates than local banks. It's perfectly safe to change your money with them, though it's probably a good idea to exchange only what you might need for the first day or two in the new country. Try not to pull out a wad of bills for all to see.

Travelers Checks

This is still the safest way to carry money during your travels, though you'll be able to exchange them only in urban areas and tourist destinations with full-service banks. There's also a bit more bureaucracy involved in exchanging travelers checks and you might be asked to show your original purchase receipt. American Express is by far the most widely accepted type of travelers check. The local American Express representative is Clark Tours (7a Avenida 14-76, Plaza Clark, Zona 9, Guatemala City, tel. 2412-4700, www.clarktours.com).

Wire Transfers

Because of the widespread phenomenon of remittances sent home by Guatemalan nationals living abroad, several companies have set up shop all over Guatemala. This may be your best bet if you happen to run short of cash during your travels. Many local banks and businesses are Western Union affiliates. For a list of these affiliates in Guatemala, visit the website at www.westernunion.com. You can also send money via American Express MoneyGram. Keep in mind these companies make their money off exorbitant fees charged for their services in addition to a poor exchange rate for the money, which you'll end up getting in local currency.

Credit Cards and ATMs

Credit cards have become more and more commonplace in Guatemala, though they are still accepted mainly in urban centers, major tourist attractions, and luxury hotels or expensive restaurants and shops. Some smaller merchants may charge a fee, usually 7 to 10 percent of the transaction amount, the justification being that they are charged this amount by the credit card companies and can't afford to absorb the cost because of their smaller sales volume. Visa and MasterCard are the most widely accepted.

ATMs in Guatemala are hooked up to international networks and most travelers have no problems accessing their bank accounts in this way. It's always a good idea to keep an eye on transactions online while you're on the road if you're able to and report any inconsistencies immediately. You will never be required to enter your pin number on a pad to enter an ATM kiosk, a common scam to steal card and PIN numbers that has fooled some travelers. Always be aware of your surroundings and try not to visit the ATM at night or unaccompanied.

You can search for Visa ATM locations in Guatemala online at http://visa.via.infonow. net/ and MasterCard ATMs at www.mastercard.com/atm. A useful listing of Banco Industrial Visa ATMs throughout Guatemala can be found at www.bi.com.gt. This will give you an idea of the availability of ATMs along your planned travel route.

COMMUNICATIONS AND MEDIA
Postal Services

Guatemala's postal service, known as El Correo, was privatized a few years back and placed in the very capable hands of a Canadian company, making it much more reliable than it once was. It's also fairly inexpensive, though a letter to the United States might take three weeks to arrive at its destination. International couriers such as Federal Express, UPS, and DHL also have a sizable presence here, along with several local companies used largely by Guatemalan expats living in the United States. The latter are substantially more affordable.

Telephone Service

Guatemala's country code is 502. There are no separate area or city codes. All phone numbers, save a few emergency numbers, are eight digits long. There are also a few toll-free numbers belonging to airlines and services that begin with 1-801. The national telephone service was privatized in 1999 and is now known as Telgua. A number of other phone companies, including Spanish Telefónica also operate here, providing some welcome competition. Each of the local phone companies have its own dialing codes for calling the United States from a land line, which will save you money. Most travelers, however, end up using any of the numerous phone centers in major tourist cities, from where you can call fairly cheaply to anywhere in the world. (These are covered in the appropriate geographical sections and are almost always housed in the same places offering Internet services.) Telgua also has call centers in major cities.

The most convenient and cheapest way to call home (and be able to call hotels and make reservations while on the road) is to have a cell phone. The most popular phone network is Tigo (www.tigo.com.gt), which likewise has the widest coverage and charges by the second, saving you money in the long run. Rates for domestic calls are about $0.16 a minute and you can call the United States for about $0.12 a minute. You can buy a phone locally, with the cheapest somewhere around $45, or bring one with you and use it in Guatemala if it's a GSM phone. The Tigo frequency is 850 MHZ. Your phone's SIM card will need to be replaced with a Tigo SIM card, available for about $7. If your phone is locked, you will need to have a

GUATEMALA CITY EMBASSIES AND CONSULATES

Most embassies and consulates tend to be open only during weekday mornings.

- **Austria:** 6a Avenida 20-25, Edificio Plaza, Zona 10, tel. 2364-3460

- **Belize:** Avenida La Reforma 8-50, Edificio El Reformador, Suite 803, Zona 9, tel. 2334-5531

- **Canada:** 13 Calle 8-44, 6th Floor, Edificio Edyma Plaza, Zona 10, tel. 2333-6102

- **Colombia:** 5a Avenida 5-55, Edificio Europlaza, Torre I, Zona 14, tel. 2385-3432

- **Costa Rica:** 1a Avenida 15-52 Zona 10, tel. 2363-1345

- **Cuba:** 13 Calle 5-72 Zona 10, tel. 2333-7627

- **El Salvador:** 5a Avenida 8-15 Zona 9, tel. 2360-7660

- **France:** Edificio Marbella, 11th Floor, 16 Calle 4-53 Zona 10, tel. 2337-3639

- **Germany:** Edificio Plaza Marítima, 20 Calle 6-20 Zona 10, tel. 2364-6700

- **Honduras:** 19 Avenida "A" 20-19 Zona 10, tel. 2366-5640

- **Israel:** 13 Avenida 14-07 Zona 10, Colonia Oakland, tel. 2363-5665

- **Italy:** 5a Avenida 8-59 Zona 14, tel. 2337-4851

- **Mexico:** 15 Calle 3-20 Zona 10, tel. 2333-7254

- **Netherlands:** 16 Calle 0-55, 13th Floor, Torre Internacional, Zona 10, tel. 2367-4761

- **Nicaragua:** 10a Avenida 14-72 Zona 10, tel. 2368-0785

- **Panama:** 10a Avenida 18-53 Zona 14, tel. 2368-2805

- **Spain:** 6a Calle 6-48 Zona 9, tel. 2379-3530

- **Sweden:** 8a Avenida 15-07 Zona 10, tel. 2333-6536

- **Switzerland:** Torre Internacional, 16 Calle 0-65 Zona 10, tel. 2367-5520

- **United Kingdom:** Torre Internacional, 16 Calle 0-65, 11th Floor, Zona 10, tel. 2367-5520

- **United States:** Avenida La Reforma 7-01 Zona 10, tel. 2331-1541

---

technician perform a *flasheo* to unlock it, costing about another $7. Most places selling cell phones can do this for you. You can buy talk time almost everywhere, available by buying cards in various denominations, which you then call in and have credited to your account. After your trip, you can put your original SIM card back in your phone.

If you're an iPhone enthusiast, or if your cell phone uses the latest 4G technology, you'll be happy to know that both Movistar (www.movistar.com.gt) and Claro (www.claro.com.gt) sell iPhones locally. All three carriers have 4G networks with various plans to suit your needs, and with prices comparable to those in the United States. These companies also offer videophone service for phones equipped with this feature.

Internet

Internet access is widely available in most cities and tourist destinations throughout the country. You'll have no trouble finding places to check your email or surf the web. Hourly rates are usually in the $1-2 range.

Newspapers and Magazines

Prensa Libre is Guatemala's most widely circulated newspaper and is highly respected. You can find the online version at www.prensalibre.com.gt. Other excellent newspapers include *Siglo XXI* (www.sigloxxi.com) and *elPeriódico* (www.elperiodico.com.gt). All of these are tabloid, rather than broadsheet, in format. A tabloid in the sense of being filled with plenty of yellow journalism, scandal, and not much else of use is *Nuestro Diario*, which nonetheless seems to be somewhat popular in the country's interior. Guatemala's respectable newspapers are an excellent source of information and make a great way to practice reading Spanish. They have a long tradition of investigative reporting and have done a wonderful job of uncovering numerous scandals Guatemala's corrupt politicians would probably get away with (at least without public knowledge) were it not for the work of these intrepid journalists. Journalism can still be a dangerous occupation in Guatemala, though press freedom has come a long way since the dark times of the civil war.

Published in Antigua, the monthly *Revue* magazine has tons of helpful tips and contact information for hotels, restaurants, and businesses in Guatemala as well as parts of Honduras and El Salvador. There are also well-written stories on topics of interest to locals and visitors alike. It's available in tourist shops, hotels, and restaurants free of charge.

Television

Guatemala has a handful of local channels, though cable TV with channels beamed in from the United States is also widely available. The country also has its own cable network, Guatevisión, with a morning show and some entertaining programs covering recreational options throughout the country.

MAPS AND TOURIST INFORMATION
Maps

Recently introduced, Mapas de Guatemala (www.mapasdeguatemala.com) makes an excellent series of beautifully illustrated full-color maps of Guatemala's main tourist regions, which also include helpful information on local businesses. The free maps are available at INGUAT as well as tourist gift shops and restaurants throughout the country. If you need a good map before leaving for Guatemala, ITMB Publishing (530 W. Broadway, Vancouver, BC,

Canada, 604/879-3621, www.itmb.com) publishes an excellent *International Travel Map of Guatemala* ($10.95), which is weatherproof and can be found at well-known bookstores in the United States.

Tourist Information

The Guatemala Tourist Commission (INGUAT) provides tourist information from its offices in major tourist areas and the country's two international airports. It is also in charge of promoting Guatemala internationally and you may see ads for Guatemala in travel magazines from time to time. Unfortunately, it's not the catchiest advertising, and chances are you missed it.

INGUAT does a fairly good job with its mandate and has been instrumental in the organization of community-based tourism providers. It also participates in international tourism fairs promoting Guatemala, provides logistical support for travel journalists covering the country for international publications, keeps tabs on hotel pricing standards, and is credited with wooing airlines to begin service to Guatemala.

INGUAT's central office is in Guatemala City's Zona 4 at 7a Avenida 1-17 and its website is www.visitguatemala.com.

WEIGHTS AND MEASURES
Time

Guatemala is six hours behind GMT and in the same time zone as U.S. Central Standard Time. Hours of daylight do not vary greatly between seasons, but daylight savings time is sometimes observed, depending on the whims of individual governments. It was observed in the summer of 2006 and has not been observed since.

Electricity

Nearly all outlets are 110 volts, 60 cycles with outlets for plugs consisting of parallel flat blades just like the ones found in the United

States, Canada, and Mexico. Power outages and electrical surges are common in rural areas, especially during unusually arid dry seasons or very wet rainy seasons in thunderstorms. Be extra careful with sensitive equipment such as laptop computers.

Measurements

Like the American and European influences on its culture, Guatemala uses a sometimes confusing mixture of weights and measures from both the metric and old English systems. Fruits and vegetables are weighed by the pound, but folks weigh themselves in kilos; gas is dispensed in gallons but distances are computed in kilometers, and so on and so forth.

Another commonly used distance measurement is the *vara,* equivalent to 0.84 meters or a little less than a yard. For measuring land areas, the *manzana* equals about 0.7 hectare or 1.7 acres and the *caballería* covers a little more than 45 hectares or 111.5 acres. The *quintal* is widely used for weighing coffee and is the equivalent of 46 kilos.

RESOURCES

Glossary

aduana: customs

agua: literally "water" but also used in reference to soda pop

agua pura: bottled water

aguardiente: cane alcohol or moonshine

aguas termales: hot springs

alcalde: mayor

alfombra: a colorful carpet made of sawdust and flowers central to Holy Week celebrations in Antigua and elsewhere in Guatemala

altense: a resident of Quetzaltenango

al tiempo: referring to drinks at room temperature

altiplano: the highlands

artesanías: handicrafts

avenida: avenue

ayudante: in cheap public buses, the man who helps the driver in collecting fares and helping passengers with baggage

bajo: lowland swampy areas of the Petén lowlands

balneario: a bathing or swimming hole

baño compartido/general: shared bath (in reference to accommodations)

baño privado: private bathroom

barranco: a ravine

baule: a leatherback turtle

billares: pool or billiards

billete: a banknote or bill

bistec: beef steak

bolo: drunk; also *borracho*

brujo: a male witch or sorcerer

cajero automático: automated teller machine (ATM)

calle: street

camioneta: a second-class bus

campesino: peasant farmer

canícula: a brief one- or two-week dry spell during the rainy summer months of July and August

cantina: a seedy bar

caoba: mahogany

casa de huéspedes: a guesthouse

cayuco: canoe

cerveza: beer

champa: thatched-roof, wall-less structure

chapín/chapina: what Guatemalans call themselves

chichicaste: a stinging plant somewhat like poison ivy

chiclero: a tapper of chewing-gum resin of the jungle Petén region

coche: a pig, not a car, as in other parts of Latin America

cofradía: traditional political-religious organization present in some highland Mayan communities

comedor: a simple eatery

corte: traditional wraparound skirt worn by Mayan women

costumbre: traditional Mayan religious practices that include offerings of flowers, candles, and sometimes animal sacrifices

coyote: a smuggler of undocumented immigrants across Mexico and into the United States

criollo: Guatemalan of Spanish heritage

cucurucho: costumed carriers of procession parade floats during Semana Santa celebrations

curandero: traditional healer or shaman

edificio: a building; used in street addresses in urban areas

encomienda: a colonial system enabling land-holders to exact tribute and labor from the local indigenous population

farmacia de turno: a pharmacy that remains open all night on a rotating basis

finca: a farm of any type but usually referring to a coffee farm

hospedaje: inexpensive family-run accommodations

huipil: traditional embroidered dress

ingenio: a sugar mill

invierno: literally "winter" but used to describe the May–October rainy season

IVA: short for *impuesto al valor agregado* (value added tax) VAT; in Guatemala it's 12 percent

ladino: a person of indigenous descent who has adopted European ways

lancha: small motorboat

latifundia: large landholding in the form of a plantation or hacienda

lavandería: laundry

machista: a male chauvinist

maquiladora: an industrial plant where clothes are assembled for reexport by cheap local labor; more commonly known in the United States as a "sweatshop"

mara: a gang, but also used to describe a "gang" in the manner referring to an agglomeration of people or a crowd

mestizo: person of mixed Spanish and Indian descent

milpa: a maize or corn plant; also sometimes used in reference to a cornfield

minifundia: small landholdings, usually in the hands of Mayan peasantry

morería: small crafts shop producing costumes and masks for traditional dancing

palapa: a high-ceilinged thatched-roof structure commonly used in restaurant or hotel architecture

parlama: green sea turtle

parque nacional: national park

pensión: inexpensive accommodations

petate: a reed mat

picop: pickup truck

Pullman: a first-class bus, though to varying degrees of newness and quality

rancho: a simple thatched structure; also sometimes referred to in its diminutive *ranchito*.

recargo: a surcharge; usually associated with credit card transactions

refacción: snack time between lunch and dinner; also on menus as *refacciones* consisting of pastries and sandwiches

repatriado: returned civil war refugee, usually from Mexico

reserva natural privada: a privately owned nature preserve

reserva protectora de manantiales: a watershed protection preserve

retablo: an altarpiece in a colonial church

revueltos: scrambled (eggs)

ron: rum

sacbe: once-paved Mayan causeways present in the modern-day lowlands of Petén and still used as footpaths

stela (stelae): pre-Columbian stone monuments, usually carved

timbre: a type of stamp sold in banks used in paying fees such as visa renewals

traje: traditional Mayan costume worn by inhabitants of individual highland villages

túmulo: a speed bump

verano: literally "summer," but usually in reference to the height of the dry season between March and the beginning of the rainy season in May

zafra: sugarcane harvest in the Pacific lowlands

zancudo: mosquito

zona: a city zone into which Guatemala's principal urban areas are divided

Spanish Phrasebook

Your Guatemalan adventure will be more fun if you use a little Spanish. Though Guatemalans may smile at your funny accent, they will certainly appreciate your halting efforts to break the ice and transform yourself from a foreigner into a potential friend.

Spanish commonly uses 30 letters—the familiar English 26, plus four straightforward additions: ch, ll, ñ, and rr, which are consonants.

PRONUNCIATION

Spanish pronunciation rules are straightforward and easy to learn, because—in contrast to English—they don't change. Spanish vowels generally sound softer than in English. (Note: The capitalized syllables below receive stronger accents.)

Vowels

a like ah, as in "hah": agua AH-gooah (water), pan PAHN (bread), and casa CAH-sah (house)

e like ay, as in "may:" mesa MAY-sah (table), tela TAY-lah (cloth), and de DAY (of, from)

i like ee, as in "need": diez dee-AYZ (10), comida ko-MEE-dah (meal), and fin FEEN (end)

o like oh, as in "go": peso PAY-soh (weight), ocho OH-choh (eight), and poco POH-koh (a bit)

u like oo, as in "cool": uno OO-noh (one), cuarto KOOAHR-toh (room), and usted oos-TAYD (you); when it follows a "q" the u is silent; when it follows an "h" or has an umlaut, it's pronounced like "w"

Consonants

b, ch, d, f, k, l, m, n, p, q, s, t, v, w, x, y, z
pronounced almost as in English; h occurs, but is silent (not pronounced at all)

c like k as in "keep": cuarto KOOAR-toh (room), corazón kor-a-SOHN (heart); when it precedes "e" or "i," pronounce c like s, as

in "sit": cerveza sayr-VAY-sah (beer), encima ayn-SEE-mah (atop).

g like g as in "gift" when it precedes "a," "o," "u," or a consonant: gato GAH-toh (cat), hago AH-goh (I do, make); otherwise, pronounce g like h as in "hat": giro HEE-roh (money order), gente HAYN-tay (people)

j like h, as in "has": jueves HOOAY-vays (Thursday), mejor may-HOR (better)

ll like y, as in "yes": toalla toh-AH-yah (towel), ellos AY-yohs (they, them)

ñ like ny, as in "canyon": año AH-nyo (year), señor SAY-nyor (Mr., sir)

r is lightly trilled, with tongue at the roof of your mouth like a very light English r, as in "ready": pero PAY-roh (but), tres TRAYS (three), cuatro KOOAH-troh (four).

rr like a Spanish r, but with much more emphasis and trill. Let your tongue flap. Practice with burro (donkey), carretera (highway), and Carrillo (proper name), then really let go with ferrocarril (railroad).

Note: The single small but common exception to all of the above is the pronunciation of Spanish **y** when it's being used as the Spanish word for "and," as in "Ron y Kathy." In such case, pronounce it like the English ee, as in "keep": Ron "ee" Kathy (Ron and Kathy).

Accent

Native English speakers often make errors of pronunciation by ignoring accented, or stressed, syllables. All Spanish vowels – **a, e, i, o,** and **u** – may carry accents determining which syllable of a word is emphasized.

The rule for accent, the relative stress given to syllables within a given word, is straightforward. If a word ends in a vowel, an n, or an s, accent the next-to-last syllable; if not, accent the last syllable.

Pronounce *gracias* GRAH-seeahs (thank

you), **orden** OHR-dayn (order), and **carretera** kah-ray-TAY-rah (highway) with stress on the next-to-last syllable.

Otherwise, accent the last syllable: **venir** vay-NEER (to come), **ferrocarril** fay-roh-cah-REEL (railroad), and **edad** ay-DAHD (age).

Exceptions to the accent rule are always marked with an accent sign: (á, é, í, ó, or ú), such as **teléfono** tay-LAY-foh-noh (telephone), **jabón** hah-BON (soap), and **rápido** RAH-pee-doh (rapid).

NUMBERS

zero cero
one uno
two dos
three tres
four cuatro
five cinco
six seis
seven siete
eight ocho
nine nueve
10 diez
11 once
12 doce
13 trece
14 catorce
15 quince
16 dieciseis
17 diecisiete
18 dieciocho
19 diecinueve
20 veinte
21 veinte y uno or veintiuno
30 treinta
40 cuarenta
50 cincuenta
60 sesenta
70 setenta
80 ochenta
90 noventa
100 cien
101 ciento y uno
200 doscientos

500 quinientos
1,000 mil
10,000 diez mil
100,000 cien mil
1,000,000 millón
one-half medio
one-third un tercio
one-fourth un cuarto

TIME

What time is it? ¿Qué hora es?
It's one o'clock. Es la una.
It's three in the afternoon. Son las tres de la tarde.
It's 4 a.m. Son las cuatro de la mañana.
six-thirty seis y media
a quarter till eleven un cuarto para las once
a quarter past five las cinco y cuarto
an hour una hora
today hoy
tomorrow mañana
yesterday ayer
a week una semana
a month un mes
a year un año
after después
before antes
last night anoche
the next day el día siguiente

DAYS OF THE WEEK

Monday Lunes
Tuesday Martes
Wednesday Miércoles
Thursday Jueves
Friday Viernes
Saturday Sábado
Sunday Domingo

MONTHS

January Enero
February Febrero
March Marzo
April Abril

May Mayo
June Junio
July Julio
August Agosto
September Septiembre
October Octubre
November Noviembre
December Diciembre

BASIC AND COURTEOUS EXPRESSIONS

Most Spanish-speaking people consider formalities important. Whenever approaching anyone for information or some other reason, do not forget the appropriate salutation–good morning, good evening, and so forth. Standing alone, the greeting hola (hello) can sound brusque.

Hello. Hola.
Good morning. Buenos días.
Good afternoon. Buenas tardes.
Good evening. Buenas noches.
How are you? ¿Cómo está usted?
Very well, thank you. Muy bien, gracias.
Okay; good. Bien.
Not okay; bad. Mal, feo.
So-so. Más o menos.
And you? ¿Y usted?
Thank you. Gracias.
Thank you very much. Muchas gracias.
You're very kind. Muy amable.
You're welcome. De nada.
Good-bye. Adios.
See you later. Hasta luego.
please por favor
yes sí
no no
I don't know. No sé.
Just a moment, please. Momentito, por favor.
Excuse me, please (when you're trying to get attention). Disculpe or Con permiso.
Excuse me (when you've made a mistake). Lo siento.
Pleased to meet you. Mucho gusto.

What is your name? ¿Cómo se llama usted?
Do you speak English? ¿Habla usted inglés?
Is English spoken here? (Does anyone here speak English?) ¿Se habla inglés?
I don't speak Spanish well. No hablo bien el español.
I don't understand. No entiendo.
How do you say...in Spanish? ¿Cómo se dice...en español?
My name is... Me llamo...
Would you like... ¿Quisiera usted...
Let's go to... Vamos a...

TERMS OF ADDRESS

When in doubt, use the formal usted (you) as a form of address.

I yo
you (formal) usted
you (familiar) tu
he/him él
she/her ella
we/us nosotros
you (plural) ustedes
they/them ellos (all males or mixed gender); ellas (all females)
Mr., sir señor
Mrs., madam señora
miss, young lady señorita
wife esposa
husband esposo
friend amigo (male); amiga (female)
sweetheart novio (male); novia (female)
son; daughter hijo; hija
brother; sister hermano; hermana
father; mother padre; madre
grandfather; grandmother abuelo; abuela

TRANSPORTATION

Where is...? ¿Dónde está...?
How far is it to...? ¿A cuánto está...?
from...to... de...a...
How many blocks? ¿Cuántas cuadras?
Where (Which) is the way to...? ¿Dónde está el camino a...?

the bus station la terminal de autobuses
the bus stop la parada de autobuses
Where is this bus going? ¿Adónde va este autobús?
the taxi stand la parada de taxis
the train station la estación de ferrocarril
the boat el barco
the airport el aeropuerto
I'd like a ticket to... Quisiera un boleto a...
first (second) class primera (segunda) clase
round-trip ida y vuelta
reservation reservación
baggage equipaje
Stop here, please. Pare aquí, por favor.
the entrance la entrada
the exit la salida
the ticket office la oficina de boletos
(very) near; far (muy) cerca; lejos
to; toward a
by; through por
from de
the right la derecha
the left la izquierda
straight ahead recto
in front en frente
beside al lado
behind atrás
the corner la esquina
the stoplight el semáforo
a turn una vuelta
right here aquí
somewhere around here por acá
right there allí
somewhere around there por allá
street; boulevard calle; bulevar
highway carretera
bridge; toll puente; peaje
address dirección
north; south norte; sur
east; west oriente (este); poniente (oeste)

ACCOMMODATIONS

hotel hotel
Is there a room? ¿Hay cuarto?

May I (may we) see it? ¿Puedo (podemos) verlo?
What is the rate? ¿Cuál es el precio?
Is that your best rate? ¿Es su mejor precio?
Is there something cheaper? ¿Hay algo más económico?
a single room un cuarto sencillo
a double room un cuarto doble
double bed cama matrimonial
twin beds camas gemelas
with private bath con baño
hot water agua caliente
shower ducha
towels toallas
soap jabón
toilet paper papel higiénico
blanket frazada; chamarra
sheets sábanas
air-conditioned aire acondicionado
fan ventilador
key llave
manager gerente

FOOD

I'm hungry. Tengo hambre.
I'm thirsty. Tengo sed.
menu lista; menú
order orden
glass vaso
fork tenedor
knife cuchillo
spoon cuchara
napkin servilleta
soft drink refresco
coffee café
tea té
drinking water agua pura; agua potable
bottled carbonated water agua mineral
bottled uncarbonated water agua sin gas
beer cerveza
wine vino
milk leche
juice jugo
cream crema

sugar azúcar
cheese queso
snack refacción
breakfast desayuno
lunch almuerzo
daily lunch special el menú del día
dinner cena
the check la cuenta
eggs huevos
bread pan
salad ensalada
fruit fruta
mango mango
watermelon sandía
papaya papaya
banana banano
apple manzana
orange naranja
plantain plátano
lime limón
fish pescado
shellfish mariscos
shrimp camarones
meat (without) (sin) carne
chicken pollo
pork puerco
beef; steak res; bistec
bacon; ham tocino; jamón
fried frito
roasted asada
barbecue; barbecued barbacoa; al carbón

SHOPPING

money dinero
money-exchange bureau casa de cambio
I would like to exchange travelers checks. Quisiera cambiar cheques de viajero.
What is the exchange rate? ¿Cuál es el tipo de cambio?
How much is the commission? ¿Cuánto cuesta la comisión?
Do you accept credit cards? ¿Aceptan tarjetas de crédito?

money order giro
How much does it cost? ¿Cuánto cuesta?
What is your final price? ¿Cuál es su último precio?
expensive caro
cheap barato; económico
more más
less menos
a little un poco
too much demasiado

HEALTH

Help me please. Ayúdeme por favor.
I am ill. Estoy enfermo.
Call a doctor. Llame un doctor.
Take me to... Lléveme a...
hospital hospital; sanatorio
drugstore farmacia
pain dolor
fever fiebre
headache dolor de cabeza
stomach ache dolor de estómago
burn quemadura
cramp calambre
nausea náusea
vomiting vomitar
medicine medicina
antibiotic antibiótico
pill; tablet pastilla
aspirin aspirina
ointment; cream pomada; crema
bandage venda
cotton algodón
sanitary napkins use brand name, e.g., Kotex
birth control pills pastillas anticonceptivas
contraceptive foam espuma anticonceptiva
condoms preservativos; condones
toothbrush cepillo dental
dental floss hilo dental
toothpaste crema dental
dentist dentista
toothache dolor de muelas

POST OFFICE AND COMMUNICATIONS

long-distance telephone teléfono de larga distancia

I would like to call... Quisiera llamar a...

collect a cobrar

station to station a quien contesta

person to person persona a persona

credit card tarjeta de crédito

post office correo

general delivery lista de correo

letter carta

stamp estampilla, timbre

postcard postal

air mail correo aéreo

registered registrado

money order giro

package; box paquete; caja

string; tape cuerda; cinta

AT THE BORDER

border frontera

customs aduana

immigration migración

tourist card tarjeta de turista

inspection inspección; revisión

passport pasaporte

profession profesión

marital status estado civil

single soltero

married; divorced casado; divorciado

widowed enviudado

insurance seguros

title título

driver's license licencia de conducir

gas station gasolinera

car carro

gasoline gasolina

unleaded sin plomo

full, please lleno, por favor

tire llanta

tire repair shop vulcanizadora or pinchazo

air aire

water agua

oil (change) (cambio de) aceite

grease grasa

My...doesn't work. Mi...no sirve.

battery batería

radiator radiador

alternator alternador

generator generador

tow truck grúa

repair shop taller mecánico

tune-up afinación or tune-up

VERBS

Verbs are the key to getting along in Spanish. They employ mostly predictable forms and come in three classes, which end in *ar, er,* and *ir,* respectively:

to buy comprar

I buy, you (he, she, it) buys compro, compra

we buy, you (they) buy compramos, compran

to eat comer

I eat, you (he, she, it) eats como, come

we eat, you (they) eat comemos, comen

to climb subir

I climb, you (he, she, it) climbs subo, sube

we climb, you (they) climb subimos, suben

Here are more (with irregularities indicated).

to do or make hacer (regular except for hago, I do or make)

to go ir (very irregular: voy, va, vamos, van)

to go (walk) andar

to love amar

to work trabajar

to want desear, querer

to need necesitar

to read leer

to write escribir

to repair reparar

to stop parar

to get off (the bus) bajar

to arrive llegar

to stay (remain) quedar

to stay (lodge) hospedar

to leave salir (regular except for salgo, I leave)

to look at mirar

to look for buscar
to give dar (regular except for doy, I give)
to carry llevar
to have tener (irregular but important: tengo, tiene, tenemos, tienen)
to come venir (similarly irregular: vengo, viene, venimos, vienen)

Spanish has two forms of "to be:"
to be estar (regular except for estoy, I am)

to be ser (very irregular: soy, es, somos, son)

Use *estar* when speaking of location or a temporary state of being: "I am at home." *"Estoy en casa." "I'm sick." "Estoy enfermo."* Use *ser* for a permanent state of being: "I am a doctor." *"Soy doctora."*

–Adapted by Al Argueta from Bruce Whipperman's *Moon Pacific Mexico.*

Suggested Reading

HISTORY AND POLITICS
Pre-Columbian History

Coe, Michael D. *Breaking the Maya Code.* New York: Thames and Hudson, 1999. Chronicles the work of several scholars involved in the eventual decipherment of the meaning behind the Mayan glyphs.

Coe, Michael D. *The Maya,* 7th edition. New York: Thames and Hudson, 2005. A classic reference manual on the Mayans and essential guide for the traveler that includes useful color plates.

Demarest, Arthur. *Ancient Maya: The Rise and Fall of a Rainforest Civilization.* Cambridge: Cambridge University Press, 2005. Written by a prominent archaeologist who has worked on numerous projects in Guatemala, this book explores the ecological aspects of the rise of Mayan civilization and the role of internecine warfare in its demise.

Harrison, Peter. *The Lords of Tikal: Rulers of an Ancient Maya City.* New York: Thames and Hudson, 2000. Traces the history of Tikal from its humble beginning to its apogee in the late 9th century A.D.

Montgomery, John. *Tikal: An Illustrated History of the Ancient Maya Capital.* New York:

Hippocrene Books, 2000. Wonderfully illustrated with photos, maps, and drawings, this is a good introduction to Tikal for the visitor and casual Mayanist.

Colonial Era

Lovell, W. George. *Conquest and Survival in Colonial Guatemala: A Historical Geography of the Cuchumatán Highlands,* 3rd edition. Kingston, Ontario: McGill-Queen's University Press, 2004. Quickly becoming a classic, this landmark work covers the Spanish conquest and the survival of the local indigenous culture despite the ravages of colonial legacies while linking the roots of the past to more recent sociopolitical conditions.

Civil War

Arnson, Cynthia J., editor. *Comparative Peace Processes in Latin America.* Washington, D.C.: Woodrow Wilson Center Press, 1999. Provides a good analysis of the peace process that led to a negotiated settlement of the civil war in Guatemala and other countries as well as issues concerning the roles of truth-telling reports, the search for justice, and reconciliation.

Burgos-Debray, Elizabeth, editor. *I, Rigoberta Menchú: An Indian Woman in Guatemala.*

London: Verso, 1984. The classic autobiography of Nobel Peace Prize winner Rigoberta Menchú.

Goldman, Francisco. *The Art of Political Murder: Who killed the Bishop?* New York: Grove/Atlantic, 2008. A fascinating look into the inner workings of Guatemala's political and justice systems *vis a vis* the murder of Bishop Juan Gerardi and its subsequent investigation. This well-researched book details the machinations involved in hiding the culprits in one of Guatemala's most notorious high-profile murders and the admirable work of a handful of investigators who sought the truth against all odds.

Grandin, Greg. *The Last Colonial Massacre: Latin America in the Cold War.* Chicago: The University of Chicago Press, 2004. This thought-provoking book argues that the Latin American Cold War was actually a struggle between two differing notions of democracy, with its main achievement being the elimination of grassroots attempts at building social democracy. It uses Guatemala as a case study and concludes, somewhat convincingly, that the version of democracy now being extolled as the best option in the war against terror is itself a product of the same.

Handy, Jim. *Revolution in the Countryside: Rural Conflict and Agrarian Reform in Guatemala, 1944–1954.* Chapel Hill: The University of North Carolina Press, 1994. A good in-depth look at the Agrarian Reform Law and the Guatemalan political scene during the Arévalo and Arbenz years.

Manz, Beatriz. *Paradise in Ashes: A Guatemalan Journey of Courage, Terror, and Hope.* Berkeley: University of California Press, 2004. Written by an anthropologist, this book centers around the Ixcán village of Santa María Tzejá, whose inhabitants were caught in the violence between the guerrillas and military during the civil war.

Perera, Víctor. *Unfinished Conquest: The Guatemalan Tragedy.* Berkeley: University of California Press, 1993. A must-read for travelers to Guatemala, covering sociopolitical aspects of the Guatemalan civil war as well as environmental issues in a well-written travel narrative style.

Sanford, Victoria. *Buried Secrets: Truth and Human Rights in Guatemala.* New York: Palgrave Macmillan, 2004. A highly recommended read with well-researched information from a number of different sources, including eyewitness testimonies from massacre survivors, interviews with members of forensic teams, human rights workers, high-ranking military officers, guerrillas, and government officials. It is an instrumental book for understanding the full scale of the genocidal civil war and the attempt to rebuild society in its aftermath.

Schlesinger, Stephen C., and Stephen Kinzer. *Bitter Fruit: The Story of the American Coup in Guatemala.* Cambridge: Harvard University Press, 2005. This is a classic book on Guatemala and its historical relationship with the United States. First published in 1982, it covers in much detail the 1954 CIA-orchestrated coup ousting Jacobo Arbenz.

Stoll, David. *Between Two Armies in the Ixil Towns of Guatemala.* New York: Columbia University Press, 1993. A controversial book postulating the theory that the Ixil Mayans of Nebaj, Chajul, and Cotzal were not so much enamored with revolutionary possibilities for social change as much as simply caught between the opposing fires of the military and guerrilla forces with widely differing sociopolitical agendas.

Stoll, David. *Rigoberta Menchú and the Story of All Poor Guatemalans.* Boulder, Colorado: Westview Press, 1999. Also quite controversial, this work directly challenges much of the testimony presented by Rigoberta Menchú in her autobiography as embellishments or fabrications while granting that the atrocities described therein were accurate depictions of events during the civil war.

Wilkinson, Daniel. *Silence on the Mountain: Stories of Terror, Betrayal, and Forgetting in Guatemala.* New York: Houghton Mifflin, 2002. Part travelogue and part history book, this is a fascinating, well-written account of the American author's experience in Guatemala; it manages to uncover many of the issues relating to the origins and unfolding of Guatemala's civil war as told by those who survived the violence.

Central America

LaFeber, Walter. *Inevitable Revolutions: The United States in Central America.* New York: W. W. Norton, 1993. Traces the historical roots of Central America's armed conflicts along with the role of U.S. hegemony in perpetuating them.

POLITICS

Grandin, Greg. *The Guatemala Reader: History, Culture, Politics (The Latin America Readers).* Duke University Press Books, 2011. An excellent resource for those wanting to explore the history and culture of Guatemala in a wide array of facets not limited solely to its dark history. It provides a well-rounded look at Guatemala in a contemporary context.

O'Neill, Kevin Lewis. *Securing the City: Neoliberalism, Space, and Insecurity in Postwar Guatemala.* Duke University Press Books, 2011. A collection of essays forming an excellent comparative study of the effects of neoliberalist approaches to postwar security in Guatemala's violent capital. Among the issues it explores are the further entrenchment of deep chasms between city and country, and the exacerbation of Guatemala's deeply rooted structures of inequality and ethnic discrimination.

TRAVELOGUES AND LITERATURE
Travelogues

Benz, Stephen Connely. *Guatemalan Journey.* Austin: University of Texas Press, 1996. A humorous, insightful, and well-written account of an American traveler's experiences living in Guatemala during the late 1980s.

Huxley, Aldous. *Beyond the Mexique Bay.* New York: Harper and Brothers Publishers, 1934. A classic take on early-20th-century travel in Guatemala by a well-known author.

Shaw, Christopher. *Sacred Monkey River: A Canoe Trip with the Gods.* New York: W. W. Norton, 2000. A superbly written adventure-travel narrative packed with historical and natural history anecdotes about the mighty Usumacinta River, which flows along the Mexico–Guatemala border.

Stephens, John Lloyd. *Incidents of Travel in Central America, Chiapas and Yucatán.* New York: Dover Publications, 1969. A classic book and a must-read for the traveler to Guatemala, also featuring the fantastic illustrations of Stephens's friend and traveling companion Frederick Catherwood. It created quite an interest in the region, particularly its Mayan sites, when it was first published in 1841.

Wright, Ronald. *Time Among the Maya: Travels in Belize, Guatemala and Mexico.* New York: Grove/Atlantic, 2000. Another good read with insights on culture, history, adventure, and anthropology by a writer with an evident love for the modern-day Mayan people.

FICTION

Goldman, Francisco. *The Long Night of White Chickens*. New York: Grove/Atlantic, 1998. This well-written novel is a tale of intrigue set in 1980s Guatemala governed by military dictatorships. It's an entertaining read and does a nice job of bridging the gap between the seemingly parallel worlds of the United States and Guatemala.

ART

Gieseman, Peter, and Ange Bourda. *Six Architects*. Bogotá: Villegas Editores, 2003. An art-photography book documenting the architecture of the Guatemala City *Seis Arquitectos* firm.

Moller, Jonathan. *Our Culture Is Our Resistance: Repression, Refuge and Healing in Guatemala*. New York: PowerHouse Books, 2004. A beautiful photographic collection of highland Mayan culture in the aftermath of the civil war with wonderful guest commentaries from Rigoberta Menchú, Francisco Goldman, and various other authors of books on Guatemala.

NATURAL HISTORY

Beletsky, Les. *Traveller's Wildlife Guides: Belize and Northern Guatemala*. Northampton: Interlink Books, 2005.

Lee, Julian C. *Field Guide to the Amphibians and Reptiles of the Maya World: The Lowlands of Mexico, Northern Guatemala and Belize*. Ithaca: Cornell University Press, 2000.

Peterson, Roger Tory, and Edward L. Chalif. *A Field Guide to Mexican Birds: Mexico, Guatemala, Belize, El Salvador*. New York: Houghton Mifflin, 1999. Describes and illustrates 1,038 species.

Primack, Richard B., et al., eds. *Timber, Tourists, and Temples: Conservation and Development in the Maya Forest of Belize, Guatemala, and Mexico*. Washington, D.C.: Island Press, 1998. Covers the delicate political and social issues implicated in conserving the region's remaining rainforests as told from the perspective of social scientists, conservationists, and biologists working in the field.

ADOPTION

Michelini, Gil. *Daddy, Come & Get Me: A Dad's Adventure Through a Guatemalan Adoption*. CreateSpace, 2012. A fascinating read chronicling a father's mission to adopt a child from Guatemala and the sacrifices endured by the child's birth mother in handing her over for adoption. The title comes from the author's dream in which he heard a child calling out these words from a mountaintop.

O'Dwyer, Jessica. *Mamalita: An Adoption Memoir*. Berkeley, Ca: Seal Press, 2010. An at times harrowing account of the difficulties in adopting a Guatemalan child vis-à-vis shady adoption agencies and bureaucratic red tape, and one woman's persistence in the face of such trials.

Internet Resources

GENERAL INFORMATION
www.prensalibre.com.gt
www.sigloxxi.com
www.elperiodico.com.gt
If you can read Spanish (or want to practice reading Spanish), Guatemala's main newspapers all have decent websites.

http://guatemalapost.com
An English-language wrap-up of news on Guatemala from various sources.

http://lanic.utexas.edu/la/ca/guatemala
The University of Texas has compounded a comprehensive list of links on everything pertaining to Guatemala.

www.revuemag.com
The highly recommended Revue magazine (in English) can be downloaded online in PDF format.

TRAVEL AND ENVIRONMENT
www.planeta.com
An excellent website with plenty of information on ecotravel in Guatemala and elsewhere in Latin America.

www.visitguatemala.com
The Guatemala Tourist Commission (INGUAT) website with a variety of information on Guatemala.

http://senderonatural.com
A Guatemalan-run website dedicated to sustainable tourism in Guatemala with a variety of good recreational options and recommended accommodations.

SPANISH LANGUAGE
www.123teachme.com
www.guatemala365.com

Both sites have reviews and rankings made by former students in the recommended language schools.

VOLUNTEERING
www.idealist.org
International volunteer website listing several opportunities in Guatemala.

www.volunteeradventures.com
Features a few Guatemala projects looking for international volunteers, mainly in the areas of wildlife conservation and opportunities to teach English.

www.entremundos.org
Quetzaltenango-based organization with tons of information on volunteer opportunities in the Western Highlands.

DESTINATION-SPECIFIC SITES
Chisec
www.puertamundomaya.com

Cobán
www.cobanav.net

Guatemala City
www.muniguate.com

Lívingston
www.livingston.com.gt

Nebaj
www.nebaj.com

Pachalum
www.pachalum.com

Quetzaltenango
www.xelawho.com
www.xelapages.com
www.xelapages.net

Semuc Champey
www.semucchampey.com

Uspantán
www.uspantan.com

Index

List of Maps

Acknowledgments

This guidebook would not have been possible without the help and inspiration of several folks to whom I owe my gratitude. First, I'd like to thank Hashem for his omnipresent love and inspiration, which are always available to help, comfort, strengthen, and encourage. I'd also like to thank my parents for their support, for planting in me a love for both Guatemala and the United States, and allowing me to experience the best of both worlds.

In Austin, I'd like to thank Shanna Offutt for providing much needed encouragement, and lots of love, along the way. My friends and former housemates Ryan Bowers and Micah Behrens I'd like to thank for their constant support and enthusiasm.

At INGUAT my thanks go to Vivian Juárez for providing logistical support. Sandra Muralles also went out of her way to make sure my travel plans went as smoothly as possible. A special shout-out goes to my drivers Yosaray Ramírez, María del Carmen Ponce, Jamil de la Cruz, and Abel Samayoa. Incidentally, if you ever need a guide in the Verapaces, give María del Carmen a call (tel. 5897-6305). She and her assistant, Jamil, amazed me with their level of professionalism.

I'd like to thank my family in Guatemala City for putting me up and providing a home away from home. My aunt, Alba Luz de Moya, selflessly gave up her office for a month so that I could put together this updated manuscript.

Also in Guatemala City, I'd like to thank Billy Bickford and Oscar Cuellar. I always have a great time at their lakeside retreat, Casa Palopó, and they are a wealth of information.

In Antigua, thanks go to John Heaton and Catherine Docter, with whom I'm glad to have been able to keep in touch via Facebook. They are an invaluable source of information on all things Guatemala. I'd also like to thank Gg Godard for helping me out with a great last-minute photo from her trip to El Mirador.

I'd like to thank all the Moon Guatemala Facebook fans and all those who have written in with their comments and suggestions for future editions.

Finally, I'd like to thank the staff at Avalon Travel, especially my editor, Elizabeth Hansen, and production coordinator, Elizabeth Jang, for all their hard work and help in making this book read and look its best.

www.moon.com

DESTINATIONS | ACTIVITIES | BLOGS | MAPS | BOOKS

MOON.COM is ready to help plan your next trip! Filled with fresh trip ideas and strategies, author interviews, informative travel blogs, a detailed map library, and descriptions of all the Moon guidebooks, Moon.com is all you need to get out and explore the world—or even places in your own backyard. While at Moon.com, sign up for our monthly e-newsletter for updates on new releases, travel tips, and expert advice from our on-the-go Moon authors. As always, when you travel with Moon, expect an experience that is uncommon and truly unique.